SPEAKING MUSICALLY

Great Artists in Conversation at
the Royal Academy of Music

Edited by
RAYMOND HOLDEN

First published in 2023 by
the Royal Academy of Music

Royal Academy of Music
Marylebone Road
London NW1 5HT

Copyright © Raymond Holden, 2023

www.ram.ac.uk

The author asserts his moral right to be identified as the author of this work.
All rights reserved. No part of this publication may be reproduced, stored in a retrieval system or transmitted in any form or by any means, electronic, mechanical, photocopying, recording or otherwise, without prior written permission of the author.

Every effort has been made to contact copyright holders. However, the publisher will be glad to rectify in future editions any inadvertent omissions brought to their attention.

ISBN 9781915635310

Also available as an ebook
ISBN 9781915635327

Designed and typeset by Tom Cabot/ketchup
Jacket design by simonlevyassociates.co.uk
Project management by whitefox
Printed and bound by CPI Group (UK) Ltd, Croydon CR0 4YY

CONTENTS

INTRODUCTION vii

THE INTERVIEWEES xii

THE INTERVIEWERS xxv

PART ONE: CONDUCTORS 1

   Sir Neville Marriner 2

   Sir Charles Mackerras 28

   Sir Colin Davis* 47

   Christoph von Dohnányi* 63

   Nikolaus Harnoncourt** 82

   Sir John Eliot Gardiner* 96

   Trevor Pinnock*** 127

   Sir Mark Elder 144

   Dame Jane Glover 161

   Oliver Knussen* 182

Semyon Bychkov* 199
Masaaki Suzuki* 219
Sian Edwards 232
Vladimir Jurowski 253
Edward Gardner 278

Part Two: Singers 305
Dame Janet Baker* 306
Dame Gwyneth Jones 319
Yvonne Minton 342
Dame Anne Evans 365
Sheila Armstrong 382
Ryland Davies and Dennis O'Neill 401
Sarah Walker 420
Dame Kiri Te Kanawa* 439
Dame Felicity Lott* 455
Dame Ann Murray 467
Yvonne Kenny 492

Part Three: Instrumentalists 517
Paul Badura-Skoda 518
Leon Fleisher 542
György Pauk 556
John Williams 575
Steven Isserlis 594
Joanna MacGregor 613
Maxim Vengerov* 633
James Ehnes 650

Part Four: Record Producers, Filmmakers and Arts Administrators 671
   Christopher Raeburn* 672
   Sir Humphrey Burton 686
   Tony Palmer 703
   Bruno Monsaingeon 731
   Roger Wright 751

Part Five: A Bicentennial Postlude: Revisiting Bruckner in Vienna 775
   Christian Thielemann** 776

Index 799

The majority of the interviews form part of the Barbirolli Lecture Series led by Raymond Holden. Exceptions are indicated according to the key:

* * Interviews led by Jonathan Freeman-Attwood as part of the Principal's Lecture Series
* ** Additional interviews led by Jonathan Freeman-Attwood
* *** An interview led by Timothy Jones as part of Barbirolli Lecture Series

INTRODUCTION

For two hundred years, the Royal Academy of Music has welcomed many of the world's greatest musicians. Whether it was at its original premises in Tenterden Street near Hanover Square or at its current building on Marylebone Road, the Academy has benefited from the musical insights and artistic generosity of a string of pre-eminent figures. Carl Maria von Weber, Felix Mendelssohn, Richard Wagner, Franz Liszt, Hans von Bülow, Clara Schumann, Richard Strauss, Sir Henry Wood, Sir Thomas Beecham and Sir John Barbirolli all either visited the Academy or worked closely with its principals, professors and students during the first 150 years of its existence. These artists did much to shape the institution's early performance and educational environments and brought with them a degree of musical expertise and intellectual gravitas that not only inspired the Academy's students and staff, but offered artistic possibilities that might otherwise have been overlooked. While these highly celebrated figures were undoubtedly some of the cultural giants who bestrode the landscape of Western art music between the early nineteenth and the late twentieth centuries, the list of performing musicians, composers, operatic directors, filmmakers and musicologists who visited the Academy during the last thirty years has been no less impactful and certainly no less impressive.

After being appointed to the Academy's staff in 2005 by its then Vice-Principal and Director of Studies, Professor Jonathan Freeman-Attwood, I quickly realised that we, as an institution, were missing a trick by not documenting the thoughts of leading artists when they came to work with our students. Clearly, great figures such as Sir Charles Mackerras, Sir Colin Davis, Leon Fleisher, Dame Kiri Te Kanawa and Maxim Vengerov were no strangers to being quizzed by eager commentators wherever they performed or appeared. But many of the interviews that they gave were either short or were affected by the particular agenda of the person or organisation doing the quizzing. In contrast, my idea was to establish an annual series of extended discussions that would be wide-ranging in their content, led by the interests of the interviewee, generous in their length and recorded for research purposes. Jonathan quickly saw the value of my suggestion and was immediately enthusiastic and supportive. That support and enthusiasm has never waned over the years, and it was he, as Principal, who commissioned me to edit a selection of these interviews, and to publish them in book form to celebrate the Bicentenary of the Royal Academy of Music in 2022.

Amongst the first to take part in the new series were the renowned English soprano Teresa Cahill and the distinguished editor and scholar Jonathan Del Mar. Sadly, these interviews were not recorded, but it was immediately clear that they were a huge popular and educational success, and that Teresa and Jonathan had enjoyed speaking openly and freely about their ideas, inspirations, ambitions and histories. More interviews with other leading figures quickly followed, and the series began to take on a life of its own. Soon known as 'The Barbirolli Lectures' after the Academy's great alumnus Sir John Barbirolli, the series rapidly became a fixed point in the institution's termly diary of public events. The unique nature of the series was also recognised outside the Academy, and was described by *The Independent* as one of London's 'top ten' lecture series in

INTRODUCTION

2013. Not only were the interviewees honest, open and frank on stage, but they were also able to continue to explore their ideas with students and members of the public at the drinks reception that followed each event. It was both amazing and inspiring to see eminent musicians such as Sir Mark Elder, Vladimir Jurowski, Dame Anne Evans, Yvonne Minton, Steven Isserlis and others engaging so enthusiastically with the Academy's young musicians over a glass of wine, and to watch those students hang on every word of advice being offered to them.

What was particularly remarkable about The Barbirolli Lectures as a whole was the willingness of leading artists like Paul Badura-Skoda, Dame Gwyneth Jones and Sir John Eliot Gardiner to travel great distances from their homes in either Europe or the English countryside to take part in the series for no financial gain. They simply wanted to share their experiences with the Academy's students and audiences, and to set the historical record straight. I'll never forget meeting Professor Badura-Skoda at the Eurostar terminal at St Pancras Station and him looking anxious about having paid 44 euros for a second-class return fare from Paris. Paul was concerned that he had spent too much, and that the expense might be too great for our budget to bear! After I assured him that it was absolutely no problem, and that our finances could stretch to that princely sum, he then produced a very expensive bottle of cognac, which he gave to me as a personal gift. It was considerably more costly than his train fare, and a typically generous and thoughtful gesture of a great and good man.

While I conducted the majority of the interviews, and was responsible for the shape and content of the series as a whole, my friends and colleagues Professors Jonathan Freeman-Attwood and Timothy Jones also led a number of events. In fact, Jonathan's interviews became something of a series within a series, and were eventually known as 'The Principal's Interview'. Very sadly, not all the artists whom I wanted for The Barbirolli Lectures lived long enough to take part, with Peter Katin,

H. C. Robbins Landon and Wolfgang Sawallisch all dying before being able to speak at the series. So, too, did Nikolaus Harnoncourt. But, fortunately, Jonathan Freeman-Attwood had conducted an extensive interview with the conductor at his home outside Salzburg for *Gramophone* in 2007, only part of which was published by the magazine later that year. As many of the issues raised during their wider recorded conversation were the same as those that Jonathan intended to ask Mr Harnoncourt at the Academy, I decided to publish the extended discussion here. I have also included an interview that Jonathan did by Zoom with the distinguished German conductor Christian Thielemann in January 2022, which Jonathan has edited himself. During that session, Mr Thielemann's ideas on Bruckner performance, and his thoughts about his forthcoming complete recording of the composer's symphonies with the Vienna Philharmonic, were discussed. As this interview was not edited by me, I have designated it a 'Postlude'.

It quickly became apparent to me when editing The Barbirolli Lectures that they represented something unique historically. Thanks to the participation of a number of leading artists who were born in the 1920s, such as Sir Neville Marriner, Christoph von Dohnányi and Leon Fleisher, the chronology of the series as a whole means that it is nothing short of a first-hand survey of performance practice during the last 100 years. The breathtaking array of great musical and historical figures that the interviewees encountered during their lives in music reads like a veritable *Who's Who* of Western, and sometimes even Eastern and Middle Eastern, culture. The ways in which artists like Artur Schnabel, Benno Moiseiwitsch, David Oistrakh, Yehudi Menuhin, George Szell, Leopold Stokowski, Zoltán Kodály and Leó Weiner affected the career paths of the interviewees are vividly brought to life in a manner that is both touching and informative. And it is immediately obvious when reading these discussions that each artist firmly believed that he or she was part of a historical performance continuum that allowed the practices of one

INTRODUCTION

generation to be distilled and passed on to the next. Even iconoclasts like Sir Charles Mackerras and Nikolaus Harnoncourt recognised the importance of their musical forebears, and openly discussed the impact that Václav Talich and Herbert von Karajan had on them. It's no exaggeration to say, then, that this book is a vital account of music-making over the last century, and one that is as personal as it is universal.

Throughout the preparation of this book, I have received enthusiastic support from the Royal Academy of Music's Principal, Professor Jonathan Freeman-Attwood, CBE. I would like to thank particularly my research assistants, Dr Margaret Dziekonski, Martyna Wlodarczyk and Dr Abigail Sin, for all their hard work in helping to present the original interviews to the public. I would also like to thank Professor Timothy Jones, Mark Racz, Nicola Mutton, Kathleen Rule, Safi Schlicht, George Chambers, Madeleine Withers, Dominic Grier, Robert Touhy, Murray Richmond, Janet Snowman, Philip White, Dr Adrian Müller, Dr Stephen Mould, Professor Daniel-Ben Pienaar, Oscar De La Roche, John Woollard, Gareth Morgan, Beverly Morgan, Amanda Forbes, Marcus Dods, Andrew Hawkins, Rachael O'Brien, David Gleeson, Andrew Lang, Alex Russell, Barra Liddy, Kirsten Cowie, Henry Kennedy, Francesco Bastanzetti and Peter Quantrill for their unstinting help, advice and kindness. I am grateful to *Gramophone* magazine for kindly allowing us to publish the extended interview with Nikolaus Harnoncourt. But my greatest debt of gratitude is to my wife, Mary, for her unfailing optimism and encouragement. She sustained me throughout this project, and without her support, this book would not have been written.

Raymond Holden, AM
Emeritus Professor of Music
Royal Academy of Music
London, 2023

THE INTERVIEWEES

PART ONE: Conductors

Sir Neville Marriner, CH, CBE (1924–2016): One of the most documented musicians in the history of recording, Sir Neville Marriner shot to fame after founding the Academy of St Martin in the Fields in 1958. Formerly a distinguished orchestral violinist and chamber musician, Sir Neville later went on to lead other major chamber and symphony orchestras in the United States and Germany. But for many viewers and listeners around the world, he will always be remembered affectionately as the conductor of the soundtrack for Miloš Forman's multi-award winning film *Amadeus*.

Sir Charles Mackerras, AC, CH, CBE (1925–2010): The Royal Academy of Music's Conductor Laureate between 2001 and 2010, Sir Charles Mackerras was one of music's great iconoclasts. With a tongue that was nearly as sharp as his incredible intellect, he never suffered fools lightly, but was always generous musically, financially and personally. His revelatory readings of Handel, Mozart, Beethoven and Janáček were acclaimed universally, and his thoughts on late eighteenth- and early nineteenth-century performance practice were both controversial and influential.

Sir Colin Davis, CH, CBE (1927–2013): As the Royal Academy of Music's International Chair of Orchestral Studies between 1986 and

THE INTERVIEWEES

2013, Sir Colin Davis helped to shape the musical lives of three generations of young musicians. Equally at home in both the opera house and the concert hall, he was particularly admired for his readings of Sibelius and Mozart. As a champion of Berlioz's music, he was instrumental in re-establishing its place in today's symphonic and operatic canons, and he was the first English conductor to perform at the Bayreuth Festival.

Christoph von Dohnányi (b. 1929): A musician with a discerning ear for intonation, Christoph von Dohnányi is renowned for the clarity and luminosity of his readings of the central European canon with the Cleveland Orchestra. As an operatic conductor, he was particularly perceptive, and shed new interpretative light on the compositions of Wagner, Strauss, Schoenberg and Berg. He had a particular affinity with the music of Mendelssohn, and his recordings of that composer's works with the Vienna Philharmonic remain benchmarks of hermeneutic excellence.

Nikolaus Harnoncourt (1929–2016): Described as 'a deliberate saboteur, but in a very positive sense' by Trevor Pinnock, Nikolaus Harnoncourt was one of the most impactful and wide-ranging musicians of the late twentieth and early twenty-first centuries. Whether it was Monteverdi, Mozart, Bruckner or Verdi, he was quick to explore new ways when interpreting their works, and was equally quick to challenge established norms. His readings of Bach's music were particularly insightful, and he was one of the first conductors to perform it within a wider historical context.

Sir John Eliot Gardiner, CBE (b. 1943): A probing musician who has explored many once-forgotten musical landscapes, Sir John Eliot Gardiner has given pioneering performances of works by Rameau, Monteverdi and Bach. He has also reassessed the music of Mozart,

Beethoven and Brahms on both period and modern instruments, and brings to his readings of those works an intellectual rigour that is both inspiring and elevating. Not given to compromise, he is a musician with strong artistic opinions, and supports those opinions with great historical and musical élan.

Trevor Pinnock, CBE (b. 1946): Appointed Principal Conductor of the Royal Academy of Music's Chamber Orchestra in 2002, Trevor Pinnock has been tireless in his support of young musicians over the last two decades. An outstanding harpsichordist, chamber musician and conductor, he has worked closely with many of the world's leading orchestras, opera houses and recording companies. With his period orchestra, The English Concert, he created a discography that was staggering in its breadth and content, and as Artistic Director and Principal Conductor of the National Arts Centre Orchestra in Ottawa, he extended his musical boundaries to include the works of his contemporaries.

Sir Mark Elder, CH, CBE (b. 1947): After accepting the Barbirolli Chair of Conducting at the Royal Academy of Music in 2009, Sir Mark Elder has led numerous outstanding performances with its Symphony Orchestra. Particularly admired for his readings of the works of Donizetti, Verdi and Wagner, he was also instrumental in restoring the musical fortunes of the English National Opera and the Hallé Orchestra as their Music Director. Now a household name thanks to his many television appearances, he is arguably today's leading interpreter of the compositions of Elgar, Delius and Vaughan Williams.

Dame Jane Glover, DBE (b. 1949): As the Royal Academy of Music's Mendelssohn Professor of Music from 2014, Dame Jane Glover was able to build on her outstanding achievements as the Academy's Director of

THE INTERVIEWEES

Opera from 2009. Her tenures as Music Director of the London Mozart Players and of Music of the Baroque in Chicago have been particularly fruitful, and she has written critically acclaimed books on Cavalli, Handel and Mozart.

Oliver Knussen, CBE (1952–2018): After being appointed the Royal Academy of Music's Richard Rodney Bennett Professor of Music in 2014, and Professor of Music at the University of London in 2016, Oliver Knussen continued to give generously of his time to students until his early and unexpected death in 2018. Much admired for his readings of Stravinsky's late works as a conductor, he was also an outstanding composer and one of music's most influential and endearing figures.

Semyon Bychkov (b. 1952): Appointed the Royal Academy of Music's Otto Klemperer Chair of Conducting in 2010, Semyon Bychkov has since gone on to conduct the Academy's students at the Duke's Hall and at the Southbank Centre. He is a master interpreter of the works of Strauss and Mahler, and is currently Chief Conductor and Music Director of the Czech Philharmonic. He was a student of the great Russian conducting pedagogue Ilya Musin, and is a strong believer in the ethical power that music exerts. As a conductor, he has a style that is inimitable, and, as an artist, he is constantly in search of new musical truths.

Masaaki Suzuki (b. 1954): As the founder and Music Director of the Bach Collegium Japan, the conductor, organist and harpsichordist Masaaki Suzuki is celebrated for his groundbreaking performances and recordings of J. S. Bach's cantatas, orchestral music and organ works. Amongst his many awards and honours are the Royal Academy of Music's prestigious Bach Prize and the City of Leipzig's Bach Medal. He is an artist who understands fully the social and ethical content of the music that he is performing, and uses his performances to explore the cultural and religious boundaries of that content.

Sian Edwards (b. 1959): Currently Head of Conducting at the Royal Academy of Music, Sian Edwards is a committed interpreter of contemporary music, and has given critically acclaimed performances with Ensemble Modern, the London Sinfonietta and Klangforum Wien. She was the first female conductor to perform at the Royal Opera House, Covent Garden, and was Music Director of the English National Opera.

Vladimir Jurowski (b. 1972): Famed for his innovative approach to programming as Principal Conductor of the London Philharmonic Orchestra, Russian-born Vladimir Jurowski also impressed as an astute and charismatic operatic conductor during his tenure as Music Director of the Glyndebourne Festival Opera. He is Principal Artist of the Orchestra of the Age of Enlightenment, a recipient of the Royal Philharmonic Society's prestigious Gold Medal and Generalmusikdirektor of the Bayerische Staatsoper. His refined interpretations represent an enquiring mind that reflect both his pan-European musical upbringing and his wide international experience as a conductor of the front rank.

Edward Gardner, OBE (b. 1974): As the Royal Academy of Music's Charles Mackerras Chair of Conducting from 2013, Edward Gardner has been unstinting in his support of young musicians. After being appointed Music Director of Glyndebourne Touring Opera in 2004, he went on to take charge of the English National Opera and the Bergen and London Philharmonic Orchestras. His readings of Witold Lutosławski's works are much admired, and he is increasingly celebrated for his interpretations of Elgar's music. He is an artist with considerable charisma, and has been fêted by critics wherever he has performed.

THE INTERVIEWEES

PART TWO: Singers

Dame Janet Baker, CH, DBE (b. 1933): One of the world's most revered and beloved mezzo-sopranos, Dame Janet Baker has a vocal timbre that is both poignant and distinctive. Her recordings with artists such as Sir Adrian Boult, Sir John Barbirolli and Sir Charles Mackerras are benchmarks of excellence that continue to amaze and to inspire, and her reading of Bach's *Matthäus-Passion* with Karl Richter remains as powerful and as moving today as it did when the discs were first heard in 1979.

Dame Gwyneth Jones, DBE (b. 1936): Undoubtedly one of the world's greatest performing artists, Dame Gwyneth Jones has sung nearly all the major Wagner, Verdi and Strauss soprano roles at all the premier opera houses. As a Straussian, she has performed all three leading female roles in both *Der Rosenkavalier* and *Elektra*, and Die Färberin and Die Kaiserin in *Die Frau ohne Schatten*. Her vast discography and filmography is both impressive and comprehensive, and includes performances with many of the greatest conductors from the last sixty years, such as Leonard Bernstein, Pierre Boulez, Carlos Kleiber, Karl Böhm and Sir Colin Davis.

Yvonne Minton, CBE (b. 1938): As an outstanding interpreter of the works of Wagner, Elgar, Mahler, Strauss and Berg, Yvonne Minton worked closely with an array of leading conductors, including Carlos Kleiber, Sir Georg Solti, Benjamin Britten and Pierre Boulez. She was particularly admired for her beauty of sound and her ability to create sensuous vocal colours. As a Mozartian, she performed and recorded with Sir John Pritchard and Otto Klemperer, and as a recording artist, her substantial Decca discography helped to secure her position as one of the truly great mezzo-sopranos of her era.

Dame Anne Evans, DBE (b. 1941): Having started her career as a Wagnerian by singing a Valkyrie, a Rhinemaiden and a Norn for a production of *Der Ring des Nibelungen* at the Grand Théâtre de Genève while still a student, she went on to perform Brünnhilde at the Bayreuth Festival under Daniel Barenboim in the late 1980s and the early 1990s. Equally at home as a Mozartian and as a Verdian, she dazzled critics and audiences with her portrayals of Countess Almaviva in *Le nozze di Figaro* and Violetta in *La traviata*.

Sheila Armstrong (b. 1942): One of the finest concert singers of her generation, Sheila Armstrong was a leading interpreter of works by Bach, Handel, Mendelssohn, Brahms, Vaughan Williams, Orff and Britten. Having started her recording career in her early twenties with Sir John Barbirolli and Leopold Stokowski, she went on to document on disc a wide repertoire with artists such as Leonard Bernstein, Sir Adrian Boult, Daniel Barenboim, André Previn, Carlo Maria Giulini and Karl Richter.

Ryland Davies (b. 1943): Famed for his work as one of opera's leading Mozart tenors, Ryland Davies was also a marvellous Handelian. His recordings of the composer's oratorios with Sir Charles Mackerras were highly praised critically, and his performances of Russian and Czech music were revelatory. During his career, he sang regularly at the Glyndebourne Festival Opera, the Royal Opera House, Covent Garden, the Metropolitan Opera, New York, the Paris Opéra and the San Francisco Opera. He is now a distinguished pedagogue and teaches at the Royal Academy of Music.

Sarah Walker, CBE (b. 1943): Rightly celebrated for her readings of new music, Sarah Walker was also highly regarded for her interpretations of Berlioz, Strauss, Schubert and Schumann. After singing the eponymous

THE INTERVIEWEES

roles in Britten's *Gloriana* and Donizetti's *Maria Stuarda*, she left the critics searching for superlatives. She famously sang in a performance of Beethoven's Ninth Symphony under Leonard Bernstein to mark the fall of the Berlin Wall in 1989, and is now greatly sought after as a vocal pedagogue.

Dame Kiri Te Kanawa, ONZ, CH, DBE, AC (b. 1944): With a voice that is both refined and vibrant, Dame Kiri Te Kanawa is an operatic superstar. After making her debut at the Royal Opera House, Covent Garden, as a Flower Maiden in Wagner's *Parsifal* in 1971, she went on to perform Countess Almaviva in Mozart's *Le nozze di Figaro* to great critical acclaim later that year. Her burnished, lyric-soprano voice meant that she was particularly well suited to the works of Strauss and Verdi. But it was her appearance singing 'Let the Bright Seraphim' from Handel's *Samson* at the wedding of Prince Charles and Lady Diana Spencer in 1981 that will always remain the general public's fondest memory of her.

Dame Felicity Lott, DBE (b. 1947): After making her debut at the English National Opera as Pamina in Mozart's *Die Zauberflöte* in 1975, Dame Felicity Lott went on to become one of the pre-eminent lyric sopranos of her age. As the Countess in Strauss's *Capriccio*, she received rave reviews wherever she performed the role, and her recordings of the composer's *Vier letzte Lieder* are some of the finest on disc. She is especially well regarded as an interpreter of French music and is an outstanding Mozartian.

Dennis O'Neill, CBE (b. 1948): With an Italianate sound that is both exciting and lyrical, Dennis O'Neill was the first choice of conductors such as Zubin Mehta and Giuseppe Sinopoli when casting the works of Verdi. His readings of Bellini's music are also outstanding, and he could be heard regularly at the Royal Opera House, Covent Garden, the

Metropolitan Opera, New York, and the Bayerische Staatsoper throughout his career. He is a committed teacher and is currently Director of the Wales International Academy of Voice.

Dame Ann Murray, DBE (b. 1949): As one of today's leading mezzo-sopranos, Dame Ann Murray has worked with many of the world's greatest conductors, such as Nikolaus Harnoncourt, Sir Charles Mackerras, Herbert von Karajan and Lorin Maazel. Her ability to master difficult *coloratura* material meant that she was an ideal Handelian and that she was naturally suited to many of the demanding roles found in Mozart's early operas. As a Straussian, her readings of Der Komponist in *Ariadne auf Naxos* and Octavian in *Der Rosenkavalier* were hailed universally.

Yvonne Kenny, AM (b. 1950): Very few singers have Yvonne Kenny's breadth of repertoire. Her reading of Aspasia in Mozart's *Mitridate, re di Ponto* under Nikolaus Harnoncourt and her rendering of Romilda in Handel's *Xerxes* under Sir Charles Mackerras were groundbreaking. She is also an outstanding operetta singer, and along with works by Henze, Previn and Bryars, she has sung Berg's challenging *Sieben frühe Lieder* and *Altenberg-Lieder* with the BBC Symphony Orchestra and Sir Andrew Davis. She is now in great demand as a teacher, and is a professor of singing at the Guildhall School of Music & Drama and a Handel and Mozart coach at the Royal Academy of Music.

PART THREE: Instrumentalists

Paul Badura-Skoda (1927–2019): One of the first major international pianists to explore the possibilities that fortepianos had to offer, Paul Badura-Skoda was also one of the most wide-ranging and engaging artists

THE INTERVIEWEES

of his generation. Whether it be as a pianist, fortepianist, accordionist, conductor, writer or editor, he constantly shed new interpretative light on all that he touched. His enthusiasms and intellect were boundless, and he was a true heir to the great Viennese artistic traditions that he held so dear.

Leon Fleisher (1928–2020): Undoubtedly one of the most influential pianists and pedagogues of the late twentieth and early twenty-first centuries, Leon Fleisher was the protégé of Alfred Hertz, Artur Schnabel and George Szell. After having his solo career cut short by the early onset of dystonia, he went on to champion the piano's left-hand repertoire before becoming a distinguished conductor. His keyboard masterclasses were always oversubscribed, and he was unstinting in his support of young artists.

György Pauk (b. 1936): A beneficiary of the great Hungarian school of violin playing through his studies with Ede Zathureczky at the Franz Liszt Academy in Budapest, György Pauk was also a student of Zoltán Kodály and Leó Weiner. After winning major competitions in Europe, he moved to the United Kingdom with the help of Yehudi Menuhin. As a soloist, he worked with Sir John Barbirolli, Sir Georg Solti, Sir Colin Davis and Sir Simon Rattle, and, as a chamber musician, he was a member of the renowned Frankl-Pauk-Kirshbaum Trio. He now teaches at the Royal Academy of Music.

John Williams, AO, OBE (b. 1941): Born in Australia, but largely raised in the United Kingdom, John Williams is the doyen of guitarists. Having had early lessons with his father, Len, he went on to become a pupil of Segovia before taking the guitar world by storm. Along with his friend and colleague Julian Bream, he did much to shape our understanding of the modern classical guitar, and to place it within a broader cultural context.

Steven Isserlis, CBE (b. 1958): A peerless interpreter of Elgar's Cello Concerto and a champion of Schumann's music, Steven Isserlis is without doubt one of today's most sought-after cellists. His readings of Bach's Cello Suites are both provocative and inspiring, and his work as a chamber musician has taken him around the world. He is a published author with Faber & Faber and is a recording artist with Hyperion.

Joanna MacGregor, CBE (b. 1959): As the Royal Academy of Music's Head of Piano, and as a Professor of the University of London, Joanna MacGregor has been an outstanding role model for two generations of young pianists. But her expertise is not confined to the keyboard, as she is also a remarkable festival director, composer, writer, broadcaster and recording artist. Her repertoire is vast and ranges from William Byrd to Thomas Adès.

Maxim Vengerov (b. 1974): As the Royal Academy of Music's Menuhin Professor of Violin between 2008 and 2018, Maxim Vengerov set new standards in string pedagogy. Drawing on his outstanding experiences as a virtuoso violinist and as a violist, he has transformed the playing of many aspiring artists at his public masterclasses. His enquiring mind also drew him to the Baroque violin and conducting, and he now works regularly as a conductor with major orchestras.

James Ehnes, CM, OM (b. 1976): With intonation that is as immaculate as his artistry, James Ehnes is one of today's leading violinists. As the Royal Academy of Music's Viotti Professor of Violin from 2015, he has made a significant contribution to string teaching through his thought-provoking masterclasses, and has inspired many young musicians to think more deeply about their developing artistry. A committed chamber musician and soloist, he has performed throughout the world, and has a discography that includes works from the Baroque to the present day.

THE INTERVIEWEES

PART FOUR: Record Producers, Filmmakers and Arts Administrators

Christopher Raeburn (1928–2009): One of the most sought-after record producers of the late twentieth century, Christopher Raeburn worked with many of the world's greatest conductors, singers and soloists. His activities at Decca set new standards in discographic excellence, and his now iconic recordings from the 1950s and the 1960s sound as fresh and vibrant today as they did sixty years ago. As a scholar, he was particularly active as a Mozartian, and was published by Cambridge University Press, *The Musical Times* and *Music & Letters*.

Sir Humphrey Burton, CBE (b. 1931): After cutting his broadcasting teeth as a trainee studio manager for BBC Radio in 1955, Sir Humphrey Burton moved to BBC Television in 1958. As a member of the production team for *Monitor*, he began to set new standards in music filmmaking. After two periods as the Corporation's Head of Music and Arts, he embarked on a distinguished career as a freelance director from 1970, and worked closely with artists such as Leonard Bernstein, Sir Georg Solti, Herbert von Karajan, Carlos Kleiber and Alfred Brendel.

Tony Palmer (b. 1941): One of the most thought-provoking and exhilarating filmmakers of the last 100 years, Tony Palmer has documented the work of artists from Lennon and Liberace to Handel and Britten. Never scared to be controversial, he has tackled many of the big issues facing musical artists and has been indefatigable in their defence. A true renaissance man, he is also a remarkably influential writer and highly regarded operatic director.

Bruno Monsaingeon (b. 1943): As a distinguished filmmaker, writer and violinist, Bruno Monsaingeon is one of France's great cultural icons. Whether it be Yehudi Menuhin, Glenn Gould, Paul Tortelier, Sviatoslav

Richter or Dietrich Fischer-Dieskau, he extracted the cultural essence of these great figures and brought it to life on film. His polished cinematic documents not only reflect his refined artistic sensibilities, but are also essential viewing for anyone interested in the development of Western art music over the last fifty years.

Roger Wright, CBE (b. 1956): Very few arts administrators have had the same depth of impact as Roger Wright. Surrounded by high-level music-making from his earliest years, he sang as a boy soprano under Sir John Barbirolli. He has been a strong advocate of new music throughout his career, and has done much to promote the works of his contemporary compatriots internationally. Having held senior positions at the British Music Information Centre, the BBC, the Cleveland Orchestra and Deutsche Grammophon, he is now reinvigorating Suffolk's musical life as Chief Executive of Britten Pears Arts, a charitable organisation that was formed after Snape Maltings merged with the Britten Pears Foundation in 2020, some five years after his interview was given.

POSTLUDE: Revisiting Bruckner in Vienna

Christian Thielemann (b. 1959): Appointed the Carl Maria von Weber Visiting Professor of Conducting at the Royal Academy of Music in 2016, Christian Thielemann is one of the last true exponents of the great central-European school of conducting. His special affinity with the music of Bruckner, Strauss and Wagner has resulted in transcendental readings of their works that have commanded the respect of musicians, audiences and critics alike. He is Chief Conductor of both the Sächsische Staatskapelle and the Salzburg Easter Festival, and holds the Order of Merit of the Federal Republic of Germany as well as Leipzig's Richard-Wagner-Preis (Richard Wagner Award).

THE INTERVIEWERS

Jonathan Freeman-Attwood, CBE: After attending the University of Toronto, Jonathan Freeman-Attwood embarked on research at Christ Church, Oxford. He served as the Royal Academy of Music's Dean of Undergraduate Studies between 1991 and 1994, before becoming Vice-Principal and Director of Studies the following year. In 2001, he was conferred Professor of the University of London, and in 2008 he was appointed Principal at the Academy. As a trumpet soloist, he has released twelve critically acclaimed solo albums, the majority of them with Linn Records. He has produced over 250 commercial recordings, many of which have won major awards for some of the world's most prestigious labels, including BIS, Chandos, Warner, Hyperion, Sony, Harmonia Mundi USA, Linn, Channel Classics and Pentatone. Published by *Gramophone*, *The New Grove Dictionary of Music and Musicians* and Cambridge University Press, he can also be heard regularly on BBC Radio. He is a trustee of several educational trusts and arts organisations, including Garsington Opera, where he chairs the Artistic Committee. He was appointed CBE in the 2018 New Year's Honours List.

Raymond Holden, AM: After studies at Sydney, Cologne and London, Raymond Holden has worked as a conductor, writer, broadcaster and lecturer. He has performed with the Philharmonia Orchestra, the Danish Radio Symphony Orchestra, the BBC Symphony Orchestra, the Orchestra of the Emilia Romagna and the New Symphony Orchestra of London. He has been published regularly by ICA, EMI and Warner Classics, the Royal Academy of Music Press, Hans Schneider Verlag

(Vienna) and Oxford, Cambridge and Yale University Presses. He has appeared on BBC Television and Radio, Servus TV (Germany), RAI Television and Radio, ABC Classic FM, 3MBS FM, 2MBS FM, SRF (Switzerland), Vision Australia Radio and Classic FM (South Africa), and has spoken at many of the world's leading festivals, universities, conservatoires and research institutes. He was conferred Professor of the University of London in February 2016 and was appointed Member of the Order of Australia (AM) in the 2019 Australian Queen's Birthday Honours List. He is currently Emeritus Professor of Music at the Royal Academy of Music, London.

Timothy Jones: After studying music at Christ Church, Oxford, Timothy Jones has worked in higher education for the last thirty years. Before being appointed Deputy Principal at the Royal Academy of Music in 2008, he held academic posts at St Peter's College and St Edmund Hall, Oxford, the University of Exeter and the Royal Northern College of Music. He has given many lectures and research seminars at universities and conservatoires throughout the world and has been published by Cambridge University Press. He is committed to public engagement and has spoken at many leading London venues, including the Royal Festival Hall, the Wigmore Hall, the Royal Albert Hall, Kings Place and the Barbican Centre. He can be heard frequently on BBC Radio 3 and he has made five programmes for the NHK television series *First Class*. He was conferred Professor of the University of London in February 2016.

PART ONE

CONDUCTORS

SIR NEVILLE MARRINER
(DAVID JOSEFOWITZ RECITAL HALL, 27 JANUARY 2012)

RAYMOND HOLDEN: It is no exaggeration to say that you've had a wonderful life in music and that you've been acclaimed critically wherever you have performed. What's it like being Sir Neville Marriner?

NEVILLE MARRINER: I have been extraordinarily fortunate to have been surrounded by extremely gifted people my entire life and they made my career for me.

RH: Let's step back in time and start at the beginning, shall we? I believe that you were born in Lincoln in 1924, came from a musical family and were first taught the violin by your father.

NM: My dad was intensely musical and would have loved to have been a professional musician. Being a pianist, and a pretty awful violinist, he took the first possible opportunity to steer me towards music. And as he always needed somebody to play with, I became a violinist from about the age of six. In those days, there was a series of local music competitions that had age restrictions: under six, under ten and so on. Consequently, everybody in Lincoln soon learned what you could and couldn't play. I was fortunate enough to win a couple of these competitions, and by the time that I was thirteen, I'd won the 'Open' category.

PART ONE: CONDUCTORS

If you did something as 'distinguished' as win a local competition back then, you were often invited to play on the radio. So, I then traipsed off to Leeds, which was the nearest centre that had a studio, to perform my competition piece there. My mother was so proud that she kept the two-guinea cheque that I was paid for many years afterwards. It was much better than having a medal!

RH: You then went on to study at the Royal College of Music before moving to the Paris Conservatoire and René Benedetti.

NM: The College was interesting, but slightly distorted because of the war. We had to spend a great deal of time underground, and, for a period, I actually lived in the basement of the Royal College of Music. My first teacher there was W. H. Reed, who was a great friend of Elgar and the Concertmaster of the London Symphony Orchestra. But what struck me first about the College was the fact that everybody was so much better than me. Having been a 'local hero' as a violinist, I suddenly realised that there were another ninety 'local heroes' who had won even better competitions. That was a bit of a shock. Sadly, after only a year with Willy Reed, he died. I then became a student of Albert Sammons, who was one of the few solo violinists that England had at the time. He, like Willy, had a facsimile of Elgar's Violin Concerto and both claimed to have written the work's first page. Regardless of the truth of that claim, there is no doubt that both violinists influenced the composer considerably.

RH: How did Paris compare to London directly after the war?

NM: You could eat very well in Paris for the price of a packet of tea in London during those years. France was poverty stricken. What I found alarming at the Conservatoire was the fact that all the teaching was done in *sol-fa* or *solfège*. This wasn't something that I'd been taught at the College and it slowed me down a little. Benedetti was a *quasi*-virtuoso player, very good, but a completely different kind of influence. But the real reason that I went to France was to experience a foreign country and to expose myself to different European styles of playing.

RH: How much of what you learned there affected your later life as a musician?

NM: Not much. But I did begin to study Bach in earnest while I was in France. Benedetti had me play from his edition of the composer's works, and those that he chose for me wouldn't have been what I would've chosen for myself.

RH: After your studies at the College and the Conservatoire, you taught for a year at Eton College. You then joined the Martin String Quartet as its second violin before founding the Virtuoso String Trio in 1949. As chamber music was clearly of some importance to you from near the start of your career, do you think that every young conductor should work in this genre?

NM: You are very exposed musically as a member of a trio and need to be very stable technically. In other words, you have to be able to play your instrument and to have a good pair of ears. You must also have a generous musical attitude when working with the other two players. A good ensemble isn't simply a group of three random musicians. On reflection, the Martin String Quartet was more influential, as the breadth of its repertoire proved a greater challenge. If you want to be a conductor, being a string player pays dividends.

PART ONE: CONDUCTORS

RH: How vital were these early chamber experiences in determining the 'Marriner sound'?

NM: I am always in search of transparency. I love to see the 'bones' of a piece and to be aware of them. But they then have to be covered with a certain warmth. This approach to sound started with the Trio and then developed with the Quartet, where the sonority had to be a little more ample. Certainly, my taste in music-making was formed during those years.

RH: How long were you active as a chamber musician?

NM: Until I was about thirty years old. But there then comes a time when you have to earn a living, as playing in a string quartet is almost a luxury professionally. Although we were quite busy, and the Quartet was paid forty guineas for a performance, there weren't that many concerts each year. It became necessary for me to have another job, resulting in the Quartet taking a back seat after I joined the London Symphony Orchestra.

RH: Around the time you founded the Virtuoso String Trio, you also established the Jacobean Ensemble with Thurston Dart. Dart was at the cutting edge of historically informed performance practice during the late 1940s and the early 1950s, and influenced many young musicians. What was he like as a man and as a musician, and how did his methods and ideas impact your approach to performance?

NM: We met during the war. After being slightly 'damaged', we ended up in a military hospital together and got to know each other as patients, rather than as musical colleagues. At the time, he was a mathematician with a keen interest in musicology. After playing together as a duo for a couple of years, he went off to Brussels to study musicology. He was a gifted keyboard player and his musicological disciplines were pretty easy to live with. His approach to ornamentation, for example, was something personal, and not something to be observed in exactly the same way every time. It had to serve a purpose and had to relate to the music being played. Unlike the harsh approach of many modern musicologists, he had a very liberal attitude. But, of course, we were complete beginners in the field. He also insisted on taking part in as many performances as possible. When we started the Academy of St Martin in the Fields, he was very keen to do Bach's 'Brandenburg' Concertos. He wanted to perform them quite differently and to alter the instrumentation. He was keen to replace the trumpet with a horn, for example. Even though our approach to these works may have been wrong, he gave us confidence. The sound I made as a violinist also appealed to Dart, as it wasn't too heavy.

RH: Towards the end of the 1940s, you taught for a while at the Royal College of Music and attended summer courses in conducting with Pierre Monteux in the United States.

NM: To be honest, I found teaching at the College to be frustrating. Everything was too safe there. I was keen to encourage a much more virtuosic attitude to string teaching. There was only one really outstanding violinist at the College, and that was Alan Loveday. When I started teaching there, I had a student who was living in East Croydon and who came up to South Kensington every day on the train to attend orchestra, chamber music and other classes. I asked if I could reorganise this particular student's timetable, as I was keen for her to enter the International Tchaikovsky Competition. I was given a dressing-down by the administration and was told that 'we are not that sort of institution'. They made it clear that they didn't approve of competitions and told me

PART ONE: CONDUCTORS

that English string playing revolved around ensembles. I was so frustrated by this attitude that I left the College after only a brief period as a teacher there. What they believed in, and what I wanted to achieve, were two different things.

RH: Did you miss teaching after that?

NM: No. I don't think that I was very good at it, and the College didn't make much of a fuss about me leaving.

RH: And of your experiences with Monteux?

NM: I went to Monteux a little late in life. I had already been a member of the London Symphony Orchestra for a period and had established the Academy by the time I attended his classes in Maine. In fact, Pierre had come to a concert by the Academy, which was something of a rarity at the time, as the orchestra had been founded for fun. Having watched me direct the orchestra from the violin, he said, 'Why don't you stand up like a man and conduct?' I replied that it had simply never occurred to me. He then suggested that I should attend his summer school in America. My journey to the United States was very laborious, with the aeroplane stopping four times before we reached New York. I started out in London and flew by way of Oostende before reaching America some days later. Apparently, the plane didn't meet the necessary safety standards to fly directly across the Atlantic. When I finally did arrive, I then took a bus to Hancock in Maine. I eventually crawled exhausted from the bus and was met by Monteux's assistant, who told me that the Maestro was waiting. My first morning on the course was alarming, as Pierre asked what I had prepared. The answer was simple: 'Nothing.' He then suggested that I might like to try conducting the Mozart symphony that I'd played under him the previous week in London. I did this, but found it very disconcerting, as Monteux sat directly in front of me and observed my every gesture. Nothing was said. I repeated the whole thing, and, again, nothing was said. Somewhat disheartened, I then returned to the little house that he had arranged for the young conductors to stay in. On the third day, the telephone rang at the cottage. It was Monteux. He said, 'It's getting fractionally better, but why do you stick your behind out when you want a *pianissimo*?' That was the first piece of criticism that I had from him, and, to this day, I can still see myself doing it. After that, things became a little more constructive. We talked about music, but not about technique. He assumed that a conductor could master beating patterns in one afternoon. The rest is your own personality. If you are an extrovert, your gestures reflect that trait. He hated what he called 'Romantic' gestures, which were designed to entertain the audience, rather than to help the orchestra. He was quite precise technically, and his movements were always made within a small frame. As far as he was concerned, the baton had to stop somewhere, and beating gestures should never be loose. He believed that every movement should have a centre of gravity. Most of what we might call 'interpretation' was done by Monteux at rehearsals. Of course, a certain amount can be indicated by your hands at the performance, but when it came to saying anything intimate about the music, he did that at the rehearsals. The orchestra then knew exactly what his intentions were, and his job at the concert was to remind the players of them.

RH: Is this a tangible example of Sir John Barbirolli's famous comment that 'a conductor is born and not made'?

NM: You can't learn musicality. Some people have it, and others don't. But you can teach conducting technique. It's easy to embarrass conducting students if you ask them what they meant by a particular gesture, or who they were trying to help with it. Technically speaking, there is quite a lot to be learned at a lesson. Any musical decisions that have to be made, must be made by oneself. It's impossible to be taught how to react to a piece of music.

RH: And, of course, there's the whole question of charisma. Can charisma be taught?

NM: First of all, it's essential to see how a young conductor manages other musicians. I was lucky, as I entered the conducting profession backwards, as it were. By the time I was active with the Academy, I was already familiar with all the musicians with whom I was working. And although we all agreed that the orchestra was to be an utterly democratic institution, it was fine as long as they all did it my way. I was happy to absorb as many observations as they were prepared to share with me, but I was never prepared to sacrifice my own musical intentions. As long as you are able to ensure that everybody's contribution is recognised, a conductor won't lose the players' confidence.

RH: May I ask something impertinent? Were you born or were you made as a conductor?

NM: I think that I was made. While I might have been blessed with a certain amount of talent, my family background meant that I wasn't a born musician. Yet there was never a moment when I thought that I *wasn't* going to be a musician. I never considered any other career. I drifted from those early, local competitions to the Royal College of Music and, later, to Paris. Apart from the war, I had really no other considerations in life.

RH: Nevertheless, the multiplicity of musical disciplines with which you have been associated has been quite remarkable.

NM: War was raging during my student years and orchestras were depleted. Consequently, students at the Royal College of Music were invited to play with the London Symphony and London Philharmonic Orchestras. I remember playing at a three-hour rehearsal with Sir Henry Wood and the London Symphony Orchestra for a Promenade Concert that lasted about four and a half hours. Things were very different in those days. Solomon was the pianist and Wood simply checked his *tempi* before dismissing him at the rehearsal. The soloist was given short shrift and everything was slightly hair-raising. Concerts were often both hilarious and embarrassing. One had to have a fairly hardy temperament to live through those years as an orchestral player. It wasn't until Herbert von Karajan took charge of the Philharmonia Orchestra that things got better.

RH: Which leads me nicely to my next question. When I was looking through the Philharmonia's personnel lists for some of its early seasons at the Royal Festival Hall, I was interested to see your name there. Amongst the concerts that you took part in was a Brahms cycle conducted by Arturo Toscanini in 1952. Renowned for extreme mood shifts, he could be as 'touchy as gunpowder', to quote the great eighteenth-century Irish tenor, Michael Kelly, about Mozart. What was Toscanini really like to work with?

NM: Those concerts were the first that Toscanini gave in London after the war, having worked closely with the BBC Symphony Orchestra during the 1930s. We were all very apprehensive about this engagement. The clarinettist, Frederick Thurston, who was also teaching at the

PART ONE: CONDUCTORS

College at the time, and something of a hardy soul, was so worked up that he was unable to eat lunch before the first rehearsal. We were all a little bit twitchy, but the rehearsals were fine in the end. Toscanini was looked after by Guido Cantelli, who was a protégé of the Maestro. He took care of Toscanini's scores and led him everywhere. When Toscanini was ushered through the doors and onto the stage by Cantelli at the first concert, the whole of the Royal Festival Hall erupted. It was an extraordinary moment, and there had never been anything like it before. Britain had not seen Toscanini for decades and tickets had been snapped up instantly. It felt like a full ten minutes before Cantelli finally settled Toscanini on the podium, and we were terrified that he'd forget the National Anthem. So, when he brought the baton down and the Anthem sounded, there was a general sense of relief in the orchestra that the old boy had got it together and that we were back in the groove. But when he brought the baton down for the second time to start the concert itself, he conducted the First Symphony instead of the 'Tragic' Overture. In a way, it made us feel less anxious knowing that somebody as grand as Toscanini could make such a silly mistake. And if you listen closely to the discs of the performance, you can hear the orchestra wobble slightly at the beginning of the 'Tragic' Overture. Looking back on the series after all these years, it's clear that the entire performance relied completely on Toscanini's personality. It had nothing to do with his baton technique.

RH: Is it true that Cantelli prepared the orchestra for those concerts?

NM: Toscanini was present for all the rehearsals, but Cantelli helped a great deal. The Maestro's English, sight and physicality weren't good by that time. Nevertheless, it was a true Toscanini performance. There's no doubt about that.

RH: You also worked with Wilhelm Furtwängler and Herbert von Karajan.

NM: I worked briefly with Furtwängler when he was recording for EMI during the early 1950s, and remember thinking at the time how much I admired the producer, Walter Legge. As EMI was still using technology that made it impossible to record little more than four minutes at a go, Legge would come out of the recording booth and say to Furtwängler, 'Maestro, I am sorry, but could you just increase the *tempo* a little so that we can fit it onto the disc.' That was quite brave. By the time that Karajan arrived in London everything had become much glossier, as we'd moved on to long-playing records. He came with a great sense of musical importance, and brought to the table a kind of sophistication that we'd never had before in orchestral playing. If you said that you'd played for Karajan in those days, you were automatically considered one step higher on the musical ladder. He transformed the Philharmonia, and it was quite unusual at the time for conductors to rehearse without a score. That, in itself, was impressive. His ear was also quite extraordinary. There were obviously set pieces where you have to tune the double basses, and when that happens, you are already digging deep into the rather thin skin of an orchestra. Yet he managed to control the orchestra so easily, which was helped enormously by his command of English.

RH: Was Legge as influential when he worked with Karajan?

NM: One of the great advantages that the Philharmonia enjoyed in the 1950s was Walter Legge. Not only did he work for EMI, but he also managed the orchestra's concerts. That meant that he was able to choose whether we performed a work in public before recording it, or to do it the other way around. The Philharmonia had the 'double-headed' advantage, so to speak, of giving the same repertoire twice. That was very unusual.

RH: I once read that as leader of the London Symphony Orchestra's second-violin section during the late 1950s and the 1960s, you were less than impressed by the standard of the playing. It seems that this spurred you on to achieve your artistic goals elsewhere, resulting famously in the founding of the Academy of St Martin in the Fields.

NM: During my time with the LSO, we began to compete successfully with the Philharmonia, as we were lucky enough to have engaged Ernest Fleischmann as General Manager. Although he was very young at the time, his ideas were sophisticated and he ensured that the orchestra engaged good conductors. The turning point for the London Symphony Orchestra came when Leopold Stokowski gave a concert with it. The orchestra suddenly realised that it *was* a good orchestra. He turned it into something very special through his own particular form of magic. But there were quite a few of us who had joined the LSO while we were comparatively young and felt that there was not enough individual responsibility required for each concert. We enjoyed the repertoire and the concerts, but we always came away feeling that it wouldn't have mattered if we'd played badly, even though we'd played well. There was no sense of ultimate accountability. Consequently, we wanted to play in a smaller group where everyone had some responsibility, and that eventually led to the founding of the Academy of St Martin in the Fields.

RH: But am I correct in saying that the great Austrian conductor, Josef Krips, did do good things with the LSO during those uncertain days, and to use your phrase, 'Put a Band-Aid on a bleeding orchestra'?

NM: Krips made a huge difference to the London Symphony Orchestra. He came from Vienna, of course, and transformed symphonic music into something more chamber-like. It was Krips who taught us how to play as an ensemble.

RH: Is it possible, then, that Krips's approach was yet another reason for founding the Academy?

NM: I think that might well be true.

RH: And as we've raised the issue of the Academy, what defines it as a group and why does it perform in London so infrequently?

NM: It's true that the orchestra does travel rather a lot. Last night, for example, we played in Budapest and in Vienna the night before. When we started the Academy fifty years ago, we considered ourselves refugees from conductors. We wanted to dominate the music ourselves, to have individual responsibility and to be able to hear each other play. For the first couple of years, we used to meet in Kensington and play for fun. At the time, John Churchill was our keyboard player, and it was he who said, 'We have to give a concert.' We were taken a little aback by this, as we didn't give concerts and only met for pleasure. He then mentioned that the church where he worked would like to have some music, which, of course, was St Martin-in-the-Fields. In the audience for our first concert was an Australian lady named Louise Dyer. At the end of the performance, this extraordinary woman mentioned to us that she had a publishing company in Paris called Éditions de l'Oiseau-Lyre and wondered if we would consider making some records. We couldn't believe our ears when she offered us £5 each for every disc we were to make, a considerable sum in those days. When our recordings did appear,

PART ONE: CONDUCTORS

they were incredibly well received. Quite ridiculous, really. Nevertheless, our discs attracted attention, and that's how the Academy started.

RH: You have famously described the works that you first recorded as being written by those 'Italian ice-cream merchants – Manfredini, Corelli, and so on.'

NM: These were pieces that you wouldn't normally expect to play, but suited our ensemble. And it was with these works that we began to examine closely the sound we actually wanted to make as a group. These compositions gave us ample opportunity to make those decisions and were the basis for our repertoire during those early years. After later documenting the music of Bach, Handel and Corelli, record companies were keen for us to perform Mozart. This meant that we had to add two oboes and a couple of horns. Then came Haydn, Beethoven, Schubert and Schumann. Things became bigger and bigger, and before we knew where we were, we were in the twentieth century. This meant that the Academy changed radically because of its expanding repertoire. As far as playing in London is concerned, we never had a sponsor until last year, which was fifty years too late. But it should never be forgotten, that if you want to present concerts, they need to be rehearsed properly. And the only reason that we fell out with the BBC was because it offered us a Promenade Concert that was to include a new work by Sir Peter Maxwell Davies. Max's piece required a minimum of ten rehearsals, but the Corporation was only prepared to pay for three. We explained that it wasn't possible for us to play even a conventional programme on three rehearsals, let alone one that was to include such a difficult work. While I recall that we did give a summer event at the Royal Festival Hall, there's not really a conveniently sized hall in London that suits an orchestra like the Academy.

RH: Did you ever consider applying for government subsidy?

NM: I was always concerned that those who controlled that type of funding would begin to get their sticky little fingers on the repertoire, personnel and related matters. We resisted that, and thanks to the large number of recordings that we made, there was a time when the Academy *almost* had money. But then we blew it by attempting to build our own concert hall. We managed to run through nearly all the money on the plans and the models alone.

RH: Amongst the 'Italian ice-cream merchants' whom I mentioned earlier was Arcangelo Corelli. For your famous recording of his *Concerti grossi*, Op. 6, you looked to some of the original sources for its preparation. Amongst the musicians involved in that recording were Christopher Hogwood and Trevor Pinnock. Could you tell me a little about that set and some of your recollections of the preparatory process?

NM: Christopher and Trevor were really very tolerant. They'd both come from a background that had a much harder attitude towards early music than me, or any of us, for that matter. By the time of those discs, the Academy had already developed its own style, and we were used to agreeing amongst ourselves the sort of sounds that we wanted to make. I remember Christopher suffering badly, as he had a more refined stylistic attitude towards the music than we did. Trevor was very kind and went along with what we were doing. Nevertheless, they both added something to the Academy's performances, and we were very grateful for their contributions. In fact, the entire history of the orchestra was built on the input of artists like Trevor and Christopher.

PART ONE: CONDUCTORS

RH: As the repertoire that we have just been discussing is now firmly the province of period instrument performers, were you ever tempted to explore early instruments, and, if so, how might that have affected the 'Marriner sound'?

NM: We did give a couple of concerts using early instruments, but the sound that I wanted was quite difficult to achieve with them. Then there were the players themselves. In those days, instrumentalists couldn't make a living by just playing early music. You can't play a string quartet in the morning and early music in the afternoon. The difference is too great. And as I've always needed a certain degree of virtuosity, we decided to compromise. When it came to a set like that of Corelli's *Concerti grossi*, the amount of preparation necessary was not sustainable if early instruments were involved, and the detail required in making the material ready was too much.

RH: Today, it's common to mix and match instruments from different periods within a single ensemble. It's not unusual, for example, to hear period timpani and trumpets playing alongside modern woodwind. What are your thoughts on this approach?

NM: I like to use period timpani, but I'm less fond of period trumpets. I once discussed the latter with a period brass player, who spoke glowingly of them. In reality, these early trumpets now all have little gadgets to help correct their intonation, otherwise the sound would be unbearable. What offends me most about these instruments is their poor intonation. When it comes to early string instruments, their sound quality doesn't suit me. I quickly lost interest in them, other than from an academic standpoint.

RH: With the sound of the Baroque still ringing in listeners' ears, you then turned your attention to early twentieth-century music. The result was a plethora of exceptional recordings of works by Stravinsky, Walton, Vaughan Williams, Britten and others. I found some of these truly breathtaking, and remember being bowled over as a schoolboy by the staggering virtuosity of the Academy's playing in Stravinsky's 'Pulcinella' Suite.

NM: I had a particular admiration for Stravinsky's neo-classicism, which suited the Academy stylistically. We also had the chance to work on some of Stravinsky's other music with the composer's protégé, Robert Craft. When Stravinsky attended one of Craft's rehearsals with us, he would make conducting gestures behind Craft's back. We had two sets of ideas for the price of one!

RH: Around that time, you also recorded an iconic set of Mozart's piano concertos with Alfred Brendel.

NM: It could be argued that Alfred has had two careers. Having started in Vienna without much distinction, where he made a series of discs for Vox, he arrived in London, where his unique style was recognised and appreciated almost instantly. One of the reasons that working with Alfred was so interesting was his inflexibility. I immediately wondered how we could fit the orchestra around him. For a long time, he wouldn't utter a word about the orchestral playing. We were never sure whether he liked it or disliked it, or whether he thought that it was too loud or too soft. When we started making recordings together, we had a sound engineer called Volker Straus, who believed that whatever was happening in the orchestra was subordinate to the piano part. Volker thought that the piano should be heard at all times, even when playing unimportant arpeggiated accompanying material. He used to drive me crazy. It took us ten years to record these concertos, as Alfred rarely played the earlier ones. He mainly performed the mature concertos in public. Nevertheless, he did have a big influence on how the Academy played Mozart. His various interpretative foibles transferred themselves to the orchestra, and although we hate to admit it, I once remember saying to Alfred that his Mozart style became our Mozart style.

RH: When I listen to your discs, there is a clear difference between how the Academy sounds when it was recorded by l'Oiseau-Lyre than when it was documented by either Argo or Philips. Was that simply down to house style?

NM: In some ways, I think it was. Someone like Alfred, who's had a great career, and who has great charisma, will come with his own piano and his own piano technician. If a recording company wants to make discs with him, it has to accept that he'll bring along his own people. An orchestra, on the other hand, is always at the mercy of a producer. If we are lucky, we might have the same person twice. This was largely true of our recordings for Philips, where our producer was Eric Smith. He was fabulous, and was always keen to accommodate everything we asked for. And while we have had some indifferent experiences over the years, there's never been an occasion where we've failed to secure something at a session. There was one famous occasion when we tried to record Strauss's *Metamorphosen*. Although it's one of my favourite pieces, the work is massive and can easily get lost in performance due to its construction. Having spent a whole day trying to record it, but getting nowhere, we decided to go out and have a very, very good meal. After we returned rather late, we sat down and started to play. The character of the piece fell into place and it came together instantly. The trouble with recording in this way was that we began to think that we should do it every time!

RH: Your discs of Schubert's symphonies with the Academy are also fascinating, particularly as they include Brian Newbould's completions of the Seventh, Tenth and 'Unfinished' Symphonies. How did this historically important set come about, and have you ever performed those completions in the concert hall?

NM: It was Brian's idea to record the works and he suggested them to Eric Smith. As it happens, I have just been asked by the orchestra in Weimar to give Brian's 'finished' 'Unfinished', but that's unusual, as most orchestras can be a bit sniffy when it comes to this type of completion. Choosing repertoire can be quite challenging these days, and programming has become something of an art. Even though I might be asked to do a particular work, I will often propose one of Brian's completions. Nevertheless, you have to be aware of local tastes and who your programme is aimed at. You must always be alert to who your audience is and what they want to hear.

RH: In those completions, how much is Newbould and how much is Schubert?

NM: Brian added very little, and most of his contribution was editorial.

RH: Amongst your very impressive discography, there are some truly wonderful recordings of operas by Mozart and Rossini. When did you become involved with opera, and what first attracted you to this corner of the repertoire?

PART ONE: CONDUCTORS

NM: My interest in opera really began when the Royal Northern College of Music invited me to conduct a student performance of Puccini's *La bohème*. I'd never worked in an opera house before and knew very little about the operatic repertoire, other than what I'd heard as an audience member. I was soon captivated by the piece and was fortunate enough to have every conductor's ideal cast. As Puccini's characters are between eighteen and twenty-five years old, each of the singers was the right age. Most of the time, you have to use older singers who don't look the part. The kids at the Northern were really fabulous. Not great voices, but alive to the drama. The only thing they couldn't do was die. The last scene was by far the most difficult, as they had no idea how to die decently. Musically, it was a completely new experience for me and I was drawn into it. I was then asked to record some operas, including those you mentioned by Mozart and Rossini. But working in the professional theatre was never a happy experience. The first company I performed with was the Los Angeles Opera for which I conducted Rossini's *La Cenerentola*. The problem with such theatres is that the director often arrives four weeks before the conductor and decides upon all the action. This can be incredibly irritating. On one occasion, I threatened to leave because of this. After the third day of a particular production, I said that I was going home. In the end, I decided to stick it out, but it was not a success. I did conduct Mozart's *Il re pastore* at Salzburg in 1989 and enjoyed that enormously.

RH: Dame Kiri Te Kanawa has described you as a 'singer's conductor', and one of her favourite collaborators. What defines a 'singer's conductor'?

NM: Generally speaking, it's one who allows the singers to have their own way. Perhaps an advantage of having been a string player is that I am very aware of how the music should be shaped. Although I don't breathe like a wind-player, I do breathe with the phrase. And while I am always conscious of what a singer's 'instrument' has to offer, I sometimes have to make compromises that are unnecessary when working with a stringed instrument. But, best of all, I am able to engage with the vocal literature. It's extraordinary.

RH: In the 1980s, you conducted the soundtrack for Miloš Forman's film *Amadeus*. How did you become involved in the project, who selected the music and was the success of that movie the reason you agreed to conduct the soundtrack for Forman's next film, *Valmont*?

NM: It all came about because Peter Shaffer, the author of the original stage version of *Amadeus*, had been chatting to Isaac Stern in America. Isaac then very kindly said to Peter, 'Why don't you talk to Neville?' I then met with Peter, Miloš Forman and the movie's producer, Saul Zaentz, at New York airport to discuss the possibility of working with them. My only precondition was that we shouldn't do anything in Hollywood. I was keen that Mozart shouldn't be placed anywhere else but Europe. They agreed with this and later visited me at my house in Devon to discuss which works should be used. In the original play, there was only about six minutes of music, but they wanted just over an hour of music in the film. We then had a very jolly weekend deciding on what should be included before reconvening at Abbey Road Studios a few months later to record our selection. Everything for the film was set down within a week. Miloš then went off to Prague and shot the film. Normally, that process is the other way around. Usually, the movie is made first and the music is added afterwards. This time, Miloš shot the film around the music, and we only had to make two corrections to the soundtrack afterwards. Sadly, when we came to

PART ONE: CONDUCTORS

Valmont, the music wasn't very good. In fact, it's pretty crummy. And if a young conductor is ever asked to conduct for a film, they should always insist on the approach that we adopted for *Amadeus*. They will then get their own way.

RH: As you are one of the most recorded musicians in history, let's turn to the nuts and bolts of the recording process for a moment. Do you involve yourself heavily in the production and editing processes like Glenn Gould and Herbert von Karajan, or are you more like George Szell, who considered recordings a tedious means to a glorious end?

NM: I enjoy recording. One of the good things about it is that you can record, say, ten minutes of music, and the whole orchestra can go into the booth and hear the result. Not only can you learn so much about yourself as a conductor, but each of the players can also learn a great deal about themselves as musicians. By the time that you make the final recording, you are giving a concert, and not just playing to the red light. This makes a recording work for me. Glenn Gould contacted me when I was conducting the Cleveland Orchestra. He suggested that we should record all of Beethoven's piano concertos together before he turned fifty. I then popped over to Toronto to see him – it was 6 o'clock in the evening and he was eating breakfast in his dressing gown – to discuss how we could do this. By about midnight, we came to the conclusion that he could only use about two and a half minutes' worth of material from every hour spent in the studio. I pointed out that the cost of the orchestra would be very expensive, if we adopted his very demanding approach. Before we eventually separated, he came up with the brilliant idea of sending me recordings of the solo material so that I could add the orchestral accompaniment afterwards. I found this suggestion very exciting, but he died before completing his part.

RH: Do you think that your passion for recording has something to do with your age, and the fact that you lived through the recording industry's ever-changing landscape during the immediate post-war years?

NM: Having been lucky enough to start making records when they were still 78rpm discs, I had the opportunity to revisit the repertoire for a second and third time as each new technological change occurred. I've made hundreds of recordings, and the act of recording has literally sustained my own career, and that of the Academy, for at least thirty years. The size of the recording industry has diminished over recent years, which makes it difficult for young artists to make an impact. Recordings are important musical visiting cards for aspiring musicians that can be sent around the world in advance. This is now impossible unless you have a lot of money. In September, we have a month set aside to make three recordings that have been sponsored entirely privately. Nevertheless, this aspect of the music profession has become very difficult and is completely different from when I started out as a young violinist.

RH: As we have spent time talking about your work with the Academy of St Martin in the Fields, let's turn to some of the other orchestras that you've led. First, let's chat a little about the Los Angeles Chamber Orchestra, which you conducted from 1969 to 1978. Founded by the cellist James Arkatov, the LACO was established to allow 'conservatory-trained players to balance studio work and teaching with pure artistic collaboration at the highest level.' What challenges did this mission statement present to you, and how did its rather specific aim affect your approach as the orchestra's Music Director?

NM: Having ignored their letters for a long time, I thought that I would investigate the orchestra. And when I did, it was extraordinary. Most of the violin section was comprised of musicians who had studied with Jascha Heifetz. The cello section were students of Gregor Piatigorsky, and the wind and brass players were all musicians from the major film studios. They were all virtuosi. But that didn't automatically mean it was a great orchestra. When you have a congregation of players who *are* so strong, it is often difficult to turn them into an ensemble.

RH: Karajan had a similar experience when he first took over the Philharmonia Orchestra. He was dismayed that the whole of the first violin section was comprised of orchestral leaders, or aspiring leaders. Barbirolli had also pointed out some years earlier that a great soloist is not necessarily a great orchestral player.

NM: You know it's a funny thing that some violin soloists enjoy playing in the section again. But if you get too many of them, the sound can be a little bit abrasive. Nevertheless, they were a remarkable lot in Hollywood, and I remained with the orchestra for nearly ten years. They were quite brilliant, but not very good with early music.

RH: Having completed a decade in Los Angeles, you moved east to take charge of the Minnesota Orchestra in 1979. What were some of the advantages and disadvantages of conducting an orchestra in America's Midwest, and how did its working practices compare to those of London orchestras?

NM: Minneapolis has always had a pretty good reputation when it comes to music and I enjoyed working with the Minnesota Orchestra. That said, the restrictions imposed by the unions there made me feel a little uncomfortable. Take touring, for example. If you were on tour, you were not allowed to rehearse the orchestra. Not even a seating rehearsal.

When I was finally granted a fifteen-minute seating rehearsal in 'important cities', I had to negotiate this with a committee of players. They then demanded to know who should decide which cities were important. Unsurprisingly, it turned out to be the same committee. When we made recordings, players had to have a twenty-minute rest-break for each hour worked. That reduced a three-hour session to two hours. I remember rehearsing Beethoven's Violin Concerto with Isaac Stern in Chicago, and just as we were about to begin the last movement, a hand reached forward from the orchestra to remind me that time was up. We simply had to stop.

RH: While still at the head of the Minnesota Orchestra, you also took charge of the Radio-Sinfonieorchester Stuttgart des SWR. Sir John Barbirolli famously rejected an offer to become Principal Conductor of the BBC Symphony Orchestra, as he had 'no intention of programming by committee.' Similarly, Sir Colin Davis once lamented the unfortunate run-ins he had with the management of the Symphonieorchester des Bayerischen Rundfunks. What are some of your memories of your time at Stuttgart, and how did you cope with the inevitable peccadillos that seem to beset large broadcasting organisations?

NM: Working for a German broadcasting organisation is very much the same as working for the BBC. In the case of the Radio-Sinfonieorchester Stuttgart, I had one administrator there whose admiration for England was so intense that we even discussed cricket. I was there for nearly six years, and although it was a long stint, it was fun. That said, I used to get slightly irritated because of the lavish way that they used their players. For every wind section, we had two principals. Of course, we had only one principal playing at a time, but if that principal fell ill, I wasn't allowed to use the other tenured principal: we had to 'import' one from another orchestra. We wasted masses of money by bringing in players from Berlin, Munich and elsewhere. I found this approach untenable.

RH: Sir John Barbirolli also performed with the Radio-Sinfonieorchester Stuttgart and gave his last performance as a Mahlerian with it in 1970. But the music of Mahler is not something with which you are normally associated. Why is that?

NM: I'm unable to take Mahler very seriously. While I have recorded a couple of his symphonies, and given a number of them in the concert hall, I've always questioned whether or not I truly believe in them. I often question the emotions that he is trying to generate and am not sure if his works are simply a kind of 'film' music. That said, I really did enjoy playing his symphonies as an orchestral musician. But when I stood up and tried to transmit these same emotions, I was concerned that I might've been doing it slightly tongue-in-cheek, and that I was not being absolutely genuine.

RH: I remember chatting some years ago about Mahler to the great German conductor Wolfgang Sawallisch, who said to me that he didn't understand why this strange man was always 'wailing on a mountain'.

NM: If you really want to feel indulgent, it's certainly possible to perform Mahler. There's that chap in America who treats himself every year by conducting a concert of the composer's music. Danny Kaye did something similar, and could also have hacked his way through a Mahler symphony. Whether or not you are doing justice to the music is another thing. But then there is also so much contemporary music that I don't understand. Perhaps I should try harder.

SIR CHARLES MACKERRAS
(DAVID JOSEFOWITZ RECITAL HALL, 9 JANUARY 2009)

RAYMOND HOLDEN: As a passionate and committed interpreter of Handel's music, you've done much to shape our understanding of how his works should be performed. Pivotal to that process was your now famous first recording of his *Music for the Royal Fireworks*. Incredibly, you made that disc for Pye at a session that began at 11pm on 13 April 1959, and that finished at 2.30am on 14 April, the bicentenary of the composer's death. How did that recording come about, and why has it proved so influential?

CHARLES MACKERRAS: Although Handel's *Fireworks Music* was quite well-known up to that time, it was only really known in Sir Hamilton Harty's arrangement of it for the modern symphony orchestra. While I knew what Handel's original score looked like, I only learned much later that it was actually to be played by a huge wind-band that consisted of twenty-four oboes, twelve bassoons, several contrabassoons, nine trumpets, nine horns and three timpanists. Along with these, Handel also wrote 'With the Side Drum' in the fourth movement, the '*La Réjouissance*'. In the composer's score, it's marked clearly that the movement should be played the first time by the trumpets and side drums, but without the horns, the second time by the oboes and horns, but without the trumpets, and, finally, by the whole ensemble. As nobody had heard it in that combination since the composer's time, I was

PART ONE: CONDUCTORS

frightened as to how the whole thing might sound, and was extremely relieved when it sounded so good on disc. Of course, to find a venue to accommodate such a large ensemble for the recording was quite a job. While there were certainly sufficient oboists in London, I knew that it would be almost impossible to bring them all together during normal working hours. We decided, therefore, that we would have to make the recording during the middle of the night. As we needed the disc to be ready for a big party to be hosted by Pye at the Battersea Festival Gardens on 14 April to celebrate the composer's bicentenary, the recording was edited that day and played as planned. To show how the music profession in London has grown and changed since that time, I recorded the *Fireworks Music* again some twenty years later at Abbey Road Studios. As there were sufficient oboists in London who were free of their normal commitments, and were willing to come along on a Sunday afternoon, it was no longer necessary to record it in the middle of the night. But I still find it remarkable that all the finest players were assembled together for the first recording, which included the great Evelyn Barbirolli, who played in the second chair between Terence MacDonagh and Sidney Sutcliffe. It was really a remarkable sight and sound.

RH: Let's chat a little about your early experiences as a musician. What was Australia like musically during the 1930s and the 1940s, and how would you describe Sydney's cultural environment during those years?

CM: The orchestra in Sydney was made permanent by the Australian Broadcasting Commission in 1932, and was an amalgam of first-class and second-rate players. So, it took some time before it became a good orchestra. The existing permanent radio orchestra had to be augmented by players who were professional, but who were mainly teachers or military bandsmen. Even though there had been visits from touring companies from abroad, such as those led by Dame Nellie Melba and others, there was practically no opera in Sydney. And except for some student performances at the New South Wales State Conservatorium of Music during my student years, there was literally no opera at all during my childhood. I remember playing works like Bizet's *Carmen* and Nicolai's *Die lustigen Weiber von Windsor* for the first time at the Conservatorium. These were considered suitable for students to perform. The Director of the Conservatorium at the time was Dr Edgar Bainton, an Englishman and a very dry old stick. He was my composition teacher for a period, but I never really got on with him, as he was something of an intellectual and quite forbidding. As a composer, he wrote in a style that was completely at odds with his character. He composed a couple of marvellous symphonies and a wonderful opera called *The Pearl Tree*, which is based on an Indian subject and has music that is very reminiscent of Delius.

RH: Given that Sydney was so far off the musical beaten track during your youth, it's surprising how many renowned artists performed there. Amongst the great conductors who travelled to Australia were Eugene Ormandy, Boyd Neel, Sir Thomas Beecham and Sir Malcolm Sargent.

CM: As a teenager, I remember hearing Richard Tauber and Lotte Lehmann, both in recital and with orchestra. It must have been very pleasant for them to have what was essentially a long holiday, as everybody travelled to Sydney by ship in those days. I also heard Sir Hamilton Harty, who began his first concert with his arrangement of Handel's *Water Music*, and George Szell, a truly tremendous experience. He conducted Walton's First Symphony, which was completely new at the time.

RH: As a young, professional musician in Sydney, you were active in a variety of disciplines. Along with your duties as Principal Oboe of the

PART ONE: CONDUCTORS

Sydney Symphony Orchestra, you were appointed the Conservatorium's professor of oboe at the age of nineteen and were engaged commercially as a composer and as an arranger.

CM: As many of my contemporaries had gone to war, and as I was too young to join up, I was able to start work as a professional musician at the age of fifteen. Along with the ABC orchestras, I played for Gilbert and Sullivan operettas, which were all the rage in Sydney and Melbourne at the time. I also played for a commercial radio station, which had on its books a famous comedian called Jack Davey, who was much loved by the Australian public. The station had a dance band, and I was soon engaged by the producers to make arrangements for it. That was my first attempt at orchestrating. I also composed some film music, but was never very good as a composer. I was not sufficiently imaginative. I wrote what the Germans call '*Kapellmeistermusik*': music that's written by conductors who have been exposed to the works of great composers and who attempt to imitate them.

RH: But, here, you are being characteristically modest, as examples of your film music can still be heard, such as the score for *The Rats of Tobruk*.

CM: That's true, but I didn't write it all. And like most film music of the time, it's rather unoriginal.

RH: As a member of the Sydney Symphony Orchestra during the 1940s, you played under Sir Eugene Goossens, whose time in Australia was blighted by a sex scandal.

CM: I'd already been appointed Principal Oboe of the Sydney Symphony Orchestra by the time Goossens arrived. I was particularly interested in him because of his brother, Léon, the famous oboist, who was fêted for his performances of Bach's *obbligati* and who had been a distinguished member of the London Philharmonic Orchestra. Although I idolised Léon for a time, I later stopped playing in his style. I found Eugene rather cold and reserved as a conductor. This was strange when you consider the music that he composed and the works that he loved and performed well. During his first visit to Sydney, which was the only time that I played under him, he performed Ravel's *Daphnis et Chloé*. This was new to the local orchestra, as it previously lacked an alto flute. But when Goossens eventually did perform it, the flute solo was played beautifully by Neville Amadio, an unforgettable memory. Goossens also conducted the Australian premiere of Stravinsky's *Le sacre du printemps*. Like Sir Adrian Boult, Goossens used a huge baton that had an equally huge handle. His beat seemed to go left, right, up and down with the flick of his wrist. I thought that playing such a rhythmically complex score like *Sacre* would be difficult with him due to his conducting style. In fact, he was perfectly suited to it, and we managed the piece very well. Of course, the work is now part of the repertoire of every Australian orchestra and they're all familiar with it.

RH: Is it true that some video footage exists of you playing the oboe under Goossens?

CM: Yes, there is. It's footage of me playing the oboe for a performance of Tchaikovsky's '*Pathétique*' Symphony under Goossens at Sydney Town Hall. This short, two-minute clip, where the oboes have little to do, can now be seen as part of a film documenting the events that led up to Goossens's removal as conductor of the Sydney Symphony Orchestra and as Director of the New South Wales State

PART ONE: CONDUCTORS

Conservatorium of Music. The scandal was to do with black magic, Satanism and so on, but was not what you would call pornography by today's standards. It's easy to forget that Goossens did some marvellous things with the Conservatorium and the Symphony Orchestra, and was the inspiration behind the building of the Sydney Opera House. But by the time that I'd returned home as a 'distinguished guest conductor from overseas', a term used by the ABC for musicians who were ex-patriot Australians, Goossens had unfortunately left. It's no exaggeration to say that the effect he had on Sydney's musical scene was absolutely immense, and that the orchestra had improved hugely thanks to him.

RH: When you arrived in Britain in 1947, you must have experienced something of a culture shock.

CM: When I left to go abroad that year, my replacement in the Sydney Symphony Orchestra was a marvellous oboist called Horace Green, who'd also played cor anglais in the London Philharmonic. At that time, Australia was not particularly proud of its culture and tried to be as British as possible. That has since changed, and, today, Australians are all trying to be as Australian as possible. The term for that is 'Ocker', an expression that represents the vulgar Australian. During my time, everything that came out of Britain was considered to be perfect. That was also true for anything that came from America, where I happened to be born. My father was an electrical engineer, and had received a bursary to study at the headquarters of General Electric in Schenectady, New York. But soon after completing his year there, my father travelled with my mother and me to England. At that time, Australians always used to refer to that as 'going home', even if they'd never been there. Do you remember that as a fellow Australian?

RH: Vividly. And although you and I are some thirty years apart in age, we even had similar school uniforms: ones that were in keeping with the 'old country'.

CM: That's true. They were made from the thickest wool and had to be worn no matter how sweltering the day was. Everything was so European that the spirit of Christmas was Santa Claus dressed for the snowiest of conditions with reindeers at the ready. Regardless of the extreme summer heat in Australia, Christmas was always considered a cold, rather than a hot, weather celebration. These days, Australians eat cold plum pudding and cold turkey for Christmas dinner. But British traditions went on for a long, long time, with the love of all things British even being extended to the arts. This meant that the majority of Australian musicians studied in the United Kingdom until the outbreak of war. After the war started, the cultural life of Australia was transformed to some extent, due to the arrival of Jewish musicians escaping from Nazi Germany. Some of these refugees had travelled by way of Vladivostok and later became quite famous in Australia. They founded, amongst other things, Musica Viva, which, at one time, was the largest employer of musicians in the world.

RH: But what of Britain in 1947?

CM: After I arrived in the United Kingdom, I was appointed Second Oboe of the Sadler's Wells Opera Orchestra, a job that also gave me a chance to do some backstage conducting. In those days, backstage conducting meant looking through a hole in the scenery, and relaying the beat to the off-stage musicians from the main conductor. The end of the first act of *Tosca* is a good example. Here the bells get going, choruses sing and cannons bang every few bars. As the cannon tells of the prison escape from the Castel Sant'Angelo, the ensemble for the whole scene rested on me. That was a particularly tricky job, as I was playing the cor anglais in the pit directly before going backstage. These days, they use television monitors. And as the singer who performed the role of Scarpia never sang it completely in time, but with a great deal of *rubato*, I once brought the cannon in too early.

RH: Shortly after arriving in London, you won a scholarship to study in Prague, where you came under the influence of the great Czech conductor Václav Talich. How did that come about?

CM: I was in a café in South Kensington one day having a cup of tea. I'd just bought a score in the local music shop of what is now known to be Dvořák's Seventh Symphony, which at the time was called the Second Symphony. I was sitting in the café looking at the miniature score that I'd just purchased when a man sitting opposite me said, 'Ah! I see you are studying the music of my country.' I started a conversation with him and told him that my ambition was to become a conductor. He then said, 'I've just come from a meeting of the British Council at which was discussed a scheme whereby six British students should be sent to Czechoslovakia to study, and six from there should be sent to study in Britain.' I should mention here that those scholarships were not restricted simply to music, but were open to all subjects. I applied for one, but read a little later that I'd not made a very good impression. Nevertheless, I still got the scholarship, after which I asked my now wife, Judy, to marry me. I then learned to my horror that I wasn't allowed to take her with me to Czechoslovakia. The scholarship was restricted to living expenses, and what I didn't know was that, unlike in British conservatoires and other Western schools of music, it wasn't possible to pay fees. Everything was free, so to speak. The scholarship paid £300 for the whole year, and it was solely for accommodation and subsistence: a reasonable sum for a student in those days. The British Council said to me that it was impossible to study and to keep a wife on that amount, so they forbade me from taking Judy. She did come, however, and joined the music academy in Prague under her maiden name.

After arriving in Czechoslovakia, I was told in no uncertain terms that it was impossible for me to study with such a distinguished conductor as Václav Talich. He'd been accused of collaborating with the Nazis during the occupation, but had just been 'rehabilitated' by the communists, even though they were not yet in power. Having overcome those accusations, he'd been appointed Artistic Director of the National Theatre and had formed a chamber orchestra. As all the players in that orchestra were marvellous but inexperienced, he scheduled a huge number of rehearsals. This meant that he was really able to train the musicians, and to make the orchestra into something that was completely outstanding. While I was first told that Talich had no time to teach me, he himself suggested that I should attend as many of his rehearsals as possible. Along with a number of other students, I made it a point of going every afternoon to hear him rehearse his chamber orchestra. To this day, I still have the notes that I took during those sessions. He was a tremendous philosopher as a conductor, and stressed the inner meaning of the music a great deal. He also discussed whether an up-bow or a down-bow was needed. As nobody was watching the clock, he had time to practise his approach, and the results were simply marvellous.

Another of our first experiences in Prague involved a young oboist who was Associate Principal of the Czech Philharmonic. He'd gone to Britain to study with Léon Goossens, and we'd met him while he was in London. He said, 'One thing that you must see while you are here in Prague is *Kát'a Kabanová* by Janáček.' I'd only heard of Janáček through playing his wind sextet, *Mládí*, and had no idea that he was such a great dramatic composer. When I heard the opening bars of *Kát'a* with its slow 6/4 chord in B flat minor swelling forth from the depths of the orchestra for the first time, I was won over.

RH: You then went on to 'discover' the two 'lost' interludes from the opera some years later.

CM: By the time we left Czechoslovakia at the end of the scholarship, the communists had taken over and we didn't go back for about twelve years. We saw many of our friends treated very badly with some even being gaoled. Talich was also treated very badly by the communists, and his chamber orchestra was threatened with 'liquidation'. It was told to get rid of him, or face being closed down. Rather than disband, the orchestra just pretended to get rid of Talich. It then invited him to rehearse them in private, which he did. He treated these rehearsals as if he were preparing the orchestra for a concert, and it then gave the performance without him. Having been sufficiently schooled by Talich, the orchestra needed no conductor; it was truly remarkable. There's still an orchestra in Prague called 'The Orchestra without a Conductor', although it occasionally plays with one, namely me.

When I did finally return to Czechoslovakia for a second time, it was not as a conductor, but as a researcher. There was, and still is, a very interesting museum of Janáček's music at Brno, where all of his autographs are held. While I was studying the original score of the *Sinfonietta* there, I noticed some writing in Janáček's hand on the back of a couple of pages that didn't belong to the piece. I then realised that these were the two 'missing' interludes from *Kát'a*: he had composed these to mask some longer scene changes for a production of the opera at the German Theatre in Prague. Although they are nice pieces, they aren't Janáček's best music. Nevertheless, it was interesting for me to discover them. Before I knew of their existence, I used to arrange a repeat of the beginning of the second scene when I conducted the opera at Sadler's Wells. I did this to cover the impossibly timed scene change there.

Here, I should explain that there was still a German-language theatre in Prague before the war. It performed operas solely in that tongue, unlike the National Theatre down by the river, where all the operas were sung in Czech. You could hear Mascagni's *Cavalleria rusticana* sung in German at one theatre, and in Czech at the other. Until German culture was destroyed as a direct consequence of the occupiers' extreme unpopularity during the war, Prague was virtually bilingual. In fact, many Czechs spoke only in German. Franz Kafka, for example, was a German speaker, despite his very Czech name. Janáček's operas were all performed in German translations by the well-known German-speaking Jewish author Max Brod. During the nineteenth century, Smetana's operas were also first heard in German. Something of a strange case, Smetana was a committed Czech nationalist, but a German-speaker. And although he learned Czech as an act of patriotism, his quintessentially Czech operas, *Libuše* and *Dalibor*, were first performed in German.

RH: And it was because Prague had a German theatre that conductors such as Otto Klemperer and Erich Kleiber began their careers there.

CM: As a student in Prague, I heard Kleiber conduct memorable performances of Beethoven's 'Eroica' and Mahler's 'Resurrection' Symphonies. In fact Mahler himself was another German-speaking Czech. And I was incredibly surprised to hear Kleiber speak Czech to the Philharmonic during their rehearsals. But, of course, he had been a young conductor at the German Theatre before the war.

PART ONE: CONDUCTORS

RH: Mahler took his Czech roots very seriously, and it was with Smetana's *Dalibor* that he made his debut as Director of the Vienna Hofoper in 1897. But let's chat a little more about Handel. Is it true that you first experienced his music as a boy in Australia?

CM: I am not sure what I heard there can be described as Handel. Of course, I was familiar with *Messiah*, but only knew it in either Mozart's arrangement, or in a version with an expanded orchestration. Ebenezer Prout's arrangement, for example, has some very interesting things in it, especially if you read his preface to the score. I was also familiar with the *Water Music*, and had even played the oboe in *Israel in Egypt*. When I was engaged to play first oboe and cor anglais in Dvořák's 'New World' Symphony for Dr Malcolm Sargent at Brisbane in 1945, I was shown a facsimile of *Messiah*'s autograph score by the renowned Handel scholar and organist Dr Robert Dalley-Scarlett. As I already had a Boosey & Hawkes score of the original *Water Music*, I thought to myself, 'How is it possible for Handel to be played with all these additions?' But, of course, that was a very long time ago. As the understanding of period performance has developed so much in the last few years, the readings of Handel that I took part in during my youth wouldn't sound very good these days.

By the time I arrived in London, the composer's operas had started to be done by the Handel Opera Society, and great care was taken in attempting to recreate an original performance style. A former Principal of the Royal Academy of Music, Sir Anthony Lewis, was quite a pioneer in that respect, and I later collaborated with him on an edition of *Semele*. My first performance of a Handel opera as Music Director of the English National Opera was also very timely. Performing *Julius Caesar* in English worked very well, as the audience was familiar with *Messiah* and many of the composer's other English oratorios. When Handel operas were done in the past, the 'battle' parts were always sung by either a bass, tenor or some other 'proper' male voice, as it never occurred to anyone that the principal soprano and mezzo-soprano parts were originally sung by *castrati*. By the time of our production, Alfred Deller had begun singing as a counter-tenor. This meant that the time was right for the main roles in Handel operas to be sung by either a counter-tenor, or a very 'forceful' woman. In the case of *Julius Caesar*, we initially cast Janet Baker, who was remarkably successful in the title role, considering what a feminine lady she is. Later, when Janet stopped singing that part, we revived it with various counter-tenors, which proved equally successful. James Bowman initially sang the role of the evil Tolomeo, and the contrast between his voice and that of Janet's was extremely suitable dramatically. James eventually sang the part of Julius Caesar himself, and very well, too. But, of course, counter-tenors are very much more at home in the lower register, which was how the part of Caesar was originally written: the famous *castrato* Senesino, who sang the role at the work's premiere in 1724, apparently had a rather low voice. But as Janet was more of a high mezzo-soprano, it was necessary for us to transfer some of the part up. As some of the *coloratura* material that she sang was originally composed somewhat lower, I had to adjust it to suit Janet's voice. This provoked a lot of controversy, and it was said that I shouldn't have interfered with Handel. I replied that Handel himself adapted his music to suit the differing voices that sang a particular role. It was not only my right but my duty to change the part so that Janet could sing it.

RH: I assume that you decorated the vocal line. How was that received critically?

CM: The whole question of embellishing and ornamenting in Handel's operas is quite a long and complicated subject. During Handel's time, an aria's *da capo* was always embellished. Yet we have very few examples of what he might have expected when it came to ornamentation. From those that we do have, we can tell exactly how the singers themselves would have decorated the material. But in the case of *Julius Caesar*, I feel that we probably went too far. Nevertheless, most of the singers were required to remain in the composer's original register, and were not asked to sing ornaments that were either higher or lower than that register. That said, there were examples of *castrati* who did have huge ranges during Handel's time. But not Senesino. He had a rather poor range, and concentrated more on the drama.

RH: And what of your approach to ornamentation and decoration in Mozart's vocal works?

CM: Handel, Vivaldi and other composers from the Baroque largely failed to notate their ornamentation. Later in the eighteenth century, however, composers, such as Mozart and Haydn, tended to write out their decorations when a singer was unable to invent their own. An excellent example of this is 'Ach, ich fühl's' from Mozart's *Die Zauberflöte*. This is a very sad and reproachful aria that is frequently performed too slowly because of all the notes it contains. And as it was composed for the seventeen-year-old Anna Gottlieb, Mozart added the ornamentation. Famous divas of the time, however, would have expected to add their own ornamentation, and wouldn't have liked a young whippersnapper like Mozart doing it for them. When Mozart was only fourteen, he composed the opera *Mitridate, re di Ponto*, which contains the beautiful aria, 'Lungi da te, mio bene'. Shortly before the first performance, the *castrato*, Sartorino, said to him, 'Listen, young man, put in a horn *obbligato* for me.' Mozart dutifully obeyed and, by so doing, recognised the primacy of the singer at the time.

RH: The examples that you return to time and again when discussing ornamentation in Mozart are 'Dove sono' from *Le nozze di Figaro* and the 'Agnus Dei' from the 'Coronation' Mass.

CM: The Countess's aria, 'Dove sono' is a typical example of an aria that starts with a slow section and that goes on to an *allegro*. There's no question in my mind that the singer would have ornamented the aria, particularly at the reprise. And how was this done? Well, I don't exactly know. What I do know, however, is that the 'Agnus Dei' from the 'Coronation' Mass has almost the same tune as 'Dove sono', even though it's in a different key, meter and register. As the 'Agnus Dei' was probably sung by a boy soprano, or at least by somebody very young, Mozart might well have added the embellishments found in that material for that reason. So, I took the ornamentation from the 'Agnus Dei' and added it to 'Dove sono'. I think that the result is quite stylish. And, by the way, as the Mass was written for Salzburg, the Latin should always be pronounced in the German manner, and not in the Italianate fashion. This also applies to Beethoven, whose *Missa solemnis* should be pronounced as if it were in German. Singers from Germany do this automatically. When I performed a Schubert Mass and the Mozart Vespers at Salzburg recently, I was very pleased that the chorus from Vienna sang it this way. But when I then did the same works in Dresden with the local opera chorus there, they asked, 'Surely, you want the Italian pronunciation?' I said, 'No. I want the German pronunciation.' They complied immediately, and sang the works quite naturally in the German manner.

RH: How much freedom do you allow singers when realising their ornamentation?

PART ONE: CONDUCTORS

CM: Some singers are very good at improvising, while others like their embellishments written out for them. When it comes to this issue, my approach is quite simple. I'll write the ornamentation if necessary, or I'll leave it to the singer if they can manage it. While only very few singers *can* manage it, they are increasingly aware of what is needed, partly thanks to the period performance movement. When I compiled the aforementioned edition of Handel's *Semele* with Sir Anthony Lewis, I added a great deal of ornamentation for the solo singers. While I regret that some of the material was over-decorated, other parts of the score are still suitable. And as I am about to conduct a student performance of the work here at the Academy, I hope that the singers will do what I suggest. If not, they can do something else.

RH: I know that one of your great musical heroes was Wilhelm Furtwängler, who famously applied Wagner's ideas on *tempo* modification and *tempo* integration. Yet your approach to these matters differs considerably from that of Furtwängler.

CM: Furtwängler's performances have always been revelatory to me. I particularly admire the sounds that he produced with the Berlin Philharmonic, and the rapt feeling that he could create in the works of Wagner, Beethoven and other German composers. But when performing Beethoven's Ninth Symphony, I take a different stance to Furtwängler. He always adopted Wagner's approach to the work, which involved a great deal of *tempo* modification. Consequently, Furtwängler's *tempi* are often either much slower or much faster than I believe to be correct. This is true of both the *Andante* and the end of the choral movement. Here, his *tempi* are either twice as fast or twice as slow as those indicated by Beethoven. Many pre-war conductors considered the composer's metronome marks to be impossibly fast and the result of either an error on his part or a faulty metronome. Recent research has since shown that the marks indicated by Beethoven were what he imagined them to be. In general, I try to conduct his symphonies more like classical works, rather than rapt German tone-poems. While I don't adopt Beethoven's metronome marks absolutely, I do something that closely approaches them.

RH: I know that a particular bugbear of yours is the *Maestoso* that directly precedes the final *Prestissimo*.

CM: Indeed it is. The *tempo* of the *Maestoso* is quite clearly marked by Beethoven. Having been *Presto* before, and then *Prestissimo* afterwards, the *tempo* should carry on at a similar pulse, even though the beat is suddenly slower. The important thing is that the *Götterfunken* that straddles the double-bar that divides the *Maestoso* and *Prestissimo* should remain at the same speed. Furtwängler performs the *Prestissimo* very fast indeed, and I was surprised by just how fast it was when I recently listened to one of his recordings of the Ninth. His speeds normally tend to be on the slow side, even though he always put great excitement into the music.

RH: What are your views on Wagner's suggestions concerning the retouching of existing orchestrations?

CM: Occasionally I do it. My view is that the listener must be able to understand the content of the music. If the orchestration is unable to achieve this due to the inability of the original instruments to play certain high notes, and if the intentions of the composer can be made clearer by putting a flute up an octave, I will make the change. A good example of this is my use of the piccolos at the end of the last movement.

PART ONE: CONDUCTORS

As the piccolo was incapable of playing all the melodic material at the time of the first performance, it had to play certain notes lower. That means that the effect of the interesting tune, which rides above the whole orchestra and chorus, is lost. To avoid this, I have the whole tune played by two piccolos. I've conducted Beethoven's Ninth Symphony twice with period orchestras and used double woodwind. As the expertise of the flute players in the Orchestra of the Age of Enlightenment means that they can play my added high notes, I say, 'Why not use them?'

RH: You also have some very strong views on how the opening of the Ninth Symphony's last movement should be played.

CM: The recitatives given to the celli and double basses should be played in the manner of a recitative, but in *tempo*. That's a very difficult instruction to observe, as the whole point of a recitative is that it's free, and *not* in *tempo*. In Beethoven's time, they tried to overcome this problem by playing the passages on a solo double bass, or by a single cello. There was a famous occasion when the renowned bassist Domenico Dragonetti was supposed to play the passage as a solo, but then didn't, as he wanted a bigger fee for performing as a soloist. The so-called *Schrekensfanfare*, or 'horror fanfare', that opens the movement should frighten and shock the listeners, so that when the bass singer says, 'Don't make these horrible sounds', and the celli and basses play the 'Ode to Joy' theme, the audience can think of something more joyful and noble.

RH: Over the years, you have conducted orchestras from many different countries that play in many different styles. How have these styles changed and developed during your career, and do you miss the former sound-worlds of some of these great orchestras?

CM: The Czech Philharmonic has changed less than the Vienna Philharmonic, which now sounds quite different when playing Mozart. When I conducted the Vienna orchestra recently in a programme of works by Schubert and Mozart, it was concerned about the way in which its Mozart style is now perceived. Of course, the strings use a lot of *vibrato* and, in my view, there's no point trying to stop orchestras from playing with that gesture, as it requires an entirely different bowing technique. Unlike the Vienna Philharmonic, the Czech Philharmonic was completely isolated from the West for many years and continued to perform in their traditional manner until relatively recently. I love the way it plays Dvořák. But the strings, as good as they are, no longer perform his music in the way that it must've been played originally. They now use a constant *vibrato*, which wouldn't have been the case in the nineteenth century. Questions also arise when it comes to *portamento*. If you listen to early recordings of the London orchestras conducted by Sir Edward Elgar, for example, you can hear audible shifting in the strings. Their constant sliding is not a planned 'artistic' effect, but the result of undue care. As Elgar clearly did nothing to prevent strings from sliding in this way, the question must surely be: 'Was it a necessary artistic gesture, or was it one that was done as a matter of course?' Somebody once described the Czech Philharmonic as 'one gigantic period orchestra'. In a way it is, although it's becoming less so, due mainly to the number of foreigners it employs. Nevertheless, it still remains one of the few orchestras to retain, at least in part, the sound-worlds of Dvořák, Janáček and Suk.

SIR COLIN DAVIS
(DAVID JOSEFOWITZ RECITAL HALL, 4 MARCH 2011)

JONATHAN FREEMAN-ATTWOOD: When you and I met recently, we discussed the education of aspiring conductors, and what they might need if they're to succeed professionally. And what we came back to time and again was the idea that for anyone who fancied a life on the podium, he or she must possess an overwhelming drive and commitment, regardless of whether or not they know what the job fully entails. How did the conducting bug take hold of you when you were young, and when did you first realise that you had been 'infected'?

COLIN DAVIS: I was about thirteen years old, and in need of being rescued from adolescence. Music then came along and gave me a terrific boost. I was passionate about it, and have been ever since. But I hadn't the faintest idea of what it demanded, or anything about it. And it has been a long journey of discovery ever since.

JF-A: Was your journey a little like that of the young Sir John Barbirolli, who shut himself in a cupboard and waved his hands around to an imaginary Beethoven's Eighth Symphony as a boy, or was it more the case of you being aware that you had to achieve a high standard on the clarinet so that you could access the conducting profession?

CD: I didn't think in either of those terms. And my 'brush' with the clarinet was so that I could play Mozart as beautifully as possible.

JF-A: Were there particular pieces that you heard during your early years that gave you a sense of artistic direction?

CD: As it happens, I was swept off my feet one school holidays by the Eighth Symphony of Beethoven. People might well ask, 'Why?' The answer is, 'Because it has such a remarkable concentration of energy.' It explodes on the ear, and it convinced me that I just had to be a musician.

JF-A: After attending Christ's Hospital as a schoolboy, you enrolled at the Royal College of Music, where you won a scholarship to study clarinet with Frederick Thurston. What was it like studying with one of the giants of the London orchestral scene, and who were some of the other big figures whom you encountered for the first time during your student years?

CD: I heard most of the leading artists from that period through the BBC Symphony Orchestra. It was still during the war, and it played in Bedford in those days. There were regular broadcasts, and Sir Adrian Boult was the conductor. He had a wonderful knack of presenting things without any fuss. And I was fortunate enough to learn so many classics from him. When I left school at the end of the war, London was flooded with musicians. I hadn't performed anything really, but knew that I just wanted to play. We played all day and all night, and we explored everything we could. And it was the people with whom I worked who taught me so much.

PART ONE: CONDUCTORS

JF-A: Some of your first experiences as a conductor were with the Kalmar Orchestra, which you co-founded with a few of your chums from the College. What was it like being put in a position of musical authority for the first time, and what lessons can a young conductor learn from working with his peers?

CD: I'd no plan when I approached this, and it just became one damned thing after another. My friends said that I should conduct something, which I did. It seemed to go well, so they suggested that we should do it again. As I was working with my mates, I had to learn to behave myself, and not to sing.

JF-A: You have often said that you learned a great deal from Boult. What attracted you to his approach?

CD: He used a stick that was very long. Too long for somebody like me. But he didn't just hang on to it to beat time, he drew with it. He painted with it, and that's what I set out to do. I felt that that was a much better way of trying to do this job. If you are going to have a stick, you shouldn't hold on to it just in case you're 'drowning'. Boult once said to me, something that he also wrote in a very slender book about conducting, that he had learned all of this from Arthur Nikisch in Leipzig. Apparently, Nikisch was extremely adept at using the baton.

JF-A: And were you able to draw any conclusions about line and *legato* from what you learned from Boult?

CD: Yes, because he didn't beat time in an aggressive way. For most music from the Classical Period, you don't need to beat time. Everybody knows when a work is in 2/4; you don't have to labour the point. You therefore have to use your stick for making music. And I still think that using a stick is the best way of managing music with an orchestra. You can do all kinds of subtle things with a baton, and then the players will begin to believe in what you are doing. The musicians like that kind of thing.

JF-A: Shortly after forming the Kalmar Orchestra, you performed Mozart's *Don Giovanni* with the Chelsea Opera Group, an amateur company of which you are still President. Was this your first engagement as an opera conductor, and what were some of the challenges you faced when conducting that company and that opera?

CD: Yes, and the challenges were huge. I knew nothing about *Don Giovanni* at the time other than its tunes. I couldn't conduct a recitative. I simply didn't know how to do it.

JF-A: As you were unable to secure work as a *répétiteur*, how might you have gone about becoming an opera conductor had you not taken charge of the Chelsea Opera Group?

CD: I don't think that I would've become one at all. For the most part, conductors are pianists.

JF-A: In 1952, you conducted the moribund original Ballets Russes before being engaged as Assistant Conductor with the BBC Scottish Symphony Orchestra in 1957. What did this job entail, and was it an important rung on the ladder to your success?

CD: Actually, it was a very difficult job, because the conductor of the orchestra, Ian Whyte, went off sick when I arrived there. I then found myself having to do pretty much everything. But I didn't know anything really. I ended up hastily learning all the music that he was going to conduct, and probably did it very badly.

JF-A: You couldn't have done it all that badly, as you replaced an indisposed Sir Thomas Beecham for a performance of *Die Zauberflöte* at Glyndebourne two and a half years later. Did that opportunity affect your perceptions as a Mozartian, and, if so, in what way?

CD: It did, because there was a language fanatic at Glyndebourne who was quite brutal with me. I learned a great deal. The journey from being a music buff to being a professional conductor is a considerable distance. I seemed to have staggered from one humiliation to another.

JF-A: That's a little hard to believe, when one considers that astonishing series of Mozart recordings that you made for Philips in the 1960s. Those discs helped forge a very identifiable Colin Davis Mozart style. And, of course, in 1960 itself, you were appointed to your first major opera post when you were made Music Director of Sadler's Wells Opera. How would you describe some of the defining musical and dramatic qualities of the company at that time, and what are your thoughts on performing opera in the vernacular?

CD: I think that performing in the vernacular is a very good idea. All other countries do it, so why shouldn't we? And it was at Sadler's Wells that I really started to learn opera. I encountered many things that I had never done before, including Wagner's *Tannhäuser*, Weber's *Der Freischütz*, Pizzetti's *Assassinio nella cattedrale* and Weill's *Aufstieg und Fall der Stadt Mahagonny*. Our production of Stravinsky's *Oedipus Rex* was very important to me. It was produced by Michel Saint-Denis, who used masks in a very stylised manner. It was very, very powerful. Then, Glen Byam Shaw came from Stratford to produce *The Rake's Progress*. That was a wonderful adventure. And, of course, everything should be an adventure and an exploration.

JF-A: If memory serves me correctly, you gave *Oedipus Rex* in 1961. What particularly attracted you to the piece?

CD: I was very much into Stravinsky at the time. I liked the jagged, uncompromising rhythms and the harsh sounds. I also liked the viciousness and the wildness of the material. I relentlessly pursued Stravinsky, much to everybody's dismay. Nobody played it much, and musicians couldn't play works like the *Symphony in Three Movements* without thinking about them. They hadn't come to terms with them by then.

JF-A: Would it be fair to say that Stravinsky is one of the few Russian composers whom you have performed?

CD: Yes. I couldn't quite take to Prokofiev, and there is a lot of Shostakovich that I've never got involved with.

JF-A: And did you perform much opera in English after leaving Sadler's Wells?

CD: No, none at all.

JF-A: Thirteen years after being appointed to the Wells, you succeeded Sir Georg Solti as Music Director of the Royal Opera House, Covent Garden. What were some of the challenges that you faced on accepting that post, and what were some of the highlights of your time as the company's artistic leader?

CD: I think the production of Wagner's *Der Ring des Nibelungen* that we did with Götz Friedrich was one of the best things I had seen. I'd never seen a *Ring* until that time. Although his use of a tilted platform that went around was very simple, you could do all kinds of things with it. *Das Rheingold* was a particularly spectacular piece of work. Steps came out from the end of the platform when you pressed a button. That's what he called the perverted *pavane*, as the gods entered Valhalla by taking two steps up and one step down. There were also some great images later on, such as when Wotan visited Erda. The platform went up, as if giving a great yawn, and she could be seen below. It was extraordinary. I had never before seen anything as dramatic as that.

JF-A: And, of course, you explored a number of works at Covent Garden that you've never returned to, such as Berg's *Lulu* and Zemlinsky's *Eine florentinische Tragödie*. How much control over the repertoire did you have both there and elsewhere, and in what ways was it reflective of your own personal performance aesthetic at the time?

CD: The recording companies decided what we were going to record, and that helped one to become a specialist in something or other.

JF-A: Was that a healthy arrangement?

CD: Not at all. But apart from recordings, I never followed that approach elsewhere. I always did things that I found interesting, such as Vaughan Williams's Sixth Symphony, or the works of Sibelius.

JF-A: And precisely how much control over the repertoire did you have at Covent Garden?

CD: This was always a bone of contention there, as we were expected to create a definitive programme of works. But when we made that programme, we were told that there wasn't enough money to perform it. Needless to say, the sponsors did have enough money for a new Rolls Royce. I told them to tell me who's got the money, to say what they want and to stop wasting our time.

JF-A: During your time at Covent Garden, you worked with two of the world's most distinguished General Managers, Sir David Webster and Sir John Tooley. What, for you, defines a good manager, and in what ways do their responsibilities affect your role as a Music Director?

CD: I suppose the best relationship that a conductor can have with a General Manager or an intendant is when he or she is a *regisseur*. You can then work on operas together and can discuss issues such as casting. That very rarely happens, however. At Covent Garden, John Tooley was not a *regisseur*; he was nothing of the kind. But he was very good at diplomacy. He was hampered because he was responsible to the board, which consisted mainly of opera lovers. And sometimes this all came apart, as there was often a discrepancy between what the opera lovers and what the professional managers wanted.

JF-A: You've also worked with some of the world's leading operatic directors. Of those, whose approach did you admire most, and how did that approach affect your understanding of opera as a genre?

PART ONE: CONDUCTORS

CD: The most successful directors were those who treated the music with respect, and who attempted to bring the music to life on stage. I was fortunate enough to be at Covent Garden with John Copley, and we have done several things together since then – including working for you here at the Academy. But he knew the music inside out, and that was a great advantage. He never tried to impose crazy ideas, which some producers do.

JF-A: As you have been associated with the operas of Mozart for many years now, what makes a good director of his works?

CD: Somebody who is in touch with life, and who understands what's going on around them. After you've spent a long time with Mozart, one gets the feeling that he actually *is* life. Everything is there. The ways in which he shades human feelings and how he represents misdemeanours are cases in point. He's the mirror of the world. And you have to enter his world, because if you impose something upon it, it doesn't function.

JF-A: To a certain extent, your career has been articulated by some extraordinary passions for particular composers. And perhaps the name that comes to mind immediately is Berlioz. In 1903, Richard Strauss, a Berlioz enthusiast, conducted the composer's centenary celebrations at the Queen's Hall to a near-empty auditorium. By 2003, that situation had changed completely, largely due to your efforts on the composer's behalf. Why are you so attracted to his music?

CD: I first heard a work by Berlioz when I was about twenty-one. It was the second part of *L'enfance du Christ*. I'd never heard music like that before. His delicate melodies and his use of the orchestra fascinated me.

I later met up with those other two Berlioz 'fanatics', David Cairns and Richard Macnutt. We then did some of the composer's works with the Chelsea Opera Group, such as *La damnation de Faust*. After that, we gave *Benvenuto Cellini* and *Les Troyens*. That was the start. And then the London Symphony Orchestra decided to present the first part of *Les Troyens*, as did the Philharmonia Orchestra.

JF-A: Do you feel that there is still a reluctance on the part of audiences to engage with Berlioz's music fully, and what, for you, are the works that reflect his genius as a composer best?

CD: There are really too many to mention. But the orchestral works are truly fantastic. *Benvenuto Cellini* deserves to be done again, but it's so fiendishly difficult and so very complicated. The problem is that you have to decide on what version you're going to play, as there isn't a definitive one. And then there is *Les Troyens*, which is going to be done at Covent Garden next season. It'll be wonderful to hear it again.

JF-A: Tell me a little more about *Les Troyens*. What is it about the piece that continues to fascinate you?

CD: It's just wonderful music. In fact, before I came here tonight I thought, 'I'll just listen to the septet.' It's so beautiful. Perhaps I find it even more beautiful now, as beauty in music is a little out of fashion today. The septet is then followed by a wonderful love duet. And if you like to be seduced by music, there it is. But I would also like to point out that whether it be Berlioz, Mozart or any other composer, it's impossible to perform their works without the orchestra and the singers being totally committed to the piece concerned. And if you listen to my live recording of the 'Chasse royale et orage' from the *Les Troyens*, you can

PART ONE: CONDUCTORS

hear just how committed they are. But why should they be, if people supposedly don't want to listen to it? I think that all of those who came to that performance will never forget it because of the way every musician actively took part in it.

JF-A: A striking feature of your career path was your work with radio orchestras, both here and abroad. Following your appointment with the BBC Scottish Symphony Orchestra, you became Chief Conductor of the BBC Symphony Orchestra in 1967. You were then later engaged as Music Director of the Symphonieorchester des Bayerischen Rundfunks. How did these two great musical institutions compare administratively?

CD: They were very different. The Bayerischen Rundfunks was a very politically biased organisation. The BBC was 'supposedly' not. The man who ran the radio in Bavaria was a member of the Christian Democratic Union. He had absolutely no interest in music at all, and was a kind of fascist. That made life very difficult. But I liked him!

JF-A: And, of course, when you took over the BBC Symphony Orchestra from Sir Malcolm Sargent, you also took over the Proms. Considering all the razzamatazz that surrounded Sargent, leading the Proms must have been something of a challenge.

CD: It's always a challenge when you take over from anybody. The first couple of years can be really difficult, as everybody remembers the way things were. This is particularly true when you succeed somebody with as strong a personality as Sargent. Nobody can be somebody else. And until you have been somewhere long enough, it doesn't really settle down.

JF-A: Like you, your distinguished predecessor at the Symphonieorchester des Bayerischen Rundfunks, Rafael Kubelík, considered it essential that a conductor should work with the orchestra as part of a team, and not behave like a martinet. You once said, 'You've got to play father to [the players]. You've got to be prepared to discuss anything with them, even their troubles or their relationships with their colleagues. I've had the oddest conversations with some of them. You've really got to like people in order to do this, which I do.' Perhaps you could elaborate on this statement, and explain how you go about managing the disparate personalities and talents that abound in orchestras and opera houses.

CD: I've never liked the tyranny of the maestro. It was not something that I could get into. The most important thing about conducting is enjoying what the other people are doing. If you can help them relax and play well, you will get a much better result than if you frighten the life out of them. I really believe that. And when I left Munich, I decided that was enough of me trying to be a Chief Conductor. The politics and the fights that are common in broadcasting companies, and the difficult attitudes of radio-orchestra musicians, prompted me to vow that I would never again take a position of power. So, when I went to the London Symphony Orchestra, I made that clear before taking the job. I was to have no power. I was not to be responsible for who was going to play, auditions or anything else. Nothing. I would simply go along and do the programmes that we'd planned. And that's why I'm still there. Because if you don't have any power, you can get anything you want out of musicians. But if you do have power, and say that 'you are not playing such and such', the musicians hate it. They hate it so much.

JF-A: How did it work when you were conducting the Sächsische Staatskapelle?

PART ONE: CONDUCTORS

CD: They now have a Music Director, but when they didn't, which was the case for many years, the orchestra simply organised themselves.

JF-A: Sibelius is a composer who is also closely associated with you. Unlike Berlioz, Sibelius has always been popular in Britain: Sir Henry Wood and Sir John Barbirolli both conducted cycles of the symphonies to critical acclaim, and the first complete recording of those works was made by Anthony Collins in the 1950s. Why is Sibelius's music so attractive to English audiences in general and to you in particular?

CD: I've no idea. It is just wonderful music. And I can't think of a better reason than that.

JF-A: But why do the British like Sibelius and the Germans don't?

CD: Because they were told that he wasn't a good composer.

JF-A: And what of the particular challenges he presents?

CD: The symphonies are a huge undertaking, as Sibelius left very few instructions as to how they should be conducted. The music seems to express so much, and you've simply got to make it work. Sometimes, he can be so dense, so heavy and so reluctant to move. You have to be able to handle all of that. He touches upon some things that other composers don't, even though I am not totally sure what those things are. But whatever they are, they're pretty dark.

JF-A: How did your recordings of Sibelius's symphonies with the Boston Symphony Orchestra come about?

CD: I think it was because they had done so much Sibelius with their former Music Director, Serge Koussevitzky, and had developed a kind of tradition.

JF-A: Was that continued with Charles Munch?

CD: No. The French have never liked Sibelius.

JF-A: When you undertook to record all of the composer's symphonies with the Boston orchestra, did you intend to work with, or even against, the Koussevitzky tradition?

CD: No, it was far simpler than that. I showed an interest in Sibelius, and Philips decided that they would record the symphonies, and that was that.

JF-A: Elgar is another composer with whom you are now synonymous, and his music has been central to your recent work with the London Symphony Orchestra. I'm curious to hear your thoughts, therefore, on Anthony Payne's elaboration of the Third Symphony, and your take on the reasons why it has yet to secure a place in the repertoire?

CD: I hope that it will be accepted more fully, as Tony has done a most extraordinary job with it. And as the sounds that Elgar and Payne created are almost identical, how the devil can one tell the difference between them? In fact, only the other day I said to the London Symphony Orchestra that it's time we played it again. And it's only by playing the elaboration that we can make the public listen to it.

PART ONE: CONDUCTORS

JF-A: As there is no performance tradition for the Third Symphony, how did you go about finding reference points in the work that helped you place it historically within the oeuvre?

CD: When I was confronted by it, I had to decide how it was supposed to go. And you have to ask, 'What's Elgar doing?' There are certain routines that he enjoys, like starting slowly before accelerating. That can be a great help when tackling the last movement and when articulating the piece as a whole. The slow movement is extremely moving and touching.

JF-A: When asked recently whether they conducted Bach, one of our postgraduate conducting students replied, 'Absolutely not, I leave that to the Bach specialists.' Having successfully released a critically acclaimed recording of Handel's *Messiah* not long ago with the London Symphony Orchestra, you clearly disagree with the view that Baroque music is the sole province of the Baroque specialist. What are your thoughts on the period performance movement, and how has it affected your approach to eighteenth-century music?

CD: I don't like that student's comment at all, but I think that it's still prevalent. All the music that was composed before Beethoven has been hijacked. And the period performance movement has now even hijacked that student. Symphony orchestras are supposedly no longer allowed to play Bach. That's nonsense. I don't see why period players should have a hold over these wonderful pieces. We're not permitted to touch them. I rather object to the foundations upon which this is built. If you've got to look up in a book how you should play a piece, you are entirely on the wrong track. When you get married, you don't go to the local library and look up what you're supposed to do.

JF-A: But you know what I am trying to get at here.

CD: Yes. You're asking, 'Should I be allowed to conduct Bach?'

JF-A: Of course, the answer is 'yes', particularly as you know how much I admire the reading of the *Matthäus-Passion* you gave in Gloucester Cathedral. These masterpieces are major achievements in Western art, and should be open to a wide approach and many perspectives. But, by way of conclusion, might we chat briefly about your remarkable commitment to young people? At the Royal Academy of Music alone, you have led no fewer than sixty projects; a considerable achievement. When did you discover that you had an affinity with aspiring musicians, and why are you so committed to them?

CD: I like young people, I must say. I like their energy, and it's such a pleasure to work with them. I also admire the speed with which they absorb things and their idealism. They're extraordinary. Who wouldn't love working with them?

CHRISTOPH VON DOHNÁNYI
(DAVID JOSEFOWITZ RECITAL HALL, 24 JUNE 2015)

JONATHAN FREEMAN-ATTWOOD: Having reached the remarkable milestone of your eighty-fifth birthday, you must find it fascinating when you look back over the professional journey that you have enjoyed. What do you recall of your formative years?

CHRISTOPH VON DOHNÁNYI: I was born and grew up in Berlin. As my father had to move around a great deal, we then went to Hamburg and Leipzig, before returning to Berlin. This meant that I had to attend about four or five schools. But the real 'event' of that time was the Thomasschule in Leipzig. I thought that I'd attended it for four years, but my wife has since discovered that I was there for less than one. It was terrible and hard. The school's windows were so high that you couldn't even look out of them. It was unbelievable. And while I found that school tough, my education was generally fine otherwise. Between my fifth birthday and the beginning of the Second World War, I was involved in a lot of music. But as soon as the war started, music became less prominent, as many other things occupied me. By the time it ended, I was fifteen years old and was not so sure that I could really make up musically for those missing six years, years that we largely spent repairing windows and roofs.

JF-A: Is it true that you also considered a career in law at one point?

CvD: Yes, that's true. I studied law first, as my mother was very much against me becoming a musician. She was from a good bourgeois family, and was concerned by what her children would do professionally. As her family included the theologian Dietrich Bonhoeffer, and a number of scientists, she was sceptical of music, so she made me play for the Thomaskantor, Karl Straube. I remember the occasion well. As I was only a child, I wasn't the least bit nervous. I simply played and left. I then waited for my mother and Straube to discuss what I did. And it was only after I'd begun to study law that my mother told me Straube had said that no matter what subject I might choose, I would inevitably become a musician.

JF-A: You then went to Munich, where you attended the Hochschule für Musik und Theater. Do you remember the kind of studies you underwent in the immediate post-war period, and what the expectations of your professors were in developing your talents?

CvD: I finished school when I was sixteen, and began studying law the same year. I was really still a kid. As I had a very quick mind and a good memory, I was able to listen to my law professor while composing music at the same time. But as I was devoting more and more of my energies to music, it soon became obvious that I should change direction. That's when I went to the Hochschule in Munich. As an institution, it was only just beginning to resurrect itself after the war. It had some staff members who had been *Mitläufer* during the Hitler period. These were people who were not really Nazis, and were not in favour of anything other than themselves. But as most of them had joined the Party, this meant that the Hochschule suffered from a staffing vacuum at the time of my enrolment. We did, however, have two very nice professors who were not particularly well trained as teachers. And as students, we had classes in chamber music, accompaniment and composition.

JF-A: As you won the Hochschule's prestigious Richard Strauss Prize, you must have been an outstanding student.

CvD: Yes. But I also said to myself that if I didn't finish my studies at an acceptable level, I would give up music. So, when I was lucky enough to win that prize, I used the money to go to the United States.

JF-A: Having arrived in America, you went on to study with your grandfather, the renowned composer and pianist Ernst von Dohnányi, at Florida State University.

CvD: I'd only met him once and barely knew him at all. But, at that first meeting, which was very nice, he played Beethoven's *Für Elise* for us, and I played a piece of my own for him. In fact, I was so young at the time that I had no idea what I'd written. One of my uncles who had perfect pitch wrote down what I'd played on the piano. It was a silly piece, but my grandfather liked it. He then gave a watch to my brother and me. And that was the only contact I had with my grandfather during my childhood, as he lived in Hungary.

JF-A: What was Ernst like as a teacher, and what did you take from him musically?

CvD: My grandfather left Hungary when the Russians arrived after the war. He went first to Cumaná in South America, where he was promised the directorship of the music school there. But when he arrived, there was only a big hole in the ground and no conservatory. He then left for Tallahassee in Florida, where he had a very nice class of students, and an equally nice, but small, house. And when I arrived there, the first question he asked, which I remember very vividly, was, 'Christoph, can you improvise?' This was something that wasn't taught to us in Munich, as it was considered to be somewhat disrespectful. I think that the loss of this skill by serious musicians was a grave mistake, as it then became the province of popular artists. The ability to improvise is very, very important, and he knew how to do it. In fact, he probably was able to improvise *too* well, as he didn't like to practise. He hated practising. But he could play a wide repertoire, and would ask, 'What would you like to hear?' He had the whole of the nineteenth-century piano oeuvre under his fingers. And I remember that he once played the whole of Beethoven's 'Appassionata' Sonata for me in the wrong key!

JF-A: I would also like to hear your thoughts on how young conductors should be trained. Artists such as Sir John Barbirolli, Herbert von Karajan and Sir Georg Solti all stressed the importance of the opera house for aspiring conductors. Do you agree with their argument and, if so, how did your early years in the theatre impact on your work in the concert hall?

CvD: I think that starting in an opera house is essential. If you start as a vocal coach, you have to be able to play the piano, act as an accompanist and understand breathing. These are all essential to music-making. Of course, nowadays, there are many conductors who start in the concert hall. It can be harder for them, but some are very successful. I am happy that I spent six years in Lübeck, where I was lucky enough to be appointed Chief Conductor at the age of twenty-seven. I was able to choose the repertoire that I wanted to give, and was also able to schedule the number of rehearsals that were needed to perform it successfully. I spoke with Herbert von Karajan about this, and he reminded me that he had spent six years in Ulm, where he had an orchestra of only thirty-eight musicians. With that small group he performed everything, including Strauss's *Salome* and *Elektra*. It was only after another three years or so in Aachen that he finally moved to Berlin. And as I'm a musician who was trained in the 'old-fashioned' way, I believe that music has singing at its core. When I was coaching and accompanying for a very well-known baritone as a young man in Germany, I had some singing lessons, even though the orchestras that I work with today might not think so. But it was very important.

JF-A: During the 1960s, you worked very closely with the Kölner Rundfunk-Sinfonie-Orchester. What were some of the advantages of working with a great German radio orchestra, and were you ever aware of the petty squabbles that inevitably come with such large and diverse institutions?

CvD: It all depends on who the manager or the administrator of the orchestra is. I was lucky, because those who held these positions in Cologne, and later in Hamburg, were artistically aware. This meant that I wasn't burdened with too many administrative matters. Quite the opposite. There were times when I had to interfere with the administration.

JF-A: Of course, Cologne was essentially a new city during the 1960s.

CvD: Yes, it was. It had been totally destroyed during the war. Before the bombings, it was a city of between 500,000 and 600,000 inhabitants, and, afterwards, that number fell to only 10,000.

JF-A: But unlike Dresden and Munich, Cologne was not rebuilt as a kind of replica of its former self. It was reconstructed as something new. Did that affect people's expectations musically and culturally?

CvD: While I was Chief Conductor of the orchestra in Cologne, Stockhausen, Boulez, Timmerman and the young Kontarskys were around, and brought with them a great deal of contemporary music.

JF-A: Was this because a new city can be a bit 'edgier' musically? And, of course, you, too, performed a great deal of new music during your Cologne period.

CvD: My performances of contemporary music in Cologne came somewhat later than the first flourish of new music in Germany. This happened while I was still a student in Munich, and where the composer, Karl Amadeus Hartmann, founded Musica Viva in 1945. He even managed to take the series to the famous Herkulessaal, where it played to sold-out houses; there had been no real contemporary music in Germany for twelve years. The same was true for modern painting. But then we could listen to everything. I hardly knew Mahler's music when I was growing up. My father once played *Das Lied von der Erde* for us in secret. It wasn't allowed, and that wasn't even contemporary music. There was no Schoenberg and no Webern. There was nothing like that. It was Karl Amadeus Hartmann who opened this all up right after the war. It was an amazing feeling. But, later, contemporary music in Germany became a little hypertrophic, and began to disconnect with the past. This normalised somewhat later, but there was certainly a period of disconnection. Nevertheless, young people went crazy for contemporary music at the time.

PART ONE: CONDUCTORS

JF-A: While you were in Cologne, did you begin to realise that you had a particular interpretative identity that you might be able to build upon in the future?

CvD: At that time, my orchestra in Cologne was the first that I led that had a high technical standard. My orchestra at Lübeck was quite good, but was not comparable to a radio orchestra, whether it be in Bavaria, Hamburg or Cologne. These ensembles were very heavily subsidised by the state, and attracted very good musicians. The Cologne orchestra certainly influenced my way of working. As a conductor, you must first establish and form a technically perfect instrument. I am not obsessed with working on an orchestra's intonation, but if it's not right, you have to fix it. And if such things are not corrected, I cannot conduct. Cologne acted as a kind of measuring-stick that showed me what could, and what could not, be achieved. But, technically speaking, I learned a lot there.

JF-A: Your ear for intonation is both famed and feared.

CvD: I'm hated for it!

JF-A: No comment! But, seriously, your understanding of balance and intonation is part of the 'Dohnányi sound'.

CvD: If you have a soloist, such as Mr Brendel or Mr Pollini, who begins to play, but finds the piano out of tune, he will rightly ask, 'Why haven't you tuned this thing?' The same is true of the orchestra: it has to be a perfectly tuned instrument. Then you can make music. But there are some conductors who will start with the music-making, but will forget about the intonation. This results in a poor sound.

JF-A: When you began your relationship with the Vienna Philharmonic, it was suggested by some that you were not the most obvious choice for that orchestra, as it was famous for its ingrained working practices.

CvD: That's not quite true. When I began to conduct in Vienna a lot, I was one of the first to perform Wagner's *Ring* from scratch. Generally, most conductors who had performed it there took over an existing production. And I remember in *Götterdämmerung* we had about 300 bars in the orchestral parts that had no rehearsal figures, which I asked to be marked in. This was because nobody had bothered to rehearse that passage in the past. With the orchestra, I also held separate rehearsals for the strings in *Das Rheingold* and the tuba in *Götterdämmerung*. The players asked for this. They wanted to rehearse. I also remember one very nice young violinist in Vienna saying to me, and this was at the time when I was already with the Cleveland Orchestra, 'Maestro, if I could play the music the way you want it, I would be in Cleveland!'

JF-A: As a conductor, you also recorded and performed a great deal of Mendelssohn's music with the Vienna Philharmonic.

CvD: When I made my recordings of the composer's works with that orchestra, I was actively discovering his music. As the criminals who ran Germany for twelve years between 1933 and 1945 prevented us from hearing his compositions, I decided to do as many of his pieces as I could when I was working at the Frankfurt Opera. Up until the age of fifteen, I had never heard a work by Mendelssohn. I was determined, therefore, to study as much of his music as possible, including *Elijah*, which I gave in Cologne. But having studied and conducted so much Mendelssohn, I was suddenly considered a 'Mendelssohn specialist'. This is very dangerous for a conductor. It seems to me that if you conduct Dvořák three times successfully, you end up being a 'Dvořák specialist'. I also took up Mahler quite late. And as I have now given some performances of his works, which I hope are good, there is now the danger of me being dubbed a 'Mahler specialist', too. Nevertheless, I did become very close to Mendelssohn during the time I was recording his works with the Vienna orchestra. Having said that, I would no longer perform his music in the way that I did back then, as I don't like the relentless approach to rhythm that I took on those discs.

JF-A: Was this because you considered Mendelssohn to be something of a conservative figure who came from a different tradition from yours?

CvD: No. When I read his scores mentally, which I am able to do, I was aware that I was encountering a tremendous genius. And because it was so clear to me that he *was* such a genius, I felt that this was his only drawback. Consequently, I would begin by studying his slow movements, a habit that I apply universally. I do this because composers always have to 'open up' in such movements. And as these movements are directly related to singing, I've always been fascinated by them. But that was twenty years ago, and as I've already said, I would conduct his symphonies totally differently today. There is a very good book by Alfred Brendel in which he warns of the danger that young people face when listening to recordings from thirty years ago, and who then believe that that is the only way those works should be performed. People should be very careful of such an approach.

JF-A: The Sinfonieorchester des Norddeutschen Rundfunks was also an important milestone in your career. Like many of the other German radio orchestras, it was established after the Second World War and is based in Hamburg, a city where great conductors, such as Gustav

Mahler, Felix Weingartner and Hans Schmidt-Isserstedt, also held posts of importance. What defines Hamburg as a cultural centre, and what were some of the differences and similarities that you experienced when working with both the Hamburg and Cologne radio orchestras?

CvD: Mahler liked Hamburg, and Hamburg liked him. My brother, Klaus, was the mayor of Hamburg for a period, and I pointed out to him that there was no square or street named after the composer. To his credit, he righted that wrong. But if I am being completely honest, Mahler was not so happy in Hamburg. And concerning the differences that I experienced with the Cologne and Hamburg orchestras, I can sum that up simply by saying that I was rather young when I was in Cologne and somewhat older when I was in Hamburg. While I was different, the orchestras were more or less the same.

JF-A: No discussion of your career would be complete without mentioning your work with the Cleveland Orchestra. How did your role as Music Director in Cleveland differ from your earlier posts in Germany, and perhaps more importantly, how different was your relationship with that orchestra from that of its previous permanent conductors?

CvD: In Cleveland, I found an orchestra that could do anything. Very often conductors are asked, 'What's the difference between American and German orchestras?' Let's take Barbirolli, who was not a success in New York, as we all know. Why? Because he took a long time to study, and refused to memorise a Beethoven symphony in two days. This didn't work in America. The Cleveland Orchestra is an ensemble that does its 'homework'. They really play very well, and can follow me easily. The opposite was true in Germany during my early days. There, they wanted me to spend time and to make music with them. And while the

PART ONE: CONDUCTORS

Americans took a different starting point, they now want conductors to spend time making music with them, too, as they have come to understand how an orchestra really works.

JF-A: But why do conductors who work with the Cleveland Orchestra always come away amazed by it?

CvD: Because it's like a terrifically well-tuned piano.

JF-A: Is that partly to do with the famously dry acoustic of Severance Hall, or was it perhaps more to do with its earlier training under George Szell?

CvD: Actually, the Cleveland musicians have a number of advantages. Take London players by contrast. They have to get up at 5.30am to be at the Royal Festival Hall by 10am. For a musician in Cleveland who lives in Shaker Heights, it might take him or her ten minutes to get to Severance Hall. And, of course, the hall is terrific. The sound heard there was not only down to Szell, but due to the venue itself. Did you know that he hated the organ, and wanted to ban the instrument from the hall? That says everything about him. But to return to the players. They also have rooms to practise in, and have individual parking spaces allocated to them. They have a wonderful life. In Cleveland, the players are only concerned with music. It's not a city that allows you to pop out to the movies. For them, it's the orchestra, chamber music and teaching from morning to night. That makes all the difference. The Cleveland Orchestra is a wonderful instrument.

JF-A: When you were appointed Principal Conductor of the Philharmonia Orchestra, you were faced with a self-governing orchestra with a history that was very different from those in Cleveland, Germany and Vienna. What attracted you to the Philharmonia, and what are some of its defining characteristics?

CvD: When I began to work with the Philharmonia Orchestra, I sensed a real partnership. But, as we all know, democracy has its problems. While the Philharmonia players recognise the authority of their conductors, the Chief Conductor also has to recognise that there is real authority in the orchestra. And the ways in which players and conductors work together in Britain is very special. The British don't know how lucky they are. To have the kind of democracy where everybody thinks that they *can't* do everything is very, very important. When I work with the Philharmonia, they offer something and I offer something. This is real co-operation. That's not the case when working with most of the American or German orchestras. The Berlin Philharmonic, for example, is not always respectful of its conductors.

JF-A: Over the years, you have made a great many recordings, resulting in your discography acting as a kind of barometer for discographic change. During the early years of your career, the recording industry was far more buoyant than it is today. Do you have strong reservations about recording, like Wilhelm Furtwängler and Sergiu Celibidache, or are you more like Herbert von Karajan and Sir John Barbirolli and embrace it unconditionally?

CvD: Recording has only one true advantage: it allows me to listen to the performances of artists from the past. Looking back historically is both very important and very interesting. It also allows me to control what I've done. These are the positive aspects of recording. But there are also lots of negative aspects, and I often feel that a great deal of copying takes place interpretatively because of it. Let me tell you a little story.

PART ONE: CONDUCTORS

Otto Klemperer recorded Wagner's *Die fliegende Holländer* here in London. I attended the sessions, as my then wife, Anja Silja, sang the role of Senta on those discs. Klemperer was very old at the time, and actually fell asleep during the duet in the second act. When the timpanist hit his drum loudly, Klemperer woke up and said, 'Bravo!' Having woken up, he then continued for a while before taking another little rest. Even though I considered Klemperer to be something of a genius, his ability to maintain his desired *tempo* was not possible in this case. Nevertheless, the recording was okay; it was fine. I then later heard a new production of the opera under a young conductor in Germany. When he got to the spot where Klemperer fell asleep in the duet, the young conductor made exactly the same *tempo* shift that Klemperer inadvertently made after he dozed off in London. And that is all I have to say about recordings.

JF-A: Let's talk a little about repertoire. As you are a distinguished interpreter of Richard Strauss's music, how do you go about preparing a work such as *Ein Heldenleben*, and in what ways have the composer's own interpretations of the tone poem affected your reading?

CvD: They haven't. There was a very famous young conductor who performed *Ein Heldenleben* with the Vienna Philharmonic at an extremely fast *tempo*. Too fast, in fact. The orchestra then said to him, 'Listen, Maestro, we can't play it at that speed.' He had listened to a disc of Strauss conducting the work, but at the wrong speed. The recording he listened to was so fast that it reproduced the work a semitone higher than written.

JF-A: But as Strauss was a master conductor, could it not be argued that the evidence found in his recordings should be taken into account, at least in part?

CvD: Of course, I have listened to those discs. But I also know that Strauss didn't care too much about what really happened while he was conducting. He must've been great when he was very young, at least up to the point when he received a letter from his father advising him not to jump around too much on the podium. Being a horn player, his father told him that all that an orchestra needs is one, two, three, four and little else. Karajan once mentioned to me that when Strauss visited him after a performance of *Elektra*, he said to the composer, 'Please tell me anything you found wrong with the performance.' To which Strauss simply replied, 'I don't remember the piece too well.' He was a composer who tended to beat time. By all means listen to his discs, but then forget them.

JF-A: Yet when one takes into consideration his achievements as a Mozartian, is there not an argument in favour of less is more?

CvD: You are correct, and what you say is very important. When I heard Karajan perform the end of the first act of *Der Rosenkavalier* with Elisabeth Schwarzkopf, it was the first time that I *didn't* cry after hearing it. And I knew that what Karajan did was right. It's not a sad story when the Marschallin talks about time and getting older. What was great about Strauss was his avoidance of exaggerated sentimentality. But for those of us who are not Strauss, it's very tempting to overdo things. Try to avoid effects and just let the music speak. And take your *tempi* from the musicians. They know what they can do well.

JF-A: A natural extension of the previous question is the old chestnut that great Straussians don't necessarily make great Mahlerians. Do you believe this to be true, and what, for you, are the fundamental differences that a performer faces when interpreting their works?

PART ONE: CONDUCTORS

CvD: We know that the relationship between Strauss and Mahler was both special and strong. Yet Mahler was totally different from Strauss. Leonard Bernstein once said something that really resonated with me: 'Mahler is not a beginning, he is an ending.' There's something to that. Mahler's symphonies were the ultimate expression of that form. After him, very little happened that was original in that particular genre. But what was common to both Strauss and Mahler, and probably to all great composers, was their ability *not* to overstate their own feelings. That doesn't mean that you have to withhold your personality when you perform their works. Of course, you have to serve the composer by observing what's on the five lines of the stave. But, when conducting Mahler, it's how you read between the lines that's most important.

JF-A: When trying to differentiate between Strauss and Mahler, is it too simplistic to say that when it comes to Mahler he is yearning for something divine, while Strauss is more of a humanist?

CvD: Strauss is something of an extrovert, while Mahler is more of an introvert. This is the case even when the opposite might appear true. But when you have a personality like Mahler who struggles with himself, your reading of his music must reflect that. In contrast, Strauss had no self-doubt.

JF-A: When you recorded Mahler's Fifth Symphony with the Cleveland Orchestra, were you influenced by the 1904 and 1905 versions of the piece, or did you simply opt for the final 1911 version?

CvD: I was particularly concerned by what was in the score, and only changed some of the dynamics. These changes were made necessary because the types of instruments that Mahler used are sometimes different from those that we use today. Other than that, I tried not to make any changes or corrections.

JF-A: In the nineteenth century, the works of Beethoven dominated the programmes of some of the world's leading orchestras. As you have recorded a remarkable cycle of the composer's symphonies with the Cleveland Orchestra, I am interested to hear your thoughts on the composer's enduring appeal, and whether or not his dominance has proven to be a double-edged sword, attracting audiences while stifling curiosity and creativity.

CvD: Beethoven is a composer who transcends interpretation. Every time I conduct one of his symphonies, I discover something new. As I am about to perform the Seventh Symphony shortly, I'll restudy it. I don't have a repertoire *per se*, as I am constantly searching for musical truths. The Second, Fourth, Sixth and Eighth Symphonies are the most difficult to interpret. And the Sixth must not be given by a conductor until he or she reaches a certain age. The Third, Fifth, Seventh and Ninth Symphonies reveal a different side of Beethoven from the even-numbered works. Beethoven, of course, was also strongly involved politically. And even when he was totally wrong, he always stood for something. His comments on Napoleon and power are a good example of that. But hovering above all of this is the genius Beethoven. Even though he might have had many faults as a human being, he defies criticism and was a tremendous figure.

JF-A: From both your discography and your concerts in London, it seems that you don't perform Bach regularly. Why is that?

CvD: It's because I never conduct Bach's music in cities or countries where there is only one way of doing it. I did perform Bach's *Matthäus-*

Passion in Cleveland with the whole orchestra, however. And the real miracle about Bach is that his music is so strong that you could play it on saxophones. It's the greatest music. It's the root of everything. But at the moment, it has been hijacked by those who think that they are right. When it comes to Bach, nobody is right. That said, I have learned a great deal from period performance musicians, and have listened to them a lot. Their approach is something that I've had to deal with personally, as I was concerned by how much of what they say is 'business', and how much is belief in what they do. Even though these players *do* perform with real belief, I'm not the kind of person who likes to look over his shoulder historically. It's not my cup of tea.

JF-A: But do you think that we are now at a point when the various schools of performance can exist side by side, and that we can be more accepting of each?

CvD: The instruments are not so important. It's the music itself that matters. Simply read the music. It's great. Thankfully, certain interpretative habits are beginning to disappear, such as the tendency to over emphasise the first note of a two-note phrase. The second note can often be just as important. And while I am unconvinced by the idea that there is only one right way to perform Bach, I am pleased that we have been able to free ourselves from certain nineteenth-century habits when giving his music.

JF-A: A composer who placed great store in the music of Bach was Arnold Schoenberg. Do you think that he's now more important as a historical figure rather than as a composer, or does his music still have something to say?

CvD: Schoenberg was the most important figure in the development of twentieth-century music. When he was asked during the war, 'Are you the Schoenberg who created the twelve-tone system?', he replied, 'Somebody had to do it!' But we know that he was a good composer, and *Verklärte Nacht* is not a bad piece.

JF-A: Are we not now in danger of dividing his music into various categories: durable Schoenberg, historically important Schoenberg and 'nice' Schoenberg?

CvD: He wouldn't have liked the idea of 'nice' Schoenberg. When I conduct Beethoven's Ninth Symphony, I usually do it without any other work in the programme. But when I was invited to give it with the Sinfonieorchester des Norddeutschen Rundfunks as part of a festival, I was asked if I could perform another work with it. Keen to couple the symphony with something substantial, I thought that either Schoenberg's *Erwartung* or *A Survivor from Warsaw* might be suitable. As the performance was to be shown on television, the broadcasting company showed me a graph of how viewing figures plummeted whenever a work by him went on air, and how those figures remained depressed even after a work like the Ninth had begun. That was the end of that programme as far as the television company was concerned. But, ironically, it also goes to show how important Schoenberg was, and is.

JF-A: Over the years, you've done much to encourage young artists. What's your advice to aspiring conductors, and what tips would you give to them so that they can avoid some of the inevitable pitfalls that lie ahead?

PART ONE: CONDUCTORS

CvD: The beginning for any conductor is hard, and it *must* be hard. We don't have an instrument to practise on. When somebody with talent is discovered these days, he or she quickly finds themselves in front of the Royal Concertgebouw, the Berlin Philharmonic or the London Symphony Orchestra. And that's a very, very hard thing to do. I would advise any young conductor to go to the smallest city that they can find and learn their conducting there. That's how I started, and I am very grateful for it. If you begin by working in a small opera house, you are able to practise and to develop certain techniques that will lead you to Vienna. In fact, when I *did* get to Vienna, I also rose through the system there. I started by conducting the Tonkünstler Orchestra before moving on to the Vienna Symphony Orchestra and, later, the Vienna Philharmonic. So, my trajectory was Lübeck, Tonkünstler, Symphony, Philharmonic. And that's the right way to do things. This was also how Barbirolli developed. He took time to study, and you can hear it. Schopenhauer once said, 'Education is what is left when you have forgotten everything you learned.' And that takes time to achieve.

NIKOLAUS HARNONCOURT
(SALZBURG, 2007)

JONATHAN FREEMAN-ATTWOOD: I was recently speaking with the counter-tenor Paul Esswood, with whom you recorded many cantatas, and I alighted on that wonderful alto aria, 'Wo zwei und drei versammlet sind' from Bach's Cantata No. 42, *Am Abend der desselbigen Sabbats*. Amazingly, he'd forgotten that particular recording with you, which astonished me, as it's one of the most beautifully shaped performances of it I know.

NIKOLAUS HARNONCOURT: Over the years, I performed a great deal with Paul, particularly in the operas of Monteverdi at Zurich. These were not only highly satisfying collaborations, but great experiences. Yesterday, I was looking through some old photos and found one with another English counter-tenor, Alfred Deller, with whom I recorded a few cantatas for Vanguard with Gustav and Marie Leonhardt and my wife.

JF-A: Yes, they are very special readings of Cantata No. 54, *Widerstehe doch der Sünde*, and Cantata No. 170, *Vergnügte Ruh, beliebte Seelenlust*, the latter with its extraordinary *obbligato* organ part.

NH: As Alice and I were just married at the time, the recordings must have been made in 1953. I remember the owner of Vanguard Records, Seymour Solomon, saying to me, 'We can't have two couples on one disc. Alice has to change her name.' And that's why she appears on the recording under her maiden name, Hoffelner.

JF-A: Throughout your career, you've returned time and again to Bach's music. Yet when I listened recently to your new recording of the *Weihnachts-Oratorium*, I was particularly struck by how much your approach has changed over the years, even when compared to your recent recording of the *Matthäus-Passion*.

NH: Could that not simply be down to the great difference between the two works? Unlike the Passions, there are comparatively few 'events' in the *Oratorium*. Instead, there are powerful mental pictures of the Christmas story to contemplate. It's a very particular kind of work and, of course, we have Bach writing in a later musical language than in the Passions.

JF-A: But there are significant differences in your approach within a single work. Take, for example, your third recording of the *Matthäus-Passion*, which is completely different from your two previous recordings of the work.

NH: I wouldn't call my second recording with the Royal Concertgebouw Orchestra a recording at all. I was asked if I would allow my 1985 radio broadcast of the work to be published in aid of the Concertgebouw, which was sinking at the time due to rotting foundations. If it *had* been a 'recording', I might have had one or two different soloists and would have asked for some retakes. When we recorded the *Matthäus-Passion* in May 2000 for release by Das Alte Werk in 2007, we took an absolutely new approach. Having intentionally forgotten what we had done previously, we gathered together all the original materials and recorded it in a church. This was not done simply for acoustical reasons, but to achieve the right atmosphere. As we had all these artefacts available to us at the recording sessions, the soloists were able to check their parts when I asked for a passage to be done in a particular way. Thus, they could see for themselves whether or not what I asked for was correct. And so the whole spirit of that performance was very different from everything that we had done before.

JF-A: As you say, the *Weihnachts-Oratorium* lacks the 'action' of the Passions and yet listeners still look for a particular kind of unity within. Both you and Alfred Dürr discuss this unity, which is not only created by conjuring up mental pictures of such things as the shepherds and other Christmas-related imagery, but also through the composer's own referencing between cantatas. But, as the work is quite long, there's always a danger of it becoming wearing on the ear, if it is not allowed time and space to breathe. Do you think that this is the reason why Bach never performed it as six consecutive cantatas?

NH: You're correct: Bach never performed the six parts in one evening. It was performed over the course of the Christmas season until Epiphany.

JF-A: Nevertheless, Bach does set up some important key relationships in the *Oratorium*. The F major in Part Four, for example, establishes a particular connection with the A major in Part Five, which, in turn, is the dominant of D major for the celebratory flourishes of the dazzling Part Six. This not only creates an outward and inner symmetry, but also establishes a strong narrative, a sense of momentum, that leads the listener inextricably towards the final cantata. I'm also very interested in the actual *sound* of your recent recording of the work. It's a fascinating blend harnessing the old and established alongside a strongly '*à la mode' galant* sensibility. Was this intentional?

PART ONE: CONDUCTORS

NH: This is *precisely* why I mentioned how different the *Oratorium* is to the *Matthäus-Passion*. In the *Passion*, there is only one *minuet* and one *sarabande*. There are no other dances. And when I was teaching the work many years ago, I always wanted a student to investigate Bach's use of dance movements in the sacred cantatas and the meaning behind their use. It's often been said that such movements are out of place in church music. Which begs the questions, 'Why do so many great oratorios conclude with *minuets*, and what, in fact, *is* a *minuet*?' And you might also like to consider the related question, 'Why do so many serious symphonies also conclude with a *minuet*?' The idea of using dances in this manner is not restricted to the eighteenth century, but can also be found in works from the nineteenth century. As we know, a symphony originally had three movements, but, all of a sudden, a *minuet* was included. Even Beethoven described his *scherzi* as *minuets*. What does this all amount to? And if we turn to Czech music, the *polka* acts as a kind of *minuet*. When I performed Dvořák's 'New World' Symphony with the Vienna Philharmonic, I was surprised to find that they had no idea where the *polkas* were to be found in the work, even though fifty per cent of the orchestra is of Czech heritage. They'd never played it as if it were a *polka* before, but have since become very aware of such things.

But to return to the *Oratorium*. Tonality is also of great importance when discussing the work. Today, it's impossible to realise the work's tonality properly, as no musician is able to adjust sufficiently to the fine differences in intonation that exist between, say, E major and F major. Yet the meaning of those tonalities remains, particularly when it comes to F major. There's always something very special about that key.

JF-A: I could tell F major was of special significance to you by your particular treatment of the horns. Your recessed approach allowed the phrasing to be quite gentle, even lyrical, rather than divisible into small units. This also allowed you to make clear its pastoral context, while ensuring that the horns avoided the pitfall of sounding like trumpets.

NH: And might I add that F major is the only tonality to boast a pure third, and that all the other tonalities in the *Oratorium* are defined by their relationship to that key. F major *is* Christmas! Thanks to that key, all is well with the world, so to speak, and that's why Bach included the horn, as it's the embodiment of F major. Whether it be A major, D major, E major, they are all related to the pastoral qualities of the work. And when Bach uses a key that's distant from F major, it's defined by its longing, or 'homesickness', for it.

JF-A: Then there's the thorny question of articulation, and how to go about realising that which was not actually written down during Bach's time. From your approach to Part Six, for example, it seems that you've made certain choices that were reminiscent of Felix Prohaska's approach in the 1950s. These would have suited the vocal style of Teresa Stich-Randall, which one hears so gloriously in the duet of Prohaska's recording of Cantata No. 78, *Jesu, der du meine Seele*.

NH: Yes, indeed. Teresa often sang in Vienna when I was a member of the Vienna Symphony Orchestra, and I did speak with her about this open and direct approach to text and style. Her way of singing was exactly what I was looking for when I recorded the *Oratorium*. I once asked her to sing with me at a concert in Paris, but that was impossible because of her schedule. Although we never actually worked together, she always remained my vocal ideal.

PART ONE: CONDUCTORS

JF-A: While you were a member of the Vienna Symphony Orchestra, you were also active in founding the Concentus Musicus Wien. This was a remarkable time. One day you might have been playing for Herbert von Karajan and, the next, you were exploring the virgin territory of period performance with your wife, Alice, Herbert Tachezi and Jürg Schaeftlein.

NH: Jürg was an old friend whom I met in the 1930s when he played the recorder as a six-year-old schoolboy. He was a year older than me and sadly died some time ago now from cancer. For a period, he was a member of the NHK Symphony Orchestra in Tokyo before returning to Vienna and the Concentus Musicus. At first, he told me that he wouldn't play the oboe, but would be happy to play Renaissance recorder with us. Nevertheless, I was keen for him to play the oboe, as we had no permanent oboist playing with the group during its early years. But he continued to reject the idea as 'impossible', because the lower pitch that we played at disturbed his sense of perfect pitch. I then discovered a fantastic, relatively unused oboe that was made in Leipzig in the 1720s, which I still own. He tested it, liked it and said, 'I'll try.' He then became a pillar of the orchestra. Schaeftlein was not the only member of Concentus to struggle with its lower pitch: Tachezi and my wife were also affected by it. When, for example, Alice hears the Vienna Philharmonic play in C major, she hears C sharp major. She can adjust to A=440, but cannot adjust to A=444. The Concentus Musicus normally plays at A=421, but when we perform Mozart's works we use A=430. Schaeftlein didn't know this when he agreed to join us as an oboist and steadfastly refused to play oboe d'amore and oboe da caccia, as he felt uncomfortable transposing from A and F.

JF-A: He wouldn't have got work in Bach's day!

NH: True. But he did play all three types of oboe by the following year. In fact, during Bach's lifetime, he would have had to play C major in *Chorton* during morning church services, which was a whole tone or a third sharper, and then in *Cammerton* in the afternoon. An even tougher task.

JF-A: When I listen to your recordings with the Concentus Musicus from the 1960s, you seem to be exploring a bigger expressive world than simply period performance. Your approach makes one redefine performances such as Herbert von Karajan's reading of the *Matthäus-Passion* from the 1950 Bachfest. That's an example of Karajan the Kapellmeister, which is an aspect of him that most listeners don't know. It's how he combined energy and lyricism with a 'front' to the note that's particularly striking. And, here, I am thinking about a type of silvery lyricism that he later achieved with the Berlin Philharmonic.

NH: I remember clearly every word he said to me about my cello playing when I auditioned for a place in the Vienna Symphony in 1952. I also remember that he was preparing Bach's Mass in B minor at the time, which was recorded partially in Vienna and partially in London. He personally led 100 rehearsals with the Singverein der Gesellschaft der Musikfreunde. He refused to leave the rehearsals to the choirmaster, and had no intention of simply stepping in at the last minute to make the recording. And, in later years, when many of the choristers were too old to sing well, he still remained loyal to it.

JF-A: Have you ever considered re-recording Bach's Mass in B minor?

NH: In principle, yes, but my schedule currently prevents it. I would also like to record some more of Haydn's operas, including *L'isola disabitata*. That, however, will depend entirely on finding a satisfactory edition of it. I've recently recorded *Die Jahreszeiten* in a new edition, which was based on Haydn's own parts. This made a huge difference to the spirit of the performance.

JF-A: Can you define that difference and what we should be looking out for?

NH: In most of the printed scores, the clarinets join the oboes in the great choruses and play in some selected solo movements. But we know that all of the major choruses should be played by the whole orchestra. We also know that Haydn conducted the work in three halls of different sizes and, on each occasion, he changed the instrumentation. It's clear, therefore, that the size of the orchestra is wholly dependent on the size of the hall. This is a principle that I have always subscribed to. Mozart's C major Symphony from Salzburg is a case in point. It was played initially with three first violins, but when it was later heard at the Hofreitschule in Vienna, it was given with twenty first violins. While this approach might not always be appropriate for Bach or Handel, it's correct for *Die Jahreszeiten*. This is confirmed when you perform the work using Haydn's own parts. And it also becomes clear from those parts that the work is not just a representation of how the changing seasons were viewed at the time, but how an individual responds to those events at different times of their lives. It explores life as a transition, and not as something that simply ends. Haydn believes that religiosity should be available to all.

JF-A: And here I am also reminded of the ways in which you approach folkloric material.

NH: I think that folkloric material is generally underestimated today. Listen to how a Japanese, American or an English player might perform the same work. If these musicians have been classically trained in one of the great conservatories, they will inevitably overlook its folkloric content. When I hear a Bruckner symphony played by a modern German or Austrian orchestra, they have no idea when a *Ländler* is being used, let alone the village from which the material originated. If you are unable to capture the correct spirit of passages, such as that which opens the slow movement of the Fifth Symphony, you shouldn't perform Bruckner.

JF-A: That has a famously low oboe note, doesn't it?

NH: It is only difficult to play on the French oboe. The three lowest oboe notes are not a problem when played on the Vienna oboe. But I would like to return briefly to the true meaning of a *minuet*, *waltz* or *polka* in Vienna, Berlin, Paris or Prague. It was impossible to annotate exactly how those works were to be played and, in many ways, having a grandfather who knows how to dance these pieces is of greater value to a young musician than any form of conservatory training.

JF-A: I would say, though, that students today are increasingly aware of the vast range of possibilities that are afforded them. Those currently attending the Royal Academy of Music, and who have heard your performances of Bruckner's symphonies, are fascinated by the depth of reference you offer.

NH: This is a consequence of my musical experiences from childhood onwards.

JF-A: Those experiences are particularly evident when I listen to how you articulate the brass in the Ninth Symphony. They have a clear and alert vocal line, but never apply glamorous opulence for its own sake.

PART ONE: CONDUCTORS

And it's also your ability to interpret what the signs and codes found in the printed score mean that also colour your reading. Indeed, I never cease to be amazed by your ability to move seamlessly between the works of Bach, Mozart, Dvořák, Bartók and Verdi.

NH: Again, it has to do with childhood. My father was musical and my mother, who was Hungarian, listened to the radio. When she heard a *czardas* being broadcast, and that was being performed correctly, she would become very excited and show me how to dance it. So, I danced a *czardas* a hundred times with musicians who knew how it should sound. As a boy, I attended a concert given by Béla Bartók at Graz in 1937. I hope to perform some of his music over the next few years.

JF-A: Why have you waited so long to conduct his works?

NH: I have felt the need for a 'passport', so to speak, to enter his world. I didn't want my Hungarian colleagues to say, 'What you did was alright, but you didn't play the *tempi* indicated by Bartók.' And this is always a difficult question, as the speeds marked by a composer are not always what they do. They are often very different.

JF-A: May I ask what you'll conduct next, or do you want that to remain a surprise?

NH: I'd like to keep it a secret, although I'd love to do the Second Violin Concerto. The problem is: I have yet to find the right violinist. When I was a member of the Vienna Symphony Orchestra, we performed it with Ede Zathureczky, and having played it with him, it's hard to imagine it any other way. The same applies to Dvořák's Cello Concerto, which I have also never performed.

JF-A: A work that I imagine would suit you marvellously is Stravinsky's *Oedipus Rex*.

NH: I know the work, as I played it under Karajan, who made a tremendous mistake at the onset of the 'Gloria'. I also played as a cellist under Stravinsky, and was again extremely surprised when he took speeds that didn't match the printed score. But I *am* going to perform *The Rake's Progress* next year.

JF-A: Are your responses to these works partly due to your upbringing, which was very rich culturally?

NH: In the 1930s, my uncle was the Director of New York's Museum of Modern Art. He was my father's brother, and a friend of all the city's leading artists, including George Gershwin. With the publication of each new work by Gershwin, my uncle would immediately send a copy to my father. And I'm sure that I was one of the first Europeans to have heard *Porgy and Bess*, as my father played it over and over again. Combine this with the fact that my mother was Hungarian, and only spoke Hungarian during the last three years of her life, and that my father was connected closely to Czechoslovakia, this meant that my youth was very rich indeed.

JF-A: Between leaving the Vienna Symphony Orchestra in 1969 and embarking on the period of your life that was dominated by the Concentus Musicus, did you ever think that your career would take the direction that it has, and have any composers become constant threads?

NH: There was never a time during my life that I didn't play Schubert, for example. And you must remember that during the early years of the

PART ONE: CONDUCTORS

Concentus, we never performed Bach's works, as we felt unready to do so. We mainly played very early music, including pieces from the Avignon Papacy. We undertook long tours of the United States, and during one of these, Stanford University refused to let us perform there because of our use of *musica ficta*. I had a fascinating discussion with Gustave Reese in New York about the subject, but Stanford was having nothing to do with it. They had their opinion and that was that. Yet when it comes to whether or not a particular cadence should resolve in the major, those issues have still to be determined. While one theorist might have a strong point of view, another will have a totally different one. And, for that very reason, we took the decision *not* to perform music earlier than Gabrieli. This saddened me greatly, as I love early music very much. That said, there are some recordings of these works with Concentus Musicus, including one with Alfred Deller performing compositions from the fourteenth century. Every second year, we also perform a concert that explores music from the period directly preceding the Baroque, which regularly includes works by Monteverdi and his immediate predecessors.

JF-A: Does the Concentus Musicus still perform consort music?

NH: No, and I am very sorry about that, as there was a time when Elizabethan music was central to the work of the group. As you might know, I recently sold my English viol, the only instrument that I've ever got rid of. When we recorded all of Purcell's fantasias, we rehearsed them for a whole year before playing them in public. But the problem with these works is the retention of seven viol players for long periods, particularly as some of the players are only required for one or two of the pieces. That can prove a logistical challenge. And you must never play only two or three of Purcell's fantasias in a concert, you must play them all.

JF-A: A question that I have often heard asked is: 'Why doesn't Nikolaus Harnoncourt record the music of Richard Strauss?'

NH: I hate Richard Strauss! I hate him because of his talent. He was the most gifted composer after Mozart, and the only works that have been the beneficiaries of that talent are *Salome* and *Elektra*. He only used his left hand while composing and never his right. By which I mean, it all came too easy to him and he preferred playing cards.

JF-A: What about Wagner?

NH: There are two or three ways into Wagner and mine would be through *Die Meistersinger von Nürnberg* and *Tristan und Isolde*. Yet I struggle with the first act of *Die Meistersinger* and feel that Wagner really wanted to write an operetta instead.

JF-A: But surely your approach to texture, and the way that you naturally respond to the interaction between voices and instruments, would benefit *Die Meistersinger* greatly.

NH: If my working day had forty-eight hours rather than twenty-four, then I would definitely perform some works by Wagner. But here I must point out that in order for me to make good music, my interests cannot be restricted to just that. My interests are very wide ranging and nobody would like my performances if I were just a musician. I don't like specialists. Players must not restrict themselves to early music, and none of the members of the Concentus Musicus is a specialist. If you don't live in your own time musically, then you are merely existing in a cultural museum. While the end result might be historically correct, it's not a living entity. The questions that should always be asked are: 'Why are we playing music by composers such as Dittersdorf and where should it be performed?' Depending on the answer, those works might be better suited to a museum or an academic seminar than to a concert hall. Only the great masterworks of art that speak to each successive generation should truly take pride of place in concert halls and opera houses. They are of paramount importance to the ways in which we live our lives. While there might well be a great deal of truth in the notion that historically informed performances enhance the understanding of a given work, that argument is only true if the result is relevant to today.

SIR JOHN ELIOT GARDINER
(DAVID JOSEFOWITZ RECITAL HALL, 21 SEPTEMBER 2012)

JONATHAN FREEMAN-ATTWOOD: With the exception of Sir Henry Wood, there are very few figures in the history of British music-making who have immersed themselves so fully in the highways and byways of music as you. You have tackled representative works from the fifteenth century onwards, and all with equal zeal. Was your eclecticism and range of musical experience down to your education and background, or was it simply a product of your artistic DNA?

JOHN ELIOT GARDINER: I don't really know. Possibly a bit of both, as I'm just naturally curious. But I admit that I've never ploughed a conventional musical furrow. I'm a rotten pianist, and although I was accepted into the National Youth Orchestra as a violinist, I did a lot better after I transferred to the viola. I sang a great deal as a treble and earned my crust as a tenor before conducting took over. My parents were both amateur musicians, and music was part of the fabric of my childhood. When I look back on it, I think of how incredibly lucky I was. Music was never something 'hooey' or rarefied at home; it was just always around. As a family, we sang grace at meals, and my parents performed Byrd's four- and five-part Masses throughout the Second World War to keep their spirits up. They also had a passion for the music of Bach, which they passed on to me from an early age. Even before I could read music properly, I knew the treble parts of his six motets pretty well off by heart. And there was always that admonishing Haussmann portrait of Bach as Kantor hanging on the wall of our house to keep one honest.

JF-A: Did you know at the time that you were destined for a career in music?

JEG: Not then, and not to start with. Music in my parents' household was always connected to the agricultural year and the cycle of the seasons. I loved everything to do with farming. We celebrated both the Christian and the pagan festivals, such as Lammas and Plough Monday. All in all, it was a pretty unusual musical upbringing, and it wasn't until I was sent away to boarding school that I discovered quite how strange it was.

JF-A: Was that in Wessex?

JEG: Yes, in Thomas Hardy country. My father was both a farmer and a planter of trees. He and his uncle planted four-and-a-half million of them in the denuded landscape of North Dorset between 1927 and the 1950s. Silviculture was my father's great love. He was also a pioneer organic farmer and a founder member of the Soil Association. He used to sing in a ringing tenor voice, either on his tractor or on his horse. My mother had a more mellifluous voice; a really beautiful contralto. She would sing arias from Bach's cantatas, and I would try to accompany her on the violin by playing the *obbligato* parts, but not terribly well! That was my first experience of those works. And then there were the talented musical friends who dropped in from time to time. Sir Thomas Armstrong, a predecessor of yours here at the Academy, and Imogen

Holst, the daughter of the composer Gustav Holst and, later, the amanuensis of Benjamin Britten, were both family friends. They would visit and sometimes conduct our choral weekends at various times of the year. Imo was quite an amazing lady who wrote a wonderful book called *Tune*. Somebody made a film of her rehearsing Bach's Mass in B minor just from the waist down, which showed her dancing while conducting. And it was from her that I learned that dance was a vital element of Baroque music. She was a great influence. She accompanied me and my sister when we sang Britten's *Friday Afternoons* at the Bryanston Summer Music School with the composer in attendance. Later, when my voice broke, I sometimes sang with her group, The Purcell Singers, at the Aldeburgh Festival.

My near namesake, the composer John Gardner, who died quite recently, was a wonderful all-round musician. I also learned a lot from him. He had a very eclectic knowledge of repertoire, ranging all the way from Guillaume de Machaut to contemporary music. But the third, and undoubtedly the most important, person to influence me was Nadia Boulanger. I was introduced to her when I was a boy of eight. She'd come to the Bryanston Summer School, later the Dartington Summer School, to lecture on Monteverdi and Stravinsky. My mother took me along. I probably hadn't much of a clue as to what she was talking about at that stage, but I vividly recall what an impressive presence she had. There was tremendous excitement at the school when its head, Sir William Glock, acquired Malipiero's new edition of the complete Monteverdi madrigals and handed out copies like newly found treasures to all the members of the course. We all sat around in a circle and sang some of these wonderful works under Mademoiselle Boulanger's direction. Even though I could just about read music, I must've decided then and there, subconsciously at least, that she was a teacher whom I would really love to learn from one day. Later, some time in my teens, I heard her lecture at the Royal College of Music. So, when I finished my academic education, I made a beeline for her and asked to study with her in Paris and Fontainebleau.

JF-A: After you finished your secondary education at Bryanston, you went up to Cambridge, where you read history and Arabic at King's College. Why not music?

JEG: History was my thing, as the music Tripos didn't look all that enticing. I had a wonderful history teacher at Bryanston, and my interest in Arabic came about because of the time I spent in the Middle East during my gap year. While I was in Lebanon, the United Nations Relief and Works Agency offered me a job writing a documentary film script on Palestinian refugee conditions. That was both an amazing and a sobering experience. And when I was not working on the script in the evenings, I had a chance to play my violin at the casino in Jounieh, a city midway between Byblos and Beirut. There, I accompanied a fantastic singer called Fairuz, who was known as the 'Lebanese nightingale'. She had a stonking voice. And as one of her accompanists, I had to sit cross-legged on a carpet with two other musicians and follow exactly what she was doing by doubling her smoky mezzo voice an octave above. Even though I only had to play on the E-string in the first or second positions, the hard thing was to mirror all her improvised ornaments. And it was essential that we matched her endless decorative 'twiddles' without 'curdling' the music or losing the overall line. I learnt a lot from that. When I arrived at Cambridge, my main passion other than music was research. I attempted to account for the historical differences that exist between Islam and Christianity. In other words, I tried to understand why the Western and Arabic worlds always get each other wrong, and how the West bears a huge responsibility and burden for instigating a great many political problems that shouldn't be there and could've been avoided. Sadly, that legacy of misunderstanding and misalliance continues to this day.

JF-A: But music was also of enormous importance to you at Cambridge. You began to develop your huge flair for getting musicians and singers together, and your passion for works that were not known widely. Monteverdi's *Vespro della Beata Vergine* is both a case in point and emblematic of what you have since done.

JEG: Looking back now, I realise what a preposterously ambitious undertaking it was to have attempted to conduct the Monteverdi *Vespers* at that stage. It all came about thanks to my Director of Studies, Sir Edmund Leach, a wonderful man and Provost of King's College and Professor of Social Anthropology at Cambridge. He called me and said, 'Look, John Eliot, you have to sort yourself out. Take a year off from the history Tripos and decide what direction your life is going to take. You have to decide whether you're going to be a musician, a farmer, a politician or an academic.' Not knowing what I was letting myself in for, I said, 'Okay, fine. I'd be glad to.' I set myself the task of forming a group to perform the *Vespers*, which was a work that was hardly known in this country and had never been performed at Cambridge. I'd first heard it some years before on the radio when Walter Goehr conducted a performance of it with the London Symphony Orchestra in York Minster. It's a hugely challenging work to organise, stage and direct, and a complex mosaic of music. The problem for me was that I'd grown up in an amateur musical home in Dorset which was light years away from the Cambridge collegiate choral culture of the time. I was a history scholar at King's and not a member of its famous choir. I wasn't a choral scholar, although they did once offer me a 'volunteer-ship'. Whenever I heard the choir perform music that I already knew – works by Tallis, Byrd,

Purcell or, worst of all, Bach – it sounded so foreign and strange to me. Although extremely polite and cultured, it struck me as rather bloodless. It lacked drama and there was no detectable emphasis on the words or the text. The King's Choir has changed a lot since those days, but, at the time, it was famed for its blend, its euphony and its perfect tuning. Actually, what I've just said is not strictly true: to my ears, they always sharpened the sevenths and the major thirds. Everything was delivered in a very genteel *mezzo piano*; never a *forte* and never a true *pianissimo*. I suppose it had much to do with the acoustic of King's College Chapel, which lent itself to a sort of 'cat-stroking' style of *legato* mush; a mush that lacked muscle, sinew and bone.

JF-A: While you were describing all of this, it occurred to me that Boulanger, whom you mentioned earlier, had no real grounding in performance practice at all. The same could be said of you. You clearly had her Monteverdi sound at the back of your mind, a sound that was a combination of the inspirational and the subliminal. It was surely an example of what was possible practically, rather than an expression of period style.

JEG: You're absolutely right. She worked by instinct rather than by the formal study of past performance practices. Nevertheless, her musicality was inevitably so profound and natural, and her results were always so convincing and persuasive. That was even true of her wonderfully idiosyncratic continuo playing on a modern piano: listen, for example, to her recording of Monteverdi's *Zefiro torna*, or her superb disc of Brahms's *Liebeslieder-Walzer* with Dinu Lipatti.

JF-A: How, then, did you develop your own critical positions on Monteverdi, rhetoric and *concitato*?

JEG: I think that as a history student, I appreciated that Monteverdi occupies a pivotal position culturally, just as Shakespeare does in terms of poetry and theatre. In fact, Monteverdi was a direct contemporary of Shakespeare, and could be said to have created something analogous to him in the world of music. Monteverdi set out to encompass in music the complete gamut of human emotions, including grief, pity, rage and intense love, in a way that previous generations of composers had not attempted. He established a system for developing what he called a *'seconda prattica'*, or 'second practice' when writing for singers and instrumentalists. And, by so doing, he extended and enriched the musical embodiment of human passions in a particularly vivid, graphic and varied way. This is not dissimilar to what Shakespeare did when he mixed raunchy comedy with high tragedy in some of his plays. In a sense, Monteverdi's concentrated, epigrammatic musical discourse in his madrigals was akin to the English metaphysical poetry of people like George Herbert and John Donne. When you read the letters of Monteverdi, it becomes clear that he was not only a thoughtful and a committed artist who was intensely proud of his craft, but that he found himself battling against social conventions in his professional life. For twenty-two years, he was employed by the Gonzaga family in Mantua, and was treated rather shoddily by them. And when he eventually did escape their court, after having given his last shirt to them musically, he took up his position at St Mark's Basilica in Venice as its *maestro di cappella*. There, he looked back ruefully at his time in Mantua, remembering the indignity he suffered in having to queue for the meagre pay that he received in recompense for all the wonderful music that he composed. When referring to his musical gifts, he comes across as somebody who could be both boastful and humble. All through his later years, he continued to explore the emotional make-up of men and women, and developed new techniques for conveying its complexity in music. In his time, he was a trail-blazer. Like Beethoven, he was a pioneer, and perhaps more so than any other composer of the early Baroque.

JF-A: Was your passion for Monteverdi and his *Vespers* the reason why you founded the Monteverdi Choir?

JEG: Absolutely. Along with period instruments, such as cornets and sackbuts, I took the people whom I could get hold of – Cambridge choral scholars, who were drilled and honed in a beautiful, but anodyne, style – and asked them to sing with engagement and passion. I wanted them to savour the articulation of the words that they were singing. This was a major readjustment for them, and they were extraordinarily indulgent and co-operative. They did their best to help me realise my target. Yet we probably fell a long way short of the unrealistic ideals I'd set for that first performance of the work on 5 March 1964. And while I'm rather relieved that no recording of it exists, it was attended by all sorts of critics and musical bigwigs who were both courteous and complimentary about it. Warts and all, it was the epiphany that I'd been looking for. And as a direct result of that performance, I took the plunge to study and to become a full-time musician.

JF-A: Clearly, Boulanger's eclecticism helped to lay the foundations of your musical style, but would it be fair to say that the time you spent studying with Thurston Dart was also of great importance to you?

JEG: Yes, indeed. Bob Dart was a mathematician who became a musician and a teacher. He had an analytical and a mathematical brain that I imagine was not unlike Bach's. As he straddled the world of performance practice and scholarship, he was the perfect person for me at that stage. And when it came to music scholarship, he really was something of a Sherlock Holmes. I spent a year studying with him at King's College London around the time that he opened a new music faculty there in the mid-1960s. He made a habit of coming to class with an armful of untitled part books of some Renaissance or Baroque piece or other, and would ask us a series of searching questions about it. He'd want to hear from us what it was about, what it was scored for, what was unusual about it, and, if possible, who composed it. In fact, we were to tell him anything and everything about the work from simply examining either its title page or its opening bars. To develop those critical tools concentrated the mind, and to be taught how to study historical materials in that manner was like grist to the mill for me. I was enthralled. Having been trained as a historian, I found it both wonderful and natural that music could be treated and analysed in this manner. Dart also possessed an instinctive musicality: it was marvellous to see and to hear him play continuo. When he was 'in the zone' as a performer, he would sometimes throw the rule book out of the window, something I found both refreshing and inspiring.

But Bob booted me out after a year, and told me to go and study in Eastern Europe just as Sir Charles Mackerras had done. He suggested that I should go to either Prague or Budapest where conductors were trained properly, as I could expect to learn nothing of use by studying in this country. Bob may well have been right. And even though I was actually offered scholarships to study in Prague and Budapest, I told him that the person whom I most wanted to study with was Nadia Boulanger. I think that Bob was rather disappointed, as he saw it as an easy option. But little did he know how tough it proved to be. My problem was: I really didn't have the necessary formal qualifications and hadn't read music at Cambridge. Although I'd been conducting choirs and orchestras since I was fifteen and eighteen respectively, and had

PART ONE: CONDUCTORS

trained and sung as a professional chorister and soloist, I hadn't yet acquired the basic 'grammar' of music. That was what I needed above all. Nadia Boulanger really put me through the grinder, and she was pitiless in the demands that she made of her students. And that applied to every sphere of musical practice, not just technique. She made you question your fundamental motives, both philosophically and morally. She wanted to know your motivation for wanting to be a musician, especially if you were keen to become a conductor. She wanted to know why you felt that you had the right to stand in front of an orchestra and to ask them to play for you in a particular way. She'd ask, 'Do you consider that you are really qualified?' Of course not. She'd set the bar so high that you really did feel that you *had* to be the master of your material. You had to know counterpoint, ear training, *solfège*, the rudiments of harmony, the psychology of conducting and the historical and stylistic development of music. You had to know all of these things before you could begin to contemplate embarking on a professional conducting career. My first year with her was a crash course during which I was confined for weeks on end to doing harmony exercises using just root-position chords, the avoidance of consecutive fifths and octaves, and the construction of satisfying melodic lines. She taught harmony as if it were a Bach chorale. Not only did you have to complete your harmony exercises on four different staves and using four different clefs, but you had to make sure that you phrased everything perfectly, so that the intersections of the lines created beautiful counterpoint. Despite my shortcomings, she somehow saw something in me worth nurturing. I learned an enormous amount from her, and I owe her a great debt of gratitude for all the often painful lessons that she taught me.

JF-A: After your two years with Boulanger, you began to work with the BBC Northern Symphony Orchestra, now the BBC Philharmonic.

What are your memories of that experience, and what were your duties with the orchestra?

JEG: I had twice attended the summer school at Canford, which was pretty much the only place in this country at the time where one could really learn practical conducting technique from a very fine musician and a skilled master of the baton: George Hurst. He was a wonderful teacher, and there were several conductors from our generation who learned a great deal from him. When I auditioned for the post of Apprentice Conductor with the BBC Northern Symphony Orchestra, George had just retired as its Principal Conductor. That proved to be a fiercely hard testing ground, as the orchestra was then a very hard-boiled, professional ensemble. It was brilliant at sight-reading, but it took no prisoners. I was amazed that all the players smoked like chimneys during the recording sessions, and that each member of the double-bass section puffed on a Meerschaum pipe. They were shrouded in a fug of smoke, and I could barely see them through the nimbus. There were two members of The King's Singers, Simon Carrington and Alastair Hume, who were friends of mine at Cambridge, and who were double-bass players in the orchestra. They said to me, 'Now look, if the principal bass player should happen to take his pipe out of his mouth, be sure not to say anything in reply or else you'll be in deep trouble.' I kept a firm eye on that pipe! Overall, it was invaluable training for me, and just the practical hands-on experience that I needed after two years of undiluted *solfège* and theory in Paris. The orchestra's programmes were mostly very conventional and would typically consist of an overture, a concerto and a symphony. Normally, as the Apprentice Conductor, you were only given the overture to conduct. If the overture lasted twelve minutes, you would be allotted ten minutes rehearsal, two minutes less than the piece lasted. That meant you had to learn how to prioritise. You had to know exactly what to go for, which bits to rehearse, what to say, what not to say, what to leave to chance and what to leave to the adrenaline and professionalism of the orchestra once the red light went on to record. These were incredibly valuable lessons to learn. Time in the music profession is costly, and you have to be really economical in your rehearsal technique. Every time you stop an orchestra to say something that you hadn't been able to convey either by gesture or by baton technique, the chances are that you will be defeated. George Hurst was very sharp on that. At the summer school in Canford, he used to sit in the front row of the woodwinds and glare at you while you were conducting. If you stopped the orchestra, other than for an absolutely crucial reason, he would say, 'Off! Next conductor!'

JF-A: By the late 1960s, you were also starting to make an impact in the theatre, and were engaged to perform Mozart's *Die Zauberflöte* at Sadler's Wells Opera in 1969. What was that experience like?

JEG: Offering me *Die Zauberflöte* was an act of pure faith on the part of Charles Mackerras, who was the company's newly appointed Music Director. He just threw me in to conduct two performances of the work at the London Coliseum. I'd only conducted one Mozart opera before with the Chelsea Opera Group, but never *Die Zauberflöte*. Nor had I ever conducted a fully staged professional production before. And I was given no orchestral rehearsals at all: just a piano rehearsal with a few of the cast. That was all a bit alarming. After I entered the pit to start the performance, I bowed, shook the leader's hand, and gave an up-beat to begin the overture. But instead of hearing a resonant semiquaver after the initial minim and pause, I heard a bullet-like hemidemisemiquaver coming at me, followed by an equally shortened long note. That was quite a shock, as Charlie had forgotten to tell me that double-dotting was his normal practice. Then, having reached the end of the overture, the first thing that I saw as the curtain went up was the Queen of the Night bestride a fork-lift truck, along with a rubber hose-pipe representing the serpent with Tamino desperately trying to avoid it. And to top it off, one of the three boys' voices cracked in Act One: they were replaced by three adult chorus ladies for Act Two! It was baptism by fire.

JF-A: In 1977, you made a deep impact with your reading of Handel's *Acis and Galatea* at the Innsbruck Festival of Early Music. This was at a time when you were also beginning to explore the music of Rameau and to become interested in period instruments. You had something to say about that music which we hadn't heard before. Where did that passion come from, and was it as a result of your time with Boulanger?

JEG: Yes, indirectly it was. I was fortunate in that I didn't learn music from the nineteenth century backwards. This was unlike so many of my colleagues for whom Beethoven to Richard Strauss by way of Mahler is the core repertoire, and who consider anything earlier as interesting, but a bit primitive. When I was growing up, Renaissance composers like Byrd and Palestrina, and three early Baroque composers – Monteverdi, Schütz and Purcell – were the dominant musical figures of my early childhood. The step to Handel and Bach was then quite natural, although perhaps rather unusual. Mozart was the summit for me at that stage. As I was not part of the English cathedral system, I never sang Wesley, Walmisley, Stainer or Dyson as a chorister. I was also extremely fortunate that George Malcolm became a good friend and mentor. He was somebody whom I revered, not only as a brilliant harpsichordist, but also as a fine conductor. As choirmaster at Westminster Cathedral in the 1960s, he drew amazing, un-English sounds from its choir. His recordings of Victoria's *Tenebrae Responsories* and of Britten's *Missa* *brevis* are just exemplary. He once said to me, 'Rameau is the man for you!' I'd never even heard of Rameau by that stage. And so when I went to study with Nadia Boulanger in 1967 and 1968, I made a point of visiting the Bibliothèque nationale, where I spent a lot of time looking at the opera manuscripts of Rameau. These are fascinating documents that represent strange and wonderful music. The first thing that I noticed was that the parts that the players used were full of *graffiti*: they were full of hilarious caricatures of the conductors, the singers and the stage staff. They also criticised both the length of an act and the opera itself. Then, I noticed in the scores that Rameau had annotated many things himself, and that he had very cramped, Gallic handwriting. I then compared his scores with the printed *Œuvres complètes*, which was published by Durand. These had been edited by famous composers such as Vincent d'Indy, Camille Saint-Saëns and Charles Malherbe. And without so much as a pardon on their side, they introduced all sorts of 'improvements' to the orchestration, along with occasional changes to the harmony that were in a completely different style to that of Rameau. So, I thought that I'd better do something about it and to make my own editions if I were to bring his operas to performance.

JF-A: Why do you no longer programme Rameau's music on a regular basis?

JEG: Because it's been taken over by all those richly endowed and highly subsidised French orchestras, the like of which don't exist in England. I still absolutely adore Rameau's music, with its sensuality and its rhythmic fluidity, and dream about conducting his operas again. Even though some of it is written out in straight quavers, its swung rhythms can sound rather like the blues, thanks to the French Baroque tradition of *notes inégales*. It has a sexy, lilting agility and suppleness about it and contains wonderfully bold harmonic excursions. I fell completely in love with Rameau's music when I was studying in Paris, and I later tried to emulate those sounds with my Monteverdi Orchestra. But we soon came up against a brick wall. You can play Bach and Handel on modern instruments and it'll sound grand and idiomatic, but when you try to play Rameau on them, you find that you are using a physical apparatus that is just too cumbersome and unsubtle. Metal strings don't react in the same supple way as gut strings when playing relaxed and lilting *inégale* music. And modern woodwinds also sound too forthright: Rameau's music needs to have a will-o'-the-wisp airiness about it and a smoky, saxophonic sensuality, especially when it comes to his use of high bassoons.

While I was studying in Paris, I came across Rameau's final opera, *Les Boréades*, a masterpiece that had never been published or performed complete before, even in Rameau's lifetime. When I went to the Bibliothèque nationale to get permission to make a copy of the autograph score, I can still recall to this day how Monsieur Lesure, the Head Librarian, looked at me piteously and asked, 'But why are you bothering with this piece? It's written by a composer at the end of his life with a clapped-out imagination. It had gone; his fantasy had gone. Poof!' I can't remember exactly what I said, but it was something like, 'Thank you, but I beg to differ.' I then went on to give the first concert performance of the work in 1975 with the wonderful musicians of the Monteverdi Orchestra. Some people who came that night and heard the music told me afterwards that they thought that Rameau should now be considered in the same breath as Bach and Handel. But even as the third member of that great triumvirate, I couldn't find a recording company that was willing to touch *Les Boréades*. Later, in 1982, I conducted the opera at the Aix-en-Provence Festival, this time with the period instruments of the English Baroque Soloists, and in a lavish, fully staged production. This came as a shock to the Parisian listeners holidaying in Aix. They brought with them their very ambivalent attitude towards their home-grown music, especially that of Rameau, but left captivated and enthusiastic. While the French seem to take to Debussy and Ravel, they can also be snooty about them. They are still rather dismissive of Berlioz, although now much less so after we gave a complete performance of *Les Troyens* at Paris's Théâtre du Châtelet in 2003. The breakthrough for Rameau came when we first presented *Les Boréades*, followed by *Hippolyte et Aricie*, in Aix and Lyon in 1982 and 1983. After that, a number of other conductors then took up these works, notably William Christie, Marc Minkowski, Emmanuelle Haïm and Sir Simon Rattle. Rameau is no longer considered an exotic curiosity. Orchestral musicians love playing his music, even young South African players, as I found out on a visit to Soweto in 1997.

JF-A: In one sense, your Monteverdi Choir has been something of an *alma mater* for you, as so much of your work starts with your understanding of singers. As the choir has now been in existence for some five decades, do you occasionally look back over its history and think how different the sound was during its early years by comparison with today?

JEG: Yes, I do. I mentioned earlier some of the difficulties that I originally faced when trying to mould singers from a totally different tradition. But what I found encouraging were the ways in which fine musicians, such as early members of The King's Singers, took to Monteverdi and began to sing it in a completely different way. They told me they felt that this degree of expressivity had not previously been asked of them. When the choir was put on a regular footing and moved to London, it was at a time when the BBC was very active in encouraging young choirs and young choral conductors to explore and to record different repertoires. It was also a time when festivals in Europe were opening up, leading to us being offered a great many engagements. Recording companies then followed suit, resulting in discs for Decca, Erato, Deutsche Grammophon and Philips. During that time, I was conducting quite a lot of Handel at the Göttingen International Handel Festival. I also received an invitation to perform at Ansbach, the Mecca of Bach festivals in Germany, and the former stamping ground of Karl Richter and his Münchener Bach-Chor. I went there for the first time in 1979 with the Monteverdi Choir and the English Baroque Soloists and returned in 1981. As German Bach interpretation at that time was very much dominated by organist-conductors, our visits to Ansbach were something of a challenge to existing trends. All of a sudden, the local audiences were confronted by English performers who sang the motets and the *Johannes-Passion* in passably good German, and who took immense care over the words, the articulation and the pronunciation. As far as the traditionalists were concerned, that was one nail in our coffin. Another was that we 'danced' to the music. So much Baroque music is dance-inflected, and if you do it in a po-faced, four-square way, you miss so much of the delight, airiness and spirituality that it contains. But I think we gradually won quite a few of the sceptics over. That was certainly the case by the time that we gave our first *Matthäus-Passion* at East Berlin's Konzerthaus in 1985. The audience contained uniformed soldiers of the Deutsche Demokratische Republik who wept with emotion. Over the years, the choir has gone from strength to strength and its numbers have been replenished by graduates of our apprentice scheme.

JF-A: A shot in the arm for those people who liked the idea of period performance, but who sometimes felt that it lacked real flesh and blood, was your recording of Bach's Mass in B minor from the mid-1980s. Not only did it reconcile many mainstream sensibilities with a historically aware approach, but it was a very strong statement about your aesthetic at the time.

JEG: I really don't believe in the 'ghettoisation' of music. Specialisation is fine as long as it's not exclusive. For me, the most important thing is to combine a search for recapturing as closely as possible the sound-world in which a composer was writing – including the sonorities that he had in his inner ear and the instruments that were available to him – with a sense of how that music can speak to us now. 'Early' music should never be the exclusive province of the antiquarian, or be just part of a cultural curiosity shop. That holds no interest for me. What interests me is whether or not any particular music of the past has 'legs'. Bach's music most certainly does, even though each generation will approach, and interpret, it differently. At the time of our recording, it felt important to demonstrate how significant differences can emerge when a period instrument orchestra joins forces with an agile chamber-choir, and how their united approach can celebrate a fresh vision of Bach's music. And if that meant doing it with an adult mixed group of singers, and with slightly larger forces than Bach could regularly count on at Leipzig, where his working conditions were often impossibly stretched, then so much the better.

JF-A: You have also worked with almost every major symphony orchestra on the planet. Was your access to these great orchestras a direct result of your increasingly close relationship with recording companies?

JEG: No.

JF-A: How did it work, then?

JEG: I've always tried hard to avoid being labelled a specialist, or just a '*baroqueu*' as the French call it. Nadia Boulanger had impregnated me with the idea that a musician must have sufficient technique and musical mastery to be able to tackle any work regardless of the style or the period. That's a very tall order, and for me as a conductor, it meant grappling with as wide a repertoire as possible. I approached it in a chronological way with the symphonic and operatic repertoires growing out of the Baroque and the Classical oeuvres. Once upon a time, symphony orchestras used to be very suspicious of anybody who came from the period instrument world. But, fortunately, I had already conducted a fair amount of symphonic work, and my early experience with the BBC Northern helped me. Orchestras have since grown much more open-minded, curious and flexible than when I was starting out. You can still come across the occasional pterodactyl, but there is now a growing number of stylistically flexible and wonderfully adaptable orchestras around today.

JF-A: You have always particularly enjoyed unlikely musical marriages. Were your recordings of Elgar's works with the Vienna Philharmonic one such marriage?

JEG: My relationship with the Vienna Philharmonic was more like an eleven-year flirtation than a marriage. First of all, they asked me to record Lehár's *Die lustige Witwe* with them. I have always had a great affection for that piece, perhaps due to the fact that my grandmother was half Austrian. I also love Vienna, and speak German with a bit of a Viennese accent. For me, the challenge was how to negotiate the operetta's corners and the idiomatic *rubati* of Lehár's music. I imagine it's a bit like driving a Formula 1 car around a chicane: you need to be very, very careful not to brake too soon and to decide when to accelerate out of the bend. You've got to know precisely how much to direct and to give, and when to lay off and to leave it to the players. If you can do that, and if the orchestra realises that you are technically on top of it, they will feel confident and will begin to enjoy it. We had a ball recording the piece. It was a great, great joy. Curiously enough, the Vienna Philharmonic had never played *Die lustige Witwe* before, as it was traditionally the province of the Volksoper. Of course, the Philharmonic's musicians knew all the tunes, but they'd never played the operetta in the theatre or the concert hall. As the recording went well, I was later invited to conduct the Philharmonic Ball and several subscription concerts.

Then, one day, the orchestral committee came to me and said, 'Maestro, we'd like to do some Elgar with you.' I felt that this could be disastrous, knowing that the composer's music didn't always go down well with European and American orchestras. I asked them, 'What have you played by Elgar so far?' To which they replied, 'We've done the Cello Concerto with Mstislav Rostropovich and the "Enigma" Variations.' I said, 'Alright, okay.' I then also said, and here I was quoting Nadia Boulanger, 'You do realise that "you will be revolting".' By which she meant, 'You will be outraged and protesting.' And, of course, they initially were! Nevertheless, we decided to tour Germany and Belgium with some works by Elgar and later to record *In the South (Alassio)*, the 'Enigma' Variations, the *Introduction and Allegro for Strings* and *Sospiri*. But my heart sank at the end of the first read-through of *In the South* when it was clear that some of the players were bamboozled by Elgar's orchestral writing: it's no secret that the Vienna Philharmonic, as wonderful as it is, is not the fastest orchestra when it comes to sight-reading. And I was also a bit disappointed when, at the end of that first read-through, the leader leant over to his desk partner and said very audibly '*Das ist beschissene, englische Musik.*' The idea had been theirs, and it was they who had invited me to conduct these works with them. Things went on like that for some time until one of the older members of the orchestra, a double-bass player, seeing that I was a bit downcast, came up to me and said, 'Maestro, please don't be offended. Our orchestra is always like this when we play contemporary music!' But, in the end, they played the whole programme really beautifully.

JF-A: Mozart is also a composer whom you have performed and recorded widely.

JEG: My first opportunity to explore Mozart's works on disc in detail was when Deutsche Grammophon asked me to record all of his keyboard concertos with the great fortepianist Malcolm Bilson, for its Archiv label. This was the first complete recording of these works using that instrument. Love or loathe the fortepiano, it becomes a very special instrument in Malcolm's hands. It upsets all our expectations of a modern piano, as its bass register is proportionally more thundery and strong, while its top register is more 'tinkly' and silvery. This means that the dialogue between the woodwinds and the keyboard is more complicit. It also means that these forces are on a more equal footing than when using modern instruments and a big Steinway. In a sense, the slow movements from these concertos are a blueprint for many of the wonderful arias found in Mozart's subsequent operas.

When it came to recording the whole cycle of Mozart's operas for Deutsche Grammophon, which I started in 1989, I devoted a whole year to each of the operas. Much to my good fortune, we hit upon a wonderful generation of vocal soloists. For *Idomeneo*, for example, we had Anthony Rolfe Johnson, Sylvia McNair and Hillevi Martinpelto. In fact, we had excellent singers for all the operas that we performed, including Júlia Várady, Anne Sofie von Otter, Bryn Terfel, Gerald Finley and Rodney Gilfry. They were a joy to work with. I did something that was slightly unusual and subversive at the time: I placed the orchestra smack in the middle of the stage in concert halls, and organised the action to take place around it. It's something that I have done many times since, even when presenting operas by Berlioz, Verdi and Weber. It's not that I'm against an orchestra pit, but, if you are doing something in a concert hall, the audience are treated to something more than just a concert performance if you place the orchestra in the centre of the platform. You are then able to weave the action in and out of the orchestra, even though it might seem rather stylised. The audience can then see the drama's orchestral 'engine room' being realised before their eyes, instead of it being hidden away in a dark chasm. And the players can 'eyeball' the singers. Stagings like these produce a different type of energy and dynamism. By performing Mozart's operas in that way, the whole experience becomes enormously enriching. You can still see the *Don Giovanni* that we did at the Amsterdam Concertgebouw in 1994 on YouTube. There, the Commendatore entered from the back of the auditorium, and had both the chorus and his private 'orchestra' of three trombones line up along the aisles. They then formed a human chain that dragged him towards Don Giovanni at the front of the stage.

JF-A: And speaking of subversive Mozart, your addition of ornaments to the woodwind parts in the *Trio* in your recording of the composer's Thirty-Ninth Symphony has divided the critics. Would you decorate it in that way now?

JEG: If done stylishly and with conviction, absolutely. Why not? There's plenty of historical justification for it. The art of improvisation and embellishment was central to Mozart's practice as a performer. So, the 'style police' don't have much of a leg to stand on! Mozart's written notation is not necessarily the complete version of what he envisioned. This is particularly true when it comes to repeated passages.

JF-A: I'd like to return to opera briefly, and to discuss your period as Music Director of the Opéra National de Lyon. Was that an important time for you?

JEG: Yes. It was a very important time for me. In 1982, I was given the opportunity to recruit, form and train a brand-new orchestra for the opera company at Lyon, France's second city. At the time, the city's symphony orchestra played in the opera pit, as well as giving concerts. To recruit an eighty-five piece orchestra was a tough assignment and a fascinating challenge. We eventually ended up with an ensemble of musicians who were, on average, twenty-three years old and who came from sixteen different countries. The very first rehearsal was quite an adventure, as nobody knew each other. To break the ice, we found a tennis ball, which we threw to each of the players. They then had to catch it and to say their names. And after we gradually go to know one another, we started to perform in various groups. I chose Haydn and Gluck as a stylistic starting point. We then moved forward chronologically, beginning with Mozart before tackling Beethoven, Weber, Rossini, Verdi, Tchaikovsky and Britten. I performed a great deal of French music, especially Berlioz, and conducted operettas by Chabrier, Offenbach and Messager, pieces that I am particularly fond of. We also gave many of the great, iconic works, such as Debussy's *Pelléas et Mélisande*.

When I came to prepare *Pelléas*, I was dismayed to find that the published edition, used throughout Europe and the United States, is littered with mistakes. If you examine the autograph at Royaumont, it's written in different coloured inks, which also indicate the successive changes that Debussy made to his score. Unlike for some other composers, you can decipher the chronology of the changes and the genesis of the composition from these annotations. You can even find out why it evolved in the way that it did. In many instances, and much to Debussy's chagrin, it was to do with the deficiencies of the players and the conductors who performed it. The opera was given its premiere at the Salle Favart by the Opéra-Comique in April 1902 under André Messager, a fine composer and conductor and a friend of Debussy. But Messager had to leave after the second performance, as he had been engaged to conduct at the Royal Opera House, Covent Garden. The chorus master then took over, but was not a great success. Debussy soon became terribly on edge about his opera and the public's response to it. As his score was so delicate and fragile, and as it was so radical at the time, he felt obliged to 'beef up' the instrumentation by doubling some of the instruments here and there. At Lyon, I felt this robbed the score of its diaphanous, chamber-like magic, so I decided to revert to the first version. This was the one that came immediately before the version with the enforced changes that Debussy made at the dress rehearsal, and for which he also composed additional interludes to cover the slow and cumbersome changes of scenery. He wrote the interludes at break-neck speed, and every time that he wrote at that speed, he tended to sound more Wagnerian than elsewhere in the opera. This prompted us to remove them, and to perform the opera with only one interval.

We also laid out the orchestra differently. Debussy was very precise about how an orchestra should be arranged. He said, 'Don't do the usual thing by using the strings as a barrier from the winds. Rather, disperse the woodwind players in amongst the strings, as if you are sowing lettuce seeds.' Once the woodwind players had got over the initial shock of not being seated next to a fellow member of their section, they quickly switched on their musical radars and raised their aural periscopes, so to speak. This was necessary as the players had to listen across the width of the orchestra pit, and to be aware of the myriad of orchestral dialogues that form and dissolve in *Pelléas et Mélisande,* which, in its original form, is very much like expanded chamber music. This was quite an experiment and was something that could only be carried out with a young orchestra that was not yet set by routine. We also took the production, with its wonderful scenic realisation by Pierre Strosser, to the Edinburgh International Festival in 1985, and a semi-staged version of the opera to the Proms with a superb cast that included José van Dam and Diana Montague in 1988. I did the opera again this year at the Opéra-Comique and reinstated the longer orchestral interludes, as I felt that I'd like to try them at least once. And, of course, I have fallen in love with them. But I still find the first version more compelling structurally and more convincing in its overall pacing.

JF-A: I would like to broaden the discussion, and to hear your thoughts about opera as a whole. You have very defined views about the traditions and sub-traditions of the genre, and have often made those views known when it comes to the works of Wagner.

JEG: If you read histories of opera and listen to its pundits, you might be left with the impression that it began as a slightly spurious recreation of ancient Greek sung and danced theatre, and that it gradually 'got better' over time. I don't think that it necessarily did. If you draw a line between Monteverdi and Wagner, you do not automatically find opera 'getting better'. It's a lot more complicated than that. Some will disagree, of course, and a lot will depend on your criteria, personal preferences and stylistic inclinations. My feeling is that opera, as invented by the Florentine Camerata, was a highly experimental, but, perforce, a primitive and an unfinished genre. It took a genius like Monteverdi to transform it into something that was structurally coherent and convincing. He created a brilliant synthesis of music and drama that was incredibly passionate and touching. Unfortunately, his achievements can only be judged by his three extant operas, even though he probably wrote between twelve and fifteen stage works, many of which have been lost. You can then see the continuation of his achievements in the works of his former student Francesco Cavalli.

But, then, two curious things happened during the course of the seventeenth century. The first was that Italian opera became increasingly episodic and formulaic. This culminated around 1700 with the closed-form operas of Vivaldi, Scarlatti and others, where the action was compressed into fast-paced recitatives with little musical interest. In these works, all the musical interest was channelled into the *da capo* arias, a form that potentially sapped all the drama and brought the action to a juddering halt. Of course, some composers, such as Bach and Handel, used ingenious devices to overcome the *da capo* problem, but this was not always the case elsewhere. Consequently, you ended up with two-speed operas, where you whizzed through the recitatives and came to a standstill in the arias. That wasn't how Monteverdi envisaged the genre. He saw it as a continuously unfolding form that was a mosaic of eliding, almost through-composed, elements. The second thing that happened was the creation of 'mutant' opera, or opera that 'jumped tracks', if you will. This resulted in the true spirit of musical drama rising to the surface in all sorts of unexpected genres during the seventeenth century. These included oratorio, certain dramatic madrigals of Monteverdi, the biblical dialogues of Schütz and the devotional *Scenas* of Purcell. Above all, it pops up in the cantatas and Passions of Bach during the early eighteenth century. But, as we all know, Bach, unlike his contemporaries – Handel, Scarlatti, Telemann, Mattheson and Rameau – never composed an opera *per se*. Yet he's arguably the most dramatic of them all, but not in a conventional, proscenium-arch way. And although Rameau operated within a highly artificial and mannered form that he had inherited from Lully, he often managed to transcend it in miraculous ways and to bridge its structural divides. To an extent, so, too, did Handel, especially once he had abandoned Italian *opera seria* in favour of dramatic oratorios in the English language. Suddenly, he finds ways to break the unvarying chain of arias and duets by introducing a chorus. The chorus then commentates on the action, and becomes a *dramatis personae* within each oratorio. It makes a huge difference to the dramatic pacing and textural variety of his works. I'm convinced that Mozart learned a huge amount from Handel, and I have a hunch, but no proof, that he also learned from Rameau, too.

JF-A: Why is Wagner missing from this ideal?

JEG: I'm sorry, but I'm a dissident who finds the whole subject of Wagner rather tedious. I don't warm to him as a human being, and I don't particularly like his libretti. I find his operas interminably long, and his musical discourse detrimental to the drama. On the many occasions that I've heard his works in the theatre, I've found problems of balance that were not really resolved. And I begin to feel suffocated when the principal singers start to yell over the orchestra.

JF-A: One of Wagner's contemporaries who has often been misunderstood is Robert Schumann. I don't think we need to be apologists for his orchestrations …

JEG: Do we not? Are you sure? Isn't he still traditionally thought to be a poor orchestrator by many of my colleagues? I don't think that's the case. I think that Schumann is often misunderstood and misrepresented.

JF-A: But, surely, he doesn't need to be retouched.

JEG: Essentially, that's true. Yet he did do quite a lot of retouching himself when he came to conduct his own symphonies. His 'Spring' Symphony, and the first version of the Fourth Symphony from the 1840s, are translucent works that must have been incredibly exciting to listen to when Mendelssohn and Ferdinand David conducted them in Leipzig. Schumann's sound palette is full of light, shade, tension, suffering and pain. When he moved to Düsseldorf ten years later, and conducted his symphonies there, he decided to revise and to 'beef up' the orchestration of the Fourth Symphony. While it's perfectly legitimate to perform that version today, as most of my colleagues prefer to do, I find it very imposing and a little heavy. For me, it lacks the transparency, elegance and fire of the original 1841 version.

JF-A: And then there's Johannes Brahms, a composer whom you have been exploring in some detail over the last four years with your own record company, SDG, and with the Orchestre Révolutionnaire et Romantique. Are you still prepared to perform these works with a 'conventional' symphony orchestra, and, if so, how might they sound?

JEG: Of course I'm always happy to perform Brahms's music with a modern symphony orchestra when the occasion arises. It's their staple, after all! But what I've relished most about giving his works with the instruments of the Orchestre Révolutionnaire et Romantique is the extra degree of colour contrasts that they elicit. This is particularly noticeable in the writing for the valveless horns, and in the added eloquence and plangency that they bring. It's just so winning. Mind you, you still need to work hard to attain that special Brahmsian *cantilena*. To that end, I implore players to 'sing' with their instruments and to 'pronounce' their lines through the woodwinds' use of embouchure and the strings' use of expressive bow articulation. You can, of course, aim for similar effects with a modern-instrument orchestra, but the upper partials become more difficult to distinguish. The density of today's instruments somehow makes that harder to achieve: not impossible, but harder. It's all part and parcel of the approach I was trying to establish when performing Brahms's symphonic cycle with the Orchestre Révolutionnaire et Romantique: I was keen to place these wonderful orchestral works within both the context of his equally wonderful, but absurdly undervalued, choral music, and of the works that he transcribed and conducted by other composers. Brahms was one of the first composer-musicologists. He looked forward to the arrival of each new volume of Bach's collected works and devoured their contents, especially the church cantatas, as soon as they were printed. Not only did he transcribe a great deal of earlier music from the Renaissance and the Baroque, but also many German folk songs, which he then wove into his own works. The two composers who influenced Brahms most before Bach were Giovanni Gabrieli and Heinrich Schütz. One hears this in the way that Brahms constructed the fabric of his symphonic music through separate, interlocking, antiphonal 'choirs'. The models for Brahms's approach were Gabrieli at St Mark's in Venice and Schütz in Dresden. And if one can somehow replicate that in the dialogic exchanges, the contrasting sonorities, the *legati* and the use of *cantabile* that he calls for between the strings, the woodwind and the brass, then I feel one is on the right track. It may sound odd, but, for me, Brahms's symphonies are essentially choral compositions without a choir.

JF-A: But, before we finish, we really must discuss the performances that you gave of Bach's complete cantatas at fifty locations during the course of a single year: your Bach pilgrimage, which has since been released on CD. If you were asked to single out one, seminal aspect of that experience, would it be practical or spiritual?

PART ONE: CONDUCTORS

JEG: To me, they are related, as I don't really see a contradiction between the two. Bach fulfilled a remarkable assignment and realised an incredible vision when he adjusted his music to the unfolding of the geophysical year – the natural and liturgical year, as it were – during his first three years as Thomaskantor in Leipzig. And by grouping three or four of his cantatas that he wrote for a particular feast day in a way that he never did, I was afforded a wonderful insight into the different approaches that he took when responding to the same liturgical and spiritual stimuli. While we simply don't have the time to discuss why Bach was the supreme composer of all time here tonight, if pressed, I would say it's all to do, both symbolically and musically, with the cross: the intersection of the vertical and the horizontal planes of organised sounds. Simultaneously, you have the horizontal – the unfolding of several interlocking melodic strands at the same time – and the vertical – the harmony and the rhythm that aligns, supports, enriches and sometimes clashes with those melodies. That, incidentally, was the way that Nadia Boulanger taught me harmony and counterpoint. And, of course, the cross is the most important symbol in Christian theology. It can't simply be a coincidence, therefore, that Bach, as a committed Lutheran, uses it as the point of intersection between the two essential planes of his music-making.

JF-A: I know that you are also very keen for us to speak briefly about Percy Grainger before we finish, a composer whom you met as a boy.

JEG: I did. And while I am aware that this might seem like descending from Mount Everest to its Himalayan foothills culturally, Grainger was one of the most striking musical originals of the early twentieth century. A maverick and a generous-minded colleague, Percy was a close friend of my great-uncle, Balfour Gardiner. They had been fellow students of

Iwan Knorr in Frankfurt am Main before the First World War, and after the conflict, Balfour gave up composing to plant trees and to help his fellow composers. In 1949, when I was six years old, Grainger arrived at our home dressed entirely in bath towels and raffia shoes. He leaped and cavorted around the garden while Balfour stood aloof in his Edwardian three-piece tweed suit. Ever since, I have been enchanted by Grainger's music, and have been impressed by its quirkiness, lyricism and daring. I adore his 'elastic scoring', his impertinent and imaginative way with folk songs and the fact that the great majority of his works last less than twelve minutes!

TREVOR PINNOCK
(DAVID JOSEFOWITZ RECITAL HALL, 14 NOVEMBER 2013)

TIMOTHY JONES: As a keyboard player and as a conductor, you've been closely associated with early music for more than half a century. But your interests are far wider than that, and it might surprise some to learn that you're really an artist of catholic taste.

TREVOR PINNOCK: I have been fighting my entire life against the habit of pigeonholing people, and the tendency of putting them into little boxes. Most listeners wouldn't know, for example, that I conducted modern works with the National Arts Centre Orchestra in Ottawa, where I was Music Director for five years in the early 1990s. While I was there, I appointed a composer-in-residence, Linda Bouchard. But I'm not a new-music specialist, and when she gave me one of her latest works to conduct, I thought, 'What have I done?' It looked like a foreign language to me. As I had a few months before I had to perform it, I thought that I'd put the score on my hall table, and would have a quick look at it every time I passed by. But each time I opened the work, it still looked like a foreign language. I then realised that I shouldn't read it vertically but horizontally. Suddenly, it all made sense, and I really learned something from this experience when it came to my response to music. When I later had a chance to meet with Linda, I was able to discuss with her what was in the score, to query some of its passages and to chat about all that I'd learned from it.

Linda then asked, 'How do you know all this?' And I said, 'It comes out of your music.' I then realised that this was exactly the same process that I use when dealing with the works of Bach and Handel. If you can identify with the source material itself through your own musical gift, you automatically gain insights into it. And if you are honest about that process, you can discover things about the work that might otherwise only be accessible through direct contact with its composer. What this exercise taught me was the importance of trust. We have to trust our musical gift. It was Albert Einstein who said that instinctive learning was a great gift, and that analytical learning was the faithful servant of that gift. He also pointed out that in the modern world we have a tendency to honour the servant, but to neglect the gift. Of course, we need to have faithful servants as musicians, but we also need to be in touch with our gift.

TJ: What are some of your earliest musical memories, and how did they help to shape you artistically?

TP: When I was two years old, I was taken to the seaside, where there was a brass band playing. My parents later told me that I made them take me out of my pushchair so that I could dance to the music until it stopped. Even then, I must've known that music was something of a life-source for me. Later, as a three-year-old, I used to climb over the garden fence so that I could walk up the hill to the house of the concert pianist Ronald Smith. I would then sit outside his door in Canterbury, and be amazed by what I heard.

TJ: Presumably, a great deal of Alkan.

TP: Yes. Absolutely. His sister then became my first piano teacher. I was completely in love with her, and was devastated when she went off to get married. I was eleven at the time. It never occurred to me that she would abandon me. As a young musician, your teacher is very important, and the centre of your life. But I also discovered that if I went down the hill that there was a building site where the workers would give me doughnuts and chips. And it was there that I experienced drinking tea for the first time: builders' tea. So, my greatest conflict as a child was whether to go up the hill or down it. It says a great deal about me.

TJ: You then became a chorister at Canterbury Cathedral.

TP: Being a chorister at the cathedral was the most amazing training. It was there that I properly learned all the disciplines of music-making and how to be a professional. I also had a great many fun colleagues there, including the young Mark Elder. Yet it was a very odd school and a most peculiar place.

TJ: What was so peculiar about it?

TP: All the teachers were either very old or very young. Luckily, I wasn't a boarder there; I was a day boy. And they were very long days indeed. We usually started at 8.30am, and finished at 6.30pm. I used to feel really tired by the end of each day, and just wanted to go home.

TJ: Was it as a chorister that you began to gravitate towards the organ?

TP: As I never found a satisfactory piano teacher after Ronald Smith's sister, I became an organist. And I am very sad that I was unable to continue my training on the piano, as I benefited greatly from it. I started with the organ in my teens, but had already become interested in early music from about the age of seven. When I was eleven or twelve,

I bought an anthology of Western music, which contained everything. The edition was appalling, but the music fascinated me. It was an absolute treasure trove.

TJ: What were your expectations of the Royal College of Music when you started there as a student aged nineteen?

TP: I had something of a crisis about a year before entering the College. I had been thrown out of school, and the cathedral organist refused to teach me any more. Strangely enough, this had a good effect on me, as I went for some lessons with Sir Nicholas Jackson in London. He had been a pupil of the great harpsichordist Gustav Leonhardt, and it was Jackson who introduced me to the harpsichord while teaching me the organ. Having been shaken by my school and cathedral experiences, I really worked hard during the year leading up to the College. I was frightened, as I couldn't imagine doing anything else other than music. The result was that I applied for scholarships to both the Royal College and the Royal Academy of Music. At the Academy, I had an argument with the examiner, so that didn't work out. But, at the College, I was offered a scholarship, and went on to do the ARCM at the same time. My organ and harpsichord teachers at the College were Ralph Downes and Millicent Silver. While Silver was not particularly historically aware, she was a marvellous teacher, and a player who could make the instrument sing. I remember spending an entire night listening over and over again to Leonhardt's recording of Bach's Second Partita before trying to copy his way of playing the work. And, of course, I 'improved' on his approach, as only a teenager can. I then thought that I would play it to Silver at my next lesson, and show her how it should be done. Within minutes of starting the Partita, I heard her shriek from the corner of the room, 'What on earth do you think you are doing?' I felt so ashamed, as I was caught out playing in a style of *rubato* that was completely Leonhardt's own. The difference was: he understood what he was doing and I didn't. That was a lesson in itself. And another good 'lesson' that she gave me was when she said, 'If that's the way you are going to do it, and I assume that it is, then I am going to make sure that you do it well.' That's the best sort of teaching.

TJ: Why have you made so many recordings as a harpsichordist, yet relatively few as an organist?

TP: Because I'm not really an organist at all. I wanted to give up the instrument while I was at the College, but was told that if I stopped playing it, my scholarship would be taken away. They thought that I wouldn't be able to make a living as a harpsichordist. I was told that I should be an organist, and that I should play the harpsichord on the side. But apart from weddings, funerals and the occasional Christmas event, I did give up the organ.

TJ: Were you still at the Royal College of Music when you began to play *continuo* with the Academy of St Martin in the Fields?

TP: No. When I was at the College, I started a group called The Galliard Trio with the flautist Stephen Preston and the cellist Anthony Pleeth. Not only did they influence me, but so did Anthony's father, William. He was a marvellous cellist, who sometimes came and played *continuo* with us. His way of shaping bass lines, and revealing their importance, has stayed with me to this day. The Academy of St Martin in the Fields came later, at about the same time that I started The English Concert. Although I undertook a couple of tours and made some recordings with the Academy, I wasn't terribly good at fitting in socially, and was not very well suited to playing with an orchestra at the time. I was too self-centred. And I remember Sir Neville Marriner coming up to me and saying that I was too 'soloistic'. He was right.

TJ: What, then, makes a good *continuo* player?

TP: Rhythm. A *continuo* is like the bass and drums in a jazz combo. It's the rhythm section of an ensemble. It also lays the harmonic foundation of a group. A *continuo*'s function is not to make fiddly little tunes, or to create clever effects. It should mould and shape the music from the bottom. In order to do that, the player has to inject energy into their playing, but not drive. As a young man, I always played slightly in front of the beat. That was dreadful. *Continuo* playing has to have an inner energy, and this applies as much to slow music as it does to fast. Whatever the type of music-making you are engaged in, whether it be as a soloist or as a member of an ensemble, it is essential to project inner energy to the audience.

TJ: What do you mean by inner energy?

TP: It's to do with presence. You have to be one with the music. And that's all that matters at that particular moment. You must be part of the music's journey. The wonderful thing about music is that joy and sadness can co-exist simultaneously. That's particularly true of Mozart, where joy and beauty often have an undercurrent of melancholy. For me, everything to do with music is a part of life. And it must surely be wonderful if we can find a place where loss, sadness and joy can live side by side, rather than being in a state of constant conflict.

TJ: In 1972, you founded The English Concert. How did that come about?

PART ONE: CONDUCTORS

TP: Tony Pleeth decided to leave the Trio that year, and it was around that time that I became fascinated by what was happening to early music abroad. Artists such as Gustav Leonhardt and Nikolaus Harnoncourt were doing interesting things with period instruments. In Britain, the Academy of St Martin in the Fields and the English Chamber Orchestra were playing early music fantastically, but I knew that they had lost their voyage of discovery. Sometimes, things have to change and new ways have to be found. You cannot simply carry on with something just because it's very good; it has to be alive with a sense of adventure. There was nothing more for them to discover, as they had discovered it all. Even though I knew that it would be down to old instruments if early music was to move forward, there were times when I doubted myself. Sometimes, what we did sounded horrible, as we hadn't worked out how to play the instruments properly. And the instruments themselves didn't seem to work. Occasionally, I thought that we should go back to the instruments that *did* work.

TJ: Was this new-found interest in period instruments a direct result of your work as a scholar?

TP: I have never considered myself a scholar, even though I do try to keep up my scholarship. I simply follow my passions. I never attended a university, or learned to do things properly. While that occasionally undermined my confidence, it also proved to be a great blessing, as it forced me to listen to the music and to keep in contact with it. This meant that I had to make real decisions, rather than draw on learned ones. Of course, I've read many old treatises, such as that by C. P. E. Bach. But it was only after I came across a technique that I had discovered for myself that I would understand fully what he was talking about. I would then mentally shout, 'Great. Bang on.' On the other hand, if he was discussing things that I hadn't encountered personally, I would probably ignore them, as they had little personal relevance. Descriptions of how *appoggiaturas* and trills should be played were useful, but most of the things contained in those early books were not always fundamental to me. Generally, the writers would discuss details, and would then proceed to disagree with each other about the exact meaning of those details.

TJ: It seems that trust and instinct are of primary importance to you.

TP: You must have trust in other people. If you are working with a musician you truly trust, you can almost be playing in different rooms and still be a successful ensemble. You don't have to see each other to work well together. And it's essential that you don't get in each other's way musically.

TJ: You once said, 'By the early 70s, we noticed that players on the Continent were becoming aware of the compromises that they were having to make on modern instruments. So, we took out original instruments because we could play them to the limit. It is always better to play right up to the limit instead of inventing some boundaries.'

TP: I still believe that passionately, and it's one of the reasons why it is very good to have old instruments. This means that the actual 'machinery' we have is made for the task. If you are extremely scrupulous about certain technical matters, you can really use old instruments. I gave a number of concerts with the wonderful modern flautist Emmanuel Pahud and the cellist and violist Jonathan Manson. It was very interesting to observe the compromises that Emmanuel had to make for the modern flute. But as he is a superb musician, he could make those compromises work. And, of course, Jonathan and I are quite happy to perform with modern instrument players who treat the music in that way. There's always a risk that when compromises are made on a modern instrument, such as when you have to lighten the sound because it seems too heavy, a *forte* will lose its brilliance and excitement. This is because it no longer challenges the limit of the instrument. The same applies to period instruments. You then have to compensate with your musicianship. I also passionately believe that there's a place for both period and new instruments. That said, some music doesn't lend itself well to modern instruments. Different musicians have different cut-off points when it comes to this issue. But if we were *never* to use modern instruments, and if we were *never* to play in different styles, then the music would be diminished. If that were the case, we would lose a whole tradition of music-making. Musicians should be honest with the music, and should play on the instruments that they have. We must avoid putting ourselves in a cultural straitjacket.

TJ: Was the style of The English Concert simply based on the sounds that the instruments made, or were you also concerned about exploring and observing ethical boundaries?

TP: The sound that we made came from within me. And although sound is very important to me, it's also important to understand that all the historical styles that we hear today are modern fabrications. None of us can, or should, claim to be 'historical'. To do so would be a false claim. And while we can't be 'historical', we can be honest with the music, and can do what we *think* past musicians might have done. We can only interpret the music through modern ears. And modern audiences are not 'authentic' either. Nevertheless, I do think that there's a place for true, diehard historical specialists who make the effort to search out sources. These are the true scientists amongst us. There's room for everybody.

TJ: And what should the role of a conservatoire be in all of this?

TP: I sometimes think that conservatoires have their students specialise in period performance too soon. While I believe that everybody should be exposed to old instruments, and have a feeling for them, I don't think that eighteen-year-olds should focus on one style of music. Students should have a solid grounding, and learn their instruments well, before deciding to specialise.

TJ: When discussing The English Concert's approach to unanimity of style and purpose, you said in 1981, 'On the whole, a well-ordered democracy invariably produces the best results. People are often surprised that I, myself, appear to spend little time directing, as such. Of course, I do direct, but I don't feel a place for it necessarily on the concert platform.'

TP: But it must be the type of democracy in which you get what you want! In the end, it was my orchestra and it was my sound. Occasionally, we had some tremendous rows, and there was a period when rehearsals were unbearable. Yet the concerts were fantastic. The performances were very tight and together. In rehearsals, we would often agree to differ as to how things should be done. And while there were a lot of creative tensions, it remained a wonderful working relationship. One of the joys of working with the orchestra's leader, Simon Standage, for eighteen years was that we were very different musicians. Completely different. This meant that we produced some of the very best, and some of the very worst, of what we did. It's always easy to talk about the successes that we have, but we have to realise that those successes don't happen without a great many failures. Anybody who is 'successful' is also able to accept their failures, to take responsibility for them and to survive them. That can be quite difficult at times, but there are always two sides to every coin. Success would be very bland without failure. You have to take the bad with the good. And as things can be so bad for performing artists at times, I often find myself asking whether I should stop tomorrow.

I have had a few experiences in my life – thankfully not many – that were completely devastating. These were often related to a failed concert, to dissatisfaction with my own playing, or to a completely demolishing criticism. These days, I don't read reviews, as even a single word from them can keep me awake at night. The critics' job is to write and ours is to play. But if you have a very bad experience, you can lose contact with who you are. You can't find yourself. It's terrifying; it's absolutely terrifying. It's happened to all performers in the past, and will happen to all good performers at some point in the future. This should be recognised as a form of trauma. And artists themselves need to be aware of this, as there's a kind of taboo about talking about such things. We don't speak much about our stage fears, especially if they are fundamental. If we did, artists would then realise that they are not alone. It's important to learn how to protect ourselves. But at the very moment when those bad experiences are taking place, you are lucky if you can hold yourself together at all.

TJ: Earlier, you mentioned the writings of C. P. E. Bach, whose symphonies you have also recorded. What is your take on his music and that of Bach's other sons?

TP: It's a bit weird, and it has all manner of stops and starts. Although we tend to think of J. S. Bach as being the end of an era, much of what

C. P. E. did was already present in his father's music. Johann Sebastian also did many peculiar things, and could also be crazy and subversive in his own writing. Wilhelm Friedemann went off the deep end, Carl Philipp did his stuff and Johann Christian managed to escape to England, where he wrote beautifully crafted and civilised music. And then there was Johann Christoph Friedrich, who also wrote some very polite music.

TJ: From a close reading of your discography, you started by recording the music of Handel, Bach, Telemann and Vivaldi before moving on to works from the late eighteenth century.

TP: That's true. I started the second phase with a small project for Deutsche Grammophon's Archiv label that involved Haydn's *Sturm und Drang* symphonies before moving on to the complete symphonies of Mozart. They allowed us time to do the Mozart project properly, and we were able to give many of the works at our concerts. Not all of the symphonies; some of the early ones were just recorded. But the company did give us time and money to do the project, which would be inconceivable today. And I'm sorry to say that I didn't realise at the time what an incredible offer it was. As I had a good orchestra, I felt that it was my right to make the discs. Nothing is one's right. It was completely the wrong way of thinking. People would now give their eye teeth for such an opportunity.

TJ: Around that time, you also recorded some of Haydn's choral works.

TP: That's such fantastic music, particularly the Stabat Mater and the 'Nelson' Mass. I have always loved the spirit and life of Haydn. Last year, I gave some special concerts of his music during which an actor read while we performed. What amazed me about those concerts were

PART ONE: CONDUCTORS

all the contrasts that we found in his scores. You could feel his spirit and vitality.

TJ: What do you say to those who consider Haydn a composer who was simply interested in wit and comedy?

TP: It's another example of people thinking in terms of pigeonholes. That kind of thing makes me so angry.

TJ: Was the choir that you used for your recording of the 'Nelson' Mass an established group?

TP: That was the first time that I had a choir, and its members were all drawn from London's wonderful pool of professional singers. That pool has always existed, and when I was a student at the Royal College of Music, it was the mainstay of such groups as the John Alldis Choir. We have always had a huge choral tradition in England, much of which was related to the universities, who kept it going. England's orchestral tradition is also remarkably disciplined, and everything that I've done musically has been based on these traditions. I was always happy to accept the best things about them, and to make them part of my own music-making. Although I might have pioneered new fields, I'm not a musical saboteur. In a way, Nikolaus Harnoncourt *was* a deliberate saboteur, but in a very positive sense. He wanted things to sound as different as possible. I had no such agenda. I just wanted to get on with music-making, and to have a voyage of discovery.

TJ: Your work with The English Concert eventually brought you to the attention of some major international ensembles, such as the Leipzig Gewandhaus Orchestra.

TP: That's a lovely orchestra with which I have performed a great deal of Mendelssohn, and with which I will be giving Beethoven's Third and Fourth Piano Concertos with Maria João Pires later this year. Maria João and I do a lot of work together with all sorts of orchestras, and we often play piano duets. There's a human aspect to music-making, which is wonderful. There's nothing quite like working with people with whom you have an affinity, such as Maria João or Maxim Vengerov. I first worked with Maxim when he played Mozart's Third Violin Concerto with me at the Salzburg Festival in 1992 as a seventeen-year-old. That was part of a matinee concert at the Stiftung Mozarteum during which Barbara Bonney sang the composer's 'Ch'io mi scordi di te?'. And what a concert that was! Maxim and I fell for each other immediately and decided to work together again as soon as possible. He was somebody who wanted to work outside the artistic box, and who wanted to transcend his Russian training. He was keen to explore all sorts of things, and decided much later that he would like to try playing the Baroque violin. I then went to stay with him in Israel, where we had a fabulous time practising. This led to a series of concerts at which we played on a Baroque violin and a harpsichord in the first half, and on a modern violin and a Steinway concert grand in the second. This stretched both of us to our limits, as I am not really a pianist; I just fiddle about with it for fun. And he's not a Baroque violinist either. Some of the concerts that we gave were quite good, but not all. Nevertheless, we survived and had a lot of fun. That year-long project was some time ago now, and although he has since suffered a burn out from playing so much, he is really a wonderful man. He now conducts, and we are still in touch.

TJ: What are your thoughts on Karl Richter's and Wanda Landowska's approaches to Bach and Handel, and what's your take on the latter's use of a Pleyel harpsichord.

PART ONE: CONDUCTORS

TP: These were musicians I learned a great deal from, and I own some wonderful recordings of Landowska playing on that instrument. When I go to America next year, I will be giving an interesting concert at the Library of Congress, where they have her restored harpsichord. As I will be performing half of the concert on it, I was told to allow two free days beforehand to come to terms with the instrument. While I've played on harpsichords with registration pedals in the past, French-system instruments are slightly different. And as I suffer from a form of dyspraxia, I often confuse right from left and up from down. This is particularly challenging when dealing with the English and French systems. If you are using an English-system instrument, you put the pedal down to get the sound, while the opposite is true for a French-system instrument. This can be a total nightmare for me. And while I admire Landowska as a pioneer, I don't like all that she did. But she had guts, and performed with great honesty. When it comes to Karl Richter, I, again, don't like everything that he did, but I do admire his commitment. I always appreciate musical commitment above rigidity of view.

TJ: What are your thoughts on that other great Richter, Sviatoslav Richter?

TP: He was a wonderful pianist who always played with incredible clarity. Although he had a great interest in old music, it was quite late in his career before he performed all the suites of Handel.

TJ: Some of your contemporaries argue that it's wrong to perform Beethoven's keyboard works on a modern piano, and that it will take an artist of Artur Schnabel's stature to make fortepianos truly viable in the modern concert hall. Do you agree with this?

TP: No. You can play Beethoven's music on a modern Steinway piano, and can do so very musically. While it is true that you can't get the same musical effects or colours that the composer was expecting from a Graf fortepiano, you can still make very good music on a contemporary grand piano. One just has to accept that this is Beethoven done in a different way. And depending on the power of the interpreter, that will either work, or it won't. It would be good if a very high-quality musician were to be associated with the fortepiano and to specialise in it. But there are big problems when it comes to this. The life of a modern, touring soloist is invariably linked to large concerts halls. These are not really compatible to the fortepiano, or the degree of specialisation that the instrument requires. It would take an exceptional artist to do this. Of course, there are some wonderful fortepianists around, such as Kristian Bezuidenhout. He gets a beautiful sound out of every instrument that I've heard him play. He gives me tremendous hope for the future.

TJ: Earlier, you mentioned the importance of orchestral sound to you. Is it possible for you to define what actually constitutes your ideal sound?

TP: Sound is always crucial, as it *is* music. But you must never accept a sound at face value. You have to be true to your own internal vision of it, and this is why you have to be able to draw that sound from the players you are directing. This can often be done through imagery. If the musicians are playing a very tight, perfunctory *staccato*, for example, you might say, 'Could you make that sound like a fat man with a generous tummy?' That way, you'll get a nice sound. It's always bad to talk about lengths of notes and particular types of articulation. It sends the wrong message. You have to picture the sound mentally and to be able to search out the music's line. This is not only true when working with period ensembles, but also when conducting modern orchestras. A beautiful sound has nothing to do with the presence or absence of *vibrato*. You must never endlessly discuss techniques such as this with the musicians. When dealing with the players, you only have about five words at your disposal before they switch off. And quite rightly so, as their job is music and not words. Sometimes, the modern halls that I played in with The English Concert were too big. This meant that we ended up compromising our style so that we could make our sound work in that particular hall. It's possible to tease out subtleties in small spaces, but that's not always possible in some of the bigger venues.

TJ: Do you find that there's a difference between directing an ensemble and conducting an orchestra?

TP: Yes, I do. With the exception of the sound that I am after, which remains much the same, the bigger the group, the more dictatorial you have to be. This is simply to do with the numbers of players involved. And, again, the less you talk the better. Music is a form of social work, it is a whole language in itself.

TJ: Are there any ambitions that you have yet to fulfil?

TP: I am not a very ambitious man. I just like music, and am very happy doing a mixture of things. I enjoy returning to orchestras that I like, and I still love the challenge of playing solo concerts. These can be very tough at times, as I am, by nature, a very nervous performer. But we must always keep in touch with our instrument, and be honest in everything that we do. I couldn't simply be a director or a conductor. That's not for me.

SIR MARK ELDER
(DAVID JOSEFOWITZ RECITAL HALL, 6 OCTOBER 2017)

RAYMOND HOLDEN: Without question, you are one of the world's leading interpreters of British music, and have championed it both in the United Kingdom and abroad. But before we discuss your views on the works of your compatriots in general, I would like to explore your thoughts on the compositions of Sir Edward Elgar. For many listeners, you are the quintessential Elgarian, and a conductor whose performance aesthetic embodies many of his artistic principles. Do you agree with those who argue that Elgar was the first great English composer, and, if so, can you quantify that greatness?

MARK ELDER: Elgar was not the first great English composer, but the first since the death of Purcell. He was very aware of European traditions and practices from his youth onwards, but quickly found his own compositional voice. Even in his earlier works there are fingerprints of a personal style that became more ubiquitous as time went by. His astonishing ability as a self-taught composer is one of his most outstanding qualities, and his thirst for musical knowledge was truly remarkable. As an outsider from Worcester, he used to get up before dawn and take the train to Paddington. From Paddington, he took another train to Upper Norwood, where he hoped to be in time for the last rehearsal for that day's concert at the Crystal Palace. After the performance, he would

PART ONE: CONDUCTORS

make his way back to Worcester, the culmination of a series of long and tiring journeys. He was always keen to hear the new work on the programme, and was terribly disappointed if he missed it. These trips were nothing short of pilgrimages, and he was always determined to hear the best orchestras in rehearsal and performance. He listened particularly to the way an orchestra sounded and how specific colours and effects were created. Being self-taught, he was constantly in search of his own poetic voice and one that represented the countryside in which he was born. He was once asked where the musical idea for the middle section of the second movement of the First Symphony came from. He replied simply that it was 'the sort of thing that one hears by the river.' What he meant was that many of his best ideas would come to him while meandering alone on his bike through the byways and highways of Worcestershire. As he said, the trees would sing to him. He was not from the musical or social establishment, but became a member through his success, the intensity of his musical imagination and his ability to be a genuine populist.

RH: You are one of the few British conductors who has recorded Elgar's three great oratorios: *The Dream of Gerontius*, *The Apostles* and *The Kingdom*. For many modern listeners, these works are challenging, both religiously and culturally. Only *The Dream of Gerontius* is performed regularly, while *The Apostles* and *The Kingdom* have largely failed to ignite the public's interest. Why do you think that is?

ME: I remember one experienced, British soprano saying to me that it was rare for her to be engaged to sing *The Kingdom*, but that she would be booked for at least three performances of *The Apostles* each year. I would've thought that it would've been the other way around, as *The Apostles* is a much bigger work than *The Kingdom* and demands so much more money and time to rehearse and to perform successfully. Concerning the works' religiosity, *The Dream of Gerontius* upset the Anglicans because Cardinal Newman's text was so Roman. But once the work had been well prepared and well performed, unlike the disastrous first performance at Birmingham in 1900, it took on an incredible power that fired the listening public's imagination. As the story of *Gerontius* is easily told, its simplicity also helped the oratorio to be accepted by audiences. Effectively, it's about a man who is at the point of death and is surrounded by well-wishers. After dying, Gerontius passes over to the other side and is supported by an angel before facing the Godhead. Elgar depicts this in music in a way that nobody else had done before. The story of *The Apostles* is much harder to describe. When Elgar came to envisage this enormous work in three parts, he was so intent on surpassing *Gerontius*, and doing something that nobody had ever done before, that he ended up being late in fulfilling his contract. So, he had to make compromises. He couldn't decide which passages from the Bible to use. He thought that if he chose sections that everybody recognised, and that were conspicuously Anglican in character, the work would be accepted more readily. Those choices influenced the compositional process of *The Apostles*. Originally, the work was going to be followed by two other parts and was to finish with the Last Judgement. What later became *The Kingdom* was originally to be part of *The Apostles*. But when he started to set the text, the notes poured from his pen. It was as if the music had been marinating for years. As he was so experienced at writing for voices and large orchestra by the time that he composed the works, he found that he had a great deal to say. He decided, therefore, to separate *The Kingdom* from *The Apostles* and to create two oratorios. It seems clear from his correspondence that the process of creating these two works prompted a nervous breakdown. He arrived at a crossroads in his career and it stopped him from writing for voices thereafter.

PART ONE: CONDUCTORS

Elgar's three great oratorios require a great deal of time, both in their preparation and in their performance. Of the three, *Gerontius* is the most straightforward in the way that the music is laid out, as self-contained choruses often lead naturally to discrete solos. In *The Apostles*, the musical technique is more like a film, fading from one scene to the next without making it particularly clear what the next scene is. You simply have to know the work and be led by the words. Elgar would take one line from one section of the Bible and juxtapose it with another passage from elsewhere. By combining these materials, he attempted to create a narrative that depicted the point at which Jesus felt assured that he had a group of acolytes who would proselytise after his Ascension. It's about the founding of Christianity and how those who believed in Christ, through their humility and dedication, could prepare themselves and others for life eternal. Elgar was profoundly affected by the story, and the music that he wrote for it is incomparably beautiful. I have to admit that I didn't always think that. I found it difficult to decide whether to do *The Apostles* or *The Kingdom* first or, indeed, whether either was really worth the effort of studying and performing at all. Having now done them, I feel slightly ashamed of those concerns. But that's often the way with big pieces. Only by living with them, doing them and committing to them do I find a way into them. It's crucial not to be sanctimonious about them; they should not be treated as church music. They are spiritual pieces about religious topics that live in the concert hall. If they can be performed in an ecclesiastical building, all well and good, but don't halve the *tempi* just because you're in the presence of God!

RH: What kind of an impact do you think a voice such as that of Dame Clara Butt would have had on the performance of Elgar's works? It's a voice-type that has simply disappeared.

ME: When I was young there were two outstanding British contraltos: Helen Watts and Norma Procter. When either was needed for low parts, such as the Angel in *Gerontius*, you knew you had the real thing. The essence of such a *tessitura* is not to do with how high or low a singer can sing, but where the colour of the voice sits naturally. Today, there are few singers who can tackle such low parts successfully: Patricia Bardon is one and Rebecca de Pont Davies is another. There were probably more when Elgar was writing, and he composed the *Sea Pictures* with Clara Butt in mind. But she never performed the first and last of the cycle, and only gave the much easier middle three. Even though Elgar knew her sound, I find it unacceptable, ugly and not at all interesting. Frankly, I am pleased that we don't have singers who sound like that any more. It may be that her appeal was more than just her sound; perhaps it was the way her personality came across as she sang. Another real contralto was Kathleen Ferrier, whose life and career were cut tragically short. She was a wonderful artist, natural and uninhibited, a real down-to-earth girl. And then there is Dame Janet Baker, a marvellous example of a great artist who has made the most of what God has given her. Unlike Butt, she sang the *Sea Pictures* complete and made a beautiful recording of them. It was difficult for her, but she is not alone in finding the *Sea Pictures* tricky: in my experience, all mezzo-sopranos and contraltos find them challenging. But, to return to Elgar's oratorios, the central problem for me is that I have to select a singer who's free, whether it's to sing the Angel in *The Dream of Gerontius* or the contralto part in *The Apostles*, and simply make it work. To avoid her singing out of tune, I beg her not to shout and not to press on her voice, especially when it rises from the lower part of the register to the higher. It's also crucial that she shouldn't be swamped by the orchestra and that I respect what she can do. There are always passages where the dynamics need to be changed. Some *crescendi* need to be less intense and some *forte* passages need to be played *piano*. If the singer has artistic credibility, and has the right understanding of the material, I can make it work. But the orchestra has to shut up!

RH: A few years ago, you conducted a London orchestra in Elgar's First Symphony, and I brought a group of postgraduate conducting students from the Royal Academy of Music to a rehearsal. The orchestra had not performed the work for fifteen years, and it was clear that a number of players were unfamiliar with the music in general and Elgar's string writing in particular. At the rehearsal break, you remarked to the students that this situation wouldn't have arisen thirty or forty years ago, as the symphony would have been a standard part of any British orchestra's repertoire. Why is that no longer the case?

ME: The answer is quite simple: orchestras only master these two huge symphonies if their principal conductors are interested in them. Otherwise, they will be relegated to occasional works for occasional seasons. The BBC Symphony Orchestra performed Elgar's symphonies frequently in the era of Sir Adrian Boult. Sir Georg Solti also gave them regularly when he was Music Director of the London Philharmonic Orchestra. It's a reflection of the taste of the Music Director, and not necessarily that of the public. Elgar's two symphonies do not make easy listening, it must be said. And even if one has heard and played them often, they are not only demanding aesthetically, but require repeated playing. A British orchestra shouldn't go for more than a year or two without performing one of them.

RH: Have you encountered resistance to Elgar's symphonies in America or Europe?

ME: I gave the first performance of Elgar's Second Symphony in Atlanta, Georgia, and the orchestra was quite nervous about it. We did two performances between which there was a day off. On the morning of the second performance, one of the players said, 'Maestro, it would be great if you could come down during intermission. We're having a bit of a party. We've got a surprise for you.' During the day off, someone in the orchestra had gone to a local patisserie and asked them to bake a sponge cake that was the size of a small table. They had it iced with a message: 'To the Atlanta Symphony Orchestra from Sir Edward Elgar: Bravo, chaps! Keep it up.' Aside from such instances, Elgar doesn't travel well. There are a few pieces that American audiences like, such as the Cello Concerto, the 'Enigma' Variations and the 'Pomp and Circumstance' Marches. But Vaughan Williams is a more popular composer. I think that this is based on prejudice. In America, choral societies adore *A Sea Symphony* and audiences love the *Tallis Fantasia* and *The Lark Ascending*. But I have conducted Delius and Bax with the Chicago Symphony Orchestra.

In 2010, I did Bax's *Spring Fire* in Manchester. It's a wonderful piece, and I find that the musicians are interested in it. All one can do is try. I find talking to the audiences about these works is important, particularly if the piece is long, or if the audience has never heard it before. Some years ago, I went one Sunday afternoon with the London Philharmonic to the newly refurbished Dome in Brighton. After performing a Mozart concerto, we gave Mahler's Sixth Symphony. As it's more than an hour long, I thought that I'd better tell them something about it. I said, 'Ladies and gentlemen, the work we're going to play is one of the greatest Romantic symphonies and a wonderful testament to Mahler's personality. It contains autobiographical parts, is a very passionate work and is rather long. It's about an hour and a quarter.' Someone in the front row then shouted, 'Oh good! I've got a bus to catch.' I said, 'I particularly hope that the gentleman in the front row who says he has a bus to catch will be able to stay for the last movement. It's half an hour long and it's very dramatic and exciting.' The reply came, 'Anything for you, Mark.' There's a great public waiting for you, if you know how to prime them.

RH: Many British conductors have conducted one of Elgar's symphonies much more frequently than the other. Sir John Pritchard concentrated on the First, whereas Sir John Barbirolli conducted 103 performances of the Second Symphony and only thirty-eight of the First. Do you have a preference?

ME: I like and perform them equally. Managements prefer the First because of its loud ending, but the Second is more mature and a greater piece overall. The challenge presented by the Second is how to bring off the long, quiet finish after the drama and brilliance of the preceding material. If audiences are unfamiliar with it, the end can be more downbeat than they were expecting. Another challenge for the conductor is Elgar's development passages. As they are often not the most distinguished parts of the symphonies, he actively encouraged conductors not to linger too long over them. Take the development section of the First Symphony's first movement: it's a little self-conscious, gauche and loud. It needs to be made less portentous and more vibrant and brilliant. It should never drag and should move on quickly to the following material. Similar problems occur in the concert overture, *In the South (Alassio)*, which is more like a symphonic poem than an overture. Because of the character of the thematic material in the middle section, it's much better if the orchestra is made to play faster than it ever thought it could. Elgar does that on his own recording, which I find particularly inspirational. If this passage is performed too earnestly, attention is drawn to its inadequacies. But if the conductor moves it along, the audience will be impressed by the sheer volume of sound and will find relief in the lovely viola solo that follows.

RH: Elgar's younger contemporary was Ralph Vaughan Williams. For many listeners, his works are representative of British cultural life, and are infused with a certain sense of Britishness. Is it possible to express such things in music?

ME: Is there such a thing as Britishness in British music? To answer that, we must consider some of the influences that shaped British music-making. As I said, Elgar was aware of the Austro-German symphonic tradition, and was equally aware of Wagner's impact on that tradition. Elgar made trips to Bayreuth to hear Wagner's works first-hand. He studied them in detail and composed his First Symphony in the key of *Parsifal*: A flat major, the only symphony by a significant composer written in that key. Vaughan Williams took a completely different path. While he lacked Elgar's inner belief as a musician, he had greater conviction as a man. Elgar was nervous, full of self-doubt and intolerable socially. As time went by, he became increasingly difficult and more unpredictable. Conversely, Vaughan Williams was grounded and the only thing that made him nervous was the possibility that he was not a good craftsman. Perhaps that's why he went to study orchestration with Maurice Ravel in his mid-thirties. As a composer, Vaughan Williams was mystical in a way that Elgar was not.

If there is anything English about Vaughan Williams's music – and I stress the word 'if' – it's his use of folk song. And it's the beauty of those songs, combined with our love of country, which prompts us to believe that his works are English. But that doesn't mean that the music in which he imbeds them is of itself English. After all, music as sound means nothing: a C major chord is just a C major chord. It's only through association and suggestion that it means whatever we want it to mean. Some years ago, I conducted a modern American piece that was inspired by the cliffs near San Diego, California. The sheer cliffs at Torrey Pines State Natural Reserve go down to the sea and waves break against them violently. To prepare the audience for the work, I explained its imagery to them. After the performance, a young man came up to me and said, 'I really enjoyed that modern piece, but I didn't think it was about the cliffs at all. For me, it was about being in a cathedral when the summer sunlight pours in through the stained-glass windows and makes lovely colours on the floor. At that moment, you can see the little particles of dust dancing in the air. That's what the music said to me.' I was touched by his reaction. I said, 'That's fantastic. Hang on to that image, be proud of it and don't be embarrassed by it. The fact that you had such a strong reaction is the most important thing.' Britons tend to be a bit uptight about Englishness in music. It's only natural that we want to have English music so that we can celebrate our love of country in sound.

But I am convinced that Elgar would have written music in the same way had he been born in Hagen, like Charles Hallé, rather than Worcester. While Elgar never used folk songs in the manner of Gustav Holst and Ralph Vaughan Williams, his works are covered with his musical fingerprints. Take, for example, his use of the seventh, a wide and expressive interval. When used in 'Nimrod', it builds intensity while creating a sense of yearning. On the other hand, triplet figures were one of Delius's most common musical traits. But by employing such devices regularly, it doesn't make them English; it's simply part of who Elgar and Delius were as musicians. When it comes to Vaughan Williams, I believe fully that he should be placed within a wider European context. It's a complete mistake to assume that an English symphony must be programmed with other English works. It's essential that the audience encounters different styles of music within a single concert. By juxtaposing Vaughan Williams with, say, Janáček, one can dispel the cosy notion of 'good old Vaughan Williams and his folk songs.' He was a modernist whose best pieces – and I consider all his symphonies among his best pieces – should be heard within as broad a context as possible.

I once conducted Ravel's Piano Concerto for the Left Hand in the same concert as Vaughan Williams's Third Symphony. Arguably the composer's best symphony, it's a work of incredible beauty and profundity. Even though it was first published as 'A Pastoral Symphony', it has nothing to do with Gloucestershire. He originally gave the work this moniker to disguise its true meaning. Like Mahler in his Third Symphony, Vaughan Williams gave each movement a descriptive title which he later withdrew, allowing the music to speak for itself. It would have been better if he hadn't employed the 'Pastoral' sobriquet in the first place, as the piece is about the terrible rape of the Belgian and French landscape during the First World War, and how that landscape was made a ghostly shadow of its former self. The music insinuates itself into our memories. It depicts the way in which the sun goes behind the clouds and casts a shroud of coldness over the land. Loneliness, emptiness and bleakness are ever present in the music. Sadly, commentators were disparaging about the symphony when it first appeared and deliberately misunderstood it. The wordless elegy sung by the off-stage soprano is particularly moving. The symphony is one of Vaughan Williams's greatest achievements and made still greater by being placed within a European context.

RH: Why does the music of Delius appeal to you so much? I know that you are particularly drawn to *Sea Drift*.

PART ONE: CONDUCTORS

ME: While I find his music especially beautiful, British orchestras generally loathe Delius. When his music appears on the stands of the Hallé in Manchester, there is always a sigh of despondency from the players. But, being British, the players' despondency is always tempered with wit and good humour. We were rehearsing the *Poème* by Chausson, for example, and I asked the players if they knew how the composer died. As the silence was deafening, I filled the void by explaining that it was terribly tragic. Chausson lived in the country and drew inspiration from going on bike rides almost every day. He would cycle through the countryside using the same route, which he knew by heart and adored. But, on his last, fatal ride, his brakes failed on the way home. He careered down a hill, went straight into a brick wall and died instantly. One player snorted, 'Pity they didn't give a bike to Delius.' When performing *Sea Drift*, the players say that they can't bear how the harmony slithers around like overcooked spaghetti. Even though they often temper their reaction by saying that they enjoy the work, they are not impressed by Delius's music in general. But I love his harmonic progressions and first got to know them when I was a student at Cambridge. I was fortunate to play bassoon in a performance of *Sea Drift* at Snape Maltings under Sir David Willcocks with John Shirley-Quirk as soloist. *Sea Drift* is about the pain of loss. The soloist describes how, as a boy, he watched birds mating. Having laid her eggs in the nest, the female bird flies off in search of food, but never comes back. In the middle of the piece, the soloist becomes the remaining bird and sings an elegy for his lost love; a beautifully poetic idea. Delius was concerned with man's relationship with the wider world. He explored the power of nature, our reliance on it and its function as a model for good. He was deeply inspired by these concepts and developed them still further in *A Song of the High Hills*. This is one of his last pieces, written for a large, wordless chorus and orchestra. It expresses the ecstasy of being on top of a Norwegian mountain on a fine summer night and being able to see for miles. It explores how a big choir can convey a sense of space by singing very quietly. The orchestra gradually takes up the musical argument, reaches an incredible climax and then dies away. Commentators who say Delius doesn't travel well are wrong. Earlier this year, I conducted the Berlin premiere of *Sea Drift* with Roderick Williams and the Rundfunkchor Berlin. The choir's English was flawless and both choir and audience adored the work.

RH: A British composer who travels better than most is Benjamin Britten. That said, I recently attended a production of his *Albert Herring* at Munich's Residenztheater that completely misunderstood the work and was at odds with its Suffolk origins and setting. As Suffolk is so central to the opera's musical and dramatic narratives, is there not a likelihood that it will always be misrepresented, misunderstood and considered somewhat parochial culturally by foreign audiences, performers and directors?

ME: If *Albert Herring* seems parochial that's a great pity. But music isn't terribly successful at describing landscapes; it's ill-equipped to describe either the countryside or the city. It does, however, describe brilliantly our responses to urban and pastoral scenes, and neither *Albert Herring* nor *Peter Grimes* need be tied to Suffolk. In their failed attempts to be more place specific, some directors have even attempted productions using a Suffolk accent. But who can truly master such an accent? Not only do the singers hate it, but it sounds horrible and unconvincing. A glass of lemonade is a glass of lemonade wherever you are. Aldeburgh beach is not the only pebbly beach in the world, and Swan Vestas can be bought in towns other than Loxford. It's perfectly possible to do works such as *Albert Herring* and *Peter Grimes* in different environments and in different cultural settings. I saw a fine performance of *Peter Grimes* in

PART ONE: CONDUCTORS

Berlin many years ago directed by Joachim Herz. He loved the piece and admired it enormously. To see an East German's view of this powerful Suffolk opera was fascinating. Herz extracted the essence of the story and showed that a myopic, bitchy, quarrelling village can exist in any country. He made clear that it was not necessary to set it where George Crabbe had written the poem, and that it had more to do with human behaviour in general than Suffolk in particular.

RH: Did you ever see Britten conduct?

ME: Not only did I see him conduct, but I performed with him. While I was an undergraduate at Cambridge, I played the bassoon in a performance of the *Spring Symphony*. The concert had been prepared by Sir David Willcocks and Britten came to work with us on the day of the concert, the same concert at which I first played in Delius's *Sea Drift*. He wore a tweed jacket, which remained buttoned, with the obligatory yellow leather pads on the elbows. He was extremely charming and calm. I remember him saying, 'I wonder whether or not you'd mind doing that little bit again for me, as I always find it rather hard.' What he was actually saying was, 'Let's do it again, as you couldn't get it right.' He was so generous in the way that he treated us and it was lovely to play for him, as he was so immediately communicative.

RH: Speaking of immediate communication, should a conductor who's going to perform a Britten opera in a non-English-speaking country insist that it should be performed in English?

ME: This depends entirely on the experience of the company, the linguistic skill of the local audience and the singers cast. Let me give you a slightly different example. If you cast a Janáček opera using only English-speaking singers, I see no reason to do it in Czech. If, on the other hand, you have four principal parts sung by leading Czech singers, then, by all means, do it in the original language. But, if that's the case, it's imperative that the rest of the cast is tireless in perfecting their Czech pronunciation. There was a company on the other side of the Atlantic that decided that if it staged a Janáček opera in translation, it wouldn't be presenting the public with the real thing. For me, this kind of 'authenticity' is fake. It's the kind of snobbery in opera that we must guard against. It's a cause for concern when people think they are getting something provincial when hearing opera in translation. Whether it's provincial or not is decided solely by the quality of the performance. And there is something else to bear in mind: audiences today are multicultural and consist of many different nationalities. The purpose of having subtitles in a performance is not just for English-speaking members of the audience, but for everybody who can manage English better than, say, German or Italian. While opera in the vernacular must always be viewed within a wider social context, the fact remains that opera should be communicated as far as possible in the language of the audience that's listening.

RH: Tell me about *Billy Budd*.

ME: It's Britten's greatest opera. Of course, I also love *Peter Grimes*, another masterpiece that received its premiere at an important moment in the musical life of our country. But I'm fascinated by the action of *Billy Budd*, what motivates its characters and what their unspoken agendas are. The issues raised are extremely interesting and it is a marvellous project to work on. Britten had a remarkable ability to set words, and the text of *Budd* is brilliant. That's not something that can be said about all his operas. I love the music in *The Rape of Lucretia* but some of the words puzzle me. Britten's collaboration with E. M. Forster was extraordinary, and, together, they created something truly remarkable. The concentration of the story, the depiction of life at sea and the way life in this tiny microcosm is developed helps to produce a highly intense sound-world.

Britten created a particular sound-world for each opera. Verdi called it *'la tinta'*. He recognised that if he represented the libretto sufficiently cogently, the music would then be absolutely right for that particular libretto. That's also true for Wagner, especially when you think of *Tannhäuser* and *Lohengrin*, two pieces I really enjoy. *Lohengrin* is the greatest German Romantic opera and a flawless piece. The sound-world at the opening of *Lohengrin* could not possibly be appropriate for *Tannhäuser*. In *Lohengrin*, the dove descending in the Prelude and Lohengrin arriving are all in A major. In the *Ring*, there are only a few small passages in that key, but nothing significant. In *Tannhäuser*, the use of key is also important, as keys really mattered to Wagner and were central to his *'tinta'*. Britten had that, too. Britten's, Wagner's and Verdi's use of key are all distinctive and are a direct result of their involvements with the text. And that's the definition of a great opera composer. The sound-world of *The Turn of the Screw*, for example, could not possibly be confused with the sound-worlds of *Albert Herring*, *Peter Grimes* or *Billy Budd*. The music in *Budd* is lean; there is no fat. When you're at sea, and living that sort of life, it's very harsh. Consequently, when Billy eventually speaks from the heart, it's all the more moving and touching. But Britten's way of describing life on board, and the cruelty and brutality of that life, is distinguished by particularly fine musical and dramatic nuancing. The harsh, and rather unfair, beating of the young novice in Act One was deliberately and carefully placed by Britten. He was concerned that if he didn't engender sympathy for any of the other characters, the audience might be less inclined to be involved in the drama. So, he invented this highly effective and beautifully written part for a young tenor. It always takes all the notices.

RH: Have you ever thought of doing *Budd* in the original four-act version?

ME: I would love to see the four-act version done once, as the great advantage of the original is that the characters have a scene earlier on the ship. When I conducted the opera at Glyndebourne, I considered the original, but decided against it. The tightness of Britten's revision, from four acts to two, works to the opera's benefit.

RH: *The Rape of Lucretia*, *Albert Herring* and *The Turn of the Screw* were all written for small spaces, but are now often performed in big theatres. How do you feel about that?

ME: The English National Opera staged *The Turn of the Screw* in my first year as Music Director. The sparseness in the writing, and the mysterious atmosphere of the opera, actually fitted the Coliseum rather well. The resonance of the space stretched the music and emphasised its beauty. That encouraged us to produce *The Rape of Lucretia*, which also benefited from the extra space. *The Rape of Lucretia* had its premiere at Glyndebourne in 1946, in a much smaller space than the present theatre. Being able to get a sense of the sound, and working out how to enrich that sound within the space while performing, was difficult. That said, the acoustic dryness of the old theatre was one of the reasons why it was so good for Mozart and Rossini, but quite difficult for anything bigger. The new house sits beautifully in terms of the repertoire that is performed there now, including large-scale works such as Verdi's *Otello* and *Simon Boccanegra*. I thought the second of these sounded less successful, but I was pleased when we gave *Budd* there. Glyndebourne continues to perform smaller-scale operas, and one shouldn't be too dogmatic about this. One should be prepared to try different things and to experiment with the spaces available.

DAME JANE GLOVER
(DAVID JOSEFOWITZ RECITAL HALL, 28 FEBRUARY 2020)

RAYMOND HOLDEN: Before we discuss your life and career in detail, I'd like to ask you a more general question that I also recently asked Sian Edwards. What do you understand the social and musical role of the conductor to be in the current political, cultural, social and economic climate, and how does it differ from that of previous generations of podium artists?

JANE GLOVER: First and foremost, I have to say that the conductor's paramount responsibilities are to the music, the musicians and the audience. That's our starting point and the lifeblood of what we do. Having said that, there's a much wider responsibility depending on whether or not a conductor is attached to a major orchestra or an important opera house. If that's the case, the conductor would be involved in a great many outreach and educational events. But it's also incumbent upon conductors to help create the next generation of musicians, which is something that exercises so many of us. Music education is now so fragile. It's always been somewhat arbitrary, and a bit of a postcode lottery. It largely depends on the whim of your local authority. It can depend on whether or not that authority wishes to invest in peripatetic teachers, or teach music at all. It's up to us as conductors to make sure that the next generation gets discovered. And as we are living in difficult times politically, the need for the arts is imperative. They are needed to make people feel better.

RH: Your point about music education is extremely sound and timely. If we compare ourselves to some of the Baltic States, where music is taught mandatorily for two hours daily, we are definitely in dereliction of our cultural duty. And as we are speaking about education, perhaps you could tell me something about your own musical upbringing.

JG: I grew up in Monmouth on the edge of Wales, and went to a good school where the teaching of music was lamentable. My family was fairly musical and regularly went to concerts, but were not professional musicians. After learning the piano, I also began to play the oboe, which meant that I was able to join some local youth orchestras. I absolutely adored being part of the county youth-orchestra system. As I was thought to have an aptitude for these instruments, it was suggested that I should do an O and A level in music. But as the teaching was so bad at my school, I never actually did my A level there. Fortunately, my parents knew somebody who studied music at university, and she tutored me privately. This meant that I was able to achieve a decent A level and to take my place at university.

RH: At the age of sixteen, you had a chance encounter with Benjamin Britten and Peter Pears before hearing them perform in concert. Were these seminal artistic and personal events, how did they affect your understanding of music at the time, and in what ways did those encounters shape your approach to the composer's works in later life?

JG: Yes, I did meet Benjamin Britten when I was sixteen, by which time I'd already discovered his music. When I was thirteen, I stumbled upon

PART ONE: CONDUCTORS

the *War Requiem* at the Three Choirs Festival at Hereford Cathedral. I had no idea what the music was, and thought that I was there to hear Elgar's *The Dream of Gerontius*. They were, in fact, rehearsing Britten's work for the next night's concert. I was immediately struck by the forces involved. Along with the boys' choir, there was a huge chorus and orchestra. This was one of the early performances of the *War Requiem* and it blew my mind! So much so that I insisted that we should go back and hear the actual concert the next night. After that, I got hold of as much of Ben's music as I could. I was passionate about it. Then, he and Pears came to give several concerts locally and stayed nearby. My father was headmaster of the school where one of the concerts was to be held, and had met both Britten and Pears on the morning of the performance. He said to them that if they needed any refreshments, they should go to the headmaster's house, where his wife would look after them. Unfortunately, my father neglected to mention this to my mother! At 4.30pm, shortly after I had arrived home from school, the doorbell rang and my mother said, 'Go and see who that is.' I opened the door, and there, on the doorstep, looking elegant and beautiful, were Ben and Peter. They looked exactly like the cover of one of the record sleeves that I had upstairs. It was amazing. And it has often been said how wonderful Benjamin Britten was with musical boys. Well, let me tell you that he was pretty amazing with the schoolgirl that found herself standing in front of him in that doorway, and who had devoured every note of his music. He talked to me and encouraged me. More to the point, he spoke to me as a musician and wanted to know about me. Somehow, he'd discovered that it was my birthday the following week and gave me a present. It was two tickets to Peter Pears's last ever performance of *Peter Grimes* at Sadler's Wells. My mind was blown for a second time! He even kept in touch with my parents and me after I left school, later inviting me to Aldeburgh, where

I took part in the Hesse Student Scheme. And it was there that I came into contact for the first time with what I effectively do now: intense music-making at a high level. I lapped it all up. As Britten was so busy conducting, composing and accompanying, I was a little shy about saying hello. But, on the last day of the scheme, I wanted to say thank you and goodbye. So I went around to his dressing room following a performance of Haydn's *Die Jahreszeiten.* Even though I hung back a little, and was standing in a corner, he spotted me and said, 'There you are! Why haven't you been to see us?' It was just the most wonderful moment, and I have loved him ever since. I adore his music, as it always feels like coming home. The story then came full circle when I gave my first performance of the *War Requiem*.

RH: You've also made some iconic recordings of Britten's works, including a remarkable disc of *Les Illuminations* with Anthony Rolfe Johnson. As the work was composed with Pears's voice in mind, and as Britten was such an outstanding performer of his own music, how hard is it to inhabit such a work and to make it your own?

JG: Tony was a most wonderful interpreter of Britten's music, and he did make it his own. If, for no other reason, because he had such a different sound from that of Peter. Tony's sound was so much more robust than Pears's, yet incredibly beautiful. His understanding of the text was also magnificent.

RH: The end of secondary education can often prove a difficult crossroads for any aspiring musician. Whether to attend a conservatoire or a university music department is a question that can be particularly vexing. Why did you opt for the latter, and how did your educational experiences at Oxford prepare you for life in the music profession?

PART ONE: CONDUCTORS

JG: This is a very important and interesting question. At one point, I did think that I was going to be an oboist, and when I was about sixteen, I did decide to be one. But I was then encouraged to go to university first before attending a conservatoire as a postgraduate student, where I could pursue the oboe fully. This is a route taken by many people. Looking back at my time at Oxford, I realise how much I owe to my immediate contemporaries there. They were a marvellous group of people, and many of them have since gone on to become conductors, such as Peter Robinson, Nicholas Cleobury and Harry Christophers. The music course at Oxford in those days was so academic that you didn't actually have to perform. We had to do all sorts of keyboard tests that I found incredibly difficult, including score reading and figured bass; precisely the things that I use to this day. And although I didn't think that I was very good at them, I did get better with time. You could opt to do performance as part of your finals, but that wasn't mandatory. Despite this craziness, we performed all the time. Consequently, we did concerts with, and for, each other.

RH: At Oxford, you made your mark as a scholar-performer with the operas of Francesco Cavalli. After conducting the first modern performance of the composer's *Rosinda* for the Oxford University Opera Club in 1973, you made your professional debut at the Wexford Festival in 1975 with his *Eritrea*, again a first modern performance. You then went on to publish your biography of Cavalli, based partially on your doctoral research, in 1978. What first attracted you to Cavalli's music, and why do you think that his works are less often performed than those of his great mentor, Claudio Monteverdi?

JG: It has to be said that one's life changes at university, and, in my case, I discovered that I wasn't such a great oboist. Nevertheless, I did begin to conduct operas at Oxford and was encouraged by my tutors to undertake a DPhil. They suggested that I should research seventeenth-century Venetian opera. I was already hooked on Monteverdi, and this was around the time that Raymond Leppard was resuscitating his operas and those of Cavalli at Glyndebourne. We all heard these and were bowled over by them. But the other thing that was happening then was that the early music movement was just getting going. That meant that you could hear period instrument performances of these works alongside those given by Raymond Leppard and the London Philharmonic Orchestra. This allowed us to question how these works might really have sounded in Venice at the time of their composition. And because of my interest in all of this, I went there to undertake my research, and it was in Venice that I was able to discover a great deal more about Cavalli. This not only resulted in me giving performances of Monteverdi's and Cavalli's operas, but also making my own performing editions of them, which I gave with period instruments.

RH: Do you think that Monteverdi still overshadows Cavalli in the public consciousness?

JG: Well, to be honest, I think that Monteverdi is the better of the two, even though I dearly love Cavalli and consider him to be a truly fantastic theatre composer. Monteverdi was one of those 'alpha-plus' composers who was just extraordinary. The fact that he wrote *Orfeo* in 1607 when opera didn't really exist – it was still an academic idea at the time – and was able to create a musico-dramatic masterpiece that shapes emotional veracity and characterisation so perfectly, is just genius. He then went on to write two very different pieces thirty years later: *Il ritorno d'Ulisse in patria* and *L'incoronazione di Poppea*. He understood fully how people think and react. When Monteverdi wrote his operas for the public theatres of Venice, he was nearly eighty years old, and was a similar age to Verdi when he wrote *Falstaff*, another work of genius by an artist nearing the end of his life. Cavalli was Monteverdi's pupil and dear friend, and learned a great deal from him. But Cavalli did have his own voice and moved the 'product' on, so to speak.

RH: An institution that has run through the fabric of your career like a red thread is the Glyndebourne Festival Opera. Having joined the company in 1979, you were appointed Music Director of its touring wing in 1981. Would you say that there is a qualitative difference between what is heard on the tour and what the company does on its main stage?

JG: I don't think so, even though the artists who perform on the tour are much younger. The system that underpins the Glyndebourne tour is founded on the principle that the young artists who cover, or understudy, the big roles in the main festival perform them on the tour. It's a wonderful training ground for aspiring singers, and it's often the case that the performances given on tour match those heard in the season itself. Funnily enough, I've just written an article for *Opera News*, the American magazine, about my very great friend Dame Felicity Lott: the whole edition is devoted to Glyndebourne. Felicity had auditioned for the Glyndebourne chorus three times and was turned down each time! She then auditioned for the role of Anne Trulove in Stravinsky's *The Rake's Progress* in front of Bernard Haitink, who immediately engaged her for the role. As she sailed through that part, the management then asked, 'Why doesn't she do the role of the Countess in Strauss's *Capriccio* on tour?' That was the first major thing that she did for the company in 1976, and succeeded Elisabeth Söderström in the part. In fact, the production had been created for Söderström. In one stroke, the management had discovered the singer who was going to be the backbone of the company for the next quarter of a century, and Felicity discovered a corner of the repertoire that was to become so important to her. That's the sort of thing that Glyndebourne does for young people.

RH: Do you think, then, that the principles of Glyndebourne's founding fathers, John Christie, Fritz Busch and Carl Ebert, are perhaps now better represented by the touring wing of the company than by the festival itself?

JG: As I haven't worked for the company recently, I'm not sure that I'm really qualified to give an opinion. But, for me, I always say that Glyndebourne was like my second *alma mater*, as I learned my trade there. I had seven or eight wonderful years with the company. I started as the most junior member of the music staff before becoming chorus master and conductor of the tour. And, of course, I was able to assist people such as Bernard Haitink and Sir Simon Rattle, not to mention being in rehearsal rooms with Sir Peter Hall, John Cox and some of the greatest artists of the period. It was such an education. The music staff was also amazing, particularly its head, Martin Isepp, who, along with Bernard Haitink, was a great mentor to me. All I can say is that I learned how to do 'it' there, and that I continue to apply the standards that the company instilled in me. And that applies to *everything* I do.

RH: During your final year with Glyndebourne Touring Opera, you accepted the post of Music Director of the London Mozart Players. While it's not uncommon today for women to hold positions of artistic authority, you were something of a trendsetter at the time. Was your gender a particular stumbling block for managements and fellow musicians during those early years, and do you think that gender equality on the podium is now a given?

PART ONE: CONDUCTORS

JG: At the time, gender *was* a stumbling block. As I was one of the very few female conductors performing then, I felt a little lonely. I tried not to think about it, as the only thing that mattered was what the music sounded like. It was tedious when journalists wanted to write about my shoes and clothes. There have certainly been occasions throughout my career when I've not been given a job because I am a woman. And I think there have also been occasions when I've been given a job because I *am* a woman. Both of those situations are lamentable. The only reason why anybody should hire me is because they believe that I'm the right person for the job. Then, if I don't do it well, they shouldn't ask me back, and, if I do, they should. Yes, it has moved on, and thank heavens that's the case. In fact, I would say that during the last two years it's changed out of all recognition. For a long time, Sian Edwards, who is some ten years younger than me, and I were the only two female conductors working consistently. Then, of course, Marin Alsop appeared on the scene and has done much to change the situation. There are now so many ways to encourage women to do this job, which all three of us have been actively involved in. But what is marvellous, and Sian and I were talking about this a couple of weeks ago, is that wherever I go in America, orchestras have been appointing women as assistant conductors. Many of these have since gone on to get truly great orchestras of their own. While Marin has yet to be appointed Music Director of one of the 'big five' orchestras in the United States, I have no doubt that she will. It's just wonderful to see all of this, and I am so thrilled that there are so many more women out there as conductors. At some point, this subject will no longer be a matter for discussion.

RH: For many years, the London Mozart Players was conducted by its founder, Harry Blech. While it's easy to forget that he had a colourful career and recorded with Nathan Milstein, Norbert Brainin and Peter

Schidlof amongst others, the orchestra never seemed to realise its full potential until you took over its direction. How did you go about shaping the ensemble in your own image?

JG: I did feel very much that I was following on from Harry. But I did have to weed out a few of the players, which was not a particularly comfortable thing to do. The orchestra was well run and well supported at the time, and being able to see the same musicians on a regular basis was extremely helpful. We also had wonderful support from the Arts Council and from British Petroleum, which sponsored ten of our concerts at the Southbank Centre annually. These days, nobody will touch a petrol company when it comes to sponsorship, but, then, that was not considered a problem. We didn't know we were born! We also received a great deal of support as a touring orchestra. These were my 'galley years', to quote Verdi. It really was quite hard work. The amount of repertoire that I absorbed and performed was enormous, particularly in the first couple of years. But one forges relationships and people begin to notice, which is why we were offered recording contracts, Proms concerts and a television series or two. The orchestra's profile rose, and it was a lovely partnership while it lasted.

RH: When I listen to your recordings with the London Mozart Players, I am always impressed by the virtuosity of the playing. This implies that the orchestra's personnel must have been very stable. Was that the case?

JG: It was extremely stable. And one of the most important things in securing that stability was the appointment of the right concertmaster. Would you like to know why I left the orchestra?

RH: I would be very keen to know why.

PART ONE: CONDUCTORS

JG: Although we were clearly on to a very good thing, we eventually became victims of our own success. As we got more and more work, the Arts Council became less generous and sponsors began to fall away. This was common in the 1980s. This meant that we began to give concerts without enough rehearsal. We also gave too many concerts where we would turn up on the day of the performance and play. You can't make good music like that. I protested about this and said that it was impossible to give a programme of Mozart symphonies in this manner. It's not fair to the composer, the musicians or the audience. The idea of driving 100 miles, rehearse for three hours, have a quick cup of coffee and a sandwich, perform and then drive home was simply unacceptable. So, my decision to leave the orchestra was one of the toughest choices that I've ever had to make. But I decided that I couldn't do it any more. I left with great sadness and with huge regret, as I stumbled a little bit professionally after that. Nevertheless, I vowed that I would never give a concert in that manner ever again, and the only time that I have broken that vow has been when I have been asked to conduct charitable performances. And one of the things that I love about my current orchestra in Chicago – Music of the Baroque – is that we rehearse properly. We *really* rehearse properly, and I am so grateful to them for that.

RH: By the time that you took over the London Mozart Players, it seems that the age of the modern, virtuoso chamber orchestra as a significant cultural and recording force was nearing its end. Although the London Mozart Players, the Münchener Bach-Orchester, the Stuttgarter Kammerorchester, the English Chamber Orchestra and the Academy of St Martin in the Fields still exist, their artistic profiles seem to be less dominant than in previous decades. As most of these were formed and were initially directed by an iconic conductor, do you think that the absence of such a figure at their musical helms has contributed to their current profiles, or do you think that the rise of period ensembles, along with the concurrent demise of the recording industry, have been contributing factors?

JG: I think that the demise of the recording industry in this context is an interesting question, as recording is now very different from thirty years ago. This doesn't mean that people aren't recording all the time, because they are. They are simply recording under very different circumstances. But to return to the other part of your question, I think that the period instrument movement has a lot to do with how the chamber orchestras you mentioned are currently perceived and received. There are now so many good period ensembles, and we have learned so much from them. What I found with the London Mozart Players, and what I have also since found with Music of the Baroque, an orchestra comprised of modern instrument players taken mainly from the Chicago Symphony and Chicago Lyric Opera Orchestras, is that the musicians in these ensembles have all been informed by the developments in period performance. I've worked with period orchestras throughout my career, and it's with these types of ensembles that I made my early recordings of Monteverdi and Cavalli. Many of the musicians in the London Mozart Players were 'cross-over' players who would perform with the Orchestra of the Age of Enlightenment one night and with us the next. Because of the way that my own orchestra in Chicago is constituted, many of the players might play Bruckner with Riccardo Muti or Wagner with Sir Andrew Davis in the morning, before coming to play Bach with me in the afternoon. But after working on Bach's music with me for only ten minutes, we have found 'our sound'. That shows how good they are as players, and how conscious they are of their identity as a group. Their loyalty as an ensemble is phenomenal, as they love the music we play. And this is particularly

PART ONE: CONDUCTORS

telling, as often their session with Music of the Baroque might be their third that day.

RH: But, when choosing to perform with a particular ensemble, is that the result of the work that you have decided to conduct? In other words, do you consciously match the sound-world of a particular orchestra with the sound-world of a particular composition?

JG: Generally, an orchestra's sound-world will already be decided by the orchestra that engages me. But let's take an obvious piece such as Handel's *Messiah*, shall we? This is a work that I have performed many times. I've conducted it with huge symphony orchestras and with small period ensembles; I've performed it with twenty-eight singers and 200 singers; and I've given it at A=440 and at A=415. Yet whether I perform the oratorio with big or small forces, or at high or low pitch, I still feel that it's 'my' *Messiah*. It's a matter of getting the big symphony orchestras to play with a period style, and to get the big choruses to sing with the clarity of a cathedral choir.

RH: When you performed *Messiah* with the Huddersfield Choral Society, for example, was it easy to reshape their established sound to match your cathedral-like ideal?

JG: The Huddersfield choir is marvellous when it comes to a piece like *Messiah*. They own it in a way. Not only can they sing the bigger choruses marvellously, but they are highly adept at singing the more *coloratura*-like passages. They are able to achieve the necessary lightness and precision that these sections require. But that's largely down to the hard work of the chorus master. I just come along at the end and have fun!

RH: I would like to return to Mozart again for a moment or two. As you directed the London Mozart Players between 1984 and 1991, it is perhaps no surprise that Mozart's music features heavily in your early discography. How would you define your Mozart style, and in what ways has it evolved and developed over the years?

JG: What I aim for in Mozart is textural lightness and clarity. We should never forget that all eighteenth-century music is based on dance, no matter however fast or slow it is. Shape is also very important. But I would aim for all of these things in every kind of music, not just Mozart.

RH: What Wagner described as *Melos*.

JG: Definitely. That's necessary, as Mozart was such a great 'tune-smith'. But, of course, he was so much more than that. His textures are also extremely interesting: look at his second violin and viola parts, for example. That cannot always be said of Haydn.

RH: When I've discussed repertoire choices with some of your conducting colleagues whose interests lie in the works of the late nineteenth and early twentieth centuries, they often divide into two categories: those who prefer the music of Mahler, and those who favour the compositions of Richard Strauss. Do you think that such a divide also exists for conductors of Haydn's and Mozart's works, and what, for you, characterises the aesthetic differences between the two composers?

JG: I think that they are just very different artists. They were great friends, of course, and, to a degree, influenced each other. It's rather like speaking about Bach and Handel. Although they were completely contemporaneous, they were also completely different. Mozart has often been described as urbane, while Haydn has been described as being more rustic. This is too simplistic, as both could be urbane and both could be rustic. What's more important is an awareness of how they treat dynamics, texture, colour and shape. If these elements are handled with care, the personalities of both composers will shine through.

RH: You once mentioned on film that 'Mozart challenges but he never defeats' and that '[he] ... was not at all an autobiographical composer.' Could we perhaps explore in greater detail what you meant by these aphorisms, and what they mean in practice?

JG: Some composers, such as Berlioz, are hugely autobiographical. By the end of one of their pieces, you practically know what they had for lunch or who stood them up at the pub! When it comes to Mozart, I've always felt that he was at his happiest when he was either composing or playing music. Music was something of an alternative universe for him, even though he would often be under great pressure to produce new works for each ensuing week's concert. But, when discussing him, I always return to the dreadful summer of 1788 when he wrote his last three symphonies for no known reason. He didn't have a commission, nobody had verbally invited him to compose them, and he wasn't travelling to Paris, Linz or Prague where a symphony was considered something of a calling card. He composed these works simply because he wanted to write music. And it was a time in his life when things couldn't have been worse. His daughter had just died and he was penniless. This prompted him to write begging letters to his fellow Freemasons in which he asked them to lend him even the smallest of sums to see him through. These are just awful to read. His wife, Constanze, was unwell, and they had to move from the centre of

Vienna to somewhere in the suburbs. He was practically suicidal and spoke openly about the 'blackness' that descended upon him. Yet he still managed to write the Thirty-Ninth, Fortieth and Forty-First Symphonies. The last of these, with its joyful and uplifting coda to the finale, is a most exhilarating piece of music. And it's almost unbelievable that a man who was in such a state emotionally could write something that uplifting. That tells me that Mozart was not an autobiographical composer, but one who used the alternative universe of music to distance himself from the day-to-day realities of life.

RH: But, surely, Mozart was autobiographical by proxy, and used some of the characters in his operas to codify his own social and demographic circumstances.

JG: Setting an operatic text is quite a different matter. My argument really relates to his activities as a composer of instrumental and orchestral music.

RH: Along with your marvellous biography of Cavalli that I mentioned earlier, you've written critically acclaimed books on Mozart and Handel. What attracts you to writing, and how do you go about finding time in your busy performance schedule to finish them?

JG: My most recent book on Handel took me ten years, largely because I was asked to become Director of Opera here at the Royal Academy of Music shortly after starting it. I was still performing around the world at the time, and it was then that I discovered that you can do two jobs at once, but not three. Consequently, I missed deadline after deadline, and the book got later and later. I am still amazed that I actually finished it, and that it can be found in bookshops. My Cavalli book was slightly

PART ONE: CONDUCTORS

different. Although it was a natural consequence of my doctoral research, I wanted to tell his story in a more readable fashion. My Mozart book, which came out years later, was the result of my daily involvement with his music, and a means by which to come to know him and his family. I felt that there was a story to tell about the women around Mozart, as they were so important to him, but rarely mentioned. This was particularly true of his wife, Constanze, who has had a bad 'press' ever since her death. That brilliant playwright Peter Shaffer wrote a wonderful play, which became a dreadful film, called *Amadeus*. The play was an interesting essay on how genius and mediocrity interact, and the relationship between Mozart and Salieri was an exceedingly good vehicle for such an essay.

While there's no question that Mozart could survive being portrayed as a sort of 'super-brat' who wrote divine music, Constanze was unable to survive the way that she was portrayed. She was seen in both the play and the movie as a vulgar airhead whose only virtue was her preparedness to sleep with Salieri if it meant that her husband could get a job. All of that was rubbish. I think that she *was* a bit of a naughty girl who liked to party, and that she shared with Mozart a slightly wacky sense of humour. But she was also a trained musician like her amazing sisters, who might be seen as a kind of musical version of the Brontës. All were remarkable singers, and all were musically literate. In fact, they had a better music education than Mozart himself. And, after he died, Constanze was responsible for getting his music into print and for keeping his name before the public. She was a tremendous businesswoman and outlived Mozart by some fifty years. Without Constanze being that incredible figure and powerhouse, we wouldn't know as much about Mozart and his music as we do. So, I was keen to tell her story. Although my book is called *Mozart's Women*, it's really my book about him.

RH: Your book on Handel – *Handel in London* – is also fascinating as it deals with the composer's work in the theatre and the ways in which he both shaped, and was shaped, by his own time. It strikes me that many contemporary composers, impresarios and performers could learn a great deal from his methods, and that society in general could gain greatly from a close reading of his pan-European approach, particularly in this post-Brexit age.

JG: It was London's great good fortune that Handel decided to settle here. His life really could have gone in so many other different directions. He was born in Halle and left home when he was about sixteen. His mother had been widowed, and he was anxious to support her financially through the income that he earned from his various jobs as an organist. He then went to Hamburg, where he learned his operatic trade, before going to Italy, where he made his name in Rome and Venice. After the great success of *Agrippina* in Venice, when he was still only in his mid-twenties, he could have gone anywhere. With such young feet that continued to itch, he could have moved to Vienna, Prague, Paris or Berlin, but, instead, he was tempted by Hanover and London. Having opted for the former, he quickly began to shine and was considered brilliant. But after taking up his post there, he told his superiors that he had been invited to work in London, and was duly given leave to travel there for a period. Of course, the Hanoverian authorities were not unhappy about this, as the local Elector knew that he would be King of England in the not-too-distant future. As Handel enjoyed a huge success with *Rinaldo* in London, he asked to be allowed to come back to Britain after he returned to Hanover, which he did a few years later. On the death of Queen Anne, George came over from Hanover and, like Handel, stayed in England. If Handel had gone somewhere else, musical life in London would have been very, very different.

PART ONE: CONDUCTORS

In my book about him, I wanted to examine the reasons why he stayed here, and what his achievements were whilst here.

RH: You are well known for flying the flag for British culture. But precisely how proactive are you in disseminating the music of your homeland abroad, and what is the appetite for British music elsewhere in the world?

JG: I do try to perform British music whenever and wherever I can. But when I've conducted Elgar's *The Dream of Gerontius* in America, for example, people will ask, 'Really? What *is* this?' That's until they actually *hear* the work, and come to understand what an extraordinary piece it is. For me, it's a great choral work and one of the greatest of all compositions. But it *is* a hard sell. Selling Elgar, Walton and our other great symphonists is very difficult in the United States. Michael Tippett's music is impossible to programme, while Britten's and Adès's works are more easily accepted.

RH: The logic behind these responses defies analysis, and must be galling for you, as you have performed a great deal of new music during your career.

JG: I love having a very broad musical palette. And when I gave the world premiere of Sir Peter Maxwell Davies's *Kommilitonen!* here at the Royal Academy of Music, it was one of the most exciting things that I've ever done. Sir David Pountney wrote the libretto and directed the performances. It was like sharing a room with Mozart and da Ponte! The students were amazing, and both the singing and the orchestral playing were of the highest standard. We played to packed houses and received five-star reviews. I wouldn't have missed the experience for anything. At the time, Max was unwell, and I received the opera like a Dickens novel:

it appeared on my desk in episodes, an act at a time. I couldn't wait for each new instalment. It was the most thrilling thing that I did as Director of Opera at the Academy.

RH: For much of your career, the BBC has never been far away. Along with the fourteen Proms that you've conducted, you were an on-screen BBC television presenter at the festival during the 1980s, hosted the television series *Orchestra with Jane Glover* and *Mozart – His Life with Music* in 1983 and 1985 respectively, appeared regularly on Radio 3 and Radio 4 and were a BBC governor between 1990 and 1995. That being so, do you feel that the Corporation continues to fulfil Sir John Reith's three founding principles – to inform, to educate and to entertain – when dealing with Western art music, and are those principles still reflected in the BBC's programming for television?

JG: While the Proms are well represented on television, it's true that we don't have enough televised music. In fact, there were fewer televised Proms last year than the year before. But it does need to be said that the BBC's commitment to music has been fabulous. Robert Ponsonby, Sir John Drummond and Sir Nicholas Kenyon were all wonderful people and all had great vision. One of the best things about the BBC is their five orchestras, two of which are based in London. One of those two London-based orchestras is the BBC Concert Orchestra, which is not only a fabulous ensemble, but an extremely versatile one. At the moment, the BBC is under threat from the government, and if the licence fee goes, and huge cuts are made, that would be disastrous, with education being particularly hard hit.

RH: What if the BBC followed the Australian Broadcasting Corporation's lead and distanced itself from its orchestras, making them financially independent? When that happened in Australia, I remember Sir Charles Mackerras saying to me that he thought that was a good thing.

JG: I don't think that the BBC orchestras would survive if that happened. Perhaps some would, but not all. While the BBC National Orchestra of Wales might manage to carry on, those based in London, Glasgow and Manchester would be unlikely to, as those centres all have other orchestras. The BBC orchestras work well with the other orchestras in those cities and often collaborate on projects together, such as in Manchester where the BBC Philharmonic recently took part in a Beethoven cycle with the Hallé. This is precisely how it should be in a city like Manchester, which has two orchestras. But, in London, where there are five other symphony orchestras and two opera orchestras, the BBC Symphony Orchestra and the BBC Concert Orchestra would struggle.

RH: One final question. Over the years, you've performed at many of the world's leading opera houses, but have yet to be appointed Music Director of a great lyric theatre. Would such a post interest you, and what might you bring to it?

JG: At this stage of my life, probably not. Had I been offered such a post twenty years ago, I might've accepted it. There is more to running an opera house than deciding what to perform and then conducting it. I don't enjoy running big things, but I do love being a guest conductor at an opera house. I prefer running smaller ensembles, and I really *do* enjoy performing.

OLIVER KNUSSEN
(DAVID JOSEFOWITZ RECITAL HALL, 26 OCTOBER 2017)

JONATHAN FREEMAN-ATTWOOD: You were given a recording of Ernest Ansermet conducting Stravinsky's *Petrushka* when you were five years old. Did you think that this was a strange gift at the time, or was it something that you considered quite normal for the son of the London Symphony Orchestra's Principal Double Bass?

OLIVER KNUSSEN: No, I didn't find it strange, as it was all that I knew. I considered it normal. It would be rather like asking Carrie Fisher what it was like growing up with Debbie Reynolds as a mum. We had a 78rpm gramophone machine at home, and I used to sit there by the hour watching Nipper the dog go round and round. There were lots of 'bits' of music around the house; by which I mean, incomplete sets of 78rpm records. This was the result of either me having sat on them, or my parents only being able to find individual discs at the shop. Consequently, I got to know sides seven and sixteen of Mahler's Second Symphony rather well! When I was about four years old, the Australian horn player Barry Tuckwell came to live with us. And it was Barry who gave me the discs of *Petrushka*. He used to tell me the ballet's story as the record played. For my sixth birthday, I was given Brahms's Second Symphony, the composer's *Ein deutsches Requiem* and Mahler's Fifth Symphony. With hindsight, Barry's gift was typical of him, and I'd give *Petrushka* to a kid, too. But much of the music that I heard on disc as a child was related to what my dad was playing in the orchestra.

JF-A: When I visited you a year or two ago at Snape, you showed me a score of Stravinsky's *Epitaphium* that you had scribbled your name on as a schoolboy. How did you come to identify then with this most rarefied of the composer's oeuvre?

OK: There was a certain moment when I discovered that there was music that my dad liked, which extended to Schoenberg and others, and that there was music that he considered beyond the pale. And late Stravinsky was definitely beyond the pale. I used to sneak out and get those scores rather than, say, Strauss's *Eine Alpensinfonie*, which my father would have completely approved of. I would also go out and buy the latest Stravinsky recording, which my dad was often involved in. That's how I got to know the composer's *Movements for Piano and Orchestra*, which is the most extreme, post-Webern work that he ever wrote. As these late compositions are very short, the scores were very cheap, which meant that I could use my pocket money to buy them. When I was ten years old, I bought the score of *Movements for Piano and Orchestra* for six shillings, and the scores of *Epitaphium* and the *Double Canon* for four shillings each. I could afford Webern, too. It was easy to like avant-garde music if you only had a paltry amount of pocket-money.

JF-A: Was your attraction to these works a result of your constant exposure to orchestral music?

OK: Entirely. I knew hardly any chamber music as a child, and continued to know very little until I was an adult. I still don't know all of Beethoven's string quartets, and I only heard a quartet by Haydn ten years ago. It's pathetic. I do know quite a bit of wind chamber music from the Classical Period, but that's only because of my work with modern music.

JF-A: Presumably, you must have attended a great many of the London Symphony Orchestra's rehearsals during your childhood.

OK: Although I had a 78rpm recording of Mozart's 'Haffner' Symphony, I took that sort of music entirely for granted. It sounded like 'ordinary' music to me: the kind that you learned at your piano lessons. Haydn's and Beethoven's slow movements also bored me. But what I used to look forward to were Stravinsky's ballets, Ravel's *Daphnis et Chloé* and Strauss's tone poems. As my boyhood coincided with Ernest Fleischmann's period as General Manager of the London Symphony Orchestra, I was very lucky growing up. He was a man of catholic taste. Pierre Monteux was Chief Conductor of the orchestra at the time, which meant that I was able to hear much of the Diaghilev repertoire. I also heard a great deal of Berlioz with him. This was before Sir Colin Davis's championing of the composer. As a child, I was not encouraged to go to concerts, but to attend rehearsals instead. Many of these were on Sunday mornings, which meant that I heard a great deal of music in an empty Royal Festival Hall. When it's full, it sounds very different: it sounds awful. And it sounded even more awful in those days than it does now. But hearing all that music in an empty hall gave me a sense of what an orchestra could sound like. This was crucial, as halls like the Royal Festival Hall 'implode' when works are loud. The acoustics just can't take it. This wasn't the case when the hall was empty, as there were places for the sound to go.

JF-A: Your father, Stuart, was the solo double-bass player for a remarkable recording of Mahler's First Symphony that Jascha Horenstein made with the London Symphony Orchestra in 1969. That was quite an event, wasn't it?

OK: At the time of that recording, Mahler's symphonies were not played very often. When orchestral musicians got to perform one of these works, it was usually for the first time. I was at the rehearsals for the second performance of the Third Symphony in England, and for the third performance of the Eighth. These works were not standard repertoire at all.

JF-A: Would it be fair to say that you have slightly obsessive tendencies? And that they express themselves in various ways, such as record collecting?

OK: Oh, yes. It's a mania that you and I share!

JF-A: And out of this experience of hearing all the great conductors of the age, one of the most important figures in your life was Leopold Stokowski.

OK: Many of the 78rpm recordings that we had at home were of the Philadelphia Orchestra conducted by Leopold Stokowski. This meant that much of the orchestral music that I heard was with him. Serge Koussevitzky with the Boston Symphony Orchestra were also favourites of my father, but the majority of the discs we owned were of Stokowski and the Philadelphia Orchestra. Their recordings set the standard for orchestral playing in the 1920s and the 1930s. The eminent German conductor Hans Schmidt-Isserstedt told my father that when Stokowski's recordings appeared in Germany for the first time, the locals thought that they had been faked electronically, as they were so good. They couldn't believe an orchestra could play like that. When I hear that the 'greatest orchestra in the world ever' then was the Berlin Philharmonic, I find myself suppressing a little giggle, as some of the orchestral playing heard on Stokowski's pre-war discs is just staggering and on another level. The *rubati* are absolutely together, as are the *portamenti*. And you can't help marvelling at the huge, arching string lines and the enormous range of colour.

My dad went to America in the late 1940s to study with a double-bass player from the Philadelphia Orchestra, and became quite absorbed by their approach. When Stokowski came to England to work with the BBC Symphony Orchestra in the early 1950s, he somehow got to know my father, who was a member of the orchestra at the time. To say that Stokowski was grand is an understatement: he was very regal. But he would, and did, accept favours from orchestral players, such as a lift back to his hotel if his own car didn't arrive. He was a very unpretentious man in private, and he became my father's friend. Stokowski had grown up in London and went to school on Marylebone High Street, opposite the Academy by the church. And even though I found him to be a very scary and an incredibly intimidating person, he loved English family life. Ours was one of two families that he 'adopted' here; the other belonged to the Polish émigré composer Andrzej Panufnik. Instead of going to posh receptions, Stokowski would divide his time in London between the two families. His sons from his marriage to the heiress Gloria Vanderbilt, Stan and Chris, were about my age. So that they could learn what it was like to live in an 'ordinary' English household, he had them come and stay with us for a month or so. Unlike Stokowski, we lived in Watford, and not in a penthouse next to the Guggenheim Museum on Fifth Avenue. While he could be very paternal, he could also be a little frightening because of his white hair, elegant way of dressing and stately bearing.

PART ONE: CONDUCTORS

JF-A: Did you speak to him about music?

OK: I tried to, but he wasn't there to talk about that. When he came over for Sunday lunch for the first time, my mother had forgotten to buy a salad. In a panic, she nipped around the corner to the local shop and bought a tin of Heinz's Russian Salad. Having enjoyed my 'mother's creation', Stokowski said, 'Jane, what's this wonderful Russian salad that you have made?' She replied blushingly, 'It was nothing; just a few things that I threw together.' Clearly impressed by the culinary treat that he'd been served, he would then always ask for 'Jane's wonderful Russian salad' every time that he came around for a meal. He also had some other gastronomic peculiarities, like insisting that he should eat every course off the same plate. He thought that it was wasteful to use too many. He could be a very strange man. Nevertheless, Stokowski did look at one of my pieces. He didn't say anything positive or negative about it, but advised me against writing so many general-pause bars. He suggested that I should insert actual pauses instead, so that conductors could decide for themselves how long each *fermata* should take.

Stokowski is still the greatest conductor that I've ever seen. Regardless of whether or not you like his performances, he had the ability to walk in front of an unfamiliar orchestra and to transform its sound within ten minutes. He managed to conjure up a huge noise from an orchestra, and it's nonsense when people say that he fluffed around at rehearsals. He always rehearsed very precisely and very quickly. This is obvious from the film of him preparing Rachmaninoff's *Rhapsody on a Theme of Paganini* with Jerome Lowenthal. He thoroughly rehearses the complete piece in a time frame that is only five minutes longer than the work itself. He worked with incredible speed, and ensured that every member of the orchestra was alert and paying attention. And if you didn't meet his standards as a player, you were reprimanded. When it came to orchestral sound, he treated the celli as if they were doubling the double basses, rather than the other way around. You can hear this in his live recording of Mahler's Second Symphony with the London Symphony Orchestra from 1963. And it should come as no surprise that my dad was thrilled by this approach. I was eleven at the time, and was present at the Royal Albert Hall to hear it. It was one of the first times that the orchestra had played the work, and the first time that it was given at the Proms. It was like a new piece.

JF-A: Along with Stokowski, you met Monteux. What was he like?

OK: Actually, I didn't meet Monteux. But I did watch him rehearse on about fifty occasions.

JF-A: Did your exposure to these renowned maestri play a part in deciding your future career path?

OK: Absolutely.

JF-A: And does that apply to conducting as well as to composing?

OK: Yes. But before we discuss that, I would like to return briefly to your question about my listening habits as a child. The works that we discussed earlier all seemed perfectly normal to me at the time. That's what music was as far as I was concerned. These works were as exciting to me as a movie about cowboys and Indians, or as a thriller would be to me now. The fact that I often listened to only some sides of a 78rpm album means that I am happy to make public some of my own compositions while they are still fragments. In fact, sometimes I even leave them like that.

PART ONE: CONDUCTORS

JF-A: Are your experiences with incomplete 78rpm albums the basis for your fondness for works such as Elgar's *Falstaff*, a piece that has a kaleidoscope of ideas and that has so many changes of direction?

OK: This might well be true, but not in any kind of intellectual way. When you are a kid, you listen to things entirely on your own terms and completely viscerally. In the case of *Falstaff*, I had no idea who the eponymous character was, or what the work was about. It was only after I read the back of an LP cover when I was about fourteen that I got to know the story. But having listened to parts of the work over and over, I can still tell you exactly what's on side four of Elgar's own recording of it.

JF-A: As a child, how did you reconcile the rather glitzy world of Stokowski and Hollywood with the *recherché* aesthetic of the modernists?

OK: Again, it wasn't a problem for me at that age, and still isn't. Every adjective that's now used to define Stokowski is based on what we are told Hollywood glitz was. In fact, the Hollywood of the period was very original and very stark. Bernard Herrmann, for example, was a friend of Stokowski, and some people could learn a thing or two from him.

JF-A: As a conductor, you use your eyes as much as your hands. Who taught you this?

OK: While the way I beat time was influenced by Leonard Bernstein, my use of eye contact comes from the older generation of conductors. Stokowski, for example, never used any fancy gestures. Of course, if he hammed it up a bit, the roof of the hall would come off. Normally, he was incredibly clear, and worked in such a way that the players had to look at his eyes. These were blue and quite frightening. Monteux, who was older than Stokowski, was a tiny Frenchman with a huge white moustache and black hair. He used a stick that was incredibly long, but moved it very little. Again, his gestures were designed so that the players had to look at his face. From the small amount of existing footage of him conducting, he looks like a diminutive French bandmaster. Yet the orchestra played incredibly. The Alsatian Charles Munch said that there were only two conductors who were masters: Wilhelm Furtwängler and Pierre Monteux. These artists could not have been more different. Like Stokowski, Monteux could achieve incredible textural clarity. When you listen to the recordings of these great figures, you can hear all the orchestral voices all the time. And these conductors achieved that without talking. I am an amateur by comparison, as I have to talk. But I have learned to do as much as possible with as little as possible. This stops me from confusing the musicians. And if there is a problem to be corrected, this approach makes total sense.

Like Stokowski, Sir Adrian Boult was a disciple of Arthur Nikisch, and used an enormous baton that had a grip covered in rubber bands. He would hold his stick between his thumb and forefinger, and would 'flip it' in an enormous arc. This meant that the players had to look at his eyes. But Boult never influenced me, as I was unsure of what he was doing. I don't want to sound hostile to change, or suggest that it should never happen, but when I see many modern conductors flinging themselves around the podium expressing every frigging feeling that they think the music contains, I find it idiotic. There's no such thing as a communistic F sharp, as Alexander Goehr has pointed out, and nor is there any such thing as an emotional E flat. Of course, there were some very good conductors who worked in this way, such as Carlos Kleiber. But, in general, most modern conductors would get the same results if they simply did nothing.

PART ONE: CONDUCTORS

JF-A: Given your eclectic tastes, it's curious that there are certain composers who fall outside your orbit of interest, such as Bach, Mozart and Beethoven. Why is that?

OK: As I discovered Mozart so late, I am embarrassed to talk about him. There are some pieces by him that I love, such as *Don Giovanni* and the last G minor Symphony. And one of the works that I can remember never not knowing is *Die Entführung aus dem Serail*. I adore that piece and still find it very, very funny. But I only properly discovered Mozart by accident when I was lying in bed one morning during my middle fifties. The 'Prague' Symphony came on the radio, and I instantly thought, 'Bloody hell, you're an idiot. Look at what you've been missing.' And I've being playing catch-up ever since. I have even managed to give myself a hernia by carrying the complete recordings of his works home from Paris on the Eurostar about twelve years ago.

JF-A: And what of Bach?

OK: I love Stokowski's transcriptions of his works, and I used to love bits of the *Johannes-Passion* as a kid. I also like *Die Kunst der Fuge*, both on the page and in Busoni's arrangement.

JF-A: But I sense you sitting on the fence a little here.

OK: I have no idea why I feel the way I do. But I am not the only person who doesn't get Bach's music and is unwilling to admit it. Every time I say what I think about Bach to people, I am told that I am wrong. I used to find his music very 'thick'. But that is less so now, thanks to original instruments. I am not a great fan of constant counterpoint and unswerving meter. It's just not my bag. There was a point when I did love some of his pieces. I remember getting the scores of the 'Brandenburg' Concertos one Christmas and being terribly excited to have received such a wonderful present. But I was soon bored rigid and went off them. It's as simple as that. Nevertheless, I do *love* Stokowski's arrangements of the Toccata and Fugue in D minor and of the Passacaglia and Fugue in C minor.

JF-A: Let's leave your dislikes and turn to your likes. Being something of an obsessive, there was a three-week period in your life when you only listened to the music of Nikolai Myaskovsky.

OK: That's true, and I then twisted the BBC's arm into letting me do three of his symphonies. I also performed one of his works with the Boston Symphony Orchestra. This made me terribly unpopular, as I would refuse to go to some places unless they would allow me to conduct one of his pieces.

JF-A: Another composer whom you adore is Mussorgsky, and of whom you have two pictures in your home.

OK: In fact, I now have one, as I gave the other to Mark-Anthony Turnage.

JF-A: What's the basis for that attraction?

OK: It started because I always loved *Pictures at an Exhibition* and *Night on the Bare Mountain*. I also had a single 78rpm disc of *Khovanshchina*, which I thought was incredible. All of these were orchestrated by Stokowski. But that was not the reason for my passion for the composer; it was after my dad brought home a recording of *Boris Godunov* that everything changed. I found the 'Coronation Scene' terrifying, and I haven't been the same since. I had never come across anything that had scared the pants off me before. Although Mussorgsky's works can be very variable, their musical language is raw invention when he's at his best. I remember going to a recital in Edinburgh with my grandmother when I was about ten or eleven years old. That night, Galina Vishnevskaya performed some of Mussorgsky's songs accompanied by her husband, Mstislav Rostropovich. Shostakovich was there, too – the only time that I actually saw him. I was knocked absolutely sideways by those songs, but can't remember why. Like the 'Coronation Scene', I found them terrifying, which is exactly the same reaction that I have when I listen to his *Sunless* song cycle. Conversely, *The Nursery* song cycle reduces me to tears, which is why I tend to avoid it. Mussorgsky has a way of getting inside characters. Most music is essentially triadic until you get to Bartók, in whose hands chords became more complex. Mussorgsky stood in sharp contrast to his contemporaries, as many of his chords are made up of four notes. They are 'added-note' chords that are often placed in strange juxtapositions. And with the exception of Mozart, I've always felt that he was the only composer who was able to tap into some previously unexplored human feelings.

JF-A: And you find this missing from works such as Verdi's *Don Carlos*?

OK: Yes, because there is something conventional about Verdi. Of course, *Falstaff* is amazing, and you can't like the 'Coronation Scene' from *Boris Godunov* and *not* like the 'Grand Inquisitor's Scene' from *Don Carlos*. And, by the way, if you place Claggart's music from Britten's *Billy Budd* side by side with the Grand Inquisitor's music, they are pretty much the same. The only difference is that one is chromatic, and the other is diatonic.

JF-A: Am I correct when I say that you met Stravinsky here at the Royal Academy of Music?

OK: I did. I shook his hand, and he wrote a message in my score. I then had an opportunity to meet him again a couple of years later when his assistant, Robert Craft, asked if I would like to pop backstage after a rehearsal. But I felt a bit embarrassed and said, 'No. I've already met him.' Afterwards, I felt *such* an idiot, and couldn't believe how stupid I'd been.

JF-A: Along with Stravinsky, the other two giants who are central to your aesthetic are Berg and Debussy. Is it possible for you to articulate their importance to you?

OK: As Stravinsky was still alive and writing pieces, he was the most exciting musical personality of my childhood and youth. Every couple of years, I would go to Boosey & Hawkes's store in Regent Street and buy what he had just composed. That was incredible. From being told the story of *Petrushka* by Barry Tuckwell to the publication of the *Requiem Canticles*, Stravinsky has been a part of my life for as long as I can remember. But Berg was a discovery of my own. The first work that I heard by him was the *Altenberg Lieder*. This was at a rehearsal for their British premiere at the Proms. I hated them. I thought that they were ghastly and a horrible noise. One birthday, I wanted to treat myself to a recording of Mahler's Ninth Symphony. So, I went to the local record shop at Watford, where they tried to charge me for a three-record set. But I knew that it was actually a two-disc set with a *free* third record. I had a hissy fit. Next to the Mahler album on the shelves was another called 'The Music of Alban Berg'. As I knew that my father would hate it, I decided to buy the Berg discs instead of the

Mahler symphony. When I got home and played the Berg recording, my world turned upside down, as the first work on it was the 'Ostinato' from the '*Lulu*' Suite.

Debussy is another composer whose music I've loved since childhood. But my understanding of it has increased with age. Richard Rodney Bennett used to say that Debussy was his favourite composer, because he couldn't understand how it was 'done'. And there is some truth in that when it comes to Debussy's music in general. You can pull his works apart and put them back together, but still be none the wiser by the end of the exercise. Take his piano *Études*, for example. His ideas in those works, and how he handles them, defy analysis. When it comes to the end of each *Étude*, it's like watching Houdini escape from a series of locks. Debussy is endlessly fascinating. As a literary character, he's similar to Berlioz. His letters and writings on Mussorgsky are a must. Debussy is very much a three-dimensional character whom you would be happy to know personally. But you still can't figure out how he did what he did. I remember hearing 'Nuages' and 'Fêtes' from *Nocturnes* conducted by Sir John Barbirolli when I was a kid. That was a real 'shivers-up-the-spine' moment: we didn't have a recording of them at home and I'd never heard them before. As a boy, Harrison Birtwistle also attended Barbirolli's concerts with the Hallé Orchestra. And it was after hearing the conductor perform Debussy's *Prélude à l'après-midi d'un faune* in Manchester that Harry had his musical epiphany. My godfather played first flute at that concert; it's all very incestuous, you know!

JF-A: Is Berlioz also important to you?

OK: Yes. My grandfather was Principal Cello of the Hallé Orchestra when Sir Hamilton Harty was its Permanent Conductor. Harty was a great Berlioz interpreter, which meant that my dad grew up knowing the composer's music. When you look at the score of 'La course à l'abîme' from *La damnation de Faust*, there is almost nothing there. It's so simple, yet so effective. A double-bass player in my dad's section once said to me that Berlioz is the only composer who never wrote anything that was ineffective. Everything on the page can be heard. And that's what I learned from his music. It's both incredibly exciting and bonkers.

JF-A: One of your other obsessions is the music of Bruckner. But, unlike him, you are also a committed miniaturist. How does this all tie up?

OK: I first heard Stravinsky's *Epitaphium* at a BBC Thursday Invitation Concert. In the early 1960s, these often consisted of old and new music. Another piece that I heard in that series was Schoenberg's *Herzegewächse*, which is written for celesta, harmonium, harp and *coloratura* soprano. Although it lasts little more than three minutes, it encompasses a whole world. And as I also liked the late works of Webern and Stravinsky, I could see no qualitative difference between their short compositions and the last two symphonies of Bruckner. The more that you look into things, the more you find. A good example of this is the music of Brahms. And having now conducted the Fifth and Eighth Symphonies of Beethoven, I think that the same is true of him.

When my father returned from a tour of the Soviet Union with the London Symphony Orchestra in 1971, he brought back two tiny postcards that depict two Ukrainian *bylinas*; they were illustrated by the Russian artist Ivan Bilibin. I still have both postcards and cherish them greatly. Last week, one fell behind the mantelpiece and I nearly went berserk. A friend who was staying with me at the time could not believe how crazy I became. I would not rest until we were able to get behind the mantelpiece and retrieve it. These miniatures mean more to me than a complete Tchaikovsky box set. The Flemish Renaissance artist Joachim Patinir is also important to me. He painted large biblical pictures that include tiny details. When I wrote my two operas with the librettist and illustrator Maurice Sendak, I used to watch him draw. As his pictures are so full of detail, they look like they have been reduced from a larger original. Yet they are very small, and often appear smaller than their actual size when reproduced in books. Maurice had a tremendous influence on me.

JF-A: I imagine, then, that the whole fabric of Sibelius's Fourth Symphony would be right up your street.

OK: Completely so. When I was about fourteen years old, I wrote an imitation of that piece from beginning to end. It was like a paraphrase. I adore the work, and would have loved to have composed it myself.

JF-A: Before we finish, I'd like to hear your memories of Benjamin Britten.

OK: When I was about seven or eight years old, my dad asked if I would like to go to the seaside. Of course, I said, 'Yes.' We then set off in the car straight after breakfast, causing me to be violently ill on the way. Having ended up at what looked like a scout hut somewhere near the coast, my dad said that I should go and speak to the man that he was pointing to, and to ask him if I could sit in on the rehearsal that was clearly about to take place. When I went up to the man and asked for permission, he replied, 'And who do you belong to?' I said, 'That's my dad over there.' He then smiled at my father and said, 'Well, just go and sit over there, and make sure that you keep quiet.' My dad then asked, 'Do you know who that is?' It was, of course, Benjamin Britten, the composer of *The Young Person's Guide to the Orchestra*, a work that I knew well. I'd never met a composer before. After the rehearsal, we then went for 'elevenses' at the Red House. I later saw Britten conduct either a Mozart or a Haydn symphony, but I can't remember which, as the music bored me rigid.

As a member of the English Opera Group's orchestra, my father also did a great deal of work for Britten in the theatre. And when it came to *Curlew River*, my dad suggested that the addition of a double-bass part to the original orchestration might 'improve' it. Britten acted on his suggestion and wrote a part for my father. The work was pioneering in many ways and required an enormous amount of preparation, as it was intended to be performed without a conductor. I went up to Suffolk for the last week of rehearsals, including the dress rehearsal. But, by the time that we arrived, Britten had rewritten a chunk of the parable, as it didn't work theatrically. The first thing that I heard on the Monday morning was the new material that he had composed during the preceding Saturday and Sunday.

SEMYON BYCHKOV
(DAVID JOSEFOWITZ RECITAL HALL, 28 MARCH 2014)

JONATHAN FREEMAN-ATTWOOD: You were born in Leningrad, now, of course, Saint Petersburg, where you attended the Glinka Choir School and the Leningrad Conservatory. What was life like in the Soviet Union during your early years, and how influential were those institutions in your development as a musician?

SEMYON BYCHKOV: They played a very important part. For all of us, the country in which we are born, the environment in which we find ourselves, and the people with whom we come into contact have an enormous influence on us. We admire them and feel loved by them. They encourage and stimulate us on our individual musical journeys. That's no different wherever you might be from. I was very fortunate to have been born into a cultural tradition and point of view that took an existential approach to art, music and literature. This was not simply about connecting human existence with the notes that we interpret, but to express our existence in as many facets as possible. That was the tradition that gave me my start in music, and the longer I live, the more I see the validity of it.

JF-A: Were you aware that Soviet music education was, in many ways, the envy of the world during your formative years?

SB: The first time I travelled abroad was to Poland when I was sixteen years old. I can't say that I was aware of how the world saw Soviet music education at the time. But, of course, the locals felt that we *were* the envy of the world. Whether or not that was really true, I'm not sure. Independent of that response, and independent of the politics, which is another subject altogether, it's interesting to consider the dichotomy that exists between what one is told to believe and the reaction of the intelligentsia. In fact, the response of the latter goes well beyond the period of Soviet power and back to pre-revolutionary times. It's genetic, passed from one generation to the next, and can be observed in both huge and tiny reactions. When the Soviet Union invaded Czechoslovakia during the 'Prague Spring', for example, the government justified the invasion by saying that it was simply honouring a request by the Czechs to help suppress an attempted anti-communist coup. I remember very clearly when it was announced. It was during a history lesson with a teacher who was both our principal and a member of the Communist Party. There was a moment when one of my classmates said something in support of the government's action, but the look on her face made it very clear that she was pained by the comment. This showed how much the intelligentsia was divided by the action, and how they disagreed and were shamed by it. So, you see, there was the 'official' façade, and then there was what the people really believed. These were times when the intelligentsia were unable to express their views as freely as they might have done had they lived in a democratic society.

JF-A: A name that is closely associated with you during your formative years was Ilya Musin, your teacher. He effectively founded a school of conducting that has since gone on to become very influential. He once said, 'A conductor must make music visible to his musicians with his hands. There are two components to conducting: expressiveness and exactness. These two components are in dialectal opposition to each other. In fact, they cancel each other out. A conductor must, therefore, find a way to bring the two together.' Do you agree with that statement?

SB: Completely. It's what conductors strive for. Conducting is a peculiar way of expressing music, as we rely on sounds made by colleagues. Our art is silent. This means that we can do more or less anything, and can then blame someone else if we don't like what we hear. But just like every instrumentalist or singer, we strive to understand what lies behind the notes. We then try to find ways of expressing that meaning. The effort in achieving that goal has no limit, and it can never be finite. It's something that is convincing at a given moment, and we are happy that it is. But, tomorrow, it will no longer feel convincing. You then have to try again. It's not about playing the right notes. It's how to play the right notes in a way that expresses the *meaning* of the piece. This is a tremendous challenge. And, of course, the two have to go together. Without an exact means of expression, the expression itself will never be quite right. The two are completely interconnected.

JF-A: When you were studying with Musin, were you aware that he was different from other conducting teachers, or were you so focused on your own artistic development that any comparisons were impossible?

SB: At the time, I was completely unaware of what was happening outside of the Soviet Union. But I was aware of the performances and recordings by great artists from abroad. As students, we were very hungry and curious for those things and those people. There was a constant and ongoing discussion of what was, or was not, convincing musically. That was, and is, absolutely normal. We also visited the classes of other pedagogues, and not simply those related to our own discipline.

Musin's class was always full of visitors whose interests were not just conducting. Pianists, singers and composers all came along. Their actual discipline didn't really matter, as conducting is only one way of expressing music. As Musin's students would also observe the classes of other teachers, it was always fascinating to compare how they approached the same subject from very different angles.

What was extraordinary about Musin was that he was genuinely the first person to formulate the art of conducting as a physical process. He was able to demonstrate how a silent gesture can invoke the character and spirit of the music while creating exactness. A gesture of a conductor has to contain the entire information that comes from the music, not only in its character, but what makes it so. In a duplet rhythm, for example, where you have two notes within a given beat, or a triplet rhythm, where you have three notes within a beat, the gesture needs to reflect the differences between each. He would demonstrate this without sound, and we were able to identify which of the rhythmic figures he was conducting. He was also the kind of pedagogue who not only taught us how to do something, but how to search for it. By way of comparison, he might say, 'You want to produce an accent here, but are you actually doing it?' Conversely, he might then ask, 'Do you want to avoid an accent, and is your gesture really designed to achieve that?' His use of contradiction was provocative, and it made us reflect on every move we made. In class, we would have two pianists playing whatever we were conducting. Whether it was a symphony by Beethoven, Brahms or Shostakovich, there would always be two colleagues playing two pianos. If their ensemble slipped, Musin would always ask, 'Was their poor ensemble the result of you being unclear, or a lack of communication on their part?' Musin constantly challenged how we studied, practised and searched out the meaning of the music. He was always encouraging and stimulating in that regard.

PART ONE: CONDUCTORS

JF-A: Concurrent with your studies with Musin, you were playing volleyball with Leningrad Dynamo. You're not the only conductor who was besotted by sport; Sir John Barbirolli was a keen boxer in his youth, and his rather bent nose was the result of his early interest in pugilism. And then there were Herbert von Karajan and Sir Georg Solti. Karajan was an avid skier and Solti loved tennis. Do you think that sport complements the study of music and helps a young conductor to come to terms with their art, both physically and psychologically?

SB: All of those. Everyone knows that a healthy spirit lives in a healthy body, and that a healthy body needs a healthy spirit. Whether it's volleyball, football or any other collective sport, it informs your character and teaches you that the match is neither won nor lost until the final whistle is blown. It teaches you not to give up or surrender, but to try and improve yourself each and every time that you are on the field of play. While that should be true of everything you do, it's especially true of music. I found the experience of playing with Leningrad Dynamo absolutely invaluable. Our coach was a tremendous man. A doctor as well as a volleyball coach, he challenged us both physically and mentally, and provided us with a foundation that helped shape our future lives.

JF-A: In which case, I will take you to a five-day cricket match sometime, which, believe me, makes Strauss's *Die Frau ohne Schatten* seem like a *minuet*! But, before that, let's return to 1973 and the Rachmaninoff Conducting Competition, which you won. What are your views on conducting competitions, and are they something that you would recommend as a matter of course?

SB: There's nothing wrong with competitions, but there is nothing right about them either. We all know of competition winners who have gone on to become extremely accomplished performers, and of those who have never been heard of again. A conducting competition is not a testament to anything, other than the fact that a particular person was noticed by a jury at a particular moment in time, and was thought to be the most convincing candidate present. There is nothing more or less to it than that. Yes, I did win the Rachmaninoff Conducting Competition, which allowed me to conduct the composer's *Symphonic Dances* in the final concert. That was a tremendous experience, which brought me to the attention of the Leningrad Philharmonic Society. I was then invited to make my debut with that great orchestra at the tender age of twenty. This was not something that is given to everybody, and from that perspective I was privileged. But if I hadn't won, I am not sure that my life would have been much different in the end.

JF-A: But your life *was* different, and very quickly so. Within two years of winning that competition, you emigrated to America, where you enrolled at the Mannes School of Music. To paraphrase Bruce Springsteen, 'You were reborn in the USA.' This must have been something of a shock, both politically and culturally. Why did you feel the need to be 'reborn' in America?

SB: It wasn't really my decision to be 'reborn'. I just needed to be free, and that's why I left the Soviet Union. When I arrived in New York, I didn't expect America to be perfect. I never considered that to be possible, and it wasn't. And I wasn't disappointed! Being 'born again' had nothing to do with religion. It was simply the realisation that I was allowed to be myself. It also meant that I was able to believe what I wanted to believe, and to be able to express those beliefs. It's one's right to do so. Culturally, my move to America was also tremendous. Suddenly, the amount of information that was available to me was overwhelming. I was now able to access musicians and orchestras that I'd only heard on recordings in the Soviet Union. This was extremely uplifting and very stimulating. I wouldn't call it a 'shock', though. I would rather liken it to being given a form of oxygen that lifts you up and allows you to explore opportunities that you had previously never thought possible.

JF-A: Having experienced American musical life for a period, you were appointed Music Director of the Orchestre de Paris in 1989. Surely, that must have been a culture shock? Known as something of a law unto itself, that orchestra proved quite a challenge for Herbert von Karajan, Sir Georg Solti and Daniel Barenboim.

SB: My nine years with the orchestra was absolutely fascinating. I first performed in France as a guest conductor at the Aix-en-Provence Festival, but spoke very little French at the time. That was something of a handicap, as there are certain ways in which one expresses oneself in every language. And that's particularly true of French. When you don't understand those nuances, you speak extremely directly. Maybe too directly. It was a tremendous learning experience. And I would say that such experiences are, in a way, indispensable. It brought me into contact with a culture that was completely foreign to me. From childhood onwards, I naturally gravitated to the music of Germany, Italy and Russia. But not to that of France. And so when I began to explore French music through the eyes of those who gave birth to it genetically, if not directly, it was revelatory.

JF-A: As Music Director of a French orchestra, did your approach to programming change?

SB: No. I was able to programme quite freely and to include works that were important to me. There was absolutely no pressure whatsoever to change my approach. What I did find stimulating was the orchestra's tradition of performing contemporary music. It was a type of contemporary music that was very new to me, mainly because of the background from which I came. For me, contemporary music had been Shostakovich, a composer who was far from contemporary in the West. I remember being asked by an interviewer when I was about to start my tenure with the Orchestre de Paris, 'So you are planning to perform Shostakovich. What's so new about him?' The very nature of the question startled me, as it was based on the premise that music *must* contain something new. I've always understood music to be an existential experience. For me, substance is of greatest relevance, as that's what we identify with. Of course, the means of expression can be new, but the question itself implied that Shostakovich invented *nothing* new. Maybe so, but the same could be said of Mozart. Yet that doesn't negate his role in the history of music. Nevertheless, I found the whole discussion particularly interesting. Of equal interest were the contacts that I made with musicians who would later become pivotal figures in my life, such as Henri Dutilleux and Luciano Berio.

JF-A: How did your first encounters with Dutilleux and Berio come about?

SB: It was different in each case. Dutilleux was an extremely admired and much-loved figure on the French contemporary scene. Even though he actually wrote relatively few works, each was of tremendous quality. He was also a renowned pedagogue, and one of the principal exponents of classical music in France. He was the 'dean', so to speak, of French contemporary music. I was extremely attracted to his works, and getting to know him personally was extremely important to me. Whenever we programmed or recorded one of his pieces, he would invariably come to all the rehearsals and recording sessions. It was clear from the conversations that I had with him about his music that it should be approached in the same way as we approach compositions from the Classical Period. You could ask him exactly how he wanted his music to be phrased and articulated. Whether he would like the notes to be extremely short, or slightly longer. And from the answers received, you were able to discover whether or not your instincts were correct. This is one of the great advantages of working with a contemporary composer. Dutilleux had a generous character and was a man of enormous culture. He was a godsend. Luciano Berio was quite different. He was a very close friend of my wife and sister-in-law, Marielle and Katia Labèque, and it was through them that I first met him. He quickly became my friend, too, and influenced my development tremendously. Like Dutilleux, he became indispensable, even though they were very different personalities.

JF-A: As you've just mentioned Marielle, dare I ask what are some of the delights and pitfalls of working with your wife?

SB: We work together whenever we can, and there are no pitfalls. Should there be?

JF-A: Absolutely not, and, of course, you recorded Mozart's Concerto for Two Pianos with Marielle and her sister, something of a rarity in your discography. Do you think of yourself as a Mozartian, and, if so, do you programme his works regularly?

SB: Yes, I do. But I don't programme his music nearly as much as I should, and not nearly as much as I want to. A reason for this is that there is so much music to do. This is one of the great challenges and dilemmas of being a conductor. And then there was the established approach to performing music of the late-eighteenth century that Katia, Marielle and I experienced, both independently and together. We were brought up speaking the language of that music in a particular way. We then became aware of the impact of historical performance practice and period instruments on that music through contact with friends such as Sir John Eliot Gardiner, Giovanni Antonini, Nikolaus Harnoncourt and Reinhard Goebel. And what is fascinating about all of this is that John Eliot Gardiner and Nikolaus Harnoncourt have read the same books, but have come to very different conclusions. This speaks a great deal about plurality, and the need for it in music. Thank God it exists!

JF-A: And that leads us nicely to my next question. Would I be right in saying that you're an artist who balances modern ideas on performance practice with those that are more established, thus creating a mutually inclusive approach?

SB: Everything has to be mutually inclusive. One of the dangers of believing in something so deeply is the possibility of becoming fanatical about it. Consequently, anything that doesn't match your point of view becomes an anathema. That's a great pity. I'm not prepared to dismiss the performances of early music by artists such as Herbert von Karajan, Wilhelm Furtwängler and others just because our position today has changed, and the ways in which we interpret this music has evolved. It was equally wrong that period instrument performers were considered charlatans when those instruments began to appear for the first time in our concert halls. That was a terrible shame, as we should never confuse the means of expression with expression itself. Things will always influence expression.

That's absolutely true. But, in the end, we should always feel privileged when we hear a convincing performance of a symphony by Mozart, whether it be on modern or period instruments. Instruments are simply instruments, and it's the people who play them who are the most important aspect of a performance. Look at Nikolaus Harnoncourt. He gives remarkable performances of early music with orchestras that play on modern instruments. When, for example, he performed Beethoven's *Missa solemnis* at the Barbican Centre with the Royal Concertgebouw Orchestra two years ago, it was a miracle.

JF-A: But the reason that performance was a miracle is that Harnoncourt has a definable core aesthetic. The same is true of you. Yours is the product of a very strong emotional compass that balances the negotiable with the non-negotiable. This is clear from the ways in which your values and approaches have changed over the years. But you've never 'bolted on' trendy gestures just to show that you are *au courant* with whatever happens to be the next new fashion in performance practice. You have always engaged in a dialogue between the big musical picture and a work's chamber-like qualities. This is particularly true of your Mahler performances. Are you conscious of this?

SB: Yes, I am quite conscious of that and am constantly striving to achieve that goal. You can never interpret a work unless you understand it as a whole. And it's the detail that makes the whole. In a way, the process of working with a score is simply the act of coming to terms with it. Imagine that you are reading a book. When you start the first page, you have no idea how it will end. But you go on reading, and eventually you get to the last page. In some cases, you might give up because it's boring. If the book grips you, you will stay with it and finish reading it. And if it grips you in a profound way, you might realise that much of it escaped you the first time you read it. You then go back to the beginning, read it again and discover other elements.

This is also true of musical interpretation, as the score itself does not change, we do. Our understanding is based on *our* life experience. The more experiences we have, the more questions we ask. Answers might not be forthcoming, but questions will be ever present. So, studying a score is always a fascinating process of discovery that we share with our audience. That being so, we must be ever vigilant when it comes to quality. Most things can be discussed. *Tempo*, dynamics and balance can all be discussed. But what's never up for discussion is quality. Conviction and devotion are necessary when approaching a work of art, as the work of art is the only thing that matters. And our devotion to that object must be of the greatest importance when we come to share it with an audience.

JF-A: One of the most important chapters in your life was your tenure with the WDR Sinfonieorchester in Cologne. With it, you recorded works by Wagner, Brahms, Mahler, Shostakovich and, of course, Strauss. When composing his tone poems, Strauss firmly believed that the symphony was a thing of the past, and that programme music was the way of the future. Nevertheless, he used eighteenth-century structures as the basis for many of his orchestral works. What are your thoughts on this, and how do you go about balancing the musical with the extra-musical?

SB: One should always be fully informed about everything one interprets. This involves the life and personality of the composer, the work itself and the cultural and historical environments that surrounded both the piece and its creator. But I do start with the premise that every work tells a story, whether it be programmatic or not. The composition might have a text, but, equally, it might simply represent an abstract story, which allows one to believe and imagine whatever one wants. Nevertheless, there's always a story, and pieces of music are, themselves, storytellers. If that's not the case, a work will lack interest. I don't have to have a literary story present to be interested in a piece of music. But if it only consists of what I call a 'play of sounds', it will only interest me for a few minutes. It won't affect me fundamentally, and there's no point to its existence. How a work *actually* affects me is a completely different thing. If a piece has a programme, but that programme is represented by music that's not particularly interesting, I am better off reading a fascinating story by a great writer. On the other hand, if a piece of music is not based on a specific story, but touches me deeply, then the work's purpose has been fulfilled. Of course, it's terribly important to know what lies behind the notes, but that's not the most important thing. Take Shostakovich, for example, a very important figure in the history of twentieth-century music. Because of the life he led, and the society within which he found himself, it's easy to reduce his works to a series of political events. But if one is completely unaware of the uprising that took place in Saint Petersburg on 9 January 1905, his Eleventh Symphony will still be affecting.

JF-A: Can the same be said for the storm section of Strauss's *Eine Alpensinfonie*?

SB: That depends on what you believe the work to be and what it represents. Is it really simply about being whipped by the wind and drenched by the rain, or is it more about being 'soaked' by life itself? That makes the discussion far more interesting. Strauss used the programme of *Eine Alpensinfonie*, and the titles for each of its subsections, as a kind of façade. They're a form of camouflage. The work is really about one's journey through life. It starts with birth and ends with man's transition into the next level of existence. What happens in between reflects the human condition. And *that's* what I find especially interesting and moving about the piece. Nature itself is a great deal more important than the sounds that depict it. On the other hand, Strauss's ability to evoke nature through sound means that we are always keen to find out how he did it.

JF-A: Another composer who was alive to nature was Gustav Mahler. Perhaps one of the greatest differences between Strauss and Mahler was their understanding of redemption. For the atheist Strauss, this was an alien concept, while for the more spiritual Mahler, it was central.

SB: It's always fascinating to reflect on two men who were diametrically opposed temperamentally, but who were quite close personally. When tackling the great existential questions, they approached them very differently, yet came to similar conclusions.

JF-A: A good example of this is how they engaged with Nietzsche's *Also sprach Zarathustra*.

SB: Historically, Strauss has often been portrayed as being very materialistic. He's regularly depicted as only being interested in playing Skat and making as much money as possible. In other words, somebody who was relatively superficial. Perhaps somebody could explain to me, then, how such a 'superficial' person could compose the *Vier letzte Lieder*, *Metamorphosen*, the 'Recognition Scene' in *Elektra* or the Trio from *Der Rosenkavalier*. These are some of the most affecting pages of music that have ever been written. So, how did somebody who was *so* 'superficial' create such works? Perhaps he did give the impression of being somewhat 'cool'. But when I look at photographs of him and see such depth in his extraordinary eyes; when I look at the Alps from his villa at Garmisch and see what he saw; and when I think about how much he suffered at the end of the Second World War, I understand fully why he composed *Metamorphosen* and the *Vier letzte Lieder*. It took a particular talent and artistic ability to create things that only he himself could create at that point in his life, a time when everything was both behind him and ahead of him. But that level of creativity was not restricted to the end of his life: he had worked consistently at that level throughout his whole career.

Mahler, on the other hand, is harder to describe. How does one describe a man who was so deeply miserable? But is all his music equally miserable? What about the Finale of the Third Symphony, which has a little subtitle that says, 'What Love Tells Me'? Here, Mahler is not referring to the love of just one person, but to a universal understanding of love with a capital 'L'. Mahler was not as self-centred as he is often portrayed. And did you know that the last movement of the Third Symphony was the first thing by Mahler that I ever heard? I was studying at the Glinka Choir School at the time, which is situated at the very heart of Leningrad and adjacent to the Palace Square. The school itself is connected to the main concert hall of the Glinka Capella, which was where the Philharmonic Orchestra rehearsed before giving its concerts at the Philharmonie. Between classes, there was often a short break during which I would always run to the orchestra's rehearsals and listen in. On this particular occasion, I arrived, but there was complete silence. Suddenly, I heard the most remarkable string sound that left me transfixed. It was the beginning of the Third Symphony's Finale. I had no idea what it was, or who it was by. But I knew that it was a miracle. So much so that I forgot to go back to class. I stayed and listened. When the rehearsal finished, I returned to school. Later that day, I was walking down the street and saw a poster that announced Mahler's Third Symphony. I'd never heard of Mahler. But it was then that my dream to conduct his Third Symphony was born. It was the direct result of those sounds. I had no idea what the work's programme was, what the subtitles were, where it was composed, or why it was written. I knew none of those things. And *that* is the answer to the meaning of music. It will either touch you, or it won't.

JF-A: That's the reason, I suspect, why you're not a committed 'completest'. You only perform works that speak directly to you and that have gotten under your skin, so to speak. There are certain pieces that you do, and then there are certain ones that you don't do. Mahler's Ninth Symphony is an example of the latter.

SB: I have cancelled it four times. What's the point!

JF-A: Is that because you consider it to be the summit of Mahler's oeuvre?

SB: No. It's not a value judgement about the piece. On each of the four occasions that I planned to conduct it, I hit a dead end with the work that left me feeling that I couldn't really perform it. It's impossible to explain. Having now announced and cancelled the symphony four times, I have decided that there is no point performing it, even though it's one of music's greatest monuments. But that doesn't mean I'll never do it. I simply don't know. And this applies to all music. There is absolutely no point performing a work from which you feel excluded, a work that you don't feel a desperate need to interpret or to express. I mentioned earlier that one thing was non-negotiable: quality. And quality can only be achieved after a work becomes part of you, when you and the symphony are one. This might take a month, or it may take a lifetime. It's impossible to tell. What's the point of performing every piece that's ever been written? Quantity is not quality.

JF-A: There's one composer I am particularly keen to discuss with you: Richard Wagner. When you were interviewed for *The Jewish Chronicle* recently, you said, 'Of course, I have ideological objections to Wagner, but not artistic ones. There's a tremendous difference. There are people who can't bear listening to his music, either because of the nature of the music itself, or because of the politics associated with it, and that has to be respected. But it should not prevent other people from worshipping his art.' While it might be possible to separate the ideological from the purely musical when performing *Tristan und Isolde* or *Lohengrin*, this is surely not the case when it comes to *Der Ring des Nibelungen*, where the political and ideological allegories that underpin the libretto are also fundamental to the score. How do you square those ethical and cultural circles?

SB: I don't try. The works that Wagner created depict existence and the universe as they actually are, both in their good and evil states. One has to accept both elements of his work, as they are all-embracing. This is why his music is still being talked about, and why we still want to hear it, depending, of course, on who you are. It all rests on how each of us responds to a particular composer. In the case of Wagner, I find many of his ideas objectionable, especially his thoughts on anti-Semitism. They are abhorrent and unacceptable. But his music is something else. Once a very dear friend asked me a question that I was unable to answer for many years. He said, 'I have often wondered why Wagner gave some of his most villainous characters some of his most beautiful music. Isn't that a contradiction?' The answer came to me when I was rehearsing Elsa's and Ortrud's duet from *Lohengrin*, some of the most sublime music ever written. On the one hand, you have Elsa, an extraordinarily pure character who is given the most beautiful and noble music, and, on the other, you have the villain Ortrud. It occurred to me that the way we view Ortrud is not the way that she sees herself. If you then put this in the context of Wagner's letters, it's clear that the suffering he inflicted on others was returned in spades. This caused him great distress. Nothing is black and white. You'll either be affected by his music, or you won't. You'll either catch the incurable virus known as 'Wagneritis', or you'll be so appalled and repulsed by his music that it will make you physically sick. It has nothing to do with the ethical and moral stances that he took, but the music that he created. Sometimes his music is so close to our life experiences that we are either able to deal with it, or we can't. It's possible to reject some of his prose writings, but still feel at one with his music.

JF-A: I would like to return to Richard Strauss for a moment and his often underrated opera *Daphne*. When you gave it some years ago at the Vienna Staatsoper, you must have been deafened by the sound of heads being scratched and critics' pencils being sharpened. It's no exaggeration to say that the Viennese were wholly baffled by your advocacy of this near-forgotten masterpiece, a work that was so dear to the composer's heart.

SB: I lived with *Daphne* for more than five years, during which time I conducted concert performances of it in Cologne, led a new production of it in Vienna, and made a recording of it for Decca. I also toured with it to the United States with Renée Fleming and the WDR Sinfonieorchester. Before that, I knew very little about the piece. When I was rehearsing the opera in Vienna, I was being constantly asked, 'What's so interesting about *Daphne*?' And I would say, 'Come and

PART ONE: CONDUCTORS

listen. You don't know it yet.' Humans have a tendency to think that if they don't know something, it's just not good enough. Schubert's *Fierrabras* is a case in point. It has often been said that Schubert isn't an opera composer. Maybe not. But when you experience that piece in a convincing performance with interpreters who truly believe in it, you cannot fail to be moved. The same is true of *Daphne*. It's not for me to try and convince people of the work's validity. It doesn't need it. What *Daphne* does is reveal Strauss in the 1930s. That is the period after *Salome*, *Elektra* and *Der Rosenkavalier*, for which he was heavily attacked for betraying avant-garde music. That wasn't true at all, as can be seen from *Die Frau ohne Schatten*.

JF-A: As you have just mentioned *Die Frau ohne Schatten*, do you think that the richness of that score is almost divorced from the fairy-tale that it is trying to support? It seems to me that if you think of the work in those terms, the sumptuous score then adds another dimension to the opera as a consequence.

SB: It's true that *Die Frau ohne Schatten* has many different layers. I hear daily that the work is an amazing musical creation that accompanies a story that nobody can possibly understand. That's a pity, as a child can understand it. It's only if you reflect on the story's themes and the characters' relationships that ideas and possibilities abound. But, essentially, the tale can easily be explained to a child, and that child will be fascinated by it. What *is* interesting for me is how everything is drawn together. It's a very polyphonic story that operates on different levels. Imagine you are watching a movie where you are observing a residential building. There are lights coming from different windows on different floors where different families live. A variety of things are going on at the same time. Somebody is having lunch, somebody is watching television, somebody is making love, somebody is fighting, and somebody is making a telephone call. It's all happening at the same time, and each is completely unaware of what the other is doing. But *we* get to see it all. And this is precisely what happens in the score of *Die Frau ohne Schatten*. Because of the sheer amount of information contained in it, we have to be constantly alert to the work's *Leitmotiven*, which represent either a specific character, relationship, situation or mood. As these motifs are often present at the same time, it's essential to find a way of harmonising them, so that they all have space and can all be revealed easily to the listener. The more you see, the more you find. And this is what makes *Die Frau ohne Schatten* so completely fascinating.

MASAAKI SUZUKI
(DAVID JOSEFOWITZ RECITAL HALL, 14 JANUARY 2020)

JONATHAN FREEMAN-ATTWOOD: When the first volume of your Bach cantatas was released in the United Kingdom in 1995, it came as a huge surprise. It was as if a man from Mars had arrived, especially as a complete series was on the cards. Previously, the only comprehensive recording of those works was by Gustav Leonhardt and Nikolaus Harnoncourt, both of whom were well-known quantities as instrumentalists and directors. Do you recall how your reading of the cantatas was received at the time?

MASAAKI SUZUKI: We were quite surprised by the reaction of Europeans and other foreigners to our approach. Bach had always been very famous and well known in Japan, even though there had never been a recording project like ours before. As Bach was very familiar to Japanese musicians, our project was a natural extension of our desire to reflect his profile there. But I had no expectations of any kind as to how Europeans might react to it.

JF-A: Twenty-five years ago, you were very conscious that some people might be surprised that a group of Japanese musicians was tackling these works. This prompted you to write: 'the God in whose service Bach laboured, and the God whom I worship are one and the same.' The fact that you needed to say this is interesting, both culturally and religiously.

MS: To be perfectly honest, I didn't mean to surprise anyone. The only thing that I really wanted to do was to keep performing Bach's cantatas, my favourite music. In fact, we started on these works quite some years before the recording project, and wanted to carry on exploring them. It was something of a continuation of what I had done as a student in Tokyo.

JF-A: And it's worth saying here that Robert von Bahr, the Swedish owner of BIS, the company that released your Bach series, showed remarkable courage when he gave you the go-ahead to undertake the project.

MS: Absolutely. It was down to his courage that it was started and finished. I am extremely grateful to him. Everywhere we go, there are now Bach fans, with Bach-Gesellschaften in every country we visit. This is truly a wonderful thing.

JF-A: What were some of the difficulties that the Japanese singers faced when tackling the German language?

MS: *Everything* was so difficult at the beginning. In Japanese, we don't separate consonants and vowels. For us, they are together. We didn't know *how* to separate them. Even though it's quite common for Japanese music students to learn a European language, that aspect of German was very challenging at the start. It wasn't uncommon, therefore, for the discs' producer to stop us and to correct the pronunciation of certain letters.

JF-A: Did that then affect your understanding of the language, especially as it impacted on issues of phrasing and articulation?

MS: Actually, we didn't attempt to be Germans. We were more concerned that the articulation of the language sat well with the instruments. Pronunciation is certainly an important part of our interpretation and performance style. That said, I've also experienced difficulties with some German choirs when trying to achieve good pronunciation. For native German speakers, their understanding of the words is often *too* easy. But, regardless of wherever you are, when it comes to aligning the words with the music, you must always be vigilant when placing every consonant, vowel and syllable. It's very important to match the pronunciation of the words with the sound of the instruments.

JF-A: Do you feel that your engagement with the German language became easier over the course of the project?

MS: Getting older helped! And we now hope that our understanding of the language is slightly better.

JF-A: By starting with the more homogenously scored earlier cantatas, were you able to establish a 'house style' relatively quickly?

MS: Before deciding to record the cantatas chronologically, we gave quite a number of them in concert. But the only early one that we performed before the recordings was Cantata No. 4, *Christ lag in Todesbanden*. Although it seemed like a good idea at the time to start the project with the earlier works because of their simpler musical narrative, the first sessions still proved taxing for the singers and the instrumentalists, as we used *Chorton*, A=465, for *Christ lag in Todesbanden*. This was the first time that the string players had used this high pitch, so the intonation proved extremely difficult for them. It was quite nightmarish to start with. And while you are right when you say that the earlier cantatas are more homogeneous, instrumentally and vocally, they are also more modest expressively. Nevertheless, they were still a challenge for us when it came to intonation.

JF-A: I remember that you once said to me that spontaneity was not your first priority when it came to the early cantatas. But then you also pointed out that spontaneity wasn't taught in Japanese schools: discipline was, but spontaneity wasn't.

MS: When it came to the cantata project, discipline was no problem. But we were always in search of spontaneity, and it took us some years before we found it.

JF-A: Was that when your realisation of Bach's musical language became so much more graphic?

MS: Yes. Exactly.

JF-A: With the exception of the Dutch bass, Peter Kooij, all the singers, and the overwhelming majority of the instrumentalists, that you used for the early volumes were Japanese. But as the project progressed, you engaged more and more European singers. Why was that?

MS: I never really cared about the nationality of the singers. I simply wanted to have very good soloists who were able to integrate with the choir. It wasn't good enough just to be soloists. It is still very hard to find good Bach singers. While some of the Japanese singers had the ability to blend with the choir, the same was also true for many of the European singers. Occasionally, I need a singer who is operatic in style. And then there are those who specialise in early music, and who are very good at the works of Buxtehude and Schütz. These singers are not always ideal when it comes to Bach's music. What's needed vocally often stands midway between the two styles. That's why it can be difficult to find the correct singers for works such as the *Matthäus-Passion* and the cantatas. And while I am very particular about the use of *vibrato*, I never discuss it during rehearsals, as it should always be part of the overall balance.

JF-A: Does the *coloratura* demanded by some of Bach's later works affect your vocal choices?

MS: Some of Bach's mature compositions are completely different in style from the earlier ones. Unlike in Mozart's choral works, the soloists have to sing throughout the movements, and the *ripieno* only joins in for some of the *tutti* sections. Those who perform in the *concertante* take the leading role the whole time. Consequently, it's really important to have very good singers with great stamina.

JF-A: The pace that you took in completing your cantata project was quite steady. Did that offer you any insights into Bach's creative process as you moved through the cantatas chronologically?

MS: It was extremely interesting to view these works sequentially. When Bach was in Mühlhausen and Weimar, he was still experimenting with new ideas. This was also true of his first year at Leipzig, where each new cantata had a different character. From his second year in Leipzig onwards, his exploration was based on the chorales, an approach that he retained for the rest of his life. This meant that the music suddenly became very complicated. And, by his third year there, his style had changed quite considerably. As a result, the works were more challenging to perform and more difficult to understand.

JF-A: Were there cantatas that you felt fell short of Bach's usual high standards and needed some special pleading?

MS: Bach had already established his own style by his early twenties. While his approach in the Mühlhausen cantatas was quite different from that which he took in the later ones, the quality of the music-making was already high. So, the works that you hear in the first volumes compare favourably with those that you hear in the later ones. There is no difference between the standard of the music. Of course, the chorale arrangements in the Neumeister collection are much simpler, and it's clear that Bach had yet to establish his style by that time. After that, his approach changed quite considerably. Not for better or for worse, just different. He always maintained his compositional quality. Naturally, you can say, 'This one is better than that one.' But those instances are the exceptions rather than the rule.

JF-A: Some years ago, Oliver Knussen confessed to me that he disliked the music of Bach, but wouldn't explain why. But when I pressed him about this a little later on, he said that it was because he felt that some of the arias were so contorted rhetorically and musically that they failed to speak to him fully. If that's the case, how do *you* convey an aria's importance to the musicians and the listeners when it has a very difficult text, a demanding *obbligato* part, and when it goes on for nine minutes?

MS: I do think that some cantata movements are very difficult to understand when performed live, such as the opening chorus from Cantata No. 77, *Du sollt Gott, deinen Herren, lieben*, or the tricky duet, 'Herr, du siehst statt guter Werke', from Cantata No. 9, *Es ist das Heil uns Kommen*. Nobody can follow all the notes in those movements. Yet Bach always had a reason for composing in the way that he did. Take the opening chorus from Cantata No. 80, *Ein feste Burg ist unser Gott*, for example. There you have a chorale with three oboes at the top, canons for basses at the bottom and an extremely complicated contrapuntal structure for the choir in between. Here, again, it is impossible to follow everything. But the reason why Bach composed in that manner was to do with the text and its close relationship to the structure. If that way of composing requires me to make a greater effort when communicating with the audience, then so be it.

JF-A: You once said that you simply concentrate on the abstract qualities of the music when you find it impossible to come to terms with the liturgical sensibilities of the words.

MS: Bach constantly struggled when attempting to balance the musical content of his cantatas with their theological structure. And while the theological structure of a particular cantata might not necessarily be reflective of his own faith, the music that he composed was always a statement of his personality. These two pillars left him in a constant state of flux.

JF-A: Because of the transformational nature of the period performance movement in recent years, musicians and singers who perform in a modern manner often feel increasingly unsure about their place in the history of Bach performance. Consequently, festivals, opera companies and symphony orchestras now play the composer's music less than ever. Is this a problem?

MS: While this is something of a challenging cultural phenomenon, it's one that will change with time. In fact, many of today's symphony and chamber orchestras *are* trying once again to play the music of Bach and other Baroque composers. These orchestras are now better informed about period performance practice and period instruments. It's no longer a battle between two schools of thought, and we should now be able to find a compromise between both approaches. I still remember a conversation that I had with Nikolaus Harnoncourt some years ago. He said that he found performing the symphonies of Mozart with a period ensemble more difficult than with a modern orchestra. This was not down to style, but due to the organisational differences between the two types of orchestra. And even though Bach is quite different from Mozart, the quality of the period instruments used doesn't guarantee the quality of the performance heard.

JF-A: Are you saying, then, that playing Bach is sometimes easier on modern instruments?

MS: Yes, I think so. It should now be possible to perform Bach with modern instruments. Probably not in the same way that Karl Richter and the Münchener Bach-Orchester did, as we are now much better informed about period performance practice.

JF-A: But can the period performers of today learn something from the historical figures of the past when it comes to interpreting Bach's music?

MS: Many historical figures played Bach's works very beautifully. The only thing that I miss is the higher registration of the organ. Apart from that, I don't find any real difference between what the singers and the musicians did or do. I have often been inspired and affected by performances such as Hermann Scherchen's reading of the Mass in B minor with the Vienna Symphony Orchestra and Ernest Ansermet's interpretation of Cantata No. 11, *Lobet Gott in seinen Reichen,* with the Orchestre de la Suisse Romande. That really is a wonderful performance. When I was young, I admired Karl Richter's recording of the Mass in B minor, but I'm less accepting of it now. What I did like was the denseness of his sound and the fervour that he achieved. His machine-gun-like approach to semiquavers was a statement of his time. But as we are all the product of a particular era, he shouldn't be criticised for that. When it comes to *tempo*, it should never be chosen for scholarly reasons, but should emerge from the rehearsal process. What you might hear when reading a score silently in your head doesn't always work in the concert hall. The most important thing is that the entire ensemble should feel comfortable.

JF-A: Let's turn our attention to works that were composed before Bach. Although you haven't given these earlier pieces nearly as frequently as your teacher, Ton Koopman, you have managed to perform some.

MS: Since there are so many extremely beautiful German cantatas that were composed pre-Bach, I wanted to make a disc called 'The Way to Bach'. This recording would have included the music of Buxtehude and Schütz. In the end, it proved impossible to realise because of time and budget constraints. You can't do everything. But I really hope to do more of these earlier works in the future.

JF-A: I'm keen to hear your thoughts on Johann Rudolph Ahle.

MS: Ahle was Bach's predecessor at Mühlhausen, and his son, Johann Georg, was also quite a well-known composer. Johann Rudolph wrote some interesting cantatas that sound quite similar to both Buxtehude and Schütz, although composed a little earlier than those by the former.

JF-A: You've just completed recording Bach's secular cantatas. Some early scholars were disparaging of these works because they mistrusted the composer's use of parody, and because they disapproved of his habit of using material that he'd already employed elsewhere. Why do you think that the secular cantatas were received in this way?

MS: I think it was mainly due to the term 'secular', although there is nothing particularly 'secular' about them. Unlike the sacred cantatas, most of the secular ones were dedicated to the Elector of Dresden's family. But, like the *Weihnachts-Oratorium*, they were probably intended to be given within a single year. Even though this practice stands in sharp contrast to Bach's approach when performing the sacred cantatas, there's no qualitative difference between the two subgenres.

JF-A: A good example of an outstanding secular cantata is *Lass, Fürstin, lass noch einen Strahl*, Cantata No. 198. Why is this composition so unique?

MS: Its uniqueness partly lies in the instrumentation that it uses: two flutes, two oboes d'amore, two violins, viola, two violas da gamba, two lutes and continuo. Bach had never used this combination before. There's also a great deal of variation between the movements, with the music itself being very dramatic. As Bach wanted to show great respect to the dead Electress, he probably wanted to compose the very best piece that he could for her.

JF-A: Whenever Bach was writing a work that was well-funded, he was always keen to display his wares fully, so to speak, often by including horns or trumpets and drums. But that wasn't the case in *Lass, Fürstin*. By being extraordinarily subtle with his orchestration in this cantata, he imbued it with a bitter-sweet funereal quality, which really draws on Passion-like elements. It's both an elegy and a celebration of a life much admired.

MS: With its constantly engaging dotted rhythm, the opening chorus is a kind of French overture. Yet its mournful character, like that of the other movements, is done so well. Bach never refers to biblical texts here. Instead, he looks to the personality of the Electress and the quality of her faith. And that's why it's appropriate to categorise this piece as a secular cantata.

JF-A: Other than Bach, who are the composers you feel closest to?

MS: I'm drawn to the music of the Classical Era and the works of Mozart and Beethoven. I am also attracted to Mendelssohn, my second favourite composer.

JF-A: Is your attraction to Mendelssohn an extension of your interest in Bach's aesthetic, or more to do with your understanding of the spiritual journey that Protestant music-making took during the early nineteenth century?

MS: While Bach and Mendelssohn each had their own approach to spirituality, there's no real difference between them. And, here, I'm not really sure what 'spirituality' actually means. Take, for example, Beethoven's *Missa solemnis*. It, too, contains deep music and is very dramatic. But it's very different from Bach. The same is true of Mozart's liturgical works. When I perform Mendelssohn, I feel freer and more expressive in a Romantic way. Even though his music is highly polyphonic, it's very easy to follow. It's really wonderful.

JF-A: You have also recorded Mozart's Mass in C minor, a piece that you seem to be wedded to. What is it about the work that attracts you?

MS: With Bach's Mass in B minor, the compositional history of the modern concert Mass began. It was then followed by Mozart's Mass in C minor and Beethoven's *Missa solemnis*. The textures of these works are all very different, and were all written by their composers for very personal reasons. There's no evidence that Bach ever performed his Mass, even though he might well have had some sort of commission to write it. And, of course, he used a great deal of material from his earlier works in its composition. In the case of Mozart, he wanted to introduce his wife, Constanze, to his father, so he wrote a beautiful aria for her in his Mass. Beethoven composed his work towards the end of his life, suggesting that he was looking forward to a life after death. This is confirmed by how he treated the end of the 'Credo', where the 'Et vitam venturi' moves ever onwards and upwards. It's extremely long. The works of these three composers are the culmination of the Mass as a form. That's not to say that there were not plenty of interesting Masses that were written before and since. But those by Bach, Mozart and Beethoven are incomparable.

JF-A: You have recently started another 'Bach journey' that will keep you busy for a further twenty years: recording the composer's complete organ music. How do you find time to practise these works?

MS: First and foremost, I am an organist. And, in fact, I intended to record the organ works before I set down the cantatas. But, somehow, the cantatas came first. Actually, playing the organ is no different from conducting a choir or directing an orchestra.

PART ONE: CONDUCTORS

JF-A: As Bach's magnificent organ oeuvre is less well known than some of his other compositions, what can be done to make these works more attractive to the public?

MS: Most of Bach's organ pieces were composed for concert performance. And when he gave them himself, he did so in a concert setting, rather than as part of a church service. Essentially, these works were a means by which to present his compositional message to an audience, so they are easy to understand. There are only a very few pieces that are difficult for listeners.

JF-A: Some might say that the best way to popularise Bach's organ works is to transcribe them for orchestra, just as Elgar and Stokowski did.

MS: I don't think that these transcriptions work well. Bach's organ music is complete in itself, and was composed quite differently from his works for harpsichord. He knew perfectly well how to compose for the organ, and his method was stylistically very close to that which he used for the cantatas. When it comes to the musical language of both, they are very similar. Having recorded all the cantatas, it's much easier for me to understand the organ pieces. Both constitute one musical world.

SIAN EDWARDS
(DAVID JOSEFOWITZ RECITAL HALL, 19 FEBRUARY 2020)

RAYMOND HOLDEN: Before we discuss your life and career in detail, I would like to ask you something more general. As this year marks the fiftieth anniversary of the death of the great British maestro Sir John Barbirolli, a musician whose cultural, social and educational influence continues to this day, what do *you* understand the societal and musical role of the conductor to be in the current political, artistic and economic climate, and how does it differ from that of previous generations of podium artists?

SIAN EDWARDS: I found it interesting that when the Wall came down in Berlin, it was Kurt Masur who was nominated as the 'leader' of East Germany during that extremely turbulent time. And as conductors are regularly involved with large numbers of people, perhaps that's the reason why Masur was considered the right person to deal with such a big event as that. Nevertheless, I do believe that an interesting change *has* taken place. When I went to study in Manchester in 1977, Barbirolli had died only seven years earlier, yet his presence was still felt. There was a real feeling that he 'owned' the city, the Free Trade Hall, the Hallé Orchestra and the Hallé Choir, and that the citizens of Manchester were 'his' people. In a way, that's now been diluted slightly. This is probably due to the fact that artists move around a great deal more than before, and that few people today have quite the same cultural grip that Barbirolli had. But I still think that conductors really represent to the public the distillation of what an orchestra does when it plays, and that's why they continue to be iconic.

RH: Perhaps this also has something to do with the cities in which many of the great conductors worked. Take Arthur Nikisch, for example. He was famously the musical head of both the Berlin Philharmonic and the Leipzig Gewandhaus Orchestra between 1895 and 1922. But his approach in Berlin was often very different from his method in Leipzig. In the case of the latter, the local Gewandhaus Orchestra was the 'only show in town', so to speak, while, in Berlin, there were a number of other prominent orchestras operating at the same time. Do you think that the responses to, and of, conductors depends on the city in which they're working?

SE: I'm sure that's the case. Even in a smaller arena, such as Frankfurt am Main, where there is a wonderful opera house that has an orchestra that runs its own concert series, as well as a local radio orchestra and the Ensemble Modern, there's a tremendous awareness of the city's musical culture. The artistic heads of each of those institutions are all well known to the local citizens and are instantly recognisable to them. In many ways that recognition is a celebration of those artists' presence in the city. That's different from a big, cosmopolitan city like London, where artistic life can be more transient.

RH: In fact, your formative years as a musician coincided with the last decade of Barbirolli's career. Tell us something about your education in the Home Counties, and how that education prepared you for a life on the podium.

SE: I'm not sure that it did! I was born in rural Sussex and went to a local primary school. It had a broken tambourine, a couple of triangles, and we used to sing from community songbooks. But we did have a piano at home, and when I was six years old, I said to my mother that I wanted to learn how to play it. She was a little worried that I might've been too young to start learning and that I would be put off by it. But I said, 'No, no. I have to do this.' This resulted in me having terrifying piano lessons from a woman called Mrs Hoare. She was the type of person who would look down in horror if you turned up with ink on your fingers from a previous lesson, and would make no effort to disguise her total disapproval of you. So, my primary school years were not marvellous musically, but I was able to learn the piano, which meant a great deal to me. My father then accepted a job in the South Midlands and took the family to Oxford, where I attended Oxford High School. During my first couple of years there, the headmistress was Mary Warnock, one of Britain's leading educationalists and philosophers. She loved music and believed fully that it was as important as sport. When I was interviewed for admission to the school, and said that I wanted to climb trees and to learn the French horn, she clearly thought that I was right for the place, even though I wasn't the least bit academic. And although I did struggle a little academically, I did learn to play the French horn on an instrument that had formerly belonged to her. The school had a fabulous musical life. I was able to continue with the piano and to make progress on the horn.

As an eleven-year-old, one's first couple of years learning the horn can be challenging. I remember that I had this enormous case in which it lived. At first, I couldn't actually lift it or walk with it without a huge struggle. It was *so* big and *so* difficult to cope with. And, to this day, I'm not sure why I originally wanted to take up the instrument. But the minute that I joined an orchestra, which was when I was about thirteen years old, everything changed. I thought that playing in an orchestra was completely wonderful. I was besotted with the Saturday-morning music school and the second orchestra of the Oxford County Youth Orchestra, which was conducted by Muir Mathieson. He was a wonderful musician who was very well known for his work as a film conductor. He had retired by that time, but would drive over to Oxford from his home at High Wycombe in his light-blue Triumph Herald, and would conduct us with a gritty Scottish accent that could be quite alarming. One of my greatest moments with the orchestra, and one of the most revelatory, was playing fourth horn in Sibelius's Second Symphony. That was really something, and it's why I am so passionate about involving young people in music. It can be life-changing.

RH: With your school years behind you, you were accepted as a student at the Royal Northern College of Music in Manchester. But was that your first choice of institution?

SE: My family loved music, but wasn't particularly musical. My parents did take me to concerts and were somewhat in awe of the public life of being a musician. They really didn't know much about how I should pursue my musical education. Nevertheless, at the age of thirteen, Oxford County Council gave me a scholarship, and when I was sixteen I began studying with Ifor James, who taught privately around the corner from the Royal Academy of Music at Nottingham Place. I'd go there every two weeks and have a lesson with him. He was a horn professor at the Academy, but was forbidden to teach his private students there, so I would go as a geeky sixteen-year-old to the basement room that he was renting two streets away for my fortnightly lesson. Suddenly, Ifor announced that he would no longer be teaching at the Academy, and that I should follow him to the Royal Northern College of Music in Manchester. That came as something of a shock, as I'd set my heart on being a student at the Academy, where I'd auditioned and had already been offered a place. As I'd only put my name on the waiting list for the Royal Northern, I had to audition there before being accepted. And as I'd never been further north than Birmingham before, Manchester was quite a culture shock when I finally arrived.

RH: In what ways did your time at Manchester shape you artistically?

SE: Being a student at the Royal Northern was a very intense experience, but Ifor James helped me enormously. Luckily, I had already played a great deal in both the school and youth orchestra environments and for Oxford University, which was always short of horns. One of my greatest assets as a horn player was that I could play quietly, which was valued greatly by conductors and other musicians. But I quickly found that I'd done too much too soon, and that I'd developed problems with my embouchure. Ifor was helpful in countering this: he was a brilliant psychologist. He had been a virtuoso cornet player from the age of three and had played extensively with many of the famous Northern brass bands. When teaching, he insisted that all his students must work from Arban's *Cornet Method*, no matter how good he or she was. So successful was that approach that he once proudly told me that he had trained twenty-one Principal Horns. He was a phenomenal teacher who allowed his students enough space to develop. Having come from an intellectual, Oxford-based background, I benefited most from meeting a series of wonderful brass players at Manchester. It was the time of the Philip Jones Brass Ensemble, and Philip was the Head of Brass at the Royal Northern. As it was also the time when you could get into music college with just two O levels, I was rubbing shoulders with many fabulous Salvation Army and Northern brass-band players who played like gods, but who had barely managed one, let alone two, O levels. That experience transformed my perception of music-making. I realised that the sound you make transcends the academic qualifications you hold. And that has lived with me to this day.

RH: At Manchester, you also came into contact with Sir Charles Groves, a conductor about whom you have spoken warmly in the past. A previous guest in this series, the Australian-born guitarist John Williams also admired Sir Charles greatly and considered him influential. What was the basis for your admiration of him, and how would you define him as a musician and as a man?

SE: I met Charles tangentially while I was studying the horn as an undergraduate. I then won a scholarship to stay at the Royal Northern as a conducting student. Charles was the conductors' senior tutor at the Royal Northern, but said to me at my first lesson, 'Of course, I don't teach conducting.' I was a little dumbstruck by this, although he did say that he would help me whenever he could. In fact, he was very encouraging, and came to many of my concerts. His wife, Hilary, was a pillar of strength for Charles, and was always very supportive of me. I attended many of his rehearsals and concerts with the Hallé Orchestra, and was struck by how shy he was. Charles was a man of few words, but his conducting was extremely eloquent. I liked it very, very much. Charles and Hilary had been tremendous artistic pioneers after the Second World War and prized music. Many of the artistic institutions that we now take for granted benefited from their energy, and they did much to resurrect British musical life during that difficult period.

RH: The last time I saw Sir Charles Groves was at the 1989 Last Night of the Proms. My teacher and dear friend Sir John Pritchard was in charge that evening, but was suffering from terminal lung cancer. As I was conducting the bugle calls that precede Henry Wood's *Fantasia on British Sea Songs* during the second part of the concert, and was in public view, I needed to change into my concert clothes at the intermission. When I popped into John's room to make that change, I could see that he was wearing an oxygen mask and breathing quite badly. I also noticed Charles Groves standing bolt upright in the corner behind him, looking for all the world like a cross between an Egyptian mummy and a naughty schoolboy. When I asked John why Charles was there, he pulled his oxygen mask to one side and gasped, 'If I die, he'll take over!' Luckily John didn't die, and Charles didn't take over. But to return to your time at Manchester. Having decided to undertake postgraduate conducting studies at the Royal Northern, you came into contact with that great musical polymath Norman Del Mar, an artist who divided his activities between the writer's desk and the conductor's podium. Were postgraduate conducting studies common at the time, and what are your memories of Mr Del Mar?

SE: As the Royal Northern admitted only one first- and one second-year conducting student annually, and as the chap who had been admitted to the second year had dropped out, I was the only conducting student at the time. Feeling slightly alone, I quickly became aware of the fact that I functioned better surrounded by other students, and that I had nobody to measure myself against. Consequently, the Royal Northern arranged with the Royal College of Music for me to attend Norman's classes in London. This involved me taking an appallingly early train from Manchester at 6.20am on Saturday mornings to Euston. From there, I would take the Northern Line to Norman's house at High Barnet, where I would have my lesson at 9.30am, a lesson that also involved his students from the College. Norman would sit in one very large armchair, and whoever arrived first sat in the chair opposite. That was usually Graeme Jenkins. The other students would sit in small chairs at Norman's feet, so to speak. Norman was always fascinated by what the scores contained, and had a repertoire the size of which I'd never really encountered before. He was particularly interested in the music of Richard Strauss, and had a living room that contained two Steinway grand pianos placed end to end. He insisted that the student conductors should play for each other from full orchestral scores. And as I was a horn player and could transpose at sight, I was elbowed into playing all the horn parts. Norman could be both encouraging and very strict with his students, so I was quite happy to be a peripheral member of the group. Nevertheless, it was always fantastic to be in his presence. I remember one memorable moment when there was a conversation about how Beethoven wrote for the horn. Understandably, I was alive to that discussion! The fact that horns and trumpets were often in one key at the time of Haydn, Mozart and Beethoven, and that they could only play a limited number of notes because of their construction, means that there are moments in the score where they appear to be 'missing'. I then suggested to Norman that perhaps we should add a few extra notes to overcome these 'omissions'. On hearing this, he rose to a great height and said, 'Are you *really* going to rewrite Beethoven, Sian?'

RH: It seems that your suggestion literally fell on deaf ears! But as important as Norman Del Mar surely was in your early education, the route you then took as a conductor led you to a series of professional crossroads that could hardly have been predicted. And it seems that at one important juncture it was the Estonian Neeme Järvi who pointed you in the right direction. How did that encounter take place, and what were the consequences of it?

SE: Between the completion of my horn studies and before beginning my conducting lessons at the Royal Northern, I auditioned for what is now known as the Kondrashin Conducting Competition in the Netherlands. It was originally called the Netherlands Radio Conductors' Course. Being a typical twenty-one-year-old, I took the boat to Holland and studied the scores on the way over. I'd bought them the day before! Not knowing what to expect, I was a little surprised to learn that 150 people were auditioning for the course. You can understand my delight, therefore, when Neeme Järvi gave me a place. Neeme had taken over the course that summer at short notice from Kirill Kondrashin, who had died suddenly from a heart attack the previous spring. This was in 1981, the same year that Neeme and his family left the Soviet Union for Britain, where he had already been appointed Principal Guest Conductor of the City of Birmingham Symphony Orchestra. But, as a member of his course, I didn't really understand fully what he was trying to teach me, as we spoke no common language. Luckily, his son, Paavo, who is also a wonderful conductor, was on hand to translate. Then, one day, Neeme became so exasperated with all of us that he did some conducting himself. It was as if someone had turned the lights on in the hall. We were able to witness some really beautiful, incredibly musical and extremely honest conducting. There was a wonderful line to what he did with the Netherlands Radio Symphony Orchestra that allowed the music to open up before us. He then apologised to us, saying that he was a little out of practice as he hadn't conducted for a while. He'd literally been living out of a suitcase for a few months. Nevertheless, it was clear to me that this was the type of conducting that I aspired to, and that I wanted to conduct like him. I then approached Neeme and said, 'How can I conduct like you?' To which he replied, 'You will have to study in Leningrad.' And although Neeme's own teacher had long since died, he thought that the other main teacher there was still working and still accepting students. I then put that piece of information in my back pocket, so to speak, and returned to the Royal Northern to continue with my postgraduate studies.

But during my second year at the Royal Northern, I really felt that I still didn't know what I was doing with my hands. I wasn't sure that the gestures that I was making actually represented the music itself. Consequently, I applied to the British Council for funding to study in Russia. The application process was very long and included an interview, the main thrust of which was whether or not I minded not having a bath for a week or two! Determined not to derail the process, I said, 'That's fine.' I was also asked if I could cope with the Russian cold and various other Soviet-related questions. To which I replied to each new implied hurdle, 'No problem.' Having done all of that, I then heard absolutely nothing for what seemed like ages. That's because it was 1983, a year that proved to be a particularly low point in British-Soviet relations, and one that saw us close to confrontation with the Soviets. Although the British Council was still keen for me to go, the Foreign Office was struggling with the number of students that it could either send to, or receive from, Russia. At the time, money was not exchanged between the two countries, and the way that the 'books were balanced' was by exchanging students. Britain used to send approximately ten students to Russia annually, one of whom was a musician, while the Soviets would send a series of middle-aged professors here. These professors would arrive under the guise of doing 'research', which usually involved 'lifting' intellectual property. The Soviets certainly had no qualms about that! Then, while I was literally flipping hamburgers at McDonald's in Manchester one day, I received a telephone call from the Foreign Office. The official said that they were still unsure when I could go to Russia, but asked if I could pop down to Whitehall on a particular Wednesday in early September. When I arrived at the Foreign Office on the appointed day, a list was read out naming the people who would be flying to the Soviet Union for ten months the following morning. My name was on that list.

RH: Having arrived in the Soviet Union, you eventually found your way to Ilya Musin, who later gave masterclasses here at the Royal Academy of Music in the 1990s, before making his British conducting debut at the Barbican Centre in 1996 with the Royal Philharmonic Orchestra, aged ninety-three.

SE: I knew nothing about Musin. In fact, very few people knew anything about him outside of the Soviet Union at the time, a time when I was one of the first Western musicians to study there. Musin was the head of the conducting department at the Leningrad Conservatory, which was comprised of about ten teachers and forty students. The department also had a full orchestra that played for three hours every morning from Monday to Saturday, and that was intended for the sole use of the conducting students. The course itself ran for five years, even though I was only there for one. Having given up any idea that I would go to Russia, I arrived there unable to speak the language. When I touched down in Moscow, where I was first sent, I realised that I didn't even know how to say 'hello'. And when I did eventually arrive in Leningrad, I was put in the class of Arvīds Jansons, the father of Mariss Jansons, as he spoke excellent English. We were always encouraged to observe the lessons of other teachers, and it soon became clear to me that I needed to study with Musin. With the help of a friend who also spoke English, I was able to contact him. We 'egged' the situation up a bit by telling him that I would have to go home if he didn't accept me as a student. Concerned that he might upset the British government if I were to be returned to England, Musin eventually agreed to take me on.

PART ONE: CONDUCTORS

RH: Would it be fair to say that Musin changed your life?

SE: Yes. Absolutely.

RH: There's a fascinating film clip of Musin giving a masterclass on Strauss's *Don Juan*, and an equally fascinating film showing George Szell teaching the same passage. As I know that you have seen both films, I am interested to hear your comments on them.

SE: I'm always in search of the underlying principle behind the music. Szell encapsulates everything that we discuss here at the Royal Academy of Music, and expresses what Musin also discussed constantly: how you prepare a sound, and what you imagine that sound to be. What's fascinating about Szell is his insistence on a compact gesture, a gesture that allows the orchestra to move. On the other hand, Musin starts the orchestra, and then goes on with it. But what separates Szell from Musin is their approach to the initial down-beat. Szell stops the hand at the bottom of the gesture, while Musin always insisted that the hand shouldn't stop. He always wanted us to keep going, as that's where the music's energy lies. The idea that one can keep everything afloat and flying along is very exciting indeed. Of course I admire George Szell, but what I got from Musin was a sense of tremendous colour. So much so that when it came to the Classical repertoire, I toned it down a little when I returned to Britain. What Musin's approach *did* do, however, was to make me live every moment of the music. I found that wonderful.

Musin was also involved in every aspect of what was taking place in the orchestra, and did so in a way that was incredibly free. The way that he increased and released tension was again very important to me. And it must never be forgotten that he was a man in his eighties when I studied with him, but one who still had a lightness and freedom of touch. Everybody in the class wanted to emulate that. He gave three classes each week, and always told us what he wanted us to learn. He was never absent, and would insist on us showing him something during at least two out of every three classes. Musin was also keen that we should conduct from memory where possible. The most important thing was that we were able to meet his expectations in each new class. That way we could move on to the next stage. But quite often he would stop us after a bar or two, take our baton, push us off the podium and imitate what we had just done. He would then proceed to show us what to do, with his remarkable lightness of touch and with his incredible energy. Consequently, we would look ninety-five years old, and he would look twenty.

RH: Having completed your first year with Musin, you returned to Britain and took part in the 1984 Leeds International Conductors Competition, which you eventually won.

SE: During that first spring with Musin, I spoke to him about the competition, which was new at the time, and whether or not I should apply for it. The stumbling block was my lack of professional experience: I needed to have worked professionally to be considered for entry. But the person running the competition was David Lloyd-Jones from Opera North. He'd learnt Russian after the war and, along with Sir Edward Downes, spoke it fluently. So Musin handwrote a beautiful letter to David saying that he had this marvellous student and could she possibly have a go? Luckily, he was completely won over and *did* let me have a go. Then Musin made it clear to me that if I was going to take part in the competition as a result of his imprimatur, I was going to have to train hard for it. In practice, this meant that I would go to his apartment

PART ONE: CONDUCTORS

for an extra lesson on the days that he wasn't teaching me at the Conservatory. He accepted no money for these sessions, and wouldn't even take a bunch of flowers as a way of saying thank you. After each lesson, his wife would make us high tea and would feed me. They knew that as a British student I was a long way from home, which meant that they were always very kind and generous to me.

RH: Having won the competition, you moved quickly from the concert hall to the opera house. After conducting Weill's challenging work *Rise and Fall of the City of Mahagonny* for Scottish Opera in 1986, you led performances of Verdi's *La traviata* at Glyndebourne in 1987, before becoming the first female conductor to perform at the Royal Opera House, Covent Garden, with Tippett's *The Knot Garden* in 1988. Had you always been interested in the lyric theatre, or was it new to you at the time?

SE: It was actually quite new to me, even though I'd done some operatic conducting at the Royal Northern, including music by Menotti, and had conducted a semi-staged student performance of Mozart's *Don Giovanni* when I was nineteen. I'm not sure that I could even pronounce Italian by then! But, in general, my experience of opera was limited, as my work as a horn player took me more towards the symphonic repertoire. And here I should mention that having won the Leeds competition, I returned to Russia and spent a second year with Musin, as I felt that I wasn't quite ready professionally. Nevertheless, Sir Simon Rattle did invite me to perform concerts in Sutton Coldfield and Kidderminster with the City of Birmingham Symphony Orchestra during that second year. Simon hadn't seen me conduct by that point, but was keen to give me a chance. I then returned to the orchestra the following summer and led some concerts during their promenade series. When Simon had to withdraw from *Mahagonny* in Scotland at short notice because his wife was ill, he suggested to the management that either I or Oliver Knussen would be suitable replacements. Of course, Ollie would have been a marvellous choice, but he wasn't free at the time. Needless to say, I was!

By the time of the Scottish engagement, I'd been taken on by a wonderful agent thanks to Sir Charles Groves. After winning the competition, I received a telephone call from Charles, who invited me to his home at Camden Square where he served me unbelievably strong tea that stuck to my teeth. Charles then asked, 'Have you got an agent?' As I hadn't, he then rang his own manager, Howard Hartog, an extremely famous London-based concert manager. I could hear Howard on the other end of the line asking, 'Who is this Sian Edwards?' Undeterred, Charles pressed Howard to take me on, and asked him when he could see me. When Howard *did* meet me, he said that he would give me a few concerts as part of a trial year with his agency. So, it was the impact of having a powerful agent, along with Simon's recommendation, that convinced Jenny Flack and Sarah Playfair of Scottish Opera to give this completely untried conductor a chance. The company had already undertaken ten days of rehearsal without Simon before I arrived, and I literally learned the opera on the job. I had an electric keyboard in my hotel room and studied each new section that I was to conduct the evening before the next day's rehearsal. It was incredibly tough. Nevertheless, it was an amazing experience, which resulted in me being invited to conduct at Glyndebourne.

RH: You were then engaged by the Royal Opera House, where your success ensured your return the following year. The great American pianist Leon Fleisher once said to me that to be invited to give a concert is one thing, but to be asked back is quite another. Would you agree with this?

PART ONE: CONDUCTORS

SE: Conducting is such a personal discipline. Being able to connect with colleagues during your first encounter with them is paramount. It's also essential to let the players and the singers know that their contributions are also truly worthwhile. If you do that, they may be happy to give you a second chance. It's very much down to chemistry, and sometimes one just has to accept that some things are just not to be. I don't think that anybody should be put off if a connection isn't made immediately.

RH: At Covent Garden, you also assisted some of the world's leading conductors, including the mercurial Carlos Kleiber, who continues to fascinate musicians and audiences to this day. What are your memories of him, and should he act as a model for young conductors?

SE: Of course he should be a role model. Every time we watch him in action, we are left smiling. But why? Because the energy that he could draw from an orchestra was remarkable. We all responded very positively to that, and young conductors can take a great deal from his methods. And while everybody will take something different from those methods, one of the first things that you notice is his eyes. He hardly ever stopped looking around the orchestra, and his use of eye contact was something that I noticed the minute I sat next to him. It was like being beside an animal that was constantly looking, but hardly ever blinking. He had a phenomenal air of control. And when I am teaching young conductors, I always say to them that they have to 'ask' the players for what they want. Kleiber always used his physicality to 'ask' the musicians to give him more: they loved him, and he loved them. Even though he could be very flamboyant, he had an underlying sense of discipline. There was never a moment when he was imprecise, and he never got in the way of the orchestra.

RH: Like Sir John Barbirolli, Carlos Kleiber didn't have perfect pitch and was not a particularly good pianist. Consequently, he struggled when learning scores. Sir Mark Elder always stresses the importance of solitude for a conductor: the time when either he or she engages intensely with the printed score, and the period when their interpretations begin to take shape. How do you go about preparing a score?

SE: You can study scores in a variety of ways. You might have a work that you know, but have never performed before. When that's the case, there's often a difference between what's on the page and what you know about the music aurally. That being so, you need to come to terms with how the piece is laid out. I am somebody who likes to understand the structure of a composition. And then there is the period after you have done all the 'mechanical' work. This is the time when you need to be able to sit with the score and to allow it to come to terms with you. That's just as important as you trying to come to terms with it. This step is often overlooked, largely due to the busyness of our lives. One of the most important aspects of my studies in the Soviet Union was the time I spent absorbing material. This was possible because I only had three conducting and two Russian lessons a week. Being able to sit with the score, and trying to understand what the composer was doing, laid the foundations for how I work now. I must admit that conductors are not the greatest people to spend extended periods with, as we need so much time to learn very complicated scores. The minute we return from being on the road, we are straight back in our studies preparing the next piece. The imaginative powers that one needs when bringing what is effectively a flat page to life is extraordinary. And that's even before you begin to consider the stylistic nuances that you need to apply to it. As well as coming to terms with what's in the score, you are constantly forming your physical idea of how the piece should go. It's a very multilayered process, and there's always a period when you just need time to be on your own.

RH: In a book of conversations with Sir Mark Elder that I published recently, he argues that some conductors are suited to being Music Directors, while others are better suited to being guest conductors. Do you think that is true?

SE: I am sure that there are people, like Sir Mark himself, who are very good at being Music Directors; by which I mean somebody who is able to cope with the everyday 'housekeeping' that an orchestra or an opera house needs. This often requires a conductor to make some difficult decisions, as Mark had to do at the English National Opera in the late 1970s and the early 1980s. It's a very tough job being a Music Director, and I think that there are probably those who have the drive to do it. Mark Elder is one such person.

RH: Do you consider yourself a champion of new music, and, if so, what artistic benchmarks do you apply before agreeing to perform an untried work?

SE: It can be a leap in the dark. Even after having looked at a score and thinking that it has merit, there's always that practical voice at the back of your mind calculating how much rehearsal time is needed, how difficult it will be to play and how quickly the musicians can absorb it. Sometimes you step back from a project because it's too ambitious within the time allocated. And it's often the case that I will be working with players who are paid by the session, which can be a problem if I think that a piece will need ten sessions, but the company can only afford three. Yet I have accepted many engagements without any clear idea of what they might entail. Even if one knows who the composer is, one never knows what new and challenging direction he or she might take next, and whether or not they will write something that's completely different from what they have done in the past. It can often be a wonderful voyage of discovery.

RH: When your name is tapped into the search box on YouTube, the viewer is offered an incredible panorama of works ranging from Mozart's Twenty-Ninth Symphony with the Sydney Symphony Orchestra to Lachenmann's *Mouvement* with Ensemble Modern. That being so, how would you describe your sound-world as a conductor?

SE: I'm not sure that I can define it easily. All I can say is that conducting the Mozart symphony was more difficult than performing the Lachenmann piece, even though *Mouvement* is a huge score that uses 'extended technique'. Effectively, the sounds you hear are not necessarily the notes you see. The players in Ensemble Modern have played the work many times before, but openly say that they very rarely get through it without making a mistake, or getting lost at some point. Even though it's a tricky work to bring off, it's a fascinating study in sound. In the end, however, it's the life that Mozart gives us that we always want to return to.

RH: For many years now, you have been active as a conducting pedagogue. What attracts you to teaching, and do you subscribe to Sir John Barbirolli's aphorism that 'conductors are born and not made, but that does not mean that they can't be refined'?

SE: I suspect that Barbirolli might have a point. It's the people who have the energy to stomach the idea of asking their friends to play for them, and who undertake the enormous amount of administrative work that's involved in mounting a concert, who eventually stand on a podium. These people will already be committed to the music and to all that it entails. Conducting might well be a self-selecting process at the beginning, but what's also interesting about conducting is that it's something that's approached by people from many different angles. Some might have successfully finished a university music course and are still in their early twenties, while others might come to it from other disciplines within the music profession. Then, of course, there are those who compose, and who enter the conducting profession via their own works. One of the reasons why conducting is so difficult to teach and to assess is the range of those who practise it. On the one hand, you might have a physical conductor like Carlos Kleiber, while, on the other hand, you might have an intellectual artist like Sir John Eliot Gardiner, a musician who has revolutionised how we now think about music. Maybe Gardiner doesn't have the 'prettiest' of hands, but he can get across exactly what he wants. So teaching conducting is a very interesting process because of its breadth and diversity.

RH: Over the years, you have done much to ensure that conducting is open to all genders, ethnicities and creeds. Was that the reason why you established the Sorrell Women Conductors Programme at the Royal Academy of Music?

SE: It's very exciting that more women are deciding to become conductors. The style of music-making that we now have in Britain is much more collaborative than ever before. In the 1950s and the 1960s, women rarely identified with conducting, as it was a time when the image of the conductor as an elderly musical autocrat was the norm. Simon Rattle broke that mould. He let it be known that one could be young and enthusiastic, while still having something worthwhile to contribute. That was certainly true in my case. But there has also been a gradual sea-change in the way that we work. The standard of musicians who are now leaving conservatoires is increasingly high. They are highly educated with an advanced understanding of style and music history. This means that they are looking for something different from what was previously on offer. They want a more collaborative approach to conducting, and I think that has been to the benefit of women conductors.

RH: To conclude, I would love to hear how *you* think that you've changed musically over the years.

SE: That's such an interesting and difficult question. One of the great problems facing any conductor is that you don't make sound and are totally reliant on the orchestra. It's often difficult, therefore, to assess one's own work and to ask for feedback. I'm sure that I must've changed over the years, but I find it hard to define that change. All I would say is that coming from the Musin school, where I was trained intensively for two years, it's taken me a number of years to process all that he offered and to make it my own. What's very interesting about being a Musin student is that our conducting styles all look totally different. That doesn't mean that there are not certain commonalities, but each conductor has gone on to express the music in his or her own way. And as one learns more and more about music, and experiences the wonderful range of repertoire on offer, one gradually learns to define one's own artistic self.

VLADIMIR JUROWSKI
(DAVID JOSEFOWITZ RECITAL HALL, 18 JANUARY 2013)

RAYMOND HOLDEN: You were born in Moscow in 1972 into what has been described as an 'intellectual family'. What was life like in the Soviet Union at that time, and how did your family differ from ordinary Muscovites?

VLADIMIR JUROWSKI: Actually, we were 'ordinary Muscovites'. I was raised at the end of the so-called 'Stagnation Era', and had the most wonderful childhood. My parents made it possible for my siblings and me not to feel the discomforts of the emerging political situation. But I do remember them growing ever fearful as I approached my teens, as Soviet troops had entered Afghanistan in 1979. A young man from a family we knew was sent and killed there, and it became increasingly clear that I might eventually be sent there too. That was the only big concern that my parents and I had. When it came to my musical and artistic education, it was more the case of observing those people who lived through, and by, art, as life was so difficult and grey. For some people, life was unbearable, and their only escape was Moscow's art scene, a scene that's now missing from the Russian capital. It was a most wonderful time for artists, regardless of the harsh environment. But despite that vibrancy, we learned, even as children, that accessing information was a huge problem. If you were given a book, for example, you had to read it overnight, as it would be passed on to someone else the next morning. Books were either handwritten or typed on an old manual machine. It was the same for music. People who had access to Western record shops were revered and seen as gods. But if you bought an album by The Beatles on the street, it would set you back an incredible 75 roubles. When you consider that bread was 5 kopeks, or 5 pence, a slice, this meant that the disc cost a staggering £75. My father earned 275 roubles as a theatre conductor. And if you were caught with a record that you *had* bought on the street – not sold on the street, but bought on the street – you would end up in jail, even as a teenager.

RH: You studied for a period at the Moscow Conservatory, which had a reputation for rigour and excellence of execution during the Soviet period. What are your memories of your time there?

VJ: The Conservatory was at the heart of the Soviet educational system from the early 1920s onwards. But, here, I must clarify the term 'conservatory'. For people in the West, it denotes a tertiary musical academy or, in German terms, a high school for music. In other words, the highest level of education that one can receive musically. But there was also the Music College of the Moscow Conservatory that instrumentalists, composers and theorists could enter at the age of fifteen; singers could enrol later, depending on how far their voices had developed. This meant that you had to leave school at the end of the eighth grade to attend the College, where you studied for four years. At the completion of those four years, you would either leave music education completely to pursue something else, or would attend the Conservatory. I only studied for three years at the College, as my family left the Soviet Union in 1990. Had I remained, I would've studied for a further year, graduated from the College as either a nineteen- or twenty-year-old and attended the Conservatory. Of course, that was if I was lucky enough *not* to have been drafted into the army. As a student at either the College or the Conservatory, you had some protection from conscription, but it was the period between the two that was problematic. People used to hide in friends' country houses, avoid answering the telephone and refuse to sign documents, just in case they were identified or discovered for the draft.

RH: Did you ever have the opportunity of hearing the conductor Yevgeny Mravinsky perform?

VJ: Unfortunately, he was in Leningrad and I was in Moscow. As he never came to Moscow during my youth, I only heard his performances live on television. But I did hear Yevgeny Svetlanov and Gennady Rozhdestvensky many times; they were the big stars of the Moscow music scene. I was also lucky enough to have heard Sviatoslav Richter. That was before he started playing by candlelight, but at the time he played from the music. He had stopped playing from memory after an ear operation, which affected his sense of perfect pitch. It was also around the time that he stopped performing with symphony orchestras. But he did play periodically with the chamber orchestra of the Moscow Conservatory. There's a video available in the West, which you can buy in America, where you can hear him play Bach's Fifth 'Brandenburg' Concerto with the orchestra. By then, he gave the impression of extreme unevenness, but that simply added to the fascination. Sometimes, you went to a concert even though you knew that it might not happen.

RH: Unfortunately, London audiences became cynical, and were disinclined to attend his concerts towards the end of his career. Was that the same in Moscow?

VJ: No. He was considered to be one of the last musical gods. The admiration and adoration that Sviatoslav Richter and Emil Gilels enjoyed meant that they remained sovereign until 1986, the year that Vladimir Horowitz returned to the Soviet Union for the first time since 1925. The balcony of the Great Hall of the Moscow Conservatory nearly collapsed under the sheer weight of people. But, sadly, I wasn't there, as I couldn't get in. For those old enough to remember, the only comparable event was when Glenn Gould visited Moscow in 1957. He gave a concert and a lecture there, which is now available on DVD. But the number of artists who came from the West to play in the Soviet Union during my youth was far less than when my father was a student at the College and the Conservatory. He would tell me stories of those times, and between 1957 and 1968, all the great orchestras and performers came to Moscow. This was the period of Nikita Khrushchev. But after Soviet troops marched into Prague in 1968, it all stopped. We were then served a diet of Sviatoslav Richter, Natalia Gutman, Leonid Kogan and Yuri Bashmet. Admittedly, this was not a bad diet, but when Mikhail Gorbachev took charge, and things began to loosen up, the Latvian violinist Gidon Kremer returned. When Kremer and the Argentinian pianist Martha Argerich played Bartók together, it felt like that there was a new world opening up for us. And things became even more interesting towards the end of the 1980s thanks to Gorbachev and *glasnost*. At one stroke, the borders opened, and information poured into the Soviet Union. Perhaps my biggest cultural shock at the time was the arrival of musicians from West Germany. They came for two weeks in 1989 and brought with them everything they had. And when they presented Karlheinz Stockhausen's electronic studio and Bernd Alois Zimmermann's *Die Soldaten* in Harry Kupfer's staging, it was as if doomsday was approaching, but in the most opportunistic manner.

PART ONE: CONDUCTORS

RH: When communism finally did fall, your family moved to Germany. That must've been something of a shock, both culturally and politically. How did you cope with the move, and what were some of the immediate differences you experienced as a young Russian living in the newly unified Germany?

VJ: We moved there in June 1990, exactly one year before the attempted 'August Coup' in Russia. In fact, we didn't emigrate, we simply went to Germany and stayed. We exited the Soviet Union with a travel permit, having left our actual passports behind. The travel document allowed us to go to the Deutsche Demokratische Republik, or DDR, which ceased to exist two months later, as did the Soviet Union the following year. As an eighteen-year-old, this was an incredible adventure, which took place at exactly the age when you are about to leave your childhood behind. In my case, I literally left it behind, as my entire childhood had been left in a country that ceased to exist shortly after we moved to Germany. I simply didn't have the papers or the necessary permission to go back. And as I was liable for military service, I was excluded from my own country for twelve years. This is how I matured. In a way, my migration, or defection if you prefer, was the act of leaving my childhood behind and starting a new life.

RH: Did your family see it as a migration or as a defection?

VJ: As my father was forty-five years old, and still didn't have an international career as a conductor, he not only saw it as his last chance but as a kind of exodus, or as an escape, if you like. The end of the Gorbachev era proved to be very dark days for the Soviet Union, and we were constantly expecting the worst. As a fascist coup and a return to hard-line communism was an ever-present threat, it seemed that the only thing to do was to escape. Of course, my parents were not only afraid for their children but, as they had defected, they were aware that there was no way back for them. For me, it was like being Alice in Wonderland: I had stepped through the looking-glass into the unknown. Yet I always thought that I'd return to the Soviet Union. Leaving my friends behind was unthinkable, particularly as I had had such a fantastic time at the College. Not only had I received the best possible education but I had established friendships and had finally found inspiration as a musician. I didn't want to leave. I only did so because my parents insisted on it, and because it seemed the only way out politically. Later, I began to understand that it was also an artistic way out, and that it opened a world of opportunities for me. But I am so grateful that I didn't leave the Soviet Union as a child. By leaving when I did, I was afforded a glimpse of the old Russian-Soviet system, which is sadly no more.

RH: After arriving in Germany, you lived for a time in Dresden before moving to Berlin.

VJ: When I arrived in Germany, I only spoke some rudimentary English and not a word of German. I soon realised that English wouldn't serve me well in East Germany. Today, the situation is very different, but, then, English was rarely spoken in Dresden. Not only did I have to learn German quickly, which was far from easy, but I had to cope with Saxon usage. As I was keen to study psychology, philosophy and music history, my first six months in Germany were absolutely horrendous. I wasn't content to study only practical subjects; I wanted to do it all. This meant that my head was constantly in a dictionary the size of a doorstop. Smartphones didn't exist at the time, which was probably a good thing. Consequently, I was forced to learn a new language while experiencing a completely different culture. As Dresden was the only Catholic city within a largely Lutheran environment, and was unable to receive Western television, it was able to preserve a culture that predated the DDR. You felt the physical presence and traditions of August II, Weber and Wagner, and were haunted by the ghosts of that little town. But as I felt that there were too many of those ghosts, I left for Berlin two years later. What struck me most about Dresden was the fact that its traditions were so alive. It was a tiny island of culture with a rather dodgy political history. Had I been raised in Leningrad rather than Moscow, I might not have been so aware of this, as Moscow was more secular, open-minded and worldly than Leningrad.

RH: While in Dresden, you took part in the masterclasses of Sir Colin Davis.

VJ: I first encountered Sir Colin Davis during the middle of my first year at the conservatorium in Dresden. He already had a long-standing relationship with the Sächsische Staatskapelle and had conducted it annually throughout the DDR period. And despite its separation from the wider world, Dresden always attracted figures from the artistic front rank. By the time of Sir Colin's masterclass, I'd already had some conducting lessons, but had never stood in front of a full symphony orchestra. Up to that point, the sole extent of my conducting experience was with one or two chamber groups. Nevertheless, I volunteered for the masterclass which involved Sibelius's Seventh Symphony, a very tricky piece that I then spent the whole of the Christmas break learning by heart. As I knew that the first part of the masterclass would be without orchestra, I practised the symphony on the piano. And when I offered to play for the class on the first day, Sir Colin took an instant liking to me. But that affection probably evaporated the next day, after he saw me trembling with nerves when conducting an orchestra for the first time. I don't remember anything at all about the experience other than he corrected a *rallentando* that I made that wasn't in the score. I'm not even sure where I slowed down, as the whole thing was like wading through a fog. After about fifteen minutes of this torture, I finally stepped down from the podium and confessed to him in English that it was my first time in front of an orchestra. He looked at me and said simply, 'Poor guy!' He then returned the following year and gave a masterclass on Beethoven's Third Symphony. Although those classes were without an orchestra, he did talk about how Otto Klemperer conducted the opening of the second movement, and his habit of playing the double-basses' grace note on the beat rather than before. He said, 'I know it's wrong, but it was such an incredible thing. It was akin to a huge ape being dropped onto the first beat.'

RH: Did you see yourself as a Russian or as a German musician at this point, or perhaps a combination of the two?

VJ: I always compare myself to a bat. As a member of the animal kingdom, it never quite made it as a bird or as a mammal: it hovers somewhere between the two. Once you've left your home country, which we Russians call our Motherland, in contrast to the Germans' Fatherland, you realise that it's impossible to find another 'mother'. You just come to terms with the fact that you've simply left your 'mother' to live somewhere else. I never tried to become a German, as I knew I would fail, and I only discovered that I was a Russian when I ended up in Germany. I always thought that I was Jewish in Russia, but, after emigrating, I realised that I was completely Russian. It was only after I started coming to England that I was constantly being asked if I felt German.

PART ONE: CONDUCTORS

RH: Your father, Mikhail, was a major influence on you. Would it be fair to say that you served your apprenticeship under him, and, if so, how were you able to balance your professional and personal relationships?

VJ: A good question, and one that I am not sure that I'm able to answer. To his huge credit, we were able to maintain a wonderful human relationship during my apprenticeship. Until then, he was simply my father and not my mentor. Once I decided that I wanted to try to become a conductor, he started to train me properly. Although his approach was very different, he knew that he could teach me a great deal, as he was the product of a very distinguished tradition. That tradition had its roots partly in Germany, and his teacher had been Leo Ginzburg, formerly Otto Klemperer's assistant at the Kroll Opera in Berlin. My father had also studied with Ilya Musin in Leningrad, and it's no exaggeration to say that Ginzburg and Musin were the two main pillars of the Russian conducting school. My father not only adopted the traditions of that school but was influenced by Rozhdestvensky after he was appointed his assistant with the Moscow Radio Symphony Orchestra. A conglomerate of a number of Russian traditions, my father then went on to combine these with those of a German Kapellmeister. As my father was such a good teacher, I found it incredibly interesting when absorbing these traditions from him. He was capable of extracting the essence of what he'd learned from his great masters, and to express that essence in very few words, a technique that many teachers are incapable of doing.

RH: Are you able to define the differences between the central European and Russian schools of conducting?

VJ: The central European school of conducting gave birth to the profession, and had its roots in the opera house. A German conductor is predominantly an operatic conductor who can extend his or her activities into the symphonic repertoire. By comparison to the central European school of conducting, the Russian school is a relatively recent phenomenon, having only been founded during the Soviet period. It was thanks to people like Hermann Scherchen, Oskar Fried, Bruno Walter, Otto Klemperer, Hans Knappertsbusch and Erich Kleiber, who performed in Russia during that era, that the school was founded.

RH: Many of the figures that you've just mentioned were closely associated with Gustav Mahler. Would it be fair to say that the Russian school of conducting had its roots in Mahler's approach?

VJ: Completely. When I was conducting in Russia recently, I performed Mahler's version of Beethoven's Third Symphony with the Saint Petersburg Philharmonic. That version had only been heard in Russia when Mahler himself conducted it at Saint Petersburg in 1906. Some of the older players in the orchestra said to me, 'You know those doublings and peculiar bowings that Mahler demands? We remember playing them when we joined the orchestra back in the 1950s and the 1960s.' How was that possible? The answer's simple. When Mahler brought his version of the 'Eroica' to Saint Petersburg, he left his marked orchestral parts behind. The parts then remained in the archives of the orchestra, and were later copied by librarians. These parts were then distributed to other orchestras, and their contents gradually became part of Soviet musical life. And that's why when you hear the Beethoven symphonies performed by Mravinsky and the young Svetlanov, they have more in common with Mahler's performance style than with that of Furtwängler and Karajan.

As a direct consequence of the Iron Curtain and the Soviet Union's separation from the West, we preserved an earlier style. This was also true of the Russian operatic tradition. These styles had completely disappeared in the West because of artists like Arturo Toscanini. They demanded that singers should follow the conductor's beat and observe the printed text. In Russia, singers continued to be very free when performing Rossini, Bellini, Donizetti and Verdi. This harked back to methods that were common during pre-revolutionary times, but had ceased to exist in the West. The Soviet school of conducting was established in the 1930s, and those who formed it did so while creating new orchestras. The founders of the Soviet-Russian school of conducting were, therefore, mainly individuals who weren't actually Russian. Unlike the central European school of conducting, which is primarily concerned with operatic performance, the Soviet tradition is principally a symphonic one. This meant that a Soviet conductor was first trained to conduct a symphony by Beethoven or Shostakovich before being expected to explore an opera. In contrast, young conductors in Germany were prepared for the profession by training as either répétiteurs or chorus masters before going on to conduct symphony orchestras.

RH: As you started in the opera house, could it be argued that you are really a central European conductor?

VJ: In that sense, yes. But I still retain some of the traits of the Russian-Soviet school. Many of the things that I learned from my father about artists like Ginzburg were only possible from a Russian. Nobody in Germany could teach me that. A conductor's posture is important to a Soviet conductor, but considerably less so to a German Kapellmeister. In Germany, they care about how you shape the beat, which is only a small part of what was taught in Russia. The Russian system was much more 'conductorial', while the German system was more concerned with the needs of the opera house.

RH: If you were asked to say which system is more relevant to the needs of today's aspiring conductors, what would your answer be?

VJ: Without question, the central European system, as the hardest thing for a conductor to do is to perform an operetta. If you can perform an operetta, you can conduct anything.

RH: Felix Weingartner also argued that conducting an operetta is essential in developing a young artist's technique, particularly when it comes to controlling the beat from the wrist.

VJ: It's good for everything and it sharpens reactions. If, for example, a singer decides to abridge the dialogue slightly, and launches straight into their next number, you have to be prepared. This happened to me at Berlin's Komische Oper during Harry Kupfer's production of *Die Fledermaus*. The counter-tenor singing Orlofsky was marvellous, but would continuously improvise the dialogue. Marvellous, but tricky. Consequently, I had to be constantly alert, both technically and musically. Luckily, the orchestra was fabulous, and could play the work in its sleep. You could give them a down-beat without an up-beat, and they would take the correct *tempo*. I only realised how difficult something like *La bohème* is once I left the Komische Oper. There, it was like pushing a button, and no matter who was in front of the orchestra, the musical juggernaut rolled on. After I left that theatre, and conducted the piece elsewhere, I realised just how tricky it is.

RH: While a member of the conducting staff at the Komische Oper, you were also appointed Principal Guest Conductor at the Teatro Comunale di Bologna. Much has been made of the artistic and administrative

PART ONE: CONDUCTORS

differences that exist between theatres in Germany and Italy, but how did those differences affect you as a young conductor?

VJ: Italy teaches a young conductor a thing or two about self-discipline, something that Italians don't possess naturally. There's never a problem with the individual players and singers, only with the institutions. Unless you have the modern equivalent of *Il Duce* in charge, they never work. Because of Mussolini's legacy, orchestral musicians behave like civil servants, and while this might not affect the quality of their music-making, it affects their state of mind. That said, my stay in Bologna was relatively smooth by comparison to my time in Naples. And while the Neapolitans really love music, I occasionally wished that I had a loaded gun while I was there. The Teatro Comunale was a very good opera house with a rich Wagner tradition. In fact, Wagner had attended performances of *Lohengrin* there, and gave his personal seal of approval to the Italian translation they used. The Bologna theatre also has a rich tradition of conductors, and amongst the great artists who performed there were Lovro von Matačić and Sergiu Celibidache. They still tell a story about Celibidache throwing his stopwatch at a bassoon player, who responded by throwing his music stand at Celibidache. I was told that story by the leader of the second violins, who had the misfortune of sitting between the two.

RH: Having survived the volatility of Italian operatic life, you moved on to the Arcadian calm of Glyndebourne. As Britain's second oldest opera company, the Glyndebourne Festival Opera was the beneficiary of a number of musical traditions thanks to the pioneering work of Fritz Busch and Vittorio Gui there in the 1930s and the 1950s respectively. Were you aware of these traditions when you took charge of the company, and in what ways has it shaped you as a musician?

VJ: Earlier, I spoke about losing one's motherland. But you can always find a second home and, for me, that's Glyndebourne. It's a unique place with a unique combination of people. Not only does it nurture goodwill and artistic aspiration, but it does so with a sense of flamboyance and independence that I find inspiring. Who, in his right mind, would build an opera house in a barn for his wife, and where else but in Britain would this happen? By the time I received the offer from Glyndebourne, I knew something of its history and had heard stories about it from Gennady Rozhdestvensky, who had conducted there in 1995 and 1996. But it was only after they said that they wanted me that I fully understood its importance. I was completely baffled by the invitation, as I had only conducted a few things in this country before receiving it. I'd performed Verdi's *Nabucco* in place of an indisposed Sir Edward Downes at Covent Garden as a twenty-three-year-old in 1996, and it was that company's Director, Nicholas Payne, who later suggested me to Glyndebourne. What I failed to realise at the time was that Glyndebourne regularly looked at what was happening elsewhere in the United Kingdom, and that was enough for them to decide in my favour. And once I understood the magnitude of the offer I'd received, I was terrified by it. Before finally saying 'yes', I took a long time to consider it. But since accepting the post, I've never regretted my decision.

RH: Central to Glyndebourne's performance aesthetic are the works of Mozart, and principal amongst these is *Don Giovanni*. Traditionally, the company performed the Prague version of the opera with some interpolations from the Vienna version. But when Klaus Tennstedt was asked to perform the work at Glyndebourne, he agreed providing that he could perform the Vienna version. When he was told that it wasn't possible to conclude the opera without the *Scena ultima*, Tennstedt decided that Glyndebourne wasn't for him. You, on the other hand, do perform the Vienna version, but retain the final sextet. This, then, begs the questions: how would you describe your Mozart style, and what characterises your approach to *Don Giovanni* in particular?

VJ: I am unable to speak about my Mozart style, as I don't have one. There's Mozart, and there are his operas. I have conducted some of these, but have yet to perform *Le nozze di Figaro* or *Così fan tutte*. I'm terrified of them, and I'll probably conduct them when I'm much older. While I've performed *Die Zauberflöte* and *Don Giovanni*, I've always felt that Mozart is the most difficult composer to conduct. That said, *Don Giovanni* is the one opera by him that I am most at ease with, due to its incredible mixture of styles. It's eclectic in the best sense of the word. It mixes the Baroque traditions of *opera seria* with the *Sturm und Drang* of the early Romantic Period. Having studied in Germany, I learned the old German way of performing *Don Giovanni* without the final scene, and, for a period, thought that was actually how the opera should be given. But after I saw the Royal Swedish Opera perform it with the final scene in Moscow in 1990, I realised that its inclusion made the opera more effective.

As *Don Giovanni* is an eighteenth-century piece, the opera needs to conclude with the *Scena ultima*. When I initially thought of doing *Don Giovanni* at Glyndebourne, I intended to use the Prague version without any interpolations, simply as Mozart first wrote it. But then the singer who was to perform Donna Elvira with us said she really wanted to sing 'Mi tradì quell'alma ingrata', an aria that Mozart later added for a soprano in Vienna. Confronted with the request, we returned, yet again, to the question of the composer's later interpolations. I found this unbearable, and tried to fight against them with all the means at my disposal. Faced with losing our Elvira, which would've been a great shame, I suggested that we should give the full Vienna version. This meant that we had to address the issue of the final scene. As its text wasn't printed in the libretti that were handed out at the opera's first performance in Vienna, it could be argued that Mozart and da Ponte cut the scene when the work was given at the Burgtheater. But it seems that a week before that performance, Mozart and da Ponte reinserted the scene while excising some of Donna Anna's and Don Ottavio's longer, more lyrical material from it. Having had a chance to study that cut, I realised that Mozart knew what he was doing. It made the opera more heartless, and that's what I thought we should do.

RH: Before the new theatre opened at Glyndebourne in 1994, the only music by Wagner that was performed there publicly was the composer's short instrumental work *Siegfried Idyll*, which was conducted by Fritz Busch before the war and by Sir John Pritchard in 1953.

VJ: While that's true, the first music by Wagner heard at Glyndebourne was not given in the theatre, but in the Organ Room in 1934. It was Beckmesser's Serenade from Act Two of *Die Meistersinger von Nürnberg* given in a private performance with the festival's founder, John Christie, singing the role of Beckmesser.

RH: Christie certainly was a keen Wagnerian, and he even tried to convince Busch that the theatre was an ideal venue for some of the composer's operas and music dramas. Busch was unconvinced, however, and neither he nor Vittorio Gui or Sir John Pritchard considered the festival a suitable venue for Wagner. They argued that it should focus largely on the music of Mozart, Rossini, Verdi and Strauss. Do you consider the inclusion of *Tristan und Isolde* and *Die Meistersinger von Nürnberg* in the theatre's repertoire to be at odds with the principles of the festival's founding fathers, or just a natural consequence of the larger, more modern theatre?

VJ: I think that the inclusion of Wagner's music is a natural extension of the festival's work. And that's particularly true if you consider *Tristan* to be a continuation of Italian operatic style within a German framework, rather than the start of something new. Both *Tristan* and *Die Meistersinger* were written for, and performed in, relatively small venues, and there is a long-standing tradition of giving those works in middle-sized German opera houses.

RH: That's true. When *Tristan* was first rehearsed, some of its early rehearsals were held in the small eighteenth-century Residenztheater in Munich, where Mozart gave *Idomeneo* for the first time in 1781. Wagner was pleased with how the work sounded in the small theatre, and it was only Richard Strauss's father, Franz, the opera's Principal Horn, who described the work as sounding like an 'old saucepan' in that space.

VJ: Perhaps Busch and Gui didn't want Wagner to be performed at Glyndebourne for ideological reasons. They wanted to get away from what they'd left behind in Europe, and probably realised that the use of big voices in the original theatre would never be successful. With the opening of the new house, such voices were possible. While I made it clear from the outset that I wanted to perform *Die Meistersinger* at Glyndebourne, it was Nicholas Snowman who decided to stage *Tristan*. I also wanted to conduct *Der fliegende Holländer* there with the Orchestra of the Age of Enlightenment. Having heard them perform Weber's *Euryanthe* with Sir Mark Elder, I thought that the OAE would be the perfect orchestra for the *Dutchman*. But as that work should be performed without an interval, where do you schedule the supper break?

And, for that reason, we were unable to programme Strauss's *Salome*, an opera that would also have proved a challenge because of its large orchestration. The inclusion of Wagner's works at Glyndebourne is far from nonsensical. I think it's a very good thing, and I hope they continue to perform them even after I am gone. But they should never stage the *Ring* cycle, which some people have already suggested. Not because of the pit, but because of the danger of turning Glyndebourne into a place of artistic worship. That would be at odds with the festival's values.

RH: Over the years, you have been associated with many directors of distinction. What for you makes a great director?

VJ: To answer your question, I need to return to my childhood and to explain why I was drawn to the theatre. I wasn't attracted to acting, but to the miracle of creating theatre: directing and producing. And not necessarily just music theatre. At one point, I did consider a career in drama. Cinema also attracted me. Had I not become a conductor, the only other thing that I would've considered becoming was a film director. The greatest virtue of any opera director is the ability to envisage and to encompass both the drama and the music. Ideally, he or she should be able to explain the music through the action. That way, they avoid violating the dramatic inspiration of the score by overlaying it with a self-invented story. They should be able to invent the story from the score. Then, when the performance takes place, the music should be further ignited by the dramatic and psychological effects that are happening on stage.

RH: Have you ever been tempted to act as both director and conductor, a dual role that Herbert von Karajan, Otto Klemperer, Gustav Mahler and Richard Strauss all occupied?

PART ONE: CONDUCTORS

VJ: Yes and no. As you are aware, directors *per se* didn't exist during Mahler's lifetime. And, with all due respect to Karajan, who was both a great conductor and a great advocate of the lyric theatre, his experiments as a director were amongst the weakest aspects of his career. As the twentieth century has produced so many incredible directors, it has meant that conductors have been able to learn from them. And they can learn certain things from us, too, such as how to read and to interpret a score. But, for me, Konstantin Stanislavski's, Michael Chekhov's and Peter Brook's books on how actors should prepare were as essential to my education as any book by a great conductor. The interviews that François Truffaut undertook with Alfred Hitchcock were later released as a book, and it's one that every conductor should read. It's all about suspense and how to manipulate your audience into feeling something. And, of course, conductors have to manipulate their orchestras into thinking they are actually doing it themselves.

RH: You are Principal Conductor of the London Philharmonic Orchestra. What's the main function of a principal conductor, and how does that function manifest itself culturally, politically and financially?

VJ: Luckily, my post with the London Philharmonic Orchestra involves mainly artistic issues, so I don't have to schmooze donors and sponsors, as some of my colleagues in America have to do. Yet, because of the way that the Arts Council is currently moving, the time may soon come when at least some schmoozing might be necessary. But the situation is very different when you are either the conductor or permanent guest conductor of a self-governing orchestra, such as the LPO or the OAE. In America and Russia, a Music Director acts as a kind of father figure, and in those countries, you have to be a father figure to a great many people, as the orchestra is like a ship that needs a rudder. The situation in London is very different. What's important here is somebody who understands the needs of musicians and how hard their lives are. A conductor must be able to inspire them, to help them and to be one of them: a *primus inter pares*. This is very much the mentality of a British orchestra, and very different from one from either Germany, America or Russia.

RH: But if one looks to the OAE as a model, defining that model can prove something of a problem, as it is chameleon-like in some ways. Is there not a danger with an orchestra such as this that the actions of the orchestra determine the reading of the conductor, rather than the conductor shaping the orchestra in his own image?

VJ: Performance is always a two-way street. Of course we have to shape the orchestra, but that depends on what's on offer to us. My philosophy is that every orchestra produces a different sound and that you should work with that sound. It doesn't make any sense, therefore, for me to try and transform them into the LPO, for example. But you can still mould your interpretation using the tools that are available. But what is the essential difference? The difference is the type of instruments being used, rather than the players themselves. It is self-evident that members of the OAE have a deep knowledge of earlier music and the instruments needed to perform that music. Their knowledge of works from the late nineteenth and early twentieth centuries is more limited, which is the opposite when it comes to an orchestra like the LPO. You bring to the rehearsal what they're missing, while learning from them at the same time. I remember having a long discussion with the OAE's Principal Clarinet, Antony Pay, about the differences in phrasing when performing either Classical or Romantic music, a discussion that completely changed my views on the music of Weber, Mendelssohn and Schubert.

PART ONE: CONDUCTORS

It's always a two-way street, and I had a fantastic adventure exploring the works of Gustav Mahler with the OAE. The orchestra brought along some incredible instruments, including some huge flutes. They called these 'elephants', not just because they could kill an elephant because they were so big, but because their heads were made from ivory. Those flutes can produce a G below middle C, which is unthinkable on a more modern instrument. And as Mahler wrote some notes in his flute parts that are below the usual register, the period instruments were revelatory. I also recently discovered wooden mutes, and I now make it a rule, regardless of the orchestra I am conducting, that the string players use them when performing nineteenth- and early twentieth-century music. These mutes completely change the sound of any orchestra. So, I do think that a conductor shapes an orchestra, as much as an orchestra influences a conductor.

RH: This leads us neatly to the question of programming. You are renowned for being both an adventurous and an innovative programmer. You made a deep impact with your series examining war and peace, and then made an equally deep impact when you mounted a festival at the Southbank Centre related to Alex Ross's book *The Rest is Noise*. I am keen to hear your thoughts on the moral, political, social, financial and musical imperatives that underpin your programming policy, and what you consider the long-term and short-term effects that those imperatives have had on your audiences and musicians.

VJ: Something that has been missing from both the minds of conductors and audiences for many years is how we should approach the works we play and hear. In the nineteenth century, programmes were built around the availability of soloists and new pieces. They would always start a programme with a big symphony and never with an overture.

The first work was substantial, while the subsequent works might have involved a singer, a pianist or a string player. The evening then concluded with an overture. Unlike today, nineteenth-century concerts might be in three or four parts. This all changed in the twentieth century, when it became common to start with an overture, continue with a concerto and conclude with a symphony, a model that has persisted until very recently. That said, there were some twentieth-century conductors, such as my mentor Gennady Rozhdestvensky, who invented programmes that were like works of art. These were constructed beautifully, and affected the ways in which we viewed certain composers. He was extremely knowledgeable about painting, and I will never forget his lecture on the art of impressionism and its impact on twentieth-century music. Having been influenced by him, and having also studied the programmes of Pierre Boulez, I came to the conclusion that I needed to do something about how concerts were presented. As my experiments with the London Philharmonic Orchestra were successful, I began to attract new audiences that were not just made up of music-lovers, but also contained scientists and those involved in commerce. While these people were undoubtedly interested in art in general, they also wanted to be stimulated emotionally and intellectually. When viewed in this way, the conductor's role is certainly that of an educator and an 'enlightener'. It's extremely important that conductors are not only experts in music-making but are capable of promoting interdisciplinary knowledge.

RH: Carlo Maria Giulini once remarked: 'when I was young I needed time to study, and now that I am old, I need time to think'; while Leonard Bernstein argued: 'it's not what the composer wants, but what I think he wants that's important.' What's your response to these aphorisms, and if you were asked for a pithy mission statement that would reflect your approach as a whole, what would it be?

VJ: While I'm not nearly the same age as these two great men when they produced these aphorisms, I would say, 'Do whatever your heart or your instinct tells you to do with the music. But remember one thing: you are not the child's parent; you are but the midwife.'

RH: Who, if anybody, was your model as a Beethoven interpreter, and what techniques have you used when revealing the composer's aesthetic intentions?

VJ: I approach Beethoven from two directions, with my first points of reference being Arnold Schoenberg and Anton von Webern. Webern's lectures on Beethoven affected the Russian tradition thanks to the Romanian composer and theorist Philipp Herschkowitz. He was one of Webern's last students, and taught a number of young musicians from the Moscow Conservatory privately. Composers such as Alfred Schnittke and Andrei Volkonsky all had lessons with Herschkowitz, and all were beneficiaries of Webern's responses to Beethoven. My second point of reference is the Orchestra of the Age of Enlightenment, and the recordings of Nikolaus Harnoncourt, Sir Roger Norrington and Sir John Eliot Gardiner. As a consequence of my discussions with the OAE about the performances of Sir Charles Mackerras and Iván Fischer, and by listening to Harnoncourt's, Norrington's and Gardiner's 'new age' recordings of the Beethoven symphonies, my approach to these works changed completely. I had originally thought of Beethoven as being a monument who stood at the heart of the central European tradition, and whose music was relatively heavy and sturdy. That impression faded completely after my encounters with the artists and orchestras I've just mentioned. I'm now trying to do the impossible by connecting the approach of Harnoncourt with that of Schoenberg and Webern.

RH: Do you consider Bach's music to be fundamental or pivotal?

VJ: Not only did I once consider Bach to be fundamental, but to be God: the God who created himself. You must understand that in Russian the word for God is '*Bog*', which is pronounced '*Boch*'. This similarity was a source of fascination for some poets, who extemporised on it at great length. But as a result of my years spent in the West, and through my conversations with artists such as Charles Mackerras, the writings of Nikolaus Harnoncourt and the works of the post-modernist conceptualist composer Vladimir Martynov, whose music can be traced back to the school of Notre Dame, I now think of Bach as being most definitely pivotal. I recently read a letter by the Italian composer and conductor Bruno Maderna, which was written only a few months before I was born. The letter is nothing short of a musical manifesto, and makes clear the need to eschew opera and other works from the standard repertoire. Instead, artists should explore the unknown compositions of Mozart, Beethoven and Schubert before extending their exploration to works that predate Machaut. For Maderna, as a modern composer, it was unthinkable that his audiences should engage with music without knowing the works of composers who preceded Bach. And now, more than ever, it's imperative for us to go back to Ockeghem, Machaut and des Prez when attempting to understand the music of Xenakis, Stockhausen and Feldman. While the works of the earlier composers can be limiting for a conductor, as there is very little for us to actually 'conduct', they are essential to study, understand and digest before we tackle the music of Bach.

PART ONE: CONDUCTORS

RH: You have always been interested in young artists, and have done much to encourage aspiring conductors. What's your advice to those who are about to embark on their professional journeys for the first time?

VJ: Don't wait until the Berlin Philharmonic telephones you. Find your own truth. Establish your own ensemble and start conducting as early as possible. I'm reminded of the wonderful letter that Peter Brook received from a young student who asked, 'How does one become a director?' Brook replied, 'One doesn't become a director. One calls oneself a director, and then finds a group of people whom he can convince that he *is* a director!' It's exactly the same when it comes to conducting. A pitfall to be avoided is restricting one's repertoire to the symphonic mainstream. It might take some considerable time for any young conductor to be contacted by an orchestra, any orchestra. I started with contemporary music written for chamber ensembles, while other conductors started with early music. But it's important to actually do *something*. That's rule number one. Rule number two is: never spend a day without learning a new score. While it's tempting to do a great deal of listening, it's also essential that conductors should learn to read a score like they read a book. This is necessary so that they can develop their 'inner ear'. But this is not to suggest that listening isn't important. Quite the contrary. Listen to everything and learn from everyone. Then ask, 'How would I perform this work differently?' Watch how musicians interact with each other during rehearsals and performances, and be aware that conducting is an interdisciplinary activity.

EDWARD GARDNER
(DAVID JOSEFOWITZ RECITAL HALL, 12 OCTOBER 2012)

RAYMOND HOLDEN: Let's talk a little about the young Edward Gardner, shall we? I believe that you were born at Gloucester in 1974 to parents who worked in the medical profession. Was music a daily feature of the Gardner household, and when did your parents discover that you were gifted artistically?

EDWARD GARDNER: My mum is a nurse and my dad is a psychologist. Although my father liked singing and making music on an amateur level, there wasn't so much music around the house. Like many male musicians then, and thankfully female musicians now, I was entered for a choristership at the local cathedral, where I sang for five or six years. It was a great training, and a great way of having a free private education.

RH: When you say 'training', what did that involve precisely?

EG: For a start, you are sight-reading music for a couple of hours every day from the age of seven or eight. That's an extraordinary thing to be doing. And although this might seem a weird thing to say, it was quite a natural environment, and there was no kind of 'sweat-shop' element about it. If you take to it, you'll love it. You are singing in amazing surroundings and immersing yourself in great music. As you are surrounded by kids who can be up to five years older than you, and who are more confident and quicker at reading than you, they bring you up musically. It's all done by a kind of osmosis without anyone really teaching you. It's wonderful, and it just happens naturally.

RH: Many of your great predecessors at the English National Opera were also boy sopranos. In fact, there is a lovely photo of Sir Charles Mackerras singing the role of Ko-Ko in Gilbert and Sullivan's *The Mikado* as an eleven-year-old in Sydney. Did you sing in any of their operettas?

EG: No, I didn't. And, of course, Charles has given a marvellous collection of his marked scores and orchestral parts to the Royal Academy of Music. He was also a wonderful supporter of the English National Opera, even after he stood down as its Music Director. He was peerless as a conductor, and had the ability to perform an extremely wide repertoire. Not only was he a trailblazer for Janáček, Mozart and Handel, but he was also a marvellous Gilbert and Sullivan interpreter. He really was extraordinary.

RH: The breadth of his knowledge was quite remarkable.

EG: Unique. He reinvented and internationalised Janáček performance. There's no question about that. He also invented a modern way of successfully performing the operas of Handel and Mozart in large opera houses.

RH: And speaking of Janáček, I know that you consulted Charles's performing material of the *Sinfonietta*, which is held here at the Academy, for a reading of the work with one of the London orchestras.

EG: It's a piece that I am hugely fond of, and there's a good story about the performance that I was actually preparing for. As you know, there are various elements of the score that have been passed down from one generation of conductors to the next. And it was Sir Mark Elder who told me that it was Charles who added a number of extra markings to the work to allow it to 'speak' in a way that only he could do. It was truly amazing to work from Charles's parts. And when I gave it with the Philharmonia Orchestra, the players insisted that they'd never played certain trills, even under Mackerras. But when you sent me his material, you were able to prove to me that they had.

RH: Being something of a musical magpie, Charles had accumulated a huge mass of research material over the years, which he used to keep in a shed at the back of his garden in St John's Wood. And being the true Australian that he was, he never lost his love of a back shed, particularly one stacked shoulder-high with musical treasures. But let's return to your next port of call: Eton College. While the school has been traditionally associated with aspiring prime ministers and royalty, it can also count leading musicians, writers and actors amongst its former students. What did you gain from your time at Eton, and what have you carried forward from it into adult life?

EG: It's a school that gives people confidence, which is no bad thing, even though some people react to that in very different ways. And the music there was amazing. I attended Eton on a music scholarship, and could never have gone there otherwise. People would come up from London, and would teach you anything you wanted. During my first term, the school knew that I was freakishly interested in Messiaen, and arranged for me to hear Yvonne Loriod play for Messiaen's eightieth

PART ONE: CONDUCTORS

birthday concert at the Queen Elizabeth Hall in 1988. Eton would always give you opportunities like that.

RH: After Eton College, you went up to Cambridge. But, by all accounts, it wasn't your cup of tea, and you are reported to have said, 'It was the only mistake – okay, not the only mistake – I've ever made. Trying to turn music into an academic pursuit I found a complete anathema. Schenkerian analysis, where people draw trees to represent a Beethoven piano sonata: I just can't understand it.' Do you still stand by those comments, or has your opinion softened with the passage of time?

EG: It was a great place to be, and I'd never do it down as an institution. Practical music-making there is very good, and I sang in a wonderful choir. Yet it tried to make music into something academic, which I found very soulless. People were writing essays from received information about operas that they'd probably never heard. It really wasn't my thing.

RH: Was your move to Cambridge a natural progression from Eton?

EG: Singing in a big-chapel choir was a kind of extension to school. And it was at Cambridge that I conducted for the first time. Thanks to the high level of the orchestras there, conductors were afforded a great many opportunities. Even if you had no idea what you were doing, which, frankly, I didn't, you could still experience what it is like to stand in front of seventy people for the first time.

RH: Which leads us nicely to your time here at the Royal Academy of Music, and your studies with Colin Metters.

EG: I really loved being at the Academy, especially after somewhere like Cambridge, which tended towards the drier side of academic musical life. I loved meeting so many practical musicians, people who were able to express themselves through their instruments and their voices. That was a revelation for me. I had three incredibly happy years here. I found Jonathan Freeman-Attwood, who was Vice-Principal and Director of Studies in those days, and all who surrounded him, to be very supportive when it came to putting on concerts. This helped in my self-development. Colin's course was very intense, and was extremely technically based. But he was a wonderful support and a marvellous advocate for his students. Every time that I conduct, I still remember things that he taught me.

RH: What should a conducting pedagogue do for an aspiring artist who is clearly predestined for a life on the podium?

EG: I truly believe that you can't make a conductor, as so much of it is personality. But what Colin gave me, which I thought about while rehearsing *Don Giovanni* today, was the ability to be acutely conscious of what my body is doing. This means that I'm very aware of my physical foibles when working with an orchestra, and how they affect my approach. As I'm really only at the start of my conducting career – I left here just twelve years ago – I feel like I am still learning. Every new concert and each passing year is an education. But having the basis for understanding what I'm doing physically is a wonderful thing.

RH: Did you give many concerts at the Academy while you were a student?

EG: Mark Wigglesworth used to come in once a term and teach us. He's a wonderful conductor and a great teacher. He advised us to perform

PART ONE: CONDUCTORS

Shostakovich's Fourteenth Symphony, as it's scored for only strings and percussion. That way, everybody would be keen to play. I acted on Mark's suggestion and programmed the work alongside Stravinsky's *Concerto for Piano and Wind Instruments*. Then I put on a concert of music by Frank Martin and Benjamin Britten at St John's Smith Square, which included the latter's *Les Illuminations* and *Nocturne*. During my time at the Academy, students were still able to book the Duke's Hall, particularly if you got in early enough. But if you put on a concert there, it's essential to programme pieces that your chums want to perform. That was what Sir Simon Rattle did when he was here. How many of his friends would've been involved in a concert of Mahler's Second Symphony before he arranged it? It's also down to force of personality. If you want your mates to turn up to rehearsals, you really have to do your spadework. I also conducted an opera for the first time while I was here: Mark-Anthony Turnage's *Twice Through the Heart*, which I gave in a double bill with another opera by a fellow alumnus. And it was incredible hubris on my part when I thought that I could light, direct and conduct the whole thing. I remember turning up and realising that if I shone a light in one direction, everyone was in shadow. But as I had absolutely no idea about such things, I quickly decided to get a lighting designer and a director in to do them properly. Even though I didn't do everything that I set out to do, I was at least able to conduct the works through. It was an amazing experience.

RH: Did the students enjoy working on the project?

EG: They did. It was a new experience for all of us. As both pieces were chamber operas, the instrumentalists were able to perform as individuals, and the singers loved the exposure they got. They're all performing professionally now, and, incredibly, we were supported fully by the institution.

RH: Do you keep in touch with your fellow students from the Academy?

EG: To a certain extent, yes, but everybody is so busy. It's lovely when you bump into someone like Simon Crawford-Phillips, with whom I did the Stravinsky concerto. We worked together again a year or two ago. And, shortly, I will be seeing the Swedish violinist Sara Trobäck, who leads the Gothenburg Symphony Orchestra. It's wonderful to retain connections like these.

RH: During your time at the Academy, you attended the Salzburg Festival. Although you were there initially to observe rehearsals, you were then asked to step in at short notice to assist Michael Gielen for a production of Alban Berg's *Lulu*. How did that come about?

EG: While I was watching a staging rehearsal of the opera, one of the *répétiteurs* became ill. Michael Gielen, who was a great, but extremely austere, Austrian conductor, then asked if I fancied taking over the next day. Having said that I would, I stayed up all night to practise the three or four pages that I was meant to play. It was a wonderful experience, even though those passages are incredibly hard to realise on the piano. Part of the skill of being a *répétiteur* is the ability to recreate the sound of an orchestra. But Berg's orchestra is like no other: it's both incredibly dense and transparent at the same time. Gielen was extremely nice about what I was doing, even though I later realised that I'd been playing the right hand in the wrong clef. He didn't notice! But works like *Lulu* can't sound 'proper' on the piano anyway. As it's meant for an orchestra, you can only reproduce an approximation.

RH: How did that opportunity affect your professional profile?

PART ONE: CONDUCTORS

EG: As a conductor, very little. But working at the Salzburg Festival gives you confidence, as the music-making there is of the highest level. To be in that environment is wonderful, and to know that I could be a *répétiteur*, musical assistant or chorus master at the Festival gave me a boost.

RH: The Salzburg Festival is very different from the Proms, and unlike any festival that takes place in the United Kingdom.

EG: Absolutely. I could go to rehearsals all day. I could watch Bernard Haitink with the Vienna Philharmonic in the morning, Simon Rattle with the Berlin Philharmonic in the afternoon and Lorin Maazel with the Symphonieorchester des Bayerischen Rundfunks in the evening. There is nowhere else in the world where you get that quality and that breadth.

RH: And Michael Gielen was a very good friend of Carlos Kleiber, a conductor whom you admire.

EG: If you ask any conductor, it's very likely that they will say that Kleiber is their favourite. It's down to the combination of things that he could do. His ear for sonority and his mercurial physicality are apparent in the famous film of Beethoven's Seventh Symphony that he made with the Royal Concertgebouw Orchestra. That's an extraordinary document. And then there was the way that he used to rehearse. He would say the most wonderful things to orchestras.

RH: Perhaps this was due to his first language being English. Although he had been born to an Austrian father in Berlin, his mother was American and he went to school in New York.

EG: That could be true. I know that when he conducted Verdi's *La traviata* at New York's Metropolitan Opera for the first time, he was disappointed by how the first-act party scene was being sung and played. To liven things up, he said, 'A bit more *Muppet Show*, please!' That was absolutely fantastic. He had such a wonderful understanding of character in music. And he must've relaxed the players with whom he worked, as he never appeared to be physically tense. Yet the control was amazing.

RH: Around the time of your Salzburg visit, you came into the orbit of Sir Mark Elder, who engaged you as the Hallé Orchestra's Assistant Conductor. I know that he has an extremely high opinion of you personally and professionally, but what did you take from him technically and interpretatively?

EG: I learned a huge amount from Mark, and I respect him more than I can say. He's an extraordinary conductor and communicator. But he was, and still is, a wonderful mentor to me. He has the ability to analyse music so clearly, and is so thoughtful about the psychology of conducting. And the more that I do professionally, the more I understand and admire his achievements.

RH: Is that because your backgrounds are so similar?

EG: Maybe. It's true that my early career path was very much like his. He's so thought-provoking and lucid about music in a way that so few people are. While many artists approach music naturally, he's unusual in that he can talk about it so freely and easily.

PART ONE: CONDUCTORS

RH: As it happens, I was at his first ever professional performance in Melbourne when he conducted Verdi's *Rigoletto* in the early 1970s. And it's his ability to draw both the musicians and the audience into a single community during a performance that's one of his defining skills. Do you think that's one of the reasons why he has been so successful with the Hallé?

EG: I think that he has made the orchestra feel really special. But it's a number of things, actually. He rehearses as well as anyone I've ever met. He gives the players the confidence they need so that they have maximum freedom in performance. As he rehearses them so intensely, they feel that they can express themselves fully in that context. It's a fantastic partnership.

RH: After the Academy, Salzburg and the Hallé, Glyndebourne Touring Opera came calling. What opportunities did it offer you as a fledgling conductor?

EG: The Glyndebourne tour usually operates between September and December, and follows the main festival. Typically, it will give a number of performances at the Sussex theatre, and will then travel around the country for approximately eight weeks. When I started with the company, I was twenty-nine years old. I then stayed with it for another three years. The first thing that I did with the troupe was Puccini's *La bohème*, which was something of a challenge, as I was still a fairly inexperienced conductor at the time. This was an amazing experience, as I got to perform the work twenty times with an excellent orchestra and with a remarkable young cast in different acoustics. I disagree with some of my colleagues when they say that they get bored in the middle of a run of performances. I think it's the greatest luxury that a conductor can be afforded. To have the opportunity to find ways of pacing these great works of art better is a gift. I absolutely loved it.

RH: Historically, Glyndebourne was always a great training ground for young artists, and was a troupe that had a true *esprit de corps*. Is that still the case?

EG: These days, every opera company, including my own, the English National Opera, is a little more international. This has become necessary so that we can engage the singers that we need. For the Glyndebourne tour, we always rehearsed for five weeks. The singers who performed the principal roles on the tour would have understudied them during the main summer festival. The cast was young and mostly British. It was great. And there was certainly an *esprit de corps*. Working in a field in Sussex is completely different from working in a metropolis like London. Looking at sheep during your tea break is marvellous.

RH: Do you now enjoy returning to Glyndebourne as a conductor at the main festival?

EG: Yes, I do. But by end of the English National Opera's season in mid-July, I've usually had enough of opera. That can be a problem. Nevertheless, I do love Glyndebourne as a place, and the quality of the work on offer there is excellent.

RH: During your Academy years, you were also Music Director of the Wokingham Choral Society. As we all know, choral societies were the backbone of British musical life for much of the nineteenth and twentieth centuries, and young conductors regularly cut their musical teeth on these groups. What did you learn from your experiences in Wokingham, and what's the future for these once-noble institutions?

EG: In one season alone, I conducted Verdi's Requiem, Szymanowski's Stabat Mater and Beethoven's Ninth Symphony with the choir. This was a great way of learning repertoire, especially big, nineteenth-century oratorios. I really enjoyed the experience. You're right, choral societies were the backbone of British amateur music-making. In fact, I'm in the middle of planning performances of Britten's *Spring Symphony* and a new piece by Jonathan Harvey with the City of Birmingham Symphony Orchestra Chorus. Amateur choirs remain fundamental to the United Kingdom's orchestral life, and our choirs are still amongst the best in the world.

RH: But should choirs that are *not* attached to great symphony orchestras be given greater support?

EG: That's hard for me to comment on, as I now rarely work with choirs that are not attached to orchestras. I'm still a Patron of the Wokingham Choral Society, and it's still going strong. The Home Counties has always been an area where choirs do well. So, too, is Huddersfield and its famous choral society. What I find particularly heart-warming are the children's and youth choirs that are attached to the orchestras in Manchester and Birmingham. When taken together with the main adult choruses in those cities, music-making becomes a very familial experience.

RH: After taking over the helm of the English National Opera in 2007, you said, 'When I started being a Music Director someone said it was two jobs. I didn't really understand what that meant until recently: you have to be a musician with your musicians, and a manager with everyone else. You can't mix the two up or you get lost.' Did you get lost?

EG: You have to be quite clinical about how you separate your professional personalities. I don't mind administrative duties, as they can help the company to become a better institution. I see the purpose of all of that. It's just the process of administration that can be very difficult. But the long-term good of the company must always remain our goal, and that's what I cling on to.

RH: A composer with whom you have a particular affinity is Benjamin Britten. After performing a critically acclaimed production of *Death in Venice* at the English National Opera, you gave an equally well-received reading of *Peter Grimes* at the Proms. What attracts you to Britten's operas, and why do they speak to you so strongly?

EG: In fact, I have something of a love-hate relationship with Britten. While I admire some of his pieces for being effective, brilliant and appealing, they don't necessarily move me when I'm conducting them. Of course, that doesn't apply to all of Britten's music. Take *Peter Grimes*, for example. It has a visceral, raw quality, which Britten never quite recaptured later on. This was probably due to his eagerness to study with Alban Berg in Vienna. There's so much of *Wozzeck* in *Peter Grimes*. It has a dark quality. The thing that unleashed something in me when it came to *Grimes* was my response to some of the recordings of it. The modern 'tradition' of recording the opera is quite English, quite respectful. But that's not the case when it comes to Britten's own discs of the piece, which are quite wild. Having heard his reading, I felt that I was given licence to find what was under the surface of the score. Britten's conducting of his own works was always pretty extraordinary. His recording of the *Sinfonia da Requiem* is a particularly raw performance.

RH: What are your thoughts on *The Turn of the Screw*?

PART ONE: CONDUCTORS

EG: As it's a chamber opera with only thirteen players and a small-ensemble cast, the role of the conductor is very different. You are essentially coaching everyone to give a performance together, which means that you are almost superfluous by the time that the opera reaches the stage. In a way, you are an observer with a piece like that. *The Turn of the Screw* is also an extraordinary piece of writing, which shows two of the elements that made Britten peerless. One is his choice of texts, and the other is the way that he emphasises key elements within those texts. The original novella hasn't the darkness of the opera. And it's remarkable to see how Britten underlines the implications of Peter Quint's character through purely musical means, and the way that he treats Mrs Grose vocally.

RH: After Sir Charles Mackerras attended one of your performances of *Der Rosenkavalier* at the English National Opera shortly before he died, he telephoned me and told me how impressed he was by your reading of the score. You also had a major triumph with the work's immediate predecessor, *Elektra*, at the Edinburgh International Festival in 2006. What makes a great Strauss interpreter, and how would you define your Strauss style?

EG: I think that you need to have five different personalities to be able to conduct Strauss successfully. As *Der Rosenkavalier* is so huge, it's a law unto itself. The first time that I conducted the opera, I felt like I was swimming around in it. It's so complicated. Although Carlos Kleiber can make it look so easy, it really isn't. It's crazy. Central to its success is how you interpret Baron Ochs's oafish mock gentry. You have to conduct the opera according to the rhythm of the words.

RH: In fact, Strauss made that very point when the young Sir Georg Solti asked him about 'the *tempo*' of the opera in the late 1940s.

EG: I was lucky enough to have had Sir John Tomlinson as Ochs for the first two occasions that I conducted the work. He's sung the role around the world, both in German and in English. I made him rehearse it over and over again, just so that I could get the inflection of it. *Elektra* is a very different thing. And while I don't love everything that Strauss wrote, I do adore *Elektra*. When I hear *Salome*, I metaphorically sit in a foetal position facing away from the stage, as I dislike it so much. And I can't get into some of the later operas such as *Capriccio* at all. But I really do like *Die Frau ohne Schatten*.

RH: Do you think that your responses might have something to do with the fact that Strauss and his librettist, Hugo von Hofmannsthal, saw their work as a natural extension of Mozart's and da Ponte's efforts? They famously described *Der Rosenkavalier* as 'their *Figaro*' and *Die Frau ohne Schatten* as 'their *Zauberflöte*'.

EG: There may well be something to that. There's something incredibly magical about *Der Rosenkavalier*. For me, the thing that links that opera with *Le nozze di Figaro* is the vanishing youth of each work's central female character: the Marschallin and the Countess. I find this incredibly moving in *Der Rosenkavalier*, and no less so in *Figaro*. *Elektra*, on the other hand, is a force of nature, and I hear a great deal of *Peter Grimes* in it.

RH: How do you pace *Elektra* so as not to exhaust the eponymous character?

EG: It's really a question of stamina. We are desperate to give *Elektra* at the English National Opera, but there are so few people who sing the title role. And even the greatest artists say that they will only perform it for three or four years internationally, as it can wreck their voices. It is an incredible act of gymnastics, and an equally incredible act of stamina. Yet the piece is all the better for it, as it has to feel like an insurmountable challenge. Not only does it have an enduring quality, it's very edgy. Strauss himself was a wonderful dichotomy. How could an outwardly calm and respectable man produce a work of such extremes?

RH: While you were saying this, I was reflecting on how Strauss performed some of his own one-act operas while he was Hofkapellmeister and Generalmusikdirektor at the Berlin Hofoper. There, he would occasionally give these works as the second part of a 'double bill', which began with one of his own tone poems, such as in 1915, when he performed *Tod und Verklärung* directly before *Salome*. Have you ever considered doing this?

EG: No. My arms would fall off! But that really was an amazing feat.

RH: It was. Performing these works in this manner would be a form of Straussian period performance practice. But there are very few ensembles today that would have the stamina to do so.

EG: A work that I do love by Strauss is his performing version of Mozart's *Idomeneo*.

RH: Thanks to that version, Strauss was able to revivify the opera. He was the first major conductor to take an interest in the piece, and without his efforts, the opera would never have come to the attention of Fritz Busch and Sir John Pritchard in the 1950s. But I would like to return to the English National Opera, if I may, and to turn our attention to its production style. It seems to me that one of the company's greatest strengths is its ability to lead the way with cutting-edge productions. Your performances of *Carmen* with the film director Sally Potter and *Aida* with the fashion designer Dame Zandra Rhodes certainly prompted comment. What, then, do you look for in a director and a designer, and how fundamental are they to your interpretation of an opera as a whole?

EG: It has to be said that the productions that you've just mentioned are two extreme examples of what we do. The directors whom I love working with most have the ability to tell me as much about the music as I can tell them about the drama. These are real collaborations. And there's no other theatre in the world that has such a breadth of great directors as the English National Opera. In one season, I might engage with Deborah Warner, Richard Jones, Sir David McVicar, David Alden and Rupert Goold. These are all outstanding artists, and the sort of people I love working with. I did *Death in Venice* with Deborah at the English National Opera and elsewhere, and have just given Martinů's *Julietta* with Richard Jones. His direction was so informed musically that he made the piece feel greater than it is. And that's a real skill!

RH: And what you have just said makes me think of John Copley, whose productions always feel like the purest physical manifestation of the music itself.

EG: Directors like John are the best sort of people to work with. But even some directors who have spent a great deal of time in the opera house are often incapable of allowing the music to speak well. One person who did allow it to sound was Terry Gilliam, with whom I gave Berlioz's *La damnation de Faust*. It was his first opera. Even though he has something of a reputation for spending money and cancelling, he completely understood that to make an image look good on stage, the music also has to sound incredible. Essentially, it's what Stravinsky said about an ideal operatic experience: 'You should see with your ears and hear with your eyes.' That's so important, and great directors get that.

RH: And speaking of hearing, the English National Opera, like the Vienna Volksoper, performs in the vernacular.

EG: This is a big topic that's been much discussed. Italian opera can be incredibly difficult to perform when not in the original language. German is quite a different matter. And, as we know, Wagner was perfectly happy to have his works given in the vernacular. Russian and French operas also work well in translation. But Italian works are the hardest to perform in another tongue, as there is a purity and romance about the language that doesn't transfer easily into English.

RH: One of the reasons I was very keen to hear your thoughts on this issue was your comment: 'Our audience [at the English National Opera] is quite unlike that of Covent Garden – it's more like a West End theatre audience.' Is this to do with your performances being sung in the vernacular, or has it more to do with your production values and choice of operas?

EG: I would say 'yes' to all of those. Our audiences expect a certain theatricality in whatever we do, and that the work's theatricality should always be in the foreground. Whereas Covent Garden, an amazing institution for which I have complete respect, has a remit that is slightly different from ours. As it employs a roster of great international singers each year, its approach to music-making is focused accordingly.

RH: Could it not be argued, therefore, that the English National Opera is something of a trendsetter when it comes to ensemble singing? If one thinks of Covent Garden in the 1950s and the 1960s, it was not uncommon for audiences to be treated to one or two superstar singers per evening supported by a series of vocal dead-legs following in their wake. Now, the quality of vocal technique across the board at Bow Street is of a uniformly high standard. Is this a direct result of both your work and that of Sir Mark Elder at the Coliseum?

EG: I think that today's audiences lust for a proper ensemble cast, and that a production should no longer be the vehicle for one great singer.

RH: I would like to return to Italian opera, if I may, and to ask you about your particularly honest and candid remarks concerning your readings of Verdi's and Puccini's operas. You once said, 'I never got *Turandot* right, and I doubt I'll try it again … [and] I think I was bit young for *Aida*, too … [Nevertheless] I was most pleased about the warm and rich and transparent sound that I got from the orchestra in *Tosca* and *Butterfly*.' What, then, is the key to interpreting the music of these composers, and who has done so successfully?

EG: Verdi and Puccini exist in two very different worlds. I think that Sir Antonio Pappano is an amazing Puccini conductor, and I would travel anywhere to hear him conduct the composer's works. Sir Mark Elder is an absolutely phenomenal Verdi interpreter, and I have learned a great deal about that composer's pieces from him. When I listen to discs of Puccini's and Verdi's works, I tend to search out those made between the 1920s and the 1950s; those that predate the warm, lush-sounding recordings of the modern age. And when it comes to the music of Richard Strauss, I am attracted to the amazing readings of Erich Kleiber and Karl Böhm.

PART ONE: CONDUCTORS

RH: And, of course, Kleiber's and Böhm's recordings of Strauss's operas mainly involved ensemble casts from the Vienna Staatsoper.

EG: That's absolutely true, and much of the success of those discs was down to how the singers were coached. They were all coached in a coherent style, and in a way that rarely happens any more. Riccardo Muti is something of an exception when it comes to this, and one of his greatest strengths is his insistence on how singers are coached. A good example of this is his recording of Bellini's *I Capuletti e i Montecchi*. There, you have some of the greatest singers in the world all singing in the same style. To have that kind of personality as a conductor today is a very difficult thing.

RH: I know that you are particularly interested in the works of Wagner, and that you began your exploration of his music with a high-profile production of *Der fliegende Holländer* at the Coliseum. Sir John Eliot Gardiner recently explained in this series why he felt that Wagner's place in the operatic hierarchy was greatly overrated. Presumably, you take a different stance. If so, how important are the composer's operas and music-dramas to you?

EG: I know that Sir John Eliot finds Wagner too right-wing, and can be quite vociferous in his dislike of the composer. I, on the other hand, adore Wagner, and am just waiting to start my journey with him. For me, he's right at the top of the operatic tree. Covent Garden has just done a magnificent *Ring* cycle, and *Die Meistersinger von Nürnberg* can cannibalise you as an audience member. Act One can be quite hard, but you could sit there for months enjoying Acts Two and Three. To be in the theatre for a piece like that is the most extraordinary experience. *Der fliegende Holländer* was a perfect beginning for me, as it sits between two worlds.

The Dutchman's own music has passages that could have come straight out of the *Ring*, while the overture and the music that surrounds his material is much more like Weber. And that's where the opera comes from: the wonderful world of high romance, a style of music that I also love.

RH: Were you comfortable with Wagner's sound-world from the beginning of your operatic career?

EG: I was, but was very shy about conducting it. I was always sure that *Holländer* would be my first attempt at performing one of his works, and that I would then move slowly through some of his other pieces.

RH: Would you ever consider conducting a complete cycle of Wagner's stage works, such as Wolfgang Sawallisch did at Munich in the early 1980s?

EG: I think Wagner's first opera, *Die Feen*, is very hard to pull off. *Rienzi* is possible, but Wagner really starts with *Der fliegende Holländer* for me.

RH: As you are clearly a man of the theatre, and as you have conducted a double bill that coupled Bartók's *Bluebeard's Castle* with Stravinsky's *Le sacre du printemps*, I find it curious that you are less than enthusiastic about conducting ballet in general. Why is that?

EG: Traditional ballet doesn't speak easily to me. I much prefer to watch modern dance. And it's the ways in which many great ballet scores are pulled around and cut that I find difficult to accept. We know that Stravinsky had many arguments about *tempo* with his choreographers, and I get incredibly irritable when his music is mistreated. Ballet conducting is really a *métier*. As you are at the mercy of your dancers, it's impossible to shape the music. You are simply 'catching' the dancers. As a means of performing music, it's not particularly large scale. When you go to the ballet at Covent Garden, the audience talks through the overture. It's clear that nobody is particularly interested in the music-making, and that winds me up.

RH: Over the last few years, symphonic music has been occupying you increasingly, and in 2010 you were appointed Principal Guest Conductor of the City of Birmingham Symphony Orchestra. How easy, or difficult, will it be for you to make a long-term interpretative mark on the orchestra?

EG: As the orchestra's wonderfully fiery Music Director, Andris Nelsons, conducts a great deal of core repertoire with it, I decided with the General Manager, Stephen Maddock, to tackle works that Andris would not ordinarily do with them. I intend to conduct Elgar and Janáček with the orchestra, and have a programme of Lutosławski and Sibelius coming up. I want the orchestra to experience musical flavours that it would not ordinarily encounter. So, yes, it's possible to make a mark.

RH: Earlier, we talked a little about Britten's operas, but you have also conducted his symphonic music to great acclaim. Some time ago, you made a wonderful recording of the Cello Symphony with Paul Watkins and the BBC Philharmonic. Of the work, and its preparation, you said: 'You can have epiphanies about your own route through a piece of music ... or a piece can reveal itself in a certain way. Britten's Cello Symphony was very difficult to find a way through, but there came a sudden point during my learning of it when I discovered its extraordinary humanity.' What did you mean by that, and how did you go about exploring this masterpiece from the 1960s?

EG: I talk to orchestras all the time about what I think a piece of music means. This is probably a result of my operatic upbringing. When I was rehearsing *Don Giovanni* this morning, I attempted to characterise some of its arias, and I don't see that that's in any way different from working with a symphony orchestra. You want to inspire musicians, and to capture their imaginations. That's how you can take a performance to another level. The Cello Symphony doesn't yield up its pleasures easily. It's very hard to programme, and can be difficult to come to terms with. The wonderful last movement, where the cello is almost submerged by the orchestral sound, is a marvellous outpouring of emotion by Britten.

RH: What did you mean when you said: 'Interpretation somehow implies wilfulness to me. I prefer to think of conducting as trying to find for yourself the composer's intentions … I think no music is exempt from different people shaping it in different ways'?

EG: Britten is very different from Mahler, for example, as we have most of the former's works conducted by him on disc. Even if I tried to conduct like Britten, not that I ever would, something different would emerge. But 'interpretation' is a difficult word. Somehow, you have to take the ego out of it, as 'interpretation' is a word that's full of ego. You have to find how the music speaks best through you as a vessel.

RH: Would you feel more comfortable with the word 'realising' when it comes to working with a score?

EG: I think that a happy medium is somewhere between the two. No matter what you are performing, it's impossible to stop your personality coming out, and nor should you.

PART ONE: CONDUCTORS

RH: Surely, this becomes even more complicated when you are trying to deal with two great musical minds, such as in your recording of Berio's realisations of Mahler's early songs.

EG: But, here, Berio manages to bury his ego, and avoids putting himself forward at all. His orchestrations are pure and beautiful. They're simply wonderful.

RH: On that disc, you also included Berio's *Rendering*, a completion of fragments from Schubert's unfinished Tenth Symphony.

EG: Schubert left extensive sketches for the Tenth Symphony, and I would say that eighty per cent of Berio's piece is Schubert. Instead of simply trying to draw together the extant sketches and complete them, Berio creates a magical composition in which other-worldly figures float to the fore before retreating. It's a marvellous work that is full of Schubert's joyfulness.

RH: You are now closely associated with the music of Lutosławski, and bring to it a transparency and luminosity that is sometimes lacking in the readings of other conductors. As your teacher, Colin Metters, is also a noted interpreter of the composer's music, how influential was he in developing your interest in Lutosławski's works, and what particularly attracts you to them?

EG: Curiously, I never discussed them with Colin. My initial route to Polish music was through Szymanowski. I heard *Król Roger* at the Proms under Simon Rattle, and was bowled over by its sound-world. I then began to explore works by other Polish composers, which led me to Lutosławski's Concerto for Orchestra. By comparison with some of his other music, it's a very well-known piece. But, for me, it's the Third Symphony that's a complete masterpiece.

RH: You are also a passionate advocate of British music, and have conducted it widely abroad. We know that the works of Elgar, Vaughan Williams and Britten struggled to be accepted by foreign orchestras and audiences throughout much of the twentieth century, but what has your experience been when presenting these works overseas today? And how willing are managements and orchestras to programme the works of contemporary British composers, such as Colin Matthews and Mark-Anthony Turnage?

EG: Newer music is not so hard to programme, as the regard for British contemporary music is incredibly high around the world. Thomas Adès's works are widely performed, and his *Tempest* is about to be given at the Metropolitan Opera in New York. But when it comes to Elgar's compositions, you have to be quite careful, as orchestras can be slow to accept them. I am about to perform *The Dream of Gerontius* in Norway, a country with a unique musical identity. It's a curious thing that countries that have unique musical identities tend to identify with each other. Finland and Sibelius is a case in point. British orchestras and audiences have always adored his music, whereas it always falls flat in Germany. The Germans have no interest in it at all, and call it second-rate music. Americans will accept the composer's big symphonies, but they don't like the Third, Fourth and Sixth. For me, it's a mission to conduct British music abroad. But it's essential that it should be placed within a wider context. Holst's *The Planets* is a good example. I consider it a spiritual, rather than a British, work, and one that is influenced by the East. I avoid performing it side by side with the 'Pomp and Circumstance' Marches. The best programme that I ever constructed around it contained Dukas's *La Péri* and Szymanowski's Stabat Mater. By placing *The Planets* within a greater pan-European context, I was able to explore three types of spirituality.

RH: Education and young people are close to your heart. Since establishing the Hallé Youth Orchestra in 2002, you have gone on to work closely with not only our students here at the Academy, but with those elsewhere in Britain and abroad. How should young people maximise their musical and educational experiences, and what should we be doing to encourage more of them into concert halls and theatres?

EG: The best way to get young people interested in music is to do it. As classical music is now largely absent from the National Curriculum in this country, it's important that performers should expose young people to it from an early age. The English National Opera is active with outreach work, and has recently built projects around *Die Zauberflöte*. And when about eighty young people came in for the dress rehearsal of the opera the other day, they were completely wild for it. The most important thing is to engage them through performance, and not to patronise them.

PART TWO

SINGERS

DAME JANET BAKER
(THE DUKE'S HALL, 17 SEPTEMBER 2010)

JONATHAN FREEMAN-ATTWOOD: After being auditioned for the part of The Angel for Sir John Barbirolli's now iconic EMI recording of Elgar's *The Dream of Gerontius*, the producer, Ronald Kinloch Anderson, wrote: 'I shall never forget the effect. It was as if the room had suddenly been illuminated by a radiant light. We [Barbirolli and I] said nothing. We had our Angel.' Although that's a lovely encomium, perhaps you could tell us in your own words a little about your early career?

JANET BAKER: Like Dietrich Fischer-Dieskau, I started by singing church music with church choirs. I sang at the regular services of the Protestant religion, which served as the background for my education. The church was there at the beginning of my life, and will be there at its end.

JF-A: If we trace the history of contralto singing from Dame Clara Butt to you by way of Kathleen Ferrier, do you think that there's a distinctive style which is quintessentially British?

JB: The idea of what a contralto and mezzo-soprano is has changed. All the young people I know are now well schooled in the operatic repertoire, and are expected to spend at least part of their working lives on stage. When I was starting, you were either an oratorio singer or an opera singer. And very rarely did the twain ever meet. This was a great pity, as it was rather like having half of your leg cut off. One of the best things about today is that you are expected to be able to do both. Perhaps not equally well, but you are expected to have experienced every kind of performance. This must be a good thing. When it comes to Clara Butt and Kathleen Ferrier, the core of their voices was seated lower down than mine. Such singers usually find the mezzo register difficult, even though it's necessary for opera. The interesting thing about being a mezzo is that you are generally equipped to perform in both the operatic and oratorio repertoires, and are not simply confined to one or the other.

JF-A: During your early years, you sang in the Glyndebourne chorus. Were you a contralto then?

JB: At Glyndebourne, I was categorised quite quickly as a 'number-two soprano'. This surprised me. Coming as a naïve young thing from Yorkshire, I thought of myself as having a deeper voice. But the member of the music staff with whom I worked there, the then-conductor of the Ambrosian Singers, John McCarthy, immediately designated me as a mezzo. While it took me a little time to adjust to this idea, I soon realised that it was a lot more interesting than being an alto *per se*.

JF-A: Three opera houses with which you were particularly associated were the Royal Opera House, Covent Garden, the English National Opera and the Glyndebourne Festival Opera. What were some of their defining qualities?

JB: I must include Scottish Opera amongst the theatres you've just named. It had a tremendous influence on the way that I was perceived when doing repertoire opera, as opposed to specialised things, such as Gluck's *Orfeo ed Euridice*. For me, I soon realised the combination of acting and singing was the ideal expression of the vocalist's art. And to have the opportunity to do that at those theatres was an education in itself. Even though all opera houses are different, there's a thread that runs through every kind of music, no matter what the period or country it comes from. That thread then acts as a kind of magnetic true north. In a sense, whatever I did was the same, as it always involved communicating a musical idea to an audience. You are, in effect, taking care of somebody else's compositional baby, whether that be when performing opera, *Lieder* or with a symphony orchestra. As you are always the servant of the composer, there's no real difference between the genres.

JF-A: What were some of the defining qualities of the repertory, *stagione* and festival theatres that you worked in?

JB: Places like Glyndebourne really spoil you, as there are not the inevitable pressures there that you find in normal opera houses. If you are working in a major theatre, you don't have the time, extravagance and freedom that is afforded you at Glyndebourne. This is particularly true when it comes to working with the same cast over an extended period. Artists come and go from time to time at theatres like Covent Garden. This means that there can often be a lack of continuity. Glyndebourne gave me something special, and given the right circumstances, it's the model of what an ideal performance environment should be. Even before the new theatre was built, it provided artists with exceptional working conditions. While such an ideal is very important, you can't expect that everywhere. This might only happen once in your life and never again. That being so, you have to create a firm base within yourself, and to know how you are going to work professionally. This involves understanding how you react to other people, and how honest you are going to be with them. While you might not always have a great deal of time to do this, you have to be clear in your own mind the direction that you are going to take as a member of a team. You can then accept anything from anybody without being untrue to your own solid foundations and how you view the world. This means that you are able to hold firm regardless of the help, or lack of help, that you might receive from others. This is very important. It doesn't mean that you are being inflexible, but it does mean that you are sure of your own technique and what you want to say. That way, it's possible for you to absorb ideas from other people very quickly without losing your own individuality.

JF-A: What were some of the challenges you faced when performing a work in the vernacular at the English National Opera, having already sung it in the original language elsewhere?

JB: It can be complicated when performing a comedy like Mozart's *Così fan tutte*. Making clear every joke in English to the audience can be great fun, particularly when you are able to respond to their reactions to those jokes. To get that kind of response is a marvellous thing. But it's not quite the same if you are singing *Così* at Covent Garden in the original language, as you don't get the same feedback. Somehow, you have to remain true to the work through the security of your own technique and your understanding of the character you are playing. If you are to learn such a score thoroughly, it requires a great deal of solitary time. And that knowledge is the only thing that a singer can rely on. You must know the work inside out and back to front. Then, very few people can dislodge you from that very firm base. To study at a place like the Royal Academy of Music will stand you in good stead when establishing such a base, and it sets the benchmark for whatever you might do later in life. No matter what language you may be singing in, you will then be better able to understand the character you are portraying; its basic truth will simply emerge. It's both helpful and marvellous to get a response from people who understand your own language, particularly in an opera that's fun. But body language and mental projection will also give you the same solidarity and purpose of idea, no matter where you are, or in whatever language you may be singing.

JF-A: You performed Vitellia in Mozart's *La clemenza di Tito* at Covent Garden under Sir John Pritchard before recording the role with Sir Colin Davis. What do you think constitutes a good Mozart singer, and what demands does his music make technically?

JB: Mozart separates the sheep from the goats. Even some established singers hit an artistic brick wall when they perform his music. They often wonder, 'Why can't I sing this material? What's going on here?' It's because Mozart is so demanding. If there is anything the least bit shaky in your technique, he will find you out. The demands he makes of singers are totally colossal. But this might also have something to do with how conductors balance modern instruments against the voice. Performing Mozart's music is only possible if a singer's technique has firm foundations. And he tests those possibilities to the limit.

JF-A: How did you prepare yourself mentally for a performance?

JB: I would always go back to my basic technique. I went to my singing teacher, Helene Isepp, all my working life until she died. She would always ask, 'What are you coming here for?' And I would reply, "For a check-up." You always need that 'other' ear as a singer, as you can't always rely on your own. You need somebody whom you can trust. If you are a student at somewhere like the Academy, you have time to think about your voice in a way that you might never have again. Being a student is a very important period in your life, as you can experiment and discover as much as possible about your own voice and how it works. It's a very precious time. When you leave education, it's like entering a factory. You don't always have the personal space to think about what you are doing. I cannot stress enough the importance of being able to hone your technique as a student. By comparison with an instrumentalist, our time as singers is short. Most instrumentalists start playing when they are knee-high. We can't do that. Everything we do has to be done within a very short time frame. If what a student's teacher is saying is echoed in a physical response, and if their technique is strong, the singer will continue to develop throughout his or her career.

JF-A: How did you go about injecting the characters you were portraying with vitality?

JB: You have to have a strong sense of inner confidence. And, of course, you are your own instrument. But developing that confidence at the age of eighteen can be problematic, as it can be very difficult to tread your own path. As a young person, you are reliant on your teacher's ear to tell you what sounds good or bad. The trick is not to lose your inner core and to have unshakeable self-confidence. The older and more experienced you become, the more unshakeable it must be. As you often have to fight against very big personalities on stage, you must never forget why you became a singer in the first place: it was because you wanted to communicate through your voice. And if you are true to the score, you can survive any conductor and any director. It's always a challenge to balance your own voice against everything that is coming at you from other people. You must be unshakeable personally, while at the same time being completely open with musicians whom you trust.

JF-A: Three great conductors whom you did trust, and with whom you had particularly fruitful relationships, were Sir Adrian Boult, Sir John Barbirolli and Sir Charles Mackerras. Can you define what made them so special?

JB: The three conductors you just mentioned were men of their time. Adrian Boult would sit back on the podium, and would extract music from you as if from a toothpaste tube. But if he considered the material that you were singing to be of lesser importance, he really wouldn't mind so much. He had a very long baton, and if you began to stray, it would be pressed into action. He had a very laid-back attitude towards singers, and would give you a lot of leeway. He left you a long rope, but would pull you in when necessary. Listening to the recording of Wagner's *Wesendonck-Lieder* that I made with him still amazes me; I don't know how he got that performance out of me. I am not generally associated with this piece, but somehow or other he made it work. Those recording sessions were blissful. He had a peculiar way of sitting, which left you feeling that you were conducting him. But it was easy, easy-going and loose, somehow.

Barbirolli was different again. He was a remarkable human being. And while he didn't have an extraordinary beat by any stretch of the imagination, his human qualities *were* extraordinary. When I was very young, I couldn't have imagined working with him at EMI's Abbey Road Studios, and I still don't know how I found myself there. The writer and critic Michael Kennedy always said that when Kathleen Ferrier died, Sir John missed her very much. While I didn't feel overwhelmed by Barbirolli, I couldn't believe that I was in that studio with him. He was funny – fun and easy – and I did many of the big pieces with him for the first time. He was also very encouraging of somebody so young, and I felt that he trusted me very much. This was a remarkable thing for a man of his age, particularly as I was somebody whom he'd just met. I felt safe with him, and also sensed a special connection. Barbirolli was a very emotional man, and if you did something that particularly touched his heart, you could see his expressions crossing his face. When that happened, he could barely go on conducting. This was such an inspiration, and I eventually grew to recognise those expressions. The sense of encouragement and self-worth that he gave me was something quite unique, particularly as I was *so* young and inexperienced at the time. Because of our strong emotional bond, we became extremely fond of each other, and I was always proud of that fact.

Charles Mackerras was something else again. He was a tremendous controller. I don't mean that he always put a musical straitjacket on you, although sometimes he did. Outwardly, he appeared to be an unemotional man, but when you got on the concert platform with him, he was able to let himself go in a way that wasn't possible in ordinary life. He suddenly became a different Charles. And it was a great, great privilege to be on stage with him. I always felt an extraordinary spiritual connection with him when performing, although he wouldn't have called it that. He could be a very strict taskmaster, and a pain in the neck when it came to ornamentation. It was terrifying when he would turn up morning after morning with something different, having had 'a wonderful idea during the night'. I was so lucky to work with so many outstanding conductors during my career. To have been let into the minds of these great musicians, and to be trusted by them, is something that will remain with me forever.

JF-A: You also worked with many of the world's leading accompanists during your career. Why did you decide to work with a variety of musical partners, rather than just one?

JB: Many years ago, it was fashionable for recital singers to stick with one accompanist. During the early part of my career, I did a great deal of broadcasting with Paul Hamburger, for example. But I wanted to benefit from different musical minds, some of whom I felt closer to than others. As the repertoire that I was singing tended to be given over and over again, it was important for me to have this variety of input. This gave me different insights into the works that I was performing. I was keen not to be stereotyped, and didn't want to close myself off from other musical ideas. It's very exciting to work with different pianists, conductors and directors, and, of course, I did have my favourites.

JF-A: The music of Johann Sebastian Bach has played an important part in your life. Even though you worked with a plethora of distinguished Bachians, including Sir David Willcocks, Carlo Maria Giulini, Sir Neville Marriner and Otto Klemperer, I am particularly interested in your recording of the *Matthäus-Passion* with Karl Richter from 1979, which you always refer to with a certain awe.

JB: Richter was great. There are times in your life when you meet a person and know immediately that the bond is exceptional. He was one such person. Although I couldn't express my musical thoughts to him in German as well as I might have liked, we just clicked. I had such an enormous respect for his Bach interpretations, even though they are now considered somewhat old-fashioned. Thankfully, we are beginning to understand that there are different ways of doing things, and that performances are only as 'authentic' as the people who give them. As Bach's music was rooted in the Church, Richter's world resonated with me and was my *raison d'être*. My performance with him had a bigger purpose, and was not something that I delivered simply to further my career before an audience. It was a great thrill to meet another musician like Karl who shared these views. When we recorded the *Matthäus-Passion*, the rich and intense sound of his Munich forces, and the tremendous feeling that the singers used when characterising the words, was accepted as a natural way of performing the piece. I find it inconceivable that anyone would sing Bach's great Passions without being involved in this way. Karl certainly was, and his approach to the composer's music was right for me.

JF-A: How different was it working with a seasoned German Bachian, having spent the greater part of your life singing the composer's music in England?

JB: When I performed the *Matthäus-Passion* annually during my early career with Paul Steinitz, I used to sing from the German version. That was the highlight of my year. But when people no longer wanted that, I found it a very sad thing. There's a place for that style of performance, provided that you observe the notes on the score. There are all sorts of ways of exploring the work's emotions, and Karl Richter was the central figure in that mould.

JF-A: You have often spoken about the need for young artists to control their energy levels during rehearsals and performances. How did you go about doing that?

JB: It's really a personal thing, as some of us have more energy than others. But I used to get very tired, as I worked so hard. I was always trying to preserve my technique. This could be stressful, and was probably one of the reasons why I retired relatively early. A singer should know his or her individual capabilities and stick to them. The same applies to repertoire. When it comes to the question of how much an individual can take, it's really a question of self-discovery. The pressure on the voice is so enormous, as you are always singing. You are either going for a lesson, studying with a *répétiteur*, rehearsing or performing. You hardly ever stop, which is why being a student at somewhere like the Academy is so important. The only period of your musical life when you'll have the space to reflect and to learn without being pursued by professional 'demons' is while you are still in education.

JF-A: What lessons did you learn in later life that you wished you'd learned earlier?

JB: I wish I'd learned to control my nerves. They haunted me until the last note of the last bar of the last work that I performed. The older you get, the more responsible you feel for younger colleagues. They don't expect you to show any professional frailty. They are the ones who are feeling nervous and look to you for support. As you don't want to let people down, situations like that can be very difficult.

JF-A: But do you think that conflicting emotions such as these added in some way to the performances that you gave?

JB: They say that you don't need nerves, but, of course, you do. Unfortunately, the vocal instrument is such that any kind of vulnerability will be reflected by it. You are at its mercy. A singer is not a machine, and the most vital part of your equipment can be affected by nerves. And it's so cruel to me that we are made this way. I never found the answer, which is why it was such a relief when I could wake up some mornings and think that I didn't have to sing that day. Yet it's now a terrible kind of death, knowing that I'll never be able to perform great works again. It's a death that I've had to come to terms with. It's a frightening thing to get up in front of the public, no matter what the circumstances are.

JF-A: What role does an agent play in the day-to-day life of a singer?

JB: I don't know any more, as I was part of an older system. The values were different then, and there wasn't the pressure that exists now. I honed my repertoire and technique throughout my working life, and was able to do this because I didn't have that pressure. Everything was more measured, and you grew technically and interpretatively as time went on. I'm not sure that's possible any more. When leaving somewhere like the Academy, it seems to me that young singers have to enter the profession fully armed, even though that's not possible. Yet if you know the material that you're supposed to sing thoroughly before your first orchestral or operatic rehearsal, nothing will disturb you. If you know your stuff, it's a rock to build on.

JF-A: As your pearls of wisdom ring so true, have you ever considered teaching in a major conservatoire?

JB: I do teach, and have given masterclasses from time to time. But I have a few concerns about them, as they can create difficulties for some singers. If you're on stage with somebody you've never met before, particularly a 'distinguished somebody', it's a formidable thing for the young person concerned. I prefer a one-to-one exploration of a score. If you are able to delve deeply into the music, and can truly come to terms with what's on the page, you then have a very powerful sense of what's involved. As not everybody does this, it can be a very rare approach. I'm not suggesting that it's impossible to achieve valuable things at a masterclass, but it's not really something for me. I like to take a great deal of time working with the scores and identifying the problems that might arise. When I'm learning a work for the first time, I like to memorise it away from the keyboard. And it's always advisable to begin studying a work a year before you have to perform it. It's also advisable to do your own translations of foreign languages. This allows you to see when the translations of others are not correctly following the musical line, and where they differ from the placement of the original language. All this is a great help.

JF-A: How do you deal with the two potentially conflicting issues of characterising a role and maintaining what is expected of you vocally?

JB: It depends on whether you think that the musical line is more important than the words that you're singing. Somebody like Maria Callas had the courage to temper her sound according to the characters she was portraying. This is a difficult and dangerous thing to do, but also extremely exciting. We're all born with a sound, and even if you don't sing correctly, the sound is yours. This is the marvellous thing about the voice, as nobody else in the world sounds exactly like you. We protect this by technique, which can beautify your natural sound to a certain extent. You can then characterise mentally, and the voice will respond to that. If your thought processes are strong enough, and if you believe in the character fully, these will colour the voice. But, if the truth be known, I absolutely hate listening to my own voice. When I listen back to the recordings that I made, I always find things that I could have done differently. Nevertheless, singing is a personal journey that gives inner joy. And if you have the opportunity to pass on that joy to other people, or simply do it for your own delight, what a lucky human being you are.

DAME GWYNETH JONES
(DAVID JOSEFOWITZ RECITAL HALL, 27 SEPTEMBER 2013)

RAYMOND HOLDEN: I am very keen to explore the phenomenon that is Dame Gwyneth Jones. Many singers have been good actors, many have had fabulous techniques, and many have had beautiful voices, but only very few have become iconic figures who attract adoring and devoted audiences wherever they appear. You are one such figure. Why do you think that is?

GWYNETH JONES: Well, what can I say! Maybe it's because I have such a large repertoire. I sing just about all the operas in my range of Wagner, Strauss, Puccini, Verdi, Beethoven and Janáček. In addition, I also sing oratorio and regularly give *Lieder* recitals. I'm very grateful to have been able to perform these roles at their 'source', so to speak. I've regularly sung the operas of Strauss in Vienna and Munich, and the music-dramas of Wagner at Bayreuth. I have frequently sung my Italian roles in Milan, Florence, Verona and Rome, where I performed *Aida* with Sir John Barbirolli in the Teatro dell'Opera in 1969. The same is true of my French roles, which I have sung in Paris. Audience members in these cities regularly travel from theatre to theatre and become friends, often staying in each other's homes. Fans from New York stay with fans in Vienna, and vice versa. They then all meet at the stage door, where they wait patiently for autographs. It's like one big, happy family that stretches across the globe. And as there are so many different composers, the fans' interests are equally diverse.

RH: Many great singers came from families who worked hard, and who were not afraid to call a spade a spade. This was certainly the case for Kathleen Ferrier, Dame Janet Baker, Dame Kiri Te Kanawa and Yvonne Minton. Was this also true of you, and, if so, how did you go about supporting yourself financially during your early years as a singer?

GJ: I came from a normal, working-class Welsh family. Unfortunately, I lost my mother when I was only three: she died from tuberculosis at the age of twenty-eight. This meant that I had to grow up without a mother, which was a great shame. Then, my father died when I was eighteen, only one hour before I received the letter notifying me that I'd been accepted to the Royal College of Music. This was quite difficult for me. I had been working as a secretary in an iron and steel foundry for a few years. In fact, I was the only secretary at the foundry, which meant that I did everything. In addition to shorthand typing and bookkeeping, I lit the fire, made the coffee and operated the telephone. I also weighed the lorries, bandaged the workers when they had accidents and organised the payroll. But this was great, as it prepared me for whatever life might throw at me. There was no television during my childhood, and telephones had to be wound up before they would operate. We didn't even have a gramophone at home. I knew nothing about concerts, and had never heard of opera. But I was always singing. Everybody sings in Wales, and that's why it's called the 'Land of Song'. When I moved to London, I used to make ends meet by working every evening at the Moo-Cow Milk Bar in Baker Street, and by living at the YWCA. I used to walk through the park to the Royal College of Music each day, as I couldn't afford the bus fare. I never had lunch, but I always seemed to

PART TWO: SINGERS

have more money than the other students. Maybe this was because I used to travel to Wales every Saturday where I would perform in a *Messiah*, or would give a concert.

When I was quite small, my father worked at the Girling's factory, and during the Second World War he was an air-raid warden. This meant that he didn't have to join up. Because he had two little girls to raise, life was quite hard for him. While he was at Girling's, my father organised concerts and dances, and brought down many of the big bands from London to play. One day, he said that there was going to be a concert at the factory, and asked whether I would like to go to it. It was a small children's choir. I was absolutely blown away by this, and was particularly impressed by the fact that they had dressed up and were acting out some of the songs. I knew instantly that that was what I wanted to do. It was my very first experience of seeing somebody sing and act simultaneously. I thought, 'I absolutely have to get into this choir.' But, before this, I had already begun to have singing lessons with a girl down the road, and went every Saturday to compete in the local eisteddfod. I was often lucky enough to win first prize, which was two and sixpence and a little crocheted badge that was hung around my neck. I also used to compete in the duet section at the local eisteddfod with another girl who had the same teacher. One day, I went along to my singing lesson and noticed that everybody was looking a bit gloomy. My teacher then said, 'I am afraid that today is going to be your last singing lesson, as I am not going to be teaching any more.' But as Jean, the girl with whom I sang duets, was so good, she was told that she was going to continue having lessons with our teacher's teacher. As I was no longer going to be singing duets, I thought it wasn't worth me going on. This gave me such a complex, as I felt that I wasn't even good enough to train as a singer.

I then thought that I wouldn't be accepted into the choir, so I persuaded a girlfriend's sister to smuggle me in. The conductor was a lady called Mrs Frieda Martin-Fullard and I sang everything that was put in front of me. But I was so intense when singing that I fainted one hot night. As I was coming to, I heard, 'Who is this horrible girl who's disturbing my rehearsal by fainting? And she's not *even* supposed to be here!' Nevertheless, I was accepted into the choir, and later performed in a group from it called Girls in Harmony. We were scheduled to sing at a working-men's club one night, but most of the soloists were ill, so we were all then asked, 'Who can sing an aria, any aria?' The others all piped up and said, 'Gwyneth can.' Mrs Martin-Fullard asked me what I could sing. The only thing that I could think of was 'I Love the Moon, I Love the Sun'. It was a big success and I had to sing it a second time. When she asked me who I was studying with, I said, 'I am not good enough to have singing lessons.' She then offered to teach me, and that's how it all started. Later, I went to another singing teacher who helped me get to London.

RH: In London, you trained at the Royal College of Music before enrolling at the Accademia Musicale Chigiana in Siena. What was life like at the College and the Accademia, and in what ways did their understanding of singing technique differ?

GJ: Their approaches to vocal technique were quite, quite different. I was delighted to be accepted by the College, and although I had had singing lessons, and had gained some experience by taking part in eisteddfods, I had done very little counterpoint and harmony. When I came to London, everything changed dramatically for me. All of a sudden, I was presented with marvellous orchestras and the Royal Opera House, Covent Garden. This meant that I could go to the opera, where I'd never been to before. I also attended the College's Opera School during my second year there. I hadn't planned to go into the

PART TWO: SINGERS

Opera School at that time, and had intended to enter it a year later. But as the person who was singing the role of La Zia Principessa in their production of Puccini's *Suor Angelica* couldn't quite manage it, they asked me if I could quickly jump in and take over. I studied the role in two days and then sang for the first time on an operatic stage. With the Opera School, I also sang Hänsel from Humperdinck's *Hänsel und Gretel*, which I thought was marvellous. I had to run around in bare feet, with patches on my trousers. I was in heaven! We then gave Bizet's *Carmen*, before finishing the course with Gluck's *Orfeo ed Euridice* in English.

I was then given a scholarship to go to Siena, where I studied with Giorgio Favaretto. As he led the *Lieder* classes, we didn't do any opera at all with him, simply *Lieder*. He was lovely, and he had all the students sit around in a big circle. He would then have each of us stand and sing in front of the class. This was a very good thing. One day, he said that he wasn't sure which student should perform at the class's final concert, and asked me to learn Dvořák's *Zigeunerlieder* by the next day. I stayed up all night and studied the songs in the bathroom. I've always been someone who just gets what's needed done. This meant that I was able to sing at the concert. Although the Accademia Chigiana was different from what I thought it would be, it was helpful for my Italian language skills. After Siena, I won a Boyce Foundation Scholarship that took me to Zurich.

RH: Was this when you joined the Opera Studio there?

GJ: Yes. It was a new era at the Opernhaus Zürich, which was called the Stadttheater at the time. When I knew that I was going to Zurich, I decided to have a couple of German lessons in London first. But when I arrived in Switzerland, to my horror, everybody spoke *Schwiizerdütsch*.

Half the time I didn't understand what was being said. While I was in Zurich, I travelled by train to Geneva every weekend for singing lessons with Maria Carpi. This was something of a challenge, as I had no money. The Austrian-born director Herbert Graf was at the Stadttheater during this period, and he had brought with him a number of American singers, including James McCracken, with whom I later recorded Verdi's *Otello* under Barbirolli, and his wife, Sandra Warfield. The Iranian-born director Lotfi Mansouri, who later became General Director of the San Francisco Opera, was also at the theatre and worked with us at the Opera Studio.

RH: How long did you remain at the Opera Studio?

GJ: I only stayed for three months instead of a year. At the end of those three months, we gave a student performance of scenes from *Orfeo ed Euridice* and Verdi's *Aida*. As I was a mezzo-soprano at the time, I sang Amneris in the Verdi excerpts. The theatre was filled with agents and opera managers from Germany, and after the performance I was offered contracts for Bremen, Ulm and several other places that I'd never heard of. Not knowing what to do, I approached Dr Graf. I told him that I'd been offered all these opportunities and asked for his advice. To my surprise, he offered me a contract for Zurich, and then listed the roles that he wanted me to sing the following season.

RH: When Graf offered you that contract, was he engaging you as a mezzo-soprano?

GJ: Yes. In fact, many dramatic sopranos start as mezzos. This is a good thing, as you build the middle and bottom of your voice while avoiding pushing the top. This means that you are not singing top Cs too soon. There's a very narrow margin between being a dramatic mezzo and being a dramatic soprano. It's whether you can hold the *tessitura* above E, F and G that matters. If you are happy to dance around this region of the voice, you can go up from there. Even though my singing teachers in both London and Geneva had been telling me for some time that I was actually a soprano, I said that we should wait, and let the transition happen slowly and naturally. But it was when Lotfi Mansouri was directing Meyerbeer's *Le prophète* at the Stadttheater that things began to change. While still a student at the Opera Studio there, I was asked to study Fidès's aria, an incredible work with difficult *coloratura* passages, and with high notes that go up to top C. As it was no problem for me to reach those notes, my singing teacher was happy for me to do it. I just loved singing the top Cs. When word got around that I was working on the aria, Herbert Graf came to see me perform it in class. He was so impressed that he told me that he wanted me to sing the role as part of the second cast in the main theatre. The only problem was that McCracken was cast in the leading role, and his wife was performing Fidès. This was neither pleasant nor easy. I arrived early for my first rehearsal, and was already seated and ready to go at 9.45am. When McCracken came in at 10am, he looked at me and said, 'What's *she* doing here?' Lotfi then explained that I would be singing the part in the second cast. McCracken then barked, 'Either she goes, or I do.' So, I left!

In Zurich, I was scheduled to sing the mezzo-soprano role of Czipra in Johann Strauss II's *Der Zigeunerbaron*. One night, the soprano who was performing Saffi, Adele Leigh, asked me to sing her chorus material for her, as she felt unwell. I thought that this was a wonderful idea. In the audience that evening was the conductor Nello Santi. The next day, he grabbed me by the arm, took me into a room, and made me sing a whole series of phrases. As I didn't yet know the soprano repertoire, I'd no idea what I was doing. But I was singing one top C after another, and having a wonderful time. He then said, '*Basta*. You will never sing with me as a mezzo again.' Instead of singing Ulrica and Azucena, he told me to go away and study Amelia from Verdi's *Un ballo in maschera*. He wanted me to prepare her two arias, and to sing them on the stage for him the following week. I did what he asked, and was then given the role in the second cast. Sir Rudolf Bing was in the audience for one of the performances, and at the end of the evening, he sent the agent Alfred Dietz rushing around to my dressing room to ask me to meet him in his hotel for breakfast the following morning. When I arrived, Bing said that he enjoyed my performance the previous night, and that he would like me to come to the Metropolitan Opera in New York. He then asked me for my repertoire list. 'You heard it last night' was my answer. As I'd literally just changed my *tessitura*, it was the only soprano role I knew!

RH: In 1963, you made your debut at the Royal Opera House, Covent Garden. Were you engaged there as a mezzo-soprano or a soprano?

GJ: Although I never got the chance to sing Fidès's aria on the Zurich stage, I sang it, along with 'O don fatale' from Verdi's *Don Carlo*, for Sir Georg Solti when I auditioned for Covent Garden. I explained to Sir Georg that I had thought of becoming a soprano, but was not quite sure when I should make the change. He then said in his marvellous Hungarian accent, 'Yes, my dear. I can hear it.' And even though I told him that I'd be content with some of the smaller roles in that register, it turned out that they'd already been cast. This meant that I was given parts like Wellgunde in Wagner's *Das Rheingold* and *Götterdämmerung*, Sister Mathilde in Poulenc's *Les dialogues des Carmélites* and Rosette in Massenet's *Manon*. Then, in 1964, I sang my first major soprano role at the Royal Opera House: Leonore in Verdi's *Il trovatore*. Leontyne Price was originally cast in the part, and I was asked to be her cover. To prepare for this, I was sent to study with Luigi Ricci in Rome, a coach who had also worked with Leontyne. Two days before the rehearsals were scheduled to begin in London, Luigi suggested that I should sing the whole role for the production's conductor, Carlo Maria Giulini, who was also in Rome. I did this, and flew to London the following day. That was the Sunday night, and on the Monday morning at 8am, Sir David Webster telephoned me to say that Leontyne had just cancelled. He said that they weren't sure who should take over the part at first, but when they spoke to Giulini, he said that he'd just heard me in Rome and thought that I would be great for the role. And that's how I made my soprano debut as Leonore in *Il trovatore*.

RH: In 1966, Bayreuth came calling. How did that come about?

GJ: Solti said that he would like me to sing Sieglinde in Wagner's *Die Walküre* during the 1965–6 season, but the company had no stage-rehearsal time to prepare me for the part. He intended to 'slot me in', so to speak. As the director was going to be Hans Hotter, Covent Garden sent me to work with him at his home in Munich. Hotter's dining room was soon transformed into Hunding's hut, and it was there that I learned the production in a week. He was so wonderful, and at the end of our time together, he said, 'I am going to Bayreuth tomorrow, and I am going to take you with me.' He then also said, 'I'd like you to sing for both Wieland and Wolfgang Wagner.' So, I had the great honour of being driven to Bayreuth by Hans Hotter. As this was something of a surprise opportunity, I wasn't sure what I should sing. But as I had been preparing Senta from Wagner's *Die fliegende Holländer*, I decided to sing her 'Ballade'. I also thought that I would sing 'D'amor sull'ali rosee' from *Il trovatore*. And that's what I did. I sang the 'Ballade' and a Verdi aria in Wagner's Festspielhaus! I was then offered the role of Sieglinde at the 1966 festival.

RH: For those of us who are not singers, what's the difference technically between singing Sieglinde and Brünnhilde, a role with which you are now particularly associated.

GJ: There is no difference. You should sing Sieglinde first, as it lies very comfortably. You then need experience to be able to perform the immensely long role of Brünnhilde. I always insisted on continuing to sing Italianate roles throughout my career. That way, I avoided being constantly forced into singing only the bigger, more dramatic parts. You must always try to keep the voice light and flexible. But there *is* a difference between the 'three Brünnhildes'. In *Die Walküre*, you must have a top C that is as safe as houses. You can't be afraid of that, and you must always warm the voice up really well. This is because you go straight on stage and the sound has to be brilliant. It requires a tremendous effort and great energy. Then comes the lower part: the 'Todesverkündigung'. For this, it is very important to have a very solid middle voice. And it's essential to develop your *piano* singing. This is essential if you want to have a long career. After *Die Walküre* comes *Siegfried*'s Brünnhilde. You start singing this part very late in the evening, and often have to lie on stage for a long period surrounded by smoke. Not only must you try not to cough, but you must be radiant. And you should place the voice as if you are singing *Il trovatore*.

RH: Does the radiance required in *Siegfried* carry over into *Götterdämmerung*?

GJ: *Götterdämmerung* has everything. If you can sing *Die Walküre* and *Siegfried*, you can sing *Götterdämmerung*. It's no problem. It's a matter of energy, and you have to have the power to be able to stand for long periods of time. A pair of comfortable shoes can be a great help! Before singing

Brünnhilde at Bayreuth, Wolfgang Wagner had been asking me for years to perform the role, as he didn't have a singer who was suitable for it. And every year I would say, 'No. Not yet, Wolfgang. I'm not quite ready.'

RH: Was it difficult to refuse Wolfgang Wagner so regularly?

GJ: You have to be able to do this throughout your career. During my second season at Covent Garden, I sang the Fourth Maid in Strauss's *Elektra* under Rudolf Kempe. And I'll never forget how the curtain swished up with the dramatic Agamemnon Motive. I'd never been so scared in my life, and I thought that I was going to drop dead on stage! That particular Maid never stops running about. Then Kempe said, 'Will you sing Elektra for me?' I told him that I was much too young to sing the part: I actually waited twenty years before I did so. When I walked onto the Probebühne of the Bayerische Staatsoper many years later to rehearse Beethoven's *Fidelio* with him, he said touchingly, 'Ah, there's my Fourth Maid.' It was incredible that he still remembered that I had sung such a small role with him all those years earlier.

RH: But to return to *Götterdämmerung*, how did you cope with its huge dimensions?

GJ: Before I finally agreed to sing Brünnhilde for Wolfgang, I had sung the title role in Strauss's *Salome* in Hamburg. This is a big sing, particularly the Final Scene. And it was during that scene one night that I thought, 'Now I can sing Brünnhilde.' I just knew that I could do it. But when Wolfgang asked me to perform the role in *Die Walküre* the following year at Bayreuth, I still said 'no'. As I had been singing Sieglinde in the same production for five years, I felt that it wouldn't be fair to the public if I suddenly switched roles. He then asked me if I was prepared to sing it in *Siegfried*. Again, I said 'no', as the part was too short. But I *was* prepared to perform Brünnhilde in *Götterdämmerung*. As I knew by then that I could sing all three Brünnhildes, I wanted to tackle the longest one first.

RH: You also sang the role of Kundry at Bayreuth. What was that like?

GJ: Performing in *Parsifal* at Bayreuth was particularly special. In the Third Act, I only had '*Dienen, Dienen*' to sing, but the acting had to be sublime. When I washed the feet and dried them with my hair, tears always rolled down my cheeks. And during the *Karfreitagszauber*, the bat always came down and flew around us in circles: there was a bat living in the Festspielhaus, and we said that Richard Wagner's soul was descending upon us. It was Wieland Wagner's production of the work, which was just incredible. His use of lighting was always marvellous. When the bat did descend, it would circle around us before flying into the audience. But, sadly, some nights the curtain came down before it was able to return to the stage.

RH: How would you describe your approach to Kundry?

GJ: What I find so important in this role is how the music and the words are combined. One must have a deep feeling for the words. The way that you express them, and your vision of them, is so important. When I work with young people, I get very annoyed if they haven't taken the trouble to translate each word. This is essential if they're to understand the text's inner meaning. They shouldn't listen to other people's recordings of Wagner's operas and music-dramas. Instead, they should find their own way of expressing the works' contents. You must always 'do your own thing'.

PART TWO: SINGERS

RH: One of your more remarkable achievements at Bayreuth was your performance of both Venus and Elisabeth in Götz Friedrich's 1972 production of *Tannhäuser*. How did you go about preparing the two roles?

GJ: Götz wanted Venus and Elisabeth to be one and the same person. They were to be two sides of the same coin, with Venus being the sexual side and Elisabeth the holy side. Of course, Elisabeth is very lyrical, while Venus is very dramatic. But if you have a solid technique, you should be able to do anything with your voice. The biggest problem was changing costumes, as the wigs and make-up were quite different. Thankfully, there is an extended interval at Bayreuth, so I was able to make some of these changes without too much difficulty.

RH: For Wagner fans worldwide, your portrayal of Brünnhilde in Patrice Chéreau's Bayreuth production of *Der Ring des Nibelungen* remains a special memory. Why do you think that production was not only so iconic, but also so contentious?

GJ: One of the reasons why that particular *Ring* was such a scandal at first was because the public had become used to the productions of Wieland and Wolfgang Wagner. The audiences were very sceptical of what they might be offered by Patrice. Wieland worked in a very minimal way with an emphasis on lighting. He placed his characters on a disc, clad them in gold and leather and had them make very grand arm gestures. Chéreau had a much more natural approach. Whether it was brutality or love, he showed the characters' emotions, and allowed them to touch each other. Previously, that had been forbidden. In Wolfgang's production of *Götterdämmerung*, I was told that under no circumstances should I look anywhere but straight ahead while singing 'Heil, Heil, Heil' as Siegfried was about to leave for his new adventures. In

Patrice's production, we touched one another and rolled on the floor. It was very moving. And the way that Wotan killed Siegmund was extremely disturbing for the public.

RH: Surely, the audiences' outrage at Chéreau's production was disingenuous, as they were equally shocked by Wieland Wagner's minimal production of the *Ring* in the 1950s.

GJ: I suppose it was because Patrice's reading was modern in a different way. Yet I didn't think that was the case at first, as my costume seemed to be quite normal. It was only at the first dress rehearsal that I suddenly realised that the men were in tuxedos and modern dress. In fact, the production was a combination of the modern and the traditional. It was probably how the characters revealed their emotions that the public found unnerving. Previously, they'd always thought that the gods were magnificent, and it had never occurred to them what terrible people they were. For them, it was fine to murder your own son, provided you remained beautiful as a god. The audience didn't want to see their gods diminished.

RH: In her memoires, the great German soprano Frida Leider described the substantial musical and theatrical differences that existed between German and Italian opera houses during the first decades of the twentieth century. What differences did you experience when you made your debut at Milan's Teatro alla Scala in 1967 as Leonora in *Il trovatore*, and how did that theatre's audience respond to you when you famously sang *Salome* there in 1974?

GJ: One big difference between Italian and German opera houses is the claque. This is where some artists pay members of the audience either to applaud them or to heckle someone else. Of course, I'd heard of it, but had never experienced it before. And when a chap came to my dressing room and said, '*Io sono il capo della claque*' ('I am the head of the claque'), I sent him away. He wanted to be paid. I was determined to earn my applause, and if I were to receive it, it was because the audience had enjoyed what I'd done. German singers won't pay the claque, and this is a problem for the Italians. The production of *Salome* that I performed in at Milan was by Jürgen Rose. This still exists in Vienna and can still be seen there. In fact, I sang in the production again recently, but this time as Herodias: I have moved on to being Salome's mother these days! Rose's production is very beautiful, but the Italians couldn't understand it. When I appeared in a flowing white dress with little white flowers in my long ringlets, the Milanese thought, 'What kind of Salome is this?' I know that, because they told me afterwards. During the 'Tanz', I developed Salome's naïve, spoilt character into a monster. To prepare for this, I worked with both a belly dancer and a ballet dancer.

RH: You're also a distinguished Octavian and a much admired Marschallin in *Der Rosenkavalier*, very different roles that demand very different vocal timbres and *tessituras*. How did you bridge those gaps, and what, for you, are the keys to performing these roles successfully?

GJ: My journey with *Der Rosenkavalier* actually started with Annina, as I always liked beginning with the small roles first. When I received a prize at the Royal College of Music, the score that I chose as my reward was *Der Rosenkavalier*. Being a poor student at the time, I thought, 'Which is the most expensive score, and which will I use the most?' Before singing the Marschallin, I performed Annina in Zurich, followed by Octavian. I did the latter first with the Royal Opera on tour in Manchester and Coventry when Covent Garden was closed for renovation, and then in a new production at the Vienna Staatsoper. This was followed by my first Marschallin in yet another new production, this time at the Bayerische Staatsoper.

RH: Were those transitions easy?

GJ: Everything's in the music. If you listen to the music, it tells you exactly how you should feel and how you should move. If you do this, you don't really need a director: it's all in the music. And if you observe Hofmannsthal's words, it's again all there. Nevertheless, when performing either Octavian or the Marschallin, you have to be aware of the quick linguistic interplay between the two characters. Having first sung Annina, I became acquainted with the opera. And then by performing Octavian before tackling the Marschallin, I was able to come to terms with the young man's feelings for the older woman. This meant that when I finally came to the Marschallin, I was able to have great empathy with Octavian's complex emotions. These are such wonderful roles, particularly Octavian. He's a boy played by a woman, before becoming a boy dressed as a girl played by a woman. It's just such fun.

RH: Multitasking in Strauss seems to be your specialism. Not only were you marvellous as Octavian and the Marschallin, but you were fêted for singing all three leading female roles in *Elektra*. Presumably, this unique achievement required considerable interpretative and technical versatility. How did you meet these challenges, and how did you go about unlocking the roles' underlying musical and dramatic characteristics?

GJ: I have actually performed four roles in *Elektra*. Don't forget the Fourth Maid that I sang at Covent Garden all those years ago! That was quite important to me. This was followed by Chrysothemis, again at the

PART TWO: SINGERS

Royal Opera House, but under Carlos Kleiber and with Birgit Nilsson in the title role. It was a remarkable night, even though Carlos's *tempi* were so incredibly fast. The same was often true of his readings of *Der Rosenkavalier*. Sometimes, I couldn't believe that I was singing so quickly. My transition into the role of Elektra was quite strange. When I was a student in Zurich, but having singing lessons in Geneva, I once went to see *Elektra* at the Grand Théâtre de Genève. It made me ill. For days afterwards, I felt that I never wanted to see the opera again. The scene between Klytaemnestra and Elektra made me feel physically sick. But when I was in my apartment in Vienna one night some years later and switched on the television – this was after I sang Chrysothemis at Covent Garden – there was a Greek play being broadcast. Even though I had no idea what it was, I was soon mesmerised by it. Suddenly, I realised that it was *Elektra*. This was a totally different *Elektra* and it was a complete revelation. I then understood that she need not be quite as neurotic as she is often portrayed on the operatic stage. She has love, and is a really wonderful character.

RH: And, of course, the role requires great vocal stamina.

GJ: You are on stage from the beginning of the opera to the end. You start with Elektra's monologue, and towards the middle of the piece you have that marvellous scene with Orest. If you have the possibility of being able to sing this *piano*, it's like medicine for the voice. And as I was able to do this, I was never tired at the end of the opera.

RH: In 1970, you performed Leonore in Beethoven's *Fidelio* at the Theater an der Wien with Leonard Bernstein. That year, you also recorded it on DVD with Karl Böhm at the Deutsche Oper Berlin. How would you describe Bernstein's and Böhm's approaches to the score, and what were some of the differences between Otto Schenk's Vienna production and that of Gustav Rudolf Sellner in Berlin?

GJ: I was only twenty-seven when I sang in those productions. We recorded it with Karl Böhm in Dresden, and they created a special set for the Dungeon Scene; the rest was filmed on the stage of the Deutsche Oper Berlin. The set was quite simple, and the Dungeon Scene on the DVD is much better than the one that we used on stage. Böhm was very precise as a conductor and had a small beat. He would only glance at you from time to time, but you knew exactly what *tempo* he wanted. He was like a metronome, and his speeds never changed. He was a very grumpy man who had the habit of picking on individuals. He even tried to pick on me in the Quintet from Wagner's *Die Meistersinger von Nürnberg* at Bayreuth in 1968. He screamed in German, 'You're dragging', and went on and on about this until the break. We thought that that was the end of it until he announced that he wanted to do the Quintet again. Everybody, including the whole chorus, were on stage by this point. To have redone the whole thing would have been the end of me, so I decided to trick him by singing it too fast. He then began to scream again in German, 'It's too fast!' So, I walked very slowly down to the footlights and said, '*Liebe* Herr Dr Böhm, I just wanted to show you that I can sing fast as well as slow.' This brought a big smile to his face. You just have to know how to deal with situations like that.

Otto Schenk's production of *Fidelio* can still be seen at the Vienna Staatsoper. He did such marvellous work as a director. And when the drawbridge came down at the end of Act Two, there was a tumult of joy from everybody on stage. In Berlin, where I was singing with James King, we were looking towards the front of the stage at this point. Then, suddenly, and as if from nowhere, there came from behind us an unbelievably beautiful voice: it was Martti Talvela as the King's Minister.

PART TWO: SINGERS

This was at the exact moment when I had to turn around and hand him the key. As I turned, I was struck by the magnificence of his white costume. He looked like a god. I'll never forget his beautiful voice and his wonderful appearance. But to return to Vienna. Lenny Bernstein was much more exuberant than Böhm. While Böhm hardly moved, Bernstein always gave big gestures. Whatever you did with Lenny, you always went away feeling that he had written the music. With him, there was only one way of doing a work. I particularly remember one rehearsal at the Theatre an der Wien. It was 10am and Lenny was ready to go. We started doing the little Trio in Act One, and there was Bernstein jumping up and down with arms outstretched. He then leapt so high that he jumped over the conductor's rostrum and landed in the first violins. He literally took off and flew through the air. I couldn't believe it.

RH: I suspect the first violins couldn't believe it, either.

GJ: You never knew what might happen next when working with Lenny. For the 1970 production, he also insisted on inserting a passage from *Leonore*, Beethoven's first version of the opera. This material is quite, quite different from the later, better-known version. I once took part in a series of performances where *Leonore* and *Fidelio* alternated on subsequent nights. In the end, I had no idea whether I was singing right or wrong! The operas take some very different musical and dramatic turns. When Lenny conducted the Dungeon Scene in *Fidelio*, he took such incredibly fast speeds that you just had to fly with him. He added a very exciting, but difficult, top C at the end of the ensemble where I pull out my pistol and sing '*und Du bis Tod!*' Then, he cut Florestan's words '*Meine Leonore, was hast du für mich getan!*' and Leonore's reply, '*Nichts, nichts, mein Florestan!*' This is a moment I just love, and a chance to catch your breath. But Lenny plunged straight into '*O namenlose Freude*'.

This was not uncommon for him. When we performed Mahler's Eighth Symphony together at the Royal Albert Hall, I remember that he came on to the stage at the rehearsal and wanted me to change parts with the other soprano, and for some of the other soloists to do the same. As we were recording the work the following evening, I said, 'Lenny, we can't do that.' But as he was such an incredible musician, he couldn't understand why that was a problem, and why we were only prepared to sing the parts that we'd learned: as the vocal lines are so different, you have to put them into your voice.

RH: Sadly, the DVD of the Vienna production is not with you as Leonore, but with Gundula Janowitz.

GJ: Yes, that is a pity, as those performances in Vienna were such an unbelievable success. But as some of my colleagues and I had already done it with Böhm on DVD, and as we had signed a contract with Deutsche Grammophon, we were unavailable to do it with Lenny. This meant that he was forced to have another cast for his DVD, which he was very upset about.

RH: Verdi and Wagner have been at the heart of your repertoire from the start of your career. But you are also a distinguished interpreter of Puccini's music, and have sung his works to great acclaim in Britain, Europe and North America. Is it true that you spent time studying the role of Turandot with Dame Eva Turner, a much admired interpreter of the part, before singing it for the Royal Opera House at the Olympic Arts Festival in Los Angeles in 1984?

GJ: Yes, that's true. Although I'd met Dame Eva only once before our sessions together, I thought it would be a good idea to speak with her, as she might be able to give me some tips about the role. We didn't actually work on vocal technique, but visiting her was quite an experience. She was a wonderful lady, and we later became very close friends. When I was working with her, she would always come up to her music room at 10am where I'd already be waiting. Being very frugal, the room was freezing, and she'd often say, 'Turn off the light, dear.' I also noticed that she was constantly using big powder puffs, and that her spectacles were always full of powder. This meant that she had trouble seeing the music when she played the piano. I would inevitably offer to clean her glasses, and when her vision was clear, she would hit a chord and shout 'immediately!' She did this so loudly that I was practically unable to produce a sound because of the shock. She stressed vocal attack, especially in passages such as 'In questa reggia', and was very particular about how the letter 'r' was pronounced. She had an incredible memory, and was great fun. I invited her to come with me to Los Angeles for the premiere of the Royal Opera House's production, which was given there before being seen in London the following season.

RH: Along with your work as a singer, you have gained something of a reputation as a stage, television and movie actress. First, let's chat briefly about your one-woman shows *O, Malvina!* and *Die Frau im Schatten*.

GJ: *O, Malvina!* was written by the journalist and critic Klaus Geitel. It's quite an interesting play, as it tells the story of Malvina Schnorr von Carolsfeld, Wagner's first Isolde. I performed it in costume, and read her letters to King Ludwig II and others on stage. The play also looked at her associations with Richard and Cosima Wagner, and was interspersed with extracts from the composer's operas and music-dramas sung by me. It really was an incredible show, and we toured with it extensively. We gave it in German, Italian, French and Catalan. When we performed it at Dresden, Klaus told me that Malvina was buried in one of the city's older graveyards. And when we went there, we discovered to our amazement that Minna, Wagner's first wife, was buried next to her.

RH: And what of *Die Frau im Schatten*?

GJ: This was about Pauline Strauss, the wife of Richard Strauss, and the idea of her being in the shadow of the composer is quite important historically.

RH: You also played the part of Malvina Schnorr von Carolsfeld in Tony Palmer's epic television series *Wagner*. This series also starred Richard Burton, Sir Ralph Richardson, Sir John Gielgud and Sir Laurence Olivier. More recently, you made a guest appearance in Dustin Hoffman's film *Quartet*, a hugely successful movie that attracted a wide and enthusiastic audience.

GJ: Dustin's movie was great fun to do, and I will never forget going into the breakfast room on the first morning. It was full of old colleagues and you really did feel like you were in a home for aging musicians! I remember being tapped on the shoulder from behind and being asked who I was. It was an old friend, but it took us both a little time before we recognised each other.

RH: In 2003, you made your debut as an opera director with Wagner's *Der fliegende Holländer* at the Deutsches Nationaltheater Weimar. How would you describe your approach as a director?

GJ: I really did enjoy the experience, and would love to produce more operas. Even though I have sung the role of Senta many times over the years, I began to look at the text differently as a director. Take Erik's dream, for example. Instead of having him on top of a mountain and dreaming of a stranger, I did it so that he actually sees the two ships arrive. He then runs back to Senta and informs her of this. And what of all those ladies who didn't remain true to the Dutchman before Senta? As they couldn't die, my solution was to have them all appear on his ship. This then reflects what the Dutchman says in the text. When I went to the management to ask how many extras I could have to play these parts, I was told that I could have as many as I needed, as they weren't very expensive to engage. But when I asked about the costumes for the twenty-five women I wanted, I was told that the theatre didn't have sufficient funds to clothe them. I said, 'That's fine, as they are all going to be naked!' Word then got around that I was going to have twenty-five naked women on stage. But as I only had their arms rising out of the sea mist and nothing else, nobody saw any naked bodies in the end. As director, I was also able to help any of the singers who had vocal and diction problems. We had a fabulous Japanese Daland, for example, whose German was not good. I went to the management to ask about arranging language lessons for him, but they said there was no money. This meant that I ended up teaching him myself. I was very careful not to embarrass or to humiliate him, and, by the end, he was delighted to have been helped. It was a great experience.

YVONNE MINTON
(DAVID JOSEFOWITZ RECITAL HALL, 1 MARCH 2013)

RAYMOND HOLDEN: Recently, I re-watched the film of Bruce Beresford's critically acclaimed 1991 production of Strauss's *Elektra* for the State Opera of South Australia in Adelaide. You were simply marvellous as Klytaemnestra in that performance. How, then, did a nice girl from Sydney end up playing one of the composer's least endearing characters?

YVONNE MINTON: Accidentally! It was one of the first times that the company had done it on stage, and it was performed alongside Strauss's *Der Rosenkavalier*.

RH: Adelaide is approximately 1,400 kilometres from Sydney, the city where you were born. But the Sydney of your youth must have been a very different place to the cosmopolitan metropolis that it is today.

YM: It's changed considerably. For a start, we didn't have all the high-rise buildings that now rather spoil the city. It was a wonderful place to grow up in. I was born in 1938 and lived in Earlwood, which meant that it was very easy for me to catch the train to Circular Quay. You could then take the ferry to Taronga Zoo, and to some of the other Sydney sights.

RH: When did the citizens of Earlwood realise that the young Yvonne Minton had talent?

PART TWO: SINGERS

YM: I don't think that they did, and probably still don't. But they may well have thought that I did well.

RH: Yet they must have been proud of the fact that you were a student at the New South Wales State Conservatorium, then the Southern Hemisphere's premiere music school.

YM: I studied with Marjorie Walker from the age of thirteen, the only teacher that I had in Australia. But she taught me privately and not at the 'Con', as the Conservatorium is known locally. I did do a number of courses there, however, such as music history. I also took an acting course at the Conservatorium, which was very interesting. It was taught by the husband of Googie Withers, John McCallum. I'd never met anyone from the theatre before, and he was rather a dashing chap. He put us through our paces, and I managed to do quite well with some of the movement exercises that he set us. These later came into their own at Covent Garden, particularly for one of my early roles there. I had to wear a gown that had been made for Margreta Elkins, who was much taller than me. As the wardrobe department refused to shorten the dress, I had to put on exceptionally high heels when I wore it on stage. At one point, I had to pivot sharply on those heels, which I did successfully thanks to John McCallum's coaching. It was considered rather impressive at the time.

RH: Margreta was certainly statuesque, and was once dubbed the 'Doris Day of Australia'. But let's return to post-war Sydney. Who were some of your musical heroes at the time?

YM: My mother and I didn't actually go to performances as such. But we played the ABC – the Australian Broadcasting Commission, as it was called back then – almost non-stop. I had a few recordings of Kathleen Ferrier, as she was one of my favourites. I also loved Marian Anderson's and Risë Stevens's voices. When I went to New York to perform in *Der Rosenkavalier*, I met Risë. It was a fantastic moment, as she had also performed Octavian at the Metropolitan Opera. And I was surprised to see that she was such a little lady.

RH: Who were some of the major artists who visited Sydney during the 1950s, and what are your memories of them?

YM: Victoria de los Ángeles came to sing at the Sydney Town Hall; she was lovely. At that time, the Town Hall was the main concert venue in Sydney.

RH: And, of course, you'd really made it as an Australian artist if you performed there. Did you ever sing at the Town Hall?

YM: I did, but only a few times. And I later gave Mahler's *Das Lied von der Erde* there when I returned home to perform in *Der Rosenkavalier*.

RH: Sir Charles Mackerras always talked about his experiences there as the youngest ever Principal Oboe of the Sydney Symphony Orchestra. And the one recording that he wanted to find from his time with the orchestra was his live performance of 'Flösst, mein Heiland' from Bach's *Weihnachts-Oratorium*. He was the oboist and the young Joan Sutherland was the echo. Were you there, by any chance?

YM: No. But my mother told me that she once stood outside in the street, so that she could hear Dame Nellie Melba sing.

PART TWO: SINGERS

RH: In fact, Melba was born Helen Porter Mitchell in the Melbourne suburb of Richmond, and had changed her name so that she was more closely identified with her hometown.

YM: And don't forget that she had that great dessert, Peach Melba, named after her.

RH: As one of Australia's other great vocal exports, have you had a dessert named after you, perhaps 'Meringue Minton'?

YM: Sadly not.

RH: Both Margreta Elkins and Dame Joan Sutherland have something in common with you: you all won major Australian singing competitions. Dame Joan won the Sun Aria Competition, while Margreta won the Mobil Quest. You, on the other hand, won the Shell Aria Competition in Canberra.

YM: It should be mentioned here that I also shared a prize board with Joan. It was for a competition that was held in the southern-Sydney suburb of Rockdale. And while I won every singing competition imaginable in Australia, not one of them had anything to do with opera. Generally, I entered folk song and sacred music competitions. At the time, my teacher was desperate for me to leave Australia and to travel to Europe. It didn't matter where I went to, as long as I left Australia! She thought that if didn't make the leap at a young age, I wouldn't do it at all. And she was probably right. Although I had saved for my trip overseas, I still entered the Shell Aria Competition. When I got to the final, I had an interview with a Mr Portnoy from Melbourne, who was quite a big name in Australia at the time. During the interview, I said that it really didn't matter if I won nothing at the competition, as I'd already saved enough to go to Europe. Being quite impressed by that, he decided *not* give the prize money to somebody who would buy a new kitchen with it, but that I should have it instead.

RH: Australia has a penchant for competitions of all kinds, and is particularly fond of eisteddfods. At one point, it sponsored more eisteddfods than Wales. Why do you think that is?

YM: I have no idea, but I entered as many of them as I could.

RH: Is it to do with the Australian need to win?

YM: It might well be. Even though the prize itself might have been only a guinea or two, that particular 'carrot' was always dangling before my eyes. You usually had a choice of which prize to accept: it could be a winner's cup, or it could be money. I always chose the guineas. Because of that, I've hardly any physical record of that period of my life. I won nearly every contralto prize, and the same was true for every sacred-song prize. As I used to arrive home sometimes quite late after some of those competitions, my mother would be in bed, and she would say, 'How did you get on, girl?' 'Oh, I got it, Mum' was my reply. But when I eventually arrived in London, it was a vastly different matter.

RH: You landed in Britain in 1961, and studied with Henry Cummings and Joan Cross.

YM: I am not really sure that you can say that I 'studied' with Henry, as he was more like a father figure to me. I don't think that he changed what I did very much, and nor did Joan. She kept telling me that I was not the least bit operatic, and used to say, 'You'll never do opera, my dear.'

PART TWO: SINGERS

RH: Both you and Joan Cross had huge repertoires, and the sheer breadth of works that the two of you performed is simply breathtaking. Was Cross a role model for you in this regard?

YM: No. But I did think that she was a remarkable lady. The very first thing that I did in London was Britten's *The Rape of Lucretia* under James Gaddarn at the City Literary Institute. I'm not sure how I managed to get the part; I suppose I must have auditioned. But unlike singers today, I did very few auditions during my career. And as it happened, the record producer Christopher Raeburn was in the audience for one of the performances. Even though he'd documented a wide repertoire, he had always wanted to record *Der Rosenkavalier*. That was one of his greatest ambitions. He knew exactly the kinds of voices and the type of cast that he wanted, and after hearing me in *The Rape of Lucretia*, he had my voice in mind. And many years later, I did record Strauss's opera with him.

RH: Christopher worked for Decca, as did John Culshaw, who also admired your voice. Consequently, your connection with Decca began soon after you arrived in London, and that connection remained important professionally to you for the rest of your career.

YM: Yes, that's true. In 1962, I was offered the slot on the BBC's *Variety Playhouse* that was reserved for those who were giving their first British broadcast. I've no memory of what I sang, but it was probably something like 'Che farò senza Euridice' by Gluck; I really had no operatic repertoire at the time. They also performed the big duet from Verdi's *Aida* with Heather Harper and Edward Byles that night, during which I sang Amneris's interjections. As the balance was so poor, and as they couldn't hear my voice, I had to get closer and closer to the microphone before I was even vaguely audible. But as a result of that first broadcast, things started to happen for me. John Culshaw asked me to sing Mercédès in a recording of Bizet's *Carmen*. I was really still too green for this, and didn't have the top notes that were needed; I think that the lady who sang the title role dubbed them in for me some time later. And, of course, I couldn't sing the French. I think the engagement was an act of kindness on John's part, and a way of helping a starving Australian. It was the first recording that I ever made.

RH: You are being characteristically modest here, and having recently reread John Culshaw's memoires, I know how highly he thought of you. And by the time of that *Carmen* recording, you had, of course, won the Kathleen Ferrier Prize for 'Best Contralto' at the International Vocalist Competition s'-Hertogenbosch in the Netherlands.

YM: The competition has changed somewhat since 1961. Then, they had different voice categories, and the Kathleen Ferrier Prize was reserved for the altos. It was quite a long process, and I was there for some weeks. But I was fortunate enough to win.

RH: It must have been special winning a prize named after Kathleen Ferrier.

YM: Absolutely. Her voice was the one that I grew up with. And it was after listening to her recording of Mahler's *Das Lied von der Erde* that I sang the work; it was very instrumental in shaping my future.

RH: Why were you attracted to Ferrier's voice?

PART TWO: SINGERS

YM: I'm not sure that I'd like Ferrier's sound so much now, but the 1950s was 'her' period. Having grown up listening to her records, I performed all the folk songs that she did. Being raised in the Presbyterian Church, I was also a church singer, and sang a great many hymns. I still love singing them, and continue to find them exhilarating. As a young musician, I joined the choir of St Stephen's Church in Macquarie Street, Sydney. That was a great experience, and even though most of the solo singing was done by the first soprano, I was able to perform a number of solos there. It had a wonderful congregation and a super minister. I ended up being booked for a lot of weddings at the church, and I also found myself singing for many of the ladies' afternoon-tea sessions. And it was at these that I sang all the material that was associated with Ferrier. The ladies loved it.

RH: Clearly, you were well suited to competitions, but are they something that you would recommend to today's aspiring artists?

YM: No. While they might seem necessary, they are not a good medium. If you win something like the Kathleen Ferrier Prize in Holland, it can be quite an important step. I also tried for the Kathleen Ferrier Award here in London, but had no success. I then decided to stop entering such things, as I was already working and really didn't need to enter any more competitions.

RH: You are now associated with the works of Mozart, Wagner, Mahler and Strauss, but your first big break came through the music of Nicholas Maw. You sang the role of Maggie Dempster at the world premiere of his *One Man Show*.

YM: Joan Cross had been asked to organise the cast for the work, and she chose me for the part. But before my engagement was confirmed, she said, 'I don't think that you are really stage material.' They did offer me the role, however, and I loved it. I just loved it.

RH: Why did she think you were unsuitable? I saw you many times on stage from the late 1970s onwards, and it was clear that you were at home there.

YM: I think it was because I just stood and sang. They probably expected at bit more animation. Today, young singers are fantastic on stage, and the education that they receive would have been of interest to me back then. The only training that I had were the classes that I took with John McCallum, which I mentioned earlier. But I was fortunate enough to have Ande Anderson, who was really kind and helpful, and John Copley at Covent Garden.

RH: After Maw's work, you continued to perform new music, and sang at the premiere of Tippett's *The Knot Garden*. How difficult was that piece?

YM: It was very, very hard. The text can be rather strange, and although Michael was a lovely chap, and could write very theatrical music, *The Knot Garden* wasn't particularly vocal. And, of course, I also sang in his *King Priam* at Covent Garden in 1967 and 1975.

RH: Having made your debut at the Royal Opera House in 1965, you appeared there regularly over the next thirty years. Were your early years with the company a good training ground?

YM: One of the advantages of being a mezzo-soprano is that you are able to do a lot of smaller things to start with. And as I was not thrown in at the deep end at Covent Garden, I was able to build my career slowly.

RH: That was also true for the young Joan Sutherland, who sang some minor roles in Wagner's *Der Ring des Nibelungen* at Covent Garden during her early years.

YM: The company would have had her singing Sieglinde in *Die Walküre* had Richard Bonynge not stepped in.

RH: Is it possible for a young singer today to have such a long-standing relationship with one major company?

YM: I am not sure that they can. Perhaps if you are a male at one of the German houses it's possible. I sang for Sir Georg Solti on several occasions, the first of which was quite early on. This was around the time that I was in contact with John Culshaw. I made a trial recording of Schumann's *Frauen-Liebe und Leben* for him, which was never released. It must have been dreadful. This was followed by the *Carmen* that I mentioned earlier, and a recording of Bellini's *Norma*. For those discs, I sang the role of Clotilda. I remember the sessions, and rehearsing with Joan Sutherland and Marilyn Horne, like it was yesterday. And I am still not sure who had the better top C! I couldn't believe my luck. I only had to sing about six words as Clotilda, but I took heart from the fact that Joan had done the same on Maria Callas's recording of the opera. And it was after this that I first sang for Solti; I was either twenty-three or twenty-four. I was studying with Henry Cummings at the time, and was worried about it. When I discussed the audition with him, he said, 'Just trust your heart. If you think that you are ready to go into a big house like Covent Garden, you do it. But if you have doubts, don't.' So, I did it.

RH: Cummings taught here at the Academy, and had been a student of Harry Plunket Greene.

YM: That's true, and Greene had written a very interesting book about singing naturally. It has nothing to do with squeezing a muscle here, or pushing a muscle there. Nothing like that. You just take a breath to the diaphragm and sing. That's all you have to do.

RH: While at Covent Garden, you were asked to sing *Das Lied von der Erde* for the ballet. And unlikely as the production might seem, it had a very long and successful history at the Royal Opera House. It was first performed there in 1965, and was given for the final time in 2007. The other mezzo-sopranos who were involved in the production included Norma Procter, Helen Watts, Bernadette Greevy and Catherine Wyn-Rogers. Presumably, this must have been challenging logistically. Did you have to sing from the orchestral pit?

YM: No. We sang from the side of the proscenium arch. I gave nine performances of it in total, and by the end of the run, I certainly knew *Das Lied von der Erde*. I wasn't prepared to like the ballet at all, but it was wonderful. Kenneth MacMillan handled it terribly cleverly, not only from a choreographic perspective, but also from a musical one.

RH: One of the conductors whom you performed the piece with was Hans Swarowsky, the teacher of Zubin Mehta and Claudio Abbado amongst others. What was he like to work with?

PART TWO: SINGERS

YM: We never really connected. He was down in the pit, and was consumed by what the dancers were doing. But I don't remember anything bad about the experience.

RH: Ballet conducting is very dancer-centric. Was there any sense that the voices had a similar importance?

YM: That never worried me. I learned to be flexible. It was a case of 'if it works, it works'. Nevertheless, it was a long sing, with the last song – 'Der Abschied' – lasting some thirty minutes.

RH: You later famously recorded *Das Lied von der Erde* with Sir Georg Solti, and it was with him that you made your debut at the Proms in 1965 as the Third Naked Virgin in Schoenberg's *Moses und Aron*. As at Covent Garden, you performed at the series for nearly thirty years, with your last appearance there being in 1994 with Vaughan Williams's *Serenade to Music*. That concert marked the fiftieth anniversary of Sir Henry Wood's death. People always speak of the Proms's 'specialness'. Do you think that there is a special atmosphere at the Proms, and how did you go about coping with the Royal Albert Hall's notoriously tricky acoustics?

YM: I've never been worried by acoustics; I just adapt to the size of the venue in which I am performing. Being a young singer at Covent Garden was really wonderful. In those days, we rehearsed on the main stage. Even piano rehearsals took place in the theatre, and they always sounded terrific. I did that every day for years. That allowed me to come to terms with the acoustic. And when you are in the Royal Albert Hall, you simply have to project. To this day, I am not sure whether or not I was successful at it. The audience *is* very special there, and the atmosphere is like nowhere else in the world.

RH: Why is that?

YM: Because the audience just love it. They are a community that attends year after year. They are like a family; a big family. They are so passionate about the Proms, and that's what you feel when you go on stage.

RH: Your concert history at the Proms is really quite special. Not only did you perform a repertoire that stretched from Monteverdi and Cavalli to Schoenberg and Stravinsky, but you also sang the works of Gilbert and Sullivan with Sir Malcolm Sargent.

YM: Sir Malcolm was truly a dapper man. There wasn't a single hair out of place, and he was always beautifully attired. This meant that you had no alternative but to sit up and take notice of him.

RH: Orchestral players were less than impressed by him personally, but they did admire him technically.

YM: He was wonderful with choirs, and he had the ability to breathe with the singers. While it is true that a great many conductors hardly look at you while you are performing, when they do, you tend to want to do your best. That was the case with Sir Malcolm.

RH: You were one of the first singers to explore the possibilities that television offered opera. You performed in broadcast performances of Tchaikovsky's *Eugene Onegin* with Dame Margaret Price and Puccini's *Gianni Schicchi* with Tito Gobbi, before being involved in a transmission of Purcell's *Dido and Aeneas* from Glyndebourne. Do you like opera on television, and are you in favour of operas being relayed directly to cinemas?

YM: Most people I know who go to these screenings love them. They think they're wonderful. But I'm not sure that I like them, as the screen directors have a tendency to zoom in on the singers. I really don't want to see their throats and tongues. And some singers really do have very strange tongues! It's not for me. But, if it educates an audience, that's another matter. And what is music if it's not '*eine heilige Kunst*' ('a holy art'), to quote Der Komponist in Strauss's *Ariadne auf Naxos*. We are very privileged living in London, and it's marvellous to be able to access all the music that's performed here. We tend to love certain works because we hear them over and over again. If we as performers hear a piece for the first time, we might think that it's beautiful. Then, when we hear it for a second time, it might seem even more beautiful. And so it goes on. This is what we must encourage the public to do, too.

RH: You were involved in Hans-Jürgen Syberberg's 1982 film of Wagner's *Parsifal*. Syberberg was something of a controversial figure who also made a contentious documentary about Winifred Wagner. His film of *Parsifal* not only combines German history with a psychological examination of the eponymous hero, but takes a commercial recording of the opera that you made and overdubs the visual action with it. Were you consulted about this?

YM: Not at all. Apparently, the filmmakers wanted to use Pierre Boulez's commercial recording of the opera, but were refused permission by Deutsche Grammophon. Eventually, we documented the work in Monaco, and considered it a normal recording project. It was only later that I learned that Syberberg had arranged for an actress to play Kundry, and for a young man, who was barely more than a boy, to play Parsifal. I've never seen the film, and from what I've heard, I know that I wouldn't enjoy it.

RH: It was one of the more novel uses of your voice.

YM: Yes. But I desperately wanted to record *Parsifal*.

RH: Thanks to your performances at Bayreuth, your name is now synonymous with that of Wagner. As the Festspielhaus's acoustics have always been a source of discussion, what's your opinion of them?

YM: I thought that they were wonderful. And as we had Carlos Kleiber in the pit for *Tristan und Isolde*, the orchestra played like gods for him.

RH: I am very interested to hear your take on Kleiber, as he could be quite tricky personally and musically.

YM: He was a very strange man, but I had no difficulties with him. While he wasn't particularly involved in the coaching process, he did give the singers notes. I didn't get many from him, and have absolutely no idea why that was. His long arms added to the work's *rubato*, which was nice and broad.

RH: Did you work with Kleiber elsewhere?

YM: Yes. I sang Octavian with him in *Der Rosenkavalier* at the Royal Opera House in 1974. But my Brangäne at Bayreuth was my first reading of that part, and, as such, I was very fresh to the role.

PART TWO: SINGERS

RH: Aside from Kleiber, what was the rest of your Bayreuth experience like?

YM: I was staying at a fantastic place called Warmensteinach. It was in the mountains and quite a drive from Bayreuth. At the time, I had very small children, and a daughter who was always waking up in the middle of the night. Fortunately, my mother was with us for one visit, and she was a great help. As it was summertime, I always took the children with me, which meant that I suffered a little from disturbed sleep. And even though we began the performances at 3pm, we still didn't finish until 11pm.

RH: Another tricky character with whom you worked was the great German conductor Otto Klemperer. With him, you recorded Dorabella in Mozart's *Così fan tutte* alongside Margaret Price as Fiordiligi.

YM: By the time he recorded *Così*, he was very frail physically, but alert mentally. And the cast that EMI had assembled was great. His *tempi* for the arias and ensembles were very broad, and on many occasions I simply took a breath and went for it. We were concerned that the recitatives would be equally slow, and we hoped to do them without him. As he was a late riser, the sessions didn't usually begin until midday, and were over by either 1 or 2pm. He was then finished for the day. So, we decided to record the recitatives at 3pm, when he would be safely tucked up in his hotel room, asleep. When we later performed the opera at the Royal Festival Hall, the one thing that he was looking forward to was seeing Lucia Popp dressed as the Notary. He kept on asking her what she was going to wear. He really was very sweet. But he did get a little cross with me in one of the duets, because he felt that I kept coming in too late. The problem was, which shaky-hand gesture were you supposed to follow?

RH: If you watch Klemperer's final, televised cycle of Beethoven's nine symphonies from the Royal Festival Hall, there's not much correlation between what his hands were doing and the sounds being produced. Yet the sound-world he created was unmistakably his own. Do you think this was all down to how he emanated his ideas?

YM: Possibly. During the concert performance of *Così fan tutte*, which was very long, he probably had a snooze or two. But as the players loved him so much, they simply carried on.

RH: As you gave a great deal of Mozart's music during your career, do you think that it's an ideal training ground for *coloratura* singers?

YM: I'd opt for Handel when it comes to this issue.

RH: Why?

YM: He's not as exposed as Mozart. In fact, I sang very few roles by him, so I am not a great exponent of his works.

RH: Yet you were known for your interpretation of 'Parto, parto' from *La clemenza di Tito*.

YM: That was *so* hard; a nightmare. When I listen back to my recording of 'Smanie implicabili' from *Così* with Klemperer, I realise how much I enjoyed making it, as I had space to sing. That was not always the case with 'Parto, parto'. The *coloratura* in that aria is something else again; I never enjoyed it. I was always more attracted to broader musical structures, such as those found in the music of Wagner, Strauss and Mahler. Broad lines suited me better than shorter rhythmic units.

PART TWO: SINGERS

RH: Were you in search of a big sound?

YM: No. I just wanted more time to breathe.

RH: As a young musician, I studied in Cologne with Sir John Pritchard, and heard you sing 'Parto, parto' there. You also performed at the city's opera house under John's great predecessor, István Kertész.

YM: Kertész really loved singers, and he had a light touch when it came to conducting. I met him when I was singing Meg in Verdi's *Falstaff*, a character who has very little to do. He asked me if I would be interested in going to Cologne and in singing Sesto in *La clemenza do Tito*, a part that I'd never even heard of at the time. The opera was rarely performed in those days, and Cologne was one of the first houses to do it. I said that I would have a look at the character, and quickly realised that the role had some wonderful moments. The recitatives are not terribly good, but the arias are lovely. So, I thought it was a good thing to do. It was always hard for me to scale the sound down, and I was never happy with the *coloratura*. I'm not made to move so quickly.

RH: Kertész was a wonderful vocal accompanist, and did a great deal of work with Lucia Popp.

YM: They were firm friends, and István's wife also sang at the theatre. I thought that everything he did was marvellous. We once discussed how he studied material, and he said to me, 'Whenever I prepare anything, I have the London Symphony Orchestra in my head; I hear them playing.'

RH: You've also sung a great deal of Bach. Is there a special technique needed when performing his music?

YM: Regardless of the music that you are performing, your technique should be the same. The composer does the rest. But, again, I do think that Bach is difficult to perform.

RH: But if you compare your sound in his music with that of some modern singers, it's much fuller and richer.

YM: I am not sure that's a good thing.

RH: And, of course, you famously recorded Bach's Mass in B minor with Karl Münchinger. Did you also work with that other great Bachian, Karl Richter?

YM: No.

RH: Was that to do with your association with Decca?

YM: It was more to do with the agents and the conductors they represented. They tended to stick together.

RH: I was struck recently by the sheer amount of Bach's music that Australian and British singers performed in the concert hall during the middle of the twentieth century. Take Helen Watts, for example. Under the guidance of Sir Malcolm Sargent, she introduced many an unfamiliar aria to her devoted Proms audiences. Were Bach's works familiar to you by the time of the Münchinger recording?

YM: I don't remember performing any of his compositions in Australia, but I did sing a lot of Handel there. When I listened to the Münchinger discs again recently, I was surprised by how good they are. It's all to do with speed. If the conductor gets the speed right, you are home and dry.

PART TWO: SINGERS

RH: You would agree with Wagner, then, when he argues that a work has one true *tempo*.

YM: Absolutely.

RH: Pierre Boulez also agreed with this, and, with him, you not only recorded Berg's *Lulu*, but also sang Gräfin Geschwitz for the first performance of the work's completed version at the Paris Opéra in 1979. That production was directed by Patrice Chéreau. What was he like to work with?

YM: He was a very interesting man. As he knew that the production was going to be filmed, he directed the opera with that in mind. He had some splendid touches, and the wonderful staircase that he created was a theatrical gift for those who had to come down it. He didn't say a lot dramatically, but the little touches he added brought out the essence of the characters we were portraying. I also sang in his production of Wagner's *Der Ring des Nibelungen* at Bayreuth. No Fricka had ever looked like that before. Her off-the-shoulder cream gown was really very striking. He liked ladies.

RH: And how did you get on with Boulez?

YM: I always got on well with Pierre. He was probably the best musician in the whole world. His ears were phenomenal, and he was a very nice man. Mind you, there were some things that I did with him that were very, very hard, and I only did them because they *were* with Pierre.

RH: Let's turn our attention to two composers with whom you are particularly closely associated: Gustav Mahler and Richard Strauss.

Would it be fair to say that Octavian was something of a signature role for you?

YM: Yes, and I think that my Octavian was better than my Klytaemnestra.

RH: As Octavian is a travesty role, did that prove difficult?

YM: It was no problem: it's just acting. It's not difficult for women to kiss on stage, and every Marschallin with whom I worked was great. They were all great. And this also applies to all the Sophies with whom I worked.

RH: What, for you, constitutes a great Strauss singer?

YM: A sense of musical broadness is essential, and so is the ability to sing big, *legato* lines.

RH: Is there a difference between being a great Mahler singer and being a great Strauss singer?

YM: Not particularly. You have to remember that you're not exactly spoiled for choice when you are a mezzo-soprano. If you don't sing Mahler, there's not a lot else to sing, unless you're very good at Bach. And as there were one or two singers ahead of me who performed Bach's music splendidly, there wasn't a great deal of opportunity for me to do it. I wasn't particularly keen to compete with them, and I much preferred to do the things that I was good at. I just fell into the Mahler repertoire.

RH: Considering the breadth and quality of the orchestral songs that you recorded, it's always puzzled me that you recorded very little *Lieder* with piano. Why was that?

PART TWO: SINGERS

YM: When I listen to some of my later discs of Mahler, I notice that my German had become increasingly better. Even though I used to speak it quite well, it was not my mother tongue. And as I was particularly painstaking when it came to expressing the content of the songs, I don't think that I could've got through a whole programme of them. I did do a few *Lieder*, but as they are very time-consuming, I never felt that I had sufficient time to devote to them. My dear friend Lucia Popp used to sing them constantly, but I was never satisfied with what I was doing.

RH: And what about oratorio? Did you perform that genre frequently?

YM: I learned how to sing through Handel's *Messiah*, and before I left Australia, I had already sung it at least ten times. That was quite impressive for someone under the age of twenty-one! And when I came to Great Britain, I more or less lived off the proceeds of my *Messiah* performances. I also gave Mendelssohn's *Elijah* many times, which I loved.

RH: No interview with Yvonne Minton would be complete without mentioning your recording of Elgar's *The Dream of Gerontius* with Benjamin Britten. What was it like working with one the world's greatest artists?

YM: I always found it interesting that when working with truly great people, I was hardly aware of them. Somehow, their greatness allowed them to slot automatically into my daily working life. And that's why I sometimes have trouble remembering that I performed with them. It was just natural. But Britten didn't like *Gerontius*, and he certainly didn't like Elgar, or the words that Cardinal Newman wrote. He recorded it for his partner, Peter Pears. Yet it is a fine recording. This was largely down to the way that Britten treated the *tempi*. Being so musical, he couldn't get them wrong. I didn't give many performances of *The Dream of Gerontius*, and I wish that I'd done more.

RH: But what you did on that recording was breathtakingly beautiful.

YM: It comes from inside the person; it all comes from inside. You internalise the words, and you constantly ask what a particular word means. Only then should you put it into your voice. That's what I've always done and, that way, I can colour them. I'm not an actress; I'm a singing actress. And that can only be achieved through the voice.

DAME ANNE EVANS
(DAVID JOSEFOWITZ RECITAL HALL, 16 NOVEMBER 2012)

RAYMOND HOLDEN: As Brünnhilde in Wagner's *Der Ring des Nibelungen* at Bayreuth during the late 1980s and early 1990s, you impressed all who heard and saw you. What was it like performing one of the composer's more demanding characters in his own theatre?

ANNE EVANS: It was both exhilarating and terrifying. And when I look again at the DVDs of those performances, I can't help thinking of the things that I could've done better.

RH: To have sung at Bayreuth must have been one of the highlights of your career, but what first attracted you to singing?

AE: Being of Welsh extraction, I sang from childhood in chapel, at eisteddfods and, later, at rugby matches, where I would stand on a table and lead the spectators in impromptu choral singing! I love rugby and am one of the Welsh team's greatest fans, particularly when they're winning. The Welsh always sing in harmony and I was brought up with that in my ears. They rarely sing in unison.

RH: Were you born in Wales?

AE: No. I was born in London to Welsh parents during the war, but my mother assured me that I was conceived in Cardiganshire. I feel very Welsh and was raised in London speaking the language. In fact, Dennis O'Neill and I sang Verdi's Requiem in Welsh together at an eisteddfod in Swansea.

RH: But why do Welsh people sing the whole time?

AE: It goes way back. You only have to think of coal miners singing in the mines and their membership of choirs. It's not dissimilar to the people of Yorkshire and their great love of choral societies. Sadly, many of those great musical institutions are now gone; a terrible loss.

RH: Where did you begin to train as a young singer?

AE: Somebody who heard me at a rugby match said, 'You haven't got a bad voice. Why don't you go and get it trained?' 'Get it *trained*', I thought. 'There's nothing wrong with it!' Nevertheless, I did decide to audition for the Royal College of Music. I sang something from Bizet's *Carmen*, as I believed that I was a mezzo-soprano at the time. I got a place there and was awarded a grant from the local council towards my fees; those were the days! My teacher was the soprano Ruth Packer. After I'd been at the College for three years, Ruth said, 'Well, darling, I think you're going to be a soprano, as you have a completely false bottom.' For my final year, I auditioned as a soprano for the Opera School, and was chosen to sing the role of Aida in excerpts from the opera of the same name. This worried me, as I felt that it might be a bit high. But Ruth told me to have a go at it anyway. I did, and I never looked back. Later that year, I sang the Aida-Amneris duet with my friend and fellow student Katherine Pring, at a concert with the

PART TWO: SINGERS

College's First Orchestra under its conductor, Sir Adrian Boult. As I'd never sung with an orchestra before, the rehearsal was particularly exciting for me. Boult told us to stand at the front of the platform, which troubled us, because we couldn't see him. When I pointed this out, he said, 'Don't worry, I'll follow you.' And that was the first, and last, time a conductor ever said that to me!

RH: After completing your studies at the Royal College of Music, you went to Geneva for a period.

AE: I did. I went to study with Maria Carpi at the Conservatoire de Musique de Genève for two years. This was with the help of a grant from the Countess of Munster Musical Trust, which I'm still associated with today as a trustee. The opera class was linked to the local opera house. Its Intendant was Dr Herbert Graf, who was also the head of the class. This meant that he gave students small parts to sing at the theatre from time to time, and it was there that I made my operatic debut as Countess Ceprano in Verdi's *Rigoletto*, followed by Annina in the composer's *La traviata*. My friend Katherine Pring was also in Geneva, and when we heard that the theatre was going to mount a new production of Wagner's *Ring* cycle directed by Graf, we 'swam' into his office and said, '*Please can we each do a Rhinemaiden?*' Not only were we cast as Rhinemaidens, but we were given roles as Valkyries and Norns, too. I was now hooked on Wagner. Graf also allowed the students to attend stage rehearsals at the theatre, which was a fantastic experience, as we learned so much by being able to watch leading singers at close quarters.

RH: Some of the singers who took part in that *Ring* were well-known Wagnerians, such as Anja Silja. What was she like?

AE: She was young and beautiful, and in *Die Walküre*, she sang her first Brünnhilde, a role not normally associated with her. Ramón Vinay, who was a great Tristan and an equally great Otello, was singing his first Wotan. Silja was more at home with Strauss's *Salome*, which she also sang at Geneva.

RH: And, of course, Silja had a close personal relationship with Wieland Wagner. Did you ever meet him?

AE: No, I never did. He was to have directed the *Salome*, but died before rehearsals started, so his widow took over the production. I remember a rehearsal for the scene where Salome kisses the mouth of Jochanaan's severed head. Silja became so emotionally involved that she flung the head to one side and rushed off into the wings. I was absolutely gobsmacked!

RH: It was around this time that you sang Verdi's Requiem with Sir John Barbirolli.

AE: That was in 1969, two years after I'd left the Royal College of Music. In those days, the four London music schools took part in an annual concert at the Royal Albert Hall, for which they provided the combined orchestra, chorus and many of the soloists. This time they put on Verdi's Requiem, and I auditioned; a nerve-racking experience. Barbirolli picked the four soloists and I was lucky enough to be chosen for the soprano part. We travelled up to Manchester to study the work with him – I still have his markings in my score – and I remember his music room was huge and freezing. Barbirolli sat there in an overcoat that went down to his ankles, and we sat there in pullovers and scarves. We knew that he kept a hip flask in his pocket, and from time to time he would disappear for a quick nip of whisky from it. As it was so cold, we could have done with a nip ourselves!

RH: How old were you when you performed with Barbirolli, and was that your Royal Albert Hall debut?

AE: I was twenty-seven, and, yes, it was my first performance at the Albert Hall. When you come out of the dressing room and enter the auditorium, you are confronted by this colossal space. It can be alarming, and all you want to do is run off in the opposite direction.

RH: I know you are committed to the training of young singers, and I also know that you believe firmly that Mozart's works are ideal pedagogic tools. Why is that?

AE: I always feel that his music is medicine for the voice. If you can sing Mozart well, you can sing practically anything. You learn from him how to float the voice, how to sing recitatives properly, how to perform long phrases and how to be aware of dynamics and vocal colours. Ruth Packer told me to go and listen to the best violinists and to see how they play long lines. That's a really important thing to do. And, of course, violinists can learn from great singers, too.

RH: An important Mozartian with whom you worked was Sir Charles Mackerras. When did you sing with him for the first time?

AE: I first met Charles when I sang Pamina with the English National Opera on tour in Liverpool. After 'clocking on' at the theatre, I got in the lift with a chap I'd never seen before. After looking me up and down, he said in an Australian accent, 'Who are you?' 'I'm Anne Evans.' I replied, 'and I'm singing Pamina tonight. Who are *you*?' 'I'm Charlie Mackerras and I'm conducting it!' He had recently been appointed the company's new Music Director. Our professional relationship blossomed after that night, and I did about sixteen different operas with him. I adored working with Charles.

RH: Singers always loved working with Mackerras, but they were often taken aback by his constantly changing ornaments. How did you cope with these?

AE: I had one terrible disaster with him. I was singing Ilia in Mozart's *Idomeneo*, an opera that I'd never sung before. Every time I went into a rehearsal he would say, 'Try this decoration.' Standing in the wings on the first night, and waiting to sing my aria, I thought, 'Does that decoration go up or down?' When I got on stage, I panicked and took a wrong turn. Everything went completely awry and I wanted to rush off in a flood of tears. I looked at the prompter for help, but he kept saying over and over, 'Deprived of my father.' I wanted to shout at him, 'It's not the words I want, you idiot, it's the notes.' At the interval, Charles was furious with me and kept asking why it went wrong. I told him about the prompter and my memory lapse. Eventually, he twigged what had happened and forgave me.

RH: Charles's repertoire was huge, and I believe you even sang an opera by Johann Christian Bach with him in 1972. How often do you hear an opera by that composer these days?

AE: Strangely enough, I was reading only last week that a theatre in Germany had just performed his *Temistocle*, the opera that I did with Charles for a BBC studio performance in Manchester with the BBC

PART TWO: SINGERS

Northern Orchestra, now the BBC Philharmonic. I sang the role of Rosanna. There was a shortage of scores and several of the other singers decided to pull out of the project. But as I was the new kid on the block, Charles pinned me down and made me do it.

RH: The music is far from easy technically.

AE: You certainly need to concentrate on your scales. As much of Rosanna's music is very florid, I practised and practised until it was okay. Afterwards, Charles said, 'Aren't you glad I made you do it? It's good for your Mozart.'

RH: At the English National Opera, you sang a great many roles. What are your memories of this period?

AE: I joined the company as a junior principal in 1968 and was paid £25 a week for singing Mimì in Puccini's *La bohème*. As I gave two performances a week, that worked out at £12.50 a performance.

RH: Along with Mimì, you sang Fiordiligi in Mozart's *Così fan tutte*, Antonia, Giulietta and Stella in Offenbach's *Les contes d'Hoffmann* and Violetta in *La traviata*. Clearly the company considered you to be a talented and versatile artist. But as a relatively young singer, performing these roles before hardened London audiences must have been unnerving.

AE: In those days, the English National Opera was made up of two companies. As one toured, the other performed at the Coliseum. They then swapped over. This meant that I could try out a new role like Violetta before singing it in London, where the opera was to be conducted by Mackerras. 'The aria's got to be fast,' he told me. 'It has to be fast and hysterical.' And that's just how I sang it. On a good day, and with a fair wind behind me, I could sing the aria's high E flat. But there was not always a fair wind to help! If Charles liked what you did, his grin would stretch from ear to ear. But if he didn't like what he heard, his head would go down and he would frown like hell.

RH: The Coliseum is a very big theatre. How did you cope with its dimensions?

AE: The important thing is never to sing into the wings or up stage. And you must never 'oversing', even though the orchestra can be very loud there.

RH: At the English National Opera, you also performed some of the smaller Wagner roles under the distinguished Wagnerian Sir Reginald Goodall. What was he like to work with?

AE: He was a wonderful coach. You could work on a role for two years with him, and, on occasion, might spend an hour and a half on just one page. This could drive you crazy, but he would say, 'If you get this page right, you'll get the rest right.' He worked in a little room nicknamed 'Valhalla' at the very top of the Royal Opera House. It had washbasins and a broom cupboard; it was the cleaners' room. I learned so much about Wagnerian style from him. He taught me how to use the text, and how to colour the music to match the composer's words. The English National Opera's *Ring* was to be sung in English, which I liked very much, as I felt that it allowed me to have a real rapport with the audience. Reggie worked on the English and German texts side by side so that the right colours could be found in both languages. He could be very grumpy, yet sweet at the same time. If he was sitting in the wings looking miserable at rehearsals, colleagues would say, 'Go and talk to him. Go and cheer him up.' He'd say, 'Hello, dear, you're the one who worked in Germany, aren't you?' I would tell him it was Switzerland, to which he'd reply, 'That's right, Germany.'

RH: Towards the end of his career, Sir Reginald had a huge cult following. Was that the case when you were working with him?

AE: Yes. It had started before I joined the company, and was the result of the famous *Die Meistersinger von Nürnberg* that he gave at Sadler's Wells, just before the company moved to the Coliseum. His speeds were always very slow. But you knew that if you could sing a role at his *tempo*, you could sing it at any speed.

RH: When did you perform Brünnhilde for the first time?

AE: I didn't start working on that role until after I'd left the English National Opera in 1979 and had gone to the Welsh National Opera, which then became my artistic home. Sir Brian McMaster, the company's general administrator, said that he wanted me to sing Brünnhilde in their forthcoming *Ring* cycle, starting with *Die Walküre*. I thought, 'That can't be right'; Sieglinde seemed to me a much better idea, as I'd sung it at the Coliseum. I remember that I was so worried about singing Brünnhilde that I didn't sign the contract until after the first night, an omission that the management failed to notice. By not signing, I thought that I could get out of it if it didn't go well. In the end, it was fine, thanks to the huge amount of preparation time that I was allocated. And if you *are* singing a great role like Brünnhilde for the first time, you must prepare it meticulously, both dramatically and musically.

RH: I was very interested to learn that when you worked on your Wagnerian roles, you explored some of your great predecessors' recordings first.

AE: Whether you are a singer, an instrumentalist or a conductor, I think it's very important to listen to renowned performers from the past, not to copy them, but to discover why they were so marvellous. One of the reasons why I was worried about singing Brünnhilde was that I didn't have a great 'organ' of a voice like Kirsten Flagstad or Birgit Nilsson. My voice was more lyric than heroic. Someone told me to listen to the recordings of the German soprano Frida Leider, a contemporary and rival of Flagstad. Doing so made me realise that there was more than one way to approach the big Wagnerian roles. If Leider were to come along today, I, for one, would drop to my knees in admiration. While it's true that lots of early singers now sound a bit old-fashioned, she doesn't. Her voice is vibrant, beautiful and full of colour. Listening to her gave me the courage to take on Brünnhilde.

RH: Five years after singing Brünnhilde in Wales, you performed the role at Bayreuth under Daniel Barenboim.

AE: By now I was a hardened Wagnerian, as I had sung eleven characters in the *Ring*, and roles such as Eva, Elsa, Elisabeth, Senta and Kundry from some of the composer's other operas. I had to audition for Barenboim in Paris, where he had taken over the Palais Garnier for an hour one lunchtime. My agent, Howard Hartog, warned me that he would probably want me to sing all the most difficult bits from the *Ring*. When I arrived at the theatre, Barenboim asked me to start with 'Ho-jo-to-ho!' from *Die Walküre*. A young lad jumped up onto the stage to play the piano, which he made sound like an orchestra. It was Antonio Pappano, who was Barenboim's assistant for the *Ring* at that time. It wasn't long before Barenboim himself took over the piano and started to make suggestions about how various passages might be phrased. 'Hang on a minute,' I said. 'Are you saying that you want me for the role at Bayreuth?' 'Oh, sure,' he replied, and went on playing as though he hadn't said anything of importance. I skipped all the way home.

RH: When you finally got to Bayreuth, what did you make of the Festspielhaus's famous acoustics?

AE: I knew something about them already, as I'd sung Helmwige, Ortlinde and the Third Norn in a previous production of the *Ring* at Bayreuth, which had been directed by Sir Peter Hall and conducted in its first year by Sir Georg Solti. But singing Brünnhilde under Barenboim was a far bigger undertaking altogether. The theatre has a huge cowl that covers quite a chunk of the pit. This means that when the conductor gives a down-beat and you begin to sing, you can sound ahead of the orchestra. It's unusual for singers to be in this position, as they are generally told by conductors that they are dragging. But if you sing fractionally behind the beat at Bayreuth, it allows the sound of the orchestra sufficient time to rise from beneath the cowl. That way, everyone ends up together. The acoustic is indeed very special: even if you sing the quietist *pianissimo*, it will carry into the auditorium.

RH: Your director at Bayreuth was Harry Kupfer. He was known for his cutting-edge productions, and famously used laser technology there for the first time in 1988. What was he like to work with, and how did you cope with the extreme physical demands that his production presented?

AE: I already knew Harry, as I'd sung two roles with him in Wales: Chrysothemis in *Elektra* and Leonore in *Fidelio*. I would've done anything for him. In rehearsal, he liked to work in a very small space, so that the characters could see each other's every expression and eye movement. It was incredibly stimulating.

RH: Having watched the production a number of times, I never cease to be amazed by the theatrical chemistry that exists between you, Siegfried Jerusalem and Sir John Tomlinson. Was that easy to achieve?

AE: You have to remember that Bayreuth is quite a small town and is about the size of Royal Tunbridge Wells. Consequently, you spend a good deal of time with your colleagues and you get to know them well. It was like one big family. And, of course, the inspirational Daniel Barenboim was there with his wife and sons, and unlike many conductors today, he always found time for an invaluable music session with each member of the cast. He also liked playing football with the orchestra!

RH: Given your experiences with the composer's music, what makes a great Wagner singer?

AE: The text and how it's used is very important. Making sure that consonants and word-endings are audible is crucial. If you look at the score, Wagner writes brilliantly for the voice. When it's in the bottom register, the orchestra is reduced to *piano*. If you follow his dynamics, the music works. The problem is that today's orchestras have become very loud. In the old days, string players used gut strings, which created a rounder sound. When Sir Simon Rattle conducted *Das Rheingold* at the Royal Albert Hall with the Orchestra of the Age of Enlightenment, I was prepared not to like it, but I thought the sound was very beautiful.

PART TWO: SINGERS

RH: Not all singers would agree with your glowing endorsement of Wagner's writing for the voice. Why do you think that some artists find his works problematic?

AE: Many of them try to compete with the orchestra and therein lies trouble. If you sing loudly all the time, it's very exhausting for audiences, who feel as though they've been hit over the head with a sledgehammer.

RH: It seems to me that there are moments in *Götterdämmerung* when Brünnhilde takes on the quality of a mezzo-soprano. Would you agree with this?

AE: Yes. As Brünnhilde, you are often telling the story in the middle or the upper-middle of the voice. If you haven't got a strong middle, or a middle that can be well projected, it's better to leave Wagner alone.

RH: As the *Ring* is incredibly demanding physically, how did you go about pacing yourself?

AE: To build up my stamina, I had a skipping rope that I used every day. The performance space for the *Ring* at Bayreuth was enormous, as Kupfer had opened the rehearsal hall behind the main stage. For my first appearance in Act Two of *Die Walküre,* I had to run from the very back of the space to the front of the stage before singing 'Ho-jo-to-ho'. It was a long way, and I found myself hyperventilating and breathless before I started to sing. A dancer at Bayreuth gave me a good tip. Before starting to run, I should take a very deep breath and hold it until I had almost reached the front. It worked, and I never ran out of breath again. I always pass on this piece of advice to my students. When singing a role like Brünnhilde, you must always remember the long journey that lies ahead of you. You must be prepared to save your most beautiful and expressive singing for the very end. The same is true when performing *Tristan und Isolde*. You must learn to pace yourself. This is really very important. I believe that in rehearsals, one should sing out all the time. You'll then know whether or not you'll be out of breath or tired when you come to sing the role on stage. That way, you can time everything.

RH: Perhaps you can answer two questions that still puzzle me about the final minutes of Kupfer's production. What's the meaning of the five television sets watched by the five differently dressed demographic groups, and how do they relate to the young boy leading the little girl off stage at the end?

AE: To be honest, I'm not sure. By then, I'd jumped into the fire! I never had an opportunity to watch the scene, either in rehearsal or in performance. But I assume that those who were looking at the television sets represented the millions around the world who were unaware of climate change. Conversely, the young people expressed the hope that the next generation might be able to save the planet from destruction. I could be quite wrong, but there were a lot of visual reminders in the production concerning the natural world's decay.

RH: When you came to perform Isolde for the first time at the Welsh National Opera with Sir Charles Mackerras in 1993, you looked to another great soprano from the past as a model: the American Lillian Nordica. Who alerted you to her, and how did she influence your understanding of the role?

AE: Again, my main influence was Frida Leider, but Nordica also played a part. Charles said that he wanted the character to sound young, fresh and influenced by the Italian school of singing. He asked me to listen to Nordica singing part of the 'Liebestod', which had been recorded live at the Metropolitan Opera, New York, on a Mapleson wax cylinder in 1903. Although Nordica can be difficult to hear, the recording is very informative if you know what you are looking for. It reminds us that she was the sort of lyrical soprano for whom Wagner wrote. He couldn't have imagined a soprano with Flagstad's weight of sound. Nordica, who uses *portamento* and places her voice very high, produces some very beautiful singing. I understood exactly what Charles meant and what he was looking for.

RH: How long did it take to prepare the role of Isolde for the first time?

AE: I learned it over a period of two years. I was doing other things during that time, but would pick up the score regularly. Sometimes it took a step forward, and at other times it took two steps back. But by the time I started production rehearsals, I was very secure, both vocally and emotionally.

RH: Having performed Isolde with the Welsh National Opera, you then went on to give it in Scotland, Dresden, Berlin, Paris and Ravello. You also performed it with Sir Antonio Pappano in Brussels in 1994. What are your memories of that?

AE: Tony knows a great deal about the voice. His father was a singing teacher and the young Pappano played the piano for his teaching sessions. He learned at his dad's knee, so to speak. Tony understands very specific aspects of singing and is very demanding. But he is also a joy to be with and great fun. While music-making should be serious, you must also be able to enjoy it. If a conductor understands that, he or she will get the best out of a singer. And speaking of lessons, I'm reminded of something that my teacher in Geneva once told me. She said that having a career in singing was like owning a great chest of drawers: you pull out a different drawer for each role you sing. Whether it be song, opera or oratorio, each work should have a different style.

RH: You counsel against singers taking Brünnhilde and Elektra into their repertoires at the same time. Why is that?

AE: I think that Elektra, like Turandot, can be a killer. It's fine if you have the right voice for it, and here I'm thinking of artists such as Birgit Nilsson and Dame Gwyneth Jones. But as *Elektra* is very heavily scored, it can be a problem for a more lyrical voice. Lorin Maazel was very keen for me to sing Elektra with him at the Salzburg Festival in the Grosses Festspielhaus, but I turned him down. I knew that the sound I made was not what people expect today. Even in the beautiful 'Recognition Scene', they still want an enormous, great, steely sound. And that's why I stuck with Chrysothemis and never sang Elektra.

RH: But you did choose to sing a role by Strauss for your final performance in 2003: the Marschallin in *Der Rosenkavalier*. What, for you, makes a great Strauss singer?

AE: Funnily enough, I always wanted to sing Octavian in that opera rather than the Marschallin, but I wasn't the right shape for a trouser-role! While the Marschallin is a more lyrical role than Elektra, you must still be able to soar over the orchestra without pushing the voice. Listen to the recordings of Ljuba Welitsch singing both Salome and Chrysothemis. For me, her voice is ideal for those roles. Whenever I hear a performance of *Salome* that's cast too heavily, I go home and

PART TWO: SINGERS

listen to Welitsch's discs of the work, as I'm sure it's the sound that Strauss had in mind.

RH: When looking through your biography, I was struck by the virtual absence of recital engagements. Why was that?

AE: I did give recitals at both the Edinburgh International Festival and the Wigmore Hall, but as I sang so much opera, I couldn't give the recital repertoire the time it needed. It's a different way of singing and a totally different way of performing.

RH: But you did give a marvellous performance of Schumann's *Frauen-Liebe und Leben*.

AE: I know that this particular song cycle is out of fashion these days, but I think it's quite wonderful. The last song, when the woman's husband has died, is especially poignant. You can't help but be touched by her anger at him for dying.

RH: You are, however, known for your interpretations of orchestral songs and are closely associated with Wagner's *Wesendonck-Lieder*. As they were written around the same time as *Tristan und Isolde*, should singers tackle them before performing *Tristan* and the *Ring*, or after they have had some experience with these works?

AE: I gave a few performances of the *Wesendonck* songs before I sang my first Isolde and enjoyed doing them. But it wasn't until after I'd sung Isolde in the theatre that I even began to understand the depths of 'Im Treibhaus' and 'Träume'. For me, this is some of the greatest music ever written.

SHEILA ARMSTRONG
(DAVID JOSEFOWITZ RECITAL HALL, 14 FEBRUARY 2014)

RAYMOND HOLDEN: I remember vividly the first time I watched you on film performing Mahler's Second Symphony with Dame Janet Baker, the London Symphony Orchestra and Leonard Bernstein at Ely Cathedral. I was completely mesmerised by it. Before we start chatting about your life and career in general, it would be marvellous if you could paint us a brief picture of what it was like working with that remarkable conductor in that magnificent cathedral.

SHEILA ARMSTRONG: It really doesn't get much better than that. I was still terribly young when we gave that performance in 1973, and Leonard Bernstein's name was one I grew up with as a student. He was legendary. To actually be there and to meet him was quite something, and I was very nervous before the first rehearsal. But he had this strange capacity for making you feel absolutely at home. It was as if I'd known him for the last twenty years. He was relaxed, casual and absolutely lovely. Yet he still had the ability to produce such remarkable music. The thing that did amuse me were his gestures, which were nearly as fully orchestrated as the score. And I noticed that in the same place in both the rehearsals and the performance, he would leap into the air. It could be so exciting when he did that, as Lenny was such a showman.

PART TWO: SINGERS

Before performing the symphony at Ely, we'd given it at the Edinburgh International Festival, a completely different atmosphere. And Dame Janet was absolutely outstanding in the fourth movement, where her *pianissimo* and control was amazing. She was also a wonderfully kind colleague, who was both caring and nurturing. When we recorded the work in Ely, it was fraught with difficulties. During the filming, one of the bulbs in the arc lights smashed, resulting in a terrible crashing sound. Having received notes saying that there were going to be bombs in the cathedral, this frightened everybody. We also had a bomb scare and the building was evacuated. But we overcame all of these things, and the final result is something that I will never forget. Mahler's Second Symphony is an incredibly inspiring piece, and if heaven is anything like it, I definitely want to go there.

RH: You were born in Northumbria in 1942, and had many of your early musical experiences in the North East. What was it like growing up there in the years directly following the Second World War?

SA: It was still very much a mining community. Most of the mines have gone now, but when I was born, there were still collieries that were functioning very profitably. I came from a poor family, and my grandfather took part in the Jarrow March. He couldn't pay the colliery-house rent, so his family of nine, including grandad and grandma, were moved into the streets. They had to go to soup kitchens to feed their children, so mine is a very poor background. I had quite a good music teacher at school, who was very interested in the recorder, and I learned to play all the various types of that instrument while I was there. We also had a very good school choir with which I sang hymns at assemblies and performed at festivals. This meant that I had a good musical education. But because it *was* a poor background, we largely made our own music.

RH: Northumbria has always been rich with folklore and folk music. Presumably this heritage influenced you during your early years, and has remained with you throughout your career. Were these the reasons why you recorded at least two albums of Northumbrian songs with Sir Thomas Allen in the 1980s?

SA: We made those discs with the Northern Sinfonia, now the Royal Northern Sinfonia, under David Haslam. He arranged the Geordie folk songs that we thoroughly enjoyed recording. And Tom, like me, is very much rooted in the North East. After making the first disc, we gave a concert of these works at Alnwick Castle. We then filmed some of the music from the second album at Durham Cathedral, as part of its 900th anniversary celebrations, before setting it down on disc. And it's true to say that Tom and I are very much Geordies at heart.

RH: I'm always fascinated to hear about my guest's musical heroes. Who influenced you during your formative years?

SA: When I realised that vocal music might be my life, my first hero was Owen Brannigan. He was a wonderful bass-baritone from Annitsford in North Tyneside. A big man with a wonderful personality, he sang Geordie folk songs like nobody else. He was somebody to look up to, and when I won the Kathleen Ferrier Award in 1965, one of the perks was to perform at the Royal Albert Hall with the Royal Choral Society. At that concert, the Principal Soloist was Owen, and much to his and our delights, he was wearing a medal that the Pope had awarded him. He was very proud of that and was just lovely. Later, my greatest hero was Dame Janet Baker. I also greatly admired Victoria de los Ángeles, who was a sweet and lovely person. When I once did a performance of Bach's *Matthäus-Passion* at Barcelona under Rafael Frühbeck de Burgos, I later learned that she had been in the audience. Thankfully, nobody told me that before the concert, otherwise I would've been an absolute mess. In my hotel room the next day, I found a box of long-stemmed yellow roses sent by her. For a lady of her stature to make such a beautiful gesture to a young singer was just amazing. That warmth and love could also be heard in her singing. Her voice and music-making had a special quality.

RH: Mr Frühbeck de Burgos had a long and distinguished career as an oratorio conductor. What was he like to work with?

SA: He was wonderful. One of the works that I enjoyed performing most with him was Mendelssohn's *Elijah*, as he treated it like an opera. Under him, it was no longer an oratorio, and there were no gaps between the movements. He performed it in one large arc, like a single stroke of the bow on a violin. It was very dramatic and brilliant.

RH: I remember that Mr Frühbeck de Burgos's name was a bit of a challenge for some London orchestral musicians. In true British style, they affectionately dubbed him 'Mr Fray Bentos' after the famous tinned-food company. But let's return to your formative years. You were a student at the Royal Academy of Music in the 1960s. What was it like in those days?

SA: When you came into the entrance hall back then, Paddy was at the security desk on the left-hand side; there wasn't one on the right. But if you then turned right, you could access the Common Room, now the Patrons' Room. The canteen was in the same place as it is now, but it was rather less sophisticated than it is today. You can now get much better food than in the 1960s, and these days you can even get a glass of wine. Things are very different. The Academy now has beautiful rehearsal rooms, and it's true to say that the facilities here are absolutely phenomenal. Students today are very lucky indeed.

RH: Who were some of your contemporaries at the Academy, and who left a lasting musical impression on you?

SA: The composer John Tavener was here at the same time as me. Even as a student, he had a striking, aquiline face and abundantly flowing hair. He used to come to lessons wearing a big cloak. And the other person whom I really loved was the wonderful trumpet player John Wilbraham. He was about six foot six and built like a barn door, but, my goodness, he was brilliant. He played his little D trumpet like nobody else. Later, when I was doing a lot of work in Munich, Karl Richter invited him to play there, as his *obbligato* trumpet-playing was fantastic.

RH: When you won the Kathleen Ferrier Award here at the Academy, were you aware of Ferrier's great achievements as an artist?

SA: Even as a child, I was aware of Ferrier, and it seemed that everybody loved her. Not only did they adore her voice, but they also adored her personality. It glowed. Even those who'd never met her loved her. Both my mother and my grandmother used to talk about her, and when I went to study with Dr John Hutchinson as a fifteen-year-old, he had a wonderful photograph of Ferrier on his grand piano. He, too, adored her, and was her first teacher before she moved on to Henry Cummings. And it was Dr Hutchinson who gave both me and her our basic techniques. It's an interesting coincidence, then, that I later went on to win the Kathleen Ferrier Award, before becoming a trustee of the prize and president of the society that celebrates her life and career. She's been a wonderful thread that has woven its way through my life.

PART TWO: SINGERS

RH: Kathleen Ferrier was also closely associated with Sir John Barbirolli, a conductor you recorded with very early on in your career. What are your memories of 'Glorious John', as Ralph Vaughan Williams famously dubbed him?

SA: I really didn't get to know Sir John well, and my only encounter with him was for a 'rehearse-record' session for HMV when we set down 'Solveig's Song' from Grieg's *Peer Gynt* in 1968. When working in this way, you have no preparatory piano rehearsal before the session itself. Instead, you rehearse the material that you are about to record with the conductor and the orchestra in the studio directly before the red light goes on for the first take. You had to be pretty good to be able to work like that, and to be able to produce a satisfactory performance in such a short space of time. After winning the Kathleen Ferrier Award, I was offered many similar engagements, probably too many for a singer of my age and experience. I remember learning whole Bach cantatas the night before I was to record them. Thank goodness I was a decent musician, otherwise I would've sunk without a trace. Other than exchanging pleasantries with Sir John in the dressing room before the session, I really didn't get to know him. But I later got to know his widow, Evelyn, who, like me, loved her garden. We had a mutual friend who not only worked on our gardens but also that of Ursula Vaughan Williams. We were all passionate about gardens.

RH: Three years before recording 'Solveig's Song', you'd made your operatic debut as Despina in Mozart's *Così fan tutte* at Sadler's Wells, a production that was given in English.

SA: I'm no longer sure how I came to be invited to sing the role in 1965, but I assume it must have been the result of an agent or a manager hearing me at one of my Academy opera performances. I was very young at the time, and I seem to recall that we gave *Così fan tutte* during my final year here. As I also sang Despina in that production, I assume that somebody from Sadler's Wells heard it. Ideally, a singer will always prefer to sing a role such as Despina in the original language. Yet there is still a great deal to be said for performing opera in the vernacular. People need to know what's going on, and that's why surtitles are so helpful. And while I understand that this issue divides my colleagues, I would still rather sing in the original language. But when opera *is* performed in the vernacular, audiences can join in in a completely different way. There is a lot to be said for both systems.

RH: Do you agree with the premise so often stated by many of your operatic colleagues that Mozart is an essential learning tool for young singers?

SA: They are absolutely right, but I wouldn't confine this premise to Mozart: I would extend it to include Handel and Bach. They are also important in different ways. Mozart's music is sensual, beautiful and has a wonderful sense of line. And the humanity found in his compositions can be absolutely breathtaking. Something like 'Deh vieni, non tardar' from the last act of *Le nozze di Figaro* not only has to be extremely quiet, but it demands a tremendous technique and poise if you are going to bring it off successfully. Bach treated his boy sopranos more like instruments, rather than with the warmth that you find in Mozart. Handel was different again. When performing his works, you have to have an outstanding technique and good breath control. You also need to know how to sing *coloratura*, and to be able to sing for extended periods using only one breath. As all of these disciplines are important, I wouldn't simply restrict technical training to Mozart.

PART TWO: SINGERS

RH: One of your more curious recordings of Mozart's music is 'Se il padre perdei' from *Idomeneo*, conducted by the Australian-born horn player Barry Tuckwell and performed with the English Chamber Orchestra. I wouldn't normally associate Mr Tuckwell with a work like *Idomeneo*.

SA: Again, I am no longer sure how it came about, and recording companies can sometimes be a law unto themselves. Barry eventually went to America and had his own orchestra. I think he wanted to branch out in much the same way as Daniel Barenboim and Vladimir Ashkenazy did. Perhaps Barry felt too confined by just playing the horn, even though he was a phenomenal virtuoso on that instrument. Roger Vignoles, Barry and I had a wonderful trio that performed works for piano, horn and soprano. While there wasn't much written for that combination at the time, we gave what did exist and travelled widely performing it.

RH: In 1966, you appeared for the first time at the Glyndebourne Festival Opera. What are your memories of that event?

SA: For a start, it's one of the most beautiful of all performance venues, and the teaching there was unique in the world. Very famous people would come and give up three months of their year – a very long time if you are famous – as they knew that they would be coached thoroughly. They didn't get paid very much while they were there, but they knew that they were investing in their future. The Glyndebourne staff was always completely dedicated to the music it was rehearsing or performing, and the company provided you with expert language coaches who made sure that you sang perfect German, Italian or French. The whole ethos of the place was wonderful. Not only was it like a family, but it was also like living in the most beautiful bubble. It was intimate, and the way you worked was just marvellous. It was really memorable. When rehearsals got a bit much, and everybody was getting a bit grouchy, we used to have lovely parties. Mary and George Christie would then produce a great big silver bowl of fantastic punch for us to enjoy. I have absolutely no idea what was in it, but it was extremely intoxicating. You certainly felt better after it. It was lovely.

RH: Did you ever work with the doyen of operatic coaches, Jani Strasser, while you were there?

SA: Yes, I did. Jani and his fabulous wig. He was short, eccentric, bald-headed and heavily bespectacled. He didn't pull any punches, and he had the habit of telling you exactly how it was. If he thought your voice was too small for a particular part, he would say so immediately. He was a great, great character, and, for a long time, the backbone of the Glyndebourne music staff.

RH: When you made your Glyndebourne debut, it was with Purcell's *Dido and Aeneas* under Sir John Pritchard. You then later recorded the work with Sir Charles Mackerras.

SA: As *Dido* was the first thing that I did at Glyndebourne, I was very nervous, particularly as I was awe-struck singing alongside Dame Janet Baker. She realised this, and because she was so kind to young singers, she took me to her rooms, cooked me a steak, fed me yoghurt and talked to me for about three hours. Gradually, I relaxed and began to see the person, and not just the wonderful figure she was. Yet she used to scare the hell out of me most nights. While John was conducting the overture, she would come on stage literally half a minute before the curtain was meant to go up. I ended up thinking silly things like, 'What if she trips over her frock and can't make it?' But she was amazing as Dido. I didn't find Charles easy to work with, mainly because he insisted on using his own ornaments. While that's fine, his choices didn't necessarily suit every voice. He was quite a difficult character to perform with, but he was a brilliant musician and an amazing man.

RH: In 1966, you also made your debut as a recording artist singing excerpts from Handel's *Messiah* with Leopold Stokowski.

SA: As for my recording of 'Solveig's Song' with Sir John Barbirolli two years later, my session with Stokowski was 'rehearse-record'. I could see him on the podium, but didn't interact with him much more than that. I didn't really meet or talk to him. We simply rehearsed my material before the red light went on. He seemed a very sweet, quiet and charming man, but his reading of 'I know that my Redeemer liveth' from *Messiah* was the slowest that I've ever sung. I thought that I was never going to get to the end of it. It was absolutely terrifying. And he insisted that I shouldn't use any ornaments, not even an *appoggiatura*. He simply wanted Handel's melody. It was also the first time that I worked with the fantastic London Symphony Orchestra, an orchestra that I always loved performing with.

RH: Around the time of your Stokowski recording, you had a diary packed full of engagements, and were managed by Emmie Tillett, one of the directors of the famous agency Ibbs and Tillett.

SA: She was a very formidable lady, and I had so much work that I could see that I was going to become ill. I couldn't cope with it and it wasn't good. And as I was only twenty-three years old, it was clear to me that I was in danger of developing technical faults and problems with the voice. With my Geordie blood coming to the fore, I decided to confront Mrs Tillett in her den, to explain to her that things were really difficult and to say that I had too much work. As most young singers would have been thrilled to bits to have been in my situation, she was quite insulted by this and said haughtily, 'What do you propose I do about it?' I suggested that she should raise my fee, so that my workload would be reduced automatically. And to my very great surprise, she did.

RH: I remember visiting Ibbs and Tillett's offices in Wigmore Street a number of times in the late 1970s, and was struck by how Dickensian it all seemed. That impression was only strengthened after meeting three of its directors, Emmie Tillett, dubbed the 'Duchess of Wigmore Street', Beryl Ball and Wilfred Stiff, names that would have been more at home in *The Pickwick Papers* than in a modern concert agency. But to return to you. Between 1966 and 1980, you sang at twenty Prom concerts, performing music ranging from J. S. Bach to Sir Michael Tippett. How did the Proms help shape your career?

SA: When you sing for the first time at the Royal Albert Hall, it's a most extraordinary experience, and when I made my debut there, the acoustic 'mushrooms' had yet to be hung from the ceiling. I sang at both the First and Last Nights, and at just about everything in between. I also performed at a Viennese Night, the Rachmaninoff Centenary Concert and at four Proms in 1973. I always felt very fortunate to be involved in these events, and it was such a special feeling to be singing on the Albert Hall stage. Given that the building is so vast, I always found it remarkable that my voice carried so beautifully. And as there is a wonderful feeling of tradition there, you cannot help but be aware of all the marvellous performers who have performed there before you. Some Prom audiences can be unpredictable. When I went on to sing at the Viennese Night, the Promenaders had made a huge banner that read, 'We love Sheila!' And, of course, at the Last Night, you have no idea what they might get up to.

PART TWO: SINGERS

RH: The Rachmaninoff Centenary Concert that you just mentioned was conducted by André Previn, one of the world's most versatile musicians, and one with whom you recorded Orff's *Carmina Burana*, a work that's now known and accepted universally. But at the time of its composition in the mid-1930s, its textual and musical content were quite shocking, causing the Nazis to designate it as '*entartete Kunst*' ('degenerate art'). As Orff was on good terms with the German government, any problems that the work faced soon disappeared, and it was staged by Oper Frankfurt for the first time in 1937. Did you ever perform the work in its original staged version, and how did you go about drawing out the theatrical elements of the score within a concert environment?

SA: I've never heard it in the theatre. But you're right, the work has to be theatrical, and that comes from the text and the colours that Orff demands from the orchestra. It's not one of my favourite pieces, and when you've sat through three days of rehearsals, you become very aware of the repetitive nature of the verses. When that happens, the work wears thin. I was always thankful when we got to the performances, and that the end was in sight.

RH: In 1973, you made your debut at the Royal Opera House, Covent Garden, singing Marzelline in Beethoven's *Fidelio* with Josef Krips, Birgit Nilsson, James King and Donald McIntyre. The following year, you revisited the role with a cast that included Helga Dernesch, Theo Adam and Jon Vickers, before appearing alongside Tito Gobbi in Verdi's *Falstaff*. Both of the 1974 performances were conducted by Sir Colin Davis, and the singers that I've just mentioned are of a kind that is increasingly rare today. What are your memories of those heady days, and why do you think that we now have so few singers with such cachet?

SA: We seem to have lost something, haven't we? When I first sang Marzelline under Krips, I was told by a member of staff that he had said in his magical Austrian accent, 'We have nobody like this in Vienna.' But he never asked me to sing there! Working with him and Birgit Nilsson was really quite overwhelming. The second time I sang the role, the cast was again wonderful, and Sir Colin rehearsed the first act quartet meticulously. Yet I do remember that Helga Dernesch had real problems singing Leonore. It's such a big sing, and in 'Abscheulicher! Wo eilst du hin?', she could never sing the top B. Her mouth was open, but nothing came out. But as the orchestration is so full at that point, very few people realised it. It was absolutely fantastic to watch.

RH: The conductor who led the first performance of the *Falstaff* production you gave in 1974 was Carlo Maria Giulini. The affection that performers and audiences had for him was unique, and it must have been a special experience recording Beethoven's Ninth Symphony with such a great artist. What was Giulini like as a human being and as a conductor, and what are some of the pitfalls that a soprano faces when singing in the composer's last symphony?

SA: Please forgive me for saying this, but the symphony is an absolute pig to sing. Like Brahms's *Ein deutsches Requiem* and Mahler's Second Symphony, you sit there for most of the evening before attempting a high B near the end. No matter how thoroughly you might've warmed up beforehand, you still feel unready. It's inhuman, and the *tessitura* is just in the break of the voice. It's really, really hard, and I always found it a difficult thing to do. I would have much preferred to have sung the whole of the *Missa solemnis* than the Ninth Symphony. And, in fact, I did sing the *Missa solemnis* and *Ein deutsches Requiem* with Giulini. He was a remarkable conductor and a true gentleman. I nearly disgraced myself when I first met him, because he *was* so courtly. When he took my hand to greet me, I was so overwhelmed and excited to see him that my hand struck him on the nose. It was so embarrassing.

RH: Berlioz's music can also be problematic to perform, and when you recorded *Les nuits d'été* with Sir Colin Davis, you only sang part of the cycle, with the rest being divided between a mezzo-soprano (Josephine Veasey), a tenor (Frank Patterson) and a bass (John Shirley-Quirk). Are you in accord with this approach, and did you ever sing the cycle in such a manner in the concert hall?

SA: Certainly not. And nor have I ever heard it performed that way before or since. The cycle really doesn't hang together when performed in that manner. But we were able to record some of Berlioz's other lovely songs on that disc, and I was happy to have done those.

RH: Your association with French music has been long and varied, and in 1968 you took part in a recording of Fauré's Requiem. The disc was made at the Salle Wagram with the Orchestre de Paris, the Edinburgh Festival Chorus, Dietrich Fischer-Dieskau and Daniel Barenboim. The discographic combination of an English soprano, a German baritone, a Scottish choir, an Argentinian-born conductor and a French orchestra must be unique. What are your recollections of those sessions?

SA: At the time of the recording, I had the feeling that Barenboim was exploring different elements and styles of music-making. The first time that I sang with Danny was for a performance of Beethoven's Ninth Symphony, after which we did various things together. I also took part in his first reading of *Ein deutsches Requiem*, which felt twice as slow as Stokowski's interpretation of 'I know that my Redeemer liveth'! The brass players thought their lips were going to drop off. It took about twenty minutes longer than usual. Danny conducted Fauré's Requiem very beautifully, and if memory serves me correctly, we performed it first at the Edinburgh International Festival before recording it in Paris. Dietrich Fischer-Dieskau was also amazing, and was one of my great heroes. He was a remarkable *Lieder* singer, and somebody who had great colour in his voice. He had superb control, and he sang the Requiem beautifully.

RH: How can a singer shed new light on a popular movement like the 'Pie Jesu'?

SA: First, I look to the words and their meaning. I am not sure that singers approach works like this in the same way any more. They are now more concerned with sound and line. I want the movement to be meaningful for the audience, so it should begin with the text. Being scored so lightly, 'Pie Jesu' is an incredibly difficult movement to sing; you are left feeling exposed and vulnerable. To sustain its soft and controlled line, you need enormous poise and remarkable breath control.

RH: Bach's music is something that you have returned to time and again throughout your career, and your recording of Cantata No. 3, *Ach Gott, wie manches Herzeleid*, with Karl Richter is particularly fascinating. Were you in sympathy with his approach to the composer's works?

SA: Karl Richter had extraordinary discipline. He understood the essence of Bach, and was in tune with the composer's tradition and style. It was as if he had been Bach in a previous life. He brought a life and vibrancy to the music that I never experienced with anybody else.

PART TWO: SINGERS

RH: When one interrogates Richter's cantata discography closely, the singers he used resembled a series of close-knit ensemble casts that shifted according to the period in which the recordings were made. Did you sense that carefully crafted ensembles were important to Richter?

SA: Yes, I did. His choir and orchestra knew him so well that he barely had to say anything to them. As you know, Richter directed from the harpsichord, and his musical intelligence was absolutely phenomenal. Outwardly, it might have seemed that he was totally consumed by the keyboard, but everything else was also directed perfectly. It was a very special thing to sing with him. But, as a person, I didn't like him.

RH: Why was that?

SA: He could be really quite cruel, and could demolish you very quickly. There was a sadistic touch to his criticism, which could be very unhelpful. Nevertheless, he was extraordinary as a musician.

RH: You've already spoken about the music of Bach and Handel, but perhaps we could dig a little deeper into your performance style when tackling their works.

SA: When I performed Bach's compositions, I treated them as if I were an instrument, an oboe or a flute, if you will, and adopted a clean, clinical feeling. But when I sang Handel's music, my approach was more robust, exciting and fiery. While I sang a lot of Bach, and loved doing it, I much preferred singing Handel. It was down to the excitement and humanity of the man, and his music is really quite sexy. When I recorded his *Semele* with Johannes Somary, I didn't find it difficult. There's something about Handel's music that just allows you to sing it. That's not the case for Bach, whose music can present certain difficulties.

RH: English music has been with you throughout your career, and, earlier, we discussed your reading of Purcell's *Dido and Aeneas*. But you've also regularly performed the works of Sullivan, Elgar, Vaughan Williams and Britten. As a Sullivan interpreter, you have either recorded or performed excerpts from *Ruddigore, Iolanthe, HMS Pinafore, The Mikado, The Sorcerer, Princess Ida, The Gondoliers* and *The Pirates of Penzance*. Sullivan's music was once fundamental to British musical life, but no longer enjoys that distinction. Why do you think that is?

SA: I honestly don't know. I find his music rather old-fashioned, and I never much liked his operettas. I didn't particularly enjoy singing the excerpts you just mentioned, and they were restricted to one recording and a single concert. For amateur operatic societies, these pieces are absolutely wonderful, as they are great fun and everybody loves doing them. But the operettas never really worked for me.

RH: In some ways, Elgar's life and work stand in sharp contrast to those of Sullivan. For many years, Elgar was a musical and religious outsider whose compositions struggled to be accepted universally. With Sir Charles Groves, you recorded Elgar's *Caractacus*, a choral work that's rarely heard today. As the British choral scene is no longer as buoyant as it once was, what's the future of such works, and how should we revivify choral singing in this country today?

SA: I suspect that the current position is partly due to so many schools no longer having a strong music tradition. This is completely different from the past and from my youth. As works like *Caractacus* are huge, they can require a large orchestra, a big choir and up to six soloists. Consequently, they are extremely expensive to put on. I find the whole situation very worrying. When I started singing, there were many recital clubs where you could go and learn how to perform. They allowed you the opportunity to hone your skills under difficult conditions before exposing yourself for the first time at the Wigmore Hall. The same was true when working with the small choirs and orchestras that existed during those years. British musical life has changed greatly during my lifetime, and the values that we had as a society, and the enjoyments that we pursued, are now dwindling sharply. It's desperately sad.

RH: With the exception of a number of committed champions, such as Sir John Barbirolli, Sir Adrian Boult, Sir Charles Groves, Bernard Haitink and André Previn, all of whom you worked with, Vaughan Williams's music has never held a central place in most conductors' repertoires. Why do you think that is, and why were you so attracted to it?

SA: I've performed a great deal of Vaughan Williams, and, for me, he is quintessentially English. But I've been assured that in America, he is revered and loved, and that recordings of his music are broadcast almost daily. That said, some British music can be problematic when given abroad. When I performed Britten's *Spring Symphony* with André and the Pittsburgh Symphony Orchestra in Pittsburgh, Philadelphia and New York, the audience actually got up and walked out in the middle of one of the contralto's most beautiful solo passages. They simply couldn't cope. The music of Beethoven and Brahms was more their thing.

RH: And, of course, Benjamin Britten's works are also closely associated with you. Did you ever meet him?

SA: Sadly not. At the end of my final year at the Academy, I arranged with a small group of friends to hire a car and to travel to Spain for a holiday. But the day before we were to set off, I received a telephone call saying that Mr Britten would like to hear me sing, and that I should be available at 10am the next morning to meet him. Being young and naïve, I had the temerity to say, 'I'm terribly sorry, I'm going on holiday tomorrow, but I'd love to sing for him when I return.' I never heard from him again.

RH: Did you perform much *Lieder* during your career, and, if so, how would you describe your approach to this genre?

SA: I loved singing *Lieder*, and when I was studying at the Academy, I worked with a wonderful teacher named Flora Nielsen. She had sung the Female Chorus at the premiere of Britten's *The Rape of Lucretia* at Glyndebourne in 1946, and was a very well-known *Lieder* interpreter. This meant that I had good grounding in the genre. Giving recitals and singing *Lieder* can be extremely difficult. When you consider that Wolf's song 'Mausfallen-Sprüchlein' is only about a minute long, and in that minute you have to create a picture and bring the text to life, you realise how difficult *Lieder* singing can be. And, in a recital, you might have twenty such songs. As *Lieder* singing can be exhausting both physically and emotionally, you have to have a very good technique to perform it. When I started working on Strauss's *Vier letzte Lieder*, it took me three years to prepare them. Every time I began to study the cycle, I would burst into tears, because they were just so beautiful.

RYLAND DAVIES AND DENNIS O'NEILL
(DAVID JOSEFOWITZ RECITAL HALL, 4 NOVEMBER 2011)

RAYMOND HOLDEN: For more than five decades, you have appeared at many of the world's great opera houses and concert halls, and have done much to fly the flag for Welsh music-making. Why do you think that your fellow countrymen are so attracted to the voice, and would it be fair to say that Wales is synonymous with singing?

RYLAND DAVIES: Singing is a beautiful disease for which there's no known cure. It's in the Welsh language, which we both had to speak and sing in at school. The vowel sounds are quite similar to Latin, and we Welsh tend to sing even when we speak.

DENNIS O'NEILL: George Bernard Shaw once described the Welsh as 'Italians in the rain', and I agree with Ryland about the vowel sounds. The Welsh accent is derived from the original language, which has no diphthongs. The sounds are written out precisely. There are some difficult consonants, such as the 'ch' and the 'll', and when we say 'no', the 'o' is elongated.

RH: Would it be fair to say that singing for the Welsh is something akin to brass-band playing for a Northerner?

DO: No. For somebody of my generation, if you were a singer, or indeed a poet, you were given great respect. And, of course, singing and poetry were disciplines that you could compete with at eisteddfods.

RD: You were also encouraged to take singing further if you reached a certain standard, particularly if you were lucky enough to be heard by someone at an eisteddfod. But both singing and brass-band playing are ways of bringing people together and of celebrating music. They are also good ways of keeping kids off the streets. I used to go to a junior youth club at my school where I learned to sing and dance The Pirate King from Gilbert and Sullivan's *The Pirates of Penzance*. As the role was a bit low for me, I sang it with difficulty. But I was big, and the organisers thought that I looked good in the part. And it has to be said that Nanki-Poo from *The Mikado* was much easier to sing when I performed it eighteen months later.

RH: We hear a great deal about Welsh male-voice choirs. Is singing in Wales predominately a male medium, or is it something that's gender-neutral?

DO: It's very much gender-neutral. You only have to look at the opera singers that come from Wales to see that. Take Dame Gwyneth Jones, for example. She is only one of many female artists who have had very big careers. The male-voice choir had its roots in mining. My grandfather was a miner, and he and his fellow miners would have to crawl on their bellies for miles underground. Singing provided them with something to do, and something that they could take to chapel on weekends.

RD: Singing would also happen at times of adversity, and was a means of keeping spirits up. The men would naturally break into harmony without necessarily being able to read a note of music. It was something within them and that was passed from generation to generation.

RH: How did you make your first steps as singers?

RD: I was good at rugby as a boy, and was about to be capped as an under-eighteen player. But when I sang at an eisteddfod, I was told that I should pursue a career as a singer. When I then went to Manchester, and met our mutual teacher, Frederic Cox, it was clear that rugby was not conducive to singing. So, that was that when it came to rugby.

DO: After singing in an eisteddfod, I, too, went to study with Frederic Cox. But my actual route to singing was somewhat different. My father was a local doctor, and when he came back from delivering babies, he would listen to Italian opera. This meant that from the youngest age, there wasn't a time that I wasn't listening to it. I simply assimilated it. He introduced me to Enrico Caruso and Beniamino Gigli, whom Ryland and I both love. Singing was in me, but I do think that the gene has to be there in the first place. Music is a language, and it can be expressed through a Welsh hymn, a Verdi aria or a Bach motet. The genre doesn't really matter.

RH: Along with Caruso and Gigli, who were some of your other early vocal idols?

RD: I also heard Jussi Björling and Mario Lanza. Lanza was a big influence on singers from our generation, and when I saw *The Great Caruso* as a nine-year-old, I said to my father, 'I'd like to sing like that.' It impressed and inspired me, and by the age of thirteen I was already a tenor. But what I didn't understand at the time was how he managed the top notes. Björling and Lanza were the singers who really stood out, and the recordings that my grandmother had of Gigli were truly inspirational. I also remember that she had a disc of Caruso accompanied by a wind band, which wasn't uncommon at the time. Something about the voice grabbed me, and as Dennis has said in his masterclasses, you always have to sing to your audiences. But to do so, you have to have a technique that doesn't damage the voice.

DO: My dad was absolutely mad about Caruso, and I thought he was marvellous too. But Gigli was something very special. Björling was also a singer I heard a great deal of on record. Another voice that impressed me was Tito Schipa. Most homes at the time wouldn't have had many of his discs, but my father did. Schipa could turn a simple Italian aria into a sophisticated *Lied*. He had a beautifully direct voice, and his tasteful approach had a huge effect on me.

RD: And when asked about Schipa, Caruso said, 'Please, all of us, don't forget to bend a knee to him.' Schipa was a great interpreter and a great singer of words.

RH: Earlier, you both mentioned Frederic Cox, who taught at the Royal Manchester College of Music, now the Royal Northern College of Music. Why were you attracted to him as young musicians, and why was he such a magnet for so many aspiring singers?

DO: Freddie was probably closer to Ryland than any of his other students.

RD: He was very honest, frank and inspirational, and had a wicked sense of humour. The way that he demonstrated the male *passaggio* to us was important, as neither of us knew how to access our head resonance.

PART TWO: SINGERS

When I auditioned for him, I sang 'Comfort ye my people' from Handel's *Messiah* and 'Questa o quella' from Verdi's *Rigoletto*. Heaven knows what the Verdi aria sounded like, but at the end of the audition he said we had enough time to repeat the recitative that preceded the Handel aria. He worked on the long E natural before taking the F sharp and the G sharp. He wanted to avoid a swell on the second syllable of the word 'Comfort'. Not only would the audience then hear the vowel sung correctly, and with only a minimal change of colour, but the notes themselves would be less taxing. I learned very quickly that if a tenor can't easily sing an F sharp or a G sharp, they're soon for the tenors' graveyard.

DO: Freddie was a master teacher, even though his own voice was very forgettable.

RD: Dennis is quite right when he says this, as he fell between a tenor and a baritone. He had studied for about seven or eight years at the Teatro alla Scala in Milan with Aureliano Pertile. Pertile was a remarkable tenor, who, like Tito Schipa, could sing *pianissimo* passages marvellously.

DO: Although we now affectionately call him 'Freddie', we always referred to him as either 'Mr Cox' or 'Professor' when we studied with him. And, later, he was Principal of the Royal Manchester College of Music. When I auditioned for him, he said in his characteristic voice, 'Yes, there's a voice there, but you really can't sing!' It was so true, and reflective of his great integrity. He dressed in a very old-fashioned manner and was extremely dignified. But he could have a sharp tongue if a student didn't show him the necessary respect. He once disarmed a pupil by saying, 'There's something odd about you. And do you know what that is? When one first meets you, one likes you.'

RD: Freddie did speak the most divine English and in a most gentlemanly manner, but when he sat at the piano, and became engrossed in the singing, his passion for all forms of music was immediately obvious. He once said to me that after studying at La Scala, he tried to be a baritone. But he immediately qualified this by adding, 'I really wouldn't like to be that sort of baritone.' It was clear that if he couldn't be truly successful singing in a *tessitura*, that was the end of it. When the Second World War broke out, he joined the Belgian Underground, and it was through his activities with that organisation that he was awarded the OBE.

RH: When I was looking through your biographies, I noticed that major international competitions were largely absent. Do you recommend competitions to young singers?

DO: Like it or not, the whole of the singing profession is highly competitive. I've little sympathy when people say that it's cruel to put young singers through competitions. First of all, we're not 'putting them through' these things, as they can decide for themselves whether or not they want to take part. All that a teacher can do is give good advice, and to be honest when a student is not ready to compete. I was once asked to adjudicate a competition that involved 247 singers in just under three days. Of those who took part, nearly 200 of them weren't up to the task, and of that 200, 180 of them had no hope of becoming a professional singer. And while their voices could change, they didn't have the 'need' to sing. This 'need' is based on a natural musical language and the ability to shape the music. To adjudicate this competition was very depressing. Yet those who managed to get to the final were all extremely good. Of course, a young singer doesn't have to win to succeed, but they should get to the final. That's when the agents and the television people turn up.

PART TWO: SINGERS

But competitions are not the start of a career, as you don't learn very much about singing from taking part in them. While they can be a good experience, they can also be very cruel.

RD: I agree completely with Dennis. But with the involvement of television, and all the razzmatazz that surrounds it, competitions now have a high profile. If you take part in BBC Cardiff Singer of the World, and you are not quite ready, that's not a good thing to do. As it happens, I once entered a competition that was held in the Royal Academy of Music's Duke's Hall. I won a scholarship at that competition, which enabled me to make my first trip to Italy. And I am proud to say that I was the first singer to win The John Christie Award at the Glyndebourne Festival Opera. This meant that I had some money to return to Italy and to study three roles with Luigi Ricci.

DO: I also worked with Ricci, and, to me, he was the spitting image of Mussolini. When I studied the Duke from *Rigoletto* with him, and came to the end of the aria we were working on, he picked up a board and threw it at my chest. Stunned, I asked, 'What did I do, Maestro?' 'Why didn't you sing the trill?' he replied. I said, 'If you want me to sing a trill, of course I will, but there's nothing in my score.' Keen to get to the bottom of this, I asked him how he knew that there should be a trill at that point. 'I'll tell you how I know. When my father, who was Verdi's preferred rehearsal pianist, played this aria with the Maestro, and I was turning the pages as a little boy, I remember Verdi going crazy and shouting when the tenor didn't sing the trill. When the tenor explained that there was nothing in the score, Verdi lost his temper again, as the publisher, Ricordi, had made a mess of it.' When the University of Chicago Press brought out a scholarly edition of the score, I must have been one of the first to buy it, and, sure enough, there was the trill.

RH: Ryland, after studying with Frederic Cox, you went on to sing at Glyndebourne. What was that like?

RD: It was a great experience, and there were some very interesting people there. I was twenty-one at the time and very young. For the 1964 season, the Glyndebourne chorus needed some fresh blood to cope with the big works that it was scheduled to perform: Verdi's *Macbeth* and Mozart's *Die Zauberflöte* and *Idomeneo*. Of the eight of us that were auditioned that year, about three or four were accepted. I was thrilled by that, but when I was called back five weeks later to sing again, I was terrified. What I didn't know was that I wasn't going to sing for the chorus master, Myer Fredman, but for that remarkable little man from Hungary, Jani Strasser. Jani spoke six languages, was Glyndebourne's Head of Music, was in charge of distributing the smaller parts and was responsible for appointing the understudies. To my great surprise, he asked me to cover one of the roles in Rossini's rarely performed opera *La pietra del paragone*. As it was to be produced by the German director Günther Rennert, I knew that it would be a wonderful opportunity to work with one of opera's great craftsmen; sadly, I'd missed working with Carl Ebert by two years. The tenor I covered was Umberto Grilli, and I prayed every night that he wouldn't be sick, as there were some passages with high B flats that I was still coming to terms with. But being in the chorus also taught me a great deal. I learned to listen to others around me, and to sing as part of a group. As an understudy, I received as much rehearsal time as the principals, which was another wonderful opportunity, as you never knew who might hear you. Many of the coaches were leading figures in their own right, such as Geoffrey Parsons and Martin Isepp. And while there was great comradery amongst the singers, there was also great competition. You had to be on your mettle, and, at the time, the music staff – the *répétiteurs* and the coaches – lived in the main house, while the rest of us had to find digs nearby.

RH: You also worked very closely with my old mentor and friend, Sir John Pritchard.

RD: He was one of my main champions during my early career, and because of his catholic abilities as a musician, he gave me many chances. He was an amazing artist who was equally at home with Mozart, Strauss and Verdi. During his early years at Glyndebourne, John had learned the German repertoire from Fritz Busch and had studied the Italian repertoire with Vittorio Gui. This meant that he had a wealth of knowledge to pass on to us.

RH: Dennis, an important turning point for you was when you attended the Opera Barga Festival in Tuscany. How did that come about?

DO: I was nineteen and was invited to attend by Peter Gellhorn. I'd never left the United Kingdom before, and was dreadfully unhappy studying at Sheffield University. Peter told me about his summer school in Tuscany, and arranged for me to have a grant of £160 to go there. This was more than enough for me to live comfortably in the late 1960s, and the experience was astonishing. By the end of the six weeks, I knew that academia was not for me, and come hell or high water, opera was what I wanted to do.

RH: At the time, were you aware that you had an Italianate timbre, and that Bellini, Donizetti and Verdi would be central to your repertoire?

DO: I knew that I had that sound, but I didn't think in those terms compositionally.

RH: When did you know that Bellini, Donizetti and Verdi would be important to you?

DO: I hoped that they would be, but I had to content myself with whatever I could sing during that period. I had yet to meet Frederic Cox, and had very little compass. But I was determined to find somebody who could teach me. I went to two or three teachers, but they simply didn't have the answers. That was the difference between Freddie and the others: if you asked him a question, he had an answer or an example to give you. It was a long and bumpy ride after I found him, but I did acquire some method. When I listen to Ryland sing Mozart, I have to ask: where are the Mozart tenors these days who can sing like that? Only the great Swedish tenor Nicolai Gedda is comparable to Ryland, as they have a remarkably similar sound. Not only is their approach healthy, but it's also Italianate. I never had that particular sound.

RH: When I recently listened to you singing a Bellini song on disc, it occurred to me that every pianist and string player could learn a great deal about line by studying his music.

DO: Like Mozart, Bellini demands much and leaves no room for compromise. His music is very difficult technically, and if you can't manage a *diminuendo* on a high C, you shouldn't perform it.

RH: To imply that you, Ryland, were simply a distinguished Mozart tenor would be to do you a great disservice. Along with the nineteenth-century Italian repertoire, you've also explored a number of Russian masterworks.

RD: I've had the pleasure of singing in the Russian language a few times, and have performed in both Tchaikovsky's *Eugene Onegin* and

PART TWO: SINGERS

Rachmaninoff's *The Bells*. I've also recently sung a lot in Czech, and both Russian and Czech are rather '*latino*' once you get past the consonants. Both languages are quite vocal.

RH: I'm keen to hear your thoughts on some of your great Welsh predecessors and contemporaries. First, I'd like to chat a little about Richard Lewis, born Thomas Thomas to Welsh parents in Manchester. We know that he had a sound that was both distinctive and influential, but did you ever meet him?

RD: I certainly did. It was during my first season at Glyndebourne when he performed the title role in *Idomeneo* there in 1964. He sang it marvellously, and the young Luciano Pavarotti was his Idamantes. This meant that I heard two very different timbres sounding from either side of the stage. I quickly realised that Richard sang with the same technique that both Dennis and I use, particularly when it came to the dreaded *passaggio*. He was brilliant and had a solid sound. But to be quite frank, as his sound was so distinctive, I wondered if he had a head cold when I first heard him. I later realised that this was his sound, in just the same way that Gigli's was very much his own. This is a very important point. Even though Dennis and I come from the same vocal 'womb', so to speak, and are from the same vocal school, we have very individual sounds. That was also true of Richard.

RH: Recently, we mourned the death of Robert Tear. For many, he was the quintessential English tenor, but, in fact, he was born in Barry in Glamorgan. Presumably, his days as a choral scholar at Cambridge, and his time as a chorister at St Paul's Cathedral, determined his future career path and sound-world.

DO: He was a really nice man and a great artist. While Bob had a very Italianate bell to his sound, he never needed to explore the extremities of his range. What we got from Bob was quintessential Bob. That was very attractive. And while he loved listening to Verdi, he felt that other people sang it better. Bob always performed the music he loved, which meant he communicated it marvellously. I once heard him sing Belmonte from Mozart's *Die Entführung aus dem Serail*. He performed it so easily and with such elegance. And he had a wickedly English sense of humour.

RD: I once heard Bob sing in Mendelssohn's *Elijah*, and was impressed by the lustiness of the voice. And had he chosen to do so, he could have gone down the same road as Dennis.

RH: No discussion about Welsh tenors would be complete without mentioning Stuart Burrows. Although he no longer performs, he remains a dominant figure thanks to his extensive discography. Central to that discography were his recordings of Mozart. What are your thoughts on Mr Burrows's work in general, and his Mozart style in particular?

RD: I once heard him say: 'I never had a teacher.' You might say that he was 'homemade'. But he had nerves of steel, and even when he performed a work that might have been a little too heavy for him, he had a go and always got through it. To paraphrase Frank Sinatra, 'He did it his way', and did so very well. When it came to the *passaggio*, it wasn't as succinct as it could have been, had he worked with Frederic Cox. But he had beautiful breath control, and you were always left wondering if he had three lungs rather than two.

PART TWO: SINGERS

DO: I remember being at the Welsh Office in Whitehall with Stuart one St David's Day. It was a terribly boring affair, and at the end of it, I asked where he was off to. As we were both going back to Cardiff, I said that I'd give him a lift to the station. We knew each other fairly well, and I always had a great respect for him. After the train had pulled out of Paddington, and was heading towards Reading, the refreshment trolley appeared. Stuart then asked me what my preferred tipple was, which, in those days, was Scotch whisky. Normally, he drank gin at that time of day, but said that he'd have a Scotch with me instead. He then turned to the attendant, and asked for two whiskies. When the chap popped a glass down in front of each of us, Stuart looked up and said, 'No, I meant two *each*.' He was adorable and had a wonderful accent. Not only was he a great man, but a very special singer. When I once asked him if he either taught or gave masterclasses, he replied in that marvellous Welsh voice, 'No. I haven't anything to say, have I?' I also once asked him what his greatest memory was. He replied, 'Oh, that's easy. The new production of the "Welsh" *Don Giovanni* at Salzburg with Herbert von Karajan, Geraint Evans and *me*!' 'Yes, but what's the great memory?' I asked again. '"Dalla sua pace"' was his reply, an aria that's terrifying to sing. He explained that, 'When Karajan put the first beat down with that fierce face of his, I was *so* scared. And after I began to sing, he laid his baton down, leaned back and waved at me to carry on.' Stuart thought that Karajan had given up on him because he was so bad. But, in fact, the opposite was true. Karajan simply wanted to get out of his way. And that's how humble Stuart is. He's a lovely, lovely man.

RH: I'm keen to hear your thoughts on the nuts and bolts of being a singer, and the day-to-day rigours involved with the profession. When learning a new role, Dennis once said, 'In terms of revving myself up [for a new part], [there's] a job of work to be done, there's a science to it, it's hard work.' What did you mean by that?

DO: There *is* a science to learning a new role, and it's a very serious business indeed. If you have the very rare possibility of doing nothing else, which is extremely unusual as a professional singer, you should read through the whole score first so that you can get a good overall understanding of it. Then, you should scientifically identify the passages that you know will be difficult, and search out the sections that will require special practice and breathing. When you've done all of that, and feel that you are ready to present the score vocally to the public without too much fear, go back to the beginning and explore it musically.

RD: My approach is similar to that of Dennis. As I was so young when I started out, I always got very excited about the music. But, with experience, I realised that it was essential to read through the complete work and to get a feel for it first. This is particularly true when it comes to the text, as it's very important to identify your character's role in the plot. You need to know whether you survive the whole thing, or get knocked off partway through. And the older I get, the more I relate to the text. I'm now a quick reader, but that wasn't always the case. I like to study well in advance of the first rehearsal, and being thorough is important to me. But to have the time to do that is a luxury. You have to grab it when you can, and you must only absorb material at the speed that the voice can take. The brain often works faster than the voice, and it's essential to embed the music into the throat's muscles. I was very pleased when I was sent a cassette of the translation and the transliterations of Lensky's material from *Eugene Onegin* before I sang it. This meant that I had time to prepare it, and to allow the text to become idiomatic.

PART TWO: SINGERS

RH: Agents are important in shaping the careers of young singers. How did you come to an agent's attention for the first time, and how did they go about marketing you?

DO: The profession has changed markedly since our early days. The recording of classical music, for example, is now run by people who formerly ran pop departments, and it's now a business that puts pressure on singers to be quick and ready. People who can survive this, such as Bryn Terfel, are very rare indeed. And there's a difference between an agent and a manager. If you are able to get a manager who understands the profession globally, and who can advise against certain things, then that can be very helpful. I was managed by Howard Hartog, who knew everybody. Puffing on his huge cigar in his high-back chair, he once said that he'd heard I'd recently sung a good *La traviata* by Verdi. I said that I did, and within seconds of hearing my answer, he was on the telephone to the Hamburg Staatsoper. My German was not good at the time, but I was able to work out that Mr Hartog got through to somebody important at the theatre, that José Carreras was not going to do *Traviata*'s opening night the following week and that he had the right man to replace him. Clearly, the Hamburg management had never heard of me, and it would have been impossible for me to have secured the engagement without Mr Hartog's intervention. That was extraordinary. And although artists might now pay ten, fifteen or twenty per cent, even when they've generated much of the work themselves, it's still necessary to have an agent.

RD: Dennis has just reminded me of the time that I sang *Messiah* in Munich with Karl Richter. As I had three or four days between performances, I thought that I'd go to see Herr Stoll, the agent who had passed on the job to me. He was an important figure in Germany who spoke good English, and while we were chatting, the phone rang. After excusing himself to take the call, he briefly interrupted his telephone conversation to ask if I knew Debussy's *Pelléas et Mélisande*. He wanted to know if I was free to sing in a new production of it at Stuttgart the following November with Silvio Varviso conducting and Götz Friedrich directing. I told him that I'd sung in a concert performance of the opera in Liverpool, and would be happy to do it. Apparently, Stuttgart wanted to do the work with a tenor, and that the German baritone Wolfgang Schöne was to sing Golaud to my Pelléas. This worked because of Wolfgang's lighter voice. If a baritone like Sir Thomas Allen were to sing Pelléas, then you'd need a heavier bass voice like that of Sir Donald McIntyre to sing Golaud. This is necessary if the true *chiaroscuro* of the piece is to be achieved. Not only was this a case of being in the right place at the right time, but it was a good example of an agent's power. Luckily, I'd already begun to make a name for myself by the time of that encounter, and had been singing for about fourteen years. But there's a point that I'd like to make here, and that I am sure Dennis will endorse. The sooner that young singers get to know themselves vocally, and to have sufficient confidence to say 'no', the better. These are important lessons to learn, and are crucial to come to terms with. And, as Dennis has said, there's a great difference between an agent and a manager. A manager will advise you, while an agent will sell you.

RH: Directors are central to any opera singer's day-to-day activities. What are your thoughts on modern production values?

DO: Both John Copley and John Cox are essentially traditionalists who know their craft. As I tend to go to more operas than I sing in these days, what I don't want to do is to sit there wishing that I'd brought a crossword puzzle to complete. While I like to be stimulated and shocked, I also need to understand what the director's point is. And there's nothing more dreadful than seeing *Lucia di Lammermoor*'s leading lady arrive on stage riding a motorbike. It's disruptive. Sir Brian McMaster was determined to take the Welsh National Opera down a modern route, and when he did, there was a twenty-five per cent drop in ticket sales. This was particularly evident when the company performed in smaller, but no less important, venues like Swansea. And I remember saying to Brian that if we were to lose the current audience, we would lose the next generation as well. This happened, and the situation never really recovered. I'm not suggesting that this was Brian's fault, far from it, but it's now a common problem.

RH: Over the years, you have worked with some of the world's greatest conductors. These have included Sir Antonio Pappano, Sir John Pritchard, Sir Colin Davis, Herbert von Karajan, Sir Georg Solti, Sir Charles Mackerras, Zubin Mehta, Daniel Barenboim, Giuseppe Sinopoli and Sir Simon Rattle. Who, amongst these, was a 'singer's conductor', and what does that moniker mean practically?

DO: Each of the artists you just named was an exceptionally talented figure, and all were different temperamentally and musically. But let me give you an example of a 'singer's conductor'. Over the last fifteen years or so, I have worked a great deal with Zubin Mehta at the Bayerische Staatsoper. And I was very flattered that whenever he did an opera by Verdi there, he'd ask for me. I always found him very flexible, and while we were performing *Il trovatore* together, I asked him about working with singers. 'It's very simple,' he said. 'If the singer is musical, I'll follow them. If not, they'll follow me.' He's an extremely elegant conductor, and one who never takes his eyes off the singers. If you take a little time, he's there with you. But if you overstep the mark, his disapproval is clear from his face and gestures. A 'singer's conductor' is one who trusts in your musicianship.

RD: And then there was Sir Charles Mackerras, who was an expert in so many genres and types of music. He was well known for his Mozart, Handel and Janáček. And although I have sung a great deal of Janáček's music over the last few years, I never performed the composer's works with Charles. If you knew your stuff, and could sing on the beat, he'd happily work with you. But he could get 'ratty' quite easily. He once said to me when recording Handel's *Judas Maccabeus*, 'Ryland, those *appoggiaturas* that we discussed at the first rehearsal, is it that you have forgotten them, or is it that you just don't want to do them?' 'Most of them are marvellous,' I said. 'But I feel that some of them are weakening Judas Maccabeus as a warrior.' I was concerned that they might have romanticised the phrase, rather than added to its sense of urgency.

RH: And, finally, what of Giuseppe Sinopoli, who recently died so suddenly?

DO: I worked with him a lot, and he was about the thirty-second conductor who claimed to have discovered me! He was a very sociable chap whose beard and small, round glasses made him look like a cross between Jesus and Schubert. I mentioned that to him thinking that he would laugh, but he didn't. Nevertheless, he was a good guy and a very decisive man. When Giuseppe invited me to audition for him, he told me to bring along Verdi's Requiem, not an easy piece to audition with. As it went well, he asked me to do a six-week tour of Germany with it. I said that I'd do as many performances as possible, and when I asked how many there were in total, he said twenty-eight! In the end, I did one. After thinking that was that, he called me again. He wanted me to go to

PART TWO: SINGERS

Hamburg and to bring along *Il trovatore*. I'd never done it before in my life. It's a terribly difficult opera, and one that needs to sit well in the throat's muscles. He then said that we were to give *Trovatore* in Munich, and that we were also going to record it. This is a good example of a conductor's power, and, of course, he had a contract with Deutsche Grammophon to back it up. But as he had a very convoluted conducting technique, he was a very difficult person to follow. It was dreadful, but I did like him very much.

SARAH WALKER
(DAVID JOSEFOWITZ RECITAL HALL, 10 FEBRUARY 2012)

RAYMOND HOLDEN: Let's kick off, shall we, with a simple question: what makes a great singer?

SARAH WALKER: That's hardly a simple question at all. Discipline, hard work and luck make a great singer. But mainly hard work and discipline. There's no magic formula. You have to do the work, and you have to have high standards.

RH: You were born at Cheltenham in 1943, and I seem to remember reading somewhere that your grandparents were members of the Hallé Choir, and that your aunt was the soprano Annie Walker. Were your parents also musical?

SW: Not particularly, although my father did enjoy music. He played the piano, but was not involved with music professionally. My darling mother was what I'd call a 'top-note fancier'. She was there for the pretty frocks and the top notes. And why not, I say. It takes all sorts, and there's nothing wrong with that. And let's face it, opera used to be based on pretty frocks and top notes. My main educational influence was really my secondary school. It was a marvellous place with a brilliant music department. I was really encouraged to get involved with music there, and it was where I began singing in choirs and playing in orchestras as a violinist. In fact, I entered the Royal College of Music as a violinist. I also took up the cello, having been inspired by Harvey Phillips. And I even managed to teach myself enough about the instrument for him to take me on as a pupil. All his students had to play Elgar's Cello Concerto. But I only managed the first page. That was it.

RH: Do you think that there was a particular moment when your parents thought that you had talent?

SW: No. I don't think that ever happened. And I don't believe it's possible to know whether somebody is talented or not. It's something that grows out of ambition and interest. But there might be a moment when you realise that your child wants to take a particular direction. When that happens, you encourage that child. I don't think that I was particularly talented. But I was musical – that was fairly obvious – and my ear was quick. While some people might start singing at sixteen, I didn't. If I had, it would've been a waste of time. My voice didn't arrive on the scene until my early twenties.

RH: Growing up in Britain in the decades directly following the Second World War must have been fascinating. Covent Garden had just been reorganised in its current guise, the recording industry was flourishing and the great conservatoires were once again accepting students from across the globe.

SW: I don't remember any of that. I was totally uninterested in opera, and I had no idea what Covent Garden was until I came up to London to study at the Royal College of Music. Even then, I wasn't interested. In Cheltenham, I was very much involved in the local music scene, and it was a marvellous place to be as a young artist. It not only had a fabulous music festival, but also a great competitive festival that I used to take part in. I entered everything possible, sometimes up to eighteen or twenty events. My headmistress got very cross about this and didn't approve. But as I won most of these events, she was forced to be quite pleased on behalf of the school, as my victories brought great credit to it. At the main music festival, I used to act as an usher. This meant that I was able to go to all the concerts and to hear works by composers such as Sir Peter Maxwell Davies and Brian Ferneyhough. It didn't mean that I learned to love contemporary music above everything else, but it did mean that I became inquisitive. My father adored the music festival, and whenever there was an opportunity to hear a piano recital, he would be there. His favourite pianist was Benno Moiseiwitsch, as he was a very unmannered player. My father didn't like lots of show and extraneous movement. He liked musicians to be still and contained. And he probably would have liked that about me, as I am that kind of performer.

RH: How did your experiences as a string player impact your approach as a singer?

SW: It didn't affect me at the time, as I wasn't singing, other than in choirs and in church. Even though the violin played a principal part in my early musical life, I didn't take it up until I was fourteen. That's much too late to do anything truly productive with it. That was a shame, as my brother and I were natural instrumentalists. We could pick up instruments and could get a sound out of them immediately. It would have been nice to have developed as a violinist, but I'm quite glad that I didn't. And as I have often said in some of my more cheeky concert biographies, that when I learned that I had to practise the fiddle for forty-six hours a day, I gave it up. But after entering the profession, I realised what an impact my string playing had on my understanding of tuning and intonation. I listened with a string-player's ear. This means that I don't hear things in terms of equal semitones, such as you might find on a piano, but according to the key I am singing in and where the note lies within the scale. There are both narrow and wide semitones. I quickly learned that this was very important.

RH: Was this a consequence of your studies at the Royal College of Music?

SW: I am sorry to say that I learned nothing about singing at the College, even though I had a great time there. I was too young. When I began singing at eighteen, I was identified as a soprano, and was given Donna Anna's aria 'Or sai chi l'onore' from Mozart's *Don Giovanni* to learn. My teacher was a wonderful pedagogue and a great woman, but she wasn't for me. My next teacher wasn't really interested, and was the kind of person who listened to whatever you happened to bring along each week. And I should point out that it was during my second year at the College that I transferred to the voice, having entered as a violinist. Such a change is probably not possible today.

RH: How would you compare your time at the Royal College of Music in the 1960s to student life today?

SW: It was extremely tame by modern standards. For a start, we didn't work nearly as hard as the students whom I now teach at the various London colleges. It's perfectly obvious to me that today's students have to work very hard. This is something that I approve of, as you are forced to face the necessities of musical life. And this can include things that might seem unimportant at first, such as historical analysis. Even though

I might've done it for A level, I don't remember anything about it. Yet it has a relevance. Apart from anything else, it makes you do something that you don't think that you can, and that you don't think is important. But you must learn to do such things to the best of your ability, as this is what performance is about for me. When I was young and given music by a composer other than Mozart, Schubert, Berlioz or Monteverdi, I would toss it aside as either rubbish or boring. But when I took the trouble to get into it, to absorb it and to make it mine, I became fascinated by it and loved it. I learned the importance of this approach early on, and it became my way into the world. It was a direct consequence of my natural curiosity.

RH: After leaving the College, you went on to study with the renowned pedagogue Vera Rózsa. Much has been written and said about her approach, but why was she such a magnet for gifted young singers?

SW: It's very difficult to sum up Vera. After she died a couple of years ago in her late nineties, I was proficient enough on the computer to transfer some old VHS tapes of her onto YouTube. I did this so that those who might be interested in Vera could learn something about her remarkable life. The six parts that I uploaded were from a wonderful Finnish television documentary that gives a tremendous flavour of her life and times. She was a woman who was almost impossible to describe and was quite unique. Her ear was faultless, and I don't mean when it simply came to hearing if a note was out of tune or not. She could hear what you were doing, where you were placing the voice, and what muscles you were using. She also had the ability to adapt to each person she was working with and to teach them differently. I don't respond to words like intercostal or soft palate, for example. I don't understand them, and they mean very little to me. But for some people, they mean a great deal. Vera understood this, and could find each singer's correct direction. She had her principles, and her musical principles were completely without fault. Vera was also incredibly curious. I once took Cage's *Aria* to her. This is written in a series of different colours, with each colour requiring an equally different vocal timbre. It's terrific fun, and one of the first truly contemporary and dangerous pieces that I took to Vera. Had I taken the work to my teacher at the College, I would have been told very firmly not to touch it. Vera's response was complete curiosity. She would ask in her marvellous Hungarian accent, 'What's this? What does this mean, darling?' She would then take me through every voice that I wanted to use, so that the sound was properly supported, was correctly produced and did no harm. It was exactly what I needed.

RH: Did Vera ever discuss her own background with you?

SW: Very little. Although she was a very private person, she did describe her upbringing in the documentary that I mentioned earlier. She talks of growing up in Hungary with her violinist father, how she studied with Zoltán Kodály, and the time that she was taken for a drive in the park by Béla Bartók. When she mentions this on the film, a photograph of Bartók appears on screen, and all you can think of is 'wow', as he was so good-looking when he was young. She remembered taking part in a competition at the conservatoire, and suddenly feeling that there were eyes boring through her. When she turned around, there was Bartók. He then congratulated her, and asked if she would accompany him to the park. She was a wonderful woman, and I spent nearly forty years with her. She was with me throughout my entire performing career. As Vera's pupils were so numerous, it is nearly impossible to list them all. And she would be the last person to tell you who they were. She would never say who was studying with her unless by mistake. Such a 'mistake' might happen if you entered her studio at the same time as another student was leaving. This was rare, however, because Vera had two rooms. You waited first in one room, before being taken into her teaching room. This was very polite. If you were an established artist, of which she had many, you might not want to be seen by someone else. Today, that's no longer the case, as we're now proud of our teachers. We are very happy to acknowledge who they are, to give credit where credit's due and to recommend them to others. When I was starting out, some singers would say, 'I've never had a lesson in my life.' And I would always think, 'So, that's the problem.'

RH: You made your debut as an opera singer in 1969 as Ottavia in Monteverdi's *L'incoronazione di Poppea* with Kent Opera, a company that no longer exists. What are your memories of that momentous event?

SW: I certainly didn't think it was momentous at the time. But, in retrospect, I suppose it was important for the company and for me personally: it was Kent Opera's first production and I met my husband at those performances. Sir Roger Norrington was the company's conductor, and continued to be so for the greater part of its existence. We performed Raymond Leppard's version of the opera, which had been given a little earlier at Glyndebourne. It was a marvellous version to perform, and I still speak of it today. It's a wonderful way of guiding somebody into Monteverdian style, and a good way of preparing for versions such as Gian Francesco Malipiero's, where the printed page can often be quite bare. I sang in three productions of *Poppea* during my twenty years with Kent Opera, including Roger Norrington's and Alan Curtis's versions of the work. In the second, I sang Poppea as a mezzo-soprano, while Nerone was sung by a soprano. This meant that the last duet finally made sense musically.

PART TWO: SINGERS

RH: Shortly after your debut with Kent Opera, you appeared at Glyndebourne. What are your memories of the Sussex house?

SW: Unlike some singers who spent many seasons at Glyndebourne, I was only there for one. This was partly due to the fact that I was engaged mainly as a chorister. I simply couldn't take the strain of being taught works parrot-fashion that I could read at sight. This was something that I simply couldn't handle. In those days, Glyndebourne was structured so that you started as a chorus member, before rising to an understudy, and, later, a principal. This was fine at the time, but I rather hope that the standard that they now expect from young musicians is greater than back then. Nevertheless, the season that I spent there was enough to give me a flavour of that wonderful place. As it's isolated and beautiful, it means that you have to concentrate. And as I was lucky enough to be there during Jani Strasser's period, it was very special.

RH: Yes, Jani was a remarkable vocal coach who had an encyclopaedic knowledge of opera.

SW: While I was at Glyndebourne, I also acted as a cover for Dame Janet Baker in Cavalli's *La Calisto*. For one of the performances, she had a prior engagement, and was scheduled to be covered by another singer. But when that singer withdrew, it was decided that I should be allowed to perform instead. That was on 11 June 1970, a very exciting day.

RH: It can never be said that Sarah Walker is afraid of a challenge. Would you risk musical life and limb again today if faced with similar situations?

SW: If you are starting out and somebody says, 'Here's a fee. Come and sing this work', you'd be mad to say 'no'. Take *Stripsody* by Cathy Berberian, for example. She had a great many works written for her during the 1960s and the 1970s, but 'compiled' this particular piece herself. In effect, it's a glossary of strip-cartoon language. Some parts of it include sounds like 'ah-choo', 'kerplunk' and 'zowee', while other parts are little stories. When it was suggested that she should notate it, an idea that seemed impossible, she teamed up with the renowned Italian artist Eugenio Carmi. They then did this by having three staves to a page: high, medium and low. These were overlaid with little drawings, words and pictorial expressions. And the very first thing that you see is a tiny Tarzan swinging towards you feet first. This prompts a series of descending wordless sounds that culminate in a sequence of onomatopoeic gymnastics.

RH: But to imply that you were simply the darling of the avant-garde would be to sell you short. You have also appeared regularly at all the major lyric theatres, including the Royal Opera House, Covent Garden, where you made your debut as Baba the Turk in Stravinsky's *The Rake's Progress* on 10 December 1982. Sir Thomas Allen recently said that every time he sings at Covent Garden, it's like 'coming home'. Do you share his affection for the theatre?

SW: It's a lovely house to be in, and I am sure Tom would agree with me when I say that there are theatres that we love, and there are others that we can't stand. Covent Garden really is highly regarded. For a start, you don't have to stay in a hotel, or struggle with an airport, if you live in London or the South East. That counts for a lot. The people there are lovely, and even before it had decent dressing rooms and all the 'mod cons' that it enjoys today, it was still wonderful.

RH: Another major theatre that has always had a special place in singers' affections is the Metropolitan Opera House, New York. You gave your

PART TWO: SINGERS

first performance there singing Micah in Handel's *Samson* with the tenor Jon Vickers on 3 February 1986. As the 'Met' is a huge theatre that can accommodate approximately 4,000 patrons, what are some of the challenges that it presents?

SW: It has a wonderful acoustic, but it was with the Chicago Lyric Opera that I performed in the United States for the first time, another extremely large theatre. I much prefer the 'Met's' horseshoe-shaped auditorium to Chicago's shoe-box disposition. You can at least see your audience when singing in New York, and it's easier to perform there than at Covent Garden. And both the 'Met' and the Royal Opera House are about 100 times easier to sing in than the English National Opera, which is really difficult. As at Covent Garden, all the people at the 'Met' are friendly, and everything that you need is taken care of. It's utterly professional. This stands in sharp contrast to the Vienna Staatsoper, which isn't so easy. In the German-speaking theatre system, you arrive, have two days' rehearsal and that's it. I sang Dido in Berlioz's *Les Troyens* at Vienna, one of the biggest roles that I've ever done. You are walked through the set and told what it's like. Then, on the night of the performance, you go on stage just before the curtain rises and the stage manager talks you through your actions. I remember being struck by the frightening set and the height of the on-stage stairs. When I mentioned this to the stage manager, she said that although they *were* very steep, I would be surrounded by a series of dancers who would lead me by the hand as I descended them. But when the curtain went up, I looked down from the top of the stairs and was confronted by the great distance to the stage floor. I was then also confronted by the even greater distance to the pit and the conductor. It was absolutely terrifying, and I still can't believe I did it. The Teatro alla Scala in Milan is another 'bad one'; a terrible place. While it might be quite a nice building to sing in, it's an awful theatre to work in. The attitude there is unacceptable and the staff couldn't care less. It has to be said that we were largely an English cast trying to perform Britten's *Peter Grimes*. And, of course, *Grimes* is a superb 'chorus opera'. But as the Italians had to sing it in English, they didn't understand a thing about it. Worse still, the choristers at La Scala aren't allowed to move and sing at the same time.

RH: From what you have said, it's clear that theatres vary markedly from place to place, but is the same true of audiences?

SW: When it comes to big houses, such as those that I have just mentioned, the short answer is 'no'. The only contact that you have with the public in such places is when individuals come backstage afterwards.

RH: What was the response of the Milanese to *Peter Grimes*?

SW: They liked it. They really liked it. It's an amazing opera and Philip Langridge was wonderful in the title role. He gave a stunning performance. The part could have been written for him.

RH: As a leading singer, you must have worked with many of the world's finest directors. Who are some of the directors you admire most, and what have you taken from them professionally?

SW: Two who immediately come to mind are Sir Jonathan Miller and Sir Nicholas Hytner. They are both extraordinary people and wonderful to work with. As singers, we now expect their kind of approach. We expect knowledge, common sense and a respect for the text. And, of course, there is John Copley, whom I have known throughout my career. He might be described as a traditionalist, but of the best kind. What he doesn't know isn't worth knowing.

RH: Do think that John's remarkable approach is because he is such a good musician?

SW: Yes. Of course it is. And that's what's missing from most directors. John is a genius, an absolute genius. And his way is a very different way of producing things. Don't ask me to be specific, because I can't. It was just something that I felt when working with him. The German director Willy Decker is another great figure. He, too, is just amazing. His production of *Peter Grimes* at Brussels was absolutely stunning, and drew audiences from around the world. It was so successful that they actually staged an extra performance. This is an incredibly difficult thing to do. If you think of how challenging it is to retain an international cast for such a performance, it really was something special. When the singers sat down with Decker at the first rehearsal to discuss their roles, he not only described the character of Grimes as a poet, but as a man who was completely out of his depth. He also pointed out that Grimes has a burning ambition that is represented by the interval of a ninth, a device used commonly by Britten and that can be heard throughout the opera. We all looked at him and thought, 'He's a director who actually *knows* what a ninth is.' We also realised that Decker knew that Britten used the interval to suggest that Grimes was striving for something he couldn't have. By using a ninth, rather than the perfect intervals of a fifth or an octave, Britten implies that the character is attempting to go one step further than he should. Decker set himself apart from many other directors by knowing this.

RH: When I interviewed the tenor Dennis O'Neill recently, we discussed modern production techniques, and he was rightly sceptical of some contemporary stagings. Do you share his concerns?

SW: I suspect that it's only a problem when people come from more conservative backgrounds. And, of course, there are those who actually enjoy such productions. Life goes on. Personally, I don't mind them.

RH: Let's leave the opera house for a moment or two and chat briefly about your work in the concert hall. You are considered universally as one of the world's pre-eminent *Lieder* singers. What first attracted you to this repertoire?

SW: I don't know why I am attracted to *Lieder*: I just love it. But that doesn't mean I love everything that's written in the genre. It took me some time to understand the greatness of Schubert, for example, and it was entirely down to Vera that I'm now so attracted to his music. And it's now a mantra of mine that Schubert belongs to the Classical, rather than to the Romantic, Period.

RH: What makes a great Schubert singer?

SW: Somebody who realises that the composer belongs to the Classical Period. It's a question of style. I would never say that Schubert or Mozart are more difficult to perform than other composers, but each has his own style and flavour. Thai cooking is very different from European. It's a question of how you balance the spices and flavours. Singers should be able to tackle contrasting styles.

PART TWO: SINGERS

RH: You are also a marvellous Schumann interpreter. Do you perform his music differently from that of Schubert?

SW: There's no difference, and that also applies to the music of Mozart and Berlioz. I don't differentiate between their works and those of others. But while my approach might not be different, there should always be a difference in sound, colour and movement. This is also true of the way that the music's dynamics, *rubati* and shape should be treated. I don't alter the way I sing, or how I position my voice box. As a classically trained singer, such things are unnecessary for any composer. The only time that you may have to alter the way you sing is when you are performing in musical theatre, or when being asked to use a microphone. These require a different technique.

RH: French song is also particularly close to your heart, and you have recorded many of Fauré's *chansons*. What attracts you to this music, and what are some of the challenges and delights of performing in French?

SW: I love performing these works, as they rather suit my nasal voice. I adore singing in French and I love Berlioz. Even though I didn't discover him until my late twenties, his music influenced me greatly. When I left the College, I didn't go straight into opera, but worked as a session singer instead. As I performed with groups like the John Alldis Choir, I encountered a wide range of music, and I remember that we worked with Sir Colin Davis on his wonderful Berlioz recordings from the late 1960s, including *Roméo et Juliette*. The British mezzo-soprano Patricia Kern was wonderful on that disc. Another fine conductor who adored French music was John Matheson, a great friend of Sir Colin. I will always remember the way that John spoke about the language, and how to treat it, when he coached us in a choral recitative from *Roméo et Juliette*. This can be quite a difficult passage to deliver with sixteen voices, as it requires both a strong sense of ensemble and a clear understanding of flexible *rubato*. When I included a French song in a recital later in my career, I would use it to warm up with. It would immediately put me 'into gear' and make me feel comfortable.

RH: *Lieder* wouldn't be *Lieder* without an accompanist, and there are three pianists whom I particularly associate with you: Graham Johnson, Roger Vignoles and Malcolm Martineau. Why are these musical partnerships so special to you?

SW: My relationship with an accompanist is very important. That said, everybody is different. Some recitalists are happy to work with any pianist, even those who might not know them so well. And, here, I am thinking of one particular person whom Graham Johnson and I heard at a summer course some time ago. When this extremely renowned recitalist came on stage and sang quite a difficult programme with a less than distinguished pianist, Graham said at one point, 'The singer is using a cheaper accompanist because they want more of the fee.' While that might sound very cutting, it was true. The pianist was in no way comparable to the singer. The audience might not have worried about it, but I wouldn't have been comfortable doing such a thing. I'm not comfortable with any pianist who doesn't understand what I am looking for and who can't support me. Dame Janet Baker once said that a ship has only one captain, and she's right. And what makes Graham such a superb accompanist is his ability to accept what some people might consider a secondary position. But he knows that's not the case, as he gains great pleasure from being able to mesh with the singer.

PART TWO: SINGERS

RH: Let's return to opera for a moment and talk about Wagner. Many singers have told me that his music often presents particular challenges for the voice. Do you think that's true?

SW: When I first performed Siegrune, it was from the wings using a megaphone in the vernacular. Amongst the lines that I had to deliver in that particular English translation was, 'I've got work to do.' I found this completely untenable, so I decided to sing the passage in the original German: 'Arbeit gab's!' It's much easier to sing, and nobody ever noticed.

RH: From what you've just said, would it be fair to assume that you're not a fan of opera in the vernacular.

SW: It depends on the translation. Kent Opera's policy was that all the works they performed should be in the language of those hearing them. I am a supporter of this. In London, we are fortunate enough to have both approaches: we can hear opera in the original language at the Royal Opera House, and we can hear it in the vernacular at the English National Opera. But I would never perform song or *Lieder* in translation, as it paints a picture through harmony. It's not dissimilar to listening to a radio play, where you have your own ideas about the characters and the story. In *Lieder* and song, it's essential to allow the harmony to lead you when coming to terms with the words. But, in opera, you do need to know what the story is about. If you have a good translation that scans wonderfully, then you are 'quids in'. Michael Irwin, who was Professor of English for many years at the University of Kent, once translated the music-hall song 'Waiting at the Church' from English into French for me, as the rest of the programme was in French. He was a genius and the translation was wonderful. If a translation comes off the tongue easily, and is immediately understandable, then singing in the vernacular is perfect.

RH: Over the years, you worked with some of the world's greatest conductors, including Carlos Kleiber. Was he as enigmatic as many of your colleagues suggest?

SW: Yes, he was. Even though he had an enormous reputation, he was a very nervous and shy person in many ways, and was treated in a ridiculous manner by managements. He was fawned upon in such a way that it allowed him to behave in a fashion that was completely unforgivable. If you were fortunate enough to work with him, you quickly realised that it wasn't him, but what was taking place around him, that was the real problem. When I was engaged to sing Annina in Strauss's *Der Rosenkavalier* under Kleiber at the Metropolitan Opera in 1990, I was telephoned by a senior casting director about a month before leaving London. He said that I might be excited to learn that Carlos Kleiber would be conducting. This meant very little to me, as I wasn't in management, and didn't understand how difficult it was to persuade him to perform. The casting director then said, 'You won't be late, will you?' I thought, 'Of course I won't be late', as the flight had already been booked. 'You won't be ill, will you?' 'I'll try not to be,' I responded bemusedly. It was soon clear that he was ringing the entire cast, an ensemble that included Dame Felicity Lott as the Marschallin, Anne Sofie von Otter as Octavian and Barbara Bonney as Sophie. It was one of the great casts and a marvellous production to be involved in. Aware that Kleiber was famous for having closed dress rehearsals, I asked the Maestro – it's always better to address such people as 'Maestro' – at the stage-orchestral rehearsal the previous day if it would be possible for my husband to watch part of the dress rehearsal. He said, 'I think that would be fine.' After I thanked him, I bumped into an important member of the management team and told him what had just been agreed. He reeled back in horror and said, 'You shouldn't have asked the Maestro that.' I apologised and told him that Kleiber was perfectly happy, and was not the least bit worried about it. But because he said 'yes' to my husband, Carlos couldn't say 'no' to anybody else, which meant that the rehearsal ended up being open.

RH: You also famously sang with Leonard Bernstein in a performance of Beethoven's Ninth Symphony on Christmas Day in 1989. This concert marked the fall of the Berlin Wall, and was probably one of the most watched concerts in the history of broadcasting. What are your memories of that event?

SW: The recording of that performance is not particularly good, and the solo quartet material at the end of the fourth movement is very slow. It was really much better at the other two performances that we gave. The Christmas Day concert was a very special occasion, which came with a great deal of emotional baggage. I remember two very mundane things about the whole thing: I'd got a cold that day, which developed into chronic pneumonia, and I'd asked through my agent on at least a dozen occasions what colour dress I should wear. I was told any colour, even though I pointed out that the concerts would be taking place over the Christmas period, and that we were singing the 'Ode to Joy'. We gave three performances of the Ninth in all: the broadcast concert on the day itself, and one on either side of it. In the end, I took three plain frocks; my favourite type. The first was a wonderful deep blue, the second was a fantastic apple green, and the third was a more celestial blue. But after I arrived, I learned that June Anderson, whom I love dearly, was going to wear black for the broadcast. I was then told by the management that

I would have to go out and buy a black dress. This was on Christmas Eve in Berlin, a city that was still suffering from the effects of its division. I thought that they were joking, as it's impossible to buy anything on Christmas Eve in Germany, let alone a black dress. In the end, I contacted a neighbour in England, who contacted another neighbour, who successfully found the only black dress I had; I don't like wearing black on the concert platform. My neighbour and the dress then had to fly Club Class to Berlin on Christmas morning. It cost a fortune.

DAME KIRI TE KANAWA
(THE DUKE'S HALL, 16 SEPTEMBER 2011)

JONATHAN FREEMAN-ATTWOOD: As a result of your connections with the Rugby World Cup, Rolex, Honda and various television networks, you have one of the most recognisable faces in the music profession. What are some of the pleasures and trials of being Dame Kiri Te Kanawa?

KIRI TE KANAWA: There are lots of pleasures and very few trials. The one thing that I really dislike is when somebody follows me around in a supermarket. You don't want people to see what you're buying. And sometimes I don't buy a particular item, as I know that I'm being watched. It can be a very difficult situation when I am trying to stock up on certain articles. But that's really the only problem. I just like getting on with my life.

JF-A: Let's go back to the beginning, shall we? You were born in New Zealand and were adopted by your parents, Tom and Nell, who seem to have been a decisive influence during your early years. Could you tell us a little about them, and some of the sacrifices that they made to further your education?

KTK: Everything that children do is similar to a puppy. They just get on and do things. But I did realise that my parents struggled, even though we never starved. I did know that I never had what my parents would've loved me to have had. But that's fine. And when I look back now, I'm not sure that I missed out on anything. My father worked on the roads, and would do things such as installing petrol tanks. That's relatively easy to do today, but, then, he had to dig the hole physically, as he couldn't afford a mechanical digger. My parents did everything with such love. They picked up this little adopted nobody, and gave me an unbelievable life. In fact, I've spoken several times about my father today, and never tire of discussing him. My mother is a different story, as the relationship between mothers and daughters can sometimes be a little problematic. She was a driving force. My father was the love of my life, and the epitome of a 'gentle giant'. He was a very proud gentleman and had great dignity. He wasn't necessarily very well educated, but he was a super, super person.

JF-A: Your first important singing teacher was Sister Mary Leo, who taught you in Auckland. From what I've read, she sounds quite a formidable woman with very clear ideas about vocal technique. What were some of those ideas, and how did she recognise that you had a voice worth training?

KTK: I'm not sure that she did recognise this, but she certainly gave me many opportunities. Her method of training was very natural, and she always ensured that I breathed correctly. She also ensured that I shouldn't sing songs that weren't right for me, and I was always paired with another singer. That really did it. Whether your partner was your best friend or your worst enemy, it made you think. If I did something wrong, or they did something better, you were spurred on to improve. That gave me a driving force, and was the basis for my competitiveness.

JF-A: In articles and biographies about you, much is made of your Maori heritage. How important is that to you, and in what ways did it manifest itself in your singing?

PART TWO: SINGERS

KTK: My Maori heritage is really the person I am. But I don't necessarily look at myself and say that I am who I am because of being Maori. My parents were from a very nice, calm tribe, but the women from that tribe were formidable. You didn't cross them and you didn't get in their way. They were the ones that had the fight in them, and that's where I got my incredible fighting strength from. It was a 'never-say-die' attitude.

JF-A: Like many important artists, you left school early to pursue your career. Dame Joan Sutherland worked as a secretary and Kathleen Ferrier worked in a telephone exchange, jobs that you, too, accepted as a young woman. Do you think that doing such jobs was important for your personal development?

KTK: At one point, I thought that was all I was going to do. Although I worked in a music shop for a while, I didn't think that there was anything else. Then, at a certain point, my parents said that they had some money for me to be trained vocally, if that's what I wanted to do. I remember thinking that singing is quite good, and that I wasn't too bad at it. So, I said, 'Okay, I'll do singing.' But, of course, I had no idea what my life's journey would be. And the distance between the sixteen-year-old that I was then, and the sixty-seven-year-old that I am now, has been long.

JF-A: During your early years in New Zealand, you always balanced art music with popular song. As you've continued to balance both genres during your career, what are some of the benefits, and indeed drawbacks, of this approach for aspiring singers?

KTK: Singers should sing songs that they love, whether that be in the bath, the shower or the concert hall. But in the field of classical music, there is a degree of integrity that should not be made fun of. When people come up to me in the street and make a warbling noise, I absolutely hate it. I'd never make a joke about any type of song. If it has beautiful words, or a beautiful tune, then that's what it's all about. When I teach I always insist that the young singers work on some sort of folk song. And after we have worked for a period on other material, I will often get them to return to that song, as it can centre their musicianship. What's required for a folk song is also required for a classical aria.

JF-A: Although there have been some outstanding opera singers from New Zealand, opera, as a genre, is not often associated with that country. What works did you hear there as a young singer, and what motivated you to turn to opera?

KTK: I've no idea. The only operas that I saw there were Mozart's *Don Giovanni* and Gershwin's *Porgy and Bess*. I saw two performances of the first and thought it was horrible. That was the only exposure to opera that I had. I never listened to any recordings of it, as they didn't exist in New Zealand. And we didn't have television there until I was fourteen. I don't know how I got the opera bug. As soon as I came to England in 1966, I visited Covent Garden as a student. I remember looking over the balcony, and there was Dame Gwyneth Jones singing in Verdi's *Don Carlos*. It was unbelievable, and from that point onwards, I just kept watching opera.

JF-A: In 1963, aged nineteen, you took part in New Zealand's Mobil Song Quest where you were placed second before winning it two years later. You then travelled to Australia, where you competed in the Sun Aria competitions in both Sydney and Melbourne. Can you tell us a little about those experiences, and your thoughts on competitions in general?

PART TWO: SINGERS

KTK: I had something of an epiphany around that time, which was repeated when I came to England. I realised that what I was doing wasn't a joke, and that there was something inside me that told me that singing was my destiny. I also realised that singing was the road I had to follow, even if I occasionally went off track. In general, competitions are extremely productive, and they can take care of young singers' immediate needs. The problem is that there's often no follow-up when it comes to agents. Winners of these events need to be offered engagements directly after their victories, as they require considerable exposure. If a young singer who already has a contract with a major opera house enters a competition, but doesn't succeed, it tells me that either he or she should never have entered the competition, or should not be employed by a theatre. I know that can be unfortunate, but that's the way it is. When I came here in 1966, I wanted to enter some competitions. I was good at them and could take the stress. But then I realised that I was at the stage of my life when entering such things was inadvisable.

JF-A: What was it like coming from New Zealand to London in the 'Swinging Sixties'?

KTK: That was the problem: it was 'the Swinging Sixties'. I didn't behave very well, and wasn't a very good student. I often say to the young singers with whom I work today, 'Don't make the mistakes I did, as you will literally carry them around with you like a sack of potatoes.' You will hear about every mistake you make again twenty, thirty or even forty years later.

JF-A: But wasn't there a time in London when it was thought that you were a mezzo-soprano?

KTK: Richard Bonynge came up to me and said, 'My dear, you are a soprano.' He then left town. This left me wondering, 'What happens now?' At that time, I really didn't have the right singing teacher.

JF-A: Wasn't there a possibility of you studying with Dame Eva Turner?

KTK: When I arrived at the London Opera Centre, the first question I was asked was, 'Who's your singing teacher?' And as my previous teacher had written to Dame Eva, somebody with whom I'd have a great deal of contact in the future, I told James Robertson, the Centre's Director, that I was going to have lessons with her. He then stood up, looked at me directly and said, 'Don't make that call.' He then left the room without another word. I was stuck, and left thinking, 'What should I do now.' Many years later, Dame Eva said to me in that distinctive voice of hers, 'Weren't we supposed to have worked together?' Feeling a little embarrassed, all I could mutter was, 'I really don't remember.' But James's advice was very good, as I ended up with a teacher who really suited me.

JF-A: A good agent is important for any aspiring artist, and the two that you had, Basil Horsfield and John Davern, both directors of Artists' International Management, were particularly supportive.

KTK: They were like a brother and an uncle all rolled up into one. They nurtured me and were simply gorgeous. Such a thing is impossible today. No one cares about singers like that any more. Agents today make young singers work extremely hard. When that's the case, I remind them that they are paying their agent's mortgage. I know that managers have to earn a living, but it's the way that they go about it that I object to. It's just not fair, and I'm often left astounded by some of the things that happen.

PART TWO: SINGERS

JF-A: How did you come to the attention of Horsfield and Davern?

KTK: While I was at the London Opera Centre, Basil telephoned me and invited me to his very posh house in Islington. I'd never seen a house quite like it before; it was wonderfully beautiful. He then said, 'I'd like to represent you.' Not quite believing it, I stammered, 'Yeah, right.' We then worked together very successfully for quite a number of years.

JF-A: How did he go about marketing the young Kiri Te Kanawa?

KTK: Basil and John knew Joan Ingpen, who was Artistic Director at Covent Garden. They mentioned to me that they wanted her to engage me as the Countess for a production of Mozart's *Le nozze di Figaro* there. I wasn't happy about this, and said that I would prefer to sing the smaller role of Barbarina instead. But in the end, I did sing the part of the Countess for a weekly fee of £50. I was then asked to accept a five-year contract, which was the best thing that ever happened to me. I wasn't concerned by the money, but I did want to be part of the Covent Garden company. Whilst there, I worked with the best vocal coaches, and was looked after by Sir John Tooley. My agents also chose the roles that I sang. Nevertheless, it was difficult, as I was tackling things that were all new to me. As people were choosing things on my behalf, I often thought, 'How am I going to learn this?' This was particularly true of Strauss's *Arabella*. When I looked at it for the first time, I thought that I'd be dead before I could come to terms with it. But I *did* learn it, and, from that point on, I came to realise how glorious it is.

JF-A: Throughout this time, you were working with the great vocal pedagogue Vera Rózsa. What attracted you to this remarkable woman, and how would you describe her approach to singing teaching?

KTK: I had found a singing teacher whom I didn't like very much, before going for lessons with Florence Norberg. After a period with her, she wrote a letter to me saying that she no longer wanted to teach me. I was absolutely devastated, and thought, 'Why? What have I done?' I knew of Vera through Anne Howells, but she said that she wouldn't teach me unless she received a letter from Florence stating clearly that she no longer wanted to work with me. I understood the protocol and was happy about that. Vera later said that Florence could see my talent emerging, but was unable to cope with it. I was prepared to accept this, yet I still felt that Norberg ended our relationship the wrong way.

JF-A: Considering the impact that Basil Horsfield and John Davern had on you professionally, what advice would you give young singers when dealing with agents?

KTK: Being an agent can be tough, but, if aspiring artists can find a teacher who will sit down with them and help them choose roles, that's one way of doing it. This is good advice if the teacher has been actively involved in the profession. Students need to be told what roles they should learn, and should not deviate from that advice. They should also be given a schedule of songs that they should learn every week or two, and to become comfortable with the language that those songs are written in. It's essential that they don't try to do too much. Don't be a superwoman!

JF-A: But you are a superwoman, and have sung with most of the world's major conductors, including Otto Klemperer, Sir John Pritchard, Sir Georg Solti, Sir Colin Davis, Sir Charles Mackerras, Lorin Maazel, Claudio Abbado, Zubin Mehta, Bernard Haitink, Leonard Bernstein and Karl Böhm.

PART TWO: SINGERS

KTK: Solti was an unbelievable conductor, who was always anxious when I sang a little sharp. This made it difficult for me whenever I had to sing on the top side of the note. That said, we were on very friendly terms, and I think that he liked me. I got on very well with his family. He could be quite hard on people, and I would find myself defusing certain situations. He was tough on everybody, and took no prisoners. But when you make music with a genius like Solti, you just tend to go with it. Everything was expressed through the tips of his fingers, and you allowed yourself to be manipulated by this incredible man. You didn't take your eyes off of his hands.

JF-A: Did you feel a sense of improvisation when working with Solti, or was his approach more pre-planned?

KTK: What he wanted was already set in his mind, even though it didn't always work out. But you always knew when he wanted to turn an interpretative corner. He never stopped looking at you. It's very exciting working with someone whose total attention is focused on you.

JF-A: Is it true that Solti wanted you to sing Sieglinde from Wagner's *Die Walküre* and you refused?

KTK: Yes. I wouldn't have had any voice left after that! My voice was too soft-grained for Wagner.

JF-A: Why do you think he was so keen for you to explore Wagner?

KTK: As much as I adored Sir Georg, he made a lot of mistakes, and, in the end, you have to protect yourself. You just don't do anything because someone wants it, and he understood that.

JF-A: If you were asked to draw a little thumbnail sketch of Otto Klemperer, what might it look like?

KTK: I did very little with him, and by the time that I did meet him, he had already suffered a debilitating stroke. But he would speak in a gruff voice, and would bark very basic instructions.

JF-A: And what did you perform with Sir Charles Mackerras?

KTK: We gave a wonderful *Arabella* together, and we also performed Gounod's *Faust*. Along with performances in Paris, I recorded Tatiana's 'Letter Scene' from Tchaikovsky's *Eugene Onegin* with him.

JF-A: You also famously recorded *West Side Story* with Leonard Bernstein. And it's immediately obvious from the film of those sessions that you loved working with microphones. You were a natural recording artist.

KTK: The microphone is your secret road to the rest of the world. You have to nurture it, to work with it and to know what to do with it.

JF-A: But who taught you that? We know that classical singers, unlike jazz artists, often find microphones tough to deal with.

KTK: When I was working with microphones, I knew that the recording's producer and engineer would be aware of the nuances I was after. I had the great good fortune of working with some of the best in the world. It's rather like working with a camera. Your eyes are constantly on it. It's a secret world that you creep into at one end, and creep out of at the other.

PART TWO: SINGERS

JF-A: Another conductor from the older generation with whom you worked was Karl Böhm.

KTK: I did Mozart's *Die Zauberflöte* with him. It was a crazy production, and he was just wonderful. The problem was that some of these great figures could be pretty horrible. They could be really, really nasty.

JF-A: Directors are central to any opera singer's day-to-day activities. Who were some of the directors who shaped your approach to stage craft most, and what is your advice to young singers when working with directors in general?

KTK: Directors I worked with included John Copley and John Cox. But for some productions, an assistant director showed me what was wanted. Young singers today must know what they want, know who the character is that they are portraying and be aware it's the one you want people to see. Don't try things out in a production too much. Always go into it with something definite in mind, but be prepared to change. More often than not, directors don't know what they're doing. Regularly, we were given a series of instructions that would change the closer we got to the first night. You may have long phrases to sing, and it can be difficult to judge the exact time it takes to get from one point on the stage to another. This is particularly true when you are dealing with emotions such as anger, love, rejection and dejection. You have to get the correct body language that will take you between those points. And when you have worked all that out, some directors change it. I was once told to sit on the floor, to which I replied, 'I don't sit on the floor!' I always found sitting down while performing uncomfortable.

JF-A: There are three opera houses with which you are closely associated: the Royal Opera House, Covent Garden, the Metropolitan Opera, New York, and the Paris Opéra. What, for you, were some of the similarities and differences between these companies?

KTK: For me, Covent Garden was a gem, and it was where I did all my training. It had a magnificent crew, and the backstage manager was strict but wonderful. The whole company was geared to what the singers were doing. And the costume department and orchestra were extraordinary. I was able to work with Sir Georg Solti and Sir Colin Davis, who were great conductors. Every moment that I had at Covent Garden was memorable. Of course, there were ups and downs, but my time there was mainly fabulous. When I think of the Paris Opéra, all I remember is strike after strike. Eighty per cent of that company's employees were not involved in artistic matters. For the small group of singers who did work there, it was very difficult. I've always had very good friends at the 'Met', and my memories of it are wonderful.

JF-A: Let's talk about some of the roles with which you are linked closely. You are rightly celebrated for your portrayals of the Countess in *Capriccio*, the eponymous heroine in *Arabella*, the Marschallin in *Der Rosenkavalier* and the Countess in *Le nozze di Figaro*, all aristocratic figures whose backstories are far removed from that of a talented young singer from far-away, provincial New Zealand. How, then, did you prepare yourself for these noble roles, and why do you think that these metamorphoses were so successful?

KTK: I always gave great consideration as to how I should portray these women. When I first came to England, there was a gentleman who looked after me. He was from New Zealand and he took me to very nice restaurants. He showed me the fineries of how to use cutlery and how to sit. I had no idea about such things at the time. And, of course, my father was a very proud man, and I feel that my pride takes me where I want to go. I'm a very proud person who is proud of what she has achieved. I always felt that I had to represent my parents, who are still very important to me, and my country. And as my country *is* so important to me, I never wanted to embarrass it by my behaviour. I always wanted to live up to what was expected of me. But I suppose I am still a country girl who loves the outdoors. I remember once doing a 'mad scene' with Ruggero Raimondi and thinking, 'I can really let go in this one.' Finding this unusual for me, Ruggero asked, 'Kiri, what are you doing?' I said, 'I'm going mad, so leave me alone!'

JF-A: Let's talk about Verdi for a moment. In 1974, you famously stepped in at very short notice for an already-ill Teresa Stratas to sing the role of Desdemona opposite Jon Vickers in *Otello* at the Metropolitan Opera. This must have been a remarkable experience. As we now know, it was a huge triumph. But how did you feel when you found out that you were about to make your New York debut in this way?

KTK: I remember Sir Colin Davis saying to me that I wasn't to go to New York, and that I must not do that particular Desdemona. He absolutely forbade me to go. At the same time, negotiations were taking place between my agents and Sir Colin that would allow me to accept the engagement. In the end, I arrived in New York about a month before the first night. I watched some of the rehearsals with Teresa, and then worked a little with Jon Vickers. But I'd been largely working with the assistant director. When it got to the dress rehearsal, Teresa was still singing absolutely beautifully. Then, after a day off, the management said that they would like me to go through the whole opera with Jon on the Friday. I thought that this was strange, as there was a matinee the next day. I didn't finish rehearsing until about 8pm on the Friday night. It was my first visit to New York and it was snowing and horrible. But I decided to go to bed early just in case, even though I fully intended to go shopping the next day. Just before I was about to set off for the shops on the Saturday morning, the telephone rang. I had a young student staying with me at the time, and I told her to tell whoever it was that I was out. It was the 'Met', and she *did* tell them that I was out! I then called my agent, who said, 'You had better get down there because you are on.' 'What do you mean I'm on?' I stuttered. This was at 11am. I then found the only cab driver in New York who didn't know where the 'Met' was. I was on 89th Street and Broadway, and when we got to 65th Street, I got out of the cab and ran across the theatre's forecourt like a crazy thing. They were waiting for me at the stage door, and asked, 'What do you want to eat?' I was given a steak! At 2.30pm, I went on stage like a bat out of hell. I thought that the only thing to do was to run on like a crazy person, which I did. But, somehow, I got through it.

JF-A: Why do you think Verdi's music suits your voice so superbly?

KTK: The soft-grained quality of my voice lent itself to the character of Desdemona. It really was the softness of my voice, and its feminine timbre, that created the colours that were necessary.

JF-A: Would you say that your triumph in New York helped your career in any way?

KTK: Yes, it did. When I speak to students today, I say, 'Never ever miss an opportunity.' And if a situation arises, they must make sure that they are singing well.

PART TWO: SINGERS

JF-A: No interview with Kiri Te Kanawa would be complete without asking about the wedding of Prince Charles and Lady Diana Spencer in 1981. For most of us, it would've been the experience of a lifetime. What are your memories of it, and why were you asked to take part?

KTK: Basil Horsfield called me on 1 April and said, 'Charlie would like you to sing at his wedding.' Never thinking for a minute that it was Prince Charles, I said, 'Charlie who?' At the time, he was a patron of the Royal Opera House, Covent Garden, and it was Sir John Tooley who put my name forward. I was then sworn to secrecy until about June; I wasn't allowed to tell anybody. While it was a wonderful secret to keep, it was tough. I couldn't believe I was so lucky.

JF-A: Did you enjoy the wedding, or did you think, 'Crikey, this is a bit *too* important'?

KTK: The build-up was quite good, so I became used to the whole idea. The only thing was, I was giving about eight performances in sixteen days of *Don Giovanni* and *Così fan tutte* before having to sing 'Let the Bright Seraphim'. I was very aware of preserving my voice.

JF-A: David Fingleton claimed in 1982 that 'Singing for Kiri is emphatically not her "life", not even her "career", but simply her "job".' Thirty years on, would you still agree with that analysis?

KTK: As he called what I did a 'job', people often take it the wrong way. But it is a job. You have to organise yourself, and to be prepared musically. Nothing is left to chance. I even write notes to myself in the middle of the night, which remind me what to put into my suitcase.

Today, I still learn material in the same way that I did at the beginning of my career.

JF-A: Over the last decade or so, you have been heavily involved in the training of young singers. What attracts you to teaching, and how do you go about imparting the wisdom that you have gained?

KTK: I don't want to teach regularly. There are all sorts of other things that I like to do. I enjoy fishing, shooting, walking, golf and tennis. I have also decided to take up painting. Even though there are a lot of things that I want to do, I also want to be able to guide students when they do the things that I did, but within the context of this difficult, modern world. Opera companies are proving more problematic than ever, and visas are becoming increasingly tricky to secure. We now have very few New Zealanders coming to Britain. There's no opera company in New Zealand, which means there's no work for singers. Of course, some have managed to overcome this and are working, but it remains a real problem. Singers often only have a narrow window of opportunity when it comes to taking their first professional steps. And I wouldn't have enjoyed the career that I've had, if the conditions then were the same as today.

DAME FELICITY LOTT
(DAVID JOSEFOWITZ RECITAL HALL, 25 SEPTEMBER 2009)

JONATHAN FREEMAN-ATTWOOD: As you are an artist who is synonymous with the lyric stage, I am curious to know when and where you heard an opera for the first time.

FELICITY LOTT: I grew up in Cheltenham, where there was no opera house. But a touring company visited the town and performed Puccini's *La bohème*. This was the first opera that I ever saw. Although we had some recordings at home, I didn't particularly want to be an opera singer, as I didn't think that that was remotely possible. I watched musicals on television, particularly those with Fred Astaire and Ginger Rogers, and sang along with *The Sound of Music* when it was shown. I came from a family of amateur musicians, who held concert parties during the war. While there was always music around the house, it wasn't necessarily opera. My father had a recording of Joan Sutherland singing some wonderful things, and we also had discs of Mozart's *Die Zauberflöte* with Lucia Popp as the Queen of the Night and Strauss's *Vier letzte Lieder* with Elisabeth Schwarzkopf. But, in general, opera was outside my sphere of experience at the time. I only sang because everybody else did.

JF-A: Do you think the recordings you had at home during your childhood sowed a musical seed that later proved fruitful?

FL: I am sure that was the case. I'd never heard anything as beautiful as Schwarzkopf's performance of Strauss's songs. While I know there are two recordings of her singing those works – and that one is better than the other – I can't remember which one we had. Nevertheless, I continue to hear it mentally, as it was the first recording of them I experienced.

JF-A: As you are an alumna of the Royal Academy of Music, I am interested to hear how the institution helped to prepare you for a life in the music profession.

FL: I came to the Academy having already completed a bachelor's degree in French, so I was a bit older than some of the other students. I was lucky enough to sing Pamina in *Die Zauberflöte* while I was here. And as I smoked quite a lot back then, which kept my voice down, I also sang Dorabella in Mozart's *Così fan tutte*. We had movement classes with the wonderful Anna Sweeney. But I don't think that I went very often, as I didn't really move! Being an oratorio singer who had given a great many performances of Handel's *Messiah* at Cheltenham, I couldn't see myself doing such things. Nevertheless, they took pity on me at the Academy and gave me some lovely parts to sing, including a Handel opera with the Principal, Sir Anthony Lewis. My teacher here was Flora Nielsen, whose range of experience not only included *Lieder*, but also the works of Strauss and Britten. The foundation of my musicianship was based on art-song, rather than opera, as my voice didn't sound Italianate. Consequently, I haven't performed any Italian operas. I'm a bit of an odd person when it comes to these things, and was jolly lucky to find works that I could fit into.

JF-A: Most successful opera singers have a turning point in their early careers that propels them to another level. Was that also the case for you?

PART TWO: SINGERS

FL: Pamina was a very lucky role for me. When I spent a year in France, I had singing lessons there, and my teacher made me learn 'Ach, ich fühl's'. She was also the person who said to me, 'Maybe if you work a bit harder, you could be a singer.' At the time, I didn't know what I was going to do with my life. I attended the Royal Academy of Music from 1969 to 1973, and then sang Pamina at the English National Opera two years later, having stepped in for an indisposed colleague. That was a lucky break for me. But there has always been a kind of *Schadenfreude*, or down-side, associated with everything that I've done. Having made my debut, I thought, 'I've made it. I've sung at the English National Opera.' As I had to jump in at the last moment, I didn't have time to worry about anything. I just had to get on and do it. Then, I was offered performances of the role on the company's tour. But when I went to the wardrobe department, I was told that they had Felicity Palmer's name on the costumes and not mine. I never *really* thought that I was good enough to make it. My life has always been like that, and still is.

JF-A: One of the defining qualities of your career has been the regard in which you have been held by great conductors. Names such as Bernard Haitink, Carlos Kleiber, Sir Charles Mackerras, Sir Andrew Davis, Neeme Järvi and Sir John Pritchard come to mind. I am interested to hear what impact these men made on you professionally, and your responses to them. Perhaps we can start with Sir John Pritchard.

FL: He was wonderful. Some conductors can make you nervous by what they do. They can be quite rigid. But 'J.P.', as he was affectionately known, was smooth and lovely. You felt like you were floating on a sea of sound. He loved singers, and was always watching what we did. He could be a bit lazy, and was a great one for the institution of afternoon tea, which usually involved a G and T – a gin and tonic! Perhaps that's a little unfair, but he was so relaxed and relaxing. He could also be very funny, and didn't take things too seriously. He never lost his temper in my experience. I did my first Marschallin from *Der Rosenkavalier* with him in Brussels. As my extraordinary costume was all black with a mantilla, he said wittily, 'Oh, my dear, you look like somebody selling cheap holidays in Majorca.' As J.P. had been a *répétiteur*, he could play the piano, and was able to work closely with the singers. And the advantage of that was very noticeable when I came to work with certain other conductors. If they were used to playing for a singer, they would breathe and make the music possible. Both J.P. and Carlos Kleiber could do that.

JF-A: Unlike Sir John, Bernard Haitink's experiences as a conductor were primarily in the concert hall before being appointed Music Director at Glyndebourne.

FL: Bernard is somebody I owe a great deal to, as he got me into Glyndebourne. When I auditioned for him there for a role in Stravinsky's *The Rake's Progress*, I was terrified. As it was the only half-decent audition that I ever did, I am endlessly grateful to Bernard. But as his experiences were essentially orchestral, he used to get very cross if anybody made a mistake. He couldn't quite bring you in, or would look up about a bar and a half early. This left you feeling that you were always a little late. He had amazing energy and strength, even though he is a very modest man. He also had tremendous control, and did fantastic performances of Sir Peter Hall's production of Mozart's *Don Giovanni* with Sir Thomas Allen in the title role and with Elizabeth Gale as Zerlina. Their reading of 'Là ci darem la mano' was one of the sexiest things I've ever seen, and the trio, where Don Giovanni kills the Commendatore, left everybody on the edge of their seat. It was unbelievable and unforgettable. Bernard's *Rake's Progress* was also amazing.

PART TWO: SINGERS

His *tempi* were great and matched perfectly the energetic and quirky music. He really was extraordinary, and I did a great many things with him. Sometimes, he would love the music so much that it became particularly expansive. When that happened, you felt like you were dying. When I did *Der Rosenkavalier* at Covent Garden with Bernard, he wanted me to sing the long phrase, '*dass ich auch einmal die alte Frau sein werd*' ('that I'll be the old woman one day, too'), in a single breath at the dress rehearsal. It felt endless, as I normally sang it with a breath in the middle. At the end of the rehearsal, a gentleman who was wearing an old anorak came backstage and said, 'Well done.' It was Carlos Kleiber. He then said that I might like to ask 'my' conductor to move on a little in that phrase. But he did point out that the way we had just done it had at least one advantage: I really *did* sound like an old woman!

JF-A: Kleiber could be quite mercurial. How did you cope with that professionally?

FL: The fact that Carlos agreed to work with me did a great deal for my confidence. When I was supposed to sing the Marschallin at the Metropolitan Opera with James Levine, I received a telephone call one day, and was asked, 'Carlos Kleiber might be taking over the performances. Will you still do them?' Of course, I said 'yes'. But there was such tension when working with him, as he was liable not to turn up, or might leave if he wasn't happy. Everybody was constantly saying that we had to be careful, as he wouldn't sign autographs, or speak to anybody. That left us feeling very nervous. But he was wonderful with Anne Sofie von Otter, Barbara Bonney and me. We had a great time, and he was very encouraging and supportive. He came to all the piano rehearsals, which some conductors don't. He also came to all of the production rehearsals, and I can still see him sitting there. It was as if he created the music anew each time. As he kept the orchestra really quiet, you felt that you could do anything. And the Trio was remarkable; it was as if he put his foot on the gas-pedal and the whole thing took flight. But he could be difficult, even though we didn't often experience it. There was a singer who was performing a small role who didn't meet his standards, and he was picky and nasty to him. Yet you often felt very free when performing with Kleiber, thanks to his detailed approach to rehearsal. He worked meticulously and knew the score inside out. He could be very minimal with his gestures, which meant that the singers and the orchestra were always alert. But he never rehearsed a work to death like some conductors do.

JF-A: Sir Charles Mackerras was something of a *sui generis* figure, whose probing mind and way of working led to revelatory performances of a different kind.

FL: The first thing that I ever did with Charles was Mozart's *Così fan tutte* at the English National Opera. That said, I might well have given some performances of *Die Zauberflöte* with him there before that – I'm not sure. *Così* was a wonderful new production by John Cox, who was one of my very favourite directors. They used to call Sir Charles 'chuck 'em up Charlie', as he was constantly cuing. You had to sing all the melismatic runs correctly, and if anything went wrong, you were given a chastising look. And he used to conduct while chewing his tongue in the side of his mouth. He was not the most charming of men and would call a spade a spade. But that's great, because being so direct meant that you knew exactly where you were. When it came to his ornamentation, I didn't like everything that he gave me; I much prefer simpler things. Sometimes, his florid decorations were too difficult or too high. Nevertheless, he did try to adapt his approach to whomsoever he was working with. When we recorded *Così fan tutte*, he had all these different ornaments for 'Per pietà', and couldn't decide which he wanted; so, we recorded it with each of them. He then chose the ones he preferred. It was very difficult. While I didn't always like doing Charles's decorations, I did like him. And he was the only conductor, apart from Carlos Kleiber, who replied to letters! When it came to *tempo*, you always felt safe and solid with Charles. His speeds were always right. Take, 'Come scoglio' from *Così*, for example. I always thought that there is only one *tempo* for each aria; the speed that I can do it at. If it's either too fast or too slow, I can't breathe. Charles got that and was wonderfully reliable.

JF-A: Neeme Järvi was very much a man of the 1980s. And it was during that decade that you did a great deal of work with him in the concert hall and the recording studio. Yet he's not a conductor whom you would naturally associate with the voice.

FL: Neeme was a big, cuddly, lovely man who was just very natural. As he was recording all of Strauss's tone poems for Chandos, the company thought it might be a good idea to record all of the composer's orchestral songs, too. He approached these without any preconceived ideas, and we recorded them all in an amazing hall in Dundee. I always seemed to be ill, so we simply went through everything twice, even when we recorded the *Vier letzte Lieder*. In any case, he never wanted to rehearse.

JF-A: The *Vier letzte Lieder* have been recorded by some of the late twentieth century's greatest sopranos, including Lisa Della Casa, Elisabeth Schwarzkopf, Dame Gwyneth Jones, Lucia Popp and Jessye Norman. Did you consider your disc of the work something of a milestone in your career, or just a natural professional progression?

FL: These *Lieder* are something of a musical mountain, as they are not only Strauss's last songs, but the last songs of their kind. They're so beautiful and so special. But you do feel a tremendous sense of responsibility when you put them on record. Even though I've sung them a number of times, Neeme made it very easy. I recorded them again later, but they didn't come out so well. This was mainly due the restrictions placed on me by the producer. I felt that I couldn't breathe.

JF-A: Would it be fair to say, then, that you are really at your best in recording sessions when you are able to do your 'own thing'?

FL: I find it very difficult to sing to a microphone. The wretched thing is so artificial. When they put the red light on, I stop breathing! I would regularly freeze up. I hated it.

JF-A: You've performed Strauss's major roles many times, and your characterisation and knowledge of them has changed over the years. With the advantage of hindsight, do you now see any connection between these characters, or are they simply a series of discrete individuals?

FL: There are tremendous similarities between the Countess in *Capriccio* and the Marschallin in *Der Rosenkavalier*. And I felt such a fool after performing *Capriccio* in Munich with Wolfgang Sawallisch. He asked me if I would like to sing in a new production of *Arabella* with him, and I told him that I didn't like the piece very much. I now shake my head in disbelief at what I said. I also like *Intermezzo*. But as I started with Octavian from *Der Rosenkavalier*, and as I sang the role for two seasons with Bernard Haitink, my reading of the Marschallin incorporates certain aspects of Octavian's personality.

PART TWO: SINGERS

JF-A: Can you define your relationships with some of the directors with whom you worked?

FL: A director who was absolutely vital for me was John Cox, as I was so awkward and shy. The first thing that I did at Glyndebourne was *Capriccio* on the 1976 tour. I wasn't long out of the Royal Academy of Music at the time, and it was a production that Elisabeth Söderström had sung very successfully at the main festival. John had set the opera in the 1920s and it was extremely beautiful. Because the work is a discussion about the relative importance of how words and music function within an operatic setting, the production was more like a play with music. And as *Capriccio* is about what we do as artists, and is such an interesting idea, I have always loved it. John understood the 'choreography' of the scenes where the Countess simply walks around the stage on her own. In many ways, that can be much more difficult than having to sing. When the wonderful *Mondscheinmusik* is heard at the beginning of the last scene, and where the Countess is wondering which of the two men she is going to choose, John managed to align one's physical gestures with each new high point in the music. This was so beautifully done and helped to direct the dramatic and musical tension to the scene's principal climatic moment. I've since sung *Capriccio* many times elsewhere, often with either little or no rehearsal, and have always been thankful that I first performed it under John's direction at Glyndebourne.

JF-A: When tensions rise between conductors and directors, singers can often be caught in the middle. How do you deal with situations like that?

FL: It's marvellous if the conductor is there for all the production rehearsals. At least that way he knows what's likely to happen, and why the director has placed me at the back of the stage at the very moment when the orchestra is at its loudest. I've been lucky enough to work on new productions where the conductor and the director have been friends, and where they have both been in attendance all the time. Today's singers tend to do what the director wants, as it's now the age of the director. They will often have you do crazy things while you are trying to sing. Of course, we will all have a go at what they want, but sometimes we just can't do it.

JF-A: Art-song has also played a huge part in your professional life, and you have worked with many of the world's leading accompanists. But it's with the pianist Graham Johnson that you seem to have a particular artistic affinity. How did that dynamic evolve?

FL: Although Graham is a little younger than me, he used to play for my lessons at the Academy. And even as a student, his knowledge was vast. He was always passionate about song, and knew a great deal about it. He had a wonderful piano teacher in Bulawayo, but was largely self-taught. He's one of those persons who remembers everything that he has read. Our ideas were very similar, and we always had great respect for what the composer wrote. But the way that we work has changed over the years, particularly when it comes to *tempo*.

JF-A: You are, and always have been, the darling of the French, and have a remarkable empathy with the French language and French song. How did this come about?

FL: In my opinion, it is very helpful – if not essential – to speak French if you are performing French song. German *Lieder* is not so difficult for an English person if they don't speak the language. As French is so subtle and so special, it requires greater mastery.

PART TWO: SINGERS

JF-A: Yet you performed very little French opera during the early part of your career.

FL: That's true, although I did do Offenbach's *La belle Hélène* with Marc Minkowski at the Théâtre du Châtelet in 2000. Marc was amazing and so inspired. And as he never did the same *tempo* twice, you really had to be on your toes. I never felt that I was suited to some of the traditional French roles, such as Micaëla in Bizet's *Carmen*. But I have sung quite a lot of French operetta in concert.

JF-A: When it comes to performance style, you are well known for your ability to shape and control your *vibrato*. How has this been perceived and received by some of those with whom you have worked?

FL: I did a lot of early music to start with, particularly Handel operas, where a wide *vibrato* was unacceptable. I've never liked an excessive use of the technique, even though it creeps in when you are trying to be heard over a loud orchestra. And, of course, you don't sing the same way when performing a work by Noël Coward as you do when singing an aria by Mozart. I was once given a good piece of advice by Sir Georg Solti when I went through the role of the Marschallin with him before singing it in public for the first time. He was so kind. And I remember saying to him that I had some difficulties with certain passages because of where the music lies vocally. He said, 'Just sing with *your* voice.' He also pointed out that I was able to do certain things that other people would love to be able to do. I had never realised that other people might have thought of me in that way. To be true to yourself, and to keep an individual sound, is very important. That's what's recognised by others, regardless of whether or not you have the most technically marvellous instrument. You are often recognised by the flaws in your voice. It's the character of the voice that is paramount. I have always been aware of style, and have tried to be stylish. This was particularly true when I was performing French music, where a big *vibrato* is inappropriate for most of it.

JF-A: What advice would you give to young singers who are about to embark on their careers?

FL: They should learn as much as they can while they still have the time to do so. And they should make sure that they see as many concerts and operas as possible. It's also essential to take advantage of all the wonderful free tickets for dress rehearsals that are on offer to them. I didn't do this, and I should've done. Students should study languages, and go to the movement classes that I avoided. And never look down your nose at the occasional engagement when somebody asks you to come and sing for nothing, or nearly nothing. You never know who might be there.

DAME ANN MURRAY
(DAVID JOSEFOWITZ RECITAL HALL, 9 JANUARY 2015)

RAYMOND HOLDEN: Being raised in Ireland in the 1950s and the 1960s must have been fascinating. What was Dublin like musically in those days?

ANN MURRAY: It was very parochial. We had, and still have, a big music festival there called the Feis Ceoil, which is something akin to an eisteddfod in Wales. It's the kind of event in which people from three to ninety-three take part. It was, and is, very much part of our culture. When I was growing up, we didn't have television, so everybody stood up and did their 'party pieces' at home. That might have been a poem, a song, or a piano composition. My mother was a fantastic pianist, and she could play anything you wanted in any key. My father sang well, and so did she. But professional opportunities were not there for someone of my mother's generation. And even when it came to me, they were not always available. That's why I had to move to Britain.

RH: When did you first know that you wanted to be a singer?

AM: My mother used to tell me that I liked imitating Deanna Durbin as a child, and would sing along with her whenever she was on the radio. We had a choir at the convent school I attended, and when the head of the Irish music inspectorate also started a choir, I joined it. I sang in my first competition at the age of four, and really began singing properly when I was about seven.

RH: Deanna Durbin was an interesting artist, who appeared with Leopold Stokowski in the 1937 film *One Hundred Men and a Girl*.

AM: She was a fantastic singer.

RH: Films such as *One Hundred Men and a Girl* are virtually unknown today. That's a great shame, as they can often serve as interesting role models for young artists.

AM: You're right. As a voice like Durbin's was beautifully clear, it can be great educationally.

RH: Who were some of your other early musical heroes?

AM: I really didn't have any, as my encounter with Deanna Durbin just happened naturally. The first opera that I ever saw was Verdi's *Aida* at the Dún Laoghaire cinema. My father took me. It starred Sophia Loren, but was sung by the wonderful Renata Tebaldi. I was then asked to sing the Shepherd Boy in Puccini's *Tosca* when singers from the Rome Opera visited Dublin in 1963.

RH: Does your passionate interest in Irish music stem from this time?

AM: I performed a great deal of Irish music in the past, and was not only educated in it, but spoke fluent Irish. Irish music was very much part of our culture, and a joy to sing. People would gather together at parties and on weekends to perform it. The honesty and beauty of the music meant that it just happened naturally.

RH: As an Australian, and as a member of the Irish diaspora, I have often wondered why Irish music travelled so well.

AM: I'm not sure. Perhaps it was because the Irish themselves travelled so well. When the Irish had to leave their country, their music went with them. Aside from cities such as Liverpool, where fifty per cent of the population is of Irish heritage, it's easy to forget that up to 50,000 Irish men and Irish women were taken to the West Indies as either voluntary or involuntary indentured servants. And that's why there are so many Irish names in the Caribbean.

RH: When you left Ireland, I believe you went to Manchester to study at the Royal Manchester College of Music.

AM: That's true, but I was supposed to go to London. My teacher in Dublin, Nancy Calthorpe, was a gracious and generous person, and realised that I needed a little more help. As she also understood that I needed to progress, she asked a compatriot of mine, Darina Gibson, for advice. I was originally going to audition for Fabian Smith at the Guildhall School of Music & Drama, but Darina suggested that I should work with a particular teacher in Manchester who seemed to be having great success with his students. My father then wrote to that gentleman in Manchester, and I was offered an audition at the Royal Manchester College of Music. When the gentleman, who looked a little like Wilfrid Hyde-White, came into the studio, he gave me a singing lesson, one of the best things that ever happened to me. He then asked, 'Have you flown over?' I thought, 'Flown? No, you must be joking.' I told him that

I'd travelled across on the boat and had arrived at 7am that morning. As it was 2.30pm by then, he wondered whether I'd be staying over in Manchester. I told him that I'd be returning to Dublin that night by boat. Slightly puzzled by all of this, he then asked where I'd been since arriving. 'I've been sitting in Piccadilly Square waiting for this' was my reply. Luckily, he offered me a place and a small bursary on the spot, which meant that I never went to London. The gentleman was, of course, Frederic Cox.

RH: Amongst Frederic Cox's students were Anne Howells, Rosalind Plowright, Ryland Davies and Dennis O'Neill. What was the secret to his success?

AM: Apart from his talent as a teacher, he had a great imagination. He never once gave me a breathing lesson or a prescriptive session. Every exercise that he set me had a reason, and was something that referred to me personally. I think that's what did it. And it was always a joy to go to his lessons, as he was so easy to learn from.

RH: What was Manchester like during your student years?

AM: I loved it. I simply loved it. I would have been lost in London, but Manchester was small enough for me to cope with. In fact, when I eventually came to London, I was terrified and didn't like it at all. Manchester was very much like Dublin. And there was a wonderful Welsh community there that came from Wrexham, and that included singers such as Arthur Davies. I had four singing lessons a week, and didn't sing anything but exercises for two years. Two of those lessons were with Mr Cox and two were with Sylvia Jacobs, his assistant. Along with acting classes, we were involved in productions of Britten's *Peter Grimes*,

PART TWO: SINGERS

Bellini's *Norma* and Mozart's *Le nozze di Figaro* and *Così fan tutte*. And I think there's even a tape recording of Rosalind Plowright, Sir John Tomlinson and me singing in *Così* from those days. I loved every minute of my time at the Royal Manchester College of Music.

RH: In 1974, you made your official debut as a professional singer.

AM: I'd won the Peter Stuyvesant Award to attend the London Opera Centre in 1972, but when they realised that I wasn't English, they took it back. By the time I'd finished at the Centre, I'd no work at all, other than the possibility of understudying the role of Rosina in Rossini's *Il barbiere di Siviglia* at the English National Opera the following November. But I was then offered the opportunity to cover Dame Janet Baker as Alceste in Gluck's work of the same name for Scottish Opera. As I knew that I'd learn a heck of a lot from that, I said 'Yes, please.' The problem was: I knew that I could sing the notes, but wasn't an Alceste in a 'month of Sundays'. About eight weeks before the production was due to start, Dame Janet withdrew. I immediately thought that this was a bit of a nuisance and considered withdrawing myself. The company's General Manager, Peter Hemmings, pointed out that this wasn't how it worked, and that I should stick with it. In place of Dame Janet, Scottish Opera was able to engage Júlia Várady – this was just before she married Dietrich Fischer-Dieskau. She was an unknown, but stunning, woman who spoke no English. She was lovely to me and we got on very well. We managed to bond, thanks to the little German that I spoke back then. On 1 September, she was scheduled to give the last performance of *Alceste* at Aldeburgh, but was unwell. So, on I went. Sir Alexander Gibson was conducting, and he was wonderful to me. I sang all the notes, and in the right order, but perhaps without the more dramatic sound that Ms Várady brought to them. Nevertheless, it was a marvellous experience, and I thought that Alex Gibson was a genius who could conduct anything. He was an absolutely wonderful conductor.

RH: Two years after you sang Alceste, you performed at the Royal Opera House, Covent Garden, for the first time.

AM: Between my debut with Scottish Opera and singing at Covent Garden, I was lucky enough to be part of Colin Graham's and Steuart Bedford's English Music Theatre Company. I felt cossetted by it and a member of a proper troupe. This suited me, as I was someone who didn't like sticking out on stage, other than when singing a role. I'm not the type of person who feels comfortable with the trappings of theatre life. At Covent Garden, I was damned if I did and damned if I didn't. If, for example, I was asked to do something that I thought might be embarrassing, I'd decline to do it. When that happened, they thought I was stupid, as I hadn't done what was asked of me. Then, I worried that if I *did* do what I was asked, I would also seem stupid. Consequently, my first couple of years at the Royal Opera House were difficult. I felt that I needed to be somewhere else to gain the necessary experience and confidence. I simply felt overwhelmed by Covent Garden.

RH: When chatting with some of your distinguished colleagues about their early years at the Royal Opera House, they often remember it as an ideal training ground. Was that your experience?

AM: No. Not at all. Even though I did my best, I didn't fare well. And that was the case until I went to Germany. As I was completely unknown there, such things didn't really bother me.

PART TWO: SINGERS

RH: I find this interesting, as most singers with whom I've worked have always had a 'soft spot' for Covent Garden. Do you?

AM: Latterly, certainly. But at the beginning, I wasn't good enough.

RH: Do you think that the newly renovated Royal Opera House is in any way different from the pre-renovated theatre?

AM: I look at it from a familial point of view: the theatre's sense of 'family' is still there. That said, the bar has gone and so, too, have many of the great characters who populated the place. It's turned into a big business, which, of course, it has to be. These days, there are a lot of ships that pass in the night. This is largely due to the reduced number of contracted singers who work there. It's now more common for the company to use talented singers from their young artists' programme in the smaller roles.

RH: Do you think that this approach has helped to raise the company's overall standard?

AM: Yes. The overall standard is wonderful, and it's now a joy and an honour to sing at the Royal Opera House.

RH: How would you compare working at Covent Garden with singing at the Metropolitan Opera, New York?

AM: I went to the 'Met' much later. I first sang there in 1984 as Sesto in Mozart's *La clemenza di Tito* conducted by James Levine. Before that, it was necessary for me to become more focused. This meant that my

New York debut was no problem, and an amazing event. I really had no time to equate it to anything else.

RH: Were you daunted by the size of the 'Met'?

AM: No. That didn't matter, as its acoustic is so beautiful. If you have a voice that's relatively well produced, it should carry. You just sing.

RH: You've given over 100 performances at Covent Garden. Which of these were particularly memorable?

AM: I sang in Strauss's *Ariadne auf Naxos*, *Der Rosenkavalier* and *Salome*, Mozart's *Le nozze di Figaro* and *Così fan tutte*, Wagner's *Götterdämmerung*, Rossini's *Mosè in Egitto*, Gounod's *Faust*, Donizetti's *La fille du regiment* and Humperdinck's *Hänsel und Gretel*, amongst others.

RH: And, of course, you made a famous recording of the last work that you just mentioned with Edita Gruberová, Dame Gwyneth Jones, Christa Ludwig, Sir Colin Davis and the Sächsische Staatskapelle for Philips. Do such recordings now feel like a long-distant memory from a once golden past?

AM: It was great fun to do and a wonderful experience. I don't know what's happened to the recording business. I suppose that its current state is due to platforms like YouTube, and the fact that everything you've sung is available only moments after you've walked on stage. Unless you are a superstar, or an artist whom the recording companies are willing to package and promote fully, the world has changed.

PART TWO: SINGERS

RH: It's nearly impossible to assemble such a remarkable cast these days. Each member of that ensemble was an iconic figure with a remarkable performance history.

AM: That's true, and that's why the Philips recording is a gem.

RH: And it's easy to forget that *Hänsel und Gretel* is a very difficult work to perform.

AM: Yes. It's a big, big sing, particularly for the Witch.

RH: Orchestrally, it's also quite tough, as it's very Wagnerian.

AM: Its orchestration is very thick indeed.

RH: In fact, Humperdinck was close to Wagner professionally and taught his only son, Siegfried, composition. This explains, at least in part, the quality, type and nature of the vocal and orchestral writing. But you've also sung a great many works by Handel.

AM: I sang Bradamante in Handel's *Alcina* at the 1979 Aix-en-Provence Festival so badly that it was nearly indescribable. In an attempt to help me through it, poor old Raymond Leppard inverted every vocal line I sang. It was really bad, and with the exception of some performances of *Messiah* that I'd given back home in Ireland, *Alcina* was the only music by Handel that I'd sung previously. Then, in the late 1980s, Sir Peter Jonas wondered if I'd be able to sing *Xerxes* at the English National Opera. As I knew that I could sing the notes comfortably, I agreed. From day one, it was clear that he was about to catapult Handel into the twentieth century. Both his production and the translation were amazing, and the buzz at the first night was fantastic. It was the first time that Handel had become the big kid on the operatic block. And thanks to the production and my wonderful colleagues, I had no trouble singing the composer's music. Christopher Robson acted marvellously, Valerie Masterson sang magnificently and Sir Charles Mackerras was a riot. The first time that we went through 'Ombra mai fu', I remember saying to Valerie that it felt either a bit fast or a bit slow; I no longer remember exactly which. She said that I should go and have a word with Sir Charles, and to ask if he could make it a 'bit easier'; not necessarily faster or slower, just a 'bit easier'. I took her advice, gingerly approached the conductor's rostrum and asked him if that were possible. Without breaking beat, he looked over his shoulder and said in his blunt, but characterful, accent, 'I'd do anything for you, but NO!'

RH: How did Sir Charles affect your Handel style in general?

AM: He was wonderful, and when we were performing 'Crude furie', it was like a race between the two of us. It was as if we were two jockeys vying to see who could go fastest. And I remember one night when the *tempo* suited us both equally, I looked down at the pit to see Sir Charles grinning approvingly and giving me a big thumbs-up. Singing arias like that, with musicians such as that, was not difficult. And once you know where your voice is going, the production and the translation also help to guide you.

RH: Sir Charles's vocal decorations in the works of Handel and Mozart often proved difficult for some singers.

AM: Not for me. They were great and no problem.

PART TWO: SINGERS

RH: You are the first singer whom I've interviewed to say that.

AM: And I remember that when we recorded *Xerxes* together, he came out with a string of monosyllabic criticisms: 'slow', 'flat', 'late' and so on. I then asked wistfully and cheekily, 'If it's so bad, how can you bear to conduct it?' 'I just grit my teeth and keep going' was his equally cheeky reply.

RH: Yes, Sir Charles was always known for his silver tongue.

AM: But he was wonderful.

RH: When interviewing renowned singers and distinguished operatic conductors, I am always keen to hear their thoughts on performing opera in the vernacular. And I have always been surprised by their strength of feeling when it comes to this matter.

AM: I must say that I am greatly in favour of it. When you have translations, such as those by Sir Nicholas Hytner and Amanda Holden, who did such a wonderful job on Handel's *Ariodante*, they make a great difference, as you are singing in English to an English-speaking audience. I've noticed, particularly in the big aria from *Ariodante*, where the eponymous character finds that he's been deceived and betrayed, that the audience identifies more closely with him if it's in translation. I have also sung Rossini's *La Cenerentola* and Offenbach's *La Périchole* in German. It's 'par for the course' in some central European theatres, and it doesn't really matter artistically whether it's in the original language or the vernacular, provided that the audience's sense of participation is enhanced.

RH: Are some works more easily performed in the vernacular than others? And here I am thinking of a work like *Götterdämmerung* being performed in Italian.

AM: Funny you should say that. My singing teacher always said that no matter what language you might be performing in, your vowel sounds should always have an Italianate base. And that it's essential to use the *legato* quality of those vowel sounds when creating that base.

RH: Handel's great contemporary was Johann Sebastian Bach. Today, his cantatas and Passions are heard regularly at the Proms, but that was not always the case. Amongst the vanguard of artists who championed his vocal works at that series were mezzo-sopranos such as Helen Watts. As you, too, are a leading mezzo-soprano who has performed the music of both Handel and Bach widely, do you adopt a different style for each?

AM: No, and I have never understood why you would do such a thing. Everything that you need to know is written on the page. The music that Bach notates is a direct consequence of the text that he is setting. Everything that we need to know in performance is contained in this kernel of information. This allows you to enter his world and to carry his vision forward through your interpretation. But when singing an aria by Bach that also has an *obbligato* oboe or flute part, you must take on a greater instrumental quality. When performing something like 'Erbarme dich' from the *Matthäus-Passion*, for example, it can only be sung according to its structure. And as it's so touching and honest in its context, it sings itself, provided that you put in the work at home.

RH: Do you find that the length and breadth of some arias by Bach are more demanding than some of those by Handel?

PART TWO: SINGERS

AM: That's certainly not the case when it comes to Ariodante's Act One aria: it seems to go on for ever. When singing Handel in the theatre, there's always the added pressure of playing a character. When performing Bach, on the other hand, your musical journey is often like that of an extra instrument, an instrument that is lucky enough to have been given words to help guide it on its journey. You are then emulsified, so to speak, into the cantata you are singing.

RH: Does this means that you sing slightly less operatically?

AM: Yes. But, in saying that, each of the sections assigned to the alto in the *Matthäus-Passion* is a *Scena* in its own right. When I am working with young artists, I try to get them to recognise this, and to get them to build their journey according to the roles they are singing. It's essential for them to know where they are going, and to act as musico-dramatic newsreaders. It's not good enough for them to sing simply what they see in the score; they have to think about what it means. And it helps if they can place the action within a modern context.

RH: Having mentioned the Proms, I am keen to hear your thoughts on the series in general. Your first performance there was at the First Night in 1977, when you took part in Vaughan Williams's *Serenade to Music* conducted by Sir Andrew Davis, and your most recent appearance was in 2012, when you sang the role of Marcellina in *Le nozze di Figaro* under Robin Ticciati. In all, you have performed at twenty-one Proms.

AM: Working at the Proms was always a combination of the marvellous and the terrifying. First Nights are exciting and Last Nights are difficult. As there's so little time for the conductor to rehearse everything at a Last Night, it can be problematic. And all of the opportunities that I have enjoyed at the Proms have come through my fantastic management team. I had a wonderful agent who was my friend, and who has worked closely with me; not for me, but *with* me. This helped me to progress and to advance my career. He advised me extremely well throughout my professional life. The pieces that I was invited to sing at the Proms were wonderful. Performing Schoenberg's *Gurrelieder* with Sir Andrew Davis was marvellous, and I remember it well. There were so many wonderful moments, and I think that the whole idea of the Promenade Concerts is unique. I am not sure that it's possible to perform such a varied repertoire anywhere else in the world. Of course, we could talk about the Vienna Philharmonic's Sunday morning subscription concerts at the Musikverein, and how the audience attends them directly after church. And we could also talk about the Bayerisches Staatsorchester's Abonnement performances during Peter Jonas's time in Munich. But they're not really comparable. The Proms are the *crème de la crème* of concerts series and are truly amazing.

RH: You are widely recognised as a distinguished Mozartian and have recently given some marvellous performances of the composer's music at the Glyndebourne Festival Opera. Did you spend much time there as a young singer?

AM: When I first auditioned for Glyndebourne, I didn't get in, and that's fine. But then, in 1979, I was invited by Raymond Leppard to sing Minerva in his performing version of Monteverdi's *Il ritorno d'Ulisse in patria*. Thirty-two years then passed before I returned to sing Marcellina in *Le nozze di Figaro*. Thankfully, I was busy elsewhere in the interim!

RH: From your chronology at Glyndebourne, you must have sung in both the old and new theatres there.

PART TWO: SINGERS

AM: Yes, I did.

RH: Was there an acoustic difference between them?

AM: The new house is much healthier for singers, and is more complementary to the voice.

RH: It's not quite as dry as the old shoebox theatre.

AM: Exactly. And the new, more spacious auditorium allows the voice to reverberate more easily.

RH: But has the theatre's increased size resulted in a diminished connection with the audience?

AM: Not really, as it is still an intimate space.

RH: And, of course, the works of Wagner are now being performed there, which would have pleased the festival's founder, John Christie, but dismayed its first Music Director, Fritz Busch. Do you think that by programming Wagner's operas and music-dramas there, Glyndebourne's founding principles have been diluted?

AM: No, I don't think so. The size of the new theatre is not much bigger than the Cuvilliés Theatre in Munich where *Tristan und Isolde* was first rehearsed.

RH: When I interviewed Dame Anne Evans recently, she was adamant that a thorough study of Mozart's works is an essential learning tool for any young singer. Do you agree?

AM: Yes, I do. I remember many years ago that I was studying one day and the telephone rang. It was Sir Georg Solti, and he said that he would like to go through *Der Rosenkavalier* with me. Stupidly, I was rather too quick to point out that he wasn't conducting the performance I was about to give. He was unconcerned by this, and replied in his highly distinctive Hungarian accent that 'I *know* I'm not conducting it, but I *want* to work with you.' And at the end of the session that I spent with Sir Georg on Strauss's opera, he said that I should sing the works of Mozart and Rossini as long as I can, as they would keep my voice young and agile.

RH: Sir Georg Solti was something of a 'Marmite' figure when it came to some of his colleagues. Nearly every singer with whom he worked adored him, while a great many orchestral players found him difficult. What was your impression of him?

AM: I sang Donna Elvira from Mozart's *Don Giovanni* with Sir Georg in London, Cologne and Hanover, with the two performances at the Royal Festival Hall being recorded. In the German cities, the audiences went absolutely wild for him before we started. It must've been twelve minutes before we could begin, and at those concerts, it was clear that the orchestra loved him too. At the end, the audience wouldn't let him go. They were really wonderful performances, and perhaps even better than those that we gave and recorded in London. They were just fantastic. Finally, he stopped and said in German, 'Ladies and Gentleman, I'm an old man. Go home.' He was so sweet and a genius. And even though he had a strange conducting technique, you always knew exactly what he wanted.

PART TWO: SINGERS

RH: Did you ever work with Sir Georg's great contemporary, Herbert von Karajan?

AM: I did, but only once. I went to Salzburg for the first time in 1981, and returned many times during the intervening Glyndebourne years. Herr von Karajan's secretary telephoned my agent and said that he knew of my work and would like to hear me. I was then called to the Grosses Festspielhaus, a huge monster of a place, to sing for him. I prepared the 'Laudamus te' from Mozart's Mass in C minor, some excerpts from *Le nozze di Figaro* and something else. I waited and waited in an empty room and was expecting a great statue of a man to turn up. When the door finally opened, this tiny, tiny person came in. I thought nothing more about it until that tiny person screamed, 'Are you going to sing or not?' I dutifully stood, sang and was told that my voice was too big for the Grosses Festspielhaus!

A little later, Karajan was performing and recording Haydn's *Die Schöpfung*, and realised that he had never given the concluding chorus with an alto soloist. When I was brought in to sing this with only one rehearsal, my colleagues were Edith Mathis, Francisco Araiza and the wonderful José van Dam. I had no score, but was given one that was normally reserved for the recording's producer: it was monstrously large and with pages that were nearly impossible to turn. Of course, I had heard the piece many times, but had never sung it before. And when they made a cut in the final recitative, I thought, 'What on earth am I going to do now?' I finally found my place and was told by Edith Mathis that I *must* sing *piano*, nothing above *piano*. But when I actually got to the passage, I screamed at the top of my lungs. I was so happy that I actually found where I was supposed to be that I simply let rip. When we got to the end, José van Dam stood up and beckoned me to join him and the other soloists at the front of the stage to acknowledge the applause. Even though I had asked him not to, he raised his arms in a triumphant manner to acknowledge my contribution. So, my sole professional encounter with Herbert von Karajan was to sing 'Amen' four times at the end of Haydn's *Die Schöpfung*. Nevertheless, I had a great time in Salzburg over the years, and sang there on more than twenty occasions.

RH: But your first experience of Salzburg was far from welcoming.

AM: I'd sung in *Le nozze di Figaro* at Aix-en-Provence the night before I was scheduled to arrive in Salzburg for the first time. And, in those days, it wasn't so easy to get from one place to another. As I finished in Aix at about midnight, I sat up all night, because I was catching a 6am flight and thought that it wasn't worth going to bed. As that flight took me to Orly, I had to cross Paris in order to catch my connecting flight at Charles de Gaulle Airport. I then flew to Munich, where I caught a cross-country bus to Salzburg. When I finally got there at 1pm, the heavens opened. I'd never seen rain like it before. The raindrops were jumping off the pavement and I was saturated. The first thing that I did was to buy a pair of Wellington boots. I then found my way to the apartment that was booked for me, only to discover that it, too, was miserable. The beds were nailed to the wall, and the owners hadn't even left a grain of salt. It was bare and horrible. I had no idea where the rehearsal venue was, and it took me some time to find it. When I finally 'swam' my way along the banks of the Salzach to the hall, my colleague said that Mr Ponnelle – the director, Jean-Pierre Ponnelle – didn't need us until tomorrow. I was not well pleased. That said, my time at Salzburg was largely blessed, as I was able to work with, and be mentored by, him. Mr Ponnelle was a genius and a great director. I was then lucky enough to collaborate regularly with him and James Levine during my first few years there. After that, I was engaged to sing *Così fan tutte* under Riccardo Muti, who was also fabulous.

RH: A conductor who made his home not far from Salzburg was Nikolaus Harnoncourt. He was a completely different kind of musical beast from those you've just mentioned, and one who was passionate about historically informed performance practice. What's your take on balancing modern vocal technique with period instruments?

AM: The first thing that I did with Mr Harnoncourt was a production of Mozart's *Lucio Silla* directed by Jean-Pierre Ponnelle. And I was surprised how quickly Mr Harnoncourt and I understood each other musically. Mr Ponnelle's production style allowed me to sing freely, and I didn't have to change my vocal technique. His methods always guided you in the correct direction, and you could easily hear what he wanted to do with the music. It was as if I had been dropped into a mixing bowl of wonderment. Consequently, I had no cause to change my general approach. Working together with such great artists will always create an interesting result. If you observe the text, it's easy to represent betrayal, sadness and happiness. Such things should come naturally.

RH: Do you consider the operas that Mozart composed before *Idomeneo* as dramatically interesting as those that he wrote later in his career?

AM: Absolutely, and they're often even more taxing than *Idomeneo*.

RH: Those who don't know Mozart's early operas often cite the Queen of the Night's arias in *Die Zauberflöte* as being amongst the most difficult in his oeuvre. But some of the material found in *Mitridate, re di Ponto* and *Lucio Silla* is not exactly a pushover.

AM: I agree. Giunia's big aria in Act Two of *Lucio Silla* is phenomenally difficult.

RH: And the writing for the tenors in these operas is also incredibly demanding.

AM: True. We should always spare a thought for whoever sings the title role in *Mitridate*.

RH: Aside from Jean-Pierre Ponnelle, who were some of the other directors who impressed you?

AM: Mr Ponnelle was unique. He spoke many languages and was an outstanding musician. His musical abilities were such that he could have conducted many of the operas that he directed. His approach to production was holistic, and he often took charge of the lighting and the costumes. He allowed me 'to fly' dramatically and musically, and he encouraged me to use my imagination. He was so exciting to work with, and was the most important director I ever encountered.

RH: Is it necessary to be a great musician to be a great director?

AM: Yes. It doesn't matter what you bring to the table as a director, as long as you know why you're doing it. A production that simply sets out to be controversial is not worthwhile: it will be a disaster. There has to be a valid reason for every decision that a director takes. And the same is true for the conductor. I remember that when I performed *Così fan tutte* with Mr Harnoncourt, his *tempo* for 'Soave il vento' was very fast at the first rehearsal. This caused me to take an audible intake of breath. He then looked up and said, 'What's the matter?' I instantly thought

PART TWO: SINGERS

that I'd overstepped the mark and that I shouldn't have made a sound. But he then explained that the accompaniment in that particular trio was not the Danube, but a little tributary, and went on to clarify what he meant by that. Like it or loathe it, he had a reason for what he did, and had thought deeply about it. His approach worked perfectly.

RH: Who amongst the younger generation of directors do you admire?

AM: Nicholas Hytner is great, David Alden can be magical and Richard Jones is extraordinary. I sang in Sir David McVicar's production of *Figaro*, and saw his reading of Britten's *The Turn of the Screw* at the English National Opera. I was bowled over by its dark and spine-chilling qualities. It was wonderful. He's a great, great talent.

RH: Earlier, you mentioned working on Strauss's *Der Rosenkavalier* with Sir Georg Solti. I am keen for you to expand on this, and to explain some of the demands that the composer's music presents to singers.

AM: The two operas that I sang most frequently by him were *Der Rosenkavalier* and *Ariadne auf Naxos*. These are 'business operas' where the fourth wall of society is removed, and where the audience becomes privy to all that's taking place within. As Der Komponist in *Ariadne*, I loved depicting his sense of professional urgency, his selfish concern for being the best that he can be, and the idea that he's still a whippersnapper who needs to grow up. And the best Musiklehrer I ever worked with was Walter Berry. He was very kind and really wonderful. As Octavian in *Der Rosenkavalier*, you are busy from start to finish and are always pushed for time. Even before the music starts, you have to enter into the Marschallin's household by walking up and down the stage and by getting used to the 'room' in which you are performing. The audience is something of a voyeur who witnesses the naked rejection of poor Octavian. It observes the fun, misery and formality of his situation, and the ridiculousness of the last act. From the early theatrical turmoil to the peace of the third act duet, the whole thing is like a huge musical washing machine that tumbles around and around before it finally comes to rest. The whole opera is so clever and wonderful, and you don't stop to think while you are in it. You start at the beginning and carry on until it's finished. And when it's finally over, you could start all over again, as you are so energised by what you've just done. It's an amazing opera.

RH: Whenever I chat to Dame Gwyneth Jones about the opera, she speaks vividly of her experiences when singing all three principal female roles. Do you think that a mezzo-soprano would also be capable of such a feat?

AM: I'm sure it's possible. When my voice was higher, I might've been able to sing the Marschallin, but I wouldn't have wanted to. I felt that as a girl on stage, I would've shown too many of my own inadequacies. I was much happier being a boy, as I was literally stepping into somebody else's boots.

RH: I would also value your thoughts on the performance of Mahler's music?

AM: It's no different from singing Strauss's music. Again, the score tells you how to perform it. *Kindertotenlieder* cannot be sung in any other way than what's on the page. When you give the *Rückert-Lieder*, the beauty and honesty of the line determines your reading. 'Ich atmet' einen linden Duft' cannot be anything other than what it is. If you paint a picture for yourself before you sing, and if you place yourself within your own domestic circumstances, you will know who you are and what you have to do. It's like being a member of a book club. We've all heard these pieces, and we all know what we like. And we also know that different audiences have different preferences. Why? Because different artists have different readings. And while it's probably both a simplistic and a stupid thing to say, compositions such as these guide you. It's not possible to do anything other than to sing them.

RH: What are your memories of performing the works of Richard Wagner?

AM: I've had only three experiences of singing his music professionally. I sang Waltraute at Covent Garden in Richard Jones's fabulous production of *Der Ring des Nibelungen* when it was conducted by Bernard Haitink. As he observed all of the composer's dynamics, I had no problem singing the part. On the strength of those performances, I was invited to give the role in Vienna. There, I sang without rehearsal, as the Staatsoper operates a repertory system. And because the theatre doesn't have a sunken pit, I walked out on stage to be confronted by an *extremely* loud orchestra. It was so loud that I screeched my way through the whole thing. It was dreadful. And at the end of my scene, I was booed loudly, which was absolutely right. I then spoke to the head of the opera house and told him that I was leaving. When Lorin Maazel later offered me the part of Brangäne in *Tristan und Isolde* at Munich, I wasn't sure that I was right for it, having had my fingers burned in Vienna. When I told him exactly what had happened at the Staatsoper, he suggested that I should go away, look at the role, and let him know. After studying the material closely, I felt that I could do it, provided that Mr Maazel followed the printed dynamics exactly. But I suggested that I should sing the role for him first, and if he didn't like what he heard, that would be the end of it. After working on it with him, and adopting some of his ideas, he said let's do it. The main rehearsal period was not a particularly pleasant experience, and I began to doubt myself. Nevertheless, I did my best. Some of the performances were fine, and some were not so fine. But because of the tensions surrounding the project, I didn't sing my best.

RH: Did you ever consider performing other Wagnerian roles, such as Erde or Kundry?

AM: No. They were too much for me. Many years ago, I was offered one of the Rhinemaidens. But as the production required me to sing naked, my agent said, 'I think we'll leave that one, shall we?'

RH: Before we finish, I'd like to discuss briefly your work as a recitalist. First, I'd like to ask you about Benjamin Britten's *Cabaret Songs*, a cycle that you have recorded.

AM: They're really like a series of little opera *Scenas*. It's essential to allow them to bubble along, and, again, everything you need to know is in the music.

RH: You've also made a remarkable recording of Schumann's *Frauen-Liebe und Leben*. What advice would you give to a young singer who is performing the cycle for the first time, and how should they go about preserving the integrity of the central narrative?

AM: I usually ask my accompanist to play the last song's postlude before we begin. That way I am able to get a sense of the cycle as a whole. Again, it's important to think in simplistic terms. If you're doing the ironing or

PART TWO: SINGERS

washing the dishes, for example, you should allow your memory to lead you through the songs. That way, you're able to identify with the central character's journey, and are aware that even though she is angry by the end of the cycle, she will happily sing it again the next day.

YVONNE KENNY
(DAVID JOSEFOWITZ RECITAL HALL, 14 OCTOBER 2016)

RAYMOND HOLDEN: I have been a great admirer of your work for many years now, and was totally bowled over by your portrayal of Aspasia in a film of Mozart's *Mitridate, re di Ponto* that was shot at the Teatro Olimpico, Vicenza, in 1986.

YVONNE KENNY: I was first offered the role for a production of the work at the Opernhaus Zürich conducted by Nikolaus Harnoncourt, and directed by the great French stylist Jean-Pierre Ponnelle. We are all now very aware of Mozart's early operas, but, at the time, the production was quite revolutionary. I first made contact with Harnoncourt through my colleague Dame Ann Murray, who also sang on the film. The great *coloratura* soprano Edita Gruberová was unable to sing in another early Mozart opera at Zurich, which left the management scratching their heads and wondering who they might engage to replace her as Giunia in *Lucio Silla*. Ann piped up and said, 'My friend Yvonne Kenny can sing it.' I'd performed it with Richard Hickox at the Spitalfields Festival with Philip Langridge, and Ann had been in the audience. Her chance remark proved quite fateful, as this was the beginning of an enormously important chapter in my life.

PART TWO: SINGERS

RH: Let's step back in time, shall we? As a fellow Australian, I'm very interested to hear your memories of Sydney in the 1950s and the 1960s. Did you find the city culturally stimulating as a young person?

YK: It was an entirely different place back then. I was born in 1950, and came from a very ordinary family in the northern Sydney suburb of Northbridge. I went to the local primary school, and it was there that the whole idea of me having a voice began. This was at odds with the culture of Sydney at the time, which largely revolved around the beach, the pool and swimming. Australian life was all sport, and I knew nothing about it. I still remember very clearly the first moment I realised that I had a voice. It was in Fourth Class when I was about ten years old. We all have one wonderful teacher in our lives, and mine was Mr Edgar Hill, an Englishman from Worcester. He loved Gilbert and Sullivan, and asked us all to audition for a school production. I dutifully went down to Classroom 4A at lunchtime and sang a few 'la-la-las'. He looked up from the piano and said, 'My goodness, you have a very nice voice.' And that's how it all began. I was cast as Tessa in *The Gondoliers*, before singing Mabel in *The Pirates of Penzance* the following year. Anyone who knows Mabel's aria will realise how high and florid it is. I was about eleven years old, and piped away in my plump bonnet and big bell skirt. But it must've been good, as I got an encore. My mother wasn't able to attend the first night, but one of her friends was there and said, 'Your little girl has got a good voice.' My mother had no idea that that was the case.

RH: Was your family particularly musical?

YK: Not really. I came from a very average family, and the extraordinary thing was that my mother was unable to sing in tune. Conversely, my aunt – her sister – had an extremely pretty singing voice. My parents separated when I was very young; I was only six at the time. Although I was brought up by my mother, my instinct is that my musical ability came from my father's side of the family. There was a lot of involvement in brass-band music, and one of my paternal grandmothers played the organ at the cathedral in Newcastle, New South Wales. But I really had no understanding of music at the time, other than seeing movies like *South Pacific* or attending shows. My father did love classical music, and I remember that he had recordings of Johann Strauss II's *Wiener Blut* and some Viennese operettas.

RH: It seems to me that nearly every Australian musician began his or her artistic life with the works of Gilbert and Sullivan. That's not only true of me, but also of Sir Charles Mackerras.

YK: Today, Australian schools stage things that are more contemporary. But, at the time, these were the works that we all performed, and it was with them that I began my life as a singer. The fact that I could sing all those runs, trills and high notes when I was eleven years old was remarkable. I've no idea how I did it; it just happened. This then continued through high school, and every time that there was a big celebration, I was always asked to sing a solo. And so it went on.

RH: Did you go to concerts and the opera during those early years?

YK: I remember very clearly that as a teenager, and this is why music education is so important, I was taken by the school to see an opera and to the Sydney Town Hall to hear a symphonic concert. These events predated the Sydney Opera House, which opened in 1973. I sang in choirs and ensembles, but as we didn't have much money, there weren't many opportunities to go to a lot of concerts. It was a very simple life, and I was

PART TWO: SINGERS

devoted to my studies. I can remember studying really hard all the way through primary school and wanting to better myself. I was determined that I was going to do well at whatever I finally decided to do.

RH: As you and I are not that dissimilar in age, one of the things that I remember about Sydney in the 1960s and the 1970s was its remarkably integrated music-education system. There were the schools' orchestral concerts and the regular visits to the Australian Opera, now Opera Australia. And then there were the schools' choral concerts. These involved bringing students in from the Outback to play and to sing in performances of such things as Handel's *Israel in Egypt* and Walton's *Belshazzar's Feast*. The students were prepared for those events by teachers from Sydney who were flown out to those remote areas, and who worked with the pupils until they were prepared enough musically to take part in the concerts at the Town Hall.

YK: Yes, I was very much part of those choral concerts at the Sydney Town Hall, which were directed by a wonderful gentleman called Terence Hunt.

RH: Terence was a truly remarkable man, and although he was a terrible conductor, he did much to shape the musical life of New South Wales for many, many years.

YK: Yes, that's right, and it was through the school system, rather than going to concerts with my mother, that a whole new world opened up for me. I remember that my father also had a recording of Smetana's *Vltava*. That disc started my great love affair with beautiful orchestral music.

RH: Am I correct when I say that after leaving school you studied science, rather than music, at university?

YK: That's absolutely correct. I worked very hard throughout my secondary-school years, and I was fortunate enough to win a Commonwealth Scholarship. If your mark at the final examination was sufficiently high enough, your whole university education was paid for by the government. That was such a gift, as I knew that I had no chance of going on to tertiary education if I didn't secure one of those scholarships. The subjects that I chose when preparing for my final year included Level One English and Level One Science, which was an unusual combination. Having been awarded the scholarship, I gained entry into the University of Sydney to study for a science degree. That was a three-year course, and I was particularly passionate about biochemistry. In fact, biochemistry and microbiology were my final-year subjects. I had no intention of having a career in music at that stage.

But at exactly the same time that I began my studies at university, I decided to have some singing lessons. I was eighteen at the time, which is the perfect age to start them. Before that, we are not physically mature enough, or settled enough, to ensure that the quality of the sound is not impaired. I then spent half an hour each week with a wonderful lady called Myra Lambert at the New South Wales State Conservatorium of Music, now the Sydney Conservatorium of Music. As I didn't actually do a music degree, my singing lessons were more like an 'additional extra' to my science studies. The first aria that I was given to sing was 'Caro nome' from Verdi's *Rigoletto*, and, from this, I gradually began to understand opera. With each new aria that I was given, I was amazed at just how beautiful the music was. I was also struck by its virtuosity, and the excitement that I felt when performing it.

RH: As a student at the New South Wales State Conservatorium, I knew Myra Lambert and remember that she was remarkably long-lived.

PART TWO: SINGERS

YK: She was one of the more important singing teachers at the Conservatorium during those years. After retiring from there, she taught at home until she was ninety-eight years old; she died seven years ago at the age of 101. I'm grateful to Myra for her tremendous kindness and her terrific sense of humour. I discovered later in life that she was quite a spiritual person. When I visited her during my trips back home to Sydney, I learned that she was interested in Eastern religions and that she was also a painter. She was a very creative person and a substantial human being. The thing that I admired most about her was that she didn't interfere with my sound. She believed that a singing teacher should facilitate a pure and natural sound through breath support, and that that sound should be as close to speech as possible.

RH: One of the Royal Academy of Music's greatest singing teachers was Manuel García. He, too, was long-lived, and also died at the age of 101. Perhaps being a great vocal pedagogue is the secret to longevity. Do you fancy going on that long?

YK: Possibly I could! Perhaps it's because teaching is incredibly inspiring; I have been doing it now for about ten years. You no longer have the stress of getting up on stage and singing yourself. But you can revisit all the music you love. One of the hardest things to confront as you approach the end of your career is the knowledge that you will no longer be performing all the big roles that you once gave. This is largely because you no longer have the physical or vocal stamina to do so. But to be able to hear beautiful young voices in your studio, and to suggest things that might help their professional journey, is inspiring. That might well be the key to a long life.

RH: You decided to study abroad at a time when Sydney was experiencing something of a musical golden period. When the Opera House opened in 1973, many of the world's greatest performers visited the city, and the local opera company was operating at a particularly high level. What impact did the Australian Opera have on you at that time?

YK: When all this was going on, I was a very young student, and I didn't perform with the Australian Opera until 1982. This was during Richard Bonynge's tenure as the company's Music Director. This 'golden time' also benefited from the presence of Dame Joan Sutherland, who gave some amazing performances. But when the Opera House actually opened, I wasn't part of it: I was a student abroad by then. This meant that I was missing during Sir Edward Downes's stewardship of the Australian Opera, a period when he raised the company to an international standard.

RH: I am regularly reminded by Sir Mark Elder, who began his professional operatic career in Australia, that you swapped apartments with him in Sydney.

YK: There were three moments in my life when it turned into something completely different. The first was when I completed my science degree. Just as I was about to get a job in a pathology department of a hospital as a biochemist, I was presented with the opportunity of singing with an amateur company called Young Opera. Its conductor, Richard Divall, was very passionate about Baroque music, and was putting on Handel's *Xerxes* at the Cell Block Theatre in Sydney's Darlinghurst. When their Romilda fell ill, Richard telephoned me and asked if I could learn the role in two days. I said, 'Yes', and then went about cramming it into my brain. That was the moment my life changed forever, as I loved the experience so much. I enjoyed performing in that opera, and Handel's music fitted my voice like a glove. At that moment, I knew that I wanted to

PART TWO: SINGERS

become an opera singer. I remember going home, and saying to my dear mother, 'I'm really sorry, Mum, but I think that I want to be an opera singer.' As that was after I was awarded my Bachelor of Science degree, my mother asked in her characteristically understated manner, 'Do you think that's a good idea?' And that was the *first* time something out of the blue totally changed my life.

The second incredible stroke of fate was when I left Australia in 1973. Even though I'm not sure whether people really believe in fate or destiny, I have found that things sometimes change on a sixpence for me. It was the academic holidays and I wasn't supposed to be anywhere near the Conservatorium. I had joined the opera course there the year after I completed my science degree, and was sharing a flat in Sydney's Neutral Bay with my great friend, the pianist and *répétiteur* Linnhe Robertson. This was the same apartment that Mark Elder later moved into. Realising that we had to pay the rent, I set off in my Mini, but encountered the Opera School's Principal, Ronal Jackson, en route. Although somewhat surprised to see me, he decided that this chance meeting was a stroke of fate, and was the ideal opportunity to ask if I was interested in accepting a scholarship to study at the La Scala Opera School in Italy. I said 'yes' immediately. As one of my fellow students had become ill, and was unable to accept the scholarship for medical reasons, it had become free. Everybody then warned me that I was far too young, and that I wouldn't be able to cope. My teacher, Myra Lambert, was also a bit anxious, as I was only twenty-two at the time. Nowadays, young people of seventeen and eighteen travel all over the world without hesitation, but, in 1973, it wasn't quite so easy. Nevertheless, I was keen to accept the offer, as it was the realisation of a childhood dream: when I was a kid in my bedroom, I was always singing with a pretend microphone in front of a mirror, knowing that one day I was going to go somewhere else.

Being terribly expensive to travel abroad at the time, I went from Sydney to Genoa on an ocean liner, and 'worked my passage' as part of my scholarship. I had to sing *Lieder* in First Class, perform popular melodies in Steerage Class, and read the news every night on the ship's closed-circuit television in my best English. This was at the time when the King of Sweden was very unwell. We would receive daily telexes about his deteriorating condition, and I remember that it took him some time to pass on. I kept announcing his imminent demise for weeks. As it was at the time when the Suez Canal was closed, we couldn't travel through it to get to the Mediterranean Sea, so we had to go by way of South Africa. It took about six weeks. When I eventually arrived in Milan, I had to audition to get into the opera school, which nobody in Sydney had realised. And the baritone who had travelled with me, and who was also supposed to attend the school, failed to be admitted. Fortunately, I did get in, but remember vividly that my Italian wasn't very good at the time. I knew this, because the auditioning panel kept giggling at it. But I did learn to speak Italian, thanks to a brilliant coach. While I was in Milan, I learned three major roles: Susanna in *Le nozze di Figaro*, Gilda in *Rigoletto* and Lucia in *Lucia di Lammermoor*. That was the beginning of my serious singing training.

RH: After you arrived in London, you had another experience that was life-changing: you sang in a performance of a relatively unknown Donizetti opera at the Queen Elizabeth Hall in October 1975.

YK: That's correct, and that was the third of the three experiences that I mentioned earlier. I left Milan with all my belongings on an overnight *couchette* train. This was a bit scary, as I only knew one person in London, and didn't have any money left. But as I decided to travel to Britain on a wing and a prayer, I was determined to make it work. While I slept on

PART TWO: SINGERS

my friend Susan Kessler's floor for a couple of nights, I practised hard and got my voice into shape. I then went and sang for Erich Vietheer, the partner of one of Australia's foremost musicians, Geoffrey Parsons. Before Erich heard me, he told Susie that he thought that I was a bit too young. He suggested to her that I should go back to Australia, and that I should come back when I was a little older. But after hearing me sing, he said, 'I think that you'd better stay.' This led to a year of intense study with both Erich and Geoffrey, and it was my great good fortune to have been involved with these musicians in London at that time.

I then auditioned for Opera Rara. This was a wonderful company that had been founded by Patric Schmid in 1970, and that mostly performed rare French and Italian operas from the nineteenth century. They engaged me as the understudy for the role of Rosmonda in Donizetti's *Rosmonda d'Inghilterra*, a part that was to be sung by the marvellous soprano Janet Price. Two days before the performance, however, she became ill. Being the excellent colleague that she was, she rang Patric to say that she couldn't sing, and that he needed to contact me, so that I would have sufficient time to prepare the role. Even though I knew it, I suddenly found myself on stage. It was a concert performance that attracted a large and important audience. As representatives of the Royal Opera House and the English National Opera were coming to the event, I knew that it was my chance to make my mark if I did a good job. I also knew that if this was not the case, I might never be heard of again. It really was *that* important. Luckily, I had sung a great deal of *bel canto* earlier in my career and Donizetti's style suited me. As I had the vocal height and agility, I can honestly say that that performance was one of the best I ever gave.

RH: How did you go about preparing such technically demanding roles during those early years?

YK: Truthfully, I'm not sure. As a mature artist and as a teacher, you tend to forget what your young voice sounded like. But as I could already sing things that were high and fast as an eleven-year-old, I do think that some singers are born with these abilities. Of course, I can help people learn how to sing such things, but that's not so straightforward. My voice has a very flexible, classical core to it, and it can move very quickly. Other artists might have a much broader core to their voice, and theirs might be better suited to more lyrical music. Each of us has a throat that fits certain composers and styles, and I was just very lucky that my natural vocal placement suited the *bel canto* repertoire.

RH: Sir John Barbirolli always used to say that conductors are born and not made. Do you think that is also true of singers?

YK: That's exactly correct. Some singers I've worked with have incredible ease when it comes to the tops of their voices, while others struggle. Every throat is different, but it's my job as a teacher to guide people, and to optimise their resonance. I'm always searching for this.

RH: After your spectacular Southbank Centre debut, what happened next?

YK: As mine had been both a hugely successful and an unexpected debut, the event was reported widely in the newspapers the next day. This meant that everybody knew my name. Around the same time, I also won the Kathleen Ferrier Award. Such things are important for young singers, as they ensure that their names are brought to the attention of those who can help them. Amongst the audience at the Queen Elizabeth Hall that night was Christopher Hunt from the Royal Opera House and Lord Harewood from the English National Opera. Both of those houses then invited me to come and to audition for them, so it was very important that I sang well. I did a very good audition for the Royal Opera House, but the day that I went to the English National Opera I wasn't very well and didn't do myself justice. Consequently, I was asked to join the former shortly after performing at the Southbank Centre. The Royal Opera was a very different company at the time. These days, singers are hired on short contracts, whereas, back then, there were between thirty-five and forty of us who were salaried. It was a true ensemble troupe.

RH: Making one's debut at the Royal Opera House must be a daunting experience, but to have done so with the world premiere of Hans Werner Henze's *We Come to the River* (*Wir erreichen den Fluss*) must surely have raised daunting to a completely new level.

YK: As that production demanded about fifty singers performing multiple roles, I didn't feel particularly exposed. I also sang the role of the Priestess in Verdi's *Aida* very early on, and similar small parts. It wasn't unlike a young artists' programme now. I was also afforded the opportunity to cover larger roles, and was eventually given a more substantial part in an opera by Mozart: Barbarina in *Le nozze di Figaro* on 1 December 1977.

RH: Apart from Henze's opera, have you performed much contemporary music?

YK: I gave one major composition about half way through my career. I'd done a lot of work in France in the 1980s, and it was there that I sang the title role in Gavin Bryars's opera, *Medea*. I had to perform half of it in French and the other half in Modern Greek; a real challenge. While I didn't do many other truly contemporary things, I did sing some of Alban Berg's works as part of a festival of his music with the BBC Symphony Orchestra and Sir Andrew Davis. We gave fragments from *Wozzeck*, the *Sieben frühe Lieder* and the *Altenberg-Lieder*, which were very elusive and difficult to learn.

RH: From a close reading of your work at the Royal Opera House, it seems that you performed there on forty-eight occasions in at least twenty-one works by thirteen composers. And what's particularly striking about your Covent Garden repertoire is its breadth and variety. This, then, raises questions about the whole *Fach* system, and the increasingly common urge to pigeonhole singers at an early age. As we know, many of opera's leading figures, such as Maria Callas, Dame Gwyneth Jones and Christa Ludwig, defied vocal designation and performed in different *tessituras*. What are your thoughts on the *Fach* system, and the consequences of it for singers?

YK: In England, we are a little more relaxed about how the operatic repertoire is divided than in the German-speaking countries. They have a much more specific idea about what roles each voice type should sing. When artists are thinking of auditioning in Germany, an important part of their preparation is how they research this issue. Even then, I have found that some theatres there unexpectedly cast the odd soprano role within an unlikely *Fach*. This was also true when I was studying in Italy; they had a completely different idea of what constitutes a *Soprano leggero*. It was really Dame Joan Sutherland and Maria Callas who changed that *tessitura* into something much more substantial and lyrical. But the Italians were absolutely specific when it came to finding the bright, high and light sound that they demanded for the works of Donizetti. Thankfully, things have changed a little with the passing of time, and it's now less specific. This is still not the case in Germany and Austria, where they continue to be definite about role types. In contrast, my repertoire is very broad, and I've constructed a website that lists all the works that I've performed over the years. I felt quite exhausted reading it, and I'm not quite sure how I managed to learn it all. But what emerges from this information is that the works that I gave were very much linked to periods within my voice's life. At the start, there were a lot of *bel canto* works. Then came the operas of Mozart, from which I performed about ten major roles. Around that time, I also began singing a great deal of Handel, followed by the works of Britten and Stravinsky. But I didn't restrict myself to opera: I also performed many oratorios and other works for voice and orchestra.

RH: One of the roles with which you are closely associated is the Marschallin in Strauss's *Der Rosenkavalier*. Would I be right in saying that that part is particularly challenging, both musically and dramatically?

YK: Absolutely. *Der Rosenkavalier* has been part of my life from near the beginning of my career. But the first role that I sang from it was Sophie under Sir Mark Elder at the English National Opera. As Sophie and the Marschallin are like the bookends of my career, I now find the conversation that takes place between them at the end of Act Three to be very touching. It brings a tear to my eye. I was very fortunate to be cast as the Marschallin, and I am thankful to Richard Strauss and Hugo von Hofmannsthal. The way that they captured the psychology of the character is just brilliant. The incredible depth of understanding that they bring to that woman's detailed and refined train of thought, and the way that they depicted the circumstances in which she found herself, is unique. In the Marschallin's monologue at the end of Act One, there's so much room for her thoughts to evolve. This is so skilful, and it is reflective of how somebody would act and respond. This is not only done harmonically, but by the ways in which Strauss set the text. And, of course, I've sung the role both in English and in German.

RH: Did you have to pace the role differently when singing it in the vernacular?

YK: I first sang the Marschallin at the English National Opera in a beautiful production by Sir Jonathan Miller. Even though I generally prefer to perform opera in the original language, I found that by singing this complex character in my own language, I was able to come to terms more easily with who she was. It was rather like performing a play. Singing successfully in the vernacular can often depend on the piece, and the situation in which it's performed. For me, the ideal is a marriage between the composer's original score and the original language text supported by surtitles. That way, there's a level of vital understanding, which works hand in hand with the beauty of the music. If this technology is not available, and if the opera being performed has a great many humorous recitatives, then singing in the vernacular can work brilliantly. A good of example of this is Handel's *Xerxes*, the opera that changed my life. Sir Nicholas Hytner's wonderful production of it at the English National Opera was in English. As he is such a skilful director, his production was not only witty and amusing, but it drew the audience into the humour and the drama of the story. We took this incredibly successful production on tour to Russia, and performed it at the Bolshoi Theatre; an interesting experience. This was at the time that Margaret Thatcher and Mikhail Gorbachev were meeting. Mrs Thatcher was very impressed and enthusiastic about the whole thing, and I seem to remember that there was a trade fair taking place at the same time. That was one of the reasons why the visit took place. But when I then sang in Martin Duncan's Italian-language production of the opera in Munich, it was equally successful, thanks to the use of surtitles. And, in a way, it felt better singing it in Italian. Both systems can work depending on the situation, but my choice, if there is a choice, is always to sing in the original language. But if you truly aspire to be an expert singer, you have to learn to use language with great refinement, nuance and delicacy.

RH: You have performed a great deal of operetta during your career. Is that better in English or in the original language?

YK: Operetta is wonderful in English, as there's often more dialogue than music. In Australia, I sang in quite a few productions of operetta, including marvellous ones of Lehár's *Die lustige Witwe* and Kálmán's *Die Csárdásfürstin*. These are big showpieces that require big personalities. You can't be too polite in operetta. You have to treat it like a showgirl, and 'sing it out, Louise'. That's what's required.

RH: Can operetta also be a good training ground for young singers?

YK: Yes, I think it can. Operetta can be very deceiving, as we think of it as being light, frivolous, fluffy and gorgeous. In fact, it requires a great deal of skill to sing it well. The orchestration is often massive and dense, which means that there's a lot of sound to sing over. It also requires great vocal flexibility and a lightness of touch. The music must be connected to the breath and should be well supported. And the text must always be clear. If all this is done successfully, then the genre can be enchanting.

RH: You also made some operetta recordings with our fellow Australian Richard Bonynge.

YK: Yes, I did. And I felt very fortunate in being able to work with him. He brings to this music a lightness of touch that's now lost. He always wants the voice to be resonant, flexible and nuanced. He's constantly in search of a sound that is tender and not too heavy. But that doesn't mean that the voice shouldn't have a substantial amount of sound. Dame Joan Sutherland is a good example of this.

RH: Dame Anne Evans has often spoken of the importance of Mozart's music in establishing a singer's technique. Do you agree with this?

YK: She is probably right. It doesn't mean that everybody has to sing only Mozart, but he's a hard taskmaster for us all. His music can expose a singer's intonation, and can be very challenging in that regard. When Mozart is sung well, people think that it's the most natural thing in the world, and that there's no technique involved. In fact, it requires an incredible amount of support, a solid core to the sound, and a high degree of homogeneity throughout the whole range of the voice. This is particularly true when it comes to the higher roles that 'sit' on top of the ensemble. These can be extremely tiring. Mozart's music can be deceptive when it's sung flexibly and lightly. It's essential to keep the air-flow consistent, so that every phrase is beautiful. There's no room for error.

RH: You regularly sang Mozart's works with Nikolaus Harnoncourt, a musician who came to opera quite late in his conducting career. Was he challenging to work with?

YK: As I explained earlier, my first experience of Harnoncourt was when I sang *Lucio Silla* with him. His background was that of a classical, ensemble musician. He then began to undertake large cycles of operas that included the works of Monteverdi at Zurich. This was with Jean-

PART TWO: SINGERS

Pierre Ponnelle, who also worked with him on some of Mozart's early operas. Having come from Australia and the United Kingdom, where Mozart was always treated elegantly, lightly and occasionally bloodlessly, I was confronted with something that was incredibly powerful. Harnoncourt's orchestral sound had great depth, and he had a horror of people singing neatly in time. He found that very dull, and always encouraged you to have a greater sense of pulse at the onset of the sound. He also wanted you to stretch the sound over bar lines, in much the same way that a jazz musician does. While he was keen for you *not* to be perfectly in time, he was eager for you to feel the text and the emotions of the text. He was more concerned that you were alive to the situations that the character was in, rather than being constricted by bar lines.

RH: Two other leading Mozartians with whom you worked closely were Sir Colin Davis and Sir Georg Solti. What are your memories of them?

YK: Even though Sir Georg was Music Director of the Royal Opera House in the period that directly preceded my appointment there, I did do a number of projects with him. A particularly memorable event was the gala concert that we gave for the Queen's birthday in 1986. This was televised live throughout the United Kingdom. I'd been asked by the company's General Director, Sir John Tooley, if I would be happy to sing the 'Presentation of the Rose' from *Der Rosenkavalier* with my friend and colleague Ann Murray. Performing this scene with Sir Georg was like an out-of-body experience. There was something about the energy that he generated in the pit, and the way that he communicated that energy, that inspired me to do things I never dreamt I could do. When it came to length of breath and matters of phrasing, he expected us to keep going, and to spin them to their maximums. And the thing was, we did it. He pushed us beyond the limits of what we thought we could do.

I was also fortunate enough to make a lovely recording with him of Mozart's *Le nozze di Figaro*. This was at a time when the London orchestras were considered to be the best in the world when it came to recording operas. I was asked to sing the role of Barbarina in a cast that also included Lucia Popp, Dame Kiri Te Kanawa and Sir Thomas Allen. Each time that I would begin a take of Barbarina's aria, Sir Georg would stop me and ask for it to be quieter. And he was right to do so. When I later listened to the completed disc, Barbarina really did sound like she was lost in the dark. As Sir Georg ensured that the aria wasn't sung too 'maturely', the end result was extremely touching.

Sir Colin Davis was Music Director of the Royal Opera House throughout my time there as a permanent member of the company. I performed a great deal of Mozart with him, and he was very demanding of me. When he saw that somebody had a natural talent, he always wanted to get the best out of that person. He worked me very, very hard. This can be a good thing, even though it can also be challenging. But I must say that the Royal Opera House was supportive of my development in a way that doesn't exist now. I can never show enough gratitude to the management of that house for the encouragement they gave me, and the continuity of roles they offered me. I am especially grateful for the language coaching that I received. There was a crazy Italian called Ubaldo Gardini who was very tough on all of us, and who worked very closely with Colin Davis at that time. There was also a wonderful German coach called Hilde Beal, and an excellent French coach called Janine Reiss. I was fortunate enough to have learned my craft at Covent Garden.

RH: Is there such a thing as a 'singer's conductor'?

YK: The answer is 'yes', but only when the conductor understands that a singer is a wind instrument. Our continuous flow of sound is not created by a bow on a string; we have to find time to breathe. A 'singer's conductor' is one who accepts that every voice has its own *tempo*, and that every artist is an individual. This means that the conductor should actively optimise the singer's sound, and to make it as beautiful as possible through their choice of *tempo* and the ways in which they shape the music. It can be very uncomfortable for a singer if a conductor takes a speed that's just a little bit too fast. This means that you are unable to breathe in time, and that your sound feels unconnected. This can happen when conductors are insensitive and have a fixed idea of how an aria should be sung. A 'singer's conductor' is one who manages to achieve what they want, while allowing the vocalist space to meet those objectives. Sir Georg was certainly a 'singer's conductor', and I think that Sir Colin was one, too. Bernard Haitink was also Music Director of the Royal Opera House during my time there, and I very much enjoyed working with him.

RH: I'm also keen to hear your thoughts on yet another fellow Australian, Sir Charles Mackerras. Many singers found his approach to vocal decoration challenging. Were you one of these?

YK: Before I speak about his use of ornamentation, I would like to say that with the possible exception of Claudio Abbado, Sir Charles was the best opera conductor I ever worked with. He was able to create the perfect shape, no matter what style of music he was performing. Of course, he was very well known for Janáček and Handel, but he was equally at home with Puccini. I once saw him do a most magnificent *Tosca*. The same was true of his Wagner. Whatever he turned his attention to, he did quite marvellously. For those of us who are Australian, he was our 'main guy'. He was always available, and gave generously of his time. This was particularly true when it came to the Australian Music Foundation. I was fortunate enough to sing the Marschallin with Sir

Charles at the San Francisco Opera, the opening night of which took place on his seventy-fifth birthday. That was one of the greatest experiences of my career. In responding to my voice, he shaped the orchestration in an elegant and translucent manner. And while it lost none of its power, it wasn't thick and heavy. It allowed the voices to shine through. I have tremendously happy memories of all my work with Sir Charles. I never had a difficult moment with him, even though he was demanding and expected perfection.

The two scores that I really treasure are Sir Charles's editions of Handel's *Semele* and *Xerxes*. In these, he indicates in a detailed and generous manner his beautiful ornamentation. His decorations are offered as suggestions as to how a singer might add variety and creativity when shaping a vocal line. And to my horror, I now hear from colleagues that these editions are no longer available. People have moved on and are now buying scores that are devoid of such material. But how do you learn to ornament if there is no model to look to? I still consider Sir Charles's decorations to be relevant and very logical. They are extremely florid and suit the voice well, particularly my own. We can all learn from this material. People now perform early music in a different way, but these scores are still valid when training young people to decorate *da capo* arias. And as we all know, this is not a straightforward skill. If I were younger, I would want to learn from someone who was as brilliant as Sir Charles Mackerras. I still use the cadenzas that he wrote for me, and regularly pass them on to my students. These cadenzas succeed wonderfully because they capture the essence of the music, the text and the character involved. Sir Charles's music-making was always joyful and it was a constant pleasure to perform under his baton. I really miss him.

RH: Before we finish, I'd like to ask a few nuts-and-bolts questions about the art and craft of singing. First, how do you go about learning a new role?

PART TWO: SINGERS

YK: When I performed Massenet's *Manon*, the first thing I did was to read Abbé Prévost's story in French. And when I sang Donizetti's *Maria Stuarda*, I read Antonia Fraser's book *Mary Queen of Scots*. This is an amazingly brilliant book from which I learned a great deal. This type of background research allows you to become involved with the characters and the story. Then, I always start with the opera's text. Learning works like Strauss's *Capriccio* and *Der Rosenkavalier* takes a very long time, so you have to be patient. Often, I'll write out sections or scenes from the text in an exercise book. I'll then translate that material with the English version carefully placed underneath the original text. This can be very time-consuming, but it does mean that I can come to terms with the flow of the words before getting involved with the nitty-gritty of the music. After that, I try to get an overview of the work's harmonic structure, and my part within it. Finally, I join both processes together.

RH: Agents are central to any performing artist's career. What were your first encounters with agents like, and what should a young artist expect from his or her management team?

YK: This is an aspect of the music profession that has changed enormously. During my early years in London, Geoffrey Parsons and Erich Vietheer were very close friends of the Austrian female entrepreneur Lies Askonas. She was a splendid person, who was not only courageous, but who had remarkably refined taste. Lies represented Geoffrey, and later accepted me into her agency. The first job that she found for me was singing the role of Frasquita for a production of Bizet's *Carmen* at the Edinburgh International Festival under Claudio Abbado. Another member of that cast was Plácido Domingo. I also had a marvellous agent in Australia called Jenifer Eddy. She had been a wonderful *coloratura* soprano at the Royal Opera House during Solti's tenure there, but had retired early for health reasons. At the time that she was representing me, people in Australia and Britain used to write to friends abroad using aerogrammes. These were quite small and coloured blue. My mother would send me one every week detailing all the family news. They were just wonderful. If Jenifer Eddy wanted to see if I was interested in singing in a performance of Bizet's *Les pêcheurs de perles* with the Victoria State Opera, for example, she'd write an aerogramme. This would go in the post, and would arrive in London about a week later. Lies would then read the aerogramme – nobody telephoned in those days, as it was so expensive – and would then write back saying that I was available. Three weeks later, there'd be an answer. Things have changed somewhat since those days. Aerogrammes now feel prehistoric, but they were commonplace in the mid-1970s. Back then, agents were very supportive when it came to developing a singer's career. If you did a good job for a theatre, and if the theatre liked you, you might be offered a second, or even a third, contract. It was not unusual for a singer to return regularly to a particular opera house over a period of four or five years. The fact that theatres were loyal to individual artists allowed agents to develop singers' careers at a very logical pace. This was paramount in ensuring vocal health, something that agents took very seriously at the time.

RH: And, finally, what are your thoughts on masterclasses and competitions?

YK: Masterclasses can be extremely helpful. If the person who is leading the masterclass is kind, compassionate and supportive of the young singer, then I think that they are very valuable. But I know that this isn't always the case. I'm completely baffled when this happens, as public learning can be a terrifying thing. And when it came to competitions, I was always a rank outsider. Nevertheless, I won the Kathleen Ferrier Award as one. As I've never been part of the mainstream, I think it's worth giving competitions a go, but not to be too discouraged if they don't work out. The hardest thing to do as a singer is to produce your best work under intense pressure. At just the moment when you need to produce a beautiful sound, your mouth might dry up, or your breath might stop. But if you can use competitions to help you learn how to cope with pressure, then they're fine. Of course, if you win a major competition, it can be the beginning of your career. The Kathleen Ferrier Award was certainly a help at the start of my professional life.

RH: And what does the future hold for Yvonne Kenny?

YK: Although I haven't performed in an opera for about five years, I do give concerts. I still enjoy the experience of getting up and entertaining people, and feeling that the audience appreciates what I have to offer. I'm very careful when preparing these events, and equally careful when choosing the repertoire for them. I've also found teaching and coaching young people to be very rewarding. It's such a joy to pass on the knowledge that I've gathered from all the wonderful people I've worked with. And while I'm certainly committed to that aim, I hope that I have the energy to carry on doing it indefinitely.

PART THREE

INSTRUMENTALISTS

PAUL BADURA-SKODA
(DAVID JOSEFOWITZ RECITAL HALL, 13 JANUARY 2012)

RAYMOND HOLDEN: Austria suffered testing times during the inter-war years. And although it was being constantly challenged politically, socially and financially by both right- and left-wing organisations, its capital city continued to enjoy a period of intense cultural activity during those dark days. As you were born in Vienna in 1927, how was your family affected musically by those events, and when did they realise that you were gifted artistically?

PAUL BADURA-SKODA: My father died as the result of a motorcycle accident when I was only four months old. That meant that my mother was a widow for most of my early life until she married Anton Skoda. He literally saved our lives during the Second World War and I admired him greatly. I adopted his name and added it to mine. And that's how I came by the name Badura-Skoda. Although we were a typical middle-class family, and music was part of our life, it was only so in a very superficial way. While everybody played the piano a little, my mother also played the guitar and sang with a lovely voice. But there was no indication that I had any special talent.

RH: Growing up in pre-war Vienna must've been both interesting and demanding. What are your memories of those years, and in what ways did the city differ from the vibrant, cosmopolitan metropolis that we know today?

PB-S: My memories go back to the time when Austria was still an independent country, before the truly black period when it became a part of Germany in 1938. After that, it was no longer Österreich, but Ostmark. Although Vienna today is buzzing with tourists and offers a great many events, I think the real cultural highlight of our history were the years between the two world wars. Franz Werfel, Stefan Zweig, Karl Kraus, Ödön von Horváth were all great poets and writers, the like of whom we no longer have. And, of course, there were great composers living in Vienna, such as Alban Berg, Hans Gál, Anton von Webern and Franz Schmidt, whose *Toccata* is in my repertoire. Then there were the renowned operetta composers, Franz Lehár and Emmerich Kálmán, and the distinguished conductors, Bruno Walter and Wilhelm Furtwängler. They were all great artists and much admired by the public. Vienna may no longer be the cultural centre of the world, but we compensate for that in other ways.

RH: From what you say, Vienna was clearly vibrant artistically during your early years. What is your first musical memory and when did you realise that music was the life for you?

PB-S: My first musical memory relates to my first piano teacher, Marta Wiesenthal. She rented a room from us that had a good piano and I remember hearing her practise Brahms's Rhapsody in G minor and Chopin's 'Revolutionary' Étude. I had no idea what these pieces were, but they remained in my memory. We also had a wind-up gramophone. As a three- or four-year-old boy, I managed to climb on to a chair and put the records on the machine without breaking them. I was unable to read at the time, but I could recognise the music I wanted to play by the colour of the label and the size of the disc. Apart from popular songs, which I can still sing today, my favourite piece was the 'Intermezzo' from Mascagni's *Cavalleria rusticana*. And that's how I developed a penchant for classical music. But I was rather a late developer when it came to attending concerts. Mrs Wiesenthal took me to a concert for the first time when I was about eight or nine years old. It was an all-Beethoven recital by Friedrich Wührer, one of the leading Austrian pianists. I remember that I found slow movements extremely boring at the time, a situation that has thankfully since changed! But when he played Op. 2 No. 3 in C major, I was just carried away. I thought that was fantastic and told Mrs Wiesenthal that I had to learn the piece. She looked at me with bewilderment and said, 'Are you crazy? You're far too young for that.' But, somehow, I managed to play it, and it's still one of my favourite sonatas.

RH: Was *this* when you realised that you were destined for a life in music?

PB-S: Absolutely not. While I was talented musically, and enjoyed playing the piano, I also had a gift for drawing and painting. I was pleased that my audiences, who were mostly family members, enjoyed my playing, but was even more pleased when they gave me candy and chocolate after my concerts, a real treat, as people were quite poor at that time. I would've been happy to have remained an amateur musician and to explore the sciences, perhaps even becoming an engineer like my birth father. Up to the age of sixteen, I was vacillating between music and technology. Even after the war, I theoretically could have entered the Technische Universität in Vienna, but, by that time, my choice had been made, and to everybody's bad luck, I am now a musician!

RH: Like you, Herbert von Karajan had an interest in technology, and, like you, was a student at the Akademie für Musik und darstellende

PART THREE: INSTRUMENTALISTS

Kunst, now the Universität für Musik und darstellende Kunst. What was life like at the Akademie during the post-war period?

PB-S: I have to correct you a little here. I attended the Konservatorium der Stadt Wien, where I studied with Viola Thern, and it wasn't until I was twenty years old, when I began to study the organ, that I attended the Akademie. So, my training as a pianist and as a conductor was at the Konservatorium. At that time, both institutions were considered equal, but the Akademie was perhaps superior for piano playing.

RH: Do any of the lessons that you learned at the Konservatorium remain with you today?

PB-S: Of course. In fact, I would say everything. I owe a great deal to the wonderful teaching that I had from the outstanding teachers there. Wilhelm Fischer, for example, who should've been dean of the university, but only became director of the Akademie because of political difficulties, gave outstanding lectures on music history – a marvellous advantage. Then there was the composer-conductor Franz Burkhart, who was a great conductor, particularly for choirs. He organised an annual children's concert, which involved about 1,000 young people singing in the Grosser Konzertsaal. He not only conducted the concerts, but arranged the music for them. These were great, great experiences. He also gave me lessons in harmony, counterpoint and composition, which later helped me understand the inner workings of music and to come to terms with what lies at the heart of works by Mozart, Beethoven, Bruckner, Mahler and Schoenberg.

RH: Perhaps what most people don't know is that you are not only a great pianist, but an exceptional accordion player.

PB-S: That was not a matter of choice! My stepfather was a good amateur musician, who played the piano, clarinet and accordion. As he wanted to play duets with his stepson, he encouraged me to take lessons on the latter. At first, I was most reluctant, because I looked down with condescension on such a popular instrument. But having found the best accordion teacher in Vienna, Herta Geisl, who had been a concert pianist, she convinced me that the instrument was worth studying. My imagination caught fire and I soon realised that it gave me fantastic opportunities. In fact, it had two great advantages over the piano. First, I could carry it with me, and, second, it has 'lungs'. These allow you to increase the volume of notes, an unachievable dream for any pianist. But, sadly, my memories of the accordion are coloured by the war, its destructive power and my removal to the country to escape the bombing. At that time, we didn't know whether or not Vienna would be spared, but fortunately only about a quarter of the city was destroyed, which was nothing compared to Berlin or Hamburg. And being sent to the country was not such a bad thing. Farmers regularly provided wedding venues for soldiers on leave and I was engaged to play the accordion at those weddings. We would then be treated to cakes and ham, all of which were forbidden at the time.

When the Soviet soldiers later arrived to plunder Vienna under the guise of being our liberators, I was able to play their music to them. As my stepfather spoke Russian well, he taught me the language and some Russian folk songs. Not only was I able to get a smile out of the Soviets, but I was able to prevent them from robbing us of anything. In fact, they even gave us goods that they'd got elsewhere. The soldiers liked my accordion playing so much that they took me to a camp where I spent three days living like a member of the Russian army. This annoyed my stepfather, who was a bit anxious about the whole thing. Having played all their favourite songs, including the

PART THREE: INSTRUMENTALISTS

Russian national anthem, to them, I was then returned to Vienna by the soldiers, laden with presents.

RH: Being somewhat addicted to Carol Reed's marvellous film *The Third Man*, I find your recording of Frossini's Tango, *Serenade Italienne*, on the accordion particularly evocative of Vienna's colourful history. Times were clearly tough during those years, but I assume you were still able to attend a great many concerts. Who were some of your musical heroes at that time, what attracted you to them, and in what ways does their influence still manifest itself in your life and work today?

PB-S: Many of my heroes were pianists, such as Wilhelm Backhaus, Friedrich Müller and Emil von Sauer. Sauer was one of the last surviving pupils of Liszt, and even at the age of seventy-nine, he could still give concerts of great perfection. To this day, his recordings of Liszt are noble and faultless guides as to how the composer should be performed, and he was one of the few pianists who never played a wrong note. And then there was Edwin Fischer, whom I first discovered through his recordings. After listening to his disc of Beethoven's 'Appassionata' Sonata, one of his finest recordings ever, I played it to one of my teachers, the pianistic genius Otto Schulhof, who said, 'That's a great pianist.' Now nearly forgotten, but a wonderful pianist in the Viennese tradition nonetheless, Schulhof could be very critical and regularly found shortcomings with Backhaus and others. But when it came to Fischer, he simply said, 'That was great.' A little later, I attended a concert given by Fischer where he conducted concertos from the keyboard with his chamber orchestra at the Mozart-Saal in Vienna's Konzerthaus. Again, it was one of the greatest musical experiences of my early years. As he could create *such* music from conducting and playing, I felt that he was a genius and I hoped to become one of his students. But as I first heard

Fischer when I was only fourteen years old, that had to wait until I joined his masterclass at the age of twenty-one.

RH: Let's chat a little about Fischer and Salzburg. Is it true that you stepped in at short notice to replace him at a concert, and that you made your local debut there as a consequence of his indisposition?

PB-S: You're absolutely correct. It's something of a special story and quite unusual. As I mentioned earlier, I was just twenty-one when I attended Fischer's masterclass in 1948. At that time, he insisted on having only nine or ten students, and I was one of those lucky few, having won a prize at the first Austrian piano competition. Apparently, I made a good impression and I remember that there was always a concert after his final masterclasses. I was the last to play at that event and chose a piece not normally associated with him: Chopin's Polonaise in A flat major. It went quite well and everybody who heard the performance thought I had promise. After the masterclass dispersed, I didn't hear from Fischer again for about a year, as I was unable to rejoin his class in 1950 due to a misunderstanding. Then, during the summer of that year, I received a telegram from Salzburg saying that Fischer was ill and that he'd recommended me as his replacement for a trio recital. Of course, Fischer not only played with his chamber orchestra at Salzburg at that time, but also with his trio, which included the violinist Wolfgang Schneiderhan, who had replaced the late Georg Kulenkampff, and the cellist Enrico Mainardi.

As the performance was scheduled for five days later, I was tremendously excited. According to the telegram, the programme had already been confirmed and two of the pieces to be performed were Beethoven's Piano Trio No. 1, which is not that difficult, and a trio by Ildebrando Pizzetti. I'd never heard of the Pizzetti work, and it was by sheer luck that the Italian Cultural Institute in Vienna had a score of the piece. There was also a third piece on the programme, which I've since forgotten. I arrived in Salzburg for the first rehearsal with Schneiderhan and Mainardi with the scores of Beethoven's and Pizzetti's works under my arm. But when Mainardi saw these scores, he told me that those pieces were not on the programme and that the concert was to be all-Brahms. With only two days before the performance, all I could think was, 'Oh, dear!' Taking me by the arm, Mainardi said, 'As you are young, we'll play Brahms's B major Trio with you. Wolfgang, you'll play a solo sonata by Bach, and I'll play one of his solo cello suites. That way, we'll have a nicely rounded programme.' To learn Brahms's B major Trio is not that easy, but I had the best coaching imaginable: Mainardi was not only a cellist, but also an excellent pianist and composer. More to the point, he knew every nuance that Edwin Fischer played and he taught me these so well that when I heard Fischer play the trio two years later, it sounded like my own interpretation! The engagement was headline news and I was thrust into a musical career as a consequence.

RH: And what a career it's been. Over the years, you have worked with many great figures, principal amongst whom must be Wilhelm Furtwängler. What was he like?

PB-S: Furtwängler was a legendary figure who transcended all others during his lifetime. It was rather late in his career when I first heard him in a concert with the Vienna Philharmonic, and it was somewhat ironic that the person who took me to that concert was my accordion teacher, Frau Geisl. I remember that it took me a while to realise the importance of Furtwängler, as he was so different from other conductors. While some conductors might beat one, two, three, four, his beat was such that only the orchestra could recognise it. Somehow he made a musical sculpture out of every note. After the war, when he conducted Mendelssohn's Overture to *Ein Sommernachtstraum*, for example, you had the feeling that the violins' *vibrato* was not simply habit, but a nuance of the greatest musical importance. Needless to say, I became one of Furtwängler's greatest admirers, but never in my wildest dreams did I expect to play with him. Two occasions did arise, however.

As I was quite well known in Vienna as a Mozart player by 1949, he invited me to perform the composer's Concerto for Two Pianos with his daughter, Dagmar Bella, who also lived in the city. She'd been a student of Wilhelm Kempff, who, in his own way, was not dissimilar to Edwin Fischer. Dagmar and I studied the score of the concerto for a whole year, and when it came to the performance, the work had become second nature. More to the point, Furtwängler treated us as equals and without any hint of condescension. Nothing along the lines of 'who are you two unknown pianists compared to me.' No arrogance whatsoever. A unique experience and a very positive one. Three years later, he invited me to play Mozart's concerto in E flat major, the so called Twenty-Second Piano Concerto. But, in the meantime, I'd met him at parties and he gave me interesting ideas and insights into music. We talked about what a musician's life should be like, and I particularly remember one piece of advice that he gave me. He said that I should try to walk for two hours every day and not to think about music. Now, walking for two hours, even in Vienna, is difficult and not really possible. Nevertheless, I've never forgotten that piece of advice.

But, in preparing myself to play the Twenty-Second Concerto with Furtwängler, I accepted an invitation to play the work in Athens a week before my concert with him. The conductor in Greece was quite good and the orchestra, although no match for the Vienna Philharmonic, was well trained. Everything seemed to go smoothly and I felt really quite happy. So, I was looking forward to giving the work again with

PART THREE: INSTRUMENTALISTS

Furtwängler in Vienna. The concert was to take place on a Saturday with the first rehearsal on the preceding Thursday morning. On the Wednesday, there was a terrible storm in Athens of the highest intensity that meant the airport had to be closed for two days. There I was in Athens knowing only too well that I'd missed my rehearsal. There was absolutely no chance of getting to Austria from Greece. Trains were out of the question, as it would've taken me thirty-six hours to get to Vienna by rail. Of course, I sent a telegram with my regrets. To my great surprise, Furtwängler said that my absence was not my fault, as it was *force majeure*. He also said that he would rearrange the rehearsal on the day of the performance so that two hours could be devoted to the concerto, which he did. The rehearsal went so smoothly that I lost all my anxieties. I suppose I sweated enough and felt anxious enough during the preceding two days that I felt absolutely relaxed, and that can be heard in the recording of the performance.

RH: You also worked with Furtwängler's nemesis, Herbert von Karajan. What was he like?

PB-S: Of course, Karajan was a much-admired musician and, undoubtedly, a great conductor. I remember the first time I heard him in Vienna. At that concert, he conducted a typical Karajan programme that included Haydn's 104th Symphony, Strauss's *Don Juan* and Brahms's First Symphony. This was truly a great event. It was the young Karajan with generous movements, unlike in later years when he became more economical physically. This made an enormous impact on the audience in Vienna. After the concert, I discussed Karajan with the Vienna Philharmonic's clarinettist, a friend of mine, who agreed that he was magnificent, but ice-cold. But I don't think that was entirely true when one remembers his performance at the New Year's Day Concert in 1987.

That was anything but cold and a reflection of his life in music. Karajan first asked me to play César Franck's *Variations symphoniques*, a decision that I wasn't particularly happy about: I would have preferred a concerto by either Brahms or Schumann. Nevertheless, I prepared the *Variations*, but unlike with Furtwängler, the rehearsals began a week before the concert. I thought that I'd play the work for Karajan and he'd say 'that's fine', with perhaps the odd suggestion here or there. That wasn't at all the case, as he started to give me piano lessons! Throughout that week, every note and every detail was scrutinised. In fact, that was yet another great experience. He was a good piano teacher, but a less good pianist.

When I was later engaged to play Mozart's Concerto for Three Pianos with him, he played the third piano. Written by Mozart for the ten-year-old daughter of Countess Antonia Lodron, Giuseppa, the part is quite simple. Nevertheless, when we performed the work with the Vienna Symphony Orchestra, the players said, 'Maestro, you must practise!' Even so, it was a great event that made a deep impression on me. Later, I realised that Karajan's way with the work was not really what the composer wanted. It took me some twenty or thirty years before I was able to return to the piece and to discover for myself what I thought Mozart intended. That's always a danger when one approaches a work for the first time with a musician who can be a strong influence. The difference between Karajan and Furtwängler was enormous.

In truth, they weren't the enemies that they're reported to have been. Yet there was an unhappy circumstance that made them so, with the Gesellschaft der Musikfreunde in Vienna being mostly responsible for their split. First of all, they had to work side by side in Berlin, with each recognising the other's greatness. Nobody, for example, doubted that Furtwängler was a genius. The difference between the two was that Furtwängler was a remarkable composer, perhaps even a great composer. Some of his works, such as his Piano Concerto, need to be revived, and when I played it to Sir Charles Mackerras, he considered it a great piece. In many ways, Furtwängler can be likened to Mahler, as both were only recognised as great conductors during their lifetimes. With both Karajan and Furtwängler, I sang in the choir for Beethoven's Ninth Symphony, and this allowed me to observe at first-hand how differently they approached music. When it came to Schiller's text, Karajan wanted it to be pronounced very clearly and he worked on the diction in detail. Then, when we performed it again a few months later under Furtwängler, he reversed the approach and demanded that it should be sung with greater *legato* and with greater smoothness.

RH: It's interesting that your clarinettist friend thought Karajan to be ice-cold. That's exactly how Karajan described George Szell, another conductor with whom you performed Mozart's Twenty-Second Piano Concerto.

PB-S: Szell was not only a great conductor, but also a great musician and an excellent pianist. Unlike Karajan, he could play and conduct concertos from the keyboard and his recording of Mozart's piano quartets is very good. By the time that I'd met Szell, I'd written *Interpreting Mozart* with my wife, Eva, which both Szell and Bruno Walter had read, a book intended for pianists only. Having read the book, Szell immediately started discussing the possibility of me playing with him in Cleveland. Szell, like Toscanini, investigated composers' autograph scores and was keen to discuss some of the problematic passages in those of Mozart. As a composer himself, he was very keen to do this and understood the importance of original material. He was also the product of the Viennese tradition that had so impacted my early childhood. And, of course, you know that it's often said of the Viennese that they're a mixture of Prussian discipline and Austrian charm. While I never experienced Szell the dictator, he had a degree of Prussian 'charm' that was often not very pleasing. Nevertheless, he could perform miracles with orchestras, particularly after he overcame his inner tension, his biggest problem. The difference between Furtwängler and Szell was intuition. With the advantage of a brilliant mind, Furtwängler felt music internally and allowed it to pour out of him. Szell, on the other hand, was firstly an intellectual, albeit a sensitive one, whose sensitivity was often obscured by his need to dominate.

RH: If one was to compare your recordings of Mozart's Twenty-Second Piano Concerto with Furtwängler and Szell, what might the difference be?

PB-S: Perhaps what defies description in the Furtwängler performance is the smoothness of the reading. But what did emerge from these performances was our realisation that there was a mistake in our book on Mozart interpretation. And this can be heard in the Szell performance. We believed that in Mozart, like in Haydn and Schubert, *Andantino* meant faster than *Andante*. But we've since found that Mozart's *Andantino* should be closer to an *Adagio* than an *Allegretto*. Unfortunately, at the time of the Szell performance, we believed that the *Andantino* should be faster. Nevertheless, the movement was still beautifully performed by him.

RH: I've something of a soft spot for the Szell reading. With hindsight, which of the two performances would you opt for today?

PB-S: Without question, the Furtwängler recording. But my preference when performing the concerto today sits somewhere between the two. And although it could be argued that Furtwängler's approach might be too Romantic, he did give the work a depth of feeling and drama that Mozart would have enjoyed.

RH: In the case of both readings, the orchestra is under the control of an artist other than the pianist. Today, it's increasingly common for pianists to direct such works from the keyboard, a skill that we also associate with you. This begs a number of questions: when did you first start working in this way; was this as a result of the influence of Edwin Fischer, who famously performed Mozart's concertos in this manner; and what are some of the advantages for both the pianist and the orchestra of performing in this fashion?

PB-S: There are advantages and disadvantages. If you're working with a conductor on the same musical wavelength, such as Furtwängler, who attempted to adapt to my approach with only two hours' rehearsal, the result was close to miraculous. With Szell it was different. We worked together for a week. Nevertheless, that was also a great pleasure, as I again felt relaxed and free. But that was not the case with Karl Böhm. He was another great conductor, but I was unable to be completely myself with him. And then there was Wolfgang Sawallisch, another fine artist, who nearly destroyed my performance of the Twenty-Second Concerto when I first performed it with the Berlin Philharmonic. For that concerto, which lasts between thirty-five and forty minutes, he gave me only thirty minutes of rehearsal. If I've time to work with a conductor, the difference between conducting from the keyboard and collaborating with another artist is hardly noticeable, as both methods then become chamber music. When I perform actual chamber music, I am the *primus inter parus* – the first amongst equals – but, when there's a conductor, we share that role. We become two firsts amongst equals! And, of course, some conductors are more equal than others.

RH: Hans von Bülow famously conducted from the keyboard. Not only did he conduct Beethoven's Fourth and Fifth Piano Concertos in that fashion, but also both of Brahms's piano concertos. Did you ever consider performing those works in that manner?

PB-S: Beethoven, yes. And I agree with Edwin Fischer when he argued that the first four concertos and the Triple Concerto can be directed from the keyboard. But the Fifth Concerto should be given with a conductor. Beethoven's own student Carl Czerny gave the same advice. Elly Ney, another great German pianist from around Fischer's time, conducted the First Concerto from the keyboard. Rudolf Buchbinder also conducts from the piano but, in his case, he also performs the Fifth Concerto this way. Along with Fischer, Bruno Walter was one of the first to direct Mozart's D minor concerto from the keyboard. This gives you space to be improvisatory, a feature of each of Fischer's performances. Furtwängler was another artist who conducted from the keyboard. But his approach was a little different from the others. Having studied a work, he didn't simply treat it like a computer printout or a photocopy. For him, every performance was slightly unique. Fischer summed it up beautifully when he said, 'The difference between two great performances can be as small as the difference between how light and shade fall on the moving hands of a wristwatch.' In the case of my own performances, I sometimes feel that the differences are more akin to the ways in which light falls on the hands of a grandfather clock!

RH: As we are talking about conducting from the keyboard, I was particularly impressed by your recording of four Mozart piano concertos that you made with the Prague Chamber Orchestra in 2006. As you're closely associated with period performance, I was interested to see that you didn't try to alter the orchestra's approach to sound production and that they continued to play in a modern manner. What are your thoughts concerning musicians who attempt to create a period sound on modern instruments, and is that something to be encouraged or discouraged?

PB-S: Naturally, I balance the orchestra in a particular way, but, in general, I like to accept an orchestra for what it has to offer. In the case of the Prague orchestra, it's the Czechs' joy when making music and their exuberance of feeling that I tried not to dampen. And then there's their ability to play with a true Mozart style. When they perform the 'Jupiter' Symphony without a conductor, this is anything but a gimmick. It's both natural and beautiful. They do, however, have very loud trumpets and drums, a sound that they share with Nikolaus Harnoncourt.

RH: Harnoncourt's sound is partially a direct result of his use of period trumpets and drums. Sir Charles Mackerras also uses these instruments in his recordings of Mozart's symphonies with the Scottish Chamber Orchestra. Yet in his earlier complete set of the symphonies with the Prague Chamber Orchestra, he continued to use modern brass and percussion.

PB-S: A true chamber orchestra needs to have a natural affinity between the players, so that they can form a unit. When I play with them it's like performing with a large string quartet, as they always select excellent players. Unlike some orchestras elsewhere, they receive no state subsidy, with their survival depending solely on sheer hard work. On occasions, they've had to play for reduced fees to guarantee their existence. This means that they've developed a certain tenacity of spirit that's missing from other more established orchestras.

RH: You are also a distinguished orchestral conductor in your own right and there's a wonderful recording of Beethoven's Second Symphony with you and the Brisbane Philharmonic Orchestra. Were you ever tempted to abandon the keyboard in favour of the baton full-time, and of all the distinguished maestri with whom you have performed, which one affected your podium style most?

PB-S: I was truly tempted at one point, but, as the Bible makes clear, beware of temptation! Unlike some keyboard-playing colleagues, I'm not an amateur conductor, but somebody who actually studied the craft. My teacher was Felix Prohaska, who was something of an all-round musician. At my first lesson with him, he had me conduct Wagner's Overture to *Der fliegende Holländer*, which introduced me to the true *métier* of being a conductor. As I mentioned earlier, I also studied with Karl Burkhart, who was a fine choral conductor. Consequently, it was soon obvious to me that orchestral and choral conducting were quite different skills. When working with choirs, you have to have a good knowledge of breathing and a different approach when securing intonation. By the time I began working with Furtwängler and Fischer, I'd already played many house concerts all over Vienna, including one at the residence of the New Zealand ambassador. A guest that evening was Josef Krips, who was the leading conductor in Vienna after the war. At that *soirée*, I read the piano part of a violin sonata at sight, which prompted Krips to remark, 'You're a born conductor.' He immediately invited me to be his assistant and offered me a job at the Vienna Staatsoper, of which he was the first Director after the war. I thought that I was dreaming! I didn't believe him, but he really meant it. I was left in a state of confusion and found myself wondering if I really should change direction. I then spoke with my piano teacher, who replied, 'Paul, are you mad! You are a pianist and you will remain a pianist.' With deepest regret, I had to tell Krips that I was unable to accept his generous offer. But it said a great deal about Krips's greatness that he was not offended in the least. As it happened, one of the first concerts that I gave in London was with him and the London Symphony Orchestra. We played Beethoven's Third Piano Concerto together, my first public performance of the work.

RH: Let's return to Mozart briefly and to your approach to ornamentation and cadenzas in his music. Do you improvise these, or are they beneficiaries of careful planning?

PB-S: Very few people are able to improvise with style. For the C minor concerto, for example, the cadenzas for that work have occupied me my entire life. Over the years, I've written some seventy versions of its cadenza before settling on one with which I could identify personally. We must always keep in mind that a cadenza should always sound like an improvisation, and it's extremely important to remember that Mozart took great care when composing cadenzas, even for those concertos that he only performed himself. Take, for example, the final concerto in B flat major. Its cadenzas contain some of the most beautiful music he wrote and fit the overall piece like a glove. And having written out these cadenzas, he also created some variants of them. This, then, encouraged me to compose cadenzas for concertos that have none by him. But I would never dare to write a cadenza for a concerto movement that already contains one by Mozart. Some other pianists take a different stance and are not quite so reverential. Some play cadenzas by Busoni, for example, but they're in a completely different style. Another reason why it's important for me to write out my own cadenzas is that I believe that composing is linked to improvisation. Improvising requires a certain skill, of course, and many artists are not able to do it, let alone document what they have improvised. As my cadenzas have been published, they've enjoyed a certain degree of success. My aim was to write something that sounds like

Mozart. And the best compliment that I can receive is for the listener to think that the cadenza is in complete sympathy with the corresponding concerto. That's not the case when it comes to cadenzas for Beethoven, but that's a completely different subject.

RH: As a passionate advocate of the Austro-German canon, it's hardly remarkable that there are many recordings of compositions by Haydn, Mozart, Beethoven and Schubert in your discography. But there are surprisingly few recordings of Bach's works. Why is that, and when performing his music, do you prefer a modern piano or a period instrument?

PB-S: I perform it on both. And, as it happens, my only substantial recording of Bach is on both types of instrument. When I recorded the partitas for the first time, it was not possible to play them on a period instrument, even though I was one of the first to perform on these unusual instruments at the beginning of the 1950s. When I was approached by Westminster Records, for which I'd already documented a wide repertoire, to record these works, I quickly became aware of the enormity of the task. The project took me six months to prepare, as I only had a limited knowledge of Bach style. But I listened to the works, both on a harpsichord and a piano, and used Edwin Fischer as my model, who could make the piano sing like a violin when conducting the composer's concertos from the keyboard. After my discs of the works were released, they were sold successfully around the world, and I was touched to learn from a listener many decades later how much these recordings meant to him personally. Then, in 1965, I bought a Kirkman harpsichord at an auction in London for a decent price. After the instrument was restored, I documented the works again. That recording won the Gran Prix du Disque, the only time I won that award. Even though the discs sold extremely well, I decided against recording more works by Bach. As his music is so deep and so profound, it takes me about six months to study just one of the preludes and fugues. With that speed of study, my life is simply too short.

RH: During your early years, you recorded a great deal of Chopin. What were some of the challenges that his music presented to you as a technician and as an interpreter during those years?

PB-S: Chopin is the soul of the piano, and with few exceptions, he devoted himself entirely to writing for that instrument. There's something mysterious about his approach. He has a singing quality and a feeling for nostalgia and melancholy. But there's also humour. I've always felt that Schubert would have loved to have met Chopin. And his music has something that you can only find in the late works of Bach, Mozart and Beethoven. But, in his first *Étude*, Chopin presents challenges that are incredibly difficult to overcome.

RH: For the musical public, the names Bösendorfer and Badura-Skoda are now synonymous. What is it about the construction and sonority of a Bösendorfer that complements your performance aesthetic so perfectly?

PB-S: It's the beauty of sound that it provides and the velvety resonance that it creates that attracts me. Of course, there are good and less good Bösendorfers, but there are never bad Bösendorfers! There's always a certain mellowness and singing quality. But I want to make it clear that while I love them, I also derive a great deal of pleasure from a good Steinway. Those two makes are without doubt the best in the world. There is one thing that you might not know, however. Shortly before the war, the BBC instigated a competition between piano manufacturers. The greatest firms were invited to send a sample of their best instruments in a variety of sizes so that their qualities could be assessed scientifically. To the surprise of the experts, Bösendorfer was the clear winner in most sizes, with the exception of one or two sizes made by Steinway. This was a totally unexpected result, and had the war not broken out, Bösendorfer would have been able to capitalise on its successes. The managing director of Bösendorfer at the time, Alexander Hüttenstrasse, explained the technical qualities of their instruments to me and compared his pianos to those of Bechstein, the instrument he felt was closest to a Steinway. He said that aside from the attack of the hammer and the vibration of the soundboard, the most important part of his instrument was the bridge. Bösendorfers were constructed in such a way that the sound does not emit immediately, but only after a slight hesitation. In other words, the time that the sound emerges after the string has been struck is perhaps one or two milliseconds later than on a Bechstein or a Steinway. And that's true. A Steinway's response is quicker than that of a Bösendorfer. This makes for a more penetrating sound when playing with an orchestra. But in the hands of young pianists, there's a danger that that sound can become metallic. There's nothing worse than a harsh tone, particularly for those of us who grew up hearing the sounds of Cortot, Backhaus, Fischer and Sauer. The Bösendorfer is, therefore, more mellow and more capable of a greater variety of sonorities.

RH: You are also famous for championing period instruments. When did you discover your passion for these instruments, and what are some of the advantages and pitfalls for the modern performer when playing them?

PB-S: Having subscribed to Darwin's theory of evolution during my youth, I used to believe that the modern piano survived because it was musically fitter than its predecessors. During my early years, I thought that fortepianos were relics from the past and should be consigned to the dustbin of music history. We were always told as students that had Bach known of the modern piano, he would have thrown his harpsichord away. And, of course, the same was said about Beethoven. But, in mitigation, it was Edwin Fischer, certainly no period performer, who had a hunch that the modern piano lacked a certain quality when it came to the performance of music from earlier periods. So, as musicians, we became increasingly curious. First, we discovered the harpsichord, which was even less well known than the fortepiano, or *Hammerclavier* as it was called. Here, I owe my interest to the great harpsichordist and fortepianist Isolde Ahlgrimm, whose coterie of connoisseurs attended concerts at her home. This affected my work at the piano and my response to Busoni's octave doubling in Bach. She performed the complete keyboard music of Mozart on the fortepiano from memory, a great achievement and a revelation. This answered many of the questions that were troubling us, specifically in relation to the realisation of Mozart's harmonies. It also clarified our understanding of the composer's use of ornaments, and the ease with which they could be played on a fortepiano.

My friend Jörg Demus and I were inspired by all of this and became true converts. The irony was that the museum that housed the greatest collection of these instruments in the world was a mere ten-minute walk from my home in Vienna. Having previously ignored that museum completely, I soon became a regular visitor and eventually a collector of period instruments. Jörg also became a collector and occasionally snapped up an instrument before me. Of course, it took me some time to get used to transferring from the action of a modern piano to that of a period instrument. But that became easier after I was able to practise regularly on Jörg's Schanz fortepiano. I was so impressed by the instrument that I said to Jörg with tongue in cheek that when he dies he should leave it to me! By return of post came a letter that said, 'I'm not dead yet, but, as I am short of money, I'll sell it to you.'

RH: Finally, what advice would you give to those young musicians who are about to embark on their careers as performing artists?

PB-S: That is a particularly difficult question to answer. Today, young pianists are confronted with a very different set of circumstances than when I was beginning. There are many more pianists being trained than directly after the war. And while many of these young people are taught well, they often lack that which was important to us: beauty of touch, phrasing and articulation. They also lack an individual sense of poetry. They need to read poetry. That's one of the things that Edwin Fischer instilled in us. He believed that music is not only a universal language, but a language that needs to be spoken and understood. It's not merely technique. Consider what *'Freude, schöner Götterfunken'* truly means. But, in practical terms, young musicians should get to know their instrument and play it well. Then, if you truly believe in music as a vocation, develop that vocation and have confidence in what you have to offer. Self-confidence is essential, but it must be confidence without arrogance.

Technically, there are so many great pianists today. Stephen Hough is fantastic. But try to avoid engaging in the sport of who can play fastest. Ensure that the piano is a source of joy. After winning the competition in Vienna, an agent came backstage and immediately offered me work. It was like something from a bad movie, a situation that's extremely rare and unlikely to happen today. For modern pianists there seems to be two possible routes forward. First, with the support of a financial sponsor, or, second, by being a prize winner at a competition. And while winning a competition can be a means to an end, it's really only the beginning. In reality, very few competitions guarantee subsequent engagements. You might be offered 100 concerts in the year directly after your victory. But what happens in the second and third

PART THREE: INSTRUMENTALISTS

years? It's being asked back that's important. It's the ability to convince the musical public that you're not simply one of the hundreds of prize winners that are produced every year, but somebody with something truly unique to offer.

LEON FLEISHER
(CONCERT ROOM, 13 NOVEMBER 2008)

RAYMOND HOLDEN: Shortly after you were born in San Francisco in 1928, the United States underwent a period of great financial and social change. Yet you went on to become one of the most important and influential pianists and pedagogues of the late twentieth and early twenty-first centuries. What was musical life like in San Francisco in the 1930s, and in what ways did it lay the foundations for your career in music?

LEON FLEISHER: Needless to say, I was very young at the time, but I was the beneficiary of one of President Roosevelt's main acts during his time in office: the Works Progress Administration (WPA). Amongst other things, it created work for unemployed musicians. Our local WPA Orchestra was founded and conducted by Alfred Hertz, who had been the conductor of the San Francisco Symphony Orchestra. One of the functions of the WPA Orchestra was to perform in schools, and, as an eight- and nine-year-old, I attended some of those concerts.

RH: Hertz, of course, was a remarkable figure, although largely forgotten today. He conducted the first American performance of Wagner's *Parsifal* at New York's Metropolitan Opera in 1903. This incurred the wrath of Cosima Wagner, who then attempted to have him blacklisted as a conductor in German opera houses. But in what ways did he influence you?

PART THREE: INSTRUMENTALISTS

LF: Funnily enough, one of the main things that I remember about him was that he was totally bald. But he did have a large, scraggy grey beard and had suffered from polio as a child: he had a limp that was very similar to that of Eugene Ormandy. He was quite fierce. Nevertheless, it was through Hertz that I met Artur Schnabel. Every time that Schnabel would visit San Francisco, he would dine with Hertz and his wife and would play bridge afterwards. Hertz was very keen for Schnabel to accept me as a student, but he swiftly rejected the idea, saying that he never accepted pupils under the age of sixteen. He was always concerned that anybody younger wouldn't be able to benefit from his approach. But, one evening, Mrs Hertz had snuck me into the house through the basement and had me sit at their piano in the living room, which was concealed by closed doors. At the end of the meal, which seemed endlessly long to me, they opened the doors, and there I was sitting at the piano. Being a gentleman, Schnabel didn't refuse to hear me. I remember playing the cadenza from the first movement of Beethoven's B flat piano concerto and a piece by Liszt. He was very sweet, and, after that, he invited me to study with him at his home at Lake Como in Italy, long before George Clooney discovered the area's delights! I went that very summer and studied with Schnabel for eight years.

RH: In the time leading up to your life-changing meeting with Schnabel, did you have much of a chance to attend concerts?

LF: As I'd just turned eight years of age, my bedtime got in the way. But I did go to concerts. I remember that my mother, who wasn't a musician, took me to a concert given by Rachmaninoff. I was seated high in the balcony of the War Memorial Opera House, and as he started to play his encores, my mother took me backstage. As she'd never been in the hall before, I'm still amazed to this day how she found her way through the labyrinth of corridors. We ended up on one of the wings of the stage that Rachmaninoff used when walking on and off the concert platform. And the interesting thing about his use of encores was that he wasn't confined to any fixed plan. But when he decided that enough was enough, he would always play his Prelude in C sharp minor. That was the signal that nothing more was to follow. I did notice that when he emerged from the wings and into the view of the public, he walked very slowly. And when he came off stage and was no longer in public view, he walked quickly. That made a great impression on me as a little boy. After about the sixth or seventh encore, he noticed me. I was very short and he was very tall. Looking down at me and pointing with an outstretched index finger, he asked with a heavy Russian accent, 'You pianist?' I looked up and nodded timidly. Looking back down at me for a second time, and again with an outstretched index finger, but while shaking his head, he said, 'Bad business'. All young pianists should take heed!

RH: Before studying with Schnabel, had you heard him perform in public?

LF: No. But I'd heard a couple of recordings.

RH: How were your lessons with Schnabel structured, and did he demonstrate at the piano?

LF: Yes. With the clouds of war gathering in Europe, he moved to New York in 1938. He lived at the Peter Stuyvesant Hotel in Room 9c, and had a Steinway concert grand in his piano studio on which his students played. He also had a small upright on which he created sounds that were infinitely more beautiful than those that any of his students made on the Steinway. What has always remained a model for me was Schnabel's practice of inviting all his students – admittedly, he never had

PART THREE: INSTRUMENTALISTS

more than a handful at a time – to be present at everybody's lessons. As there were three or four of us, this meant that we heard three or four times the repertoire. Lessons would last two and a half or three hours; sometimes longer. Former students, some of my now lost respected colleagues, such as Sir Clifford Curzon and Rudolf Firkušný, would show up when they were in town and join the class. This style of teaching, where individual students were not always the focus of attention, and where you were able to observe others, was highly informative. One really began to gain an overview of music and to come to the realisation that we all share the same challenges and problems. It reinforced in me the idea that music is universal and that it transcends national boundaries. It was an extraordinary learning experience and has been my model throughout my entire life as a teacher.

RH: Did Schnabel have any preferences or biases when selecting repertoire for his students?

LF: Unsurprisingly, he favoured Beethoven, Brahms and Liszt and was not particularly fond of Debussy, Ravel or Russian composers. And he became quite exercised when I brought along Rachmaninoff's *Rhapsody on a Theme of Paganini*. Not once, but twice! He thought of himself primarily as a composer and wrote music that was quite atonal. In later life, he confined himself to what he called 'music that was better than what could be played'. A prime example of this is Mozart's Rondo in A minor. The rest was subject to what he said was 'sleek capacity'. You had in Britain one of his greatest, and youngest, students: Maria Curcio. A most extraordinary lady who was both inspiring and passionate. When teaching, Schnabel tended to work in great detail, but he didn't like hearing the same piece twice in succession. He felt that he'd told you everything that he'd learned about the work during his sixty or so years of experience in one session, and simply didn't want to repeat himself. But he was perfectly happy for a student to bring a piece back after a year or two. You must remember that we didn't have tape recorders in those days, and I remember as a young man staggering out of his studio inebriated by information and inspiration after one of his three-hour sessions. I was overcome. He was the most consistently inspiring, and inspired, musician that I've ever known. He really took you to another place as a student. He took you out of yourself into a whole new realm. It is such a pity that we spend our lives in a defensive posture, which requires of us so much energy and time. Today, we can't even step into an elevator without being bombarded with sound. It's remarkable to think that most of the great composers had no newspapers, television or cellphones. They had time to explore the various dimensions of their humanity. We don't have time any more.

RH: Another great figure with whom you worked closely was George Szell. In what ways did his personality and musicianship act as a guiding influence during your early years as a professional musician?

LF: Szell had a fierce reputation, and was also something of a fierce person. He was tall, with piercing pale-blue eyes that sat behind 'Cokebottle' glasses. These only served to magnify his stare. His standards were incredibly high, and anyone who agreed to work with him, whether an orchestral musician, soloist or recording producer, had to understand that he would demand of them standards that were similar to his. If that wasn't the case, he'd let them know. He was scary to play with, and was known for pushing soloists off the piano stool and showing them how a work should be played. People such as Clifford Curzon, Rudolf Serkin and Glenn Gould were all subject to this behaviour. But, for some reason, he never did that to me: something that I still find unfathomable.

PART THREE: INSTRUMENTALISTS

I was introduced to Szell by Schnabel, and perhaps that carried a certain weight. I know that he adored Schnabel.

RH: One of the things that's always struck me when listening to your recordings with Szell is their chamber-music-like quality. Your recording of Beethoven's 'Emperor' Concerto with him is a case in point.

LF: I remember that when we recorded Schumann's Piano Concerto, he and I spent more than two hours studying the first movement together directly before the session began. I was then about to begin rehearsing the second movement with him when he said, 'It's not necessary to discuss the opening of this movement, as I've trained my orchestra to respond to whatever rhythmic nuances you might make at the beginning.' I thought 'fine.' So, after we finished recording the first movement, I decided to test his readiness and immediately played the figure that opens the second movement. Needless to say, neither he nor the orchestra was ready, and it was one of the only times I saw him break into a great big smile! He could have a wonderful, but juvenile, sense of humour. When we were playing Brahms's Second Piano Concerto, he'd arranged with the Principal Horn, Mike (Myron) Bloom, to play his opening figure a semitone higher. He carried on like that until the entry of the strings, whereupon it was clear to all and sundry that he'd played a 'tonal' prank on the whole orchestra.

RH: One of Szell's defining musical characteristics was his ability to affect the sound of an orchestra, and to shape it in his own interpretative image.

LF: During the 1950s and the 1960s, the Berlin Philharmonic was known for its late response to a conductor's down-beat. And I remember that when Szell and I played a concerto with them, their lateness of attack prompted him to repeat his down-beat five or six times before he could bend them to his will. Only after that was he satisfied. But the orchestra had the final word, and at the performance, they reverted to their old habit of playing well after the beat.

RH: As a conductor yourself, were you affected interpretatively and technically by Szell?

LF: The simple answer is 'yes'. I've never tried to analyse it and I never will. But I try to be nice to my players!

RH: Who else amongst the long list of great conductors with whom you've worked has made a deep impression on you?

LF: I played many times with Pierre Monteux. When I was growing up in San Francisco, he was the conductor of the orchestra there, having succeeded Alfred Hertz. And in all my travels, I've never met any professional musician who played under Monteux who's had *any* negative word to say about him. The good Lord could come down and become Music Director of any major orchestra, and there'd be somebody who would grumble after two weeks. Without question, Monteux was the most professional, prepared and gentlemanly conductor I ever encountered. I must've played on no fewer than eighty occasions with him, including works by Rachmaninoff and Franck. In fact, most of the concertos that I played during the early years of my career, I performed with him for the first time. He's rightly remembered for giving the first performances of Stravinsky's *Le sacre du printemps* and Ravel's *Daphnis et Chloé*.

RH: You've conducted a great many orchestras in a great many countries. Have you noticed a significant difference in the sounds that they produce?

PART THREE: INSTRUMENTALISTS

LF: Less and less. Today, you're not considered a success as a conductor unless you have at least two, preferably three, orchestras on different continents. Even as a Music Director, many of these conductors devote a maximum of only twelve weeks to each of their orchestras. This has the effect of homogenising the sound of orchestras, wherever they may be found. That said, there are a few orchestras that have retained their individuality.

RH: Has the Cleveland Orchestra retained anything of Szell's sound?

LF: It's been a long time since he died. He was known as '*Pa* Szell' and his successor, Lorin Maazel, was known as '*Ma*-azel'. And while there are no longer any players from his era still in the orchestra, it continues to be defined by his discipline and standards. I remember recording Beethoven's Second Piano Concerto, and at the end of the first movement's orchestral exposition, one of his hands appeared in front of my face, indicating that I shouldn't start the solo exposition. He then picked up the telephone, told the producer in the booth that he wasn't happy, and said that he wanted to do the whole passage again. Having repeated the section, he again held his hand up and again indicated that I shouldn't play. He said to the producer, 'I'm still not happy.' I could hear what displeased him, but, by that time, I'd developed a relationship with him that allowed me to speak to him about such matters. I went up to him and said, 'I think that what's missing is a sense of the *debonair*.' He loved the idea. And the first thing that he said to the orchestra on remounting the podium was, 'Gentlemen, more *debonair*.' You can hear the difference: it was more *debonair*! The opening *tutti* of the Second Concerto sounds like Charlie Chaplin on the Champs-Élysées.

Szell not only spoke, but he'd listen. He never had a son of his own, and I was something of a surrogate in that regard. It always struck me that Szell's wife, Helen, must've been a remarkable woman. She would've had to have been. Whenever I visited Cleveland to perform, I stayed with a friend who was a professor of comparative religion. After one particular concert, my friend gave a party to which the Szells and members of the orchestra were invited. In the midst of this party, I suddenly heard a loud voice say, 'Helen, tell us: what's it like being married to a god?' Silence descended, with all eyes turning to Szell, who was munching his way through a plate of food in a corner. After a short pause, Helen replied, 'Well, Horace, it's really rather difficult, because before a concert he won't have sex, after a concert he can't and, as you know, he gives six concerts a week!'

RH: As an artist whose career has spanned more than six decades, you're uniquely placed to comment on how the music profession has developed during that time. What are some of the most significant changes, and were those changes for the better?

LF: When I was young, there were two main management companies in the United States: Columbia Artists and National Concert and Artists Management. Each had a concert circuit that their artists would perform on: Community Concerts for Columbia and Synod Concerts for NCAM. Communities who wanted to have concerts in their small town, for example, would collect as much money as possible, approach one of the two management companies and ask who they could afford to engage based on the sum collected. Programming could be problematic. I remember Columbia Artists told my friend Eugene Istomin, a wonderful artist, that he couldn't play Schumann's *Carnaval*, as it was too long for provincial audiences. Eugene dutifully agreed and played it in reduced form. These agencies were also unhappy when I played Bach. It was a real dumbing down. Thank goodness that these circuits no longer exist in the same way. With the proliferation of radio, television, CD technology and iPods, it's become possible to play enterprising programmes to better informed audiences.

RH: Along with Eugene Istomin, who were some of the other American pianists of your generation that you admired and respected?

LF: Without question, the greatest pianistic talent of our generation was William Kapell. His was a fabulous gift. And, of course, there was Byron Janis. But I'm also impressed by the next generation of pianists, such as Murray Perahia, Daniel Barenboim and Sir András Schiff.

RH: But many of your contemporaries had their careers cut short. Were the concert circuits that you mentioned earlier in some way responsible for this?

LF: No, I don't think so. The circuit tours allowed us to try out new pieces, so that when you performed in New York, for example, you weren't playing something for the first time. One of my colleagues, Gary Graffman, who has also been stricken with focal dystonia, now also plays only the literature composed for the left hand. And if I have any advice for young people, it would be this: do not over-practise. Everyone succumbs to Horowitz's sound when they listen to him on records: that unique, clangorous sound he was able to modulate with his hands. But you have to remember that his piano was 'doctored' to his taste. This meant that it was adjusted so that the action was very, very light. You could've blown on the keys and they would've gone down! His piano also had very hardened hammers, so that he could make this 'fire-engine-type' sound with the minimum of effort. One of his greatest qualities was his ability to modulate his sound, particularly when he was playing *pianissimo*. When you heard him in person, it could take you two minutes to adjust to that sound. But no pianist today wants to make that kind of sound. And very often we now play on a 'dead' piano in a 'dead' room.

It has to be remembered that the muscles in the hand are small and that you must never play through pain. Footballers might be able to do this, but musicians shouldn't. Nobody can concentrate productively for more than five hours. But some younger players insist on going on for seven, eight or even nine hours. This results in mindless work. They're just sitting there 'pumping ivory'. And that's the worst thing they should do. There's no cure for dystonia. While physicians are able to deal partially with the symptoms, and have identified the part of the brain from which the condition emerges, musicians themselves are reluctant to admit to the symptoms. They're concerned that if they do, they'll not be offered any engagements. Pianists then try to disguise it by announcing that they're indisposed for anything *but* dystonia. If there are physical abnormalities that you don't understand, find a doctor who is aware that there's not only such a thing as dystonia, but also focal dystonia. There's nothing worse than not knowing what's happening to one's self physically, and not understanding how to deal with the situation. From everything that we know about Robert Schumann, it's clear that he had dystonia. All his efforts to stretch or counteract his uncontrollable and involuntary muscle function simply meant that it went from bad to worse.

RH: Having had to focus your attention on repertoire written for the left hand, did you uncover any new or lost works that were of great value musically?

LF: Some of the works written for left hand alone are absolutely superb. One of the greatest pieces, whether it's written for five fingers or fifty fingers, is Ravel's Left-Hand Concerto. It's just a straight-out masterpiece.

PART THREE: INSTRUMENTALISTS

Benjamin Britten wrote a marvellous work called *Diversions for Piano Left Hand and Orchestra,* which was recorded by both Julius Katchen and myself. Then there's Prokofiev's Fourth Piano Concerto. But I find Strauss's works for the left hand not so good. There are also works by Korngold and Franz Schmidt, whose Brahms-like concerto has melodies that are evocative of the South Pacific. Schmidt also wrote three quintets for the left hand: one for string quartet and piano left hand, and two that involved clarinet and piano left hand. These chamber works are very good pieces. With both humility and pride, I've also been the object of a few works that have helped to expand the repertoire. The Boston Symphony Orchestra commissioned a work, and Gunther Schuller has written a concerto for three hands, which I've performed with Lorin Hollander. William Bolcom also wrote a fun piece that's divided into two parts. Each part is played separately before performing both sections simultaneously! I also gave the first performance of a left-hand concerto by Hindemith that had been lost for decades. There were rumours that it existed, but nobody had any proof. It was only after Paul Wittgenstein's widow died a few years ago that it was discovered amongst her belongings. Hindemith had written it in 1923, when he was at the peak of his powers, and after the publishers gained access to the manuscript, they called me and invited me to perform it. I then played it for the first time about four years ago with Sir Simon Rattle.

RH: While you've now come to terms with the condition that changed the course of your career, how long did it take for you to identify that you were suffering from dystonia?

LF: Almost thirty years. My doctors had no idea what was wrong with me, but were willing to experiment. I tried everything from aromatherapy to Zen Buddhism. It wasn't until the middle of the 1990s that a friend of mine alerted me to a programme at the National Institutes of Health in Washington DC. During the thirty or so years that I suffered from the condition, there was not a day that went by that didn't involve some form of experimentation on my part. My muscles had grown so contracted that I was unable to make an indentation when I pressed my finger into my arm: it had become like petrified wood. My wife found me a thing called 'Rolf Therapy'. Most people would describe it as massage, but that's not accurate. It's a way of stretching the very fibre of the contracted tissue and restoring it to its normal length. I attended Rolf Therapy sessions twice a week for a year before my arm recovered some of its plasticity. This, combined with Botox injections, then began to have an effect. Rolfing is very healthy. The latest thing is neurotherapy. This involves placing your bad hand behind a mirror while situating your good hand in front of the mirror. You then pretend that what you see in the mirror is your bad hand, and then attempt to fool the brain by activating your good hand. This is often the basis for phantom-limb therapy, where people still have pain in limbs that are missing. That seems to be promising; I like the idea of fooling the brain. But it was Botox that's been of the greatest help, and immediately after my first injection, I began to play as I did thirty-one years earlier.

RH: Returning to music for a moment, what's your preferred instrument?

LF: I like a Steinway. There are a few great American Steinways, but the general level of Steinways made in Hamburg is probably better.

RH: If asked to speak generally about music-making over the last twenty or so years, how would you describe it?

PART THREE: INSTRUMENTALISTS

LF: The word that comes to mind is 'globalisation'. But this is not restricted to pianists; it's also true of conductors. If there's one thing that defines young players today, it's their need to demonstrate how much they're affected by the music they're playing. They don't seem to realise that the more they writhe and move about, the guiltier they are of distracting from the music. There's a tripartite relationship between composer, performer and listener. We seem to need a 'star' today, and many people are quite eager to be 'stars'. But the only 'star' in this tripartite relationship is the music. The performer is the vessel, or channel, through which the composer communicates with the listener. And if we simply sit there and watch somebody act out the music, rather like show business, then that's a complete misunderstanding and misrepresentation of our function as performers. We are indispensable, but we are not the 'star'. Without us, music is just a series of dots on a piece of paper. We bring those dots to life.

GYÖRGY PAUK
(DAVID JOSEFOWITZ RECITAL HALL, 23 OCTOBER 2015)

Raymond Holden: Recently, I was alerted to a marvellous film of you on the internet playing Brahms's Violin Concerto in Paris. You were clearly very young at the time. How did that performance come about?

György Pauk: It was a gala concert that was arranged after I won the Jacques Thibaud Competition two weeks earlier. And, by chance, I, too, only received a copy of the video recently. This was a very pleasant surprise, as I hadn't realised that it had been televised. But, sadly, four or five minutes are missing from the beginning of the first movement.

RH: You were born in Budapest in 1936 at a time of political turmoil, both domestically and internationally. What was family life like in the Pauk household during those tumultuous years, and how did they affect the young György?

GP: My family were musicians. My mother was a professional pianist, and she played a great deal of chamber music at home with a great many violinists. This meant that I heard the sound of the violin from the very beginning of my life accompanied by my mother. I was later told that when I was about three years old I was out walking with my parents when a stranger said, 'Do you know what your little boy is singing?'

PART THREE: INSTRUMENTALISTS

They replied instantly, 'Yes, of course we do. It's Mendelssohn's Violin Concerto.' It was something that I'd heard my mother play many times with her colleagues at home.

RH: Do you retain any memories of Budapest from those early years?

GP: I do. Even though it was a very difficult period politically, I had a pleasant time for the first four or five years of my life. At the age of five and a half, I started to play the violin. And it was my great good fortune to have in our building a very well-known violin teacher. Then, the war came. Hungary was one of the last countries to be occupied by the German army, but, from the beginning of 1944 onwards, my life became particularly hard. I remember having to hide in the cellar to avoid the effects of non-stop bombing. The fear of bombing and being in the cellar was just awful. To make matters worse, my father had been taken to a labour camp in 1942: I never saw him again. I was less than six years old when I lost my father. Then, two years later, my mother was also taken away, and that was the last time I saw her, too. Luckily, I had a grandmother: my mother's mother. She brought me up and took care of me until I left Hungary some years later.

RH: This must have been a dreadful period for you. But, somehow, you managed to carry on as an aspiring musician. Are you able to describe how you developed during those early years?

GP: I knew that I had talent and that I loved music. I also sang a great deal, which is very important for any musician to do. My love of singing has stayed with me all my life, and I'm still very passionate about opera. I studied with Zoltán Kodály, and the Kodály Method of music education was based on everybody singing. This helped me a great deal when it came to intonation, and was also very useful when it came to my violin playing in general. I always recommend the Kodály Method to my students, and I'm constantly asking them to sing. Not only does that allow you to come to terms with yourself musically, but it also helps your phrasing. It means that you breathe when you have to breathe.

RH: Were you ever tempted to take up another instrument, or was the violin your one true musical love?

GP: No. It's always been the violin for me.

RH: The immediate post-war years must also have been very tough for you.

GP: They were, but it was already understood that I had talent. And because I'd lost my parents, I was given a lot of help by the communist state, and was lucky enough to have been awarded the highest scholarships. I managed somehow until I left for the West, and today is the fifty-ninth anniversary of the Hungarian Revolution in 1956. Just before that took place, I'd travelled to Italy and had won the Paganini Competition in Genova. I then returned to Budapest the day before the revolution broke out. My stay in Italy was my first experience of Western life, and the first time I experienced a free country. This was incredibly important to me, as I essentially grew up in a prison. Hungarians had no idea what was happening in the West.

RH: For many people, especially for those living in Eastern Europe, the Second World War didn't end until the fall of the Berlin Wall in 1989.

PART THREE: INSTRUMENTALISTS

GP: That's true. Dates like the Hungarian Revolution and the fall of the Berlin Wall are ones that you will always remember. And when the second happened, I was giving a concert in Düsseldorf with Witold Lutosławski conducting. When I was in Italy for the Paganini Competition, I wasn't allowed to play any performances, as my visa was restricted. But it was at that moment that I knew I had to leave Hungary and to live in the West.

RH: Let's step back a stage, shall we? Clearly, you were developing at speed as a musician during the war years, and entered the Franz Liszt Academy in Budapest at the age of twelve. What are your memories of the Academy at that time?

GP: It was like attending church. Times were tough politically, but the Academy was outstanding as a music school. All my teachers were great musicians, and I was very lucky to have studied there. Sadly, it's no longer the same.

RH: Are you able to articulate why the Franz Liszt Academy has changed so much?

GP: It's down to the personalities. All of the teachers I studied with are dead. They were my idols, particularly Ede Zathureczky. And don't forget I also studied with Zoltán Kodály and Leó Weiner. Zathureczky was one of the last outstanding exponents of the great Hungarian school of violin playing. This had begun with Joseph Joachim and was continued by Jenő Hubay. I was looking for a father figure at the time, and Zathureczky fulfilled that. I was thirteen years old when I was accepted into his class, which was very rare indeed. He had never taken on such a young musician before. My classmates were all in their twenties, and there I was turning up in short trousers. I adored Zathureczky because he was a great musician and a great human being. And it was for those reasons that he was my childhood idol.

RH: I am fascinated by the whole idea of 'schools of playing'. Is there really such a thing as the Hungarian school of violin playing, and, if so, what defines it?

GP: I certainly hope that there is. I believe that I'm part of it, and I'm keen to pass it on to my pupils. Perhaps one of the defining features of the Hungarian school is tone production. And then there is the co-ordination between the left and right hands. These allow us a variety of sounds that have beauty and colour, and can only be achieved by the violinist and not the instrument. And that's what I learned from Zathureczky. He left Hungary a little earlier than me and became a professor in Bloomington, Indiana. Sadly, his time there was very short and he died little more than a year after being appointed. He was very young.

RH: Do you see many heirs to this school of playing amongst the younger generation of violinists?

GP: As I've taught hundreds of students during my long career, they've been the beneficiaries of its traditions. What worries me is the general standard of violin playing internationally: it's not very good. And what worries me even more is that the style of playing has not changed over the last fifty years.

RH: I would like to return to Zoltán Kodály for moment. What defined him as a teacher?

PART THREE: INSTRUMENTALISTS

GP: He was a phenomenal musician, but a bad teacher. He always assumed that all his students already knew what he was talking about. We never did. He spoke on such a high level that he left his students behind. And that's why he wasn't a good teacher. Besides playing the violin at the Franz Liszt Academy, I had to play chamber music and to learn the piano. These were compulsory. As a student, I had a string quartet that carried my name, and I asked Kodály to listen to us a couple of times. He had wonderful ideas and was very helpful. But, as a teacher, he only taught me Hungarian folk music, which my fellow students and I never took very seriously.

RH: Kodály shared a love of Hungarian folk music with Béla Bartók. Did he speak to you much about Bartók?

GP: No. And it was surprising that he didn't. But it had nothing to do with rivalry, as Bartók was already dead by that time and as they were great friends. Zathureczky also knew Bartók, and played with him for the first time when he was twenty-two years old. This meant that I was able to absorb what Bartók had to offer through Zathureczky. When I was about seventeen or eighteen, Zathureczky taught me Bartók's Sonata for Solo Violin and the Second Violin Concerto. And, on reflection, I'm now completely unsure how I could have understood the sonata at that age. Nevertheless, it was a great help to me, because he actually knew Bartók.

RH: Leó Weiner was a completely different kettle of fish. As a teacher, he was considerably more impactful, particularly when it came to chamber music.

GP: Weiner was simply one of the greatest Hungarian music teachers. He was also a composer, but his works weren't particularly interesting.

Artists such as Antal Doráti and Sir Georg Solti were influenced by him, but by the time that I studied with Weiner, he was an old man. When my quartet went to his house, he never watched the clock and our lessons lasted for hours. By the end of these marathon sessions, we were dead tired, but he was still raring to go. And, to this day, I can still remember the advice he gave us when playing the quartets of Beethoven and Schubert.

RH: Earlier, you mentioned the 1956 Hungarian Revolution. Am I correct when I say that you left for the Netherlands directly after it?

GP: Yes. I had some friends in the Netherlands, which is a lovely country. It's still like a second home to me. In fact, I first went for a short while to France as a refugee in 1958, before moving on to Holland. And, here, I must mention Yehudi Menuhin, who changed my life, both in Hungary and in the Netherlands. When he went to Hungary to give some concerts in 1956, I was introduced to him by Zathureczky. I was able to play for Menuhin during that visit, and two years later I visited him backstage in the artists' room after a concert in Holland. He looked straight at me and recognised me immediately. He asked, 'What are you doing in Amsterdam?' Although I told him that I was very happy there, he insisted that I should go to London. It took me a couple of years to make the move, and when I did, Yehudi sent a recommendation to the Home Office on my behalf. Because Britain was full of refugees at the time, I wouldn't have been allowed in without Menuhin's recommendation, as I only had a Dutch refugee passport. This was in 1961. Before deciding to come to London permanently, I'd already auditioned for the BBC. In those days, you couldn't broadcast for the Corporation unless you'd done an official audition for it. I passed the test, and was soon asked to record Tchaikovsky's Violin Concerto with the London

PART THREE: INSTRUMENTALISTS

Philharmonic Orchestra. This was a wonderful introduction to the British capital, and a couple of months later I moved here permanently with my wife. And from the very first time I set foot on English soil, I felt that I was home.

RH: Those early years in the United Kingdom can't have been easy financially. But as you'd won a number of competitions by that time, were they of benefit to you?

GP: Competitions are not my favourite subject, but they were quite different then. By the time I'd arrived in England, I'd already won three major competitions. And one very wise lady in Genova said to me that I shouldn't take all my prize money back to Hungary after the Paganini Competition. Instead, I should leave some of it in an Italian bank. Had the Hungarian Revolution not broken out, I'm not sure what would have happened to me. But at least I had some money saved in Italy. When I won the Jacques Thibaud Competition, it was of some considerable importance, as its adjudicators included David Oistrakh and Henryk Szeryng. This opened the door to a great many concerts, including quite a lot in England. But starting a new life in a new country was not easy. Luckily, I knew some people, and, of course, there was Yehudi Menuhin. He introduced me to some very important contacts, and just being in London in the 1960s and 1970s was remarkable. It was buzzing musically. Artists such as Daniel Barenboim, Vladimir Ashkenazy and Fou Ts'ong all lived here. We even played football together! As London *was* simply wonderful, it was very important for a young artist to be at the centre of it all.

RH: What's your take on musical life in London today?

GP: London is still the capital of the musical world. The competition facing artists today is bigger, yet classical music is no longer as popular as it was in my day.

RH: Why do you think that is?

GP: It has to do with the amount of television and other electronic media that's now available. When I made my debut at the Wigmore Hall in 1962, every artist had to pay for his or her first concert there. But the next day there were five reviews. That would be unthinkable today. At the time, you knew that all the major papers would send a critic. And if you had good reviews, you also knew that they would be a great boost for your career.

RH: A Wigmore Hall debut was an important event up until the late 1970s. Do you think that it still carries the same cachet?

GP: No. Now it's all to do with public relations. If you play a concert at the Wigmore Hall today that's not advertised and arranged properly, and without the right people in attendance, you've wasted your money. After my debut there, all the London and provincial orchestras became interested in me and offered me engagements. Because of these concerts, I met, and worked with, many of Europe's and Britain's greatest conductors, including Antal Doráti, Sir Georg Solti, Sir John Barbirolli, Sir Adrian Boult, Sir Malcolm Sargent, Sir Charles Groves, Sir John Pritchard, Sir Colin Davis and Sir Andrew Davis. Consequently, I started to become very well-known in the United Kingdom. I was also fortunate enough to have an excellent management team: Ingpen & Williams Ltd. But there was one man who liked me very much, and who was not only my manager but my advisor: Howard Hartog. He had many conductors on his books, and was instrumental in coupling me with artists like Pierre Boulez. And here I must also mention another conductor who was very helpful to me at the start of my career: Harry Blech, the founder of the London Mozart Players. During my early years in London, the orchestra played monthly at the Royal Festival Hall. Harry loved my playing, and invited me almost annually to play with his ensemble at the Southbank Centre. Because of this association, I was dubbed the 'London Mozart *Player*', a title I am very proud of.

RH: You play on a Stradivarius violin.

GP: Yes, and I've been very lucky with the instruments that I've played on from my Amsterdam years onwards. Just before a competition in 1959, I was lent a very beautiful Guadagnini by a well-known dealer in Holland, Max Möller. I explained to him that I was about to play in the competition, but didn't have a good instrument. He then arranged for me to have that beautiful fiddle, which I used for about three years. I continued to play on it until I arrived in Britain, but just before my Wigmore Hall recital, I was asked to return it. Luck was again on my side, however, and some people I knew arranged for me to have a good Amati for my debut. It was then organised that another Guadagnini should be bought for me, which I then used for many years. When Solti took over the Chicago Symphony Orchestra, he invited me to perform with him during his first season as Music Director. This was my American debut, and a very important engagement for me. The concert was a success and I was immediately invited to perform with the orchestra again the following season. After the concert, an important violin collector came to the artists' room and introduced himself. I'd heard of him, and knew of his collection. He told me that he liked my playing very much and would like to show me some of his violins. This gentleman then visited my hotel room carrying two Stradivarius and two Guarneri violins, which he asked me to try. So, I played and he listened. This carried on for quite a long time until he finally asked me which instrument I preferred. After mulling over the various merits of each of the four violins, I settled on a Stradivarius. And, to my surprise, he said that I could use it to perform on. I nearly fainted. The violin was the 'Massart' Stradivarius from 1714, which I still play to this day. But I was concerned by what might happen should he die, or should the loan be withdrawn for some reason. I then asked him if I could buy the instrument from him, and although he was initially reluctant, he finally agreed.

RH: With that instrument, you later made a disc of Handel's violin sonatas. What's your take on period performance in general and the Baroque violin in particular?

GP: I'm very interested in these subjects. After I made the Handel recording, I then performed Bach's sonatas for violin with a harpsichord as the accompanying instrument. In my opinion, the harpsichord doesn't work with a modern violin. When we were making the Handel disc, we had constant problems with tuning, as the pitch of the harpsichord was continually dropping. We had to stop every fifteen minutes to do something about it. I believe fully that a modern violin should be coupled with a piano. When I recorded the Handel sonatas, I wasn't particularly interested in Baroque music. My interest in it began to blossom after I started working with the young Sir Simon Rattle. At the time, he was only in his twenties, but was very interested in works from that era. He urged me to think about it, which encouraged me to listen to a great many period performances. But, to be quite honest, I don't like listening to Baroque instruments. Nevertheless, I've thought about this issue a great deal, and feel that we need to find a middle ground between historically informed playing and modern style. In my search for this middle ground, I've listened to many performances by leading Baroque violinists and performers. And I now think that I've come up with a solution. When we played works by Bach, Mozart and Schubert in the past, we did so very slowly. If you observe what Bach says about an *Adagio* from one of his solo sonatas, for example, it should be performed in four beats to the bar, rather than in eight. The difference between playing such a movement in a slow four, rather than a fast eight, is substantial. And then there is the question of *vibrato*. When I listen to my own recordings of eighteenth-century music, there's too much *vibrato*. It makes the music sound too sweet.

RH: As you've just mentioned Mozart, tell me about your recordings of his concerti?

GP: I recorded the Fifth Concerto with the Württemberg Chamber Orchestra for Vox Turnabout, and, later, all five concertos with the Franz Liszt Chamber Orchestra for Hungaroton. In all honesty, I don't like listening to myself, and the last time I heard the Württemberg Chamber Orchestra disc was more than twenty-five years ago. I remember that it was a fairly charming performance, but the slow movements in the complete set are too slow. And there's far too much *vibrato*. I've changed musically quite a bit since those days.

RH: As you have now raised the issue of *vibrato* twice, can you expand on it a little more?

GP: When I am working with students, they nearly all arrive having established a basic technical know-how. But sound production can be difficult when playing on a modern instrument. This problem doesn't exist when playing on Baroque violins, as players of those instruments use small bows, play fast and have one kind of colour. On a modern instrument, the balance between the left and right hands can be problematic. It's important to be aware of the relationship between the left-hand's *vibrato* and the weight needed for the right. I learned this from the Hungarian school of violin playing. The sound must have a singing quality, and I always compare it with the human voice.

RH: How, then, do you justify your heritage as a Hungarian violinist with your thoughts on the performance of eighteenth-century music?

GP: Simple. I've changed. And I think that I've changed for the better. As I said, I am in search of a middle way, a way that takes into consideration sound production and *tempo*. I want the sound to be more alive than it used to be.

RH: You've also recorded Mozart's complete sonatas for violin and piano. Did you play them all in the concert hall first?

GP: No, but I'd played them all as a student. I was offered the opportunity to record them when I was twenty-two years old, a fantastic project. But by the time I came to record them for the BBC, I'd changed a great deal. What's missing from the earlier set is my ability to make the music breathe, but I was very young at the time. It's essential to make the music breathe in much the same way as you would when speaking. My later recordings of these works are much more colourful and alive.

RH: Of the Frankl-Pauk-Kirshbaum Trio, which was a very big part of your musical life, Annette Moreau wrote in *The Independent* in 2011: 'The team of Peter Frankl (piano), Gyorgy [sic] Pauk (violin) and Ralph

PART THREE: INSTRUMENTALISTS

Kirshbaum (cello) will not have had to fight over who played second fiddle but if the understanding of Kreisler's remark is that chamber music allows egos to be gracefully laid aside, 25 years of togetherness by Frankl, Pauk and Kirshbaum shows an astonishing welding of friendship and music-making.' What was the key to the Trio's success, and what were some of its defining musical qualities?

GP: The Trio was formed because of a producer at the BBC who's now dead. By the time of its formation, Frankl and I had recorded practically all the violin and piano repertoire. The producer said that she was very keen for us to continue, but felt that we needed a cellist. She then offered to find us the right person. And the artist she found was a much younger American cellist who had made his Wigmore Hall debut in 1970. After we met and sat down to play for half an hour, we knew that we'd found our cellist: Ralph Kirshbaum. While my solo career was of greatest importance to me, chamber music was, and still is, of considerable significance. All three members of the Trio had major careers as soloists, but we took our chamber music performances very seriously indeed. We usually reserved three or four weeks a year for trio concerts, and our first public performance together was at the Edinburgh International Festival. We then did a great deal for the BBC. But in those days, the Corporation was completely different from what it is today. Initially, we were offered seven programmes comprising of seven Mozart trios coupled with seven Romantic trios. Over the next thirty years, we played throughout the United Kingdom, North America and Europe, and gave cycles of the Beethoven, Schubert and Brahms trios. We recorded many of these, and at one series of six concerts, we performed seven of Beethoven's trios alongside his complete violin and cello sonatas. This was an incredible opportunity.

RH: Another important cycle that you recorded was Schubert's music for violin and piano. These works are extremely attractive, but they seem to be programmed less frequently than sonatas by Mozart and Beethoven. What challenges do Schubert's works present?

GP: To be able to play Schubert well can be even more difficult than playing Mozart. You must have complete control over your instrument and a variety of colours. But, first and foremost, you have to be aware that nearly everything Schubert wrote was tragic. His music distils his tragic life. It's also essential to understand what constitutes Viennese music, and to be conscious of what every accent means. And you must be able to breathe with the music, even before you begin to play. For a young person, there's nothing more difficult than playing Schubert's music, and, for a violinist, his works are hard to play technically. Before you perform the two trios, the quintet and the octet, it's crucial to understand what demands the composer will make of you as a violinist.

RH: The disc of Bartók's Violin Sonatas that you recorded with Jenő Jandó at the Unitarian Church in Budapest is particularly interesting. By recording these works in Budapest, were you in some way reaffirming both your own roots and those of the sonatas?

GP: In fact, we were actually returning to Bartók's roots, as he converted to Unitarianism in 1916. But the disc that you mention had nothing to do with the composer being Hungarian. It had more to do with Naxos's propensity to record in Hungary at the time. The disc of the sonatas, and the one that includes the Sonata for Solo Violin, were made in a tiny church within a big block of flats. Aside from the occasional sound coming from a neighbouring apartment, there was very little extraneous noise. And in that tiny church was a bust of Bartók, which stood directly in front of me as I played his music. As I said earlier, my relationship with the composer's works dates back to my student years, and they have travelled with me throughout my entire life.

RH: On the same disc as Bartók's Violin Sonatas are his *Contrasts*, which you recorded in the later, three-movement version. Have you ever played them in the earlier, two-movement version, as recorded by Bartók, Joseph Szigeti and Benny Goodman?

GP: No, and I didn't even know that there was a two-movement version. Over the years, I recorded *Contrasts* on several occasions, and have played it with many different clarinettists. But to return to the first of the two sonatas, it's a huge piece. It lasts about thirty-five minutes and I have always found that it pairs marvellously well with Beethoven. I also have my students play Bartók's music, as they can gain greatly from my experience of it. If you are to play works like the two sonatas, then you have to have a very good pianist. And for the first sonata, you really must have a pianist of the front rank. Bartók and Szigeti, whom you just mentioned, famously played at the Library of Congress in Washington in 1940, and when I gave a concert there many years later, all I could think of was how honoured I was to be able to perform on the same stage as they did. A memory like that remains with you all your life.

RH: You are clearly committed to Hungarian music, but do you still return regularly to Budapest?

GP: Not any more, as I no longer perform. But I used to go there quite a lot.

RH: Were those trips important to you?

GP: Yes, they were. As I'd made a big career in the West, I was being constantly asked to visit. Yet, for seventeen years, I didn't dare return because of the unstable political situation there. After I was eventually persuaded to go, I must have visited forty or fifty times. But because I'd succeeded in the West, expectations were always very high, and this made performing quite difficult. Along with established masterpieces, I played a great deal of twentieth-century music in Hungary, which was not very popular at the time. I performed works by Alban Berg, Lutosławski and Bartók, and premiered music by some of the leading local composers. Twentieth-century music has always been a very important part of my life.

RH: That's undoubtedly true when one examines the list of composers you performed during your career. And along with the names that you've just mentioned, we should also add Sir Michael Tippett and Krzysztof Penderecki. But amongst the many great twentieth- and twenty-first-century composers with whom you've worked, was there one with whom you had a particular artistic affinity?

GP: Witold Lutosławski.

RH: Why was that?

GP: For me, he was one of the great twentieth-century composers. Through my manager, Howard Hartog, I was asked to give the first London performance of Lutosławski's Violin Concerto. That performance was given only a couple of months after the work received its world premiere in Basel. And it was at the British concert that I met the composer for the first time. I just adored him as a man and as a musician. He was one of the greatest musicians I ever met, and was very good at conducting his own works. After that, he invited me to perform with him many times elsewhere, and I played his concerto around the world. I also gave the first British performance of *Subito*, but this was after Lutosławski had already died.

RH: Tell me about your relationship with Tippett.

GP: Again, I met Tippett through Howard Hartog, who was also the composer's manager. The Triple Concerto for three solo string instruments is something of a rarity, and I played the solo violin part at its world premiere. This was at the Proms under Sir Colin Davis, someone I'd played with on many occasions by the time of that concert. Colin was a great admirer of Michael's music, and performed a great deal of it. Meeting Tippett again for that premiere was a wonderful experience, and one that was full of joy.

RH: Over the years, you've worked with many of the world's greatest conductors. Who amongst them impressed you most, and what, for you, defines a great conductor?

GP: I've played with hundreds of conductors throughout the world. But the number of great conductors amongst those hundreds is small. Perhaps the greatest with whom I worked were Barbirolli, Solti, Doráti and Colin Davis. And then there was Simon Rattle, who was unknown when I first met him. I played for his first performance of Beethoven's Violin Concerto. We did the work on five consecutive occasions, and he was so eager to learn. In later years, I worked with Simon many times, and he was always very helpful when it came to pieces like those of Berg. Finnish conductors were often violinists, and I played with Paavo Berglund for the first time in Australia. He then invited me to play in

Finland, which was my local debut there. Something that was common to all the great figures with whom I performed was their urge to discuss the music with me first. When I worked with Solti, for example, he invited me to his house, where we played through the piece, and where he marked his score in line with what we discussed. It's simply not good enough for a conductor just to follow a soloist. The truly great amongst them sense what you want and act accordingly. Solti understood this, and when we performed together, it was as if we were breathing together. The same was true when I worked with Simon Rattle. Another conductor with whom I performed a great deal was Iván Fischer. I toured with him and the Budapest Festival Orchestra throughout Europe and North America. When we played Bartók's music together, it felt like the most perfectly fitting glove. We understood each other musically and personally. And time is essential. The number of concerts that I gave in the United Kingdom where I simply rehearsed in the afternoon and played in the evening is too many to count. This is not really music-making, and it's impossible to come to an agreement artistically. That was not the case when I worked with a truly great conductor. There was always time to prepare.

JOHN WILLIAMS
(DAVID JOSEFOWITZ RECITAL HALL, 15 NOVEMBER 2013)

RAYMOND HOLDEN: Although you were born in Australia in 1941, your father's roots were embedded firmly in British soil. Len came from a well-established East End family and was something of a musical jack-of-all-trades during his younger years. Could you tell us about his early activities, and the ways in which they defined his character and later career?

JOHN WILLIAMS: My dad was raised within a mile of Bow Bells, so he was a real cockney. His father had been a cabinet-maker, and his Aunt Belle taught him a bit of piano. But during his late teens, he got together with a number of friends, formed a group and played some early dance-band music. During the 1930s, he taught and worked in London as what we'd now call a 'session guitarist'. He was indeed a jack-of-all-trades. He was also very interested in real jazz and the classical guitar. He worshipped, as everyone did then, Segovia, and began learning classical guitar in the 1930s from Mario Maccaferri. Maccaferri was not only celebrated for having designed the 'cut-out' guitar that Django Reinhardt played on, but was also a very notable classical guitarist at the time. He'd come from Italy to England before finally settling in America. My father also worked at the music store John Alvey Turner, which sent him to Australia shortly before the outbreak of the Second World War. He arrived in Melbourne with his first wife, Phyllis, in 1939, where he designed the Aristone, the Australian equivalent of the American Epiphone guitar. While there, he worked at Sutton's music store and played for The ABC Showband.

RH: Melbourne is now a great city, but it was a very different place at that time. It must have been something of a culture shock for your father after cosmopolitan London.

JW: It was, and that was probably one of the reasons why we returned to England. Melbourne was very quiet in those days, but he did love Australia and the Australian character. After getting off the ship from Britain, my father's first encounter with an Australian was when a huge chap took him by the lapels of his jacket and gently lifted him off his feet. The chap then said, 'That's a bloody nice suit you've got', before lowering him to the ground. After wishing my dad 'G'day', the man went off. Although my father was never given to novelty for novelty's sake, he was always keen to do something new.

RH: Melbourne doesn't seem to have been Phyllis's cup of tea, as she returned fairly quickly to Britain.

JW: That's true, but they parted as very good friends. We always kept in touch with her, and she later married a member of the Royal Navy. When they emigrated to New Zealand, I would visit her if I was there on tour.

RH: Your father then met your mother, Melaan, whose background was quite different from that of Len. Her father, William Ah Ket, was born in Melbourne, and was the first Chinese-Australian to be called to the Bar.

PART THREE: INSTRUMENTALISTS

JW: Like many other Chinese families during the 1850s and the 1860s, my grandfather's parents moved to northern Victoria during the gold-rush years. A first generation Chinese-Australian, my grandfather worked his way up to become a very prominent barrister before eventually becoming a King's Council. He was also a Freemason and an advocate for the Chinese community. My grandmother was equally amazing. For a white, Anglo-Saxon woman to marry somebody who was Chinese in the second decade of the twentieth century was pretty extraordinary. And this reminds me of a trip to Australia in the 1970s during which the ABC's concerts' manager told me that he had something to show me. He said that he was a collector of postcards, and that he had three or four that were addressed to a Bertie Young of Wangaratta in north-eastern Victoria. This was a region where many people with the name Ket lived, the Anglicised version of my grandfather's name. Bertie was my grandfather's sister, and the postcards had been sent from China while he was representing Chinese people in Australia for the first Sun Yat-sen republican government. It so happened that the ABC's concerts' manager had heard me mention the name Ah Ket the previous day in an interview, and had noticed that the postcards were signed 'Willie Ah Ket'. They were addressed to his sister, Bertie, and were sent during my grandparents' honeymoon.

RH: Len and Melaan had quite an unusual lifestyle for a conservative city like Melbourne in the 1940s. They had left-wing sympathies, and were closely associated with Montsalvat, an artists' colony in the Melbourne suburb of Eltham.

JW: I'm not really sure how they met, but when they wanted to return to London in 1952, it was necessary for my parents to get married; I was one of two witnesses at their wedding at Kew in Victoria. Earlier, my father had met the famous Australian jewellery maker Mitcham Skipper when he popped into Sutton's music shop to discuss his nephew, Sebastian Jorgensen. Like Skipper, Sebastian played the guitar, and it was the Jorgensen family who had founded Montsalvat. And it was through this connection that we got to know about the artists' colony. Sebastian was two years older than me, and we both used to learn the guitar from my dad. When we lived in Brighton Road, St Kilda, Sebastian often came to stay with us on weekends, and, on others, we'd go to Montsalvat. As a place, it was very free, open and culturally dynamic. It was the type of atmosphere that my parents were attracted to.

RH: Your father's employment history in Australia was remarkably varied. Along with being a musician, he also worked as a counsellor and as a zoo-keeper.

JW: When my father and his first wife arrived in Melbourne, they had no money, so he needed to do something just to 'earn a crust'. For a short while, one of the things that he did was to act as a self-appointed 'psychologist'. He took a little room somewhere off Elizabeth Street, and called himself something very English. And while I think that the surname he chose was 'Johnson', I do remember that the given name he adopted was 'Ormerod'. He then worked as a zoo-keeper during his last year in Australia. He'd always loved animals, and as a child I had a dog, a sulphur-crested cockatoo called 'Jerry' and various other animals.

RH: Clearly, your father's approach and interests were fundamental to you taking up the guitar. But were his ideas also the foundation of your technique and musicianship?

PART THREE: INSTRUMENTALISTS

JW: His approach was 100 per cent crucial for what I did. And as any string player will tell you, it's those early years that are the most important. If you've been taught wrongly, there'll often be a great deal to undo. I learned from my father from the age of four, and he was extremely clever psychologically. He would never tell me to practise three hours a day, and I never practised more than half an hour a day until we returned to London. My father's teaching was always very good and correct, and his understanding of tone and hand positions were pure Segovia. Like my father, I have quite a big thumb, whereas Segovia's was smaller and could bend a little more. A smaller, slightly bent thumb is quite good for the classic Segovia hand position, but a bigger thumb, like mine or my father's, tends to stick out too far when using Segovia's approach. This can create all sorts of other problems. I've always had to practise, but if you've been taught well, things often come naturally. If something falls naturally for my hand, I don't necessarily have to practise it. This means that I don't have to warm up for two or three hours before I perform.

RH: As you progressed very quickly on the guitar as a child, was that the motivation for the family to return to Britain?

JW: That and a teaching job that my father had accepted. My parents were also very keen to meet and to hear the jazz guitarist Django Reinhardt. As there had been a great deal of support for the Chinese revolution amongst the Australian left-wing, my father had been a member of the Communist Party for a time before returning to England. During the war, many Australians also feared that the Japanese were going to invade, which meant our garage was stacked high with tinned food. At one point, my father and a mate even stole a huge tarpaulin from a railway yard so that they could wrap up the provisions and head for the bush. That was their way of dealing with any possible Japanese invasion. But as there was no invasion, we ended up with a garage full of tinned food! When we arrived back in Britain in the January or the February of 1952, there was still rationing and everything felt very rainy and dark. My father wanted to start a guitar school in London, which many guitarists will now know as the Spanish Guitar Centre. It opened first in Little Newport Street before moving to Cranbourn Street. Sadly, Reinhardt had died before we could hear him, but we did meet Segovia. That introduction was made through a guitarist friend in Manchester: Terry Usher. I played a couple of pieces for Segovia at the Piccadilly Hotel there and he was very pleased. He then asked my father to return a couple of days later to discuss the things that I should study. My dad then wrote down the whole of the Segovia scale system, which only includes the major and melodic-minor scales. I learned that he'd written all this down after he'd arrived back in London. He also told me that Segovia would say 'empty' when referring to open strings.

RH: You were a pupil at Friern Barnet Grammar School for a period before being accepted as a student at both the Royal College of Music and the Accademia Musicale Chigiana in Siena.

JW: In fact, I went to the local secondary modern before enrolling at Friern Barnet Grammar School. I also attended the great summer school at the Chigiana in Siena, which holds classes in singing, conducting, opera and orchestral studies. When it came to the guitar, it was not like some other summer schools, which are devoted solely to that instrument. I'm very sceptical of these and much prefer summer schools that are more global in their approach. When I first went to Siena in 1953, Segovia had just undergone an eye operation. But the great Venezuelan guitarist Alirio Díaz was there, and I was able to establish a lifelong friendship with him. I then played my first concerto at Siena in 1956 with a Portuguese conductor. Zubin Mehta was a student conductor at the same concert, and Benjamin Zander, Rohan de Saram and Daniel Barenboim, a boyhood friend, were also there. Siena was a fantastic experience and a very important part of my early years. I was there annually between 1953 and 1956, and returned again in 1958 and 1960. Segovia was there in 1954. There were guitarists from all over the world, and to make friends with them was very formative for me.

RH: Tell me about the composer Stephen Dodgson, whom I also met during my first year in Britain. I remember that he had a very nice house in Barnes, South West London.

JW: I first met Stephen in 1955 when I joined the junior department of the Royal College of Music. He taught me keyboard harmony, but I don't think he was very impressed by my attempts at it. By the time I attended the College's senior department, I knew him very well. I really liked his guitar music, which was quite sharp and unconventional. This was before the serialism of the Darmstadt School in the late 1950s and the 1960s, which came and went. One of the first things that I did by Stephen was his First Guitar Concerto, which I gave in either 1958 or 1959 with Walter Goehr, the father of the composer Alexander Goehr, conducting. It had been composed in 1956, but for some reason hadn't been performed until I played it. I haven't played everything that Stephen has written for the guitar, but I did record his *Partita* and First Concerto in 1964 and 1967. On occasions, I would sit next to Stephen at the piano while he was composing. He would absolutely live the small rhythmic figures that he was writing, and I can still see him doing so when I hear the *Partita*. The most recent work of his that I've played a lot is *The Midst of Life* from 1994. It's a wonderful piece.

RH: Segovia was keen for you to participate in the 1956 Concours international d'exécution musicale de Genève. Why did you decide against taking part?

JW: The fact that the guitar had been accepted by a major competition was of great importance to Segovia. But he thought that he could 'fix' it so that I would win the competition. In other words, he thought that he could nobble the jury. But my father was very against competitions, and for very good reasons. When I was fifteen and about to sit my O levels, which I didn't do, he thought that it was time for me to go to college. This was quite important for him, even though he was not an establishment man. By nature, he was anti-establishment and self-educated, but always knew the important thing to do. He was very intelligent and very respectful of certain basic issues, even if that meant that he had to work within a system that he didn't like. He thought, therefore, that I should go to the Royal College of Music rather than to try and win a competition that might result in twenty concerts and a few hundred quid. And I still believe that he was right today. Segovia was furious, however, and my mother disagreed with my father. For all her left-wing ideas, my mother still had a latent authoritarian mind. She respected authority, and, as an Australian abroad, was slightly overwhelmed by the culture and the musical personalities that she encountered in Britain and in Europe. My mother also acted as chaperone to a young lady who later became Segovia's third wife. This meant that there was quite a bit of history between them. A rift then appeared between my father and Segovia after my dad visited his hotel and confronted him. The whole episode didn't reflect well on Segovia either, as he summoned me to say, 'I have to tell you that I am no longer your teacher, and when you are older, I'll tell you why I detest your father.' As a fifteen-year-old, I was more puzzled than hurt by this.

Nevertheless, I used to keep quiet about it for a long time, and didn't repeat it until about twenty years ago. Not for any personal reason, but just in case it might be misinterpreted. I was always concerned that some people might think that Segovia's comment was why I could be critical of him. It had nothing to do with it.

RH: In the 1960s, you toured the Soviet Union and the United States in quick succession. What were your impressions of both countries, and were you of the often expressed view that the Soviet system was more conducive for the arts in general and music in particular?

JW: From what I gathered, the Soviet system was fantastic, even though some people were either critical or defensive of it. The locals could be ashamed of their very cramped living quarters, which meant that you didn't get invited into their homes. This was often misinterpreted as them being frightened of the secret police. That was not the case: it was more to do with the individual's sense of pride. I went to the Soviet Union because of an engineer who had worked on the Tchaikovsky Concert Hall, the hall in which I later played. He'd approached Ibbs and Tillett, and had sent the agency a photograph of himself in a public concert hall with an enlarged copy of my first record cover. He then visited Gosconcert, the Soviet's state-run concert organisation, and suggested that it should invite me to play in Russia. Could you imagine somebody popping into the Arts Council today to suggest such a thing? As I was going to earn quite a few roubles that I was unable to spend in the West, and as my mother always wanted to go to the Soviet Union, I suggested that she should come with me.

I went to Estonia, Lithuania and Latvia, and my mother came for the final two weeks of the tour in Leningrad and Moscow. This was in 1962, and coincided with Stephen Dodgson's trip to the Soviet Union with a group of British composers. Not only was I able to meet up with him, but my mother and I were able to attend the premiere of Leonid Yakobson's restaged version of Khachaturian's *Spartacus* with Nikita Khrushchev in attendance. There were always stories at that time of visitors being spied on, which was clearly not always the case. Our interpreter said that she was excited to attend *Spartacus*, but asked if we wouldn't mind if she didn't come along, as her sister was graduating from university. When we said that she should go to the graduation, she was concerned that if anything should happen to us, her office wouldn't approve. But we said that we had the address of the hotel written down, and that we could get a taxi there after the performance. In the end, it was all fine. Mstislav Rostropovich used to say that the Soviet System was great, as he could play in little Russian towns and in the cities of Siberia. But for somebody of Rostropovich's stature, the system proved frustrating, and that's why it collapsed. America has no system and there are no rules. If you are lucky enough to make it, then you've made it. But it's not so good for the ones who can't.

RH: In America, you had a long relationship with CBS, and made a number of recordings for the company. Why were you so attracted to the studio?

JW: To be completely honest, I don't think that my best playing is on record. That said, I really like recording, and am very interested in the recording process. My ideal is when a recording closely represents the sound I make. That might sound easy, but it's not. And it can't be solved by simply using a good pair of microphones. That might result in an adequate job, but I am interested in an amazing job.

PART THREE: INSTRUMENTALISTS

RH: Is that why you have been very selective when working with engineers and producers? A producer with whom you worked closely was Paul Myers. How would you describe your working relationship with him?

JW: Paul helped me enormously as a young and inexperienced recording artist. We got along wonderfully well and I learned a lot from him. When I set down Stephen Dodgson's *Partita* with him in New York in 1964, the recording required quite a lot of editing. But, as a general rule, I don't like editing from take to take unless it's absolutely necessary. Of course, there are exceptions, such as when recording with an orchestra.

RH: Over the years, you have been associated with many great conductors, and had a particularly close personal and professional relationship with Sir Charles Groves. Why were you so drawn to him as a man and as a musician?

JW: He was just a lovely man, and not only did I play with him in Liverpool, but I also made a couple of concerto recordings with him, including Dodgson's First Guitar Concerto.

RH: I was at a performance of Mahler's Seventh Symphony the other night, and when the orchestral guitar started to play, I thought of you. Have you ever played orchestral guitar?

JW: I have, and when Sir John Pritchard gave the world premiere of Hans Werner Henze's *Elegy for Young Lovers* at Glyndebourne in 1961, I performed in that. I also played in Rossini's *Il barbiere di Siviglia* at Covent Garden under Carlo Maria Giulini.

RH: Julian Bream has been your close friend and colleague for some sixty years, and your performances and recordings with him have always been popular and critical successes. In what ways do you differ from him technically and musically, and why do you think that your partnership has been so successful?

JW: Julian is eight years older than me, and the first time that I ever encountered Rodrigo's *Concierto de Aranjuez* was when I heard him play its second and third movements after we moved to England. I then went to see him perform at the Tottenham Municipal Baths. He used to come to parties at my flat in New Cavendish Street, and it was he who suggested that we should form a duo. And as one of my oldest friends, the South-African-born filmmaker Christopher Nupen, had already made two films with Julian by the late 1960s, we all go back a long way. But even today, there are some listeners who prefer Julian to me. This is quite ironic considering the relationship that Julian and I have. Yet it's understandable, as we are both very different. I tend to push on with things musically and like the rhythm to be fairly constant. That doesn't mean that I play slow pieces quickly, but I do like rhythmic compositions to move on. Conversely, Julian tends to dwell. But when we perform together, we both think that this creates a terrific dynamic. When we listen to other duos play the same works as us, we notice that they fly through them as if they're so easy. Because of our very different personalities, Julian and I think very creatively when we play. And I don't want to hear people who perform together to play like identical twins, regardless of their instruments. This defeats the purpose of a duet, particularly as music is all about personality and communication. One of Christopher's early films, *Double Concerto*, with Vladimir Ashkenazy and Daniel Barenboim, was remarkable for showing their totally different ways of playing the piano. And Julian and I are even more different than that.

PART THREE: INSTRUMENTALISTS

RH: Would it be fair to say that you have stretched the guitar's repertoire chronologically forward, while Mr Bream has stretched it historically backwards?

JW: I wouldn't necessarily say that, as there are many ways of going forward. Julian, for example, would put his heart and soul into learning a long, modern work like Henze's *Royal Winter Music*. That's something I'd never have the patience to do. Yet it's true that when it comes to lute music, he does go further back than me. After Julian's automobile accident in 1984, he showed a degree of determination that I don't have. Then again, I once sat in our holiday house in France for two weeks listening to sixty records of African music. Julian would never do that. Sometimes, musical taste has little to do with the music you necessarily like. I once recorded Leo Brouwer's First Guitar Concerto, which is written in an aleatoric manner and is more 'contemporary' than some other contemporary music. And it's a false idea that I don't like new music. It's more to do with what the work actually is.

RH: Both you and Julian Bream have performed and recorded transcriptions. What's the essence of a good transcription?

JW: It depends on the transcription, of course, but they should be able to stand on their own merits and not simply be a copy of the original. There's a tendency, possibly out of respect, to squeeze in as many notes as possible from the original into a transcription. This is something of a musical blind alley. If the original was written for the piano, then it's impossible to play all the notes on the guitar. It's important to think about the character of the piece and how it should come over. Let me give you an example. Granados's *Valses poéticos* is a beautiful piano piece. I was introduced to the work by Paul Myers after he recorded it with

Alicia de Larrocha in the 1960s. I recorded all but two of the eight movements, as I couldn't work out a way to transcribe the other two faithfully. Subsequently, I did the complete set, and recorded all eight movements. But as the sections need to feel continuous, the biggest problem was how to transition from key to key without retuning the guitar in performance. The real bugbear was the waltz in D minor. As the movement before is in F major, and the one after is in B flat major, it was necessary to retune the guitar for the D minor waltz. This totally destroyed the flow of the overall piece. So, when I started to play them again two or three years ago, I decided to find a key that gives the same feeling without having to retune. I opted for A minor. This meant that when I went from F major to A minor to B flat major, I was able to do so without retuning the guitar. Some people might say that this is a questionable alteration, but, in fact, it actually realises the musical feeling of the original without breaking the flow of the work.

RH: Do you consider it an ethical and an artistic priority for performing artists to champion the works of their contemporaries?

JW: As a general principle, no. Performers should play music that they really like, and if that happens to be new music, fine.

RH: Presumably, you are sent scores of new music regularly. Where do you draw the line?

JW: Let me take you back a generation or so to the BBC's Thursday Invitation Concerts, dubbed the 'Thursday Irritation Concerts' by many of us who had to play in them. It could be argued that it's the duty of the BBC to give composers airtime, and to hire performers to play their works. But this is where the line becomes blurred. As a musician, I don't feel it a duty to play something simply because it's new or to help a composer. To do so would be very patronising. And with the exception of the Thursday Invitation Concerts, I've never done this. While I loved playing at those events, the works that I gave were something akin to crossword puzzles or chess problems. It was more a sound thing for me, rather than a musical one. It was nice to be able to play the notes and to create the complicated sounds. To make something decent out of the compositions was important to me, even though I didn't think that they meant much culturally or emotionally. But, as a general rule, every piece that I've played by a contemporary composer has been one that I've really liked.

RH: You've championed contemporary Australian composers for much of your career. In what ways do their works exhibit musical fingerprints that define them as being quintessentially Australian?

JW: Peter Sculthorpe's music is, for example, very Australian. He's inspired by the geology, culture, history and traditions of the Northern Territory and its links with the archipelago of Indonesia. In fact, he extends his interests to Japan, and is a lover of Japanese theatre and Japanese theatre music. Yet, when representing the spirit of Australia, he wouldn't necessarily link it to Australia *per se*, or to the fact that he's Australian. For me, it's the slow harmonic rhythm of his music that makes it Australian. His works are not descriptive, and they don't describe the Northern Territory. Like an impressionist painter, he's simply expressing his reaction to it. Perhaps it's for these reasons that he's extremely underrated in Britain. That's a shame, as a great deal of his music is seriously great. Today, we are obsessed with complexity, and we think that a lot of harmony and quick harmonic change are good things. If a work doesn't have these qualities, then it's thought to be lacking in some way. This is a seriously flawed idea. When I react to Peter's music, I do so in a very organic way. I respond to the tree and not to the leaves.

RH: Over the years, you have been associated with a number of luthiers. For a period, you preferred the guitars of Ignacio Fleta, but now you play on an instrument made by the reclusive Australian maker Greg Smallman. What are some of the constructional hallmarks that define his instruments?

JW: I first met Greg in 1979 when I was in Sydney to do some teaching. He and a friend of his had a couple of guitars with them, and they wanted to know what I thought of them. This happens to me quite often. But if you've something constructive to say, and suggest a valid criticism, the maker always has an excuse. Politeness forbids one from saying, 'Well, why did you bring it to me, then?' Yet when I made a critical comment to Greg, he was refreshingly honest. He said, 'The Fleta is such a fantastic instrument that I don't know why we bother.' I was very impressed by his attitude. He then made contact again a couple of days later and said, 'I've been thinking. Is there anything about the Fleta that could be improved?' I thought that was an interesting question, from an interesting man who had an interesting way of putting things. And because of his great respect for the Fleta, we were able to get started. I do like the Fleta's lovely rich bass, a quality that doesn't appeal to some guitarists. But the instrument can feel a bit stiff. Even by the second half of a concert, when the Fleta has usually warmed up, the first five frets of the first string can still be a bit stiff and hard. With this as his starting point, Greg began to develop his lattice top.

Traditionally, guitars have used the fan-like struts that were introduced by the Spanish luthier Antonio de Torres Jurado in the middle of the nineteenth century. While earlier guitars did have a full tone, they were somewhat quieter. Torres developed his system to meet the Spanish need to make the instrument project more, but the result was a rather more percussive guitar than most previous instruments. Fleta constructed his guitars within that tradition, a tradition that remains the Bible for many players. Greg's lattice brace resembles the simple strutting of early nineteenth-century instruments, where there were only one or two cross braces. Steel-string guitars, and other popular versions of the instrument, don't use fan strutting. This means that they sustain better and are less percussive. Not only do Greg's guitars sustain the sound well, but they have lighter tops that react like the skin of a drum. This allows the player to feel the sound and to sustain it more intimately while performing.

RH: As an Australian who has lived in Britain for the majority of his life, I am always asked if I feel more British than Australian. I'm sure that you've also been asked a similar question. How do you respond to it?

JW: I usually answer rather glibly by saying that I am neither Australian nor English, but a Londoner. And even that's not completely true, as I spend half my time in Cornwall. But if I had to jump one way or the other, I'd have to say that I'm an Australian, even though I love England and the English. When we left Australia in 1952, it was far from ethnically diverse, a situation that remained largely unchanged until the early 1970s. This made me feel very uncomfortable. What I love about England and Europe is their cultural mix, the lifeblood of any society. But Australians are brilliant at seeing through the class system. Not only are they open, but they have humour.

RH: Television and film helped to make John Williams into a household name, and your appearances with Eric Sykes, Val Doonican and Les

Dawson did much in putting the classical guitar before the general public. How did the critics and the public react to those appearances, and where do you think the guitar's future lies?

JW: Val Doonican and Eric Sykes both adored the guitar, and I met Eric at the beginning of the 1960s when we were guests on the Billy Cotton Band Show. I played, and Eric did his act. This involved him sitting at a desk ostensibly 'practising' his guitar. He used to mime to Segovia's recording of Bach's *Gavotte*, and could play well enough to do so convincingly. We got chatting during the filming, and he contacted me again some time later. He wanted to know if we could do something together that was not dissimilar to his Segovia routine. When we did this, I would play off stage, and he would again mime to the music perfectly. And no matter what the show was, he would always ensure that I had an opportunity to play a proper classical solo. The same was true when I worked with Val Doonican. Yet when I took part in shows like these during the 1960s and the 1970s, many thought that it was a very bad idea. It's hard to believe how snobbish some people were and still are. To be able to play Bach's *Gavotte* to 18 million viewers on a Saturday night cannot be a bad thing. As the shows were broadcast live, they could be a bit nerve-racking. But what a way for audiences to hear the classical guitar for the first time.

The guitar, as championed by Segovia, has been a fantastic addition to the world of classical music. It built on the nineteenth-century tradition of having composers write for it, and I hope that this approach continues. But I believe that there is another dimension for the instrument that is both culturally and socially important, and that allows it to act as a kind of fifth columnist in the best and most creative way. Thanks to the modern digital age, our ability to absorb and to understand other musical cultures has risen to a level that was unimaginable thirty years ago. Simon Broughton, for example, who edits *Soul Lives* and broadcasts on BBC Radio 3, makes programmes that include everything from Japanese drummers to the music of Outer Mongolia. They're fantastic. The plucked string of the guitar is a universal sound that is quite unique. Unlike a woodwind instrument or a piano, you are still able to shape the guitar's sound as it dies away, thanks to such things as *vibrato*. This quality is shared by the Japanese koto, the Indian sitar and the West African kora. I believe that the future of music depends upon European music taking its place alongside other musical cultures. European music is not the only musical culture, and it's certainly not the best. No single musical culture is the best. Music has come full circle, and we're now able to acknowledge that each culture has developed at its own pace. As the sound of the guitar can connect in a very real way with these other cultures, it can act as a fifth columnist. That's its future.

STEVEN ISSERLIS
(DAVID JOSEFOWITZ RECITAL HALL, 20 FEBRUARY 2015)

RAYMOND HOLDEN: You are one of the most-travelled musicians working today, and, for many, the doyen of modern cellists. Your repertoire is extensive, and you've never been afraid to challenge audiences' musical conceptions and misconceptions wherever you've performed. As you tour so much, what's an average week like for you, and what might that involve?

STEVEN ISSERLIS: Last week I was in Zurich, and next week I'm in Salzburg and Basel. This week, I am in London practising lots of Beethoven, as I am about to perform all of his sonatas. I'm also currently trying to get Bach's Cello Suites back into my fingers, as I foolishly agreed to play them for the first time in eight years. After recording them, I thought, 'Great, I don't have to play them any more', not because I don't love, adore and worship them, but because I find them terrifying to play. And although I thought that I wouldn't have to perform them again, Mr John Gilhooly of the Wigmore Hall is extremely tenacious, and a very hard man to say 'no' to. So, I finally said 'yes', and will be playing them at the hall next year. Mainly, I've been thinking about Beethoven and tuning my cello down to A=430, which is supposedly Classical pitch; something of a myth, actually. But that's the pitch that Robert Levin tunes his fortepianos to when we play together, the pitch at which those instruments respond best. I'll be playing on pure gut strings and with a light bow. Some aspects of touring life I really don't like, particularly when it comes to nerves and jet lag. But the thought of spending a week with Bach and Beethoven is not such a bad prospect. That, I like.

RH: Would it be fair to say that music has been ever present throughout your family's history?

SI: My grandfather was born in Moldova, but was really Russian-Jewish. As a pianist, he studied with Sergei Taneyev, who also taught Rachmaninoff, Medtner and Scriabin. Something of a child prodigy, my grandfather was either the youngest person to win the Moscow Conservatory's Gold Medal, or the youngest professor to be appointed there. As a composer, he studied for a year in Paris with Charles-Marie Widor, before being one of twelve Soviet musicians who were given permission by Lenin to travel abroad with their families for six months in 1922. Lenin thought that this was a great way of spreading the word about the cultural oasis that was the Soviet Union. This was a good idea except that none of the twelve ever returned! Having been amongst the last musicians to be allowed to leave the Soviet Union, my grandfather planned to go to America, where he'd been some time earlier thanks to the recommendation of Scriabin. But, having given a successful concert in Vienna *en route*, he decided to remain there with my grandmother and my five-year-old father. They then started to look for an apartment and eventually found one owned by a 102-year-old *Hausfrau*. She seemed extremely friendly until my grandfather said, 'Is it okay for me to practise here?' 'No,' she replied, 'I hate musicians.' A strange comment coming from a Viennese. In an attempt to get to the bottom of this, my grandfather then asked, 'Why do you hate musicians?' 'Because when I was a little girl, my aunt had a lodger who was a filthy old man who used to spit all over the floor.' My grandfather asked, 'Who was that?' 'Beethoven' was her reply. So, my father actually met somebody who'd met Beethoven.

RH: How, then, did your family get to London?

SI: In 1938, my grandfather was invited to tour Britain for the first time, and within a week of arriving, the *Anschluss* happened. After deciding to stay here, he then spent several months trying to bring my father and grandmother over from Austria.

RH: You were born twenty years later, and after attending the City of London School, you went on to study in Scotland and America.

SI: I was a pupil of Jane Cowan, who had studied with Emanuel Feuermann and Donald Tovey. She was a great, but eccentric, lady who came with a good musical pedigree. Although she could be quite scary at times, she had charisma. I began studying with Jane when I was ten, and even returned for lessons with her after I went to America at the age of seventeen. She was my main teacher. After sitting my O levels, I left school when I was fourteen. I then studied with Jane in London for another year, before following her to Scotland. There, I continued to work with her for another two years. I'm very pleased that I didn't go to a specialist music school, as there's always the danger of receiving an unbalanced education. I went to a normal school.

RH: What attracted you to America at such an early age?

SI: Jane Cowan was very loath to let me go there, as she thought I'd be corrupted. The one person she did like was Gregor Piatigorsky. I then raised the money necessary to study with him in Los Angeles, and even passed my driving test to make my stay there a little easier. A pointless exercise, as it turned out, as I haven't been behind the wheel of a car for well over thirty years. I'm something of a danger to traffic! After studying with Piatigorsky that summer in Zurich, I was all set to join him in America, but then the news came that he'd died. Before that, I'd met Steven Doane at a competition in Bristol when I was sixteen, the last major competition that I took part in. After I introduced him to my teacher in Scotland, he introduced me to his in America. And that's how I ended up studying with Richard Kapuscinski at the Oberlin Conservatory of Music between 1976 and 1978.

RH: Aside from Piatigorsky, who were some of your other early musical heroes?

SI: Two cellists whom I admire are Pablo Casals and Daniil Shafran. I loved them when I was little and I love them today. I particularly admired Shafran when I was a teenager, but now that I'm older, I'm increasingly drawn to Casals. There are others, of course, such as Paul Tortelier. As a little boy, I used to listen to Schumann's Cello Concerto played by various artists, but, at the time, I thought it a bit of an odd piece that I didn't really understand and couldn't easily remember. When I discovered Casals's recording of the concerto, that all changed, and I was suddenly able to remember the whole work. Casals made sense of the music, and I love his depth and truth. Shafran was very different. He was like a Russian folk singer who happened to play the cello, and it's his freedom and fantasy that I admire.

RH: Can you identify a major turning point in your career?

SI: I seem to have emerged gradually, and it was through the recommendations of other musicians, rather than through competitions, that my career progressed. As I said earlier, the last major competition that I took part in was in Bristol, where I got to the second round. After that, I was always knocked out in the first stage. I decided thereafter that competitions were a bad thing. I've a similar response to critics who give me bad reviews, as opposed to those who give me good reviews. The latter are clearly geniuses! *The Protecting Veil* by John Tavener gave my career a lift, but it was through the help of colleagues, such as Olli Mustonen, who introduced me to his agents, HarrisonParrott, and Joshua Bell, another great friend, that my career developed.

RH: From the information found on your website, it seems that you programme in blocks. In January, for example, concertos dominate, while in February and March, you'll be devoting your time to the Beethoven project that we discussed earlier. Why do you programme in that way?

SI: It just happens. I'm very happy to play the same concerto for three weeks running, but that's quite a rare occurrence. The concerto you're referring to is that by Walton, which I'm asked to play regularly. I adore the work, but many listeners don't know it. And when three consecutive orchestras asked me to play it, I was able to introduce it to a wider audience. The Beethoven cycle that I'm performing with Robert Levin will be given four times. Giving the cycle four times in a row is very helpful for me, as the cello has to be set up in a particular way to meet the demands of playing with a fortepiano.

RH: Presumably, you are one of the few cellists who alternates between period and modern styles.

PART THREE: INSTRUMENTALISTS

SI: It's become increasingly common, and I don't see a huge difference between the two. I play on gut strings most of time, which, of course, is something that's associated with the period instrument movement. When I began learning the cello, the use of gut strings was not as rare as one might think. My teacher always played on them, and some of the older generation, such as William Pleeth, Jacqueline du Pré's teacher, also used gut strings. Although they weren't fashionable for a time, I've stuck with them. I don't find it difficult to alternate between period and modern instruments. The analogy I always use relates to Shakespeare. It's of little consequence whether you perform *King Lear* or *Hamlet* with the original pronunciation, as Lear still falls out with his daughters and Hamlet still murders his uncle.

RH: A recording of yours that I find particularly intriguing is that of Beethoven's Horn Sonata arranged for cello. Does it sit well on the cello?

SI: Fairly well, but not brilliantly. But you can still tell that it's Beethoven. There's also a transcription for cello and piano of his String Trio, Op. 3, numbered Op. 64. That's a truly bad arrangement, and can't be by Beethoven.

RH: Over the last fifty years or so, transcriptions have fallen from favour. What are your thoughts on the genre in general, and are you happy to play them at live concerts?

SI: Of course, particularly as the transcription of the Horn Sonata is by the composer, a work that I love. And what I usually do as an encore is my transcription of his 'Mandolin' Variations in D major. But in the case of some transcriptions, you lose too much and they shouldn't be done. I used to play a transcription of Brahms's First Violin Sonata, but it was obvious to me that it was better on the violin. Whereas Schumann's Third Violin Sonata, which I transcribed for cello myself, sounds to me just as good on the cello as it does on the violin, and I hope that my transcription brings something to the piece that's missing in the original. It's just a matter of quality.

RH: Curiously, Benjamin Britten sanctions the use of a cello instead of the horn when playing his *Serenade for Tenor, Horn and Strings* domestically. Have you ever performed the piece on the cello?

SI: No, as the horn is essential to the work. It's a completely different matter when it comes to Beethoven's sonata. In Britten's work, his magical use of the horn means that I could never imagine the cello replacing it.

RH: You play on a Stradivarius. What are your thoughts on Norbert Brainin's thesis that instruments by Stradivarius, and here he was referring specifically to violins, resonate better at A=432?

SI: That's interesting, as he never played flat. I once performed Mozart's Quintet in G minor with Brainin playing first violin and with Joshua Bell playing second. Afterwards, Norbert said to Joshua, 'I'm thinking of selling my violin; you should try it.' Joshua did so, and it was amazing. He then asked, 'How much do you want to sell it for?' Norbert replied, 'For you, £5 million.' A mere snip.

RH: Your recording of Bach's Cello Suites is remarkable for many reasons, not the least of which is your treatment of the Prelude to the First Suite, where you played from various manuscripts and editions. Where do you stand on the debate concerning Anna Magdalena's involvement in the composition of them?

PART THREE: INSTRUMENTALISTS

SI: There's no evidence whatsoever that Anna Magdalena wrote the suites. It's also been suggested that Bach's first wife, Maria Barbara, probably committed suicide, because she'd found out that he was having an affair with Anna Magdalena. I didn't quite understand the logic behind all of this. I recently read an interview with the principal advocate of these ideas in an Italian newspaper, where he said his favourite performance of the suites was mine. Although I felt very guilty, I can't accept his theory. As in Beethoven's cello sonatas, there's a great deal of humour in Bach's suites. And side by side with this humour, there are moments of great profundity. Every note is so human. I'd never swap Beethoven's Cello Sonatas for his Violin Sonatas, and I wouldn't swap Bach's Cello Suites for his Violin Sonatas. As great as the violin works surely are, they're far more academic than the Cello Suites. Perhaps 'academic' is a slightly stupid word when discussing such sublime works of genius, but as the Cello Suites are so human, they talk to you.

RH: Recording works that were once lost, but since rediscovered, is a thread that runs through a number of your discs. Haydn's Cello Concerto No. 1 in C major is a case in point. Rediscovered in 1961 by Oldřich Pulkert at the Prague National Museum, the concerto's cello part is alternately marked '*solo*' and '*tutti*'. This suggests that it might have been performed by a front-desk cellist when given for the first time at Esterházy. Have you ever considered performing the work in this manner, and in what ways does Haydn's writing for the cello in the C major concerto differ from that in the later D major concerto?

SI: I wouldn't play it from the front desk, but I would play along with the orchestral celli in the *tutti* passages. Perhaps more interesting in this regard are Boccherini's concertos, or at least the two that I play. In these, there's no bass line while the solo cello is playing. At those moments, the bass line is found in the violas, or even the second violins. This implies that Boccherini was the only cellist available, and that he had a cello-bass line for the *tutti* passages. It's a beautiful effect and I love Boccherini. Haydn's D major concerto was usually played in a bowdlerised version.

RH: Was that because the first movement's exposition was thought to be too long?

SI: Perhaps. But any excision is unnecessary, as the work is wonderful as it is.

RH: Would you agree that Haydn's two concertos occupy two different sound-worlds?

SI: In some ways, the C major is the great Classical concerto, as it's wonderful and full of virtuosity. The D major is more operatic, with many more 'singable' melodies. While the concertos are very different, they both have a certain radiant joy. And having recently played them a week apart, their differences and similarities were clearly apparent to me.

RH: Have you ever played them both on the same programme?

SI: I have, and, of course, audiences love Haydn. It's wonderful. There's a nice little trick that I do in the D major concerto. Haydn was always keen to show off his Esterházy orchestra, and at the end of the last movement, the oboes and horns finally get their big moment. I now ask them to stand and play, and they're always quite happy to do so. The violins also get their moment to show off, as I also get them to stand up. By the end, almost all of us are standing, a situation that Haydn would've approved of.

PART THREE: INSTRUMENTALISTS

RH: A composition that *was* conceived with a front-desk player in mind was Strauss's *Don Quixote*. Have you ever performed this work from the front desk, or do you think that would detract from the cello part's virtuosic qualities?

SI: I sometimes sit directly in front of the cellos, as I have to play along with them for much of the work. But, of course, that depends on the disposition of the orchestra and the placement of the second violins. It's not a cello concerto, but a marvellous piece to play.

RH: When Strauss conducted the work himself, he performed it with both a front-desk player and a soloist. When asked to give the work in London in 1899, he was offered £30 by the Philharmonic Society, but turned it down not only because it was a derisory fee, but because he was concerned that the Society's cellist, W. H. Squire, might not be up to the job with only one full orchestral rehearsal.

SI: Of course, there are some section leaders that are wonderful cellists. And both approaches are not so different, as they each require the player to face out to be heard.

RH: I was thinking more of the piece's narrative and how Don Quixote is perceived as an antihero.

SI: Don't forget that it's not only the cello who represents Don Quixote. He's also represented by other members of the orchestra. It's not like the cello *is* Don Quixote – it is when it's playing solo – but many other instruments also occupy that role. I'd love to do the piece with a film of the story. There are not many pieces that I'd like to add a video to, but in the case of *Don Quixote*, every bar describes a specific event in the book. You could make a wonderful animated, or even non-animated, film of it. I'd love to do that, and have already spoken to various people about it. But, so far, it's gone nowhere.

RH: Have you ever played Strauss's Cello Sonata, which was written when he was a teenager and dedicated to the renowned Czech cellist Hanuš Wihan?

SI: I've recorded it with Stephen Hough. I also recorded the *Romanze*, which is a beautiful work. Strauss is not my favourite composer, but I did make an all-Strauss disc. And while I like the cello music, I loathe *Salome*. I hated it when I saw it. But *Don Quixote*, which I've recorded twice – first with Edo de Waart and, later, with Lorin Maazel – is great. And as I said, the *Romanze* is very beautiful.

RH: A composer who influenced the young Strauss was Robert Schumann, an artist about whom you made a documentary. What attracts you to his music?

SI: I loved the name Schumann as a little boy, and I remember picking up a volume of his letters while I was waiting for my lesson with my teacher at her house in Ladbroke Grove. I thought, 'What a beautiful way of writing.' Consequently, I became more and more interested in the composer. As I got older, I found his music incredibly touching.

RH: Do you share the unease of some conductors when it comes to his orchestral technique?

SI: No. What I'm uneasy about is the wisdom of those conductors, as there are no problems with his approach. When his works are performed on original instruments, the orchestration sounds wonderful. I don't know what all the fuss is about. Shostakovich re-orchestrated the Cello Concerto, and later wished he hadn't. It's perfect as it is. Some people say Schumann was a miniaturist: they're wrong. The symphonies are wonderful. Perhaps the greatest problem for Schumann is that he can't be pigeonholed. He took so many different directions, especially towards the end of his life. He was steeped in the classics as a choral conductor, and he performed works by Orlande de Lassus and Heinrich Schütz, amongst others. And yet he was also a modernist who was writing incredibly forward-looking music at the end of his life. He's something of a problem for the critics, as they have trouble understanding him. If they identify one aspect of Schumann, they then find that the opposite is also true.

RH: You made a film of Schumann's Cello Concerto when you were quite young.

SI: We recorded the sound first, and then mimed to our first edit elsewhere. The venue seemed like a bunker. It was a very sinister place with a horrible history. It had been a factory where prisoners were made to build submarines during the Second World War. When some of the prisoners died, some of their remains were incorporated into the building. In contrast to the concerto, it was a weird place that was both dramatic and striking. As the venue was soaking wet, which was a great problem, I decided to play on a modern cello that I'd borrowed. And although I was overdubbing, I was still actually playing. The sound recording with Christoph Eschenbach was later released commercially with a few minor changes.

RH: In your liner notes for your recording of Brahms's Cello Sonatas with your friend Stephen Hough, you wrote of the First Sonata: 'Brahms [stakes] his claim as the greatest "classical romantic" [*sic*] composer of chamber music.' What do you mean by that?

SI: I find Brahms a very interesting figure, and am most attracted to his early and late works. The effect of watching Schumann deteriorate, and falling in love with the composer's widow, was both traumatic and horrifying, resulting in Brahms growing a beard, both physically and musically. If you perform the earlier version of the B major trio, which I prefer, you encounter quotes from songs that Clara loved. But after Schumann's death, these are removed, and Brahms becomes a Classical composer. It's only towards the end of his life that he returns to being experimental. I love the Cello Sonatas, but they are very Classical. You could call the First Sonata an 'historical sonata'. The first movement, which is my favourite movement from both the sonatas, is glorious. It embodies the idea of a Romantic-Classical sonata, while the second movement is a tribute to Haydn and Mozart. It also references Schubert and Beethoven – the *Scherzo* from the Sonata in A major – with the last movement quoting Bach through its fugal writing. The Sonata in F major is gloriously Romantic, but, again, constructed completely classically. And it's only in works like the late piano pieces and the Clarinet Quintet that I feel that Brahms fully recovers his experimental edge.

RH: A striking aspect of your Brahms recording, and for that matter many of your other discs, is its format. Along with Brahms's sonatas, the disc contains works by Dvořák and Suk, effectively creating a well-programmed recital in digital form. The same is true of your discs of Martinů's and Adès's works. How much control do you have over the final product, and is your holistic approach something you would recommend to other artists?

PART THREE: INSTRUMENTALISTS

SI: I choose the repertoire to be recorded. The label for which I record most is Hyperion, and Simon Perry who runs it said rather gloomily the other day, 'I've given up arguing about repertoire with you, Steven, as you'll never give way.' Which I suppose is true. If you want to record something that's not going to sell, it's not fair on the company. But I always have in mind what people might like, and what I like. There has to be a balance. The disc that I made containing Adès's music was completely against Hyperion's principles, as it contained the music of five different composers. It really was like a recital programme. But I pointed out that the link was Adès, as the other four composers – Liszt, Fauré, Kurtág and Janáček – were all major influences on him. To make this clear, we finished the disc with Adès's piece. There always has to be an idea behind such a project. And then there is my latest disc with Stephen Hough, which not only contains works by Mendelssohn and Grieg, but also Stephen's own sonata for cello and piano left hand. It really was something of a struggle to justify that recording's combination of composers in my sleeve notes!

RH: Your sleeve notes are always beautifully written and engaging. Do you think that they're part of the whole experience of recording, and do you also think that all artists should be able to put into words their understanding of a particular piece?

SI: It's important to put into words what you feel about a piece and your understanding of its history. It's a fascinating process, regardless of whether or not it influences the way you play the work. One should be interested in the composer who wrote the music. Nobody else is able to describe what I see in those pieces as accurately as I can, and it makes complete sense for me to write about them. One should always read about the work that one's about to play. My teacher was a keen advocate of that. When I first started playing the Walton Concerto, she made me read Sacheverell Sitwell, as she thought it would give me an introduction to Walton's world. Although I can't say how exactly, it was extremely helpful in alerting me to the aesthetic that 'enshrouded' him. Writing sleeve notes is hard work, but I enjoy it. I've just finished the notes for my disc of Bach's gamba sonatas, which are not that easy to write about. But it was interesting to research the material in that way.

RH: You've also written two books for young people. What prompted you to explore this genre?

SI: The first book was for my son, who'd just started to become interested in classical music at the time. Excitedly, he said to me, 'Daddy, I heard some Schumann today.' As it turned out, it was Beethoven. I wanted to find a book for him that would tell him the stories of the great composers, but that proved difficult. I had some tapes that had come from Canada called *Beethoven Lives Upstairs* and *Mr Bach Comes to Call*. Of course, they were fantasies, but he liked them. And I liked them, too. But as I considered the real stories to be fascinating enough, I felt that there was no need to make them into fantasies. I then wrote a chapter about Beethoven on 'spec', and Faber & Faber accepted it. That's how *Beethoven Threw the Stew* came about. They then commissioned the second book, and would now like a third. But I simply don't have the time to write a new book, and, if I did, it would be for adults. I do have one in mind, but I'm not sure that I'll ever get around to writing it.

RH: As you have recorded and performed Dvořák's music widely, I'm keen to hear your take on his compositional style, and whether or not you consider his music to be quintessentially Czech.

PART THREE: INSTRUMENTALISTS

SI: He certainly thought it was, and if he saw his name spelled without the correct accents in a shop window, he'd go into that shop and pencil them in himself. He was a true patriot, and he constantly referred to himself as a Czech, even though he wrote in German. Dvořák was one of the first composers to incorporate folk music into symphonic form, and that was probably one of the reasons why Brahms held him in such high regard.

RH: Your recording of Dvořák's Cello Concerto includes an alternative ending to the last movement. Why did you decide to include it on the disc?

SI: When he was writing his concerto, Dvořák heard that his beloved sister-in-law, Josefina, was ill. And in the middle of the slow movement, he inserts a reference to the song of his that she loved most. Having completed the concerto, he returned to Prague and learned that she'd died. In response to her death, he wrote an alternative *coda*, which makes the last movement much longer and much more beautiful. Even though I've recorded the original ending, I can't believe that he would've preferred it to the later one. The earlier version just doesn't work, and is really only included on my disc as an 'appendix'.

RH: As you are a master interpreter of Elgar's Cello Concerto, do you sense foreign audiences are still reluctant to accept the composer's music fully?

SI: Less now than previously. When I performed the concerto with the Berlin Philharmonic for the first time, they hadn't played it for ten years. They were on tenterhooks, which is rather good, as it made me feel a bit more relaxed. But I've had problems with conductors when performing the work abroad. There was a particular conductor in America who told the orchestra that certain passages were like eating cucumber sandwiches and drinking tea with the vicar. Imagine saying such a thing about such great, universal music. I've never understood what the problem is. When I played Elgar's Piano Quintet at Salzburg last summer, I was slightly worried that the audience wouldn't like it. But they loved the work. And well they should: it's a masterpiece. The Cello Concerto is endlessly moving.

RH: I remember discussing your interpretation of the Cello Concerto with the filmmaker Tony Palmer, who considered it completely unique. How would you compare your interpretation with those of Beatrice Harrison and Jacqueline du Pré?

SI: Their performances are very much in the moment, and perhaps the best way to describe their approaches to the concerto is that they play it in a 'first-person way'. Their recordings are wonderful, and I love them both equally. But, for me, the concerto is the work of an old man looking back through a poem of regret. He's reflecting on all that he's lost with an incredible aching sadness. The *coda* to the last movement is particularly moving. It's both so beautiful and incredibly sad.

RH: A piece that was given its premiere two years before Elgar's concerto was Bloch's *Schelomo*, a work that was reflective of the crisis that the world faced at the time. What message should we take from these two great works?

SI: As they are music, perhaps we should simply be moved by them. All music should sound like new music, as if it's just been composed, or being composed as you're playing it. For works like those by Elgar and

Bloch, it's unfortunate that performance traditions have grown up around them. This can often result in self-indulgent interpretations. The form in Elgar's piece is much clearer than in Bloch's, which is really a rhapsody. In order to give the latter structure, the player has to be very disciplined, and must follow all of the composer's markings. In both works, there's an annotation on almost every note, an instruction that you have to follow. They're not there by accident. As beautiful as *Schelomo* is, I prefer *From Jewish Life*. *Schelomo* has been described as being akin to a Hollywood score. But it influenced Hollywood, and not the other way around. And as it's about King Solomon, it has to have wisdom and dignity.

RH: From a close reading of your discography, it seems that man's inhumanity to man is a trope that links many of your discs. Was that your intention?

SI: First and foremost, my recordings are of music I like. But when it comes to my discs of Messiaen's *Quatuor pour la fin du temps* and Shostakovich's Second Piano Trio, the issue of man's inhumanity to man is certainly present in those pieces. And my recording of Shostakovich's and Prokofiev's cello concertos does consider the idea of good versus evil, but that's simply because the works themselves address those issues. I'm also personally convinced that Bach's Cello Suites portray the life of Christ, which I find an inspiring thought. But it doesn't affect the way I play those works; it just inspires me. The content of the score is the music, and my emotional response to it in no way affects how I approach it technically.

RH: How do you go about preparing a work for performance?

SI: I often start by working through a piece at the piano and analysing it structurally. If you don't know what the different subjects are, it's like reading a novel and not knowing who the main characters are and what happens to them. That's why I work at the piano for several hours. It allows me to see the piece from above and to understand its shape. Unless it's an incredibly complicated modern work, I find that a day or two is usually enough to prepare a chamber music programme, provided that I am playing with friends I know well and that we are all properly prepared. Either you're on the same wavelength, or you're not. It's rather like when you meet somebody at a party and you immediately start talking to them. You find that you've everything to talk about. Conversely, you can meet another person and struggle even to talk about the weather. It's like that with musicians. Some are on the same wavelength as you, and some aren't. It's a conversation.

RH: Earlier, we touched on the issue of touring. Can you expand on this a little?

SI: The greatest problem is being away from home, particularly if you are in a relationship or have children. Jet lag and waking in the middle of the night is horrible. You can hear the clock ticking, and you know that you have a rehearsal in a few hours and a concert after that. It's not a nice feeling, but you learn to cope with it. But it's also marvellous to have friends around the world. I do tend to judge countries by their audiences and their food. That's what matters most! But, joking aside, no matter what happens, music must always come first. Not your career, not your agent and not your audience. If you start playing for them, and not for the music itself, then you're lost.

JOANNA MACGREGOR
(DAVID JOSEFOWITZ RECITAL HALL, 9 JANUARY 2017)

RAYMOND HOLDEN: Concert pianist, festival director, recording artist, writer, broadcaster, conductor, composer, pedagogue and impresario are all activities that are inextricably linked to the name Joanna MacGregor. This breathtaking compendium of skills and talents represents all that's best about being a great international artist. But how did it all begin, and in what ways did your formative experiences help shape the mature Joanna MacGregor?

JOANNA MACGREGOR: My early years were really quite unusual. I didn't attend school until I was eleven, which was a very good idea! I've since realised that if you can stay out of the system until you're eleven, it can't get you back. And when I finally went to school, I couldn't believe that I was sitting in a classroom with a teacher who was telling us what to think and what to write; up until that point, I'd largely been self-taught. My father worked nights, and when he returned in the morning, I'd be there to let him in at about 6.30am. And the first question that he'd always ask was, 'Have you been studying?' I'd reply dutifully, 'Yes, yes, yes!' My mother played the piano, and she gave me very informal piano lessons. The majority of my education came from reading books, which was something that really appealed to me. It prepared me for the need to be on my own: the ability to work, read and study. This is what pianists do, as they're not members of an orchestra. But along with the ability to be rather solitary, pianists also have to be ebullient enough to step on stage.

RH: Many conductors whom I've interviewed over the years have talked about both the importance and problems of solitude. Is the ability to be solitary an essential part of being a musician?

JM: Yes, and I don't think that being solitary is a problem at all. It's fabulous to be on your own with a piece of music. I can't think of anything better than sitting at the piano and studying what you're about to play. As a musician, you have to travel a great deal by yourself. In some ways, this compensates for when you're performing. When you're rehearsing with an orchestra, you're often with people you don't know very well. And after the concert, you'll also meet many people you don't know well. So, to be solitary can be a nice balance.

RH: Like many renowned artists before and since, you studied with Professor Christopher Elton, your distinguish predecessor here at the Royal Academy of Music. What are your memories of those years with him?

JM: As I only ever had two teachers, the first being my mother, Chris was incredibly impactful. When I started having lessons with him, he, too, was very young. It's easy to forget that he wasn't the legendary figure that he now is. He was yet to become Head of Piano at the Academy, and was a *young* professor who was very active as an examiner for the Associated Board of the Royal Schools of Music and as a private teacher. Looking back, it's now clear to me that Chris was cutting his teeth as a teacher, and I know that he thought I was very unusual!

PART THREE: INSTRUMENTALISTS

RH: How did your experiences with Professor Elton help shape your later activities?

JM: Students at the Academy are shocked when I tell them that I had my last piano lesson when I was twenty-two. These days, students continue lessons for much longer, but, back then, it was common to stop earlier and to move into the world of work. I started studying with Chris when I was seventeen, but I was a student at Cambridge and not at the Academy. I used to take the early train from Cambridge, have a lesson at Chris's home every three or four weeks, and then catch the late train back to university. After I finished my degree there, I said to him rather timorously, 'I'd like to have a go at becoming a pianist.' I'd like to stress here that for any young musician there will always be some key figures in their lives, and that they should stick with them. In my life, there was the great record producer James Mallinson, who produced many of my recordings when I was younger. He'd often argue with me about how I was approaching a work, but I stuck with him. Another important figure was the Radio 3 producer Nigel Wilkinson. I also met him when I was young, and he'll be producing my new recording of Chopin's mazurkas. And then there is my long-standing agent, David Sigall, whom I have been with for nearly twenty years.

Long-standing relationships such as these represent people you can trust, who will tell you the truth and who will help you grow as a person and as a musician. If you want a career, you want it to be a long career. You don't want to be one of those people who wins a competition, has a brilliant four or five years and is never heard of again. What you want is a career that's on a long, slow-burning trajectory, and that allows you to get better and better and to do more and more things. That will make you an increasingly interesting musician. In order to do that, you have to have mentors and *compadres* along the way. It's essential to resist the urge to chop and change personally. If you *are* an interesting musician, it's only natural that you'll chop and change professionally. But to be taken up constantly by new people means that they are unlikely to know you, or your history. It's important to recognise who's important and loyal to you, as those people don't come along every five minutes.

RH: If we consider musicians such as Sir Charles Mackerras and Sir John Pritchard, they left school in their middle teens and entered the music profession. The next generation of artists tended to finish an undergraduate degree before working professionally. And, today, it's common for young musicians to continue their formal studies well into their middle twenties. Do you think that extending their education in this manner is beneficial?

JM: For me, continuing to study in that way is just putting off the 'evil hour' of having to enter the uncertainties of the world! Every student at a conservatory is there to be a performer and a musician, but there does come a point when you just have to get out there and start doing it. The Royal Academy of Music is very good at encouraging students to do this. Staff members are excellent at offering contacts and developing people professionally. I watched the film *An American in Paris* recently, which stars Oscar Levant playing a pianist on a continuous fellowship. And he says in the film something like, 'I know that I've had ten years of American fellowships, and that they're about to run out: I might have to start giving concerts!'

RH: As it happens, Oscar Levant was a tremendous pianist and, like you, made a wonderful recording of Gershwin's *Rhapsody in Blue*. Your recording of the work is with Carl Davis and the London Symphony Orchestra. How did that disc come about?

PART THREE: INSTRUMENTALISTS

JM: When I was in my late teens, I had a recording contract with Collins Classics, which was a major label at one point. The company signed me up as a kind of 'house pianist' and were keen to make a lot of recordings. The first discs I made for them were Britten's Piano Concerto with the English Chamber Orchestra and Steuart Bedford, and music by Satie, which they thought would sell well. I nearly drove myself mad learning sixty minutes of Satie's music, which translates into about sixty pieces, as his compositions are so tiny! Quite soon after that, I recorded *Rhapsody in Blue* with Carl Davis and the London Symphony Orchestra. The orchestra was just amazing: absolutely incredible. We recorded the jazz band version of *Rhapsody* followed by Gershwin's Piano Concerto. After the sessions, we performed both works at the Barbican Centre, which is really the wrong way around. That was back in the heyday when companies were recording all the time. It has now slowed down somewhat, and you now perform things many times before recording them. Carl Davis was fantastic, as he knew that repertoire inside out. The same was true of the LSO, which had a brass section that was sensational.

RH: In the 1960s and the 1970s, London was a cultural magnet that attracted the world's greatest artists, and was a hotbed of musical innovation and artistic subversion. What are your recollections of those times, and who were some of the big figures who caught your attention?

JM: I was fortunate enough to hear many of the legendary pianists, as they were still playing at that time. Some of them were in their seventies and eighties: Emil Gilels, Claudio Arrau, Vladimir Horowitz, Sviatoslav Richter and Shura Cherkassky, artists who now seem historic. I grew up musically going to the Royal Festival Hall and sitting in the cheap seats. Those musicians made a deep impression, as I realised that I was witnessing the end of a golden age of pianism. Watching them was like watching old warriors. I remember hearing Arrau, who must have been in his mid-eighties, play Schumann and Beethoven. Even though he'd lost some power, you knew you were watching an artist with a lifetime of experience, repertoire, touring and expertise. Each of these great figures had a different sound.

RH: In the case of Arrau, his sound was a direct result of how he managed his arm weight.

JM: Yes, but it was also affected by his sense of spaciousness. And these artists were not part of an 'industry'.

RH: A question today's students often ask about the pianists you've just mentioned is: 'were they as great as they now seem?' Or, for those of us from an older generation, are we simply looking back at them through rose-tinted glasses?

JM: They're not rose-tinted glasses at all! I was young when I heard them, and they seemed like rugged individuals who had earned their spurs. They were remarkable intellects, as well as great players. They had character, athleticism and scholarship. One can't ask for anything more than that.

RH: Up until the 1980s, the majority of London's concert life took place in a few central, iconic venues. That has changed significantly. Has that affected the music profession?

JM: I was very fond of both the Royal Festival Hall and the Queen Elizabeth Hall, which I associated with contemporary music and the

PART THREE: INSTRUMENTALISTS

London Sinfonietta. I saw Pierre Boulez and Sir Peter Maxwell Davies at the Roundhouse, and I went to the Proms at the Royal Albert Hall from the age of sixteen. For some reason, I didn't go to the Wigmore Hall back then.

RH: There was also a time when the Wigmore Hall used to be booked by musicians who wanted to make their London debut.

JM: And I made my debut there, too! But it has changed since then, and has become very international.

RH: For those of us with longer legs, the seating in the Wigmore Hall is something of a challenge. After being opened as the Bechstein Hall in 1901, it changed its name during the First World War and was refurbished in 2004. Sadly, the disposition of the seating remained largely the same after the refurbishment, an arrangement that might have been ideal for the average Edwardian, but less so for those of us born after the Second World War. Nevertheless, I've always considered the hall's acoustic to be one of the best in the world.

JM: I agree. I think that it's a fantastic acoustic, and for pianists playing there, you have to play to it. You have to come to terms with what the acoustic is, and to understand how it reverberates. It's essential to be aware that it's a very big piano in quite a small hall. And you must be in control of the sound. Everyone loves being on stage at the Wigmore Hall: it's like being in the middle of a little golden box.

RH: A number of our more outstanding former students took an educational route that was not dissimilar to yours: undergraduate studies at the University of Cambridge followed by postgraduate studies here at the Royal Academy of Music. What are some of the benefits of that path, and is it one that you'd recommend today?

JM: Not necessarily now. When I was young, conservatoires didn't offer much in the way of academic studies, and I was absolutely desperate for an academic education. I knew intuitively that I lacked a certain knowledge. I was a composer then, and I was keen for something that would help me with the hard grind. But that's all changed, and you can now go to a conservatoire and have a fantastic academic education. Cambridge is still a great place to study, not least of all for the interesting people that you will meet there.

RH: Did you, and do you, consider Britain the equal of Germany and Russia when it comes to producing pianists?

JM: When I was a student, I knew people who left to go and study in Moscow. It was the 'done thing' at the time. It has since changed, with students now gravitating to Western Europe and London. There was a sound and a tradition that was associated with Moscow and made attractive by the Russian pianists we heard on stage.

RH: But, of course, Soviet pianists dominated many competitions until the 1980s. Take the first Sydney International Piano Competition in 1977, for example, where the winner and the runner-up were both from the Soviet Union.

JM: Was that not to do with the Cold War? There's always a story behind a story. Perhaps we no longer have the wider political implications that accompanied Van Cliburn's and Barry Douglas's wins at the International Tchaikovsky Competition in 1958 and 1986.

PART THREE: INSTRUMENTALISTS

RH: Is the International Tchaikovsky Competition as prestigious as it once was?

JM: I'm sure it is if you win it! If a student is keen to enter a piano competition, the one thing that they should ask themselves is: 'How will I feel if I don't get through the first round?' And if you know that you'll feel fine about that, then by all means enter. At the very least, you might get to travel to an interesting city. If, on the other hand, the answer is: 'I'll be devastated if I don't get through', for God's sake don't do it. It's not a given that somebody with talent will automatically progress. I won one competition at the start of my career: the Young Concert Artists Trust. The best piece of advice that was given to me was from Stephen Kovacevich. He said, 'On a good day, of course you could win the Leeds International Piano Competition; any of us could. But the problem is: it might not be your good day, or the luck of the gods might not be with you.' He spoke very pragmatically about competitions and why they're there. The greatest problem facing them is their ubiquity; there are too many of them. Some people thrive on competitions, while others find them a rather damaging experience. There are examples of fine pianists who've never won a competition.

RH: After the Academy, you took part in masterclasses with Jorge Bolet, a musician who had a particular affinity with the music of Liszt.

JM: Yes, I did. I was invited to Jorge Bolet's masterclasses at Fort Worth, Texas, when I was twenty-two. And as unlikely as this might seem, I played Rachmaninoff's Second Piano Sonata and, I think, Scriabin's Sixth Sonata to him. He was a proper old-school pianist. He had huge hands, a huge technique and a big sound.

RH: Where do you stand on the Liszt-Chopin debate? Are you an artist who feels that Liszt sacrifices content for surface and that Chopin is a greater synthesis of the two?

JM: Liszt has been completely re-evaluated, and one of the people who led this re-evaluation is Alfred Brendel. He's done a great deal for Liszt's reputation. Liszt was surely one of the most generous, interesting, vivacious and fun people to have been with. If any of us had been his student, we would've realised that he was a fantastic teacher. Chopin disliked teaching, and it would've been a horrible experience playing for him. Chopin and Liszt were profoundly different. Liszt was extremely generous to fellow composers, which can be confirmed not only by his numerous transcriptions of other people's works, but also by his conducting.

RH: You're absolutely correct about Liszt. You only have to think of his generosity in conducting the premiere of Wagner's *Lohengrin* at Weimar in 1850. This was at a time when the Leipzig-born composer was exiled in Switzerland. Weimar then became something of a cultural magnet, with many musicians flocking there to learn from the Master.

JM: And Liszt gave the second-ever performance of *Tristan und Isolde*. He conducted the work from the autograph score. Can you imagine what that must've done to his eyesight? He had a complicated and a messy family life, too, including his daughter, Cosima, who married Hans von Bülow before becoming the mistress, and later wife, of Richard Wagner.

RH: One of the reasons why I raised this issue is to do with your forthcoming recording of Chopin's mazurkas. Why have you chosen these works to document in preference to some of the composer's other pieces?

PART THREE: INSTRUMENTALISTS

JM: I was Artistic Director of the Bath International Music Festival when it was Chopin's bicentenary in 2010. I was keen to perform the mazurkas complete, but chronologically, rather than in their published order. I wanted to track the composer's thought processes, the way in which each new, jewel-like mazurka emerged and his handling of emotional memory. Those works are an unusual example of a composer returning again and again to a tiny form. A similar example is György Kurtág, who returns repeatedly to miniature structures in *Játékok*, which are quite autobiographical. When I eventually played fifty-seven mazurkas at Bath, I started at 10am and finished at 1.30pm with two intervals! I've given this programme several times, and we will be recording the works in Aldeburgh, an old stamping ground of mine.

RH: Over the years, I've had the chance to speak with a number of leading pianists in this series, such as Paul Badura-Skoda and Leon Fleisher, about their preferred choice of instrument. Would I be correct in saying that you're an artist who's fond of a Steinway?

JM: You are absolutely right, but I'm even more specific than that: I prefer older Steinways from the 1960s and the 1970s, as they're very different from the ones being made today. They have a bigger dynamic range and greater colour, but they are much harder to control and are much heavier to play. Modern Steinways have a more compressed sound, plastic keys and a shallower key depth. While this sounds quite 'nerdy', I find the compression similar to a radio broadcast and a little less interesting. It's harder to achieve a greater emotional range.

When I was much younger, I made many recordings on older Steinways. I adore these pianos, particularly the one that they have from the 1970s at Snape, where we recorded Britten's Piano Concerto. I also recorded sonatas by Charles Ives and Samuel Barber on it, pieces that require a 'rock-like' sound. With Collins Classics, it seemed like we were making a new disc every two months; I nearly died! Bartók was followed by Scarlatti, which, in turn, was followed by Bach's 'French' Suites. It was a lot of work. But there will always be a period in a young pianist's life, usually between their early twenties and their mid-thirties, when they'll play a wide repertoire and learn so much. They will play a great many concerts and make numerous recordings. But there comes a point when you're barely able to hang on by your fingernails. The same is true of young conductors. They consume repertoire and accept one engagement after another.

RH: Your disc of Scarlatti's sonatas is particularly fascinating. Whilst it's clear that you are masterful in extracting marvellous colours and nuances from the modern piano in that recording, I'm interested to know whether you've ever been tempted to explore period instruments, such as fortepianos and harpsichords, and what criteria you used when selecting the sonatas for the CD.

JM: I had fortepiano lessons when I was at Cambridge and nearly destroyed the instrument! I've always thought that I would be a good clavichord player, as it's a much tougher and more eccentric instrument. But I'm admiring of harpsichordists and early keyboard players, some of whom are good friends, and I'm especially interested in the repertoire that they play. I recently performed Book One of Bach's *Das wohltemperierte Klavier*, and that was a good excuse for me to listen to many recordings of the work, which I love doing. I rediscovered Rosalyn Tureck's discs from the 1970s. She has gone out of fashion, but the recording is mesmeric. Her background as an early keyboard player shines through thanks to the creativity of her phrasing, which is intricate. She makes everybody else sound quite timid because of the big decisions she adopts. A modern instrument is mighty and exciting, and can give the player a great deal. But pianists can be guilty of not engaging their brains in the same way as some early instrument players do! When it came to Scarlatti's sonatas, I bought the complete set of the 555 published sonatas, as I was initially unsure which ones to choose. When I saw Horowitz play them in London in the early 1980s, he started with a set of six sonatas and played the one in A flat major first. That was an immediate choice for me, so that I could relive the excitement of hearing him. But, apart from that, I had no fixed ideas. I enjoyed playing them through before deciding.

RH: For young and established pianists alike, repertoire building and repertoire management are crucial issues. From your diary for the early part of next year, it appears that you're balancing a major recording project with recitals and concerto performances. How did you go about creating this schedule?

JM: The only difference between one's younger self and one's older self is that you take far more risks when you're older! You become much more dangerous in your approach and have a greater sense of individuality. When you're young, you're concerned with hitting the right notes in the right order, getting a good review in *Gramophone* and not offending too many people. I was mainly worried about practising seven or eight hours a day, giving concerts and building repertoire. It's got rather more complicated now, as I am responsible for the artistic and educational sides of the Dartington Summer School and Festival, as well as mentoring pianists here at the Academy as Head of Piano. When it comes to building a diary these days, sometimes it can be related simply to what's next on the schedule. This month, I'll be teaching at the Academy, performing a Schubert recital at Liverpool, liaising about the

Chopin disc and flying to South Africa for a tour. As an older musician, it's necessary to carry a great many different programmes in your head.

RH: But how do you keep those programmes fresh?

JM: I've never found repeating repertoire boring. Perhaps it's because music written for the piano is so difficult and rich. I was talking about this during the audition period here at the Academy. One of my colleagues was rhapsodising about the time when all he thought of was the harmony, and how he was able to dig deeper and deeper into the music. It's impossible to get bored. If you're about to play Schubert's impromptus, for example, they're just too difficult to become complacent about. And then there's the task of sifting through the various editions.

RH: You play a great deal of French music. What attracts you to French music in general, and what are some of its defining features?

JM: I'm attracted to certain French composers who are at different ends of the compositional spectrum: Messiaen and Boulez at one end, and Satie and some eighteenth-century composers like Couperin at the other. I'm also attracted to extremes. Again, at one end, the miniature, which can be deceptively simple, and here I include John Cage with Satie, and, at the other end, furious, loud and complex music, such as pieces by Messiaen, Boulez and Charles Ives. So, it's more to do with types of music.

RH: You've also made a marvellous recording of Ravel's *Valses nobles et sentimentales*. What do they mean to you, and are they a pastiche, a homage or a parody?

PART THREE: INSTRUMENTALISTS

JM: I suppose the work is about melancholic memory, something that it has in common with Chopin's mazurkas. It captures the rhythm of the waltz, while revealing Ravel's complex, multilayered psychology.

RH: Along with Ravel, you're also closely associated with the music of Messiaen, whom you mentioned earlier. In what ways does he challenge our assumed cultural and artistic norms, and is it necessary to come to terms with his understanding of religiosity to perform his works successfully?

JM: Would you ask the same question about Bach?

RH: Absolutely.

JM: Bach's choice of keys can be an expression of faith. Redemption, salvation and death are all represented through his tonal choices. You don't have to share the composer's beliefs, but you do have to have a knowledge of them. The same is true of John Cage, who expressed his values, often related to Zen Buddhism, in his music. If a performer doesn't understand these, his music might make less sense.

RH: That being the case, could it not be argued that the compositions of Cage, and for that matter Messiaen, were simply the expressions of a certain point in the historical continuum?

JM: No. John Cage was a genius. Cage and Messiaen both died in 1992, and neither has dated in any way. The first piece of Messiaen that I played was *Quatuor pour la fin du temps*. This was while I was a student here at the Academy. When I opened the score for the first time, I'd never seen chords like them: the piano part is written on three and four staves. But having struggled with the *Quatuor*, and then with *Vingt* *regards* and the *Turangalîla-Symphonie*, I realised that playing Messiaen's harmonies was no different from playing a C major chord: it was his code, and I needed to crack it. I respect his theological and spiritual beliefs, and the way they inform his rhythm and architecture.

RH: As you've performed all twenty-seven of Mozart's piano concertos, did your global reading of these works enhance your understanding of him as a composer? And perhaps more importantly, do you have any plans to record any of his concertos in the future?

JM: I love playing and directing the concertos, and I've spoken with the Britten Sinfonia about recording them. Their range of form, colour and orchestration is unsurpassed, and they are challenging technically. Mozart's mercurial changes of mood blow playfully and changeably across the score like the weather of western Ireland. The concertos really are like a voice at the piano.

RH: I know that you've conducted from the keyboard in the past. What attracts you to working in this way?

JM: I'm tempted to say 'power', but that's far from the case! It's a good skill to have. It teaches pianists how to communicate, and how to engage in dialogue with an orchestra's strings and woodwind. It also means that the pianist has to know the orchestral score inside out.

RH: Have you ever thought of giving up the piano to take up the baton full time?

JM: Everybody should know what it feels like to conduct; it can be pretty scary. I've done it a lot, and sometimes with unusual repertoire, such as Mozart's *Maurerische Trauermusik*. Conducting is part of being a musician, like composing or improvising.

RH: Why have you returned again and again to the works of Johann Sebastian Bach?

JM: He's something of a touchstone for pianists, as he makes you use your brain in a particular way. So much of Bach is evident in the works of other composers, and he can be found in Messiaen, Piazzolla, Schumann and Beethoven. Almost anything a pianist touches is influenced by Bach, and it's essential to know those influences. You can develop great skills in musical analysis by studying Bach, which are transferable.

RH: For young musicians about to enter the profession, how important are agents and how did you first come to their attention?

JM: These days, artists can promote themselves very easily. This can be done to a high quality, and their work can be made available to a wide audience. It's now possible to make recordings that are viable commercially. That slightly alleviates the pressure of having to find an agent *at all costs*. That said, agents are very significant for two reasons. First, they know people that young musicians can't possibly know, such as managing directors of orchestras and concert halls. And, secondly, it returns to the idea of having a professional partner, someone who will talk to you about you as a musician, and who will nurture you artistically. As a fledgling pianist, it's easy to make mistakes. You might choose the wrong repertoire, or suggest an inappropriate programme. You might want to do too much too quickly, or enter a competition that wouldn't suit you. Agents can be incredibly helpful, but your teacher is also important.

They often have had, or continue to have, big careers. Their advice is invaluable, and they know what they're talking about when it comes to career management. I met my agent, David Sigall, after I completed a three-year apprenticeship with the Young Concert Artists Trust, and I learnt so much from him.

RH: You are also a respected composer. How do you balance that role with your work as a performing artist and as a teacher?

JM: I write music for myself to play, or for the orchestras and musicians I am working with. But you can be just as creative when you curate a programme, a concert series, a festival or a recording label. Each of these is an important and a creative thing to do. It's not new: Edwin Fischer, Wilhelm Kempff, Daniel Barenboim and Martha Argerich have all done similar things at Berlin, Verbier and elsewhere. And it's a marvellous way for young artists to get their careers going.

RH: In the case of Kempff, a truly fascinating character, he wasn't only a great Beethoven interpreter, but was also a forward-thinking composer. Are your works as cutting-edge as his?

JM: I love the cadenzas that he composed for Beethoven's Fourth Piano Concerto! I'm not sure I know what cutting-edge means nowadays, but I'm writing a ballet for the choreographer Kim Brandstrup, which is being 'workshopped' in New York. It's a mixture of medieval music and electronica.

RH: You're also a fine writer. Along with a wonderful radio play about Satie that starred Jim Broadbent, you've written a number of books on piano pedagogy for younger players. And then there are your liner notes

PART THREE: INSTRUMENTALISTS

for your CDs, which are a delight to read. Is this an attempt to link the educational, artistic and historical elements of the artistic process, and should all musicians develop literary skills such as yours?

JM: All performers should write their own programme notes, as it really makes you think about the music you've chosen to play. I'd really like to write a book about practising, and about being alone with one's instrument. This is one of the most profound aspects of being a musician and of being a person. We all practise under difficult circumstances, and how you practise is who you are. Audiences think you are the person they see on stage, but that's only the tip of the figurative iceberg.

RH: And, of course, in Britain orchestral musicians have to be able to sight-read quickly and accurately, a practised skill and not a God-given gift.

JM: It's the same for pianists. One of the ways to improve is by playing a lot of chamber music and by working with singers. When I was a teenager, I worked for dance and music-theatre companies for pocket money. A good sight-reader is someone who can predict and understand what's going to happen next.

RH: Over the years, you've run a string of music festivals and have been indefatigable in helping the careers of young musicians. What have been some of the joys and pitfalls that you have experienced along the way?

JM: Often there's some politics involved in running a festival! I'm not overly keen on fundraising, but I'm enough of a politician to address these matters. You have to have energy, and be prepared to understand marketing and audience development. It's always best to take responsibility for the entirety of an event's concept. And, up to a point, you must be willing to think about public relations. It might not be something that you thought you'd have to do when you were practising your Beethoven sonata, but it's important to be aware of. But the upside is the thrill of inviting artists you admire, of setting up new collaborations and relationships, and of exploring artistic ideas.

RH: You also run your own recording label, Sound Circus. How much control do you have over the end product?

JM: I started the label more than twenty years ago, and it has evolved to include a variety of artists, composers, orchestras, jazz players and world music. I'm responsible for everything!

RH: Is there an ambition yet to be fulfilled?

JM: There are still many works that I'd like to play. I'm currently going through a real Schubert phase and I'm playing a great deal of Beethoven. I've recorded Bach's 'Goldberg' Variations, *Die Kunst der Fuge* and the 'French' Suites, but I'd love to record the complete *Das wohltemperierte Klavier*. I want to carry on playing and directing Mozart's pianos concertos, and I want to write my own concerto.

RH: Do you have an urge to record all of Beethoven's piano sonatas and concertos?

JM: While I love playing them, I'm not fussed by the idea of recording all the concertos. The Second, Fourth and Fifth Concertos are really the ones I like playing. And although I'm not a 'completest', I *will* play all the sonatas!

MAXIM VENGEROV
(DAVID JOSEFOWITZ RECITAL HALL, 30 SEPTEMBER 2015)

JONATHAN FREEMAN-ATTWOOD: You're only forty, but have already delighted and enthralled at least three generations of listeners. It seems like you've been with us forever. As you gave your first concert at Novosibirsk in Siberia when you were only five years old, does that now seem like another world?

MAXIM VENGEROV: Siberia *does* seem such a long time ago and such a long way away. It was nearly forty years ago. But, in some ways, it feels like yesterday. I vividly remember my first violin lesson with my first violin teacher, Galina Turchaninova. And I also remember thinking at the time that I was a little bit different from the other kids. I felt very fortunate to be able to play the violin, as I knew what I'd be doing for the rest of my life.

JF-A: It's an interesting phenomenon that industrial cities, such as Novosibirsk, are often centres of musical excellence. That was certainly true of Leipzig, Milan and Manchester. Do you think that the environment in which you were raised played much of a part in your musical development?

MV: The world is a place of wonder, and we often wonder why certain places become dominant musically. Italy once led the operatic world, while Russia produced a series of outstanding string players. But it shouldn't be forgotten that the Russian school of string playing owed a great deal to Henryk Wieniawski, the legendary Polish violinist who studied in Paris. He came to Russia at the invitation of Anton Rubinstein, and taught at the Moscow and Saint Petersburg conservatories. Those appointments were amongst his greatest achievements and were fundamental to his legacy in Russia. And that's why I have always felt so lucky that two of my teachers – Galina Turchaninova and Zakhar Bron – came from that tradition, a tradition that also included Leopold Auer and Pyotr Stolyarsky. Without this, I wouldn't be who I am today.

JF-A: Am I correct in thinking that your mother sang and conducted and that your father was a professional oboist?

MV: That's correct. My father was an oboist in the Novosibirsk Philharmonic Orchestra. At the time, there was also an enormous opera house in Novosibirsk that was one of the biggest in the world. It had five thousand seats. Most of the city's musical infrastructure was pretty much put in place during and after the Second World War. When the siege of Leningrad began in 1941, the city's Philharmonic Orchestra took refuge in Novosibirsk. Some of the orchestra stayed on after the blockade was lifted, and it was there that my father and mother met.

JF-A: You mentioned earlier that you knew what you were going to do for the rest of your life when you were only five years old. Is that really true?

MV: If a boy of five from Britain, Western Europe or the United States said that, we might either smile or laugh. But not when it comes from a child born in Siberia. I'm not sure that I had a choice. And, don't forget, it was bloody cold in Siberia. I had to practise with gloves on. My teacher

PART THREE: INSTRUMENTALISTS

did point out, however, that if I could practise with gloves on, I could definitely do better without them!

JF-A: After beginning your studies in Novosibirsk, you then moved to Moscow. How did that come about?

MV: I moved to Moscow to study at the Conservatory's Central Music School. I was about seven at the time and was accompanied there by my grandparents, as my mother simply couldn't abandon her job in Siberia. So, my parents remained in Novosibirsk, while I went with my grandparents to study in Moscow. I stayed there for three years, during which time my grandfather unfortunately became very ill. As a result, we had to go back to Novosibirsk, and that's when I began studying with Zakhar Bron.

JF-A: How would you describe Bron's approach to teaching the violin?

MV: I learned to play the violin in much the same way that a child learns to eat or dance. I simply picked up the instrument and made my first steps with it. It became part of my body. It was an extension of my left and right hands. When I went to Bron, he offered me something that I needed at that time: resistance. As a ten-year-old, I would play Mendelssohn's Violin Concerto for him, and he would say, 'This is not the way to play. You have to play differently.' And he'd explain how it should be done. But then I'd ask, 'Why do I have to play it like that?' To which he'd reply, 'While you are studying in my class, you are going to play the way I tell you!' It was a disciplined approach, as he probably thought I needed taming. But then he said to me, 'Would you like to play Paganini's First Concerto? It's a wonderful work, and how would you like to play it in Moscow?' I thought that was great. To go from Siberia to Moscow, how wonderful. But the bad news was that I had to play it the following week. I went home, prepared the work, and played it for him the next day from beginning to end. He said, 'Very good, but I expect you to be able to play it from memory by tomorrow.' I returned to his studio the next day, but was still playing from the music. This then prompted him to say, 'Well, if you bring it back to me for a third day with the music, I'll just assume you're not talented enough.'

JF-A: Bron's approach was nothing if not brutal. But it obviously appealed to you, for when he came to teach here at the Royal Academy of Music, you followed him. You were a mere fourteen years old at the time.

MV: But would I teach like Bron today? Absolutely not. For me, music must always be associated with love. You should always want to sing with your violin and to give joy. Nevertheless, Bron's driven approach meant that I made progress, and, ultimately, that allowed me to play throughout the world.

JF-A: During your early years, you won first prize at the International Karol Lipiński and Henryk Wieniawski Young Violinists Competition, and later triumphed at the Carl Flesch International Violin Competition. What are your memories of those successes, and are you an advocate of competitions for young instrumentalists in general?

MV: Thirty years ago, if you didn't win a competition, you didn't make it professionally. Today, it would be fair to say that competitions have advantages and disadvantages. I entered the Lipiński-Wieniawski competition when I was ten years old. But having arrived in Lublin, I couldn't have cared less how many competitors there were, or who played best: I just wanted to enjoy myself. So much so that when they announced the result, I wasn't even in the hall. I was in a nearby restaurant, enjoying its wonderful cakes. I could have eaten them all! Nevertheless, I was lucky enough to win first prize. By contrast, I was considerably more mature when I entered the Flesch Competition. Along with the other competitors, I was given lodgings in some kind of hostel here in London. My room was incredibly small, and only had space for one tiny bed. I could barely fit my suitcase in there, let alone practise. I had to stand bolt upright so as to avoid hitting the walls with my bow. In the adjacent rooms, two of my fellow competitors were constantly, and simultaneously, practising Tchaikovsky's Violin Concerto. They were so good technically that I quickly became very nervous. I didn't sleep a wink during the competition, and never expected to win. But, thank God, I did. Nevertheless, it was a struggle for me, as I thought that everyone else was so good. Being nervous for a competition is never a good thing, and should never be encouraged. I believe that a competition should be more of a festival for young people, where they can enjoy meeting and learning from each other. The result doesn't matter. Whether or not a competitor wins is of little consequence. It's more important that they take part. By so doing, they're able to see and to hear other violinists, and to compare themselves with them. They're also able to present their art in a variety of styles, and to play works from a variety of periods, whether they be by Bach, Mozart or contemporary composers. So, yes, I think that competitions are a good thing, and I encourage young people to go and play in them.

JF-A: As a consequence of your competition successes, you came to the attention of the recording industry. You have won prize after prize as a recording artist, and have documented music ranging from the Baroque to the present day. What attracts you to recording, and how does your approach in the studio differ from your approach in the concert hall?

MV: For me, recording is a real art, and stands in sharp contrast to concertising, which can be so ephemeral. Recordings offer a degree of intimacy with the performer and the performance, and allow greater access to the details and purity of the music. If we listen to a great symphony at home, we can actually hear every orchestral voice, voices that might be lost if we were to be sitting in the tenth or twentieth row of a concert hall. Nobody coughs and nobody distracts you when you are listening at home. There's only the music. But, of course, live and studio performances are both important. The ability to record myself from a very young age was a driving force. When my father left the Soviet Union for the first time to tour Italy with the Novosibirsk Philharmonic Orchestra, he returned with a tape recorder. I was delighted with this and immediately started recording whatever I played. I would play a phrase, and then I would listen to it. All of a sudden I could hear myself and could make some objective criticisms about what I was doing. I would then record the passage again, and would try to do it better. I would then repeat the process until I couldn't play the passage more perfectly.

I was lucky enough to be invited to record with the Soviet company Melodiya from the age of ten. Amongst the label's artists were some wonderful soloists and conductors, such as David Oistrakh, Sviatoslav Richter and Yevgeny Mravinsky. These were legendary figures. I spent three days in the studio, and remember coming out a very different musician. It certainly improved me. And when I listened to the final tape, I couldn't believe my ears. It had been edited marvellously. It was wonderful, and just the way I imagined it! Then, for my next concert, I rehearsed with the pianist and tried to imitate what I had achieved in that recording. It must have worked, as people said, 'My God, you're so much better now. What have you been doing?' Musicians should use recordings to advance their skills, and to better what they do. It's like looking in a mirror.

PART THREE: INSTRUMENTALISTS

JF-A: But it could be argued that recording is, to a greater or lesser extent, a kind of public-relations exercise, and that creativity and artistic integrity can be lost when recordings are copied and parodied in the concert hall.

MV: Let's chat about public relations, shall we? It's a good subject. When I signed my first recording contract with Teldec, I was sixteen years old. My first disc for the company was with Zubin Mehta and the Israel Philharmonic, and the second was of sonatas chosen by me. These were works by Beethoven, Mendelssohn and Brahms. The company was absolutely against this, as they felt that I was too young for such repertoire and that I should record something virtuosic instead. But I was not going to be put off and said, 'I insist. I want to become a good musician, so, for me, it's important to record repertoire that is serious and classical.' I got my way, but when the disc was released, there was no publicity of any kind in the shops. Over the next two or three years, I would contact Teldec regularly and ask, 'Why do I see pictures of so many other violinists hanging on the walls of record shops, including some of your own artists, and not me? Not only does it make me jealous, but nobody will buy my CD.' The reply I received was, 'Don't worry. Your CDs are selling well, because you don't need publicity!'

But I'd like to speak for a moment or two about other reasons why recordings are important. For most listeners, they're the main ways in which they come to know a musician artistically. If you meet someone for the first time, and then they telephone you the next day, you'll instantly recognise their voice. Without prompting, you'll say, 'Oh, that's you, James', or 'that's you, Helen.' Every musician also has a distinctive voice when he or she plays. When we hear Fritz Kreisler, we instantly know that it's him. The same is true of orchestras and conductors. It's very important that these distinctions should be maintained. We strive for technical perfection these days, which is a good thing, but it's only a means to an end. It's far more important to find your own voice and that of the composer. The next step is how you combine the two.

JF-A: Of all the great artists with whom you are associated, Mstislav Rostropovich seems to be of particular importance. Together, you've recorded works by Shchedrin, Stravinsky, Tchaikovsky, Prokofiev, Shostakovich, Walton, Britten and Beethoven. Would it be fair to say that he's the most influential figure in your adult musical life, and that your reading of Beethoven's Violin Concerto with him has a special place in your affections?

MV: It's been my great good fortune to have collaborated with Maestro Rostropovich for so many years. Thanks to him, I was introduced to the miracle of music. He was never dogmatic about interpretation, but just offered his view on a particular piece or composer. And it must never be forgotten that he worked closely with so many great composers himself, including Shostakovich, Prokofiev and Britten. As many of these major figures wrote works specifically for him, his understanding of their compositions was unique. He literally thought like the composer. I learnt a great deal from him; not only as an instrumentalist, but also as a conductor. Thanks to him, I was able see beneath the skin of the composer. And this was no less true when we came to perform Beethoven's Violin Concerto. When we recorded the work with the London Symphony Orchestra after performing it live at the Barbican Centre, I asked, 'Maestro, why is the *tempo* so much slower today?' He said wisely, 'Because yesterday was yesterday and today is today.' And it's much harder to play that concerto slower than it is to play it faster. Nevertheless, it felt so right to play it at the slower speed. It gave us extra space, and we were able to say many more things. It allowed us to meditate musically, and to rid ourselves of our preconceptions. It also allowed us to enjoy a completely new understanding of the work. Today, we perceive music differently. Thanks to new technology and the internet, everything is so fast. But when Beethoven wrote his concerto, there was a totally different pace of life. People reacted differently. They had more time to feel and to anticipate. And what's miraculous about music is its ability to take us back to those times. We really can go '*Back to the Future*'.

JF-A: It's clear from what you've just said that you think deeply about the purpose of music, and how it has developed and changed over the last seventy or eighty years. As an artist, do you feel a certain responsibility as to how music should be perceived, received and curated?

MV: As you were asking that question, I immediately thought of my idol, Fritz Kreisler. He said, 'Every musician has the right to call himself a musical priest.' And I think that's true, as we not only have to present, but be advocates for, the incredible legacy that has been left to us. In our modest way, every musician must invest in society. People must be given time to relax and to reflect on their emotions. Not only must they be given time to consider what has happened during the day that has just passed, but also what has occurred during the preceding months. That can be done through the beauty of music, which can also carry us into the future. This applies both to classical and folk music, the purest form of music. Tchaikovsky once said, 'Music belongs to the people. Composers just edit it.' And this is the main reason why we play it.

JF-A: Can we talk a little more about Rostropovich? Are you able to articulate precisely why his effect on you was so profound?

MV: I remember my very first lesson with the Maestro. I arrived and played Shostakovich's First Violin Concerto for him. But instead of getting straight down to business, he said, 'Maxim, let's go and find a restaurant.' The meal took over three hours, and he talked about anything and everything. He told me stories about his life with the great composers, which were incredibly inspirational. It was such an unexpected treat to spend precious time with a musician whom I admired since childhood. Time just stopped, and the three hours went by in a flash. When we finally returned to his room and began the lesson, he said, 'When you make music, it's not only important how you play, but also what you are thinking about while you play.' And that's true, as your thought process is the medium of communication. Our thoughts are translated through the music. The act of playing is just a physical exercise; it means nothing, even when we play the greatest of works. Rostropovich would always connect musical content with some kind of image. Consequently, the music immediately comes to life and is much stronger. As Rostropovich was so modest himself, he made me feel his equal. He had a similar reaction when he worked with Shostakovich. He told me how humbled he felt in Shostakovich's presence, and how the composer was so simple and straightforward with him. I think that this is true of all great geniuses. You're able to learn from them because you are able to connect with them. When I performed Shostakovich's First Concerto with Rostropovich, his advice when tackling its famous cadenza was, 'Maxim, you must think of this as if you are a marathon runner. You have to pace yourself, or otherwise you'll quickly become too tired and never reach your goal.' And of the next movement, he said simply, but wittily, 'It's like a fire in a madhouse.'

JF-A: Perhaps you could talk about your relationships with some of the other major conductors with whom you worked. I am particularly interested to hear your thoughts on Daniel Barenboim.

PART THREE: INSTRUMENTALISTS

MV: Before signing my recording contract with Teldec, I rather grandly demanded to work with Daniel Barenboim, Mstislav Rostropovich, Kurt Masur, Zubin Mehta and Claudio Abbado. I did this as I was eager to learn from them. I needed to find, and to define, my own distinctive musical voice. But that can only be done after laying a strong musical foundation. Playing with all these wonderful conductors was a precious time for me. But missing from the list I just mentioned was Carlo Maria Giulini, one of the greatest conductors of all time, and Lorin Maazel. Every time I worked with these great figures, I would literally surrender my *tempi* and the interpretation to them. I would say, 'Please, let me follow you.' Those were wonderful experiences, as I not only learned the way that they made music, but was able to observe their facial expressions. I could actually see how they were feeling, and could almost hear their thoughts. I also worked in this way with Barenboim. We made a lot of music together. Along with sonatas for violin and piano, we played chamber music with Yo-Yo Ma, and recorded quite a few CDs. My experiences with Barenboim were quite different from my encounters with Rostropovich. Unlike Rostropovich, Barenboim told me what to do. It was almost like I had to do what he said, and that there was no other way. I felt that it was his way or the highway. But I learned a great deal from this type of discipline. You can't become a general before being a good foot-soldier first.

JF-A: You made a famous recording of Sibelius's Violin Concerto with Barenboim and the Chicago Symphony Orchestra. Was this a work that you'd studied with Bron?

MV: Actually, no. I never did it with Bron. I played the concerto with Barenboim for the first time when I was twenty. As I had a free day before the first rehearsal, I played it for him privately. He crushed me.

He totally crushed me. He said, 'You play in tune, and if not technically perfect, close to it. But my question is: "Why?"' I then asked him, 'Maestro, please tell me, how can I improve what I'm doing?' He said, 'Take the orchestral score home, study it, and then bring it back tomorrow. We'll talk and rehearse then.' I didn't really know what to do. So, I put my violin aside, and started studying the score. It changed my interpretation immediately. I soon had completely different ideas about *tempo*, melodic development and structure. After our first rehearsal, he looked at me and said, 'Well, that's a good start.'

JF-A: Is it fair to say that it freed you up?

MV: Yes, it did.

JF-A: Some musicians might have been destroyed by this approach, but not you.

MV: Barenboim always forced me to think. I learned to think like the composer, and not just horizontally. This is only natural when playing a one- or two-line instrument such as the violin. But to be able to feel profoundly what the composer's intentions were, and how the piece was written, you need to think like a composer, and not like a violinist. Barenboim planted that seed.

JF-A: You were also quick to expand other areas of your musicianship, including improvisation and Baroque string style.

MV: My willingness to learn is part of my character. It's just the way I am. I've always needed to look over the horizon, and to see what might be possible tomorrow. I've never been content with today's successes. While tomorrow is tomorrow and today is today, you must always do the best you can. But as music is endless, you can't embrace everything. Nevertheless, by the age of twenty-two, I'd become particularly curious about period instruments and Baroque style. As a consequence, I met my wonderful friend Trevor Pinnock, who invited me to perform with him. I played on a period instrument, and he played on a harpsichord. But as I'd learned something new from him, I suggested that he should try something new for me. I proposed that we should play some Beethoven sonatas in the 'traditional' way, using a grand piano. And we did just that.

JF-A: It must have been like going back to school in one respect. Were these new experiences a way of learning more about yourself?

MV: Absolutely. It was essential for me personally to become a well-rounded musician. As I always knew that the violin was my mother tongue, I was forever searching for things that would allow me to speak more effectively with it. I quickly realised that if I didn't know the full score of Brahms's Violin Concerto, for example, I would be missing out on so many things: I wouldn't actually be playing Brahms's concerto, but simply a piece for virtuoso violin and orchestra. I took the full score and started to study it. Then, when I played Bach, I was curious to search out source materials, and to learn how his music was performed during his lifetime and on what instrument. This meant that I had to learn a completely different technique, which has since influenced my style when performing Mozart and Beethoven.

JF-A: But you've always been something of a musical maverick and have never shied away from pushing artistic boundaries. Yusupov's *Viola Tango Rock Concerto* is a case in point. For that work, you bought, and played on, a five-string, sea-blue Violectra electric instrument.

MV: That was at a time when my 'other self' was challenging some of my long-held ideas. While I never doubted that classical music was my true calling, I thought that the electric instrument would give me something extra. I was very curious about rock music at the time and had studied improvisation with Didier Lockwood, a student of Stéphane Grappelli. It was my dream from the age of five to learn how to improvise, and I have always had a deep admiration for people who can do it in a jazz style.

JF-A: Can we briefly touch on the viola? I know that you don't play it any more, but there was a time when it was of great importance to you. What made you want to undertake this additional challenge?

MV: Don't laugh, but my interest in the viola began after I performed Brahms's Violin Concerto with Claudio Abbado and the Berlin Philharmonic. When I later listened to a recording of that concert, I thought that my violin sounded 'squeaky'. As it seemed to lack certain colours, I thought that the best way to overcome this was by playing on an instrument with a deeper voice. Ideally, that would've been the cello, but I couldn't learn it fast enough. The viola was the next best thing. Having made the decision to make this addition to my skill set, I recorded Walton's Viola Concerto. This came about because Rostropovich had asked me to record Britten's Violin Concerto, a piece that I love. And as we needed a work to complete the CD, Walton's composition seemed like the ideal choice.

JF-A: Along with Britten and Walton, another English composer who attracts you is Elgar. His works have always been well received in Russia, and you've regularly played his violin sonata.

PART THREE: INSTRUMENTALISTS

MV: I think that the Russians and the English are connected spiritually and emotionally. We clearly understand each other, and I've always been amazed at how British audiences have taken Tchaikovsky and Shostakovich to their hearts. Of course, the merits of Elgar's music are recognised everywhere, but I don't think that his works are played with particular regularity in Russia. There's a sense of profundity that we connect with. And that's why I adore the beautiful musical landscapes that can be found in his violin sonata.

JF-A: Can we return to Bach for a moment? Many young violinists find his music challenging for a variety of reasons, and struggle to decide whether or not they should play it in a modern or period manner.

MV: When we talk about Bach style, it is difficult to tap into anything in particular. I remember Rostropovich saying to me, 'Maxim, it really doesn't matter how we *actually* play today, as performance style is always changing. Today, it might be fashionable to play in a Romantic style, and to use a great deal of *vibrato*, but, tomorrow, that might be regarded as total nonsense.' The day after tomorrow, something else will be in fashion. But what remains constant is the composer. Performers are always secondary. And this is why I think that you have to play Bach according to your own particular insights. Bach is a unique composer who has universal appeal and whose works operate on different levels. Even those listeners who have never experienced classical music before will connect immediately to his compositions. Those hearing them for the first time might say, 'My God, this is beautiful music; it's incredible.' That's the first layer. The second layer is textural and appeals to musicians who are relatively new to Bach's music. The third layer is attractive to musicians who are more academically and scientifically minded, while the fourth and most important layer allows us to follow our own instincts. There's no doubt that

Bach is a very complex composer. When I begin explaining him to students, I always start with one of his more accessible works, and gradually build on that foundation. Bach needs time and maturity. Rostropovich made this clear when he said to me, 'Don't make the mistake I did. I recorded Bach when I was thirty years old, and I regret it.'

JF-A: Let's chat briefly about your work as a teacher. When did you first realise that you were a great teacher, and was this part of a reflective process that had its roots in your own musical education?

MV: I regard teaching as the most responsible part of the music profession, as it's not dissimilar to being a doctor. If you give the wrong advice, it can change a student's life for ever. And that's why I'm extra careful and concentrate my efforts completely when I teach. I first recognised that I loved teaching when I found myself needing to share what I'd learned, and when I realised that I wanted to help others. I began to teach privately when I was studying in Germany, as I had to pay for my apartment. This was lent to us by a well-established family whose child I taught. But as he was my first student, I thought that he needed to be at least as good as Heifetz! I was extremely demanding of him, and his parents put a stop to that immediately. I teach very differently today.

JF-A: You're now greatly sought after as a conductor. How has this affected your approach as a violinist?

MV: I find it impossible to separate conducting from violin playing. It's one and the same. And although music is one language, that doesn't mean there aren't different ways of speaking it. When I play a major concerto, such as that by Brahms, I always think symphonically. And when I play Beethoven's Violin Concerto, I approach it as if it were a symphony with an *obbligato* violin part. But as I now conduct regularly, the way I colour a work and interact with an orchestra has changed. And it certainly helps to be able to speak the same language as the conductor when you are working with them as a soloist. I'm also fascinated by the possibilities that conducting has to offer. Much like playing the violin or the piano, conducting is a craft that has to be mastered. When rehearsing an orchestra, the players become familiar with the conductor's demands through the gestures they make, and not through the words they speak. Of course, there'll be times when you have to stop and say a few things, but mainly you are able to connect with the orchestra through your hands. This is the most miraculous feeling, as it's almost telepathic. But this can only happen when you trust the orchestra and the orchestra trusts you. As every member of the orchestra will have a view as to how a work should be played, a conductor is needed so that the process of music-making can be facilitated. To do this, the conductor's technique has to be crystal clear, and that's why I decided to study the craft with Yuri Simonov in Moscow. I've now worked with him for five years on symphonic music, and have just begun a two-your course with him on operatic conducting. That doesn't necessarily mean that I want to conduct operas in the future, or to give up playing the violin. But being both a violinist and a conductor can be challenging, as each uses very different muscle groups.

JF-A: Would you say conducting has affected the way you approach the violin technically?

MV: Of course. But it's also helped to shape my understanding of music. I now have a greater awareness of a work's harmonic nuances, structure, and instrumentation.

JAMES EHNES
(DAVID JOSEFOWITZ RECITAL HALL, 11 JANUARY 2016)

RAYMOND HOLDEN: As a performing artist, you're remarkably well documented, and, over the years, a number of your concerts have appeared on film. While that medium offers you the chance to reach a wide and curious audience, it must also have its drawbacks.

JAMES EHNES: When you learn that a particular live performance will be filmed, it seems like a great idea. Then you find out that the company will put it on their website, which then leads to the performance being shown on YouTube. That can be unnerving, particularly when I don't know the conductor and I don't know the orchestra. And before you know it, you're on television playing Sibelius's Violin Concerto. But, of course, it's nice to have a souvenir of a particular event. We're in the business of dealing with an art form that's so ephemeral. There's nothing of permanence. Yet a recording or a film is something that can remind you of who you were at a particular point in time.

RH: Your father was a trumpeter and your mother was a ballerina. Can we assume, therefore, that music was part of your life from the beginning?

JE: There was a lot of music. My parents met when my mother was dancing on stage and my father was playing in the pit. Although they were

PART THREE: INSTRUMENTALISTS

Americans, my father accepted a post teaching trumpet at Brandon University in Manitoba, Canada, and my mother ran what was basically a satellite school for the Royal Winnipeg Ballet. They thought that they would stay for a couple of years, as it was the ideal place to start a family, but, in the end, they stayed for nearly forty years. Between my mother running her choreography classes for her students, and my father's activities as an orchestral musician, there was always music in the house. That not only introduced me to all kinds of different instruments, but it kept me out of trouble. Where I grew up is a very cold part of the country, and I'm not a cold weather person. I now live near Sarasota and am a Floridian by choice. Long cold winters in Brandon could be demanding and we lived in a house with old floor radiators. But boys being boys, I occasionally got up to mischief. To settle me down, my parents would sit me on top of a radiator, where it was nice and warm, would put a record on the turntable and would place the speaker right beside me. I'd sit there and listen. They knew that as long as they turned the record over at the end of each side, it would keep me out of their hair for the whole afternoon.

RH: What attracted you to the violin and not the trumpet?

JE: That's something of a family mystery, and no one has been able to give me a good answer for that. Having heard mainly orchestral music, I would've been introduced to the sounds of most instruments. But it must have been something in the violin that was very special to me. And since I didn't attend many concerts, how did I know which instruments made which sounds? I do remember seeing Itzhak Perlman on *Sesame Street* and thinking, 'This guy is just the coolest guy ever.' I still think that. That might have been how I made my connection with the violin. My parents also remember that there was a picture of a violin on the wall of a friend's house and recall me saying, 'That's what I want.' I knew that the object in the picture made the sound that I had in my ear. So, it could have been one of any number of things that attracted me to the violin. But it was very much my decision to play that particular instrument.

RH: Brandon had a vibrant cultural life. Were you aware of this as a boy, and what impact did it have on you?

JE: Brandon is a fascinating place. It's not a big city, but bigger today than when I grew up there. When I was a kid, it must've had a population of approximately 35,000 people. Although not big, it serves a large area. It's more than 150 miles in each direction before you get to anything else. Brandon has to service a great deal more than a town of its size would normally cater for. For that reason, there were a lot of interesting things that happened there. Without question, the university is a big part of Brandon, and it's what makes the city what it is. There were always a lot of really fascinating people there. We were exposed to all sorts of interesting stimuli, but we also felt that the best route to enjoying a creative life was to leave. While I still go back as often as I can justify – usually about once a year – I return less often these days, as my parents now live near me in Florida.

RH: Having started to play the violin at the age of four, you had lessons with Francis Chaplin at the age of nine, before eventually ending up at Juilliard in New York.

JE: Beginning at four was something that was decided by an early manager, who felt that the younger I started, the better. I was given a violin that year for Christmas, and as my birthday is 27 January, I was effectively five years old when I received it. My father was the greatest influence on me from a purely musical standpoint. With him, I spent the most time, and worked most closely. As he was not a violinist, my early training on the instrument was with students from the university. It seemed like I had a different teacher every year, as they were always graduating. My father's closest friend at Brandon was Francis Chaplin, who'd become something of a legendary Canadian violinist and pedagogue. My father never took advantage of that friendship, and withstood the urge to have him listen to his son. To suggest that I was a really gifted eight-year-old to Chaplin wasn't something my parents would do. When I was playing at a local festival at Brandon, I was heard by one of the adjudicators, and it was she who recommended me to Francis.

Having listened to me, Chaplin offered to take me on as a student, which was quite something, as all his other students were older and at the university. After starting to work with him, he became very much more than just a violin teacher. As a close friend of the family, Francis gave me lots of time, and would always schedule my lessons at the end of the day. He felt that that way I was able to go home from school before going over to the university, where the lesson would go on for as long as we wanted. We might then go out for dinner, or go to the golf course. There, we'd hit some golf balls, before going back to his house to listen to records, after which my father would collect me. It was just great. Then there was Donald Henry, the piano teacher at the university, who offered to play with me; another amazing opportunity. The people I spent the most time with were Francis Chaplin, Donald Henry and my father. Even at the time, I knew that that was a little unusual, as they were generationally at a very different stage of life than me. But we had a great time together. Francis Chaplin had been a student of Ivan Galamian, and had studied at the Meadowmount School and Juilliard. As they were places he knew, and as I was thirteen by then, he suggested that I should attend the summer school at Meadowmount. There, I met Sally Thomas, another former student of Galamian. After four summers with her at Meadowmount, it seemed only natural that I should continue working with her at Juilliard. Consequently, I've only had two violin teachers, both of whom studied with the same person. While that might not seem like a well-rounded background for a violinist, the thing I appreciated most about my teachers was their lack of dogma. Both were capable of taking a student of moderate ability and to make them as good as they could be. But when they had students who could offer a little more, they had a great way of setting boundaries, while allowing enough freedom for the person to learn by themselves.

RH: Is that how you also work as a teacher?

JE: I only give masterclasses. If I had to work with students week after week, I'm not quite sure what kind of teacher I'd be.

RH: Have you ever considered devoting more time to teaching?

JE: It wouldn't be the right thing for me to do at the moment. Although I find it enjoyable and rewarding, it can be very tiring. With everything that's going on in my life, I often rationalise my decision not to teach by saying that I've neither the time nor the energy to commit to it. But when I think about it more, it's really something that I don't want to do at the moment.

RH: But do you consider yourself a role model?

JE: From a pedagogical standpoint, the 'masterclass-type teacher' is a very valuable person to have in one's life. I've always found masterclasses to be extremely helpful. Whether I was playing for a well-known teacher, or, more often, a well-known performer, the fact that they would hear me for twenty minutes, and would then work with me for another twenty-five, was very helpful. As they knew nothing of my background, and had no preconceptions about my playing, that allowed them to think very freshly about what they heard. I'd like to think that when giving masterclasses, I'm able to give a perspective that comes from a different place, a perspective based on what I do. If something doesn't go quite right, I'd never say, 'Well, I know that they can actually do that', or, maybe, 'They can do it better than that most of the time.' Such comments don't address problems. I come to the student's work from a very 'separate' place.

RH: Who were some of your musical heroes?

JE: As Brandon was definitely off the beaten path, Itzhak Perlman and Pinchas Zukerman were never going to perform there; it just simply wouldn't happen. They didn't even go to Winnipeg. But I did hear Isaac Stern play there. Essentially, I got to know the playing of great violinists from recordings. In one sense, that was limiting, and it would have been great to have been in a place like London where you could hear everybody live. But on the other hand, it meant that whether living or long dead, the violinists I heard on disc all occupied the same place in my world. I sometimes talk to young people growing up in big cities today, and the only violinists that they're really aware of, or care about, are those that had recently played in their cities. The artists that I listened to when growing up were both modern violinists and past masters. But those whom I listened to most were Fritz Kreisler, Jascha Heifetz and Itzhak Perlman. Nevertheless, I was also exposed to a great many other players. Francis Chaplin had a fabulous record collection, and he thought that it was important for me to hear as many different people as possible. We'd listen to just about everybody. If an LP recording of a violinist had been made between about 1950 and 1985, it was likely that he had it. I heard a lot of different players.

RH: Students often find the choice they have overwhelming and confusing. There are a number of online platforms that offer a vast array of recordings at the click of a mouse. But is that any more beneficial musically than going to a record shop, paying your $10 for a disc, taking it home and listening to it time and again?

JE: Both approaches have distinct advantages. It's a very interesting question, and I'm not sure that I can give a definitive answer as to which is the more beneficial. One of the great problems in the modern world is multitasking: having everything available at the click of a button. Consequently, there's not always the need to invest in the act of study in quite the same way that it was in the past. If, for example, you had a recording of Brahms's Violin Concerto, and you knew every aspect of that disc because you only had six recordings in your collection, you *really* listened to it. You didn't listen to it while either checking Facebook, texting a friend or jogging in the park. You sat there and you listened. You really got to know the recording. But I also don't want to sound like some old fuddy-duddy who says, 'Back in my day', as the disadvantage of the earlier approach was that by constantly listening to the same recording of Brahms's Violin Concerto over and over again, audiences were affected by what they'd heard when attending concerts. People who went to concerts a generation or two ago, and who considered themselves to be musically literate, only wanted to hear something that sounded like their recording. You'd hear them say, 'He played that far too fast.' Did that mean that it was too fast in relation to the printed text, or simply faster than on the recording they owned? Whereas, today, people might sit at their computer and sample twenty-five different recordings, and if they don't hear a performance that sounds totally different from the others, they might say that that person has no imagination. That has really made a difference to the way people now listen.

RH: At Juilliard, you won the Peter Mennin Prize, after which you went on to win other competitions. What's your reaction to competitions in general, and are they necessary for young artists to progress through the music profession?

JE: No. All any artist wants to do is to find an opportunity to play in a format where people will listen. How one gets to that format varies considerably. There are a lot of different ways. I never entered any of the major competitions, such as the Tchaikovsky, the Queen Elizabeth or the Indianapolis. Admittedly, I was a jury member for the Tchaikovsky, but I didn't have to play. That's a much better way to experience a competition. I can recommend that, and they pay you to be there! My parents and teachers were very wise when selecting competitions for me. If I won some money, that was great and always handy. But it was more important to look for competitions that gave me opportunities. The first time I played with the Montreal Symphony Orchestra was the result of a competition. I was thirteen years old. Similarly, the first time I played with the Quebec Symphony, the National Arts Centre and the Minnesota Symphony Orchestras were all as a result of these opportunities. Canada is a funny place. Politically speaking, if you're from Brandon, you're from nowhere. You're not from Toronto, Calgary, Vancouver or French Canada. You're from nowhere. That's harsh, but true. In order to get noticed, it takes some effort.

RII: I'm particularly interested to hear a little more about your first performance with the Montreal Symphony Orchestra. As you were just thirteen years old, were you considered something of a child prodigy?

JE: The concept of being a child prodigy is very relative. Strangely, I don't have a clear memory of the performance, but I do remember the trip very clearly. I played Ravel's *Tzigane*. I recall that my whole family came, along with some extended family members who travelled up from the United States. We all stayed at a friend's house, and that those friends had two sons who were of a similar age to my brother and me. We all began horsing around. They had a basketball hoop in their driveway, and the night before the concert, I was hit by a rebound from the hoop that knocked the middle finger of my left hand very badly. I didn't tell anybody. I thought that if I was to be a very good boy, I'd wake up in the morning and it wouldn't hurt too much. It's funny the way you think when you are thirteen. I said to myself, 'I have been looking forward to this my whole life' – as if that's a long time when you're thirteen – 'And I did something stupid to put this in jeopardy. I can't let this opportunity pass me by.' By focusing on that, I was able to calm my nerves, and to take the stress out of the actual performance itself. As it happened, my hand felt fine, probably due to the adrenaline, and I just really enjoyed the experience.

RH: Can we talk a little about your instrument? You play on a Stradivarius. What attracts you to the sound of that violin, in preference, say, to an Amati?

JE: I first saw my violin in November 1996 – a Stradivarius from 1715 – and have been playing on it regularly since September 1999. I'd been playing on a violin that was on loan from the Canada Council for the Arts, which has a wonderful collection of instruments that's now quite extensive. In fact, I was loaned their instrument as a consequence of winning a competition, the only instrument in their collection at the time. This gave me the opportunity to play on a not particularly good Stradivarius, an instrument that had experienced various troubles during its life. It was the 1717 Stradivarius known as the Windsor-Weinstein, an instrument that's now sounding better than when I had it. But it was my first chance to play regularly on an instrument that was very special, even if it wasn't the best of the best. There's something about the tonal priorities of 'Strads' that really speaks to me. I'm a complete nerd when it comes to violins. And whether they be good or bad instruments, I just like looking at them. But 'Strads' have always been something special to me. Stradivarius was clearly in search of something. You can play on twenty 'Strads' from his 'golden period' and they all have a great deal in common, particularly if all are healthy and well set up. They're all remarkably similar in what he was trying to achieve. The combination of an infinitely refined and dense core of sound, with very large dynamic range, is something that speaks to me. There's also a certain brightness to 'Strads': it is like a shimmer.

RH: An interesting addition to your discography is *Homage*, a recording where you compare the tonal qualities of various violins, particularly those made by Stradivarius and Guarneri. How would you best summarise the differences between the two makers?

JE: When I listen to that disc, the difference that strikes me immediately is that when I play on a Stradivarius, it sounds like me, as it's the instrument that I normally play on.

RH: But how much of the instrument is really you? When one listens to Dennis Brain play Britten's *Serenade for Tenor, Horn and Strings*, first on a piston-valve, French-made F horn, and, later, on a rotary-valve, German-made single B-flat horn, the sounds are very different.

JE: This project created something of a psychological dilemma. The instruments were all part of the same collection. There were six 'Strads', three Guarneris and some violas. As a player, your first instinct with an instrument is always to ask, 'How do I use that tool to do what I want it to do?' But, on the other hand, the entire point of the CD was for them to sound different. That's a very unnatural thing to do as a violinist.

RH: How much, then, did the psychology of the project affect the sound of the instruments heard?

JE: When choosing the pieces for the CD, I tried to find works that would fit what I thought were the innate personalities of the instruments. I then played each excerpt in a manner that was in keeping with the way that I'd generally play it. I quickly realised that to a very small extent, you do become a different player. At three different points in my career, I spent short periods of time playing on Guarneri violins: the 'Haddock' from 1734, the 'Russian' from 1740 and the 'Carrodus' from 1743. I loved them all very much, but, ultimately, I didn't sound quite the way *I* wanted to sound. I was too tempted by the instrument to play it the way that it wanted to be played. The response of people who reached out to me personally was another amazing thing about the project. As it was all recorded in high fidelity, audio enthusiasts would write to me about the amplifiers, preamps, cables and speakers that they were using: frankly, things that I had little understanding of. But by telling me this, they were making clear to me that they had the 'street cred' to write about the sound quality of the discs. Equally, I received a similar number of letters from people who were keen to point out how different these violins sounded. And then there were those who wrote to say, 'I couldn't hear a difference at all. Not a single difference.' That's not to suggest that the people who couldn't hear a difference didn't have good ears. It simply suggests that different people listen in different ways. Some years later, I downloaded the comparison tracks onto my wife's iPod and set it to shuffle. To my delight, I could identify which instrument was which. I felt quite proud of myself for being able to spot the difference.

RH: Have you ever thought about investigating the Baroque violin? And what are your thoughts on Norbert Brainin's thesis that 'Strads' resonate better when they're strung with gut strings and are tuned to the lower pitch of A=432?

JE: It's true that the instruments do resonate differently. But I'm not sure that I'm ready to say that they resonate better. 'Strads' were the most coveted instruments amongst the upper classes, but when it came to performing violinists, they also used those made by Amati, Steiner and many others. When the violin was modernised through greater string tension, it was the instruments of Stradivarius and Guarneri that gained greater prominence. If I tune my instrument down, there's something wonderful about the warmth and resonance that it achieves. On the other hand, when the instrument is set up properly at modern pitch, it has capabilities that other instruments just simply don't have. It all depends on what you want to do with the instrument. Increasing the tension on an instrument, adding steel strings to it and raising its pitch were not things that happened by accident. They were done on purpose. All instruments have been developed, and often for good reason. Some of my favourite musicians play in a historically informed manner, and I love listening to early instruments. And when such instruments are played in an appropriate space, they make perfect sense. I don't often play in small spaces, but when I do, I have to work hard with my instrument to make sense of that environment. One of the major advantages of a modern setup on a truly great violin is that it allows the player a wider range of options. With proper training and proper skill, it's then possible to approximate closely earlier sound-worlds. Whereas when instruments are not set up in that manner, it's impossible to make even the vaguest approximation of what's now possible.

RH: Tell me about your disc of Bach's accompanied sonatas.

JE: After documenting Bach's solo sonatas and partitas, I recorded his sonatas for violin and harpsichord with Luc Beauséjour. From the very beginning of that project, Luc would say with tongue in cheek, 'You're making me a very unpopular person in some circles.' He knew that he was breaking an unwritten rule by working with me. Musicians live in a very strange world, where we tend to speak only to each other. We often only speak of where a particular accent should be placed in a piece by Schubert, for example. These are issues that are ultimately completely meaningless to people who simply want to listen to music and to enjoy it. Whether it's Bach, Tchaikovsky or the music of today, I like to remain open-minded when listening to other people play. Concerning my own work, not only do I need to be able to justify it intellectually to me and me alone, but I also have to make it accessible to a broad audience.

RH: When recording or playing Bach, do you feel that you differentiate stylistically between the solo sonatas, the partitas and the accompanied works?

JE: My recording of the D minor Partita was made some sixteen or seventeen years ago, and I'm not sure that I'd play it that way now. The only thing that you can do when making a recording is to try and document how you feel about a piece at the moment of recording. It's easy to think that a work should go a particular way when you grow up with the recordings of old masters who are now long gone. We see it as a permanent document of that artist's lifetime's thought and contemplation about every detail of the composition in question. Actually, the disc might only represent how he felt on a particular Wednesday in 1950. Did he feel good; did he feel bad; was he rested; was he healthy? The recording only reflects what needed to be said on that day. Clearly, that doesn't answer your question about whether a harpsichord informs how I play Bach. But the different stimuli that we're exposed to at any given time make us who we are. No matter what approach you take to a recording, it should sound like you're committed to it.

RH: But in contrast to the recordings of the solo sonatas and partitas by Jascha Heifetz and Nathan Milstein, who play each set sequentially, you alternate between sonata and partita on your discs. Was that your decision to structure the recording in that way, and, if so, would you take that approach in the concert hall?

JE: If I perform the set in the concert hall, I arrange it slightly differently. Over the next few years, I'll be playing these works a great deal. Previously, I had the habit of playing a few of them frequently and some not at all. I began to miss those that I hadn't been performing, and felt that I was being a little bit lazy by simply playing the same ones over and over again. The E major Partita is a very useful piece to have at your fingertips due to its length, public acceptance and ease of access. So, too, is the D minor Partita. And I prefer to play the Chaconne as part of the work as a whole. Concerning how I ordered them on the CDs, I was affected by a beautiful manuscript that also ordered them in that manner. I thought that it made complete sense. But when performing them in concert, it's very difficult to play anything after the D minor Partita. If I play the whole cycle, I end with that work. Truthfully, they could be played in any order, and the music will still speak wonderfully.

RH: Many violinists talk about a 'Bach style' and a 'Mozart sound'. Are there really such things?

JE: What people are saying when they talk about a 'Bach style' is: 'If you play it the way I like it, then you have a Bach style, and, if you don't, then you don't.' And, of course, sound is tremendously important in music. For me, the violin is a beautiful instrument that can make a variety of sounds that are emotionally affecting. And I find it frankly confusing when I come across players who argue that sound is not particularly high on their list of priorities. Without a beautiful sound, what's the point? But, of course, that's a matter of personal taste. There are many things that can be achieved on a violin, and 'beauty is in the eye of the beholder'.

RH: But it has to be said, your intonation is virtually faultless, a quality you share with Heifetz and Perlman. Is that the kind of sound you find ideal?

JE: That's very kind of you to say. I look for a refined sound with purity at its core. And those qualities are also of importance when choosing an instrument. An instrument's core of sound should be pure, exciting and very even. Its default sound should reflect the middle of any tonal characteristic. Then, if it's a great violin, it has variety on both sides of that core. I don't want to be pushed in a direction that I might not necessarily want to go in by a particular instrument. Something I value most about a violin is that when I play a Mozart concerto one week, followed by a Bartók concerto the next, people will say that the violin is right for the repertoire they're hearing. And, more importantly, that I can feel that it's the right violin for the repertoire being performed. While the works being played are very different, the violin should be capable of coping with both, as its default position should be neutral. Some instruments are capable of remarkable things the first time you touch them. This can be intoxicating. But, ultimately, the better tool is the instrument that gives you a palette of possibilities while not painting the picture itself.

RH: What are your thoughts on textual fidelity, and what is your take on Leopold Auer's and Jascha Heifetz's use of cuts in Tchaikovsky's Violin Concerto?

JE: As we know, Auer was offered the premiere of the concerto, but turned it down. Later, he came to regret that decision, and prepared an edition that took some major liberties with the text. Specifically, there are a number of cuts in the last movement. I grew up listening to the piece with those cuts and played it that way myself for many years. I now play it in a way that is closer to the published text than most people. I've kind of gone full circle with the work. The fact is, it's a great piece, and if it's played with commitment, it's simply going to succeed. It's fantastic. Although I grew up playing it with some cuts, I didn't give it with all the cuts that Auer suggested in the first movement. I did play some things in the cadenza up the octave and I did make some cuts in the last movement. As I got to know Tchaikovsky's music better, particularly his chamber music, and here I am thinking of the Piano Trio, which is often played with cuts, I quickly realised that a great deal of important material was being lost. I now take the position that if there's a passage that I think should be cut, or that leaves me uncertain, it's probably my fault and not the composer's. I'm either going to play what he wrote, and decipher whatever mysteries the work contains, or simply not play it.

RH: You made a marvellous recording of Tchaikovsky's Violin Concerto with Vladimir Ashkenazy, along with some of the composer's works for piano and violin. What was it like working with Mr Ashkenazy on Russian music?

JE: I like working with him no matter what the repertoire. Sadly, he no longer plays the piano as much as he did. His arthritis keeps him from playing for extended periods of time. Luckily for recording purposes, he was still willing to play and continues to make beautiful piano recordings. The Tchaikovsky concerto was one of the first things that I played with him some years ago. As Music Director of the Sydney Symphony Orchestra, he invited me to play the work with him in Australia, and as the orchestra has its own label, we were able to make a disc of it together. I'd never recorded it before and it was a little intense. We recorded the concerto live in the Sydney Opera House, and as many of the people who attend concerts there are tourists, audience noise can be a problem. It wasn't easy. We also recorded the *Valse-Scherzo* and *Sérénade mélancolique*. These were not programmed, but were given as encores at different concerts. Recording these works was particularly thrilling for me, as I grew up listening to Vladimir's LPs of piano music.

RH: Your regular duo partner is Andrew Armstrong. What's the basis for that partnership?

JE: Andy is one of my best friends and is like family to me. There are a few people with whom I work regularly, and these people are my closest friends. For me, life is too short to spend that kind of intense time with someone I really don't care for. Andy and I met when we were students, but we became friends after he won a competition as a young man in Miami. Some lovely older people ran a concert series there and would periodically invite him to play concerts for them. I'd moved to Florida in the fall of 2001 and took a call from this Andrew Armstrong, whom I had met, but barely knew at the time. He told me that he'd been asked to give a concert in Miami and wanted it to be a violin recital. We had such fun and we went on to give similar concerts over the next three years. We found this rewarding musically and decided to play together regularly.

RH: Your partnership with Mr Armstrong has resulted in some remarkable recordings. One of my particular favourites contains transcriptions of some of Strauss's *Lieder*.

JE: A challenge when making these recordings was how best to search out and maintain the musical line, while retaining the meaning of the poetry without the use of words. In 'Wiegenlied' that wasn't such a problem, as it's such a lyrical song. But in 'Morgen', it is necessary to say something, but you don't have the luxury of the words when doing so.

RH: Perhaps the polar opposite to those works is Bartók's Sonata for Solo Violin, which was commissioned by Yehudi Menuhin in the 1940s.

JE: It's a very, very difficult piece to play and contains so many different challenges, both for the violinist and the listener. But I'm now no longer able to judge the challenges it presents to listeners, as I know the piece so well. I've been playing a great deal of Bartók over the last six or seven years, including quite a number of all-Bartók programmes. The violin is the ideal instrument when surveying his music. But it's essential to play with clean intonation, otherwise it begins to disintegrate musically. Although he could be chromatic and harmonically progressive, he was a tonal composer, whether he liked it or not. Even when a cluster of intervals explode, they are comfortably consonant. In the Solo Sonata, there are definitely places where the dissonances are intentionally pungent. But when these are balanced against its periods of harmonic clarity, its harmonic language becomes easier to understand. In terms of its actual construction and pacing, that comes naturally. Although it's in four movements, it's very much one thought. But it's essential to know where you've come from, and where you're going to.

RH: You also play Bartók's Viola Concerto and Berlioz's *Harold en Italie*. As a violinist, how difficult is it when swapping to the viola, and should all violists play on the violin from time to time?

JE: I think that there are some people whose physicality makes it easier to switch between the two than others. There are things to be learned from playing both instruments and I find that rewarding. I have large hands, and when I first started playing the viola when I was about eighteen years old, I found it easy to go from the violin to the viola. But when I went back to the violin, it felt like a little toy that was difficult to cope with. That's no longer a particular problem, and the change now feels quite natural.

RH: Have you ever thought of putting the bow down and taking up the baton?

JE: No. When directing things like Vivaldi's *Le quattro stagioni* or Mozart's concertos from the violin, there's very little conducting to do.

PART THREE: INSTRUMENTALISTS

The few occasions where I have actually just conducted, I found it both rewarding and frustrating. At this stage in my life, I enjoy the tactile aspect of playing an instrument.

RH: You've also performed a great deal as a string quartet player. How hard is it for you to include chamber music in your schedule?

JE: I actively ensure that chamber music is included in my itinerary, and I am Artistic Director of the Seattle Chamber Music Society. That organisation holds two festivals, which involve programming and performing. My quartet is one of the really great joys of my life, but scheduling for it can be a total nightmare. Nevertheless, my colleagues and I just love it so much that we find ways to make it work. As we all have such varied workloads, simply blocking out certain parts of the year never quite works. Yet, somehow, we always manage to identify a few periods in a year where we do nothing but perform together.

RH: Something that most listeners might not know is that you're also an excellent pianist. Do you still play the piano publicly?

JE: I used to play quite a bit, but have since retired, so to speak. I recorded Adams's *Hallelujah Junction* with my friend and old roommate Andrew Russo, which we also played on a short tour. That was a fun experience and I was keen to continue playing the piano. But when my daughter was born, something had to give, and, sadly, it had to be the piano.

PART FOUR

RECORD PRODUCERS, FILMMAKERS AND ARTS ADMINISTRATORS

CHRISTOPHER RAEBURN
(DAVID JOSEFOWITZ RECITAL HALL, 26 SEPTEMBER 2008)

JONATHAN FREEMAN-ATTWOOD: You began your career as a producer in the 1950s, arguably the heyday for the recording industry. This was a time when Decca, EMI, Deutsche Grammophon, CBS and RCA were setting new standards and breaking new ground. What defined those years for you?

CHRISTOPHER RAEBURN: Those early years saw the beginning of long-playing records, and we were experimenting with stereo. As far as Decca was concerned, this meant establishing an almost completely new catalogue, and that the sky was the limit.

JF-A: While it seems that the world was your oyster when it came to repertoire, was that also the case when it came to choosing artists?

CR: Not altogether, as Decca had their own. That was also true of HMV and Columbia. This meant that you might have a figure like Maria Callas working exclusively for the 'opposition', while Renata Tebaldi was one of ours. Then you might have a singer such as Giuseppe Di Stefano, who was eventually shared by us and EMI. And while exclusivity was a problem, we were able to handpick between half and two-thirds of the major artists who were performing at the time.

PART FOUR: PRODUCERS/FILMMAKERS/ADMINISTRATORS

JF-A: Each recording company was known for having a particular house style in the decades following the Second World War. What defined Decca's approach, and was their house style attractive to certain artists?

CR: I don't think our house style was attractive to artists *per se*, as the way that Decca eventually worked as a team didn't happen until the late 1950s. Originally, the head of our Artists and Management Department was the violinist and orchestral 'fixer' Victor Olof. He always got on well with all the engineers, and was dubbed 'The Baron'.

JF-A: If he was 'The Baron', how would you describe EMI's Walter Legge?

CR: He was a creative dictator.

JF-A: I'm pleased that you said that and not me. But being a producer when you joined Decca was quite a new concept, as your passport at the time described you as a 'Music Director'.

CR: Correct.

JF-A: Your interests have always been very theatrical, and when Decca began to use stereo, you could document operas in a completely new way. This meant that the recordings that used this new process often required more than one producer.

CR: And that was also true for some of the later recordings we made. When I was first engaged by Decca, it was largely because of my enthusiasm for all things theatrical. The idea of stereo operatic recordings had only just started during my early years with the company. One of the first experimental stereo sets was of Lehár's *Die lustige Witwe*, which

Decca made on behalf of RCA. Then came a huge order for five operas to be made in Rome during the summer of 1958. I was tasked to create what might be called 'productions' for those recordings. The idea was to reflect on disc the movement that you might see on stage.

JF-A: This is an approach that we now associate closely with Decca. You can literally feel, and sense, the movement of the singers, thanks to the way you and your colleagues worked with the emerging stereophonic technology. Today, this would be considered problematic, but, at the time, it was remarkable for its realism.

CR: We could explore absolutely anything. And by the time that this was all happening, John Culshaw had arrived on the scene. He was prepared to stick his neck out, and we were given huge scope for experimentation.

JF-A: Culshaw's approach must have been revelatory. But did his proactive manner with the singers prove unsettling at first?

CR: That's absolutely true. Singers were very used to having their own microphone, standing still and doing their own thing. John's style obviously put them off their stroke a bit, but the intelligent ones amongst them were prepared to have a go.

JF-A: I seem to remember that you were sent into battle very early on over a Verdi opera.

CR: When we recorded the composer's *La forza del destino* for RCA, Zinka Milanov must have been nearly sixty. In the first crowd scene, where Leonora is dressed as a student, Verdi says that she must stand '*a parte*', meaning that she should be separated from the other cast members and definitely be off to the side. This kind of instruction was ideal for stereo. But when I asked Milanov to observe the composer's instruction, her imperious response was, 'I have to be in the centre, as I have the tune.' In 'Pace, pace, mio Dio', Leonore starts with a recitative during which I wanted Milanov to run in from the side. And with an even greater sense of defiance, she said, 'If you make me move even one more step, I'll cut your beard off.'

JF-A: Would it be fair to say that by the time of Sir Georg Solti's famous recording of Wagner's *Der Ring des Nibelungen*, many of the singers were used to this new way of working?

CR: Solti's *Ring* recording was slightly different, because my co-engineer thought that I was really going over the top. So much so that he complained to John Culshaw about me and demanded that I be dismissed by Decca. But John was determined to judge the matter for himself, as he had faith in me. Having considered the situation, he agreed that we should have an extra person on stage, and that that person should act as a guide for the singers and as a go-between for the studio and the booth. The idea of having an extra producer on stage, therefore, was the direct result of me *not* getting the sack, and *Das Rheingold* was the first time that we worked in that way.

JF-A: As you were young at the time, this must have been a valuable learning experience. It must also have allowed you direct access to many distinguished artists whose careers had begun around the beginning of the twentieth century. And, here, I am thinking of figures such as Hans Knappertsbusch, Pierre Monteux and Tullio Serafin.

CR: Working with these men was a tremendous musical education, and, for me, Knappertsbusch was the greatest of all Wagnerians. Monteux was a wonderful conductor of the French repertoire, and Serafin was an outstanding interpreter of Puccini's operas. Serafin was slightly younger than Arturo Toscanini, but more sympathetic to the singers. And when it came to recording opera, that sympathy was of tremendous importance. Unlike Toscanini, who was anything but a benign dictator, Serafin was somebody who rehearsed singers in an understanding manner.

JF-A: Then we come to your discs of Strauss's *Ariadne auf Naxos* from 1958. This was the first time that you were the 'commander-in-chief' of a recording, rather than its 'adjutant'. And by the time of those discs, you were steeped in Viennese culture, as you had already lived in the Austrian capital for some time. As the sessions' 'commander-in-chief', your responsibilities were global, and involved hand-picking many of the singers for the smaller roles.

CR: We made the recording for RCA. They had cast Jan Peerce as Bacchus, Leonie Rysanek as Ariadne and Roberta Peters as Zerbinetta. But for the part of Der Komponist, they'd engaged a young American singer who was far from a star. As I knew that Sena Jurinac was the greatest Komponist of the age, I pushed and pushed until she was given the role. While casting the secondary characters, I learned of a young baritone whom I wanted for both the Harlequin and the Musiklehrer. His name was Walter Berry. He was completely unknown at the time.

JF-A: These days, the choices you had to make while recording *Ariadne* would be divided between about ten people.

CR: That's true, and while I didn't have to make any of the financial decisions, I do remember that the whole project cost £17,000. Today, that would scarcely cover two sessions.

PART FOUR: PRODUCERS/FILMMAKERS/ADMINISTRATORS

JF-A: Decca, EMI and Deutsche Grammophon all had artists under contract, which meant that they were committed to them. Was this a good way of working?

CR: Yes. Amongst the Italians, Decca had Renata Tebaldi and Mario Del Monaco as house artists, and both were very popular with the public. Later, Birgit Nilsson was put under contract by us, as we wanted her to sing Brünnhilde in Solti's *Ring*. At the time, it was common practice for Decca to sign somebody up for practical reasons, and not just because they happened to be a hugely popular artist. This meant that we were sometimes faced with a *quid pro quo*, and that we had to use an artist who might not be satisfactory for a particular part.

JF-A: When you look back at the 1958 *Ariadne*, are you proud of the final result?

CR: The fact that it was theatre, and not simply a studio recording, was very important for me. And to be able to cast strong singers for roles such as the Harlequin meant that the quality was good overall.

JF-A: You began your illustrious career without ever having seen a producer at work. As you had no template to follow, did you ever feel at sea?

CR: I simply drifted in, and sheer good fortune did the rest. I had no clear method.

JF-A: During the latter part of your career, the constellation of great musical stars with whom you worked included Cecilia Bartoli, Vladimir Ashkenazy, Kyung-Wha Chung and Sir András Schiff. Your personal and professional relationships with these artists were of great importance to both you and them. How did you create such positive artistic connections with these musicians?

CR: I think that my first record with Ashkenazy was a Chopin disc. As we got on very well from the outset, and were on friendly terms, it was possible to create a good working relationship. But I should point out that at Decca, producers tended to work with a variety of musicians, rather than being tied to one particular artist. There were exceptions, of course, such as when recording cycles, like the complete Mozart piano concertos. When that was the case, the producer usually remained stable.

JF-A: You were particularly well known for your work with singers, and you were somebody Decca would turn to if there was a problem. What was the secret of your success?

CR: It's essential to have sympathy for the singer, both as an artist and as a person. You have to know them, and they have to trust you. If that's the case, it's a great, great help.

JF-A: What was your policy when, for example, the Principal Clarinet of the Vienna Philharmonic might ask to listen to his solo again, even though the session clock is ticking down?

CR: You have to say that you are terribly sorry, and that he or she will have to wait until the end. The Vienna Philharmonic often spent the first half of each session 'sleep-walking' their way through their material. But, then, something marvellous would happen, and the last forty-five minutes would be magical. Conversely, English orchestras always worked hard and professionally from the start. This meant that you

PART FOUR: PRODUCERS/FILMMAKERS/ADMINISTRATORS

didn't experience the vast qualitative difference within one session that you encountered in Vienna.

JF-A: For many audiophiles, Decca and Mozart are synonymous. And as a passionate advocate of the composer's music, you've documented a great many of his works, including the sonatas for piano and violin with Radu Lupu and Szymon Goldberg.

CR: I enjoyed that project hugely, and it was a great privilege to do.

JF-A: But your fascination for Mozart is not just restricted to recording, you've also been active as a researcher.

CR: I am very interested in the first productions of the composer's operas, and have examined them from a theatrical perspective. I then began to look more generally at what happened in Vienna's theatres during the late eighteenth century.

JF-A: You also did some revelatory work on the Count's aria from Act Three of *Le nozze di Figaro*.

CR: Yes. I found this particularly interesting. Having looked at the score in Florence, I realised that Alfred Einstein had overlooked the aria, and that nobody else had done any work on it. After 'discovering' it, I then convinced Dietrich Fischer-Dieskau to record it. This was part of an 'improvised' disc of less well-known arias by Mozart and Haydn that was appropriately called *Haydn & Mozart discoveries*.

JF-A: Presumably, one of the advantages of working for a big label such as Decca was that you could risk recording young artists and be their mentor. And one of the great risks that you took was to document the then unknown Spanish mezzo-soprano Teresa Berganza.

CR: We set down her first British-made disc of Rossini arias in 1959, and while she was relatively new to the recording scene, her engagement was not as risky as it seemed. She'd made her Glyndebourne debut the year before as Cherubino in *Le nozze di Figaro* under Hans Schmidt-Isserstedt, and it was that debut which really piqued my curiosity.

JF-A: You then recorded her singing Fiordiligi's aria 'Per pietà, ben mio' from *Così fan tutte*.

CR: Previously, she had only sung the role of Dorabella in that opera, and had never performed the part of Fiordiligi. But as I thought that she was ideally suited to the latter's arias, I asked whether or not she could manage them. Luckily, we had the great good fortune of having Sir John Pritchard as the disc's conductor, an expert with this music.

JF-A: You once worked with the renowned Austrian conductor Herbert von Karajan, a committed audiophile who had strong ideas on record production.

CR: I quickly realised that I would not only have to know the score intimately, but to know the man, if I were to deal with him successfully. And as we had so many fascinating technological 'toys' in the booth for him to play with, I also knew that he was less difficult with English producers than he was with our German-speaking colleagues. But as he would never keep to a session's pre-arranged schedule, and as the full cast was nearly always present, the possibilities available to him were legion. He might rehearse one passage, but then immediately decide to

PART FOUR: PRODUCERS/FILMMAKERS/ADMINISTRATORS

record another. Unlike most other conductors, Karajan would do whatever he wanted to do within the time allocated. When we were recording Puccini's *Madama Butterfly*, I decided to expand my team and to work out a code. If it looked like he was taking a particular direction, I might pick up the studio phone and say, 'Contingency C'. This meant that the team had to jump quickly to whatever technical or musical possibility Karajan might opt for. In the end, we were largely able to anticipate what he might do.

JF-A: This must have been quite demanding when it came to the final edit.

CR: Yes. I found that I had to make very comprehensive notes.

JF-A: Producers have a code of conduct that they should honour, and central to that code is discretion. Nevertheless, we've all been at sessions where things have not gone according to plan. As Luciano Pavarotti could prove problematic, you ended up being something of a Henry-Kissinger-like figure when dealing with him.

CR: When Pavarotti arrived on the scene, it was really quite a joy. Previously, many of the roles that he sang were performed by Del Monaco, who could be like a bull in a musical china shop. Pavarotti was a more refined singer with a very good voice and marvellous diction. I was delighted by this, particularly when working with Italian operas that required the text to be understandable. He also had an innate musicality, and was definitely very musical. But he did struggle when learning a role. Plácido Domingo could read a full score, and could probably reduce it at the piano. He was a fantastic professional musician. But that was not the case for Luciano. He could follow a vocal score, but it was difficult for him to learn it.

JF-A: Was this because he was so busy professionally, or was it because he was defensive musically?

CR: I think that he was always on the defensive, and there was definitely a lazy side to him. He wouldn't easily apply himself to studying, and problems arose when we opened cuts. When we came to record Donizetti's *Lucia di Lammermoor*, an opera that he'd sung for many years, he wasn't well prepared. About six months before the sessions, we told him that we were going to include the famous tenor and baritone duet, a *Scena* that was new to him. We had a most marvellous *répétiteur* called Nina Walker, and she did her best with Luciano. But as he was not good about it, things became very difficult and he was poorly behaved. The recording's conductor, Richard Bonynge, was very fair with Luciano, but the person who drummed the material into him was another member of the music staff, who sat him down and behaved like a prison wardress.

JF-A: Was it true that Sir John Pritchard worked successfully with Pavarotti?

CR: Luciano adored Pritchard. They had worked together at Glyndebourne in 1964, when Pavarotti had sung Idamante in Mozart's *Idomeneo*. Years later, we recorded the opera with Pritchard, but with Luciano in the title role. Pavarotti was thrilled to have Sir John as the discs' conductor. And at the sessions, Pavarotti had the habit of dishing out advice, particularly to Leo Nucci, who was singing the part of Idamante. Pritchard was very, very good with Pavarotti.

JF-A: You are still active as a producer, and have recently been working with Cecilia Bartoli. Do you consider her one of your 'discoveries'?

PART FOUR: PRODUCERS/FILMMAKERS/ADMINISTRATORS

CR: When she was nineteen, I heard her in an audition when nobody else was particularly interested. She seemed to me to be ideal for Rosina in Rossini's *Il barbiere di Siviglia*. It was very exciting.

JF-A: Was it difficult convincing your colleagues at Decca that she was a young artist worth listening to?

CR: I recommended her to Ray Minshull, who was the company's Head of Music. He asked to have a tape of her singing, but was happy to take me at my word, and to plan some things for her to do. He was tremendously helpful and supportive.

JF-A: Recently, you've been working with the Austrian mezzo-soprano Angelika Kirchschlager.

CR: To record *Lieder* with her is very special.

JF-A: You are now a freelance producer. Does this give you some advantages that you might not have enjoyed at Decca?

CR: The way that I conduct a session today is no different from the way that I did it in the past. But I'm now able to work with people I *want* to work with. And, today, people very kindly ask if I would like to produce their records. I no longer have to work with contracted artists, and I've enjoyed my years as a freelancer enormously.

JF-A: During the course of your career, you have witnessed the emergence of a wide range of technologies. How did these innovations affect your abilities and approach as a producer, and which of these did you find preferable in achieving your artistic aims?

CR: I still long for the hiss of a 78rpm record! And while vinyl discs could sound like Rice Krispies, CDs were at least quiet and a very good medium. Yet the transferring of older formats onto CD has not always been successful. This is due, at least in part, to irresponsible engineering, where the original tapes are often remastered, rather than transferred directly. This causes listeners to complain that the CD version is not as good as the long-playing original. And then there's the addition of echo. This is a very dangerous thing to do. Natural acoustics should always be respected. It's also dangerous to look to pop music as a model, as it has nothing to do with the recording of classical music. We are brought up nowadays believing that the meters are the gods of the booth. This is a mistake, as the sole criterion for excellence must always be our own ears.

JF-A: When it comes to the final product, who decides on which takes to use?

CR: I have often made choices that the artist might query. And while there is always room for discussion, if I feel strongly about a particular take, I will explain why I believe my choice to be the best. Sometimes the musician will accept that, and on other occasions he or she will have their own subjective reason for wanting something else. This is understandable, and they should always have the final say, as their name is the one that goes on the recording.

JF-A: Before we finish, I know that you would like to alert the public to an artist who was particularly close to your heart: the versatile French singer Régine Crespin.

CR: Yes, I do. She was a fantastic Marschallin in Strauss's *Der Rosenkavalier*, a great Sieglinde and Brünnhilde in Wagner's *Der Ring*

PART FOUR: PRODUCERS/FILMMAKERS/ADMINISTRATORS

des Nibelungen and a wonderful Carmen in Bizet's opera of the same name. She was also a marvellous interpreter of Berlioz's and Ravel's works. And when you first broached the idea of me taking part in this interview, you kindly said that I could mention a musical wild card who meant a great deal to me, but who might not mean quite so much to others. Régine Crespin is that person.

SIR HUMPHREY BURTON
(DAVID JOSEFOWITZ RECITAL HALL, 15 MARCH 2016)

RAYMOND HOLDEN: As you are one of the world's greatest and most influential filmmakers, it's easy to forget that you are also a marvellous writer, a distinguished broadcaster and a fine musician. Your achievements are many, and your legacy is second to none. But, in this interview, I'd like to focus on your work with that other great polymath Yehudi Menuhin, a musician who's been part of your life since boyhood, and who was born a century ago in 1916. Did you ever encounter him personally, and what attracted you to him as a biographical subject?

HUMPHREY BURTON: I first met Menuhin in 1959 when I was a junior director on the BBC arts programme *Monitor*. He'd just come to live in London, and when he came to the Maida Vale Studios, his second wife, Diana, came too. I can remember vividly that she peeled lychees throughout the session. I'd never seen a lychee, let alone tasted one, before. This was an early example of Yehudi latching onto 'green' subjects and simply eating vegetables. We probably only had carrots for lunch! Yehudi was talking about Bartók on that programme, a composer I love. I wanted very much to hear about the commissioning of the Sonata for Solo Violin. The composer had heard Menuhin play something else, and was so inspired by that performance that he accepted the commission. Yehudi said that as Bartók was ill, he only wanted him to write a solo

PART FOUR: PRODUCERS/FILMMAKERS/ADMINISTRATORS

sonata. It ended up being one of the most important works of its kind ever written. Concerning the second part of your question, I felt compelled to write Yehudi's biography, and did a series of programmes for his eightieth birthday for Classic FM. That was effectively an overview of his entire life, and when he later died very suddenly, I accelerated the work that I'd already started. He had a fantastically colourful life.

RH: Another Hungarian with whom Menuhin worked was the conductor Antal Doráti. He, too, was a great interpreter of Bartók's music. Didn't they meet on a ship to Australia?

HB: They did. Doráti was conducting a ballet there, and it was Antal who introduced Yehudi to Bartók.

RH: I've always found Doráti an interesting conductor, and one of the very few to move successfully from the ballet pit to the concert platform.

HB: That's true. Another was Sir Georg Solti, whose first job was also as a ballet conductor. The movie of Mendelssohn's Violin Concerto that Yehudi shot with Doráti was the only actual film that he ever made. He did a great deal of television, but no other films. The Mendelssohn document was made using 35mm film, and was shot just after his second marriage in 1947. I always like to show it whenever I speak about Menuhin, even though he looks a little uncomfortable and it doesn't show his freedom of movement. And, of course, the Mendelssohn concerto was one of his visiting cards.

RH: You mentioned meeting Yehudi in 1959, but when did you first hear him play?

HB: I had a pre-war 78rpm recording of him playing Kreisler's *Praeludium and Allegro* with the pianist Marcel Gazelle. It's an absolutely wonderful piece. I was about twelve years old at the time. Then I heard him play Bartók's Violin Concerto on the radio at my school. It was a nasty little electric radio in the middle of the room, and there was nobody else there. This was in 1945, and it inspired me. In fact, it was the single most inspirational piece of music that I'd ever heard.

RH: I remember seeing Menuhin perform as a conductor at the Sydney Opera House after it opened in 1973, and hearing him again in London towards the end of the 1970s at the Royal Albert Hall. The programme that Sunday afternoon included both the Mendelssohn and the Beethoven violin concertos.

HB: He always had a strong feeling for Australia, and first went there as part of a world tour in 1937. And, of course, his first wife, Nola Nicholas, was also Australian.

RH: Before we talk about Nola, let's chat a little about his early years, shall we?

HB: His mother wanted him to be somebody very special from the word go. Both his parents had been immigrants from Palestine, and, before that, from Tsarist Russia. Many people in the early 1900s went from there to what they hoped was the 'Promised Land'. This didn't always work out, so quite a few of them moved on to America. Yehudi's parents, Moshe and Marutha, had met in Haifa before travelling separately to the United States. When Moshe heard that Marutha was staying in Chicago, he wrote to her. She then returned from Chicago to New York, where they kissed on Grand Central Station. If I were a feature

PART FOUR: PRODUCERS/FILMMAKERS/ADMINISTRATORS

filmmaker, this would've made a wonderful opening sequence. The couple then married, got pregnant and looked for a nice set of rooms in the Bronx. The new apartment's landlady told them that it was ideal for them, as it was close to shops, a park and transport. 'Best of all,' she remarked, 'there were no Jews' there. Marutha then said, 'But we are Jews!' To ram the point home, the couple called their first child Yehudi, which literally means 'the Jew'. It was an attempt at nailing their colours to the mast from the start.

Marutha was a remarkable woman, and she was determined that her firstborn should do something very special. They took Yehudi to concerts when he was only two or three. Apparently, he looked down from the balcony and said that he wanted to play the 'thing' that the concertmaster had. Within three years of that experience, that concertmaster was actually teaching the young Yehudi. When Menuhin was about two, the family moved from the Bronx to San Francisco, where Moshe ran all the Hebrew schools. This meant that he was able to establish an extensive network of contacts. Yehudi was taken first to a Viennese violin teacher, whom he hated: Sigmund Anker. He only stayed with him for six weeks. Nevertheless, one of the first things that I did when I started my biography of Menuhin was to go to San Francisco and look up his name. There were only three Ankers in the telephone book, and the first number I called was the violinist's daughter. Eighty years on, she was still angry that Yehudi had failed to acknowledge the early impact of her father on him. As it was clear that the boy had talent, the Menuhins were then able to persuade the concertmaster who had so excited the two- or three-year-old Yehudi to take him on as a student. Louis Persinger was that concertmaster. But he was reluctant to accept the young Menuhin, as he didn't teach children. Marutha and Moshe persisted, however, and were able to change his mind. Persinger had led the Berlin Philharmonic under Arthur Nikisch before being appointed concertmaster of the San Francisco Symphony Orchestra. And I have always felt that Persinger saw in the young Menuhin a little of himself. By six and a half, Yehudi was already playing concerts, and there were soon photographs of this chubby little chap making musical waves in the papers. Persinger wanted Yehudi to have all the solo triumphs that had eluded him as a boy. The family lived in San Francisco until Yehudi was about ten, and it was at that point that Persinger said he could do no more for the child. Menuhin had to go to Europe.

RH: In many ways, Menuhin was something of a pioneer as a recording artist. Do his recordings still have merit today?

HB: Yehudi recorded for the first time in 1927, which was very near the beginning of the electrical-recording era. Previously, discs were recorded and reproduced through an acoustic horn. The kind of repertoire that he revelled in at the time was exactly what the recording companies wanted to sell: salon pieces. Today, we are confronted with a repertoire that's largely serious and 'highbrow'. In the first two decades of the twentieth century, however, every fiddle player performed a series of musical 'marshmallows' in the second half of their programmes. These followed the meatier works of Beethoven or Haydn in the first part of the concert. And the very first disc that Menuhin made was the *Allegro* by Viotti. This was recorded when he was eleven years old and is quite remarkable. Some people say that he was at his best during his teenage period. But he wasn't just flashy; his interpretations also had soul. And I don't mean by this that he cultivated it just to make an effect. He wasn't like a tragic actor who could cry at will; he was a man who instinctively felt emotion. He once told me that when he heard Nathan Milstein play Tchaikovsky's *Sérénade mélancolique*, he felt that he – Menuhin – was carrying the cares of the world on his shoulders. That

PART FOUR: PRODUCERS/FILMMAKERS/ADMINISTRATORS

feeling for humanity then spilled over into his later life. It was astonishing. He always played from the heart as a youth, and that's why he was dubbed the 'Miracle Boy'. When Yehudi later went to Paris with his two sisters, Hephzibah and Yaltah, the girls auditioned for a piano teacher there who said that he couldn't teach them because they were too young. That was until he heard them play. The teacher then said, 'Madame Menuhin has a womb that is a *veritable conservatoire*.' Yet there was nothing musical in the family genes. When I met the hundred-year-old Mrs Menuhin, she told me she wasn't particularly musical. But she did say that her husband loved singing Hasidic songs when driving around the countryside. And, amazingly, Moshe had an electric car in 1923, which he never drove more than 15 mph.

RH: I've always been puzzled by the sheer number of violin teachers that Menuhin had. Along with Sigmund Anker and Louis Persinger, he studied with Eugène Ysaÿe, Adolf Busch and George Enescu, all very different artists with equally different styles of playing.

HB: Persinger had always taught Menuhin through real music, rather than through technical exercises. Persinger had studied with Ysaÿe in his youth, and it was he who sent Yehudi to the Belgian violinist. Menuhin didn't want to work with Ysaÿe, however, as he thought that he was too old. He wanted to study with George Enescu, the great Romanian musician who had played in San Francisco. But when Yehudi met Enescu, George said that he didn't teach, and even if he did, he was about to go on tour the next day at 8am. Unwilling to take 'no' for an answer, Yehudi said that he needed him, and persuaded Enescu to hear him the following morning at 7am. Menuhin's persistence paid off, and he was taken on by his hero. He then went to live with the Romanian for the summer as a ten-year-old. From the start, Enescu felt that Menuhin had so much to give instinctively. And as Enescu later claimed that he'd learned as much from Yehudi as Menuhin had learned from him, he never took a penny from the young violinist. Whether or not that's true is debatable. But what Enescu *didn't* approve of was Menuhin's lack of discipline. Yehudi would come to each new lesson with a different set of fingerings and bowings. He was then told that he wouldn't be able to sustain a career like this, and that he'd have to develop a routine. Enescu suggested that Menuhin should study with Busch, who would be able to instil in Yehudi the necessary discipline to pursue a career. Adolf was the brother of the conductor Fritz Busch, and lived in Basel because he couldn't abide the Nazis. And by the time that Menuhin had finished with Busch, he had a real musical pedigree. He couldn't have asked for a better technical and interpretative training. But the fact that he lived only with his own family, that his parents wouldn't let him play games, that they refused to allow him to cross the street by himself and that he never had any girl-friends was a real problem. Not only was he precious personally to Moshe and Marutha, but he was also valuable to them financially. He earned great sums of money for the family from touring.

RH: And speaking of girlfriends, it was only after the Australian conductor Sir Bernard Heinze introduced Nola Nicholas and her brother, Lindsay, to Yehudi after a concert at London's Royal Albert Hall that romance blossomed. What's your take on that meeting?

HB: It was an astonishing encounter. The two young Australians were the children of the scientist who had invented Aspro during the First World War. He'd made a fortune and had sent them on a tour of Europe in 1938. They both went to the dressing room after the concert, and Yehudi quickly started to chat very vividly with Nola. By coincidence or not, they were staying in the same hotel, and went off to a party together the next day. Nola's brother, Lindsay, who was older and very handsome, then took a shine to Hephzibah. Within months of that meeting, both couples were married. Yehudi and Hephzibah were particularly keen to get away from their mother and father, as they had been so dominated by them. Not to be outdone, little Yaltah then got married at the age of sixteen. But that marriage didn't work out because of the sexual orientation of her husband. Nevertheless, it was clear to all that the Menuhin children's childhoods were well and truly over.

RH: During the Second World War, Menuhin spent a great deal of time playing to the troops. How did this affect him personally and professionally?

HB: He once said that it wasn't until the war that he had a chance to meet 'ordinary' people. Even after he married in 1938, and was living in California, he continued to tour for about eight or nine months of the year. This carried on until the end of 1941, when the United States entered the war. But as he had two children by then, he wasn't called up immediately. Keen to do his bit, he would find out where the nearest military base was to wherever he was performing and would play to the troops. He also offered his services more generally, and was flown out to the Aleutian Islands before being sent on to Hawaii. Today, Honolulu might be something of a holiday resort, but, then, it was a staging post for the war in the Pacific. He played to two different groups of people on the island: marines, who were about to embark on the airborne invasion of Guam, and the wounded. He'd seen a mile-long queue of ambulances bringing injured servicemen to hospital. He wrote very touchingly about this, and described how he would walk through each ward and play to the men there. It was a true manifestation of his belief that music acts as succour for people in need.

RH: And, here, one should spare a thought for Menuhin's long-suffering pianist, Adolph Baller. He accompanied Yehudi on many of these journeys, and was often faced with very poor instruments. Inevitably, the keys would stick or freeze because of the humidity or the cold.

HB: After the Nazis took charge of Germany in 1933, Menuhin refused to play there. But he was keen to perform elsewhere in Europe, and once managed to talk his way onto a Royal Air Force bomber that flew him across the Atlantic. In Britain, he gave concerts at Scapa Flow, Liverpool, Birmingham and London. He went all over the shop, and even played for the Free French at the Royal Albert Hall. After performing in London in 1944, Yehudi managed to get a lift to Antwerp, where he played the day after the city was liberated. The room that he performed in had been the headquarters of the Gestapo until the day before. He then moved on to Brussels before 'hitchhiking' by plane to Paris. There, he met all his old friends from Ville-d'Avray, where he'd lived before the war, and where there's soon to be a Menuhin Festival. When he first performed in Paris as a boy, Yehudi played under the great French conductor Paul Paray at concerts that were organised very quickly. That was still the case during the war, and within days of arriving in the French capital, he played Mendelssohn's Violin Concerto and Lalo's *Symphonie espagnole*.

RH: During Yehudi's wartime visits to Europe, he met his second wife, Diana. In what ways did Menuhin's second marriage shape him personally and professionally?

HB: We could spend hours on this! Diana totally changed the way that Yehudi's life played out. He was unhappy in his first marriage to Nola, as they'd married very young and didn't really share the same interests. In contrast, Diana's mother, Evelyn Gould, was a great social 'lioness' before

PART FOUR: PRODUCERS/FILMMAKERS/ADMINISTRATORS

the war, and who numbered the great German conductor Wilhelm Furtwängler amongst her admirers. As Evelyn had a wonderful salon, Diana grew up surrounded by music. She was invited to dance with Pavlova and Diaghilev, but both died before that could happen. Yehudi also loved dance, and while he was in London in 1944, Diana's mother arranged a lunch and invited him. He duly went, and that's when he and Diana met for the first time. The couple married in 1947 and lived in California for eight years. But Diana realised that Yehudi's heart was in Europe, so they settled in Highgate, North London, in 1959. They also put down roots in Gstaad in Switzerland, and, for a time, in Italy. And Diana was also with him at a particularly crucial moment in his life.

Before they married in 1947, Yehudi and Diana travelled together to Berlin, where Menuhin was to give some charity concerts with Wilhelm Furtwängler for a Jewish organisation. But it all went sour for a time. For some reason, Menuhin always wanted to re-establish Furtwängler's political and social credibility, even though they had never actually played together. It seems that Yehudi had always felt very close to Furtwängler because of Diana's mother, and because the German had been best man at Diana's sister's wedding to the Hungarian pianist Louis Kentner. Amongst the concerts that Yehudi was to play in Berlin was one at the Tivoli Cinema for displaced persons from a camp outside Berlin. As most of the camp's residents were Jewish, and as the camp newspaper had called upon its readers to boycott the concert because it claimed that Menuhin's previous audience contained two former SS men, less than fifty residents attended. Encouraged by Diana, Yehudi then visited the camp and attempted to explain his position. He was then booed and sneered at, even though he made a very beautiful speech. The residents felt that Menuhin was a traitor to his race. But he told them that he was Jewish, and that he did what he believed to be right. Yehudi also explained that Jewish people should not act with revenge in their hearts, but should be proud to be who they were. If revenge was sought, he argued, the Jewish race would be no better than those who tried to exterminate it. Little by little the speech won the people over, and he eventually gained the support of those who had been shouting 'collaborator' and 'traitor'. Later, the journalist who wrote the piece in the camp newspaper visited Yehudi at his hotel and apologised. The incident had a happy ending.

RH: Menuhin also supported Furtwängler's attempt at being appointed Music Director of the Chicago Symphony Orchestra in 1949. But because of an outcry by artists like Arthur Rubinstein, Isaac Stern, Arturo Toscanini and George Szell, Furtwängler's appointment fell at the first hurdle.

HB: I've never got to the bottom of why Yehudi was so stubborn in fighting for Furtwängler. The whole of the Jewish-American musical community refused to play in Germany because of the Holocaust, and they also accused Menuhin of being a bad Jew because of his defence of the conductor.

RH: When one takes a broader view of the post-Holocaust period in Germany, it can be a very confusing picture. Otto Klemperer, for example, returned to Germany quite soon after the end of the war, but never suffered the same criticism as Menuhin.

HB: True. And Yehudi also used his celebrity to fight outside of the musical world for other ethical and moral causes. When he went to South Africa in 1950, for example, he attacked apartheid by playing in the townships after being told that black and coloured South Africans were forbidden from attending his scheduled concerts. Later, when he

PART FOUR: PRODUCERS/FILMMAKERS/ADMINISTRATORS

was visiting the Soviet Union, and when he was president of UNESCO's International Music Council, he confronted the Soviets in the Kremlin over their treatment of dissidents. Then, in Israel's Knesset during the 1990s, he lectured the country's leaders over their unacceptable approach to the Arab minority.

RH: His relationship with the Israeli state was never smooth.

HB: It certainly wasn't. Menachem Begin even sent Yehudi letters saying that he would bomb him should he give a concert in Israel. Menuhin *did* give a concert and he *wasn't* bombed.

RH: Yehudi's relationship with Hollywood was also fascinating. Do you not think that he missed an educational trick by not engaging with it more?

HB: Before the war, Moshe didn't want Yehudi to have anything to do with Hollywood, but he did give the first televised concert in Los Angeles after the conflict. Once television was really established, he did embrace that medium fully. When I ran music on BBC Television, we started a series called *Masterclass* immediately after the launch of BBC Two. The very first show was with Paul Tortelier, followed by programmes with Daniel Barenboim and Yehudi Menuhin. Menuhin's six different masterclasses were divided into six different stages, from Manoug Parikian at the top to the young Nigel Kennedy at the bottom. A decade later, Menuhin televised a whole method of teaching. This type of programming hasn't caught on.

RH: Currently, art music on free-to-air television is very fragmentary. Is there now anyone at the BBC who does what you once did?

HB: Alas, no. It's different now. It is more populist and less educational. But, for me, education can also be very entertaining if it's done well. When Yehudi made his film of Mendelssohn's Violin Concerto, the man who produced it wanted to send 16mm copies of it, along with other films of Menuhin in recital, to cinemas throughout America, and not just to the big cities. Rather like the famous beer advertisement, the promoter was going to send music to the places that other musicians couldn't reach. And when Yehudi founded Live Music Now in the 1970s, he wanted to use the organisation educationally. He paid young professionals to play in places like prisons, hospices and old-folks' homes, places where good music was not always accessible.

RH: Menuhin was always keen to embrace the music of other cultures, specifically that of India. I was interested to learn that when he played as a soloist with the Bombay Symphony Orchestra under Mehli Mehta, Zubin's father, Yehudi was keen for the musicians to engage with their own culture rather than with Western art music. I found this both paradoxical and slightly hypocritical. Why did Yehudi become so involved with Indian cultural life?

HB: In a word, 'yoga'. He discovered it in 1951 when he picked up a book in a waiting room and learned how it might help him relax. And when he went to India, he put an advertisement in a local newspaper that read, 'Virtuoso seeks guru'. He then 'auditioned' half a dozen people before settling on B. K. S. Iyengar from Pune. Iyengar later came to England at Yehudi's invitation, and went on to established clinics in Paris and the United States. He then became one of the most sought-after yoga practitioners in the West. While Menuhin was in India, he also had supper with Pandit Nehru. Keen to see what Yehudi had learned from Iyengar, Nehru suggested that he should show him what he could do. Menuhin

PART FOUR: PRODUCERS/FILMMAKERS/ADMINISTRATORS

then proceeded to stand on his head in full evening dress, followed by Nehru himself. While both the great fiddle player and the great statesmen were on their respective heads, the major-domo entered the room and announced, 'Dinner is served.'

RH: Menuhin then got involved with the great French jazz violinist Stéphane Grappelli. Both Indian music and jazz require highly developed improvisatory skills. How expert was Yehudi as an improviser?

HB: Here, we must step back in time to when he was in Romania, and when he met gypsies playing in a market square there. Menuhin always loved the sound of improvised music, its lack of exact intonation and its use of *portamenti*. He then spent ten years, and a great many television programmes, a number of which I was involved with, talking about Indian music. George Harrison and other members of The Beatles later took it up before it largely disappeared from our screens. It was a passing phase. Yehudi always liked improvising, but he never quite got it. Perhaps he came closest to it when he was performing Indian music. He not only played it at the Bath Festival, but also at the General Assembly Hall of the United Nations. A few years later, Michael Parkinson's producer heard that Yehudi was keen on improvising. The producer then had the brilliant idea of putting Menuhin together with the fiddle player who used to perform with the guitarist Django Reinhardt at the Hot Club de France before the war: Stéphane Grappelli. And the first time that Menuhin and Grappelli played together was on Parkinson's television programme on Christmas night in 1971.

RH: When that broadcast took place, much of the viewing audience would've known who Menuhin was. It's unlikely that the same percentage of today's public would know who Janine Jansen or James Ehnes are, even though they are artists of the front rank.

HB: True, particularly when it comes to the middle classes. For donkey's years, Menuhin used to write to *The Times* each month. He always backed worthy causes and even helped to start a health-food restaurant. Well before they became fashionable, he fought for all the things that we now take for granted as part of a 'green' lifestyle. He even had two experimental electric cars that were always breaking down. This meant that his passengers had to get out at the bottom of Highgate Hill and help push them to the top. They were huge vehicles that he'd imported from America.

RH: When did Menuhin take up conducting?

HB: He started by leading performances from the concertmaster's position with his chamber orchestra. But he then became bolder. His management team also realised that if his name was listed as conductor on concert posters, they'd sell lots of tickets. Brand 'Menuhin' was probably the biggest ever invented, and was always sure-fire box office. He was never on the same technical level as Leonard Bernstein or Herbert von Karajan as a conductor, but the musicians enjoyed working with him. As he'd performed with great figures such as Furtwängler, Busch and Willem Mengelberg, he always had something interesting to say. Not only did he have strong working relationships with the Royal Philharmonic Orchestra, the Philharmonia Hungarica and the Sinfonia Varsovia, but he made dozens of symphonic recordings, including cycles of the Beethoven and Schubert symphonies. Today, he tends to be pushed aside as a conductor, but I had a healthy respect for him.

PART FOUR: PRODUCERS/FILMMAKERS/ADMINISTRATORS

RH: Menuhin was constantly open to learning, and when he established the Menuhin School in the 1960s, it came as no surprise. Was this a means of exploring his own past?

HB: I think that he was keen to ensure that young virtuosi with a similar talent to his, and highly gifted children in general, were not segregated like he had been. As well as concentrated teaching in their chosen instruments, he wanted the students to have a good formal education, healthy food, plenty of fresh air and team games. And the school has flourished because it *is* so good. When Mrs Thatcher was Secretary of State for Education and Science, she gave the school a special standing in this country, along with the Royal Ballet School and one or two other specialist schools. While some people might object to such institutions, the proof is in the pudding. Tasmin Little, Nicola Benedetti and Nigel Kennedy all benefited from this type of education.

RH: The breadth of Menuhin's other educational activities was remarkable, including the idea of a European Cultural Parliament where cultural minorities from across the continent could engage with one another. Did any of his wider educational activities have any lasting impact?

HB: Of course, the European movement is still going strong, even though we don't take to it so much in Britain. Don't forget that there's a foundation in Brussels that helps Roma children from five or six different countries to understand their music and to come to terms with the importance of their culture. There are also foundations, competitions and festivals in places like Switzerland that still carry his name. I believe fully that he's still impactful across a broad educational spectrum.

RH: Menuhin died in Berlin in 1999, and shortly after his death Kaddish was said for him by Rabbi David Goldberg. What were the foundations of Yehudi's belief system?

HB: At his memorial service at St Paul's Cathedral, there were contributions from the Christian, Jewish, Muslim and Indian faiths. He obviously believed in a spiritual power, and when he was asked by Cliff Michelmore whether he believed in a god, he said, 'I believe in a universal power, which integrates everything. All the elements, all life, inorganic or organic. There is this universe which hangs together on basic laws. And we will never know the mysteries which are all around us.'

TONY PALMER

(DAVID JOSEFOWITZ RECITAL HALL, 14 NOVEMBER 2014)

RAYMOND HOLDEN: You've published at least eight books, made countless films on a variety of topics, directed operas at major theatres and have written for *The New York Times*, *The Times*, *Punch* and *Life*. Very little seems to daunt you. Is there anything that you can't do?

TONY PALMER: Peter Pears once told me that the only thing that Benjamin Britten could do in the kitchen was to watch an egg boil and to watch toast burn. Since telling me that, I've learned how to cook an egg and how to make toast!

RH: Can we now add 'chef' to your great list of achievements?

TP: Yes, I can now do that, too!

RH: You were born in London towards the end of 1941. What was life like growing up in the post-Blitz capital?

TP: I didn't grow up in London, as I was 'shipped out' of the city almost immediately. I'm still not quite sure why that was the case. I was brought up by my godparents, and I didn't really know my parents until I was about seven. I was fortunate in that my godfather was a railway engineer.

With his partner, Nigel Gresley, he built the famous 'Mallard', which was the fastest thing on wheels at the time. Gresley died the year that I was born, and he left his desk to my godfather. When he died in 1968, he then left the desk to me, one of my proudest possessions. When I finally acquired this lovely roll-top object, I looked in the large middle drawer, and there were all of Gresley's original sketches for the 'Mallard', which I've since given to the National Railway Museum in York. I now have a marvellous photograph of me standing in front of this gigantic locomotive with the sketches displayed beside me. Being a railway engineer, my godfather was then sent to Cornwall, which is now my home, and where he worked at a place called Goonhilly Downs. There, he developed a sophisticated form of radar. So, I had something of a split childhood that was divided between Doncaster, where the railway works were, Cornwall and Cambridge, where I later attended university.

RH: At Cambridge, you were president of The Marlowe Society for a period.

TP: That was rather odd, as I went to Cambridge on a scholarship to read Moral Sciences, an intimidating-sounding subject. Effectively, it's the opposite of Natural Sciences. It's all those so-called scientific subjects that are non-empirical. It was founded at the beginning of the last century by the philosopher G. E. Moore, and its most famous teacher was Bertrand Russell. Its most famous pupil, and later one of its greatest teachers, was Ludwig Wittgenstein. That gives you a flavour of my background at Cambridge, and as I knew a little about mathematics, that's what I seemed destined to do. I wasn't remotely interested in the arts, but I did have a friend at university who came from a similar lower-middle-class background, and who also went to a grammar school. His name was Trevor Nunn. As he was very particular about who should

PART FOUR: PRODUCERS/FILMMAKERS/ADMINISTRATORS

take over The Marlowe Society, he thought of me. And that's how I 'inherited' it. In fact, at Cambridge, I had no intention of doing what I now do; that happened entirely by accident.

RH: How did that change come about?

TP: I had a friend at Oxford who was several years older than me: the stage director Patrick Garland. After he left university, he got a post at the BBC. He then telephoned me one day and asked if I'd like a holiday job. I jumped at the chance and said 'yes'. The previous long vacation, I'd packed butter at Sainsbury's. That was the other thing that I was really good at: I could look at a big block of butter and cut it exactly into one-pound portions. When I later joined the BBC, I put that skill on my curriculum vitae. The guy interviewing me thought that I was making it up, so I decided to call his bluff. I said, 'No. Challenge me!' But to return to Patrick. One of his first major assignments was to make a film about the Salzburg Festival. That was in 1964. As I spoke a little German, and was already acquainted with Salzburg, he asked me to assist him. Even though I would effectively be the project's tea boy and odd-jobs man, it still sounded preferable to sitting in the basement at Sainsbury's, chopping butter. On the third day in Salzburg, we were to film in the famous Festung Hohensalzburg, which overlooks the city, and my job was to get the extremely heavy film equipment up there. Having managed to drag everything up the very steep incline that leads to the Festung, I then sat in a corner, completely knackered, hoping that the whole thing would go away. But what Patrick was filming was quite extraordinary. No further than two metres from me was Oskar Kokoschka. He was giving an art class to students, who were drawing a naked girl. As she was probably one of the most beautiful women I'd ever seen, I still remember thinking, 'There's Oskar Kokoschka with a very beautiful naked lady, and I am being paid for this.' It was a far cry from the academic life that I thought I was destined for. And I also remember thinking, 'This is money for jam. This is the future.' That's why I decided to make films. From that moment on, I thought, 'To hell with being an academic; this is much more interesting.'

A few years ago, I was making a film about the great South African playwright Athol Fugard, and was able to interview Nelson Mandela. Uncharacteristically, I was asked to provide the questions beforehand. Normally, I'd never do that. Instead, I'd usually suggest to an interviewee that we should meet, have a conversation, and work from there. But as it *was* Nelson Mandela, and as he *was* very old at the time, I sent him three very predictable questions in advance. On the day of the filming, we erected what is known in the trade as an 'idiot board' behind the camera and me. This displayed Mandela's answers. As he was quite frail by the time of the interview, and as Athol Fugard meant an enormous amount to him, it was understandable that he wanted to organise his thoughts. He was keen to ensure that whatever he said was exactly what he meant. One of the questions that I asked him was: 'Can you tell me how important Athol Fugard was to you when you were on Robben Island?' After starting with, 'When I was on Robben Island', Mandela suddenly paused. Concerned that he'd forgotten what he wanted to say, I turned around and began looking at the 'idiot board', thinking that he couldn't see it. But he then said, 'I'll tell you a story. When we were on the boat first going over to the island after being found guilty, the guards said to us, "Don't worry about a thing. You will be here for about five years, be released and emerge a hero. You'll then be surrounded by glamorous women who will want your autograph, amongst other things".' At which point Mandela leant forward and said, 'I'm still looking for the women!' I always think how lucky I was to be there with him, and what a joy he was.

PART FOUR: PRODUCERS/FILMMAKERS/ADMINISTRATORS

RH: Let's talk about Ken Russell and Sir Jonathan Miller. Am I correct in saying that you came into their orbits fairly early on?

TP: By the time I was interviewed for a job at the BBC, I knew of Ken Russell and had seen his Elgar and Bartók films, the second of which I thought was very powerful indeed. I said in the interview that if there was any chance of working with him, that's what I'd like to do. I was then assigned to Ken, effectively as his producer. This meant that I did everything that he didn't fancy. He was wonderful. One evening, he telephoned quite late and said that he wanted to do a scene the next morning in Hyde Park, a scene that I knew didn't exist in the original script. He wanted the Household Cavalry to come rushing across the park, hoped that I could arrange it and told me to be there at 8am. That was Ken. We also made a film called *Isadora*, which was enormous fun. I learned two things from him that were incredibly important to me. First, never put music in the background, and to always treat it with the respect that it deserves. If you are making a film about a composer, try and understand what the composer is saying. I profoundly believe that every note that a composer puts on the page tells us something. What that something might be can often be a completely different matter, but what it most certainly is not, is simply a series of dots and dashes on the page. The second thing that Ken sort of hinted at, but wasn't necessarily very good at, was how to drive the narrative of a film through music. When I made a piece with Maria Callas much later on, for example, you see her talking and singing. What she sings comments on what she says, and vice versa. The two are absolutely intermeshed. Music then drives the narrative of the film. I definitely learned this from Ken.

Nominally, I was the producer on Jonathan Miller's film *Alice in Wonderland*, which was broadcast again quite recently on television. It's curious, given his quite deserved later reputation as an opera director, that he once said to me, 'You know a bit about music, but I don't know anything at all.' This was very Jonathan-like, and I quickly realised that I was being led into the spider's web. He went on to say, 'Could you organise us some concerts to go to?' I agreed, and arranged for us to attend a concert at the Royal Festival Hall. Jonathan then told me to book a box, which I did. When I picked him up from his home at Gloucester Crescent, he emerged carrying about six books wrapped in a string bag. I asked him what they were for. He said, 'In case I get bored, I can read a book.' After we arrived at the hall, we took our places in one of its grand boxes. I sat at the front trying to concentrate, while Jonathan sat at the back ostentatiously reading. The person performing that night was Ravi Shankar, and when he came on stage with his troupe, it took at least ten minutes for them to tune their instruments. When the tuning-up came to an end, I suddenly felt a hand on my shoulder from behind. 'That's it. That's the music we need. Perfect. Perfect,' said Jonathan. I tried to tell him that the players were simply tuning up, but he still insisted that it was 'Perfect. Perfect' for the film. In the end, Ravi Shankar actually did record the music for *Alice in Wonderland*. But what I thought that was again very Jonathan-like was when *Life* came to do a huge cover story about the film. When he and I were interviewed by the magazine, he delivered a lengthy intellectual dissertation on what he understood the story to be about. For him, it reflected the autumn of the British Empire, and the sound of the sitar was central to that image. The problem was: Jonathan invented the whole thing. All he'd heard was Ravi Shankar and his ensemble tuning up, and that was that.

RH: Between 1966 and 1969, you made twelve films, a remarkable statistic. One of these was a truly iconic document: *Benjamin Britten & His Festival*.

PART FOUR: PRODUCERS/FILMMAKERS/ADMINISTRATORS

TP: I was incredibly lucky to have 'inherited' the film, which was originally to have been directed by Humphrey Burton. Benjamin Britten and the BBC had a slightly fractious relationship. There had been a short black-and-white film made in 1958 by the wonderful director John Schlesinger, which Britten had taken against. Nobody knew quite why Britten felt that way, but he did, and he wouldn't have the BBC anywhere near Aldeburgh. He didn't mind working in a BBC studio, but if the Corporation wanted to do a project that involved anything personal about him, he would refuse to take part. When *Benjamin Britten & His Festival* was made in 1967, the original Snape Maltings was about to be opened by the Queen. As it was to be something of a state occasion, Britten was eventually persuaded to allow cameras in to cover the event. Being not quite the project's tea boy, I was taken down to Aldeburgh by Humphrey to meet Britten, whom I'd met briefly once before. Over the next few weeks, I got to know him quite well while Humphrey planned what we were going to do.

The filming was due to start on the Monday, but shortly after lunch on the previous Wednesday, there was a knock on my hotel-room door. The manager said that I was wanted on the telephone downstairs. It was Humphrey Burton. He said, 'Don't panic. I've just been fired by the BBC.' Apparently, it had been leaked by the *Evening Standard* that he, Frank Muir and one or two others were leaving the Corporation to set up London Weekend Television. Considered traitors by the BBC, their punishment was to clear their desks and to leave. Humphrey went on to say, 'I'm not sure what's going to happen, but you stay there.' After returning to my room, and feeling slightly nervous, I heard yet another knock on the door. There was a second telephone call for me downstairs. It was Huw Wheldon. Not only was he very Welsh, but he was also very 'military'. Huw had created the BBC's music and arts ethos singlehandedly and was a truly amazing man. He said, 'Palmer. Wheldon. The cavalry's coming. Stay there.' I wasn't planning to go anywhere. Half an hour later, there was a third knock on my door. I told the manager that no matter who it was, I wasn't going downstairs again. He said, 'I think you'll want to take this call.' It was 'Mr Britten'. The composer said that he'd heard what had happened, and suggested that I might like to go to his house for tea and discuss it. I could hardly say 'no', so off I went to the Red House. I remember that at this particular tea, Ben was pouring while Peter was cutting a very nice fruit cake. But they were also giggling the whole time, and all they kept saying was, 'Don't worry, we'll get you through it.' They were absolutely wonderful, and they did get me through it.

After Britten died in 1976, Pears asked me if I would make, if not the official film about Ben, but a second one, which was later called *Benjamin Britten: A Time There Was…*. This piece was really about their love affair, an extremely emotional thing for Peter to talk about. He had never spoken about it in the past, but was now willing to speak openly about their homosexual relationship. During the course of this, I asked Peter if he remembered the tea that we had all those years ago. As he said that he did, I then asked why the two of them had been giggling throughout it. 'Oh,' he said, 'it was a bit naughty, and we should have told you. We never wanted to make the film. But as Humphrey had been fired, and as it was clear that you had absolutely no idea what you were doing, we thought that we could tell you exactly what to do.' They were right. After all, it was my first film.

RH: A marvellous moment in that film is when Sviatoslav Richter and Benjamin Britten are playing the last movement of Mozart's Sonata for Two Pianos.

TP: Richter never wanted to be filmed, and I had to beg him to take part in the project. In those days, we used celluloid and the exposure was quite

PART FOUR: PRODUCERS/FILMMAKERS/ADMINISTRATORS

slow. This meant that you needed a great deal of light, which he also didn't like, or any of the other paraphernalia necessary for filming music. I discussed this with Britten, and he said that he'd tell me exactly what to do. As he needed to rehearse the sonata with Richter, Ben said that I should be on stage at Snape and be ready to start filming as soon as the two of them came through the door at 3pm. Having got our two cameras set up, I stood there nervously at the appointed time. The doors then opened and in came Richter. I was the first person that he saw, and if looks could kill, I would've been dead meat. But as Britten was right behind him, he grabbed Richter by the arm, frogmarched him up the stage and sat him down. Richter clearly decided that this was a bit much, so he decided to trip Britten up in the sonata by speeding up and slowing down and by leaping from passage to passage. Richter did this to see if Britten could stay with him. He was trying to humiliate Ben in the nicest possible way. But as Britten was such a phenomenal pianist, that was never going to happen. Hence, all the grins and smiles from Ben, who was able to predict exactly which bar Richter was going to jump to next.

After the festival film was finished, there was a screening of it at the old BBC studios in Lime Grove. Britten and Pears were invited, and Huw Wheldon and I joined them. As it *was* my first film, Ben and Peter were absolutely right: I had no idea what I was doing. I'd busked most of it and hoped for the best. When I was editing the section that included the 'Deo Gracias' from *A Ceremony of Carols*, for example, I'd removed two bars from the end of the work, and hoped that nobody would notice. During the screening, I was seated next to Britten, but withstood the urge to ask him whether or not he was enjoying it. When the passage with the missing two bars was about to happen, I thought a well-placed cough might be just the thing to cover my indiscretion. I was in such a sweat, but the passage flew by before I could do anything. There was a nice luncheon after the screening during which Ben and

Peter were quite complimentary about the film. Before Britten and Pears left Lime Grove in the BBC limousine, Peter gave me a big hug and thanked Huw for everything. Ben had been nice about the film, and after speaking to Huw, he, too, gave me a big hug and kiss. I thought that I'd got away with it. But just as he was about to step into the car, Ben turned around, looked at me and said, 'I actually think it's better without those two bars.'

RH: Your second film, *All My Loving*, was an examination of rock and roll in the 1960s, and was made at a time of considerable political unrest.

TP: The film was made during the heyday of rock and roll. As I'd been writing about the genre for quite some while, I was asked to make a film about it. I knew from friends who performed this music that they felt very strongly about the direction the world was taking at the time. Of course, everybody thinks that the music of their youth represents some kind of golden period, but the popular music of the late 1960s really was absolutely extraordinary and still lives with us today. For reasons that I've yet to fathom, *All My Loving* was the first film of its type to be networked in America. Suddenly, from being a tea boy, I was a golden boy. That's always fatal! The idea for *All My Loving* came from John Lennon, who was more or less my best friend during those years. He had taken me out to lunch, during which we ate an awful lot of brown rice, and said, 'Now that you are in the BBC, you've got to use this to our advantage.' I didn't quite understand what he meant until he said, 'There are all kinds of wonderful musicians who can't get on to the BBC. Either they don't want to appear on *Juke Box Jury*, or they don't want to be seen behind gyrating nubiles.' Lennon was right. If you were Jimi Hendrix, for example, you wouldn't want to be seen behind a group of bright young things gyrating in the foreground. John said that he would give

PART FOUR: PRODUCERS/FILMMAKERS/ADMINISTRATORS

me a list of people to shoot and the title of the film. All I had to do was to ensure that it was broadcast. And that's why the piece is called *All My Loving*. Groups and solo artists like Cream, Pink Floyd, Jimi Hendrix and Frank Zappa had never been seen on television before. Our intention was to reflect what these people felt and said; it was a direct attack on the governments of the day, both here and in the United States. When the BBC management saw the film for the first time, it was so horrified that it put it on a shelf for nine months and left it there. It was then decided that the film should be aired after BBC TV's *Epilogue*, which was usually given by a Christian minister. As we knew that the Corporation's tactic was designed to hide the piece, John arranged for a great deal of pre-publicity, which ensured a vast audience. Even though I was then sued by Mrs Mary Whitehouse, the first of four such legal encounters with her, I felt that it was incumbent on me to reflect exactly what these artists had to say.

While working on *All My Loving*, I realised that I'd made a total hash of editing it after seeing Stanley Kubrick's *2001: A Space Odyssey*. Kubrick's film had just opened, and I went to see it again and again. In all, I saw it about six times in a week. The most important thing about the film for me was the first twenty-five minutes when nobody says a word. You don't get lost. That's because the music is extremely powerful and is used to drive the narrative of the film. I then realised that it was entirely possible to construct something that depended entirely on image and music. Having seen how the two media could be dovetailed in order to tell a story, I went straight back to my cutting room, junked what I'd done and started again. I then began to construct a film based entirely on the music's narrative drive and the images that we had. In every film since, I have categorically refused to have any kind of narration. Clearly, you can have a narration in general documentaries, but to have one in the average film on music is laziness. It tells the audience what to think, rather than allowing it to decide for itself. And the latter is absolutely the case with *All My Loving*. Lennon and I bet a pound before the film was broadcast. I said that the 'quality' newspapers would rubbish it, and that the popular-music press would go crazy for it. He thought I was wrong, and said that the reverse would be true. He was right. The 'pop' press rubbished it, and, to this day, I still receive academic essays examining the piece in detail. I simply told it like it was. I felt that that was the necessary thing to do. There's an interesting corollary to this story. After *All My Loving* was screened, I went to the BBC Christmas party, where I was confronted by the broadcaster David Jacobs, whom I'd never met before. He jabbed his finger at me and said before disappearing, 'Young man, you've ruined my career.' I had no idea what he was talking about. Then another colleague asked, 'What have you said to David Jacobs? He has just left the room and slammed the door.' Unsure of what I'd done, I was told that within days of *All My Loving* being broadcast, *Juke Box Jury*, Jacobs's programme, had been cancelled. It seems that the BBC finally realised that the show had nothing to do with what these particularly articulate, popular artists were saying, both through their words and their music. I felt that I'd struck a blow for freedom at the BBC.

RH: A work closely associated with *2001: A Space Odyssey* is Strauss's *Also sprach Zarathustra*. When you came to make your film about the Salzburg Festival in 2006, you used some footage showing the great Austrian maestro Herbert von Karajan conducting the opening of Strauss's 1896 masterpiece.

TP: In my Salzburg film, I was able to use a lot of material that I'd collected over the years. We'd tried for a long time to make a film with Karajan, but he was always very reluctant. But we did manage to film

PART FOUR: PRODUCERS/FILMMAKERS/ADMINISTRATORS

three or four sections, which were just breathtaking. He gave me no instructions whatsoever. He just wanted to know where the camera was, and how we were going to record the sound. What I tried to do when shooting the opening of the tone poem was to concentrate on Karajan's face. I'd learned the importance of this from one of my other great mentors, Ingmar Bergman. He was once asked what single, characteristic attribute defined his films. He said, 'The face.' 'Always watch the face. Everything is in the face.' I also remembering him saying this to me, and that's what we tried to do with Karajan.

RH: That clip captures the essence of Karajan. It reflects accurately his sound-world, his refined conducting technique and his devotion to his hometown of Salzburg.

TP: In the film, there's a section that shows him conducting the end of Beethoven's Ninth Symphony with the Vienna Philharmonic. It's absolutely electrifying. We had cameras everywhere, but we simply had to watch his face. Every element and aspiration of the music was registered in it. He was able to convey these qualities to the orchestra, which is why the performance is so exciting. Another section of the film that I'll never ever forget is him rehearsing the third movement of the Ninth Symphony with the orchestra. He effectively gave a half-hour masterclass to the violins on which string to use and on how to place the bow. It totally changed the sound, and, remarkably, the players accepted what he had to say willingly. Sadly, we could only use five or six minutes from this 'masterclass' in the final film. We all know Karajan's reputation, but there was considerably more to him than that.

RH: Absolutely. To dismiss Karajan, as some people do, is a big mistake. His particular artistic vision did much to shape the performance environment of his age. The other great figure who helped to shape that age was the man that Karajan wittily called 'Mr Music': Leonard Bernstein. Your 1971 film *Four Ways to Say Farewell*, which you made with Humphrey Burton, charts Bernstein's journey when preparing and performing Mahler's Ninth Symphony with the Vienna Philharmonic. What was Bernstein like to work with?

TP: Bernstein wasn't always easy, and between Humphrey and me, we filmed all the Beethoven symphonies with him. We alternated between directing and editing. Quite early on, Bernstein came to look at a rough cut of Beethoven's Second Symphony, which I was editing. The video tape hadn't been going for more than two or three minutes before I could hear him begin to mutter. Then, he screamed, 'Stop this rubbish! Did you edit this, or did Humphrey?' I told him that I did. Still white with rage, he screamed over and over, 'How can you do this to me?' He was very angry and very loud. Eventually, I plucked up the courage to ask, 'Do what?' 'I'm not conducting in "sync". What have you done to me?' he shouted. To calm matters down, I said that I was terribly sorry and that I'd re-edit the section by the next day. Bernstein then stormed out and slammed the door. He did come back the following day, but all I did was show him the material that we shot using the one camera that was devoted entirely to him. I naughtily told Bernstein that I had re-edited the section so that it now focused solely on him and so that it was completely in 'sync'. He then looked at the new clip, realised his outrageous *faux pas* and apologised. It was clear to him that the delay between sight and sound was purely down to the orchestra playing behind his extremely expressive beat. Bernstein's physicality always conveyed the power and majesty of the music. In fact, when we edited him, we were able to adjust the material so that when he gave a down-beat, the orchestra sounded with it.

PART FOUR: PRODUCERS/FILMMAKERS/ADMINISTRATORS

I remember one terrible evening when we were working with Bernstein on Mahler's compositions. He suddenly became very tearful and we couldn't understand why. What we didn't realise at the time was that he'd received terrible reviews for his *MASS: A Theatre Piece for Singers, Players and Dancers*. He felt absolutely crushed by the work's reception. He wanted to be Mahler: he wanted to be a great composer. He didn't much care about being a magnificent conductor. Eventually, he admitted to being depressed by all of this, and began to relax a bit. It was at that point I said, 'If I had written any single song in *West Side Story*, I'd be in heaven.' He finally got the point and begrudgingly said, 'I suppose so.' It was easy for him to forget just how astonishing works like *West Side Story* and *Candide* are, and that he was a phenomenal pianist like Britten. But it still wasn't good enough for Bernstein.

And, here, I'd like to return to Benjamin Britten for a moment or two, if I may. I once asked him in an interview, who, amongst the *other* great composers, interested him. He said, 'I'm not a great composer, and I wish people would stop saying so.' 'But who do *you* consider a great composer?' I asked. 'Schubert' was his immediate reply. Then, during the course of a fascinating conversation about the greatness of Schubert, I realised why Britten *couldn't* consider himself to be a great composer. If you are a composer, or a creative artist of any kind, you are in the shadow of titanic figures. As you will always measure your work against theirs, it's nearly impossible for composers like Britten to get anything into perspective. They are riddled with every conceivable kind of insecurity. I then had the temerity to say to Ben, 'Don't you think that Schubert was also riddled with similar insecurities?' I can't think of any great creative artist with whom I have dealt, and I have dealt with quite a few over the years, who was in any sense confident about what they've done. I would say that Britten was one of the greatest pianists I ever had the good fortunate to hear. Yet, even when he gave a recital of his own music with Peter Pears, he couldn't go on stage unless he drank a tumbler full of whisky first. Not a sip, a tumbler full. If his stomach was empty, he would then be sick in the dressing room. Only after that would he go out and play. I have footage of Britten where he is about to perform and his hands are shaking like a leaf. In my most recent Britten film, *Nocturne*, Dame Janet Baker tells an amazing story. After singing with Ben at a concert, they both returned to the stage to take a bow. Janet remembers trembling with nerves as she came back on to the platform, only to find that Britten was also shaking after taking her hand. They were both absolutely petrified. And all this was *after* the concert. The extent to which great artists can be hopelessly unsure of what they do, and the manner by which they do it, goes quite a long way in creating their own special magic.

One of the most remarkable things about Britten, and his facility to compose, was the way in which he accepted a commission for an opera. First, he would ask when the premiere was scheduled for. If the piece was to open in February 1973, say, and that he'd accepted the commission in 1968, he'd then work out that he could start composing six months before the 1973 deadline. He actually did this for at least one of his operas, and began composing it six months to the day before opening night. But he also knew that the parts and the vocal scores had to be copied, printed and delivered, so that the singers and musicians could learn their material. It was all mapped out and done. And even though he could write at a phenomenal speed, he needed that map. The *War Requiem* is probably the most famous example of all. That particular piece was his fourth attempt at writing a grand choral work: he wanted to compose something similar after both the bombing of Hiroshima and the death of Gandhi. The *War Requiem* was commissioned two and a half years before the first performance, which was in May 1962. I know, because I was there. Britten began work on the piece in the November

PART FOUR: PRODUCERS/FILMMAKERS/ADMINISTRATORS

of the previous year. Even though he'd sketched out the words in one of his school books many years before, the actual placing of the notes on the page didn't happen until the end of 1961. He wrote the work section by section, and sent off each part after it was completed. There was no notion of seeing how the whole work panned out before dispatching it. His copyist, Imogen Holst, said that he could compose thirty pages of full score in a day. His handwriting on the whole was fairly neat, but it was Imogen's task to add some of the details. It was a phenomenal production line.

RH: But you, too, are something of a creative production line. Just take your books, for example. You wrote five books in six years, everything from Charles II to Liberace.

TP: It was a period when I was bored with making films. They weren't much fun, and I blame Julian Bream, in the nicest possible way, for my temporary change of direction. Julian was approaching his fiftieth birthday, and his wonderful agent, Martin Campbell-White, said, 'I'm sick and tired of Julian telling me that he's going to write his autobiography. His fiftieth birthday is approaching, and he's not going to do it. Would you go and help him?' I went down to Wiltshire to see Julian and to ask what he'd like to do. After telling me that he had a great many stories that he'd like to tell, I suggested that I should go on tour with him. I'd been on tour with Led Zeppelin, so why not go on tour with Julian Bream? And that's why the book's called *A Life on the Road*. In it, I simply describe what happened during his three-week tour in Italy. I then 'fleshed' this out with other biographical information. There was one wonderful night, for example, when a promoter said to Julian that it was time to go on stage. Right to be distrustful of Italian impresarios, Julian said, 'I'm not going on stage until you pay me in cash.' Having obviously already agreed this with the promoter, Julian was confronted with a huge stack of lira. I asked if he would like me to look after it, but he said 'no'. He then stuffed the banknotes into his guitar, walked out on stage, bowed to the audience, winked at me and began to play. In the book, I also mentioned that he had two voices: his stage voice, which is frightfully proper, and his day-to-day cockney voice. When I delivered the manuscript to Julian, he didn't comment at all. Martin considered it safe, so off it went to the publisher. I then got a tirade from Julian saying that I'd betrayed his trust and that I'd written stuff that wasn't true. As Julian clearly hated the book, I was both surprised and amused when Dame Peggy Ashcroft, somebody I knew extremely well, and who was also a close friend of Julian, telephoned me the following November to say, 'I've heard that Julian has been berating you and berating the book. Is that true?' I said 'yes', and that he and I were probably not friends at the moment. Peggy then said, 'I was at his house the other day, and he has fifty copies that he's signing as Christmas presents.' I went to see him a short while ago to talk about his autobiography, which he still hasn't written. This would be for his eightieth birthday. I told him that the book would be a wonderful thing, and that I'd love to help.

RH: Tell me about Liberace.

TP: Somebody once asked me in the early 1970s, 'Have you ever thought of making a film about Liberace?' At the time, I thought he was a bit of a joke. But as the chap who asked the question said I might find the idea interesting, I decided to fly to Warwick, Rhode Island, where Liberace was playing. As his career had nosedived, and as his television series had ceased, he was mainly 'on the road' during that period. After checking in at my own hotel, I went down to the swimming pool at Liberace's, where I found the American talent agent Seymour Heller, the pianist's manager.

PART FOUR: PRODUCERS/FILMMAKERS/ADMINISTRATORS

He asked what I wanted to do and how I wanted to do it. He also invited me to the concert and suggested that we should talk afterwards. Suddenly, Liberace appeared, whom I'd never met. After we shook hands and sat down, his first question was, 'Where are you staying?' When I told him which hotel it was, he said, 'You can't stay there.' He then turned to Seymour and said, 'Book him into the best suite in this hotel at my expense.' It really was a swish place. At the concert that evening, there was a queue a mile long. Not only did the 'blue-rinse set' turn out, but a complete cross-section of the public. That struck me as extraordinary, and for two and a half hours, I've never laughed so much. He was a wonderful entertainer and very funny. Of course, he was wearing all his jewels, which he showed to a woman in the front row. With his trademark smile and customary wit, he then said, 'Do you like them, dear? Good, because you've paid for them.' The show was a series of non-stop gags.

I became pretty close to Liberace during the filming, and was incensed by the Michael Douglas film. In that movie, Douglas minces all the time, but, in my experience, Liberace never did. I knew that he was gay, but he never thrust it in your face. In fact, he always wanted to get married and to have children; his eight dogs acted as a kind of surrogate family. It's true that he tried to adopt his young chauffeur, as Liberace hoped that the young man would be the son that he never had. And when I was filming Liberace, he showed us some of his absolutely magnificent *objets d'art*, including an extraordinary onyx table. When shooting him at his home, we were still using celluloid and a great many lights. To get the shot we needed, I suggested that we put a light on the corner of the table. He was happy with this, and as he walked and talked to camera, he said that this is one of the largest onyx tables in existence. Within seconds of saying that, there came a loud cracking sound. I looked back at the light, only to see that it had shattered the table. When Liberace also looked back at it, all he said was, 'I think we'd better do that again.'

I was mortified by what had just happened, and when we retook the shot with him yet again walking and talking to camera, he sighed, 'And this is one of the largest onyx tables in existence, which is also cracked.'

I don't want to say that my film rescued Liberace's career, as that would be completely untrue. But when it was shown on American television, his career did take off again. Towards the end of his life, it was phenomenal to see him at the Radio City Music Hall. At that gigantic venue, he gave two weeks of consecutive shows, all of which were sold out. At one point, I was staying with him in Las Vegas, and he said that it had been a terrible year. I asked him why. He said it was because he could no longer face wearing all those heavy costumes. He then told me that he'd 'slimmed down' and was wearing more modest outfits. I was puzzled as to why this was a problem. He explained that because audiences always wanted the full Liberace experience, his income had dropped by several million dollars.

RH: Another major television series that you directed in the 1970s was *All You Need is Love*. This seventeen-part series was one of the most comprehensive overviews of popular music to date, and explores, amongst others, the Royal Academy of Music's Sir Elton John, one of our most generous and enthusiastic supporters.

TP: Elton is an incredibly generous human being. And, again, this series was John Lennon's idea. We met by accident in New York, having not seen each other for two or three years. He had the unnerving habit of catching you off guard with the first thing he'd say. On this occasion, his first words were, 'What are you doing that's useful?' Not 'Great to see you', but 'What are you doing that's useful?' He then said 'lunch', which meant more brown rice. During the meal, John was adamant that I should do a multi-episode series on American popular music. As it was

PART FOUR: PRODUCERS/FILMMAKERS/ADMINISTRATORS

one of the most important cultural phenomena of the twentieth century, he felt that it should be given the same weight as Kenneth Clark's *Civilisation*, Jacob Bronowski's *The Ascent of Man* and Alistair Cooke's *America*. I agreed immediately and we began to make a list of subgenres that needed to be investigated: ragtime, blues, soul music and so on. He then said that he had to go, and shot off towards the door. Just as he reached it, he turned and said, 'I have the perfect title for you.' 'What's that?' I asked. 'Call it *All You Need is Love.*' I looked a bit worried, but he said that I had his permission to use it. When the DVD box set finally came out a few years ago in America, we were required to do what's called a 'title search'. Even though I told the lawyers that the phrase was really common parlance, they insisted that a search was still necessary. Interestingly, we found that The Beatles had never taken out any copyright or a trademark relating to the title, but two organisations had: one was a brothel in Amsterdam, and the other was the maker of *risqué* lingerie in Hong Kong!

We found when making the series that it didn't matter which subgenre of popular music that we chose to investigate, the same curve happened. Take country and western music, for example. Having heard the music performed in concert, a radio executive might put it on the radio live. The audience grows immediately. A record producer then hears the broadcast and makes a disc of it. The audience grows still further until it cascades out of control. Recording-company executives then get involved at this point and exploit it mercilessly until it no longer has any meaning. And it's only rare individuals, such as Bob Dylan and Leonard Cohen, who have managed to hang on to their innate intimacy, which is why they are so remarkable. But what was common to all the styles that we tackled was that they all started out very simply and with the intention of telling people something. We know that was the case for Scott Joplin and his marvellous opera,

Treemonisha. But because of his ethnicity and social situation, nobody would perform it. In fact, we staged a segment from it in 1975 for the series. Ragtime was Joplin's attempt at imitating string quartets. We know this from his letters, and that's why his music is so complicated. And there's a vast gulf between the ragtime of Scott Joplin and Irving Berlin's song *Alexander's Ragtime Band*. While Berlin's song was not ragtime, it did make money. Joplin's original, on the other hand, was washed away by the tidal filth of commercialism until comparatively recently. Whether it be the blues, jazz, ragtime or rock and roll, people are singing about their conditions and circumstances. These styles have nothing to do with the popular, televised award shows that now dominate the airwaves. They came later and tended to destroy the music. So, it's not only great classical composers, such as Dmitri Shostakovich, who are telling us something.

RH: Speaking of Shostakovich, you made a film about him called *Testimony*.

TP: When I shot that film with Sir Ben Kingsley as Shostakovich in 1987, I was puzzled by one thing: why had the composer's opera *Lady Macbeth of the Mtsensk District* offended so many people? As we know, Stalin had gone to see it, and, within a few days, *Pravda* had denounced it. Shostakovich then lived in fear for his life. At night, he would sit by his front door with a suitcase strapped to his arm that contained the beginnings of his Fifth Symphony. He knew from what had happened to some of his friends, who had been taken out and shot, that he, too, would have about four or five days in prison before being murdered. Since he composed at such great speed, he also knew that he would be able to sketch out the symphony during those days. I then discovered that there was, in fact, eighteen months between the first performance

PART FOUR: PRODUCERS/FILMMAKERS/ADMINISTRATORS

of *Lady Macbeth* and when Stalin had gone to see it. I had no idea that that was the case. We then began to check on the number of performances that the opera had received, and discovered that in Russia alone, let alone in the United States, where it was also performed during that period, that there were more performances of the piece than of the collected works of Puccini, Verdi and Wagner combined. I found that incredible. Eventually, the penny dropped. If you are a poet, and you write a line saying that Stalin was a bad man, it can be read and easily understood. But if you write a tune that says it, it can be awfully difficult to prove.

Effectively, Shostakovich got away with it, even though every note of every opera, symphony and string quartet that he composed described life in Russia at the time. There's nothing and nobody else quite like him, perhaps with the exception of a figure like Boris Pasternak. History is endlessly rewritten, and even today, we really don't know what happened during the Stalinist era. When we were finishing *Testimony*, I wanted two captions at the end. The first was going to state the number and types of works written by Shostakovich, and the second was to enumerate the vast number of murders that Stalin perpetrated during peace time. In the case of the latter, we weren't sure what that number was. I slightly knew the wonderful historian Robert Conquest, and asked him if he could suggest a figure. He said that nobody actually knew, and this was in the late 1980s. He did say, however, that if we were to put between 15 million and 45 million people, nobody would be able to contradict us. We opted for 30 million. Stalin murdered six times the population of Switzerland in peace time. Don't ever tell me that a creative artist such as Shostakovich isn't trying to tell us something. Composers like him are our witness and that's their importance.

I am currently working on a film about Lina Prokofiev, Sergei's first wife. Shostakovich, Khachaturian and Prokofiev were all famously denounced by the Soviet Union's Minister of Culture, Andrei Zhdanov, in January 1948 in the Great Hall of the Kremlin. During the course of this denunciation, the manuscript of Shostakovich's Ninth Symphony was actually torn up in front of him. This was intended as a way of humiliating him. When his son, Maxim, was about ten years old, he, too, was forced to stand in front of his classmates and to denounce his father. Maxim later told me that it still upsets him. In some ways, Prokofiev was more interesting. His wife, Lina, who was born in Spain, had parted from Sergei before 1948, but was still married to him until the beginning of that year. After the denunciation, the MGB, the forerunner of the KGB, arrested Lina and tortured her for nine months. Her diaries and letters have finally come to light, and it was horrendous. The MGB was trying to get her to admit that Sergei was a spy for the CIA; Sergei and Lina had lived in the United States during the 1920s and 1930s before returning to Russia. The Soviets knew that none of this was true, but it was their way of getting at the composer. And, of course, Prokofiev felt terrible that his former wife was being persecuted in this manner. He was devastated. After nine months, the MGB gave up trying to get Lina to admit Sergei's supposed guilt and threw her into a gulag for twenty years. Eventually, she was released, oddly enough after the intervention of Shostakovich, who had appealed to the authorities at the behest of Lina's two sons during what is now known as the 'Khrushchev Thaw'.

Then, clever old Shostakovich suggested that it might be a good idea if the Soviets sent Lina around the world as a kind of ambassador for Prokofiev's music. But what I didn't mention earlier about my time as a 'tea boy' at the BBC was that I was also the production assistant for Kenneth MacMillan's staging of Prokofiev's *Romeo and Juliet* with Dame Margot Fonteyn and Rudolf Nureyev. And what I didn't know at the time was that Mrs Prokofiev had been in the audience. But I *did*

PART FOUR: PRODUCERS/FILMMAKERS/ADMINISTRATORS

know that she was at the first complete performance of the composer's *War and Peace* at Sadler's Wells in 1972, which I also attended. She eventually came to London to live permanently and where she later died. According to her diaries, almost the last person she saw, apart from her two sons, was Margot Fonteyn. The dancer thanked Lina for what she'd done for her. Lina replied, 'I have to thank you for what you did for us.' Until that famous production of *Romeo and Juliet*, people knew the music, but had never seen the ballet. There had been no tradition of giving the work in the theatre. Now, it's seen all over the world, thanks largely to MacMillan's pioneering production.

RH: You have also been active as an opera director and famously produced Wagner's *Parsifal* at the Mariinsky Theatre with Valery Gergiev and Plácido Domingo in 1997.

TP: The initiative was Gergiev's, as he had seen my film on Richard Wagner with Richard Burton. By the time that he'd seen that piece, Valery had his feet well and truly under the table at the Mariinsky Theatre, and had begun to take control of its artistic direction. Having also learned that I'd already directed some operas, Gergiev decided to invite me to produce *Parsifal* there. As the opera had never been performed without cuts on a Russian stage before, the big question we then faced was: how would the local audience take to the work, even if they knew the music? To ease the way, I suggested that we should set it in a Russian village. I then also suggested that when the village woke up, it should be to a traditional Russian Easter, but set to the music of Richard Wagner. In other words, as the curtain rose, the audience would see a Russian village with everybody dressed as local peasants. Valery wasn't so sure about this, but Plácido saw the point immediately. We even had the ushers wear Russian peasant clothing, which they thought was a bit downmarket. But when the village awoke on stage, it was less like a Russian Easter service than a Black Mass.

At the first night, I sat in the audience so that I could judge the audience's reaction. About halfway through the first act, I heard the sound of shuffling and was convinced that the public was leaving. It was quite loud, but I was determined not to look around. At the end of the act, I went backstage only to find Valery slumped in a chair looking miserable. Domingo, on the other hand, was excited and was convinced that everything was going wonderfully well. Nothing seems to faze Plácido. Then Valery asked, 'Did you hear all that shuffling? Were they leaving?' 'I didn't dare look' was my reply. Gergiev then summoned my interpreter, who now works in public relations at Moscow's Bolshoi Theatre, and asked in Russian why there was so much shuffling in the auditorium. It seems that when the 'Mass' got going, many of the ladies fell to their knees and began to cross themselves. And I must tell you that our Second Flower Maiden was the then unknown Anna Netrebko. We also had three complete Russian casts for the production, as the theatre didn't have the wherewithal to bring artists from abroad if any of the principals fell ill. The production was successful, and remained in the Mariinsky's repertoire until 2012.

RH: Am I correct when I say that it was Gergiev who suggested that you should make a film about Rachmaninoff?

TP: Yes. In the middle of rehearsing *Parsifal*, Gergiev suddenly asked me what I knew about Rachmaninoff, and whether I also knew of the composer's relationship with the Mariinsky Theatre. I had to admit that I didn't. I then learned from Valery that Rachmaninoff had conducted the premiere of his Second Symphony there, along with some of his other works. Gergiev became so excited by all this that I agreed to make the film

PART FOUR: PRODUCERS/FILMMAKERS/ADMINISTRATORS

if he took charge of the music. As Valery is notoriously busy, I made him shake hands on it there and then. On returning to Britain, I realised what a spot I'd landed myself in. After contacting Boosey & Hawkes, I was able to confirm that the composer's grandson, Alexander, was still alive, that he was notoriously difficult to deal with, and that he didn't want anything to do with his grandfather other than to collect the royalties. With the help of the publishers, I was able to arrange to meet Alexander at the composer's house, Villa Senar, on the shores of Lake Lucerne. To my surprise, he then offered to pick me up from the airport at Zurich and to take me to lunch in the mountains. In the briefing notes that I was given, I was told that under no circumstances should I mention the movie *Shine*. But after several bottles of wine, Alexander leant across the table and asked, 'What did you think of *Shine*?' While trying to think of something diplomatic to say, Alexander then said, 'It made me a lot of money.'

RH: Your film on Rachmaninoff was ultimately called *The Harvest of Sorrow*, and the narrator was Sir John Gielguld. Ironically, he also played David Helfgott's piano professor at the Royal College of Music in *Shine*. Was that intentional?

TP: Actually, no. When Alexander eventually took me to Villa Senar, he showed me a cupboard full of Rachmaninoff's unpublished letters. He had written these to his two daughters from both America and the villa in an attempt to explain what had happened before 1917 – the composer had to flee Russia, as the Bolsheviks had destroyed his home, Ivanovka, during the October Revolution. To this day, some of these letters have yet to be published in English. Then Alexander showed me a second cupboard that contained all of Rachmaninoff's home movies. As you can imagine, I made a beeline for it, but was blocked by the grandson, who slammed the door shut before saying, 'We'll have to talk about this first.'

One of the problems when working on any film is how to construct it using some sort of narrative device. I suddenly realised that we could build a narration from these unpublished letters. To make this work, I needed someone who could sound both old enough and dignified enough to do the letters justice. I'd worked with Gielgud a number of times over the years, but he was already in his mid-nineties by the time of my film. Nevertheless, I decided to telephone him and to ask how he was. 'Creaky' was his reply. After he agreed to be the film's narrator, I sat him down and got him to read the letters. He was pretty frail. When we had finished recording them, Gielgud stood up and said that he had seen Rachmaninoff perform in London. I knew that the composer had played here in 1938 and suggested that date. Gielgud quickly corrected me and said, 'Dear boy, don't be so foolish. It was 1910.' I then asked him if he still remembered the performance. Always up for a good story, John went on to say, 'Rachmaninoff came on a bit late, ignored the audience, sat down and played. At the end of the first piece, he ignored the applause and moved straight on to the next work. He continued in this way throughout the recital until he got to the end. He then got up, bowed quickly to the piano and left.' And there's a wonderful line in one of Rachmaninoff's letters that captures his sense of public indifference. It reads something like: 'And no matter what I put in the programme, all the audience wants is that damned Prelude in C sharp minor. Damn them, Damn them.'

BRUNO MONSAINGEON
(DAVID JOSEFOWITZ RECITAL HALL, 14 JANUARY 2014)

RAYMOND HOLDEN: You are one of the great musical polymaths of our age. Not only are you a pre-eminent filmmaker, but you are a remarkable writer and violinist. How did such a gifted young string player turn into one of today's most significant cinematic and televisual figures?

BRUNO MONSAINGEON: It's to do with what I *don't* have. There are so many ways of communicating one's love of music. Performing, composing and writing are to name but three. I had no talent for composing, but I wanted to create something that would survive me. And that's one of the main reasons why I got into film. I'm convinced that it can convey as much emotion as any piece of music. This can be done through documentaries and correctly filmed performances. Yet the circumstances surrounding my journey are somewhat more complicated. After spending about a year playing concertos and sonatas in television studios for a French broadcaster, I wrote to Glenn Gould. When we got together, he said to me, 'Why are you wasting your time performing in public, when making films is so much more creative?' I wasn't so sure about that at the time, but during the nearly ten years that we worked together, he influenced me enormously.

RH: Tell me about the young Bruno Monsaingeon.

BM: I was 'ignited' by the violin at the age of four or five. The event that changed my life was hearing an old recording of Yehudi Menuhin playing Joachim's transcriptions of Brahms's *Ungarische Tänze*. I remember shivering when I heard them. I had no idea who Brahms was, let alone who Menuhin was, but I was 'ignited' by them. I decided then and there to become a musician.

RH: Every time I speak with Paul Badura-Skoda, I immediately think of Vienna. And when we speak, Paris appears before me. What was the French capital like during your youth, and what impact did it have on you artistically?

BM: None at all. I don't know that I am particularly French: it doesn't really come up. Although I visited England early on, I've never lived here, and I fell in love with Russia when I was young, largely because of David Oistrakh. All these influences were more important to me than living in Paris, even though it was exciting and full of opportunities. There's nothing specifically French about my passions or interests.

RH: Is it a mere coincidence, then, that many of your films have a Parisian element to them?

BM: It's interesting that you feel that, as I've made very few films in France or with French musicians.

RH: I've always believed that many of the early music films from the 1930s, such as those showing Felix Weingartner, Fritz Busch, Willem Mengelberg and Sir Adrian Boult conducting, are valuable educationally and are revelatory artistically. Do you consider these artefacts to be important culturally and socially?

PART FOUR: PRODUCERS/FILMMAKERS/ADMINISTRATORS

BM: I would hope that they are. But the person who directly influenced my desire to film music was the American theoretical physicist Robert Oppenheimer. When I was about nine years old, I heard him speak on a television programme. I understood absolutely nothing that he said. Not a word! Yet his thought processes were apparent to me. And this was something that was central to me when I began working with Glenn Gould, especially when it came to our films on Bach. I was extremely aware of the things that would *not* be understandable on first hearing, or even after several hearings, by the general public. Not only was I keen to avoid the need for the viewer to be a specialist in music when watching the films, I was also keen to transfer my emotions into something more universal. I was conscious of the fact that if Glenn and I were talking about the extremely intricate harmonic evolution of a fugue, or the philosophical implications of fugue writing, it wouldn't be immediately understood. But people could still watch the film and be fascinated by the brilliance of Gould's thinking on the subject. That's why Oppenheimer was important to me.

RH: French musical filmmakers led the way during the 1930s and the 1940s, and Tobis-Klangfilm's experiments at Épinay-sur-Seine with Mengelberg and the Concertgebouw Orchestra in 1931 were groundbreaking. Why are the French so fascinated by film, and was the example that I've just mentioned a natural extension of the pioneering work of the famous Lumière brothers?

BM: Your question is very intriguing, and I would like to answer it in a slightly circuitous manner. A few years ago, I read a book by Leon Goldensohn called *The Nuremberg Interviews*. The writer was an American psychiatrist who was sent to Germany to monitor the mental health of the defendants during the Nuremberg trials. He later published his interviews with Hans Frank, Hermann Göring and Joachim von Ribbentrop, amongst others. When one of the defendants said that he thought the Führer was a charming person until about 1940, and that his only real disappointment with him was his horrible taste in music, I found the whole discussion unbelievable. And while these men were clearly criminals, they were German politicians, who considered their country to be at the forefront of musical culture. If they'd been Italians, their focus might well have been painting, or, if English, their interests might've been literature. Whereas in France, one of its main cultural phenomena is cinema. And perhaps that's why Tobias-Klangfilm's document is a direct consequence of the Lumière brothers. Movies are an essential part of French culture.

RH: During the same period, musical filmmaking in the United States took a different direction. Films such as *One Hundred Men and a Girl*, *Fantasia* and *Carnegie Hall* offered cinemagoers high quality music-making within either a comedic or a melodramatic context. Although Leopold Stokowski was common to all three movies, artists such as Bruno Walter, Jascha Heifetz, Lily Pons, Fritz Reiner, Arthur Rubinstein, Jan Peerce, Gregor Piatigorsky and Artur Rodziński also took part in the latter. What's your reaction to such films, and do you think that they are still important cultural commentaries?

BM: The art of filming music is an essential ingredient. Over the years, it's mostly been the province of television, and has often suffered because of the terrible results of direct transmission. These transmissions were regularly subjected to arbitrary changes of shots and a lack of intellectual consideration, leading to a kind of sabotage of the perception of music. That which constitutes cinema – lighting, movement and carefully planned shots – must always be taken into account when filming music. Only then can the act of seeing music being performed add to

PART FOUR: PRODUCERS/FILMMAKERS/ADMINISTRATORS

our emotional response to it. If not, there's no point to filming music, other than to document a great cultural event. And, of course, such great events have often been filmed as a pretext rather than for musical reasons. I remember when Maria Callas sang in Puccini's *Tosca* at the Paris Opéra. The reason for filming her in the title role was because President René Coty attended the performance. The criterion for deciding on whether or not to document this event had nothing to do with Callas, but everything to do with the attendance of a now forgotten president. Such things are extremely odd, and result in television largely failing to fulfil its vocation.

RH: Herbert von Karajan was a musician who was quick to recognise the importance of film, and an early influence on him was the great French director Henri-Georges Clouzot. They documented a number of works together, including Schumann's Fourth Symphony, Verdi's Requiem, Mozart's Fifth Violin Concerto, Beethoven's Fifth Symphony and Dvořák's Ninth Symphony. Did these films influence you in any way?

BM: They influenced me tremendously. That said, I find the film of Mozart's Fifth Violin Concerto with Yehudi Menuhin quite disgraceful, even though I'm totally taken by Yehudi's playing. The framing of the violin is completely insensitive, and the cadenza in the first movement is focused primarily on Karajan! The set that was chosen is an example of disgustingly sugary Viennese kitsch taste. Yet these things have done little to damage the Clouzot myth. But when he and Karajan worked together on the Schumann symphony, the result was flabbergasting.

RH: If a viewer encounters Karajan's and Clouzot's masterful films of the Schumann and Beethoven symphonies first, it would be completely understandable if they were left scratching their heads after watching the Mozart concerto. Do you think that film was something of a 'mad moment' on Clouzot's part?

BM: The Schumann and Beethoven films were imaginative, and it's a case of 'hats off' when it comes to those. And what Karajan did on his own without Clouzot in Beethoven's Sixth and Seventh Symphonies is wonderful. He understands fully how to stage music for the camera. Every shot is done separately with an orchestra that's set up to meet the expressive needs of the camera. It's a marvellous thing. Karajan was a visionary who did some really imaginative work. And very few musicians have given thought to transmitting music in this way.

RH: Perhaps you could answer a question that has worried me for some time about Clouzot's and Karajan's film of Beethoven's Fifth Symphony. At one point, the flutes and the oboes appear to swap their positions on stage. Was there a technical reason for this?

BM: It was probably done out of necessity. Something similar occurred when I was filming Tchaikovsky's First Piano Concerto with Viktoria Postnikova as soloist, and with Gennady Rozhdestvensky conducting the Leningrad Philharmonic Orchestra. We spent two weeks shooting one movement of the work. During that time, I had the whole orchestra and the Philharmonic Hall at my disposal. It was something of a dictatorial system that Karajan also enjoyed. He had the Berlin Philharmonic at his beck and call. If you want to achieve the proper relationship that exists between the conductor and the timpanist, for example, you have to reappraise their placement with every shot. When you do that, it's an extremely expressive way of showing music. If such a change is done for the purpose of expression, and if you are keen to help the viewer come to terms with what they are seeing, any procedure is justified.

PART FOUR: PRODUCERS/FILMMAKERS/ADMINISTRATORS

RH: You were very close to Yehudi Menuhin, both personally and professionally, and your films introduced him to a new generation of concertgoers. How would you define Menuhin ethically and musically, and why were your films about him so important to you personally?

BM: First and foremost, I wanted to show the musical side of his genius. I then hoped that his humanitarian side would emerge naturally. I considered him to be a 'natural genius', two words that normally don't stand easily together. And while there was nothing abnormal about him, the ease with which he addressed the music that he was performing, and the violin that he was playing, was miraculous. His love of music was divine, and no other violinist has ever transmitted that love to such an incandescent degree. From my earliest years, he's been important to me, both as a person and as a violinist. And it was always my intention to show Yehudi's greatness as a musician.

RH: You spent much of today searching through the Menuhin Collection here at the Royal Academy of Music. Did you find anything of interest?

BM: I found a film of Stravinsky's Violin Concerto that we made together in New York in 1981. The work was not one that sat naturally within Yehudi's standard repertoire. He learned the piece specifically for the film, which I thought was lost. Thankfully, I found its master tape here, and I now hope to publish it. The collection also contains many scores that were marked by him. This annotated material reveals a man who was constantly questioning his own performance style. And when you examine his bowings and fingerings, you can literally hear his sound. I made many films with Yehudi over the years, particularly in Russia. And it's my great hope that during the centenary of his birth in 2016 that they'll be re-released. Some of them have not been seen since the end of the 1980s due to various contractual reasons. Having now secured the rights, I hope that they can be made available to the public.

RH: Nadia Boulanger was another great figure who influenced you. Not only did you document her on film, but you wrote a book about her.

BM: She was my first attempt at making a film, rather than just a television programme. But my skills as a filmmaker at that time didn't allow me to reflect her personality fully; the piece is really that of a 'debutante'. There was something about Boulanger that I always found extremely touching. Despite her rigour, and her often terrifying discipline, she could still abandon herself to the joy of music. And I've often wondered why she acquired such an iconic status. Was it simply that she was the right person at the right time? I don't know. Even though she was extremely old when I made my film about her, she continued to display the same vigour and rigour that she showed in her youth. It was very strange. Every Wednesday, from about the first decade of the twentieth century until her death in 1979, her teaching sessions at her salon were part of Paris's musical life. Edgard Varèse, Quincy Jones, Astor Piazzolla or Igor Stravinsky might be in attendance and might be submitted to an analysis of a Bach cantata. She had a room that contained two pianos and an organ, and that was constantly full of people. She was the grand priestess of music who spread its good word to her students. And those students came from all nations and were of all ages.

Boulanger was born in 1887, and I completed my film of her when she was ninety-two years old. When one remembers that her father was born in 1815, her immediate lineage dates back to the time of Beethoven and Schubert. In contrast, Nadia's sister, Lili, a winner of the Prix de Rome in composition, died very young in 1918. After her death, there

PART FOUR: PRODUCERS/FILMMAKERS/ADMINISTRATORS

was an annual ceremony in Paris that was organised by Nadia and that you were obliged to attend. These were amazing. When everyone was seated in the huge church, she would enter accompanied by her 'ladies-in-waiting'. At the end of the service, all there were compelled to give her their condolences. This continued for seventy years after Lili's demise. Nevertheless, Nadia continued to have an open and transparent mind when it came to each new trend in contemporary music. She knew the music of Pierre Boulez and of Iannis Xenakis, although she remained closer to the sound-worlds of Igor Stravinsky and Béla Bartók.

RH: Boulanger was also something of a magnet for young American musicians, and I remember reading somewhere that she taught more than 600 of them during her career. When Leonard Bernstein visited her, he used to say wittily that he was off to the '*Boulangerie*', and when you watch her teaching with *solfège* it can be something of a challenging experience.

BM: The French cellist Paul Tortelier once said to me that although he thought *solfège* to be a wonderful system, he'd come up with an alternative one. In his method, all the notes found on the piano's white keys finish with an 'ah' sound – dah, rah, mah, fah and so on – while those found on the black keys finish with an 'oh' sound. If you sing the beginning of the first movement of Mozart's Fortieth Symphony using Tortelier's approach, for example, it would sound: moh, rah, rah/moh, rah, rah/moh, rah, rah, soh etc.

RH: Over the years, I've had the great pleasure of meeting, knowing and teaching three generations of Torteliers: Paul, Yan Pascal and Maxime. And it seems to me that Paul, with his distinctive good looks, his outgoing personality and his sovereign musicianship, was every filmmaker's dream subject.

BM: Curiously, Tortelier was much better known in England than he was in France.

RH: Really?

BM: There's no question about that. And there's also no doubt that the English were not only attracted to him as a cellist and as a musician, but also because of his Maurice-Chevalier-like French accent. He had a tremendous following in the United Kingdom right from the start. When we made our film together in 1972, I was a beginner. While I found him quite intimidating and very opinionated, I was attracted by his anarchic and revolutionary convictions. He was great fun to work with, and despite certain reservations I have about our films together, I have approved them for release. There are lots of things in them that are very primitive from a filmmaking perspective. I also find their structure to be a little artificial. Yet when you see him playing Bach, his glorious phrasing, and the meaning that he gives to each note, is extraordinary. When I say that the films seem artificial, I'm referring primarily to the overall structure of the three episodes. The underlying idea of the whole project was that each episode should be linked to one of the elements of nature: water, fire and earth. It was necessary to structure the overall piece somehow, and although I now feel it to be a bit artificial, Tortelier is revealed in a genuine fashion. I'm still struck by the remarkable quality of his sound and lyricism. Unlike many musicians with whom I've worked, he never had the urge to compete. You always felt that there was something important in his music-making, and that he couldn't care less what people thought of him. I found that very endearing.

RH: When filming around the world, many of the countries that you've worked in owe a great deal to French culture, such as Poland, Russia and

PART FOUR: PRODUCERS/FILMMAKERS/ADMINISTRATORS

Canada. Was nationality a stimulus when working with people such as Piotr Anderszewski, David Oistrakh and Glenn Gould?

BM: Nationality is not that important. Oistrakh was another artist who was essential to me, not only as a violinist, but also as a man. I heard Oistrakh for the first time when I was nine. I was totally bowled over by his playing and went backstage to meet him. The programme included works by Tartini, Prokofiev, Franck and Szymanowski. I remember every single note of that concert. When I did go backstage, I was unable to communicate with him, as he didn't speak a word of French. I immediately decided to learn to speak Russian. This did much to shape my life.

RH: Oistrakh suffered greatly under the Soviet system. Yet I've heard it argued that his talents might not have been realised fully had he *not* operated within that system. Is that a correct assessment?

BM: He did suffer greatly at the hands of the Soviets, and he did accept things that were completely unacceptable. My own vision of Russia is nuanced by what happened then and what continues to happen today. While it's true that Oistrakh suffered quietly and silently for much of his life, the Soviet system also had some positive aspects. If you were a great musician, and were willing to accept certain rules, you didn't have to promote yourself or to fight against possible opponents. You could find everything that you needed when expressing music. This meant that you were able to be a musician in the purest sense of the word. And as Oistrakh *was* a pure musician, his circumstances are difficult to assess today. But there's no doubt that he went through horrible times. I was lucky enough to have played a great deal with the outstanding American pianist Julius Katchen. He took me to the Pablo Casals Festival in Prades, where we spent a wonderful week. Oistrakh was also there, and alone. After he rented a small Peugeot, we then travelled through the Pyrénées and had a fabulous time together. There was, however, one unspoken condition: under no circumstances were we to discuss anything to do with the Soviet system. The only slight disappointment I had with Oistrakh was when he and Katchen were rehearsing Beethoven's 'Kreutzer' Sonata. It was prodigious. But at the end of the first movement, Oistrakh had recourse to my abilities as an interpreter and asked me to ask Julius if it was possible to have a short break, as he wanted to watch the second half of the football World Cup!

RH: I'd like to turn your attention to Glenn Gould and Sviatoslav Richter. Both had an external fragility that stood in sharp contrast to their inner core of artistic strength. Was this paradox attractive to you as a filmmaker?

BM: It's true that Gould was socially remote and that he had inner strength. He had complete control over what he wanted to do, and despite all the rumours and temptations, he remained true to himself. He was totally consistent. When he decided to withdraw from concert life in his early thirties, it was far from certain that the direction he was about to take would be successful. If you want to make recordings for a company like CBS, how do you convince it to allow you to do so if you are unwilling to promote your discs publicly? And while that might be fine when it comes to Bach, what happens when it comes to Schoenberg and Hindemith? Artists need to be present to market their wares, otherwise things simply don't sell. While Gould never wavered from his artistic position, he once said wittily that if Wall Street were ever to fail, he'd have to record the Tchaikovsky and Grieg piano concertos! Our collaboration during the last ten years of his life was extraordinary. We worked with tremendous dedication. It was ideal, and do you know why? It was

PART FOUR: PRODUCERS/FILMMAKERS/ADMINISTRATORS

because he was both a great comedic actor and a tremendous musician. This meant that he always had an awareness of the dramatic structure that I wanted to achieve.

After making our first films together, Glenn and I started on a huge project that explored the works of Bach. And the only reason why the project ended with the 'Goldberg' Variations was because Glenn died suddenly. We still had so much more to do. On one of my many trips to Toronto – I was commuting between Paris and Toronto more or less monthly – I arrived late one afternoon. After I checked into my hotel room, I received a telephone call, having barely had time to close the door. It was Glenn. He then proceeded to tell me that his spies had told him that I was in town, and that he would like me to pop down to the street, where he was waiting for me in his car. But then he said to me, 'Bruno, I am so sorry. We can't work together immediately, as I have to go to my apartment and practise.' On hearing the word 'practise', I was astounded and asked, 'Are you ill?', as the whole concept of practising was an anathema to him. He then said, 'No. But I'm going to record Webern's *Konzert für neun Instrumente* next week.' In keeping with his normal approach, he'd learned the whole work mentally and away from the piano. But as he couldn't separate the piano from the other instruments, he realised that he had to go to the keyboard in order to *unlearn* those instruments. He then played me the *Konzert*'s entire piano part around midnight in his apartment. For Glenn Gould the genius, the instrument simply didn't count. He dictated his mental processes to the piano, and it obeyed through his remarkable technical mastery.

If ever the word 'genius' were applicable to an interpreter, it would be to Glenn. Very few others would suit that designation; he was unquestionably and overpoweringly a genius! Glenn had remarkable musical intelligence, and not only was his knowledge of music unfathomable, but his intensity was almost terrifying. He knew all of Bach's cantatas from memory, and had the entire outputs of Wagner and Strauss at his fingertips. Having read a work, it was instantly committed to memory. I remember once working with Glenn in New York for three months. We would normally finish filming at about 3am, and would remain in the studio for another hour until he could take me back to my hotel in his car. During these journeys, he'd love to play guessing games. On the radio one night, there was a piece that neither of us could identify. It was a string quartet, but not one that I'd ever heard. We tossed around a number of possibilities, including quartets by Grieg and Tchaikovsky, but were certain that it was none of these. When the two movements that we heard came to an end, we learned that it was an early work by Mendelssohn. The next afternoon, Glenn went straight to the piano and played them from memory. And, don't forget, he'd listened to those movements while talking to me in the car. That was the kind of polyphonic mind he had.

RH: Let's move on to Sviatoslav Richter, a notoriously reclusive figure. How did you manage to get him to work so closely with you?

BM: Curiously, there was nothing easier for me than getting to Richter. But considering his aversion to microphones and cameras, it was a miracle that it happened at all. I was confronted by a very old, tired and extremely moving person. We'd known each other for about twenty-five years, and he would occasionally come to my place in Paris. And when he was on board with the project, it became very important to him. There was definitely something innocent and saintly about Richter, and I only introduced the camera after nearly three years of working with him: he had a remarkably expressive face. We started by meeting on a daily basis at the Majestic Hotel in Paris, where I would have Richter speak into a microphone. And there were some striking moments at

PART FOUR: PRODUCERS/FILMMAKERS/ADMINISTRATORS

those sessions. He once asked me if I knew the filmmaker Andrei Konchalovsky. When I said that I did, Richter grumbled, 'He pretends to be a friend of mine. But what kind of friend writes that I've got fingers like sausages, and that they can't tell the difference between the black and the white notes? What kind of friend is that?' At which point, Richter looked very sad before violently shaking his hand and demanding, 'Are *these* sausages?' I had no camera to record this fantastic moment. It was horribly frustrating.

After about a year and a half of working with Richter, I was finally able to introduce the camera. Up to that point, there had to be no notion of making a film or writing a book. Everything had to lack definition, and there could be no one else around. Yet his innocence when connecting with the camera was quite staggering. One day in Antibes, after we had been working all afternoon, we went for a drive in his car with his female assistant, Milena Borromeo, and his companion, Nina Dorliak. As Richter didn't drive, I took charge of the car, but was given detailed directions by him. He knew every road and restaurant. Not only was he knowledgeable about the beautiful scenery, but he knew each of the factories and foundries. And by the time we were settled in the restaurant of his choice, he was in good form. That was fine, but this created a problem for filming, as Richter was usually at his worst when the South of France's beautiful light was at its best. And, after all, my aim was to create a lovely piece about him. In the restaurant that night, he asked me if he had told me a certain episode regarding Shostakovich's Ninth Symphony. In fact, he'd talked to me about the work on audio tape some two years earlier. But I said, 'No, Maestro', as I wanted him to talk about it on film the next day. Needless to say, there was no way I could refrain him, so he proceeded to tell me how the composer telephoned him after finishing the symphony and had asked him to sight-read the work at the piano with him from the manuscript. As Shostakovich had the unnerving habit of getting faster and faster, Richter said the experience was horrible. After they'd finished working, the composer started pouring copious amounts of cognac and they became totally drunk. Then, around midnight, Shostakovich suddenly became desperate to kick Richter out of the apartment. It seems that Madame Shostakovich had returned and that the composer wanted the pianist to disappear for some reason. Richter quickly left, went into the street, and fell in the gutter – it was midwinter in Russia and snowy. The great pianist then spent the rest of the night drunk and lying in the gutter. After regaining some degree of consciousness around six or seven o'clock in the morning, he found his way to the home of his former teacher, Heinrich Neuhaus. After looking Richter up and down, Madame Neuhaus proceeded to pour him yet more wine. It took Richter two days to recover from this somewhat surreal experience. The whole story was very amusing and extremely colourful. Yet when I sat him down the next day to recapture it on film, he looked at me as if I were a complete idiot. He said, 'But we've already talked about this last night.' As the presence, or absence, of the camera made no impression on him whatsoever, the moment was lost. There were days when it was completely impossible for me to get anything out of him. And there were other days when he would say nothing more than either 'yes' or 'no'.

RH: Your nine films and book, available in one beautifully presented large box set, on the great German singer Dietrich Fischer-Dieskau must surely be the definitive study of this amazing artist. How did you go about creating this remarkable biographical synthesis?

BM: Two of the most important things to establish first when embarking on a project such as that are trust and confidence. This can take years. But, in the case of Fischer-Dieskau, we'd known each other for two decades. On 2 January 1993, I received a letter from him that said

PART FOUR: PRODUCERS/FILMMAKERS/ADMINISTRATORS

he had ended his career two days earlier – on 31 December 1992 – and that we could now proceed with my filmed portrait of him. I then spent part of the next twelve months with him at his home in Berlin, while also carrying out most of my research for the project. One particular episode was especially touching. At his home, he showed me a video of Brahms's *Die schöne Magelone* in which he not only sang, but also recited the texts of the songs between each of the *Lieder*. It was a magical performance, but filmed horribly. As an encore, he gave the composer's 'Feldeinsamkeit'. It was so moving. Afterwards, he said to me, with that rigorous self-criticism for which he was famous, 'I should've stopped earlier.' Such comments allow you to establish the kind of relationship necessary for the type of project that we intended to achieve. And having established that relationship, the end result was extraordinary. I started by filming some music with him. As these were events that were specifically designed for the camera, I decided to avoid opera. I often find masterclasses and recitals ideal for my needs, as they have a dramatic structure. I don't like filming reality, I like transposing reality, as that leads to a *deeper* reality. Consequently, we didn't start with the portrait, which is called '*Die Stimme der Seele*' ('The Voice of the Soul') in German and *Autumn Journey* in English, but with the music. Later, we worked with his wife, the great Hungarian-born soprano Júlia Várady, who sacrificed part of her career for him.

While I was working with Fischer-Dieskau in Berlin, an interesting incident happened. After I finished doing the French and English subtitles for the Richter film, my producer told me that he needed a translation for the German version. But since Germans are notoriously adverse to subtitles, he also told me that the German version would have to be dubbed. As it had taken me thirteen months to get the film right, and to achieve the correct rhythm, I was appalled by the idea of replacing Richter's wonderfully undulating voice. Sensing my reluctance, my producer then said that if I didn't direct the voice-over myself, the Germans would do it on their own. Faced with this *fait accompli*, I decided to find a suitable actor. I then had the crazy idea of writing to Carlos Kleiber. I told him that, as my idea was *so* crazy, I immediately thought of him and wondered if he would like to be the voice of Sviatoslav Richter. Along with the letter, I sent him a copy of the film and the libretto in Russian, French, English and German. I really didn't expect an answer, but, to my surprise, I had already received one by the time that I'd returned home two days later. Kleiber wrote that it would be a criminal offence to overdub such a sovereign artist as Richter. I then called Fischer-Dieskau and asked him to help me with the German version. He agreed, and prepared the whole thing with the same care that he would devote to a *Lieder* recital. He needed very little direction, and the German version is really very good. But that was not the end of the matter. Carlos Kleiber wrote to me again shortly afterwards. He said that he had now spent twenty days with the Richter film, and if I could wait, he would find a solution to my dilemma. In the end, he admitted defeat, and said that there was no solution. In the interim, I wrote to him again, thanked him for his help, and suggested that we should meet the next time I was in Munich. I then realised that he probably felt that he was being led into a trap. And his last letter to me read, '*Ich bin Kapellmeister in Ruhestand* ('I am a retired conductor') and I want to die without my name appearing on any disc, film or book. Incidentally, I know nothing about conducting. When I was young, I asked Toscanini and Stokowski, and they, too, said that they knew nothing about conducting. The only person in recent years who knew what conducting is about was Herbert von Karajan. With all best wishes, Carlos Kleiber.'

RH: Many of the artists we have spoken about are now historical figures from a glorious musical past. But you are also passionately interested in

PART FOUR: PRODUCERS/FILMMAKERS/ADMINISTRATORS

today's artists, and have made a series of films about the Polish pianist Piotr Anderszewski, including one called *Piotr Anderszewski: Voyageur intranquille*, which makes reference to Mozart's *Die Zauberflöte*.

BM: I have a tendency in my filmmaking to blur the lines between documentary and feature film. The Anderszewski piece is staged on board a train, with the train being symbolic of his activities. It took about six years to make, and the material relating to *Die Zauberflöte* was only included late on. I was staying at a friend's house near Paris one weekend, and it was there that Piotr played the whole of the *Die Zauberflöte* to me from memory, having learned it the day before. It was at that very moment that I decided the opera would be the *Leitmotiv* of the film. Many of the sequences relating to Mozart's work were shot in Portugal, which was also the train's last stop after journeying through Warsaw, Budapest, Paris, London and other European capitals. *Die Zauberflöte* acts, therefore, as a structural device between the episodes.

RH: It seems to me that your Anderszewski film is not only about time, but also about some of the seminal demographic and ethnic differences that still plague Europe. And it's the scene in the market near the end of the film, where you show the pianist with his Hungarian grandmother, which should act as a wake-up call for us all. That being so, do you see yourself both as a musical and as a social commentator?

BM: The very fact that I'm deeply interested in countries that were once linked closely to the former Soviet Union is certainly a central element of my work. But still I find the emotions of music to be of the greatest importance to me. While I don't make sociological films *per se*, matters pertaining to society and history are a central part of any film's dramatic structure. And I believe fully that a film must have a very strong dramatic structure. If it doesn't, it has limited appeal and remains simply a series of musical issues loosely strung together. I want my work to impact musicians and the public alike. And I had some evidence that that's the case after my film on Richter was replayed during the night some years ago on ARTE. When I visited a shop the next day, the boy who was stacking the shelves said that he'd watched it. He knew that it was about a musician, a Russian musician, but didn't know what a pianist was. Yet he was riveted by it. Then, speaking in strongly worded French slang, he said that Richter was like a prisoner who was coming to the end of his sentence, and who wanted to confess his crimes. I was staggered to hear that, as the young man had absolutely nothing to do with music. This was by far the most compelling comment that I've heard made about any of my films. Trying to modulate one's own emotions and responses, and to make them into something more universal and significant, is the one real challenge with which I like to be confronted.

ROGER WRIGHT
(DAVID JOSEFOWITZ RECITAL HALL, 1 MAY 2015)

RAYMOND HOLDEN: Having worked administratively and artistically with such great institutions as the British Music Information Centre, the BBC Symphony Orchestra, the Cleveland Orchestra, Deutsche Grammophon, BBC Radio 3, the Proms and Britten Pears Arts, you have done much to shape the musical landscapes of Britain, the United States and Europe. But your musical journey started in Manchester, where you were born in 1956. As your brother is the distinguished pianist and conductor Simon Wright, can we assume that you came from a musical family?

ROGER WRIGHT: Simon is one of the best and most natural musicians I know, and I was blessed to have him as an elder brother. It was because of Simon that there was a lot of music around the house, and as our father was a clergyman, we were also surrounded by a great deal of church music. This meant that a love of music was instilled in us from quite early on, and Manchester was a really important part of that process.

RH: To have two leading musicians from the one family implies a real familial interest in the arts.

RW: There was one leading musician and one 'suit'! But, in all seriousness, there are wonderful musicians, and then there are people like me who are fortunate enough to play music a little. And, here, I am not being unduly modest. The family were music lovers and subscribers to the Hallé Orchestra. Growing up, we not only had the joy of hearing that orchestra, but also the BBC Northern Symphony Orchestra, as it was then known. And as Simon and I were lucky enough to attend Chetham's School, the advantage of such an environment was very telling.

RH: Over the years, I've worked with many people who have either attended or taught at Chetham's. What was it like when you were there?

RW: Chetham's was tiny at the time, and its transformation is one of the great marvels of music education. When Simon and I were there, it had about 200 boys. And as the age range was from six to eighteen, you can imagine just how small the class sizes were. It had a genuine family atmosphere. Yet it really wasn't at all good academically, even though it did have a strong sense of purpose. But it was very collegial and it had a great atmosphere. Chetham's always had a good musical tradition, even before it became a specialist music school, which was something of a 'sink or swim' moment for it. Some people, like Peter Donohoe and Simon, left before that happened, and went on to have musical careers. To give you an idea of how much the school changed, let me use me as an example. Up to the point when it began to specialise, I led the orchestra's cello section. Within a year of that change, not only was I gradually moved to the back of the section, but I finally ended up playing percussion next to Wayne Marshall. He told me quite correctly that I had no rhythm and had no business being there either! Nevertheless, the school's environment was very special, and when it became co-educational, it grew still further. Looking back now, Chetham's transformation must have been very difficult, and I was in the upper school's third year when that happened.

RH: Was it simply financial necessity that prompted the change?

RW: Yes. The question of how an independent, bluecoat school of that size could survive must have been central in shaping its future. And although it did build on a good music tradition, it was, in the best sense, of a non-professional, amateur kind. Norman Cocker, who was organist at Manchester Cathedral at the time, used to write music for Chetham's, which acted as a kind of informal choir-school for the cathedral. As the individual players from Chetham's gradually improved, he would edit, and make more complicated, existing pieces to reflect the students' increasing abilities. This was a great privilege to be a part of.

RH: Are you an advocate of specialist music schools in general?

RW: They're a really strong environment in which a specialist training can flourish. Of course, I'm aware that that's also something of a generalisation. But it's essential to have the right kind of teaching for that kind of environment. In the early days of Chetham's, the hothousing of young talent largely eclipsed academic training. If you create an environment in which there is an assumption that people will simply go on to a career in music, and if they are given little else academically so early on in life, it narrows possibilities. Trying to get the right balance is something that specialist schools struggle with. Nevertheless, the basic principle is a positive one, and they are a good means of developing special talents of all sorts, whether they be music or football.

RH: When you were growing up in Manchester, it was alive culturally and benefited from the presence of Sir John Barbirolli. Did you ever see him conduct?

RW: I did see Barbirolli perform, and I was terrified of him. Yet you knew that you were in the presence of an extremely magnetic personality. I was fortunate enough to perform with him as a member of the boys' choir in Mahler's Third Symphony. If you ask me what it was like to sing with Dame Janet Baker and the Hallé Orchestra in the Free Trade Hall, I can't really remember, other than being utterly petrified to be on the same stage as Sir John Barbirolli. He might well have been small in stature, but he was big in personality. As Simon was the *répétiteur* for the Hallé Choir from a very young age, I used to go along to some of their rehearsals. I can remember turning pages for him and listening to Barbirolli mumble instructions. I could never understand what he said, but Simon had learned to interpret his gestures. And one of the standard lines that popped out of Barbirolli's mouth was 'Marvellous cello tune, this.' He would then sing it in his inimitable way. But he was utterly magnetic. And, of course, much of what we remember is enhanced once we acquire a certain degree of knowledge. I can now think back to Barbirolli's performances of Sibelius with greater understanding, thanks to what I have since learned. It was a very special time. Manchester audiences were always very proud of Barbirolli's readings of Sibelius, and when Sir Charles Groves brought the Royal Liverpool Philharmonic to the Free Trade Hall to perform the composer's Second Symphony, I heard one member of the Hallé audience ask, 'Why have they brought our music?' While the physical distance between Manchester and Liverpool is only relatively short, Hallé audience members would never have dreamed of going to the Liverpool Philharmonic. And if you went to the Manchester City Art Gallery, you

PART FOUR: PRODUCERS/FILMMAKERS/ADMINISTRATORS

might never go to Liverpool's Walker Art Gallery. The East Lancashire Road was something of a psychological dividing line between the two cities. Along with Barbirolli, I saw Sir Adrian Boult with the Hallé Orchestra and István Kertész just before he died. He was such a wonderful conductor. But when you're young, you are unable to explain why such experiences are so important to you. They clearly mean something, but only later can you articulate why they were such special occasions.

RH: Barbirolli was a huge cricket fan and scheduled his first tour of Australia around the 1950–1 Ashes series. As you are also a lover of the sport, and are a keen supporter of Lancashire County Cricket Club, what can musicians learn from sportsmen and sportswomen?

RW: There are some clear comparisons, and preparation and focus are two really obvious ones. Public pressure also links the worlds of sport and music. And if you listen to how some star sportspersons talk about their work, and the psychology of what they have to deal with, there are some very interesting parallels.

RH: Is it also to do with immediacy of response?

RW: Yes, I think it is. The ability to co-ordinate hand and eye quickly is essential. But it's also about speed of development. This is something that both sportspersons and musicians talk about. They're in it for the long haul. There might be a sort of 'growth spurt', so to speak, when it comes to technique, but then there's a point at which you will plateau for whatever reason. That's probably quite important. It allows you time to take stock musically before moving on again. There will always be the urge to improve, but if you feel that you've achieved all that is possible as either a sportsperson or as a musician, then you're in a very bad place.

RH: After Chetham's, you read music at Royal Holloway, University of London. With the exception of Percy Pitt in the 1920s, you must be one of the very few directors of music and controllers of Radio 3 at the BBC who didn't attend Oxbridge.

RW: 'Manchester boy makes good!' But, in all seriousness, this is not a particularly important issue. It's true, though, that I was one of the few who actually read music at university. And it has to be said that I had some incredibly distinguished predecessors. Sir William Glock is a good example. He was never controller of Radio 3, but he was director of the Proms and director of music. But to suggest that William was lacking in some way because he didn't actually study music at university would be wrong. He was a wonderful pianist and had a fantastic mind. He was the person who revolutionised the Proms, and thereby Radio 3. And because of his connection to Pierre Boulez, he also helped to shape orchestral life in this country. But as we are talking about education, I'd like to return to Chetham's for a moment, if I may? There was one member of staff there who spotted that I was particularly interested in contemporary music and was keen to find new and different repertoire. Quite often on Fridays, he would slip recordings and scores to me as if they were in a figurative brown-paper envelope containing forbidden goodies. These included Berg's Chamber Concerto, Penderecki's *Threnody for the Victims of Hiroshima*, Britten's *War Requiem* and Schoenberg's Chamber Symphony. It was a whole range of things that were not on the syllabus. There was a slightly anarchic element to the whole thing, and it was if he was saying, 'You're not really supposed to be looking at these, but you might just like to take a peek anyway.' With hindsight, he did a wonderful thing. He opened up a world for me that I might otherwise never have experienced. The fact that it was something that I shouldn't be studying encouraged me to

PART FOUR: PRODUCERS/FILMMAKERS/ADMINISTRATORS

explore it further. That man was Robert MacFarlane. I owe a huge amount to him, and because of what he did, I've never lost the urge to discover new things.

RH: When you enrolled at Royal Holloway, did you intend to become a music administrator?

RW: No. I had no idea what I was going to do. A commentator for *Test Match Special* would have been high on my list of chosen occupations at the time! I simply fell into things. After my music degree, I did a sabbatical year as president of the student union. This was a very good learning tool when it came to administrative work. At one point, I was also interested in teaching, and had considered postgraduate studies in it. I then sent the usual embarrassing letters that young people write to places like the Royal Opera House, asking for work. I also wrote to the British Music Information Centre, which I'd used as a student. It was a treasure trove and a truly special place to visit. I could access scores and recordings there that were free at the point of use and that were unavailable elsewhere. It also housed a library of off-air recordings of British music. To my surprise, I received a letter back from it, thanking me for my application for the post of librarian. I didn't know that there was a vacancy for the job, but I happily accepted an invitation to be interviewed for it anyway. After being appointed, I rose quickly through the ranks over the next few years. I went from librarian, to manager, to director. This is pretty impressive, until you realise that there was only me on the staff. But, still, the title changed, and that was no bad thing. That was a wonderful time for me, as I was able to learn so much about the music industry by working there. Whether it be composers, festivals, publishers or performers, they all had links with the centre. We then started to put on concerts in what was then the BMIC premises, 10

Stratford Place near Bond Street. Eventually, we staged about two or three concerts a week. These increased our visitor base, and it became a really lively space.

RH: Do you think that conservatoires should offer a degree in music administration?

RW: I am a great believer in just getting out and doing something. But that's based on what I was fortunate enough to have done. There are certain core skills that can be taught, but as much as anything else, it's knowing about the job. It should be made clear what a particular position entails, because when somebody takes up a post after being an undergraduate, they will have no idea what the profession is really like.

RH: How did you go about marketing British works, and do you envisage a time when they will stand shoulder to shoulder with the German, French, Italian and Russian canons?

RW: I certainly hope so. I heard Daniel Barenboim perform Elgar's Second Symphony with the Staatskapelle Berlin recently. And when you hear an orchestra like that play the symphony, you are left in no doubt that it's not only important music, but international music. We, as a nation, tend to beat ourselves up when it comes to such things.

RH: But Barenboim has been a passionate Elgarian for many years. And I suspect that if he weren't at the helm of that orchestra, it would never have committed itself to the symphony.

RW: You always need people who are powerful advocates. When I was trying to convince a particular conductor to do a piece at the Proms or

PART FOUR: PRODUCERS/FILMMAKERS/ADMINISTRATORS

with the BBC Symphony Orchestra, the sure-fire way of making certain that it *wasn't* going to happen was when they would say something like, 'Well, if that's what you want. Then under those circumstances I'll do it.' I would then say, 'Only do it if you are really passionate about it.' That's why Bernard Haitink's cycle of the Vaughan Williams symphonies is so fantastic, and why André Previn's work on behalf of English music was so marvellous. Advocates such as these are very important. But many British commentators are often negative about the music of their compatriots simply because it's a received opinion. These opinions are often based on absolutely nothing. When I've been asked about programming British music at the Proms in the past, and said that we were going to feature pieces by Frank Bridge, John Foulds, Havergal Brian, Sir Arnold Bax or Sir Hubert Parry, the response was often, 'Yes, but those are second-rates works.' I'd then ask, 'When was the last time you heard a symphony by Parry?' The answer was always, 'I don't think that I have.' Received opinion dictated that such works were second-rate. But to over-claim on behalf of British music is also a bad thing. As we are in a world in which we have to make a case for these compositions, we often become unreal in our support of them. British music societies are often guilty of this. It's just as bad to over-claim as it is to be too critical. Not everything that Havergal Brian wrote is a great piece. But it was worth dusting off his 'Gothic' Symphony and performing it under the best possible circumstances. That way, people could assess it. There are, of course, a great many British works that should be spoken up for, and it's important to make clear that these pieces should be heard. Listeners can then find their own way.

RH: It has often been suggested that British music is eclectic. Do you agree with this suggestion, and, if not, what are some of its unique characteristics?

RW: The minute you find a defining characteristic in one composer's work, another will do something completely different. We must be careful not to generalise. But I do think that we are currently enjoying a golden age of British composition. This is not only to do with the quality of the work, but also to do with the range of the work taking place. You'd be hard pushed to find anything to connect Brian Ferneyhough, Gavin Bryars, Michael Finnissy, Sir George Benjamin and Julian Anderson other than that they are all British composers and are all expert in their own way. But they do not represent one genre or one compositional style. We now have an explosion of styles that are all of a very high quality. It's not one sound-world. If you go back fifty or sixty years, the musical language had greater commonality. Even then, the sound-world of Frank Bridge's late string quartets was very different from that of E. J. Moeran. A work like Parry's Fifth Symphony does much to fill out the musical landscape, and helps to remind us what a great composer Elgar was. To appreciate the grandeur of the Alps, it often helps to admire the beauty of the foothills first.

RH: During your time at the BMIC, you were also active as a writer and as a reviewer. Did you ever feel that there was a conflict of interest when dealing with performing musicians professionally?

RW: I quickly realised that being a music critic was futile and I didn't do it for long. When I was at Royal Holloway, I wrote for the *Windsor & Eton Express* and the *Staines & Egham News*, before doing some work for the *Financial Times*. I thought that it was a curious job, and felt much more comfortable reviewing opera productions. While I regularly questioned what I was really doing, I always tried to find something positive to say. I always felt that I was spreading the word and communicating, and that's why broadcasting came to interest me. If you are passionate about some-

PART FOUR: PRODUCERS/FILMMAKERS/ADMINISTRATORS

thing, be it the Lancashire County Cricket Club or a really bad joke, you want to share it with people. And as I'm passionate about music, I always looked for different means to disseminate that passion. We're now in a world in which sharing is done in a way that was unthinkable before.

RH: Was your urge to share one of the reasons why you accepted the post of Senior Producer with the BBC Symphony Orchestra?

RW: The reason for my move to the BBC was straightforward: Sir John Drummond created that post and was kind enough to ask me to do it. Previously, one person would book the conductor, another would organise the programmes and yet another would engage the soloists. The senior sound engineers would then look after the balance in the studio, while other members of the team would handle the editing, writing and reading of the script. As John quickly realised that a programme's original idea could become completely lost by this process, he was keen to streamline it. My job was to plan what the Symphony Orchestra did with its conductors and to produce the sessions. But the problem was: I had no training for this whatsoever. The first session that I produced was with Gennady Rozhdestvensky, a conductor not given to rehearsing. One of the works on the programme was a Bach transcription by Elgar. This had already been planned before my appointment, and I felt like a lamb to the slaughter when I was sent to the Maida Vale Studios as producer. I suggested to Rozhdestvensky that it might be a good idea for the orchestra to play a short passage for balance reasons. But he mumbled something unhelpful and insisted that the red light should go straight on. That was a real baptism by fire.

RH: The geography of the BBC Symphony Orchestra's management team must have been challenging. You were based in Great Portland

Street, while other members of the team were housed at the Maida Vale Studios.

RW: Looking back, it now seems very strange that the BBC orchestras, the Proms and Radio 3 were all in separate parts of the Corporation. This was partially to do with the geography of the management structure, and partially to do with various tensions surrounding the Symphony Orchestra. And some of the creative questions that were asked then are still being asked today. Should the BBC orchestras broadcast live; should they dominate Radio 3's schedule; and should we continue to invest in such a costly resource? The combined cost of the BBC orchestras is about £25 million, and one in fifty of all BBC employees is a musician. But if you were to take away the BBC orchestras from the United Kingdom's musical life, it would look very different. The only symphony orchestra in Wales is run by the Corporation, and if its funding was withdrawn from the Ulster Orchestra, it wouldn't exist. The BBC Scottish Symphony Orchestra plays throughout Scotland, and the BBC Philharmonic is Salford's orchestra. And then there's the BBC Concert Orchestra. It's probably the most popular orchestra in the world, thanks to the size of its audience on Radio 2. It's a mistake to think that the Corporation's orchestras duplicate much the same material to much the same audience. That's far from the truth, as they are such a rich resource. When I was first appointed to the BBC, the general standard of its orchestras was a little uneven. But thanks to the quality and range of conductors that are now working with them, they are all doing marvellously. It's also important to remember that the BBC's licence fee helps to fund these musicians, and is crucial when planning the Proms.

PART FOUR: PRODUCERS/FILMMAKERS/ADMINISTRATORS

RH: In the early twentieth century, the BBC was a role model for broadcasting organisations in Australia, South Africa and New Zealand. But in 2007, all the Australian Broadcasting Corporation's orchestras were made independent of it. While that was quite controversial at the time, some artists, such as Sir Charles Mackerras, supported the move. Do you think that the BBC might now look to the ABC as an exemplar, and set its orchestras adrift, too?

RW: No, I don't. You have to remember that the BBC originally had dozens of orchestras. But aside from the Ulster Orchestra, it now only has five. In the past, the Corporation funded ensembles such as the BBC Studio Strings, the Langham Chamber Orchestra, the BBC Training Orchestra and the BBC Northern Dance Orchestra. It's very easy for us to forget this when discussing the future of the five remaining ensembles. I can tell you that at the very top of the BBC there's huge support for what the orchestras and the BBC Singers do and the distinctiveness of their work. Might it change? Possibly. But that would depend on what happens next with the licence fee.

RH: Should the BBC Symphony Orchestra have a different function and remit from other major London orchestras?

RW: It's true that the BBC Symphony Orchestra's programming could be even more distinctive than it currently is. It could be playing Xenakis, Dallapiccola and James Dillon daily. Yet we know that in order to build the sound, ensemble and training of an orchestra, you need to play Haydn, Mozart, Beethoven and Brahms. That's a natural part of what an orchestra should do. Where the programmatic balance sits is always going to be up for discussion. But it's also incredibly important that the orchestra should play its part in the dissemination of new and unfamiliar works. Let's look at Sir John Pritchard's tenure with the orchestra as an example. There were certain pieces that I asked him to do that he really didn't want to perform as Chief Conductor. And as you were his personal musical assistant, he probably told you more about that than he told me. But there were also things that he recognised as being an important part of the BBC's function. And if you compare the BBC Scottish Symphony Orchestra's programmes to those of the Royal Scottish National Orchestra, they operate within very different spaces. That's part of the ecology of music, an ecology that shifts over time.

RH: Sir John Barbirolli was asked on a number of occasions to take charge of the BBC Symphony Orchestra, but refused to do so because he didn't want to 'programme by committee', to quote his wife, Evelyn, precisely. Was there a committee of programmers during your time at the Corporation?

RW: In the past, there were such things as score-reading committees, but these had gone by the time I joined the BBC. It was latterly more about personal relationships, and I remember once mistakenly programming Vaughan Williams's Fifth Symphony for a concert with Sir John Pritchard.

RH: He was not a fan of Vaughan Williams's music.

RW: That's true, and I still can't work out how it happened. I would never have scheduled the work without talking to him first. When I asked whether he'd ever conducted the work, he replied, 'I once did do the symphony, but I don't want to renew my acquaintance with it', a response that was typically 'Pritchardian' and elegant. Even though programming committees were a thing of the past, there was an under-

PART FOUR: PRODUCERS/FILMMAKERS/ADMINISTRATORS

standing that the BBC Symphony Orchestra had to be different. And as it couldn't look like other London orchestras, that's when we occasionally felt like we were between a rock and a hard place. It is very easy to empty a hall if a programme is unattractive.

RH: I do remember your period with the orchestra and how you worked with both Sir John Drummond and Sir John Pritchard. There was a great deal of give and take and a high level of respect between all parties. The standard of the orchestra improved greatly during those years, thanks in no small part to you.

RW: I have to say that was largely down to the work of Pritchard and Boulez, who were regulars in the studio at the time.

RH: While that's characteristically modest of you, it was also the result of how you managed these great artists. A good example of this was the Strauss-Mozart series that you organised in 1989 as part of John's final season as Chief Conductor with the orchestra. It was also your last series as Senior Producer before moving on to the Cleveland Orchestra.

RW: That series comes into the category of 'not avoiding the obvious'. Before my time at the BBC, colleagues had asked Pritchard to do a great many things. Being the good servant that he was, he would often agree, but there were other times when he would simply stamp his foot and refuse. He conducted Henze's Sixth Symphony, for example, a piece that he didn't feel particularly close to. But he did it extremely convincingly, and turned its musical corners very elegantly. Yet nobody had ever asked him to do a Strauss-Mozart series. And if there was anybody to do such a series, it was him. The interleaving of the two composers' works really saw him at his best, and the concerts were magical.

RH: After the BBC, you moved to America to become Artistic Administrator of the Cleveland Orchestra in 1989.

RW: The Cleveland Orchestra is a wonderful ensemble. The city itself was the third largest in the United States until its circumstances changed, causing it to become smaller. And without its quiet pride, it could easily have gone the way of Detroit. In many ways, Cleveland is not dissimilar to Manchester in that regard. Like some other smallish cities, the only reason for musicians to go there was to be a member of the local orchestra. This meant that the players quickly formed a collective bond. While they might have a little teaching at the Cleveland Institute of Music, there's no opera, freelance or film work. Their sole focus is the orchestra. The players' schedule would usually involve a rehearsal on a Tuesday, two rehearsals on a Wednesday, and a general rehearsal on a Thursday. These were followed by concerts on Thursday, Friday and Saturday nights. As all the players were involved in every type of event, such as educational and Christmas concerts, there was a keen sense of unity. And the spirit of George Szell, the orchestra's celebrated Music Director between 1946 and 1970, was ever present. There were still players in the orchestra who wore jackets and ties on tour because Mr Szell said they had to. This was nearly twenty years after Szell's death and the appointment of two subsequent Music Directors: Lorin Maazel and Christoph von Dohnányi. I remember asking the orchestra's Principal Oboe, John Mack, what the transition from Szell to Maazel was like. 'Let's just say there was a great difference between *Pa* Szell and *Ma*-azel' was his reply.

    A special feature of the Cleveland Orchestra is its clarity of sound. And the balance between the strings, brass and woodwind is also very natural. This is partly due to Severance Hall's rather dry acoustic. But as the hall is so dry, the orchestra really relishes the opportunity of playing

PART FOUR: PRODUCERS/FILMMAKERS/ADMINISTRATORS

in other more resonate venues, such as Boston's Symphony Hall. Conversely, when the Boston Symphony Orchestra visits Cleveland, it has difficulty adapting to the less generous acoustic of Severance Hall. My time in Cleveland also provided me with a fascinating opportunity to see how American orchestras worked. I was particularly interested in their subscription series, and to see how the players reacted when giving the same programme three times in a week. This was a completely different approach from the BBC Symphony Orchestra, which would perform and record a concert, broadcast it and then move on to the next event. While the ability to work quickly is a defining feature of a British orchestra, the opportunity to repeat a programme several times can also be of benefit to an ensemble. And, of course, the salary of American orchestral musicians is considerably higher than that of British players. The Cleveland Orchestra receives no public funding, but relies instead on endowments, ticket income and individual donations. It's a completely different financial model from Britain. As the Cleveland Orchestra is a remarkable ensemble with a special history, it was a great privilege to work with it.

RH: The American funding model has caught the attention of various British governments over the years. Do you think that it's one that might work here?

RW: As the history of British and American arts institutions is completely different, it would be difficult to adopt that model in the United Kingdom. Taxation is structured differently, and there is a different kind of disposable income. If you look at the Cleveland Orchestra's donors, they are more or less the same families who have been giving since the 1920s and the 1930s. They share a connection and a sense of pride. And if you are in a place like Cleveland, there's only one orchestra. This automatically strengthens the bond that I just mentioned. But then you are also more beholden to specific donors than you are here. Although our system can be problematic in all sorts of ways, it can also be a successful one. The combination of public funds and private giving works very well. This means that you are not too dependent on state funding when the public purse becomes problematic, and that you are not entirely at the whim of private donors and sponsors.

RH: The flaws in the American model become particularly obvious when interest rates hit rock bottom. The value of some orchestral endowments have fallen through the floor recently, and are a real cause for concern.

RW: True. This has proven very difficult, and has resulted in a number of American orchestras going under.

RH: How would you describe your working relationships with the Cleveland Orchestra's conductors?

RW: In Cleveland, we usually had a twenty-six-week season with only one programme a week. We also had a summer season that took place at the Blossom Music Center, a wonderful outdoor space with a fantastic acoustic. This was a completely different scenario from the BBC Symphony Orchestra, which never had a standard programming pattern. After planning my first three or four seasons in Cleveland, I quickly came to terms with it. It was also good to be able to introduce new conductors to the local audience. And as they were there for at least a week at a time, and as there wasn't much else for them to do other than to rehearse and to perform, I was able to get to know them pretty well.

PART FOUR: PRODUCERS/FILMMAKERS/ADMINISTRATORS

RH: Did you continue to work closely with Pierre Boulez in Cleveland?

RW: Boulez has been one of the constants of my career, and it has been a great privilege to know him. I've worked with him at both the BBC Symphony and Cleveland Orchestras, and when Szell died in 1970, he was named Artistic Advisor of the latter for a couple of years. This was concurrent with his duties as Music Director of the New York Philharmonic. I then worked with him at Deutsche Grammophon, and remain in contact with him to this day. Not only is he very special to me, but he was adored by the Cleveland Orchestra. It is often the nature of orchestral life that the players love their guest conductors more than they love their Music Directors. They can see too much of some people, and tend to gravitate to the last person with whom they worked. This is entirely understandable. Boulez's ear, conducting technique and sense of precision was something that matched the exactness and balance of the Cleveland Orchestra. When I then went to work for Deutsche Grammophon, and signed Boulez to an exclusive contract, his recordings of Debussy and Ravel with the Cleveland Orchestra were marvellous.

RH: In 1992, you moved to Hamburg and became Executive Director and Vice-President of Deutsche Grammophon. Of the recordings that were made by the company during that period, which do you remember most fondly?

RW: Boulez's disc of Debussy's *La mer* with the Cleveland Orchestra was extraordinary. And I could happily spend many hours talking about his work. The lazy notion that Boulez's music-making is detached is nonsense. Just listen to the accuracy, balance and internal energy of his recordings. They're very exciting. The first project that I was involved in at Deutsche Grammophon was a DVD of Debussy's *Pelléas et Mélisande* conducted by Boulez and directed by Peter Stein. This was a wonderful production that was staged at the Welsh National Opera and that was conducted with incredible control. The same is true of Boulez's readings of Stravinsky's *Le sacre du printemps*. Other conductors are wilder and some are less accurate. This 'rawness' is considered to be more authentic by some listeners. But if you play the notes correctly and balance it well, as Boulez does, the work remains wonderfully fresh. I once remember seeing some footage of him rehearing Sir Harrison Birtwistle's *The Triumph of Time* with the BBC Symphony Orchestra. At one point, there's a huge climax where a series of horn clusters sound. He then stops the orchestra, asks the horns to play their note clusters separately and corrects their mistakes. You can immediately see the musicians looking at each other and asking, 'How does he do that?' Oliver Knussen's disc of Stravinsky's late works is also quite special. It's one of the great recordings, and he had an ear very much like that of Boulez.

During my time at Deutsche Grammophon, the company was releasing in excess of 100 new discs a year. This may well have been the end of the golden period of recording. It was soon obvious that that world was changing rapidly, and that the model had changed completely. And one of the reasons why that was a good thing is because primacy has now returned to live music. In the past, you would make a recording and would then go on the road to try and sell it. That's no longer the case, as the market is completely saturated. It's now much more like the pop-music model. And it's very easy for us to take a black-and-white stance when it comes to this issue. If you're asked whether specialist music schools, new concert halls and the modern, international recording business are good or bad things, we are often unable to have a nuanced conversation about them. And if I were to say that a new concert hall for London is a really bad idea, for example, I might well be

PART FOUR: PRODUCERS/FILMMAKERS/ADMINISTRATORS

dubbed 'anti Sir Simon Rattle'. This would be a ridiculous position to take. As this is often down to the way things are reported, there isn't the space to have a subtle dialogue about such matters. Consequently, everything becomes black and white. You're either for it, or you're against it. Yet the world isn't that straightforward. That doesn't mean to say that we are all 'grey' people, but we do need space and context if we are to have these discussions. We have to look for the positives in our world, as audiences will always support confident messages.

RH: Since 1995, the use of the internet has increased one hundredfold. As a natural consequence of that increase, there has been a sharp decline in CD sales and CD outlets around the world. For musicians, this has been compared to the arrival of the microphone in the late 1920s, and the subsequent mass unemployment of cinema musicians that so devastated the profession after the advent of the 'talkies'. Do you think that we are facing a similar crisis today?

RW: As I now live in Suffolk, coming to London can be a bit of a shock to the senses. But it also means that I can hear the Staatskapelle Berlin and Martha Argerich and can see the Royal Festival Hall buzzing with people. And if you are from elsewhere in the world, you might think that it's fantastic that the building is so alive. It has to be said that the Queen Elizabeth Hall doesn't look its best at the moment, but anybody who attended the recent concert there by the National Youth Choir would have come away thinking that there's nothing wrong with the world after hearing it. The choristers learned their fourteen pieces in a week; a real achievement. It didn't matter that the acoustic wasn't great, or that the food wasn't so good. You left the hall thinking that this is a really lively space. What matters most is the content and the quality of what's happening in the venue. Nobody came away from the first performance of *Le sacre du printemps* at the Théâtre des Champs-Élysées thinking that the acoustic was a bit dry. They left marvelling at the experience. While quality is paramount, I do worry that younger audiences' attention spans are diminishing. And although I do think that it's great that we encourage young people to play and sing, we also need to train them to listen. In a way, we no longer need the old market for CDs, as there's now so much music available to us. And, inevitably, we will find our own way. But what we do need are knowledgeable friends, and not online-shopping companies' algorithms to help guide us.

RH: Can we assume, therefore, that Sir John Reith's three founding principles for the BBC – to inform, to educate and to entertain – are still valid?

RW: Yes. And, to this day, nobody has come up with anything better. To make the good popular, and the popular good, might sound a bit cheesy, but it's not a bad starting place.

RH: How, then, have you put this into practice at your new job in Aldeburgh with Britten Pears Arts?

RW: The Aldeburgh model shouldn't work at all. If I went to Harvard Business School and asked them for a really strong business model for an arts organisation based on three halls seating 850, 350 and 200 people on the edge of nowhere, and a programme of world-class events involving young artists, prison concerts and a groundbreaking dementia scheme, the academics in Boston would be left scratching their heads. It shouldn't work, but it does. Much like the Proms, the circumstances surrounding the series may have changed, but the vision has remained largely intact. Would what we do have worked had Benjamin Britten

PART FOUR: PRODUCERS/FILMMAKERS/ADMINISTRATORS

not been from Suffolk? Probably not. Young artists' schemes are two a penny these days, but when Britten and Peter Pears were discussing them in the late 1950s and the 1960s, they were quite revolutionary. New music, young artists and community work were at the very heart of what Britten started in 1948. And the exciting thing for me is to realise his vision in a modern world with its ever-changing circumstances. We have a marvellous audience at Aldeburgh Snape, and the town itself is such an inspiration. It's a joy to work there, and the future is very exciting.

The second problem is that the published texts from Bruckner's lifetime often deviate from his manuscript scores, and so there has been a lot of guesswork and speculation as to how much Bruckner was involved in those publications during his life. Then coming out of that, of course, between the wars the *Gesamtausgabe* – the critical edition – which initially was helmed by Robert Haas, and then, of course, the re-examined scores were edited by Leopold Nowak.

The point of mentioning this is that every symphony has its own story. Another crucial point is there are editions we have considered being more 'authentic' Bruckner than others – but they have changed hugely over the century because of taste and new scholarship. And the whole matter is likely to continue and evolve further. We are constantly reassessing how or whether Bruckner wanted particular changes. Was he persuaded to make those changes by his friends or did he genuinely agree and initiate them? Maybe some changes were made without his permission. As an example of modern scholarship, we now know, in the Fourth Symphony, that Bruckner had *far* more control of the editorial process with the first publication than we ever knew before. We always assumed that everything was decided by other people, and that changes our perspective of the traditional approach we've had in the past about the 'goodies' and 'baddies' in this story.

On the back of this summary, do you see the Bruckner editorial problem as a desperate issue and a distracting challenge, or a real opportunity to communicate the spirit of the composer as you understand it?

CT: The Bruckner edition problem is very much up to the conductor's taste because, as you described it, it's so complicated and illogical that you would never know which was really changed, or what he wanted to change. You have some security in the First Symphony that he had the 'Linz' version and the 'Vienna' version. That is simply what he did.

that he solves, because he beats four instead of two. I must confess that I stole some things from him. For example, in the beginning of the Eighth, I stay in four with the triplets, where everybody conducts in two. And when I see it with him in four, I keep the four, because the triplet then doesn't run away. Karajan did it in two and the triplet doesn't run away! More importantly, Wand was never *steril* because he had this *Fluidum* [aura] in his person which always conveyed good health in his musicianship. And everybody would admire him, as he would stand there for one hour and a half conducting from memory. He was always incredibly safe in the way he held a performance in his hands. You never had the impression that he was weak, or that he would somehow lose his energy. It was so well prepared. That is a kind of *Gesamtkunstwerk* [a complete artwork] which is hard won and to be respected and learned from. Overall, I have very few reservations about Günter Wand.

JF-A: I want to move into the subject of editions, and by talking about them, return to the idea of the interpretative implications of what version to choose. Just for those who don't know what the 'Bruckner problem' is, I'll give a quick survey.

CT: Okay, good!

JF-A: The first category is, you might say, caused by Bruckner himself, because he made several different versions and revisions of some of his symphonies. We can single out the First Symphony, which we have just briefly touched upon; the Third Symphony, which has many different versions; the Fourth and, of course, the Eighth Symphony, which is *sui generis*, because Hermann Levi, a mentor, looked at the first version and he was very disappointed, and Bruckner completely rewrote it. The version from 1890 is the one that we use now.

realisation of new dialogues that often get lost. It's partly about balance, but also a fluidity which comes from trust?

CT: I tell you why. The orchestra and I have known each other for such a long time, and we play so much opera together. Don't forget opera playing! I think I've played more opera in Vienna than in Dresden. If you do *Tristan*, the *Ring* or *Die Frau ohne Schatten* in two productions or whatever, they know you so well, and I know them so well. I am completely relaxed. It's such a trust you have in them that you encourage them to find something you don't expect. There are these musical dialogues that lead to new perspectives. It's a rare thing to achieve. It's very rare.

JF-A: Just thinking a little about a performance aesthetic, there are certain people who will find that Bruckner with Christian Thielemann is a kind of reconciliation between what, simplistically, could be said to be 'Wagnerian' in sensibility, but kept within the bounds of Bruckner's profound religiosity. But it's not born from, say, Günter Wand's building blocks, those cathedral-like views, even though you clearly choose to adopt degrees of that approach, but only selectively.

CT: You have noticed that. You have a very good ear. I don't want to say that I criticise Mr Wand, but I think sometimes he is too cold. Sometimes, in my opinion, he has so much experience that he knows it already, in advance: every bar, how he is going to do this and that, and he becomes a kind of *Lehrbuch* [textbook] of instructions for doing a Bruckner symphony. So, he shows me how one can do a Bruckner symphony. And, for me, it's a little bit too unspontaneous. On the other hand, I must say I am watching him and his films. Sometimes when he beats in four, where everybody beats two, I see the sense as there are little rhythmical things interpretation sounds like a mathematical proof. It's not spontaneous any more. I had a piano teacher when I was very young and he would say it has to become 'your second nature'. So, it's in your bones in a certain moment and you live that moment.

JF-A: I sense when listening to these performances – I listened to Number Four most recently – that you resist releasing energy too soon. If you don't, you just hit your head against the wall for an hour!

CT: Yes, and that's the same with every Bruckner symphony. He usually begins softly and has a big *crescendo*, and then the main theme comes from somewhere. If you overdo that, you are in a bad position from the start, because you have already used up too much energy and power. It is *not* like the 'Tristan' Prelude, for example, where you know you cannot think about Acts One and Two and Three when you conduct it. It has to go from zero to 300, 500 or 1,000 at once. But that's only in the beginning, and then you have to cut back. And then to off you go with Acts One, Two and Three.

For a Bruckner symphony, you have this problem, too. It's very nice that a Bruckner symphony is not as long as *Tristan* or *Meistersinger*! But you learn to use a red warning lamp in your head for the musical aspects that can be too much. Only then can you get an inner sense of the whole *Landschaft* [landscape] in front of you. You have to overview the whole symphony before you start, and before I conduct I usually have a mental run-through. Where is it going? There. Okay. You have to be freed up for music-making and offer it 'in the moment'. Without that, it will not breathe with naturalness and spontaneity.

JF-A: One of the things I hear (and you may tell me I am wrong) in the Vienna recordings is a strong attention to the inner parts, and a it, precision. It's mostly about perfecting the same rhythm, and you achieve it because there are so many wonderful musicians, they just make music immediately. But sometimes you tend to forget that there is a *Doppelpunktierung* [double-dotted note] or *scharf punktiert* [sharply dotted], so that the staccato is longer or shorter, which has to be distinguished. Then, the string sound in the Musikverein encourages you to play very softly. You can do things with *pianissimi* which you cannot do in Dresden, because it's a large opera house, not a concert hall like the Philharmonie in Berlin. And in Vienna your experience always depends on where you are standing. My position in front of the orchestra in Vienna is a particular thing; usually, as you know, the strings and the winds are far away from each other. In Vienna, they have this unusual seating where the orchestra is spread out to the sides. In the middle you have the first flute and the first oboe, very close to each other. You could shake hands without moving hardly at all! The orchestra and I hear them very well. We have wonderful contact and the means to watch each other very carefully. So, the whole sound is very special to that environment.

And how does the interpretation develop? It develops because you get calmer. It becomes more about pacing. Indeed, more and more about pacing. It's a training from Wagner operas, and yet also from the Bruckner mistakes that you've made before. To start with, you have to analyse which *forte* or *fortissimo* is a real *fortissimo* even in the beginning. But you should also think of the end of the climaxes which will come much later, as we know. In an *Adagio*, like in the Seventh or Eighth Symphonies, you must wait patiently until you reach a certain point. And when you reach that point, you have to be listening to what you want to keep for the end of the symphony. So, in the best case, you should save one and a half per cent for the end. This sounds very much as if you calculate it but, of course, that cannot be, otherwise your multiple alterations. I am especially riveted by the performance practices of the Fifth Symphony going back to Karl Böhm and Hans Knappertsbusch. I have some questions there which I won't pre-empt now, but we will come to. So, to the first point. Having recorded so much Bruckner in Dresden – you have recorded some of the symphonies more than once, and have performed Bruckner in other contexts with other orchestras, like Berlin – how did this Vienna series come about, and what stage have you got to?

CT: Originally, the Vienna Philharmonic wanted to do a Bruckner cycle, but they hadn't decided with whom. Somebody had the idea to ask me, but I was not free. So, I decided to rearrange my whole calendar, and fortunately it worked out.

JF-A: How many had you done?

CT: I've done the Fourth, Fifth, Seventh and Eighth a lot. The First I had only conducted once, in the early version – the 'Linz' version – with the Sächsische Staatskapelle. But in this current cycle I wanted to perform the 'Vienna' version of the First, which Bruckner revised over twenty years after the 'Linz' version.

JF-A: In general terms, how would you describe the evolution of your Bruckner interpretations from Dresden to Vienna? Have you found that the context of Vienna encourages you towards a certain performance aesthetic or approach?

CT: Yes and no, because Dresden and Vienna are quite similar orchestras. You rehearse with them in the same kind of way. It's interesting. If you come to these two orchestras, you rehearse very much on, let's call

CHRISTIAN THIELEMANN

(ZOOM MEETING, 20 JANUARY 2022)
EDITED BY JONATHAN FREEMAN-ATTWOOD

JONATHAN FREEMAN-ATTWOOD: In the pandemic, you started a magnificent cycle of Bruckner symphonies in Vienna when nobody else was doing any playing at all! When I last had a chance to talk to you about Bruckner, in the summer of 2020, you said that you were just about to record the Eighth Symphony, and I remembered saying, 'But there's no music going on, Christian! How can you do this?' Since then, you've recorded the Third, the Fourth, and, recently, the Second Symphonies.

CHRISTIAN THIELEMANN: Yes, and all done in an empty Musikverein! It's so wonderful to record there.

JF-A: In this interview, I want to focus on three broad areas. I know many of your Bruckner performances, and mainly those from Dresden. First, I'd like to explore initially how your ideas have evolved over the years. The second concerns the particular challenges (and opportunities) of how the complications of Bruckner's texts can have such a strong role in the creative process. And, thirdly, some specific considerations on three symphonies that raise important issues: the First Symphony, the so-called 'Linz', and in particular Bruckner's own 1891 version, and whether Bruckner's changes improve or diminish the original vision; and this obviously affects the Third and Fourth Symphonies with their

PART FIVE

A BICENTENNIAL POSTLUDE: REVISITING BRUCKNER IN VIENNA

PART FIVE: A BICENTENNIAL POSTLUDE

There is also a supporting letter he wrote that he wanted to make sense again of this wonderful piece.

JF-A: Maybe this is the time to clarify the order of his early symphonic works and where the confusions lie.

CT: The problem starts with the so-called *Studien Symphonie* [Study Symphony in F minor]. It was his first symphony and he was not satisfied. He said, 'I will put it in my desk and leave it there.' It is the work commonly called Number '00'. Then, logically, you would assume Number '0' in D minor would be the next one, and so people think it's really Number One. It's not Number One because Number One is Number One: the 'Linz' Symphony in C minor – the first one written after Number '00'. The next piece he composed after Number One is Number '0' in D minor. I think you can see that it is written *'Symphonie Nummer Zwei in D moll'*, which is very interesting because the C minor symphony (which is now called Number Two) was called Number Three. For some reason, though, Bruckner was also unsatisfied with Number Zero. I think he scratched it out on the paper, but you can still see that it was Number Two. Then, came this word in German *'annulliert'* or 'cancelled'. Cancelled has nothing to do with zero, but *'annulliert klingt auf Deutsch wie Null'* ['annulliert sounds like zero in German']. It was forgotten, but not totally forgotten, because we know that there is a letter, or a remark, that he always liked this symphony very much, and kept it until his last days in his *Schreibtisch* [desk]. It was always with him, as he was not so convinced that it was so wrong. Somehow, there are mysteries about this 'Null'. So, it got the name 'Null', and it confuses everybody because they think it's before the First Symphony. So, then we move forward to Number Two, the C minor. Then, we have Number Three with all its interesting versions. And onwards we go.

JF-A: So, we can look forward to eleven Bruckner symphonies, instead of the usual nine! On the Third you have changed your allegiance on various editions over the years.

CT: The first time I did the Third, I performed the very first version, and I was very unsatisfied with myself and with the whole piece, because I thought, 'Something's wrong here.' 'Something is not in the pot in which it is cooking', as we say in German. I think that there is also a recording of the concert in the archives of the Munich Philharmonic. But I would not do this score again.

JF-A: There is also the last version, another 'Vienna' version from 1890 – another revision at the end of Bruckner's life, when he was concurrently working on the Ninth Symphony.

CT: He shortened it, and it is this version most of my colleagues do. I am a little bit shocked about that because it is too short. Therefore, I took the second version. And we then come to the point we spoke of earlier at the beginning: editions have very much to do with the taste of the conductor. Most interesting is the Fourth Symphony. It's the 'happy' symphony. It was conceived as a 'happy' piece. Unfortunately, the last movement is not happy. It's like music for a mystery movie.

JF-A: It feels a real struggle sometimes after the open, naturalistic, almost bucolic world of the first three movements.

CT: *Ja*. It has an atmosphere of going to a dark garden, with funny noises from everywhere (where probably somebody comes out with a knife!). It's so disorienting. It's like one of these horror movies, and it starts with this odd idea, which has nothing to do with the rest of the symphony. And, so, there are different versions of the last movement, one which is called '*Volksfest*' ['folk festival'] which is very strange: happy *Fest* for the people. Because he felt that his last movement would not fit with the rest of the symphony. We will, by the way, also record the *Volksfest*. When we are through with the Sixth and Ninth, we have a recording period fixed in which we will play the long version of the *Adagio* of the Third. By the way, when you hear the *Volksfest* finale for the first time, you think it cannot be true. Is it really Bruckner? Oh, yes! You recognise the main theme, and then the ending is quite similar. It's a real adventure. So, we will do these two extra movements.

JF-A: There is another *Scherzo* of the Fourth that you could do!

CT: The Fourth has seven versions. Seven! It's a total nightmare. The editorial questions are endlessly problematic, although it is regarded as the most popular one. I think the more you get into the symphony, the more you get insecure, and, again, you have to choose which version you think is best. We don't have so many letters or remarks on this by Bruckner. Richard Strauss, when he was presented with the whole of *Der Rosenkavalier*, which he was about to conduct in a small German theatre, said 'but what's that?' 'It's one of the cuts you made.' They said, '*Ja*, but Herr Professor, we studied in preparation that you would conduct the whole *Rosenkavalier*.' He said, 'No. I refuse, I don't know my own music any more.' And that's probably what happened with Bruckner that he would say, 'Oh, my God. I wrote *that*? I cannot remember it, as I have done so many other symphonies.' Such is the case with the Fourth and Third. The Fifth has a different set of problems because of the length of the piece and the tempo *Angaben* [declarations] were changed drastically by the Schalk brothers.

JF-A: We'll come back to the Fifth Symphony! But let's stick with the idea of Bruckner thinking, 'God, did I write this music?' There's also probably an element where he heard performances of his music – and we know that he did hear performances of the Fourth (though he never heard a performance of the Fifth, and I think that he only heard two movements of the Sixth in a two-piano version) – and the publications, maybe, incorporate some of the expressive marks and *tempo* indications that he reconsidered, on reflection, from the performances he experienced.

One other idea that I want to plant is that, aesthetically, when Haas's edition presented the symphonies in their 'autograph' form, many of these performance indications were banished, as there are so few. Was it a deliberate ploy to promote a kind of pure, original text; in other words, the spirit of the 'holy Bruckner' is now available, stripped of all the vulgarities that were added either by him or his 'misguided' friends?

CT: I like Haas very much. Nowak was the collaborator of Haas, and they were on very good terms. Often people think that as Haas was thrown out because of his Nazi Party membership during World War Two, nobody would speak to him any more. But this was not the case. Nowak was always his collaborator, and, in a certain way, continued Haas's work. He didn't agree with everything. For example, in the Eighth, Haas did something which I think is the best he could do, as there are always these gaps in the last movement. (I think between letters OO and PP.) Also, there are a few bars where you realise it is not connected, but if you hear the whole reprise, which is similar to the exposition, you find that it has equilibrium. In the *Adagio*, for me, I cannot believe that Nowak would cut one of these most beautiful *crescendi* out of this movement. I mean, how could he? He probably had his reasons, but I think that this was something 'put into' the score. So, people said that it's a mixture between the different versions. Yes and no.

PART FIVE: A BICENTENNIAL POSTLUDE

It is very interesting that Günter Wand, who knew *really* well what he was doing, always did Haas. And Karajan, although I think in the beginning he did Nowak, then went with Haas. Furtwängler also did Haas. There are many conductors who like Haas more, even if we know that it's somehow 'incorrect', but musically 'correct'. From the point of science, it's not correct, but musically it's just wonderful. Therefore, I took this version. If you hear the very first version of the Eighth, now discarded by performers, the first movement finishes with this enormous *crescendo* and *fortissimo*. It's clear that it is too much and already uses up the forces you need in the last movement. So, it is very good that it is cut, and from the point of dramaturgy, it's much better. The more that I get into this Bruckner business, the more I realise, as I told you before, that very often you cannot really get a 'right' answer, because we don't have the sources and all the material you need to be certain. What you *can* get is a trust about your own instincts and taste.

JF-A: There are so many layers of interpreting taste according to the text. I happen to much prefer the Haas version of the Second Symphony, because Nowak's cuts are really problematic. I don't like the end of Nowak in the Eighth Symphony. Somehow the voicing is not as noble as Haas. I am always disappointed when I listen to this point in Giulini's recording of the Eighth and you hear all those Nowak things that don't seem to be quite right. But that's just my taste. It's not right or wrong, as you say.

CT: It's so wonderful that we can refer to taste. If you listen to Furtwängler's conducting of the Ninth, or of Bruckner in general, with his *tempo* changes, it's so radical! Isn't that wonderful? If he convinces you in his Mozart, then we say that is enough! A Mozart purist would say, 'Oh, my God, that's not Mozart.' But if I hear it played by Horowitz, I might say that it's just how I want to hear it. Let's be illogical. Let's be unpredictable.

JF-A: Here is the most illogical thing that I want to ask you. It's about the Fifth Symphony and why I wanted to delay discussing it until now. I was listening to the 1959 recording of Hans Knappertsbusch in the Schalk version with the Vienna Philharmonic, which is full of some of those absolutely outrageous orchestrations, particularly in the first and the last movements, and not to mention the radical cuts. One thing that I find absolutely fascinating is Knappertsbusch's mastery of the overall *tempo* structure, the *Landschaft* and the colour, even though the text is so awful. You have two things happening in parallel: a kind of Brucknerian 'authenticity', whatever that means, through Knappertsbusch's inspired vision. At the same time, exercising it with an edition that seems so far removed from the spirit of Bruckner. It's the kind of contradiction that could only happen with Bruckner.

CT: It also has to do with being a very convincing conductor. It can convince you with Günter Wand with his way. It can convince you with Knappertsbusch. It essentially depends on how deeply you want to get into this music, if you have the sensitivity for these symphonies. Some people say, 'I don't want to do Bruckner because I think it's boring, and I don't know what to do with it.' Others are simply 'in it' from the start. Knappertsbusch with his *Parsifal* and Wagner experience is effortlessly at the heart of the music and I think that it's mostly the fact that he's a Wagner and a Brahms conductor. If you do those two, you will probably do Bruckner.

Listen to Furtwängler conducting the Fifth, by the way. It's so fast and then there are the cuts and these *Beckenschläger* [cymbal hits]. Shocking in a certain way. Shocking. But even there, he is convincing. I must say, in a certain way, I don't like it very much, and it's probably the only Furtwängler recording I have reservations about. The Schalk gang changed the *tempi*, and they would write '*Allegro molto vivace*', or '*Allegro con brio*'. Wild things going on, but it should *not* be that wild.

PART FIVE: A BICENTENNIAL POSTLUDE

JF-A: What's emerging in this discussion is how the aesthetic, and the persuasiveness and advocacy, of certain conductors repositions the hierarchy of the edition problem, and a classic case of this is the First. When I heard the 'Vienna' version of the First Symphony with the Berlin Radio Symphony Orchestra with Chailly – it's an old recording, back in, I suppose, the late 1980s – I was appalled by it, because I had a younger man's view that here is this post-Schubertian creation, Classical in resonance still, and Bruckner imposes in the 'Vienna' version a late-Romantic language of the Seventh and Eighth Symphonies on a canvas that doesn't need it. That, in one sense, still worries me, but *you* play it and it then makes more sense. And I don't understand why it makes sense!

CT: I tell you why. It's like with Beethoven. You conduct Number One by Beethoven when you have done all nine symphonies and then you have more to say. With the development in Bruckner himself, he wanted to change the First. If you listen to what we recorded, the *Langsam* or *Sehr Langsam* or *so weiter* [etc.], it feels hard to know how to arrive at this *tempo*. You cannot play it faster than very slow. It must be an *Übergang* [transition], and I must confess that it was one of the most difficult and interesting weeks that I had, because we had five rehearsals with the Vienna Philharmonic and a chance to delve into it deeply. The harmonies often give the impression in the First that they are wrong. There are these 'wrong notes', and so I asked the brass, 'Would you please play *piano* and slow. And I would like to know who is playing this wrong note.' Then the third horn says, 'I have this C.' But with the conviction that it must be *Gesanglich* [lyrical] and it must be sung, you soon find out that this is really, like *Tristan* – a dissonance going to a dissonance, and going to another dissonance, and going to yet a further dissonance. And going to the end, it then opens up and you get to C major and it all makes sense. The First has one of the most interesting endings of the symphonies. But it takes you a long time, and if you approach it as a kind of youthful Bruckner drive-through, then you are on the wrong side. If I start too fast and I come to the tenth bar and think, 'Oh, my God, how can I distinguish the first *Punktierung* [dotted note] with the double *Punktierung*?' then I'm too fast. In that week, I went to my hotel and I was not satisfied. What can I do? The next day I said, 'Okay, well we will just play it a little bit slower.' As the orchestra didn't know it so well, it was quite lucky for me. And so we developed it together.

JF-A: Are you absolutely certain the 'Vienna' version of the First Symphony is an improvement and not just an alternative?

CT: The 'Vienna' version has some vastly improved instrumentation changes. It is just more refined. And the very end is unbeatable, the same kind of ecstatic experience as Number Seven or Eight in its later version. It is so wonderful. Having done both versions, I would always go back to 'Vienna'. We are invited to Linz, and we will play the 'Vienna' version there!

JF-A: Returning briefly to the Fifth, this doesn't really have a complex editorial history, does it?

CT: Number Five is an enigma as a work, but it's not because of the edition as there is only one – apart from the Schalk version which we've just cast aside.

JF-A: So, even with just one edition, what is the enigma for you?

PART FIVE: A BICENTENNIAL POSTLUDE

CT: I always had the impression that it is all leading to this enormous climax. But after one and a half hours, you cannot do it because the orchestra gets so tired. That means that you need to find a way for it to function. You must ask the orchestra all the time – even in the big eruptions in the last movement – always to leave three or four per cent for the very end, which in any case should never be too loud but a clear and full *fortissimo*, which is just sensational when it is played in a round sound. That's what you have to care for above all in this work: unfolding the direction and sound without any unnecessary force.

JF-A: In the 1960s and the 1970s, probably also in the 1980s and the 1990s, performances of this work were often made of granite. And, of course, there is a structural Holy Grail about certain aspects of the piece and out of that comes its perceived austerity. But, within that austerity, a deep-seated lyricism is waiting to be released.

CT: *Ja*, and it lies in the chorale, which is so *cantabile*. It is helpful to think about what the Fifth would have been in Bruckner's time. One hundred years after Strauss's *Die Frau ohne Schatten*, we look back to who sang the premiere, and you find out that Strauss had quite lyrical voices because the so-called Strauss voices did not exist, just as the so-called Wagner voices did not exist in Wagner's time. So, it is the same with Bruckner. We know that the orchestra's strings were not too powerful. The whole brass was not so powerful. I often think back to the times when the orchestras did not play so loudly.

JF-A: And with gut strings and a different concept of projection?

CT: *Ja, ja*. And I think there is the caricature of this kind of Teutonic aggression, even if he was Austrian! For some people it is the same. It has to do with misinterpretation, and with a misunderstanding of the grandeur of this music. Grandeur does not mean that it was just empty show. It has to be a grandeur that is filled with *Gefühl* [feeling] or sentiment, or with *lyrischen Geschichten* [lyrical stories]. The *Nebel* [mist], the Bruckner mist, a kind of mysterious fog. *Ja*, it is a fog that you must somehow go through. It's a little bit foggy, but you see there are buildings all around.

JF-A: Now, in terms of other aspects of this, I want to turn briefly to Karl Böhm's recording of the Fifth in 1938 with the Sächsische Staatskapelle. What interests me about it is not so much Böhm's taste, or his technical way of thinking, but that somehow in 1938, we still perceive something in the performance practice of Bruckner that, maybe, tells us a little bit more about Bruckner style in the early twentieth century. Of course, you get this with Abendroth and a few other people of that era. But you get quite a seismic shift with Haitink, Karajan, Giulini and others more recently towards, generally, a more monumental Bruckner.

CT: It may also be because there were only a few Bruckner conductors before the 1960s. Bruckner was never very popular. Mahler was neglected, but then he became so popular so fast. I don't think that Bruckner is really popular. You might know Number Four and Number Seven a little bit, but Mahler is much more popular than Bruckner.

JF-A: Yet there is still a sense of people wanting to discover, even if they are unsure about it, the values of Bruckner as if they suspect there are important truths there. If you put Bruckner's Seventh, Eighth or Ninth Symphonies, or the Fifth, on at the Proms, you will get 5,000 people in that hall, just like that. You'll do the same with Mahler, but I think that Bruckner just has a different kind of pull. Maybe a Bruckner symphony is more a pilgrimage and journey than the presentation of a theatrical cosmos of a Mahler symphony.

CT: I actually think Bruckner is becoming more and more fashionable, because times are becoming more hectic. Life is always a big confusion, now with the Coronavirus and political uncertainty, *und so weiter, und so weiter* [and so on]. People like to sit down and search for a kind of quietness and peace, a rediscovery of our centre. For me, probably this is religious in a certain way. It's like you go to the church for the Christmas service – die *Weihnachtsgeschichte ist immer dieselbe* [the Christmas story is always the same]. This is the same repetition, and that is what people need to hold on to in order to find a certainty.

JF-A: A sense of the 'daily bread'? Bruckner explores a 'space' that is increasingly remote in terms of people's day-to-day expectations. Bruckner somehow takes us on a journey within a fascinating range of time frames, which is quite unlike anything else. Audiences sense something deeply honest and reassuring about it somehow; it washes through us in some way.

CT: It is indeed honest, *aber ehrlich* [but noble]. Wagner wants to seduce us, and Mahler too, and they want us to join them in their special worlds. Bruckner is from another world where he's not trying to sell us his music. He comes from a different planet and is inviting us to observe his music simply for what it is.

JF-A: Bruckner asks so many questions, and even as an affirmation of faith he's not giving you an answer. He's giving you a view. He wants you to find it. And so we must move on to the Sixth.

CT: Number Six doesn't bring any textual problems. It feels a very different piece from any of the others, not least because it begins with this very unusual rhythm. It is one of the most beautiful things he wrote, and the slow movement is just divine. It's very strange that the Sixth is not that popular compared to some of the others.

JF-A: There is something about these granite-like harmonic shelves, but circumnavigated by these enigmatic and elusive 'mists' we were talking about. Why do you think Bruckner moved from the Fifth back to a symphony that was relatively – I am not going to use the word 'Classical' – unambitious, in architecture at least.

CT: Because after Number Five, he feared that if he continued in this way, it would be too exhausting for him. Bruckner said how much he suffered doing the Finale of the Fifth. It's a little bit like after Beethoven's 'Eroica', the next is Number Four, which is a simpler creation in a certain way. I think this is the same here: after Number Five, Number Six is his *Entspannung* [relaxation].

JF-A: Seven, of course, in terms of text again, is not as problematic as others.

CT: Not at all. Not at all.

JF-A: You do, however, have the question of whether to put in the cymbal clash in the slow movement.

CT: First, he has a cross over the note, and then he writes under it '*gilt nicht*' [does not apply]. What does that mean? The cross '*gilt nicht*', or the whole thing. It's a double negation. '*Nein nein*' means '*Ja*'. I must say that I did it without the cymbal, but you sense something is missing. It must be allowed, Jonathan, to say 'excuse me, it's my taste to include it. I like it.' There is no letter, no proof, and we cannot take the phone and call him as Bruckner is in heaven. It's our choice.

JF-A: Technically, we have a choice in the Eighth, and not just the Haas or Nowak choice. We have already noted the 1887 version, which he completely recast. Of course, this is a symphony of a totally different scope. Bruckner is taking you on, and not just harmonically, another kind of journey, another kind of world. He is going deep into the recesses of his aural imagination, and with huge courage and boldness, out comes this new vision of a late-Romantic symphony. And yet, when we look back at the 1887 version, there is a reticence and a lack of cohesion. I think it's just amazing that Levi managed to see that it was not the complete package.

CT: Yes, it's not the complete package. This was a period when Bruckner was increasingly influenced by many people. They would constantly *hack* [chop] on him, and would say, 'Anton, avoid this, and don't do that.' He was a very sensitive man, and he put this terrible ending to the first movement, which I mentioned earlier, but the ending in the new version, the one that is always done today, is one of the great moments in symphonic music. There are three climaxes in the whole symphony: the *reprise* [recapitulation] from the *Ersten Satz* [first movement], the climax of the *Adagio*, and the very end where the sun blazes! He has written two *Sonnenaufgänge* [sunrises]. One is Number Four – the end of Number Four – and the end of Number Eight. I can never decide for myself which one I like more!

JF-A: With the slow movement of Eight, you've got the rising motif, that sense of redemption. The whole symphony is poised at that point, like a swing turning back. Isn't it the fulcrum?

CT: A member of the Vienna Philharmonic told me years ago that they have a tradition that they let one player in the double-bass section play the octave *tiefer* [deeper]. Only one plays the bottom D flat. One *hört es kaum* [barely hears it] but you know that there is something different.

JF-A: Getting to Number Nine …

CT: *Ja*, and I am studying it thoroughly now, and I will do it first in Dresden in February, and then again in Vienna and in Salzburg. Let's start with the very end as he intended it, although we almost always end with the *Adagio* as a kind of swansong. You know that the plan for the Finale was that Bruckner said that he wanted to make the combination of a six-voice fugue: his biggest creation on the fugue side he had ever done, and he wanted to use several themes from his symphonies. When you listen carefully to the very end, the last eight bars of the *Adagio* gives you an idea of what he wanted to prepare, because it is derived from Number Seven, and in the original key. Isn't that strange that the last movement of Number Nine is written in E major, but when it starts, you don't have the slightest idea in which key it is? It is atonal in a certain way. It goes to D major through all these strange excursions, and you don't know what the key is. And then it comes back to this E major, which is truly wonderful. You have a D minor work and the *langsamer Satz* [slow movement] is in E major. *Sehr komisch, sehr komisch* [very comical].

JF-A: Bruckner, of course, had already used material from the Seventh Symphony elsewhere – in the Te Deum. I think I'm right that there is a small quote from the Seventh in that huge *Helgoland* piece, too. But the interesting thing about the Finale is that we have 200-odd folio sheets, and yet there just isn't quite enough there to reconstruct it.

PART FIVE: A BICENTENNIAL POSTLUDE

CT: I heard several of them, and I heard what some of my colleagues did after this divine *Adagio*, but the only fascinating thing of the beginning is this *wunderbare Choral* [wonderful chorale], one of the best chorales Bruckner wrote.

JF-A: There is that supreme chromatic shift as it descends.

CT: *Ja,* just wonderful, but you know what was strange? Before we went on a trip to Japan, I asked my library, 'Please give me two or three of these reconstructions. I would like to read them on the plane, because I cannot sleep. I would just love to read them.' And I go to the plane and on the list of music there is the Rattle recording of Number Nine with the Finale! So, I had the score and could even listen to it, and I did that, but I was so shocked about the poor quality of the reconstruction and the D major end. Primitive. You can get furious about that. How could somebody do that? I think Harnoncourt was very clever. Before you play Number Nine, after the *Adagio* you don't want to hear anything. He would do it the other way around, start with these sketches of the fourth movement, and say, 'Listen. We have this and we have that and that's it.' In any case, Bruckner knew that he would not be able to follow his plan in the way he wanted.

JF-A: You can be certain that the size of the ambition, and the layers of craft that would have had to have gone into twenty-five minutes of music of that complexity, would have taken him another two years at least – and he knew he didn't have that time.

CT: *Ja.* It's a killer writing a movement like that. Already, I think he remembered the experience with Number Five. That was killer number one. And I think he said it would exceed that challenge.

JF-A: Like a good Catholic, he was prepared to put himself through the pain!

CT: *Ja, genau.* [exactly] For me, it's okay. Bruckner Nine with the *Adagio* ending is the only way. I will play it, though, with the Te Deum after Number Nine in Dresden. I want to try it once, even if I am not convinced that it is a good idea. I will try it.

JF-A: Do you like the Te Deum?

CT: I love it, except for the terrible ending. We have programmed it now for the Dresden commemoration concert for 13 and 14 February. It is a very moving moment. Nobody applauds, everybody stands up when the piece is over, I count to forty-five and then everybody leaves. Please come and see that once!

INDEX

Abbado, Claudio, 352, 446, 511, 513, 643, 646
Abbey Road Studios, 22, 29, 312
ABC Showband, 576
Abendroth, Hermann, 792
Academy of St Martin in the Fields, 6, 13, 14, 15, 16, 18, 19, 24, 131, 133, 171
Accademia Musicale Chigiana, 322–3, 580, 581
Adam, Theo, 393
Adams, John, 669; *Hallelujah Junction*, 669
Adès, Thomas, 179, 302, 606, 607; *Tempest*, 302
Ah Ket, William, 576–7
Ahle, Johann Georg, 227
Ahle, Johann Rudolph, 227
Ahlgrimm, Isolde, 539
Aix-en-Provence Festival, 110, 205, 475, 484
Akademie für Musik und darstellende Kunst (see Universität für Musik und darstellende Kunst Wien)
Aldeburgh Festival, 98, 163, 471
Aldeburgh Snape (Suffolk), 772, 773
Alden, David, 294, 487
Alkan, Charles-Valentin, 128
Allen, Sir Thomas, 384, 416, 428, 458, 510
Alnwick Castle, 384
Alsop, Marin, 169
Amadeus (film), 22, 23, 177

Amadio, Neville, 32
Amati violins, 565, 658, 661
Ambrosian Singers, 307
An American in Paris, 616
Anderson, Ande, 350
Anderson, Julian, 760
Anderson, June, 437
Anderson, Marian, 344
Anderszewski, Piotr, 741, 749
Ángeles, Victoria de los, 344, 384
Anker, Sigmund, 689, 691
Anne (Queen of Great Britain), 178
Ansermet, Ernest, 182, 226
Antonini, Giovanni, 208
Araiza, Francisco, 483
Arban, Jean-Baptiste, 236; *Cornet Method*, 236
Archiv (Deutsche Grammophon), 116, 138
Argerich, Martha, 256, 630, 771
Argo, 19
Aristone guitar, 576
Arkatov, James, 24
Armstrong, Andrew, 666–7
Armstrong, Sheila, 382–400
Armstrong, Sir Thomas, 97
Arrau, Claudio, 617, 618
ARTE, 750
Artists' International Management, 444
Arts Council (Great Britain), 170, 171, 271, 583
Ashcroft, Dame Peggy, 720

Ashkenazy, Vladimir, 389, 563, 586, 666, 677, 678
Askonas, Lies, 513
Aspro, 692
Associated Board of the Royal Schools of Music, 614
Astaire, Fred, 455
Atlanta Symphony Orchestra, 150
Auer, Leopold, 634, 665
August II (Elector of Saxony), 259
'August Coup' (Russia), 257
Australian Broadcasting Commission (see Australian Broadcasting Corporation)
Australian Broadcasting Corporation (ABC), 29, 31, 33, 180, 343, 576, 577, 763
Australian Opera, The, 495, 498
Avignon Papacy, 93

Bach, Anna Magdalena, 600–1
Bach, Carl Philipp Emanuel, 133, 137, 138
Bach, Johann Christian, 138, 370–1; *Temistocle*, 370–1
Bach, Johann Sebastian, 4, 6, 15, 32, 61, 62, 78, 79, 82, 83, 84, 85, 86, 87, 88, 89, 91, 93, 96, 97, 98, 101, 103, 105, 108, 110, 112, 113, 121, 124, 125, 128, 130, 137, 138, 140, 172, 174, 191, 219–31, 255, 276, 314, 315, 344, 359, 360, 362, 384, 387, 388, 392, 396, 397, 398, 403, 478, 479, 525, 536, 537, 539, 550, 566, 567, 592, 594, 595, 600–1, 606, 608, 611, 624, 627, 629, 632, 637, 645, 647, 648, 662, 663, 664, 733, 738, 740, 742, 743–4, 761; Toccata and Fugue in D minor (arr. Stokowski), 192; Passacaglia and Fugue in C minor (arr. Stokowski), 192; 'Brandenburg' Concertos, 6, 192, 255; 'Brandenburg' Concerto No. 5, 255; Cantata No. 3, 396; Cantata No. 4, 221; Cantata No. 9, 224; Cantata No. 11, 226; Cantata No. 42, 82; Cantata No. 54, 82; Cantata No. 77, 224; Cantata No. 78, 86; Cantata No. 80, 225; Cantata No. 170, 82; Cantata No. 198, 228; Cello Suites, 525, 594, 600–1, 611; *Das wohltemperierte Klavier*, 624, 632; *Die Kunst der Fuge*, 632; 'French' Suites, 624, 632; *Gavotte*, 592; 'Goldberg' Variations, 632, 743; *Johannes-Passion*, 112, 191; Mass in B minor, 88, 98, 112, 226, 227, 230, 360; *Matthäus-Passion*, 62, 78–9, 83, 85, 88, 112, 223, 314, 315, 384, 478, 479; organ works, 230, 231; *Weihnachts-Oratorium*, 83, 84, 85, 86, 228, 344; gamba sonatas, 608; solos keyboard partitas, 130, 536; solo violin sonatas and partitas, 662, 663, 664; accompanied violin sonatas, 662
Bach, Maria Barbara, 601
Bach, Wilhelm Friedemann, 138
Bachfest (Vienna), 88
Backhaus, Wilhelm, 523, 538
Badura-Skoda, Eva, 529; *Interpreting Mozart*, 529
Badura-Skoda, Paul, 518–41, 623, 732; *Interpreting Mozart*, 529
Bahr, Robert von, 220
Bainton, Dr Edgar, 30; *Pearl Tree, The*, 30
Baker, Dame Janet, 40, 148, 306–18, 320, 382–3, 384, 390, 427, 434, 471, 718, 754
Ball, Beryl, 392
Baller, Adolph, 694
Ballets Russes, 50

INDEX

Barber, Samuel, 623
Barbican Centre (London), 209, 242, 617, 640
Barbirolli, Lady (Evelyn), 29
Barbirolli, Sir John, 8, 25, 26–7, 47, 59, 66, 72, 74, 81, 151, 195, 203, 232–3, 248, 250, 306, 312–13, 319, 324, 368–9, 387, 391, 399, 502, 564, 573, 754–5, 764
Bardon, Patricia, 148
Barenboim, Daniel, 205, 374, 375, 376, 389, 395, 396, 417, 551, 563, 581, 586, 630, 642–4, 697, 758
Bartók, Béla, 91, 193, 256, 298, 425, 561, 570, 571, 572, 574, 624, 665, 667–8, 686–7, 688, 707, 739; *Bluebeard's Castle*, 298; *Contrasts*, 571; Sonata for Solo Violin, 561, 570, 667, 686; Viola Concerto, 668; Violin Concerto No. 2, 91, 561; violin sonatas, 570, 571; violin concertos, 665, 688
Bartoli, Cecilia, 677, 682–3
Bashmet, Yuri, 256
Bath International Music Festival, 623, 699
Battersea Festival Gardens, 29
Bax, Sir Arnold, 150, 759; *Spring Fire*, 150
Bayerische Staatsoper, 329, 334, 417, 419, 462
Bayerische Staatsorchester, 480
Bayreuth Festival Opera, 152, 319, 327, 329, 330, 331, 336, 356, 357, 361, 365, 374, 375, 376, 377
BBC (British Broadcasting Corporation), 15, 26, 57, 111, 180, 181, 192, 347, 370, 407, 537, 562, 568, 569, 588–9, 593, 686, 697, 705, 707, 709–14, 726, 751, 756, 758, 759, 761–5, 766, 772
BBC Cardiff Singer of the World, 407

BBC Concert Orchestra, 180, 181, 762
BBC National Orchestra of Wales, 181
BBC Northern Dance Orchestra, 763
BBC Northern Symphony Orchestra (see BBC Philharmonic)
BBC Philharmonic, 105, 106, 114, 181, 299, 370–1, 752, 762
BBC Proms, 10, 15, 57, 120, 170, 180, 188, 194, 237, 285, 290, 301, 353, 354, 360, 392, 478, 479, 480, 573, 619, 751, 756, 758, 759, 762, 772, 792
BBC Radio 2, 762
BBC Radio 3, 180, 593, 615, 751, 756, 762
BBC Radio 4, 180
BBC Scottish Symphony Orchestra, 50, 57, 762, 764
BBC Singers, 763
BBC Studio Strings, 763
BBC Symphony Orchestra, 10, 26, 48, 57, 149, 181, 186, 504, 751, 759, 761–2, 763–5, 767, 768, 769, 770
BBC Television, 686, 697, 713
BBC Thursday Invitation Concerts, 196, 588–9
BBC Training Orchestra, 763
BBC Two (television), 180, 697
Beal, Hilde, 510
Beatles, The, 254, 699, 723
Beauséjour, Luc, 662
Bechstein Hall (London) (see Wigmore Hall)
Bechstein pianos, 538
Bedford, Steuart, 472, 617
Beecham, Sir Thomas, 30, 51
Beethoven, Ludwig van, 15, 23, 26, 38, 42, 43–5, 47, 48, 61, 65, 66, 72, 78, 80, 85, 103, 108, 118, 140, 141, 142, 181, 183, 184, 191, 196, 202, 209, 229–30, 239, 260, 262, 263, 275, 276, 281, 285, 289, 319, 329, 335–8, 358, 393–4, 394–5, 399, 437–8, 520, 521,

801

Beethoven, Ludwig van *cont.*
523, 524–5, 529, 532, 533, 535, 536, 537, 539, 543, 545, 547, 549, 562, 569, 570, 571, 573, 594, 595, 596, 598, 599, 600, 601, 606, 608, 618, 629, 630, 632, 639, 640–41, 645, 648–9, 688, 690, 700, 715, 716, 735–6, 738, 742, 763, 789, 794; Piano Sonata No. 3, 520; Piano Sonata No. 23 ('Appassionata'), 66, 523; cello sonatas, 569, 594, 598, 601, 606; Piano Concerto No. 1, 532; Piano Concerto No. 2, 543, 549, 632; Piano Concerto No. 3, 140, 535; Piano Concerto No. 4, 140, 532, 630, 632; Piano Concerto No. 5 ('Emperor'), 532, 547, 632; Triple Concerto, 532; *Fidelio*, 329, 335–8, 393–4, 393; *Für Elise*, 65; Horn Sonata, 599, 600; Sonata for Piano and Violin No. 9 ('Kreutzer'), 742; *Leonore*, 337; *Missa solemnis*, 42, 209, 229–30, 394; piano concertos, 23, 140, 532, 535, 543, 549, 630, 632; Piano Trio No. 1, 524–5; Symphony No. 1, 789; Symphony No. 2, 78, 533, 716; Symphony No. 3 ('Eroica'), 38, 78, 260, 262, 794; Symphony No. 4, 78; Symphony No. 5, 78, 196, 735–6; Symphony No. 6 ('Pastoral'), 78, 736; Symphony No. 7, 78, 285, 736; Symphony No. 8, 47, 48, 78, 196; Symphony No. 9 ('Choral'), 43–5, 78, 80, 289, 394–5, 437–8, 529, 715; Violin Concerto, 26, 573, 640–41, 648–9, 688; String Trio, Op. 3, 599; String Trio, Op. 3 (arr. cello and piano, Op. 64), 599; violin sonatas, 569, 601, 645; Variations for Mandolin and Piano, 599; piano sonatas, 632, 281; string quartets, 183
Beethoven Lives Upstairs, 608
Began, Menachem, 697
Belgian Underground (Resistance), 406
Bell, Joshua, 598, 600
Bella, Dagmar, 526
Bellini, Vincenzo, 263, 297, 351, 409, 410, 471; *I Capuletti e i Montecchi*, 297; *Norma*, 351, 471
Benedetti, Nicola, 701
Benedetti, René, 3, 4
Benjamin, Sir George, 760
Bennett, Richard Rodney, 195
Berberian, Cathy, 427–8; *Stripsody*, 427–8
Beresford, Bruce, 342
Berg, Alban, 53, 194–5, 284, 290, 361, 504, 519, 572–3, 756; *Lulu*, 53, 284, 361; '*Lulu*' Suite, 195; *Altenberg Lieder*, 194, 504; *Sieben frühe Lieder*, 504; *Wozzeck*, 290, 504; Chamber Concerto, 756
Berganza, Teresa, 680
Berglund, Paavo, 573–4
Bergman, Ingmar, 715
Berio, Luciano, 206, 207, 301; *Rendering*, 301
Berlin, Irving, 724; *Alexander's Ragtime Band*, 724
Berlin Hofoper, 293
Berlin Philharmonic, 74, 81, 88, 233, 277, 285, 531, 547–8, 609, 646, 689, 736
Berlin Radio Symphony Orchestra, 789
Berlin Wall, 232, 437–8, 558, 559
Berlioz, Hector, 55, 56–7, 59, 111, 117, 118, 175, 184, 195–6, 294, 395, 424, 429, 433–4, 668, 685; *Benvenuto Cellini*, 56; *Harold en Italie*, 668; *L'enfance du Christ*, 55; *La damnation de Faust*, 56, 196, 294; *Le nuits d'été*, 395; *Les Troyens*, 56–7, 111, 429; *Roméo et Juliette*, 433–4

INDEX

Bernardi, Francesco (see Senesino)
Bernstein, Leonard, 77, 189, 274, 335, 337, 338, 382–3, 437, 446, 448, 700, 716–17, 739; *West Side Story*, 448, 717; *MASS: A Theatre Piece for Singers, Players and Dancers*, 717; *Candide*, 717
Berry, Walter, 487, 676
Bezuidenhout, Kristian, 142
Bibliothèque national (Paris), 109, 110
Bilibin, Ivan, 196
Billy Cotton Band Show, 592
Bilson, Malcolm, 116
Bing, Sir Rudolf, 326
Birtwistle, Sir Harrison, 195, 770; *Triumph of Time, The*, 770
BIS, 220
Bizet, Georges, 30, 323, 348, 366, 465, 513, 514, 685; *Carmen*, 30, 323, 348, 366, 465, 513, 685; *Les pêcheurs de perles*, 514
Björling, Jussi, 403, 404
Blech, Harry, 169, 565
Bloch, Ernest, 610–1; *Schelomo*, 610; *From Jewish Life*, 611
Bloom, Myron (Mike), 547
Blossom Music Centre (Cleveland), 768
Boccherini, Luigi, 601, 602
Böhm, Karl, 296, 297, 335, 336, 337, 338, 446, 449, 531, 777, 792
Bolcom, William, 553
Bolet, Jorge, 621
Bolsheviks, 729
Bolshoi Theatre, 506, 728
Bombay Symphony Orchestra, 698
Bonhoeffer, Dietrich, 64
Bonney, Barbara, 140, 436, 459
Bonynge, Richard, 351, 444, 498, 507, 682
Boosey & Hawkes, 39, 194, 729
Borromeo, Milena, 745

Bösendorfer pianos, 537, 538
Boston Symphony Orchestra, 59, 60, 185, 192, 553, 767
Bouchard, Linda, 127–8
Boulanger, Lili, 738–9
Boulanger, Nadia, 98–9, 101, 103–5, 108, 109, 114, 115, 125, 738–9
Boulez, Pierre, 68, 274, 355, 361, 565, 619, 626, 739, 756, 765, 769–70
Boult, Sir Adrian, 32, 48–9, 149, 190, 312, 367, 399, 564, 732, 755
Bowman, James, 40
Boyce Foundation, 323
Brahms, Johannes, 10, 11, 101, 123–4, 182, 196, 202, 210, 394, 399, 519, 525, 527, 528, 532, 545, 547, 553, 556, 569, 599, 605–6, 609, 639, 645, 646, 648, 656, 732, 747, 763, 788; cello sonatas, 605–6; *Die schöne Magelone*, 747; 'Feldeinsamkeit', 747; *Ein deutsches Requiem*, 182, 394; *Liebeslieder-Walzer*, 101; Piano Concerto No. 2, 547; Piano Trio in B major, 525, 606; piano concertos, 532; Rhapsody in G minor, 519; Symphony No. 1, 11, 527; Symphony No. 2, 182; 'Tragic' Overture, 11; *Ungarische Tänze* (trans. Joachim), 732; Violin Concerto, 556, 645, 646, 648, 656; Violin Sonata No. 1, 599; Cello Sonata No. 1, 606; Clarinet Quintet, 606
Brain, Dennis, 659
Brainin, Norbert, 169, 600, 661
Brandon University (Canada), 651, 652
Brandstrup, Kim, 630
Brannigan, Owen, 384
Bream, Julian, 586, 587, 719–20
Brendel, Alfred, 18, 19, 69, 71, 622
Brian, Havergal, 759; Symphony No. 1 ('Gothic'), 759

Bridge, Frank, 759, 760
Brighton Dome, 150
Brisbane Philharmonic Orchestra, 534
British Council, 35, 36, 241
British Music Information Centre, 751, 757–8, 760
British Petroleum (BP), 170
Britten, Benjamin, 18, 98, 108–9, 118, 156, 157, 158–9, 160, 162, 163, 164, 179, 193, 197–8, 283, 289, 290–91, 294, 299, 300, 302, 347, 363–4, 398, 399–400, 430, 431, 456, 470, 487, 490, 505, 553, 600, 617, 623, 640, 646, 659–60, 703, 708–12, 717–9, 751, 756, 772–3; *Albert Herring*, 156, 159, 160; *Billy Budd*, 158–9, 160, 193; *Cabaret Songs*, 490; Cello Symphony, 299, 300; *Ceremony of Carols, A*, 711; *Curlew River*, 198; *Death in Venice*, 290, 294; *Diversions for Piano Left Hand and Orchestra*, 553; *Friday Afternoons*, 98; *Les Illuminations*, 164, 283; *Missa brevis*, 108–9; *Nocturne*, 283; *Peter Grimes*, 156, 158, 159, 163, 290, 292, 430, 431, 470; Piano Concerto, 617, 623; *Serenade for Tenor, Horn and Strings*, 600, 659–60; *Spring Symphony*, 157, 289, 399; *Rape of Lucretia, The*, 158, 160, 347, 400; *Turn of the Screw, The*, 159, 160, 290–91, 487; Violin Concerto, 646; *War Requiem*, 163, 164, 718–9, 756; *Young Person's Guide to the Orchestra, The*, 197–8; *Sinfonia da Requiem*, 290
Britten Pears Arts, 751, 772
Britten Sinfonia, 628
Broadbent, Jim, 630
Brod, Max, 38
Bron, Zakhar, 634, 635, 636, 643
Bronowski, Jacob, 723; *Ascent of Man, The*, 723
Brontë sisters, 177
Brook, Sir Peter, 271, 277
Broughton, Simon, 593
Brouwer, Leo, 587; Guitar Concerto No. 1, 587
Bruckner, Anton, 90, 172, 196, 521, 776–98; Symphony No. 1, 776, 777, 781–2, 783, 789–91; Symphony No. 2, 776, 783, 787; Symphony No. 3, 776, 781, 783, 784, 785; Symphony No. 4, 776, 777, 779, 781, 782, 784, 785, 786, 792, 795; Symphony No. 5, 90, 777, 785, 786, 788, 790, 791–2, 794, 797; Symphony No. 6, 785, 786, 793–4; Symphony No. 7, 777, 778, 789, 790, 792, 794, 796; Symphony No. 8, 776, 777, 778, 781, 786, 787, 789, 790, 792, 795; Symphony No. 9, 90, 784, 785, 787, 792, 796, 797, 798; Symphony No. 00, 783; Te Deum, 796, 798; *Helgoland*, 796
Bryanston School, 98, 99
Bryanston Summer School, 98
Bryars, Gavin, 503, 760; *Medea*, 503
Buchbinder, Rudolf, 532
Budapest Festival Orchestra, 574
Bülow, Hans von, 532, 622
Burgtheater (Vienna), 268
Burkhardt, Franz, 521
Burkhardt, Karl, 534
Burrows, Stuart, 412, 413
Burton, Sir Humphrey, 686–702, 709, 710, 716
Burton Richard, 340, 727
Busch, Adolf, 691, 692
Busch, Fritz, 168, 265, 268, 269, 293, 409, 481, 692, 700, 732
Busoni, Ferruccio, 191, 535, 539
Butt, Dame Clara, 147, 148, 306, 307
Buxtehude, Dieterich, 222, 227
Byam Shaw, Glen, 52

INDEX

Bychkov, Semyon, 199–218
Byles, Edward, 347
Byrd, William, 96, 100, 108; Mass for Four Voices, 96; Mass for Five Voices, 96

Cage, John, 425, 626, 627; *Aria*, 425
Callas, Maria, 318, 351, 504, 672, 707, 735
Calthorpe, Nancy, 469
Cambridge, University of, 99, 100, 103, 104, 106, 155, 157, 281, 282, 411, 615, 619, 620, 624, 704, 705
Campbell-White, Martin, 719–20
Canada Council for the Arts, 658
Canford Summer School, 106, 107
Cantelli, Guido, 11
Canterbury Cathedral, 129
Carl Flesch International Violin Competition, 636–7
Carmi, Eugenio, 428
Carnegie Hall (film), 734
Carpi, Maria, 324, 367, 380
Carreras, José, 415
Carrington, Simon, 106
Caruso, Enrico, 403, 404
Casals, Pablo, 597,
Casa Ricordi, 407
Cavalli, Francesco, 121, 165, 166, 167, 172, 176, 354, 427; *Eritrea*, 165; *La Calisto*, 427; *Rosinda*, 165
CBS, 584, 672, 742
Celibidache, Sergiu, 74, 265
Cell Block Theatre (Sydney), 498
Čermáková, Josefina, 609
Chailly, Riccardo, 789
Chandos, 461–2
Chaplin, Charlie, 549
Chaplin, Francis, 652, 653, 655
Charles, Prince of Wales, 453
Charles II (King of England, Scotland and Ireland), 719

Charles de Gaulle Airport (Paris), 484
Chausson, Ernest, 155; *Poème*, 155
Chekhov, Michael, 271
Chelsea Opera Group, 50, 56, 107
Chéreau, Patrice, 331, 332, 361
Cherkassky, Shura, 617
Chetham's School, 752–3, 756
Chevalier, Maurice, 740
Chicago Lyric Opera, 429
Chicago Lyric Opera Orchestra, 172
Chicago Symphony Orchestra, 150, 172, 565, 643, 696
Chopin, Frédéric, 519, 524, 537, 622–3, 626, 627, 678; Étude, Op. 10 No. 12 ('Revolutionary'), 519; Étude, Op. 10 No. 1, 537; Polonaise in A flat major, 524; mazurkas, 615, 622–3, 627
Christ, Jesus, 147, 418, 611
Christian Democratic Union (Germany), 57
Christie, Sir George, 390
Christie, Sir John, 168, 268, 481
Christie, Lady (Mary), 390
Christie, William, 110
Christophers, Harry, 165
Christ's Hospital, 48
Chung, Kyung-Wha, 677
Churchill, John, 14
City Literary Institute, 347
City of Birmingham Symphony Orchestra, 240, 245, 289, 299
City of Birmingham Symphony Orchestra Chorus, 289
City of London School, 596
Clark, Kenneth, 723; *Civilisation*, 723
Classic FM, 687
Cleobury, Nicholas, 165
Cleveland Orchestra, 23, 70, 72–3, 77–8, 549, 550, 751, 765, 766–9
Cliburn, Van, 620
Clooney, George, 543

Clouzot, Henri-Georges, 735–6
Cocker, Norman, 753
Cohen, Leonard, 723
Coliseum (London), 107, 160, 296, 297, 371, 372, 373
Collins, Anthony, 59
Collins Classics, 617, 624
Columbia Artists, 550
Columbia Records, 672
Communist Party (Australia), 579
Communist Party (USSR), 200
Community Concerts (USA), 550
Concentus Musicus Wien, 87–8, 92–4
Concertgebouw (Amsterdam), 83, 117
Concertgebouw Orchestra (see Royal Concertgebouw Orchestra)
Concours international d'exécution musicale de Genève, 582
Conquest, Robert, 725
Conservatoire de Musique de Genève, 367
Cooke, Alistair, 723; *America*, 723
Copley, John, 55, 294, 350, 416, 431, 449
Corelli, Arcangelo, 15, 16, 17; *Concerto Grossi*, Op. 6, 16, 17
Cortot, Alfred, 538
Coty, René, 735
Countess of Munster Musical Trust, 367
Couperin, François, 626
Cowan, Jane, 596, 604
Coward, Sir Noël, 465
Cox, Frederic, 403, 404, 405–6, 408, 410, 412, 470
Cox, John, 168, 416, 449, 460, 463
Craft, Robert, 18, 194
Crawford-Phillips, Simon, 284
Cream, 713
Crespin, Régine, 684, 685
Cross, Joan, 346, 347, 350
Culshaw, John, 347, 348, 351, 674, 675

Cummings, Henry, 346, 351, 386
Curcio, Maria, 545
Curtis, Alan, 426
Curzon, Sir Clifford, 545, 546
Cuvilliés Theatre (see Residenztheater, Munich)
Czech Philharmonic, 36, 46
Czerny, Carl, 532

Dallapiccola, Luigi, 763
Dalley-Scarlett, Robert, 39
Dam, José van, 120, 483
Dart, Thurston, 5–6, 103–4
Dartington Summer School, 98, 625
Darwin, Charles, 538
Davern, John, 444, 445, 446
Davey, Jack, 31
David, Ferdinand, 123
Davies, Arthur, 470
Davies, Sir Peter Maxwell, 15, 179, 422, 619; *Kommilitonen!*, 179
Davies, Ryland, 401–19, 470
Davis, Sir Andrew, 172, 457, 479, 480, 504, 564
Davis, Carl, 616–7
Davis, Sir Colin, 26, 47–62, 184, 259, 310, 393–4, 395, 417, 433, 446, 450, 451, 474, 509–11, 564, 573
Dawson, Les, 591–2
Day, Doris, 343
Debussy, Claude, 111, 118, 119, 120, 194–5, 416, 545, 769–70; *La mer*, 769; *Nocturnes*, 195; *Pelléas et Mélisande*, 118, 119, 120, 416, 770; *Études*, 195; *Prélude à l'après-midi d'un faune*, 195
Decca, 112, 216, 347, 360, 672–5, 677, 678, 679, 683
Decker, Willy, 431
Delius, Frederick, 30, 150, 153–7; *Sea Drift*, 154, 155, 156, 157; *Song of the High Hills, A*, 155, 156

INDEX

Della Casa, Lisa, 461
Deller, Alfred, 40, 82, 93
Del Mar, Norman, 238, 239
Del Monaco, Mario, 677, 681
Demus, Jörg, 539
Dernesch, Helga, 393, 394
Deutsche Grammophon, 112, 116, 138, 338, 355, 419, 672, 677, 751, 769–70
Deutsche Oper Berlin, 335, 336
Deutsches Nationaltheater Weimar, 340
Diaghilev, Sergei, 695
Diana, Princess of Wales, 453
Dickens, Charles, 179, 392
Die Frau im Schatten (play), 339–40
Dietz, Alfred, 326
Dillon, James, 763
d'Indy, Vincent, 109
Di Stefano, Giuseppe, 672
Dittersdorf, Carl Ditters von, 95
Divall, Richard, 498
Doane, Steven, 597
Dodgson, Stephen, 581, 583, 585; Guitar Concerto No. 1, 581, 585; *Partita*, 581, 585; *Midst of Life, The*, 581
Dohnányi, Christoph von, 63–81, 766
Dohnányi, Ernst von, 65–6
Dohnányi, Klaus von, 72
Domingo, Plácido, 513, 681, 727–8
Donizetti, Gaetano, 262, 409, 410, 417, 474, 500, 501, 504, 513, 682; *La fille du regiment*, 474; *Rosmonda d'Inghilterra*, 501; *Maria Stuarda*, 513; *Lucia di Lammermoor*, 417, 500, 682
Donne, John, 102
Donohoe, Peter, 752
Doonican, Val, 591–2
Doráti, Antal, 562, 564, 573, 687
Dorliak, Nina, 745
Douglas, Barry, 620

Douglas, Michael, 721
Downes, Sir Edward, 244, 266, 498
Downes, Ralph, 130
Dragonetti, Domenico, 45
Drummond, Sir John, 180, 761, 765
Dukas, Paul, 303; *La Péri*, 303
Duke's Hall (Royal Academy of Music, London), The, 407
Duncan, Martin, 507
Durban, Deanna, 467–8
Dürr, Alfred, 84
Dutilleux, Henri, 206, 207
Dvořák, Antonín, 35, 39, 46, 71, 85, 91, 323, 606, 608–9, 735; Cello Concerto, 91, 609; Symphony No. 9 ('New World'), 39, 85, 735; Symphony No. 7, 35; *Zigeunerlieder*, 323
Dyer, Louise, 14
Dylan, Bob, 723
Dyson, George, 108

Ebert, Carl, 168, 408
Eddy, Jenifer, 513, 514
Edinburgh Festival Chorus, 395, 396
Edinburgh International Festival, 120, 291, 381, 383, 396, 513, 569
Éditions de l'Oiseau-Lyre, 14, 19
Éditions Durand, 109
Edwards, Sian, 161, 169, 232–52
Ehnes, James, 650–69, 700
Einstein, Albert, 128
Einstein, Alfred, 679
Elder, Sir Mark, 129, 144–60, 248, 249, 269, 280, 286, 287, 296, 498, 499, 505
Elgar, Sir Edward, 3, 46, 60–1, 114–5, 144–53, 163, 179, 189, 230, 231, 299, 302, 306, 363–4, 398, 421, 609, 610–1, 646–7, 707, 758, 760–1; *Caractacus*, 398; Cello Concerto, 115, 150, 421, 609, 610–1, 761;

807

Elgar, Sir Edward *cont.*
  'Enigma' Variations, 115, 150, 153; *Falstaff*, 189; *In the South (Alassio)*, 115, 151–2; *Introduction and Allegro for Strings*, 115; *Kingdom, The*, 145, 147; Piano Quintet, 610; 'Pomp and Circumstance' Marches, 150, 302; *Sea Pictures*, 148; *Sospiri*, 115; Symphony No. 1, 145, 149, 151, 152; Symphony No. 2, 149, 150, 151, 758; Symphony No. 3 (completed Payne), 60–1; *Apostles, The*, 145–8; *Dream of Gerontius, The*, 145–8, 163, 179, 302, 306, 363–4; Violin Concerto, 3; Violin Sonata, 646–7
Elizabeth II (Queen of the United Kingdom), 709
Elkins, Margreta, 343, 345
Elton, Christopher, 614, 615
Ely Cathedral, 382–3
EMI, 12, 306, 312, 357, 672, 673, 677
Enescu, George, 691, 692
English Baroque Soloists, 110, 112,
English Chamber Orchestra, 133, 171, 389, 617
English Concert, The, 131, 132, 135, 136, 139, 143
English Music Theatre Company, 472
English National Opera, 39, 160, 249, 279, 288, 289–96, 303, 309, 369, 371–3, 429, 435, 457, 460, 471, 475, 487, 501–3, 505, 506
English Opera Group, 198
Ensemble Modern, 233, 250
Epilogue (BBC Television), 713
Epiphone guitar, 576
Erato, 112
Eschenbach, Christoph, 605
Esswood, Paul, 82
Esterházy Orchestra, 602
Esterházy Palace, 601
Eton College, 4, 280, 281

European Cultural Parliament, 701
Evans, Dame Anne, 365–81, 481, 508
Evans, Sir Geraint, 413
Evening Standard, 709

Faber & Faber, 608
Fairuz (Nouhad Wadie' Haddad), 99
Fantasia, 734
Fauré, Gabriel, 395–6, 433, 607; Requiem, 395–6
Feis Ceoil (Ireland), 467
Feldman, Morton, 276
Ferneyhough, Brian, 422, 760
Ferrier, Kathleen, 148, 306–7, 312, 320, 344, 348–9, 386, 387, 441
Festung Hohensalzburg, 705
Feuermann, Emanuel, 596
Financial Times, 760
Fingleton, David, 453
Finley, Gerald, 116
Finnissy, Michael, 760
Firkušný, Rudolf, 545
Fischer, Edwin, 523–6, 531–2, 534, 536, 538–40, 630
Fischer, Iván, 275, 574
Fischer, Wilhelm, 521
Fischer-Dieskau, Dietrich, 306, 395–6, 471, 679, 746–8
Fisher, Carrie, 182
Flack, Jenny, 246
Flagstad, Kirsten, 374, 379
Fleischmann, Ernest, 13, 184
Fleisher, Leon, 246, 542–55, 623
Fleming, Renée, 216
Fleta, Ignacio, 590, 591
Florentine Camerata, 120
Florida State University, 65, 66
Fonteyn, Dame Margot, 726, 727
Foreman, Miloš, 22, 177; *Amadeus*, 22, 23, 177; *Valmont*, 22–3
Forster, Edward Morgan (E. M.), 158
Foulds, John, 759

INDEX

Franck, César, 528, 548, 741; *Variations symphoniques*, 528
Frank, Hans, 734
Frankl-Pauk-Kirshbaum Trio, 568–9
Frankl, Peter, 568–9
Franz Liszt Academy (Budapest), 559, 561
Franz Liszt Chamber Orchestra, 567
Fraser, Lady Antonia, 513; *Mary Queen of Scots*, 513
Fredman, Myer, 408
Free French, 694
Freeman-Attwood, Jonathan, 282
Free Trade Hall (Manchester), 232, 754
Fried, Oskar, 262
Friedrich, Götz, 53, 331, 416
Friern Barnet Grammar School, 580
Frossini, Pietro, 523; *Serenade Italienne*, 523
Frühbeck de Burgos, Rafael, 384, 385
Fugard, Athol, 706
Furtwängler, Wilhelm, 12, 43–4, 74, 190, 208, 262, 519, 525–9, 530, 531, 532, 534, 695–6, 700, 787, 788; Piano Concerto, 528

Gabrieli, Giovanni, 93, 124
Gaddarn, James, 347
Gál, Hans, 519
Galamian, Ivan, 653, 654
Gale, Elizabeth, 458
Gandhi, Mohandas ('Mahatma'), 718
García, Manuel, 497
Gardiner, Balfour, 125–6
Gardiner, Sir John Eliot, 96–126, 208, 251, 275, 297
Gardner, Edward, 278–303
Gardner, John, 98
Garland, Patrick, 705
Gazelle, Marcel, 688
Gedda, Nicolai, 410

Geisl, Herta, 522, 525
Geitel, Klaus, 339, 340; *O, Malvina!*, 339
Gellhorn, Peter, 409
General Assembly Hall of the United Nations, 699
General Electric, 33
George I (King of Great Britain and Ireland and Elector of Hanover), 178
Gergiev, Valery, 727–8
German Theatre (Prague), 38
Gershwin, George, 92, 442, 616–17; *Porgy and Bess*, 92, 442; *Rhapsody in Blue*, 616–17; Piano Concerto, 617
Gesellschaft der Musikfreunde (Vienna), 528
Gestapo, 694
Gibson, Sir Alexander, 471, 472
Gibson, Darina, 469
Gielen, Michael, 284, 285
Gielgud, Sir John, 340, 729–30
Gigli, Beniamino, 403, 404, 411
Gilbert, Sir William Schwenck (W. S.) (see Gilbert and Sullivan)
Gilbert and Sullivan, 31, 279, 354, 398, 402, 493, 494; *Gondoliers, The*, 398, 493; *Mikado, The*, 279, 398; *Pirates of Penzance, The*, 398, 402, 493; *Ruddigore*, 398; *Iolanthe*, 398; *HMS Pinafore*, 398; *Sorcerer, The*, 398; *Princess Ida*, 398;
Gilels, Emil, 256, 617
Gilfry, Rodney, 116
Gilhooly, John, 594
Gilliam, Terry, 294
Ginzburg, Leo, 261, 263
Girling (factory in Wales), 321
Girls in Harmony, 322
Giulini, Carlo Maria, 274, 314, 327, 394, 585, 643, 787, 792

Glinka Capella, 213
Glinka Choir School, 199, 213
Glock, Sir William, 98, 756
Gloucester Cathedral, 62, 278
Glover, Dame Jane, 161–81; *Mozart's Women*, 177; *Handel in London*, 178
Gluck, Christoph Willibald (Ritter von), 118, 307, 322–3, 347, 471; *Orfeo ed Euridice*, 307, 323; 'Che farò senza Euridice', 347; *Alceste*, 471
Glyndebourne Festival Opera, 51, 160, 166, 167, 168, 245, 246, 265–70, 288, 307, 308, 355, 389, 390, 400, 407, 408, 409, 426, 427, 458, 463, 480, 481, 483, 585, 680, 682
Glyndebourne Touring Opera, 167, 168, 287–8
Gobbi, Tito, 354, 393
Goebel, Reinhard, 208
Goehr, Alexander, 190, 581
Goehr, Walter, 100, 581
Goldberg, David, 702
Goldberg, Szymon, 679
Goldensohn, Leon, 733–4; *Nuremberg Interviews, The*, 733–4
Gonzaga family (Mantua), 102
Goodall, Sir Reginald, 372, 373
Goodman, Benny, 571
Goold, Rupert, 294
Goossens, Sir Eugene, 31, 32, 33
Goossens, Léon, 32, 36
Gorbachev, Mikhail, 256, 257, 506
Göring, Hermann, 734
Gosconcert, 583
Gothenburg Symphony Orchestra, 284
Göttingen International Handel Festival, 112
Gottlieb, Anna, 41
Gould, Diana, 686, 694–5
Gould, Evelyn, 694–5
Gould, Glenn, 23, 256, 546, 731, 733, 741–3

Gounod, Charles, 448, 474; *Faust*, 448, 474
Graf fortepiano, 142
Graf, Herbert, 324, 325, 367
Graffman, Gary, 551
Graham, Colin, 472
Grainger, Percy, 125, 126
Gramophone, 625
Granados, Enrique, 587–8; *Valses poéticos*, 587–8
Grand Central Station (New York), 688
Grand Théâtre de Genève, 335
Gran Prix du Disque, 536
Grappelli, Stéphane, 646, 699
Green, Horace, 33
Greevy, Bernadette, 352
Gresley, Nigel, 704
Grieg, Edvard, 387, 607, 742, 744; *Peer Gynt*, 387; Piano Concerto, 742
Grilli, Umberto, 408
Grosser Konzertsaal (Vienna), 521
Grosses Festspielhaus (Salzburg), 380, 483
Groves, Sir Charles, 237, 238, 246, 398, 399, 564, 585, 754
Groves, Lady (Hilary), 237
Gruberová, Edita, 474, 492
Guadagnini violins, 565
Guarneri violins and violas, 566, 659, 660, 661
Guggenheim Museum (New York), 186
Gui, Vittorio, 265, 268, 269, 409
Guildhall School of Music & Drama (London), 469
Gutman, Natalia, 256

Haas, Robert, 782, 786, 787, 795
Haïm, Emmanuelle, 111
Haitink, Sir Bernard, 167–8, 285, 399, 446, 457–9, 462, 489, 511, 759, 792

INDEX

Hall, Sir Peter, 168, 375, 458
Hallé, Sir Charles, 153
Hallé Choir, 232, 420, 754
Hallé Orchestra, 155, 181, 195, 232, 237, 286–7, 752, 754–5
Hallé Youth Orchestra, 303
Hamburg Staatsoper, 329, 415, 419
Hamburger, Paul, 314
Handel, George Frideric, 15, 28, 29, 30, 39, 40, 41, 43, 61, 89, 108, 110, 112, 121, 122, 128, 138, 140, 141, 173, 174, 176, 178, 279, 321, 358, 360, 363, 388, 391, 397, 398, 405, 418, 429, 453, 456, 465, 475, 476, 477, 478, 479, 495, 498, 505, 506, 511, 512, 566; *Acis and Galatea*, 108; *Agrippina*, 178; *Alcina*, 475; *Ariodante*, 477, 479; *Israel in Egypt*, 39, 495; *Judas Maccabeus*, 418; *Julius Caesar*, 39, 40, 41; *Messiah*, 61, 173, 321, 363, 391, 405, 456, 475; *Messiah* (arr. Mozart), 39; *Music for the Royal Fireworks*, 28, 29; *Rinaldo*, 178; *Samson*, 429, 453; *Semele*, 39, 43, 397, 512; violin sonatas, 566; *Water Music* (arr. Harty), 30; *Water Music*, 39; *Xerxes*, 475, 476, 477, 498, 506, 512
Handel Opera Society, 39
Hardy, Thomas, 97
Harewood, Lord, (George Lascelles), 502
Harnoncourt, Alice, 82, 83, 87
Harnoncourt, Nikolaus, 82–95, 133, 139, 208–9, 219, 226, 275, 276, 485, 486, 492, 508–9, 533, 797
Harper, Heather, 347
Harrison, Beatrice, 610
Harrison, George, 699
HarrisonParrott, 598
Hartmann, Karl Amadeus, 68
Hartog, Howard, 246, 374, 415, 564, 572, 573

Harty, Sir Hamilton, 28, 30, 195
Harvard Business School, 772
Harvey, Jonathan, 289
Haslam, David, 384
Haussmann, Elias Gottlob, 97
Haydn, Joseph, 15, 41, 88, 89, 118, 138, 139, 164, 174–5, 183, 184, 198, 239, 483, 484, 527, 530, 536, 601, 602, 606, 679, 690, 763; Cello Concerto No. 1 in C major, 601–2; Cello Concerto No. 2 in D major, 601–2; *Die Jahreszeiten*, 89, 164; *Die Schöpfung*, 483, 484; *L'isola disabitata*, 88; 'Nelson' Mass, 138, 139; Stabat Mater, 138; *Sturm und Drang* symphonies, 138; Symphony No. 104 ('London'), 527
Heifetz, Jascha, 25, 648, 655, 663, 664, 665, 734
Heinze, Sir Bernard, 692
Helfgott, David, 729
Heller, Seymour, 720–1
Hemmings, Peter, 471
Hendrix, Jimmy, 712–3
Henry, Donald, 653
Henze, Hans Werner, 503, 585, 587, 765; *We Come to the River* (*Wir erreichen den Fluss*), 503; *Elegy for Young Lovers*, 585; *Royal Winter Music*, 587; Symphony No. 6, 765
Herbert, George, 102
Herkulessaal (Munich), 68
Herrmann, Bernard, 189
Herschkowitz, Philipp, 275
Hertz, Alfred, 542, 543, 548
Herz, Joachim, 157
Hesse Student Scheme (Aldeburgh), 164
Hickox, Richard, 492
Hill, Edgar, 493
Hindemith, Paul, 553, 742
Hitchcock, Sir Alfred, 271

Hitler, Adolf, 64
HMV, 387, 672
Hoare, Mrs, 234
Hochschule für Musik und Theater (Munich), 64–5
Hoffman, Dustin, 340; *Quartet*, 340
Hofmannsthal, Hugo von, 292, 334, 505
Hogwood, Christopher, 16
Holden, Amanda, 477
Hollander, Lorin, 553
Holmes, Sherlock, 104
Holst, Gustav, 98, 153, 302, 303; *Planets, The*, 302, 303
Holst, Imogen, 97–8, 719
Horenstein, Jascha, 184
Horne, Marilyn, 351
Horowitz, Vladimir, 256, 551, 617, 625, 787
Horsfield, Basil, 444, 445, 446, 453
Horváth, Ödön von, 519
Hot Club de France, 699
Hotter, Hans, 327
Houdini, Harry, 195
Hough, Sir Stephen, 540, 604, 605, 607
Household Cavalry, 707
Howells, Anne, 446, 470
Hubay, Jenő, 559
Huddersfield Choral Society, 173, 289
Hume, Alastair, 106
Humperdinck, Engelbert, 323, 474, 475; *Hänsel und Gretel*, 323, 474, 475
Hungarian Revolution, 558, 559, 562, 563
Hungaroton, 567
Hunt, Christopher, 502
Hunt, Terence, 495
Hurst, George, 106, 107
Hutchinson, John, 386
Hüttenstrasse, Alexander, 538

Hyde-White, Wilfrid, 469
Hyperion, 607
Hytner, Sir Nicholas, 430, 477, 487, 506

Ibbs and Tillett, 391, 392, 583
Ingpen, Joan, 445
Ingpen & Williams Ltd., 564
Innsbruck Festival of Early Music, 108
International Tchaikovsky Competition, 6, 620, 621, 657
International Violin Competition of Indianapolis, 657
International Vocalists Competition s'-Hertogenbosch, 348
Irwin, Michael, 435
Isepp, Helene, 310
Isepp, Martin, 168, 408
Israel Philharmonic Orchestra, 639
Isserlis, Steven, 594–612
Istomin, Eugene, 550, 551
Italian Cultural Institute (Vienna), 525
Ives, Charles, 623, 626
Iyengar, B. K. S., 698

Jackson, Sir Nicholas, 130
Jackson, Ronal, 499
Jacobean Ensemble, 5
Jacobs, David, 714
Jacobs, Sylvia, 470
Jacques Thibaud Competition, 556, 563
James, Ifor, 235, 236
Janáček, Leoš, 36, 37, 38, 46, 154, 157–8, 279–80, 299, 319, 418, 511, 607; *Káťa Kabanová*, 36, 37; *Mládí*, 36; *Sinfonietta*, 37, 279–80
Jandó, Jenő, 570
Janis, Byron, 551
Janowitz, Gundula, 338
Jansen, Janine, 700
Jansons, Arvīds, 242

INDEX

Jansons, Mariss, 242
Jarrow March, 383
Järvi, Neeme, 239, 240, 457, 461, 462
Jenkins, Graeme, 239
Jerusalem, Siegfried, 376
Jewish Chronicle, The, 215
Joachim, Joseph, 559, 732
John, Sir Elton, 722
John Alldis Choir, 139, 433
John Alvey Turner Music Shop (London), 575
John Christie Award, The, 407
Johnson, Graham, 434, 464
Jonas, Sir Peter, 475, 480
Jones, Dame Gwyneth, 319–41, 380, 402, 442, 461, 474, 488, 504
Jones, Philip, 236
Jones, Quincy, 738
Jones, Richard, 294, 489
Joplin, Scott, 723–4; *Treemonisha*, 724
Jorgensen, Sebastian, 578
Juilliard School, The, 652, 653, 654, 657
Juke Box Jury, 712, 714
Jurinac, Sena, 676
Jurowski, Mikhail, 254, 257, 261
Jurowski, Vladimir, 253–77

Kafka, Franz, 38
Kálmán, Emmerich, 507, 519; *Die Csárdásfürstin*, 507
Kalmar Orchestra, 49, 50
Kapell, William, 551
Kapuscinski, Richard, 597
Karajan, Herbert von, 10, 12, 23, 25, 66, 67, 74, 76, 87, 88, 92, 203, 205, 208, 262, 270, 271, 413, 417, 483, 484, 520, 527–9, 680, 681, 700, 714–16, 735–6, 748, 781, 787, 792
Karol Lipiński and Henryk Wieniawski Young Violinists Competition, 636–7

Katchen, Julius, 553, 741, 742
Kathleen Ferrier Award, 349, 384, 386, 387, 502, 515
Kathleen Ferrier Prize (Netherlands), 348, 349
Kelly, Michael, 10
Kempe, Rudolf, 329
Kempff, Wilhelm, 526, 630
Kennedy, Michael, 312
Kennedy, Nigel, 697, 701
Kenny, Yvonne, 492–515
Kent Opera, 426, 427, 435
Kent, University of, 435
Kentner, Louis, 695
Kenyon, Sir Nicholas, 180
Kern, Patricia, 433
Kertész, István, 359, 755
Kessler, Susan, 501
KGB (formerly MGB), 726
Khachaturian, Aram, 584, 725; *Spartacus*, 584
Khrushchev, Nikita, 256, 584
'Khrushchev's Thaw', 726
King, James, 393
King's College (University of Cambridge), 100, 101
King's College (University of London), 104
King's College Chapel (University of Cambridge), 101
King's Singers, The, 111
Kingsley, Sir Ben, 724
Kinloch Anderson, Ronald, 306
Kirkman harpsichord, 536
Kirshbaum, Ralph, 568–9
Kissinger, Henry, 681
Kleiber, Carlos, 190, 247–8, 251, 285–6, 291, 335, 356, 357, 436–7, 457–60, 461, 748
Kleiber, Erich, 38, 262, 296–7
Klemperer, Otto, 38, 75, 260, 261, 262, 270, 314, 357–8, 446, 448, 696

Knappertsbusch, Hans, 262, 675, 777, 788
Knorr, Iwan, 126
Knussen, Jane, 187
Knussen, Oliver, 182–98, 224, 246, 770
Knussen, Stuart, 184–6, 188, 195–8
Kodály, Zoltán, 425, 557–61
Kodály Method, 557–8
Kogan, Leonid, 256
Kokoschka, Oscar, 705
Kölner Rundfunk-Sinfonie-Orchester (see WDR Sinfonieorchester)
Komische Oper (Berlin), 264
Konchalovsky, Andrei, 745
Kondrashin Conducting Competition, 240
Kondrashin, Kirill, 240
Konservatorium der Stadt Wien, 521
Kontarsky, Alfons, 68
Kontarsky, Aloys, 68
Konzerthaus (East Berlin), 112
Konzerthaus (Vienna), 523
Kooij, Peter, 222
Koopman, Ton, 227
Korngold, Erich Wolfgang, 553
Koussevitzky, Serge, 60, 185
Kovacevich, Stephen, 621
Kraus, Karl, 519
Kreisler, Fritz, 569, 639, 641, 655, 688; *Praeludium and Allegro*, 688
Kremer, Gidon, 256
Kremlin, 697
Kremlin, Great Hall of, 726
Krips, Josef, 13, 14, 393–4, 534, 535
Kubelík, Rafael, 58
Kubrick, Stanley, 713–4; *2001: A Space Odyssey*, 713, 714
Kulenkampff, Georg, 524
Kupfer, Harry, 256, 264, 375–8
Kurtág, György, 607, 623; *Játékok*, 623

Labèque, Katia, 207, 208
Labèque, Marielle, 207, 208
Lachenmann, Helmut, 250; *Mouvement*, 250
Lalo, Édouard, 694; *Symphonie espagnole*, 694
Lambert, Myra, 496–7, 499
Lancashire County Cricket Club, 755, 761
Landowska, Wanda, 140, 141
Langham Chamber Orchestra, 763
Langridge, Philip, 430, 492
Lanza, Mario, 403, 404
Larrocha, Alicia de, 588
Lassus, Orlande de, 605
Leach, Sir Edmund, 100
Leeds International Conductors Competition, 244, 245
Leeds International Piano Competition, 621
Legge, Walter, 12, 673
Lehár, Franz, 114, 115, 507, 519, 673; *Die lustige Witwe*, 114, 115, 507, 673
Lehmann, Lotte, 30
Leider, Frida, 332, 374, 378
Leigh, Adele, 325
Leipzig Gewandhaus Orchestra, 139–40, 233
Leningrad Conservatory, 199, 242
Leningrad Dynamo, 203
Leningrad Philharmonic Orchestra, 262, 634, 736
Leningrad Philharmonic Society, 204
Lennon, John, 712, 713, 714, 722–3
Leonhardt, Gustav, 82, 130, 131, 133, 219
Leonhardt, Marie, 82
Leppard, Raymond, 166, 426, 475, 480
Lesure, François, 110
Levant, Oscar, 616
Levi, Hermann, 781, 795
Levin, Robert, 594, 598
Levine, James, 459, 473, 484

INDEX

Lewis, Sir Anthony, 39, 43, 456
Lewis, Richard, 411
Liberace, 719, 720–2
Library of Congress (Washington DC), 141, 571
Life, 703, 708
Lime Grove Studios, 711, 712
Little, Tasmin, 701
Liszt, Franz, 523, 543, 545, 607, 621, 622
Live Music Now, 698
Lloyd-Jones, David, 244
Lockwood, Didier, 646
Lodron, Countess Antonia, 528
Lodron, Giuseppa, 528
London Mozart Players, 168–74, 565
London Opera Centre, 444, 445, 471
London Philharmonic Orchestra, 10, 32, 33, 149, 166, 271, 272, 274, 562–3
London Sinfonietta, 619
London Symphony Orchestra, 3, 5, 7, 10, 13, 14, 56, 58, 60, 61, 81, 100, 184, 185, 188, 196, 359, 382, 391, 535, 616, 617, 640
London Weekend Television, 709
Loren, Sophia, 468
Loriod, Yvonne, 280–1
Los Angeles Chamber Orchestra, 24–5
Los Angeles Opera, 21
Lott, Dame Felicity, 167, 436, 455–66
Loveday, Alan, 6
Lowenthal, Jerome, 187
Ludwig II (King of Bavaria), 339
Ludwig, Christa, 474, 504
Lully, Jean-Baptiste, 121
Lumière, August, 733–4
Lumière, Louis, 733–4
Lupu, Radu, 679
Lutosławski, Witold, 299, 301, 302, 559, 572, 573; Concerto for Orchestra, 301; Symphony No. 3, 302

Maazel, Lorin, 285, 380, 446, 489, 549, 604, 643, 766
Maccaferri, Mario, 575
MacDonagh, Terence, 29
MacFarlane, Robert, 757
MacGregor, Joanna, 613–32
Machaut, Guillaume de, 98, 576
Mack, John, 766
Mackerras, Sir Charles, 28–46, 104, 107, 181, 275, 276, 279–80, 291, 312, 313, 344, 369–70, 371, 372, 378, 379, 390–1, 417, 418, 446, 448, 457, 460–1, 476–7, 494, 511–12, 529, 533, 616, 763; *Rats of Tobruk, The*, 31
Mackerras, Lady (Judy), 35, 36
MacMillan, Kenneth, 352, 726, 727
Maddock, Stephen, 299
Maderna, Bruno, 276
Mahler, Gustav, 27, 38, 39, 68, 71, 72, 76, 77, 108, 150, 154, 174, 182, 184–5, 188, 194, 209, 210, 212–14, 262, 270–1, 273, 283, 300, 301, 338, 344, 348, 349, 352–3, 358, 361, 362, 363, 382–3, 394, 488, 521, 529, 585, 716, 717, 754, 792–3; Symphony No. 1, 184–5; Symphony No. 2 ('Resurrection'), 38, 182, 188, 283, 382–3, 394; Symphony No. 3, 154, 185, 213–4, 754; Symphony No. 5, 77, 182; Symphony No. 6, 150; Symphony No. 7, 585; Symphony No. 8, 338; Symphony No. 9, 194, 214, 716; *Das Lied von der Erde*, 68, 344, 348, 352–3; *Kindertotenlieder*, 488; *Rückert-Lieder*, 488
Maida Vale Studios, 686, 761
Mainardi, Enrico, 524, 525
Majestic Hotel (Paris), 744
Malcolm, George, 108
Malherbe, Charles, 109
Malipiero, Gian Francesco, 98, 426

Mallard, The, 704
Mallinson, James, 615
Manchester Cathedral, 753
Manchester City Art Gallery, 754
Mandela, Nelson, 706
Manfredini, Francesco, 15
Mannes School of Music (New York), 204
Manson, Jonathan, 134, 135
Mansouri, Lotfi, 324, 325
Mariinsky Theatre (Saint Petersburg), 727–8
Marlowe Society, The, 704, 705
Marriner, Sir Neville, 2–27, 132, 314
Marshall, Wayne, 752
Martin, Frank, 283
Martineau, Malcolm, 434
Martin-Fullard, Frieda, 322
Martinpelto, Hillevi, 116
Martin String Quartet, 4, 5
Martinů, Bohuslav, 294, 606; *Julietta*, 294
Martynov, Vladimir, 276
Mary Leo, Sister, 440
Mascagni, Pietro, 38, 520; *Cavalleria rusticana*, 38, 520
Massenet, Jules, 326, 513; *Manon*, 326, 513
Masterclass (BBC Television), 697
Masterson, Valerie, 476
Masur, Kurt, 232, 643
Matačić, Lovro von, 265
Matheson, John, 433–4
Mathieson, Muir, 235
Mathis, Edith, 483
Mattheson, Johann, 121
Matthews, Colin, 302
Maw, Nicholas, 349–50; *One Man Show*, 349–50
McCallum, John, 343, 350
McCarthy, John, 307
McCracken, James, 323, 325

McIntyre, Donald, 393, 416
McMaster, Sir Brian, 373, 417
McNair, Sylvia, 116
McVicar, Sir David, 294, 487
Meadowmount School, 653, 654
Medtner, Nikolai, 595
Mehta, Mehli, 698
Mehta, Zubin, 352, 417, 446, 581, 639, 643, 698
Melba, Dame Nellie, 30, 344–5
Melodiya, 638
Mendelssohn, Felix, 70, 71, 123, 140, 229, 272, 363, 385, 412, 526, 557, 607, 635, 639, 687, 688, 694, 698, 744; *Elijah*, 70, 363, 385, 412; Overture to *Ein Sommernachtstraum*, 526; Violin Concerto, 557, 635, 687, 688, 694, 698
Mengelberg, Willem, 700, 732, 733
Menuhin, Diana (see Diana Gould)
Menuhin, Hephzibah, 691, 693
Menuhin, Marutha, 688, 689, 691, 692
Menuhin, Moshe, 688, 689, 691, 692, 697
Menuhin, Nola (see Nola Nicholas)
Menuhin, Yaltah, 691, 693
Menuhin, Yehudi, 562, 563, 667, 686–702, 732, 735, 737–8
Messager, André, 118, 119
Messiaen, Olivier, 280–1, 611, 626, 627–8, 629; *Quatuor pour la fin du temps*, 611, 627; *Vingt regards*, 627–8; *Turangalîla-Symphonie*, 627
Metropolitan Opera (New York), 286, 302, 326, 344, 379, 428, 429, 436–7, 450, 451–2, 459, 473, 474, 542
Metters, Colin, 281, 282, 301
Meyerbeer, Giacomo, 325; *Le prophète*, 325
MGB (later KGB), 726
Michelmore, Cliff, 702
Milanov, Zinka, 674–5

Miller, Sir Jonathan, 430, 506, 707–8; *Alice in Wonderland*, 707–8
Milstein, Nathan, 169, 663, 690
Minkowski, Marc, 111, 465
Minnesota Orchestra, 25–6, 657
Minshull, Ray, 683
Minton, Yvonne, 320, 342–64
Mobil Song Quest (Australia), 345,
Mobil Song Quest (New Zealand), 442
Moeran, Ernest John (E. J.), 760
Möller, Max, 565
Monitor, 686
Monsaingeon, Bruno, 731–50; *Piotr Anderszewski: Voyageur intranquille*, 749; *Die Stimme der Seele* (English version: *Autumn Journey*), 747
Montague, Diana, 120
Monteux, Pierre, 6–8, 184, 188, 190, 548, 675–6
Monteverdi, Claudio, 82, 93, 98, 100, 101, 102–3, 108, 111, 120, 121, 165–7, 172, 354, 423, 426, 480, 508; *Il ritorno d'Ulisse in patria*, 166; *Il ritorno d'Ulisse in patria* (ed. Leppard), 480; *L'incoronazione di Poppea*, 166, 426; *L'incoronazione di Poppea* (ed. Norrington), 426; *L'incoronazione di Poppea* (ed. Curtis), 426; *L'incoronazione di Poppea* (ed. Malipiero), 426; madrigals, 98, 102, 121; *Orfeo*, 166; *Vespro della Beata Vergine*, 100, 103; *Zefiro torna*, 101
Monteverdi Choir, 103, 111, 112
Monteverdi Orchestra, 110
Montreal Symphony Orchestra, 658
Montsalvat (Eltham, Victoria), 577–8
Moo-Cow Milk Bar (London), 320
Moore, George Edward, 704
Moscow Conservatory, 245, 254, 255, 275, 634

Moscow Conservatory, Central Music School of, 635
Moscow Conservatory, Gold Medal of, 595
Moscow Conservatory, Great Hall of, 256
Moscow Conservatory, Music College of, 254, 255, 256, 258
Moscow Conservatory, Chamber Orchestra of, 255
Moscow Radio Symphony Orchestra, 261
Mozart, Constanze, 175, 177, 230
Mozart, Wolfgang, 7, 10, 15, 18, 19, 20, 21, 22, 39, 41, 42, 46, 48, 50, 51, 55, 56, 76, 87, 89, 91, 94, 107–8, 116, 117, 118, 122, 132, 138, 140, 150, 160, 171, 174, 175, 176, 177, 179, 180, 184, 191, 193, 198, 206, 207, 209, 223, 226, 229, 230, 239, 245, 250, 266–7, 268, 269, 276, 279, 282, 292, 293, 300, 303, 309, 310, 349, 357–8, 369, 370, 371, 387–8, 389, 408, 409, 410, 412, 413, 418, 423, 424, 432, 433, 442, 445, 449, 450, 453, 455–6, 458, 460–61, 465, 471, 473, 474, 476, 479, 480, 481, 482, 483–4, 485, 486, 487, 492, 500, 503, 505, 508, 509, 510, 521, 526, 527, 528, 529, 530, 531, 532, 533, 535, 536, 537, 539, 545, 565, 567, 568, 569, 570, 600, 606, 628, 629, 632, 637, 645, 664, 665, 668, 678, 679, 680, 682, 710–1, 735–6, 739, 749, 763, 765, 787; *Così fan tutte*, 267, 309, 357–8, 371, 387–8, 453, 456, 460–61, 471, 474, 485, 486, 680; *Die Entführung aus dem Serail*, 191, 412; *Die Zauberflöte*, 41, 51, 107–8, 267, 292, 303, 369–70, 408, 449, 455–6, 460, 485, 749; *Don Giovanni*, 50, 117, 191, 245, 266–7, 282, 300, 413, 423, 442, 453, 458, 482; *Idomeneo*,

Mozart, Wolfgang *cont.*
116, 269, 370, 389, 408, 411, 485, 682; *Idomeneo* (arr. Richard Strauss), 293; *Il re pastore*, 21; *La clemenza di Tito*, 310, 358, 473; *Le nozze di Figaro*, 42, 267, 292, 388, 445, 450, 471, 474, 479, 480, 483–4, 487, 500, 503, 510, 679, 680; *Lucio Silla*, 485, 486, 492, 508; *Mitridate, re di Ponto,* 41, 485, 486, 492; Piano Concerto No. 20, 532; Piano Concerto No. 22, 526, 527, 529, 530, 531; Concerto for Three Pianos ('Lodron'), 528; Concerto for Two Pianos, 207, 526; piano concertos, 18, 116, 531, 532, 628, 632, 678; piano quartets, 529; Rondo in A minor, 545; Sonata for Two Pianos, 710–1; Quintet in G minor, 600; Symphony No. 29, 250; Symphony No. 34, 89; Symphony No. 35 ('Haffner'), 184; Symphony No. 38 ('Prague'), 191; Symphony No. 39, 117, 176; Symphony No. 40, 176, 739; Symphony No. 41 ('Jupiter'), 176, 533; Mass in C minor, 230, 483; 'Coronation' Mass, 42; Vespers, 42; *Maurerische Trauermusik*, 629; Violin Concerto No. 3, 140; Violin Concerto No. 5, 567, 735–6; violin concertos, 567, 665, 668; violin sonatas, 568; 'Ch'io mi scordi di te', 140
Mozart-Saal (Konzerthaus, Vienna), 523
Mravinsky, Yevgeny, 255, 262, 638
Mr Bach Comes to Call, 608
Muir, Frank, 709
Müller, Friedrich, 523
Munch, Charles, 60, 190
Münchener Bach-Chor, 112
Münchener Bach-Orchester, 171, 226
Münchinger, Karl, 360

Munich Philharmonic, 784
Murray, Dame Ann, 467–91, 492, 509
Museum of Modern Art (New York), 92
Music of the Baroque (Chicago), 171–3
Musica Viva (Australia), 34
Musica Viva (Munich), 68
Musikverein (Vienna), 480, 776, 778
Musin, Ilya, 200–203, 242–5, 252, 261
Mussolini, Benito, 265
Mussorgsky, Modest, 192, 193, 195; *Boris Godunov*, 192, 193; *Khovanshchina*, 192; *Night on the Bare Mountain*, 192; *Nursery, The*, 193; *Pictures at an Exhibition*, 192; *Sunless*, 193
Mustonen, Olli, 598
Muti, Riccardo, 172, 297, 485
Myaskovsky, Nikolai, 192
Myers, Paul, 585, 587

National Arts Centre Orchestra (Ottawa), 127, 657
National Concert and Artists Management, 550
National Curriculum (England and Wales), 303
National Institutes of Health (Washington DC), 554
National Railway Museum (York), 704
National Theatre (Prague), 38
National Youth Choir (Great Britain), 771
National Youth Orchestra (Great Britain), 96
Naxos, 570
Nazi Party (Germany), 34, 36, 64–5, 393, 692, 694, 695, 786
Neel, Boyd, 30
Nehru, Pandit, 698, 699
Nelsons, Andris, 299
Netherlands Radio Conductors' Course, 240

INDEX

Netherlands Radio Symphony Orchestra, 240
Netrebko, Anna, 728
Neuhaus, Heinrich, 746
Neuhaus, Zinaida, 746
Neumeister Collection, 224
Newbould, Brian, 20
Newcastle Cathedral (New South Wales, Australia), 694
Newman, John Henry, 146, 363
New South Wales State Conservatorium of Music (see Sydney Conservatorium of Music)
New Year's Day Concert (Vienna), 527
New York Philharmonic, 769
New York Times, The, 703
Ney, Elly, 532
NHK Symphony Orchestra, 87
Nicholas, Lindsay, 692, 693
Nicholas, Nola, 688, 692, 693
Nicolai, Otto, 30; *Die lustigen Weiber von Windsor*, 30
Nielsen, Flora, 400, 456
Nietzsche, Friedrich, 212; *Also sprach Zarathustra*, 212
Nikisch, Arthur, 49, 190, 233, 689
Nilsson, Birgit, 335, 374, 380, 393, 394, 677
Norberg, Florence, 446
Nordica, Lillian, 378, 379
Norman, Jessye, 461
Norrington, Sir Roger, 275, 426
Novosibirsk Philharmonic Orchestra, 634, 638
Nowak, Leopold, 782, 786, 787, 795
Nucci, Leo, 682
Nunn, Sir Trevor, 704–5
Nupen, Christopher, 586; *Double Concerto*, 586
Nuremberg Trials, 733–4
Nureyev, Rudolf, 726

Oberlin Conservatory of Music (Ohio), 597
Ockeghem, Johannes, 276
October Revolution, 729
Oistrakh, David, 563, 638, 732, 741, 742
Offenbach, Jacques, 118, 371, 465, 477; *Les contes d'Hoffmann*, 371; *La belle Hélène*, 465; *La Périchole*, 477
Olivier, Sir Laurence, 340
Olof, Victor, 673
Olympic Arts Festival (Los Angeles), 338
One Hundred Men and a Girl, 468, 734
O'Neill, Dennis, 366, 401–19, 432, 470
Opera Australia (see Australian Opera, The)
Opera Barga Festival, 409
Opéra-Comique, 119, 120
Opéra National de Lyon, 118, 119
Opera News, 167
Opera Rara, 501
Oper Frankfurt, 70, 393
Opernhaus Zürich, 82, 323, 324, 325, 492
Oppenheimer, Robert, 733
Orchestra of the Age of Enlightenment, 45, 172, 269, 271–3, 275, 376
Orchestre de la Suisse Romande, 226–7
Orchestre de Paris, 205, 206, 395
Orchestre Révolutionnaire et Romantique, 123, 124
Orff, Carl, 393; *Carmina Burana*, 393
Orly Airport (Paris), 484
Ormandy, Eugene, 30, 543
Otter, Anne Sofie von, 116, 436, 459
Oxford, University of, 164, 165, 166, 236, 705
Oxford County Council, 235
Oxford County Youth Orchestra, 235
Oxford High School, 234
Oxford University Opera Club, 165

Pablo Casals Festival (Prades), 741
Packer, Ruth, 366
Paganini, Niccolò, 635; Violin Concerto No. 1, 635
Paganini Competition (Geneva), 558, 559, 563
Pahud, Emmanuel, 134
Palais Garnier, 374
Palestrina, Giovanni Pierluigi da, 108
Palmer, Felicity, 457
Palmer, Tony, 340, 610, 703–30; *All My Loving*, 712–14; *All You Need is Love*, 722–4; *Benjamin Britten & His Festival*, 708, 709; *Benjamin Britten: A Time There Was …*, 710; *Wagner*, 340, 727; *Testimony*, 724–5; *The Harvest of Sorrow*, 729–30; *Four Ways to Say Farewell*, 716; *Nocturne*, 718; *A Life on the Road*, 719–20; *The World Of Liberace*, 720–2
Panufnik, Andrzej, 186
Pappano, Sir Antonio, 296, 375, 379, 417
Paray, Paul, 694
Parikian, Manoug, 697
Paris Conservatoire, 3, 4
Paris Opéra, 361, 450, 735
Parkinson, Sir Michael, 699
Parry, Sir Hubert, 759, 760; Symphony No. 5, 760
Parsons, Geoffrey, 408, 501, 513
Pasternak, Boris, 725
Patinir, Joachim, 197
Patterson, Frank, 395
Pauk, György, 556–74
Pavarotti, Luciano, 411, 681, 682
Pavlova, Anna, 695
Pay, Antony, 272
Payne, Anthony, 60–1
Payne, Nicholas, 266
Pears, Sir Peter, 162, 163, 164, 363, 703, 710, 711, 712, 718, 773

Peerce, Jan, 676, 734
Penderecki, Krzysztof, 572, 756; *Threnody for the Victims of Hiroshima*, 756
Perahia, Sir Murray, 551
Perlman, Itzhak, 651, 655, 664
Perry, Simon, 607
Persinger, Louis, 689, 690, 691
Pertile, Aureliano, 405
Peter Mennin Prize, 657
Peters, Roberta, 676
Peter Stuyvesant Award, 471
Peter Stuyvesant Hotel (New York), 544
Philadelphia Orchestra, 185, 186
Philharmonia Hungarica, 700
Philharmonia Orchestra, 10, 12, 13, 25, 56, 73–4, 280, 700
Philharmonic Hall (Leningrad) (see Philharmonie [Leningrad])
Philharmonic Society of London (see Royal Philharmonic Society of London)
Philharmonie (Berlin), 778
Philharmonie (Leningrad), 213, 736
Philip Jones Brass Ensemble, 236
Philips, 19, 51, 60, 112, 474, 475
Phillips, Harvey, 421
Piatigorsky, Gregor, 596–7, 734
Piazzolla, Astor, 629, 738
Piccadilly Hotel (Manchester), 580
Pickwick Papers, The, 392
Pink Floyd, 713
Pinnock, Trevor, 16, 127–43, 645
Pires, Maria João, 140
Pittsburgh Symphony Orchestra, 399
Pizzetti, Ildebrando, 51, 524, 525; *Assassinio nella cattedrale*, 51
Playfair, Sarah, 246
Pleeth, Anthony, 131, 133
Pleeth, William, 131, 599
Pleyel harpsichord, 140

INDEX

Plowright, Rosalind, 470, 471
Plunket Greene, Harry, 352
Pollini, Maurizio, 69
Ponnelle, Jean-Pierre, 484, 485, 486, 492, 508–9
Pons, Lily, 734
Ponsonby, Robert, 180
Pont Davies, Rebecca de, 148
Ponte, Lorenzo da, 179, 268, 292
Popp, Lucia, 357, 359, 363, 455, 461, 510
Portnoy, Mr, 345
Postnikova, Viktoria, 736
Potter, Sally, 294
Poulenc, Francis, 326; *Les dialogues des Carmélites*, 326
Pountney, Sir David, 179
Prague Chamber Orchestra, 532–3
Prague National Museum, 601
Prague Spring, 200
Pravda, 724
Pré, Jacqueline du, 599, 610
Preston, Stephen, 131
Previn, André, 393, 399, 759
Prévost, Abbé, 513
Prez, Josquin de, 276
Price, Janet, 501
Price, Leontyne, 326
Price, Dame Margaret, 354, 357
Pring, Katherine, 366, 367
Pritchard, Sir John, 151, 237, 268, 293, 310, 359, 390, 409, 417, 446, 457–8, 564, 585, 616, 680, 682, 764, 765
Prix de Rome, 738
Procter, Norma, 148, 352
Prohaska, Felix, 86, 534
Prokofiev, Lina, 725–7
Prokofiev, Sergei, 52, 553, 611, 640, 725, 726–7, 741; Piano Concerto No. 4, 553; Cello Concerto, 611; *Romeo and Juliet*, 726; *War and Peace*, 727
Puccini, Giacomo, 21, 34, 264, 287, 296, 319, 323, 338–9, 354, 371, 455, 468, 511, 676, 681, 725, 735; *Gianni Schicchi*, 354; *La bohème*, 21, 264, 287, 371, 455; *Madama Butterfly*, 296, 681; *Suor Angelica*, 323; *Tosca*, 34, 296, 468, 511, 735; *Turandot*, 296, 338–9
Pulkert, Oldřich, 601
Punch, 703
Purcell, Henry, 93, 101, 108, 121, 144, 355, 390, 398; fantasias, 93; *Dido and Aeneas*, 355, 390, 398
Purcell Singers, The, 98
Pye, 28, 29

Quartet, 340
Quebec Symphony Orchestra, 657
Queen Elisabeth Competition (Brussels), 657
Queen Elizabeth Hall (London), 281, 500, 502, 618, 771
Queen's Hall (London), 55

Rachmaninoff, Alexander, 729
Rachmaninoff, Sergei, 187, 392, 393, 411, 543, 544, 545, 548, 595, 621, 728–30; *Bells, The*, 411; Piano Sonata No. 2, 621; *Rhapsody on a Theme of Paganini*, 187, 545; Prelude in C sharp minor, 544, 730; Symphony No. 2, 728
Rachmaninoff Centenary Concert, 392, 393
Rachmaninoff Conducting Competition, 203, 204
Radio City Music Hall, 722
Radio-Sinfonieorchester Stuttgart des SWR, 26
Raeburn, Christopher, 347, 672–85
Raimondi, Ruggero, 451
Rameau, Jean-Philippe, 108, 109, 110, 111, 121, 122; *Hippolyte et Aricie*, 111; *Les Boréades*, 110, 111

Rattle, Sir Simon, 111, 168, 245, 246, 251, 283, 285, 301, 376, 417, 553, 566, 573–4, 771, 797
Ravel, Maurice, 32, 111, 152, 154, 184, 545, 548, 552–3, 626–7, 658, 685, 769; *Daphnis et Chloé*, 32, 184, 548; Piano Concerto for the Left Hand, 154, 552–3; *Tzigane*, 658; *Valses nobles et sentimentales*, 626–7
RCA, 672, 674, 676
Red House (Suffolk), 198, 710
Reed, Carol, 523
Reed, William Henry (W. H.), 3
Reese, Gustav, 93
Reiner, Fritz, 734
Reinhardt, Django, 575, 579, 580, 699
Reiss, Janine, 510
Reith, Sir John, 180, 772
Rennert, Günther, 408
Residenztheater (Munich), 156, 269, 481
Reynolds, Debbie, 182
Rhodes, Dame Zandra, 294
Ribbentrop, Joachim von, 734
Ricci, Luigi, 326–7, 407
Richardson, Sir Ralph, 340
Richard Strauss Prize, 65
Richter, Karl, 112, 140, 141, 226, 227, 314–5, 360, 386, 396–7, 415
Richter, Sviatoslav, 141, 255, 256, 617, 638, 710–1, 742, 744–6, 747–8, 750
Ricordi (see Casa Ricordi)
Robben Island, 706
Robertson, James, 444
Robertson, Linnhe, 499
Robinson, Peter, 165
Robson, Christopher, 476
Rodrigo, Joaquín, 586; *Concierto de Aranjuez*, 586
Rodziński, Artur, 734
Rogers, Ginger, 455
Rolf Therapy, 554

Rolfe Johnson, Anthony, 116, 164
Roosevelt, Franklin Delano, 542
Rose, Jürgen, 333
Ross, Alex, 273; *The Rest is Noise*, 273
Rossini, Gioachino Antonio, 20, 21, 118, 160, 263, 268, 408, 471, 474, 477, 482, 585, 680, 683; *Il barbiere di Siviglia*, 471, 585, 683; *La Cenerentola*, 21, 477; *La pietra del paragone*, 408; *Mosè in Egitto*, 474
Rostropovich, Mstislav, 115, 193, 584, 640–3, 646, 647, 648
Roundhouse (London), 619
Royal Academy of Music (London), 39, 55, 62, 90, 130, 149, 176, 179, 194, 235, 242, 243, 251, 279, 281–4, 287, 309, 385–6, 388, 407, 456–7, 463, 464, 497, 614–6, 620, 625, 626, 636, 722, 737
Royal Air Force, 694
Royal Albert Hall (London), 188, 338, 353–4, 368–9, 376, 384, 392, 619, 688, 692, 694
Royal Ballet School, 701
Royal Choral Society, 384
Royal College of Music (London), 3, 6, 7, 9, 10, 48, 99, 130, 131, 139, 238, 320, 322, 323, 333, 366–8, 421, 423, 424, 433, 580, 581, 582, 729
Royal Concertgebouw Orchestra, 81, 83, 209, 285, 733
Royal Festival Hall (London), 10, 11, 15, 73, 184, 357–8, 482, 565, 617–18, 708, 771
Royal Holloway (University of London), 756, 757, 760
Royal Liverpool Philharmonic Orchestra, 754
Royal Manchester College of Music (see Royal Northern College of Music)
Royal Navy, 576

INDEX

Royal Northern College of Music, 21, 235, 236–8, 240, 241, 245, 404, 405, 469, 470, 471

Royal Northern Sinfonia, 384

Royal Opera House, Covent Garden, 52–6, 119, 245, 246, 247, 266, 295, 296, 297, 299, 307, 308, 309, 322, 326, 327, 329, 333, 334, 335, 338, 339, 343, 350, 351, 352, 353, 356, 372, 393–4, 421, 428, 429, 435, 442, 445, 450, 453, 459, 472, 473, 474, 489, 501, 502, 503, 504, 509, 510, 511, 513, 585, 757

Royal Philharmonic Orchestra, 242, 700

Royal Philharmonic Society of London, 603

Royal Scottish National Orchestra, 764

Royal Swedish Opera, 267

Royal Winnipeg Ballet, 651

Rozhdestvensky, Gennady, 255, 261, 266, 274, 736, 761

Rózsa, Vera, 424, 425, 426, 445, 446

Rubinstein, Anton, 634

Rubinstein, Arthur, 696, 734

Rundfunkchor Berlin, 156

Russell, Bertrand, 704

Russell, Ken, 707; *Isadora*, 707

Russo, Andrew, 669

Rysanek, Leonie, 676

Sächsische Staatskapelle, 58, 259–60, 474, 777, 792

Sadler's Wells Opera, 34, 38, 51, 52, 107, 163, 373, 387, 388

Sadler's Wells Opera Orchestra, 34

Sainsbury's, 705

Saint-Denis, Michel, 51

St Mark's Basilica (Venice), 102, 224

St Paul's Cathedral (London), 411, 702

Saint Petersburg Philharmonic (see Leningrad Philharmonic)

Saint Petersburg Conservatory, 634

Saint-Saëns, Camille, 109

St Stephen's Church (Sydney), 349

Salieri, Antonio, 177

Salle Favart (Paris), 119

Salle Wagram (Paris), 395

Salzburg Festival, 21, 42, 140, 284, 285, 286, 287, 380, 413, 483, 484, 524, 610, 705, 714

Sammons, Albert, 3

San Francisco Opera, 324, 512

San Francisco Symphony Orchestra, 542, 548, 690

Santi, Nello, 325–6

Saram, Rohan de, 581

Sargent, Sir Malcolm, 30, 39, 57, 354, 360, 564

Satie, Erik, 617, 626, 630

Sauer, Emil von, 523, 538

Sawallisch, Wolfgang, 27, 298, 462, 531

Scarlatti, Alessandro, 121

Scarlatti, Domenico, 121, 624, 625; Sonata in A flat major, 625

Schaeftlein, Jürg, 87

Schalk, Franz, 785, 788

Schalk, Josef, 785, 788

Schanz fortepiano, 539

Schenk, Otto, 336

Schenker, Heinrich, 281

Scherchen, Hermann, 226, 262

Schidlof, Peter, 169–70

Schiff, Sir András, 551, 677

Schiller, Friedrich, 529; *An die Freude*, 529, 540

Schipa, Tito, 404, 405

Schmid, Patric, 501

Schmidt, Franz, 519, 553; *Toccata*, 519

Schmidt-Isserstedt, Hans, 72, 185, 680

Schnabel, Artur, 141, 543–7

Schneiderhan, Wolfgang, 524, 525

Schnittke, Alfred, 275

Schnorr von Carolsfeld, Malvina, 339

Schoenberg, Arnold, 68, 79, 80, 183, 196, 275, 276, 353, 354, 480, 521, 742, 756; *Survivor from Warsaw, A*, 80; Chamber Symphony, 756; *Erwartung*, 80; *Gurrelieder*, 480; *Herzegewächse*, 196; *Moses und Aron*, 353; *Verklärte Nacht*, 80

Schöne, Wolfgang, 416

Schopenhauer, Arthur, 81

Schubert, Franz, 15, 20, 42, 46, 92, 217, 272, 276, 301, 418, 424, 432, 433, 530, 536, 537, 562, 567, 569, 570, 606, 625, 626, 632, 662, 700, 717, 738, 789; *Fierrabras*, 217; Symphony No. 7 (completed Newbould), 20; Symphony No. 8 ('Unfinished') (completed Newbould), 20; Symphony No. 10, 301; Symphony No. 10 (completed Newbould), 20; impromptus, 626; symphonies, 700

Schulhof, Otto, 523

Schuller, Gunther, 553

Schumann, Clara, 606

Schumann, Robert, 15, 122–3, 351, 381, 433, 490, 528, 547, 550, 552, 597, 600, 604–5, 606, 608, 618, 629, 735, 736; *Carnaval*, 550; Cello Concerto, 597; Cello Concerto (arr. Shostakovich), 605; *Frauen-Liebe und Leben*, 351, 381, 490; Piano Concerto, 547; Symphony No. 1 ('Spring'), 123; Symphony No. 4, 123, 735; Violin Sonata No. 3, 600

Schütz, Heinrich, 108, 121, 124, 222, 227, 605

Schwarzkopf, Elisabeth, 76, 455, 456, 461

Scottish Chamber Orchestra, 533

Scottish Opera, 245, 246, 307, 471, 472

Scriabin, Alexander, 595, 621; Piano Sonata No. 6, 621

Sculthorpe, Peter, 589–90

SDG (records), 123

Seattle Chamber Music Society, 669

Segovia, Andrés, 575, 579–83, 592

Sellner, Gustav Rudolf, 336

Sendak, Maurice, 197

Senesino (Francesco Bernardi), 40, 41

Serafin, Tullio, 675, 676

Serkin, Rudolf, 546

Sesame Street, 651

Severance Hall (Cleveland), 73, 766–7

Shaffer, Peter, 22, 177

Shafran, Daniil, 597

Shakespeare, William, 102, 599; *King Lear*, 599; *Hamlet*, 599

Shankar, Ravi, 708

Shaw, George Bernard, 401

Shchedrin, Rodion, 640

Sheffield, University of, 409

Shell Aria Competition, 345

Shine, 729

Shirley-Quirk, John, 155, 395

Shostakovich, Dmitri, 52, 193, 202, 206, 210, 211, 263, 283, 605, 611, 640, 642, 647, 724–6, 745–6; Piano Trio No. 2, 611; Violin Concerto No. 1, 642; *Lady Macbeth of the Mtsensk District*, 724, 725; Symphony No. 5, 724; Symphony No. 9, 726, 745–6; Symphony No. 14, 283

Shostakovich, Maxim, 726

Shostakovich, Nina, 746

Sibelius, Jean, 53, 59–60, 197, 235, 259, 299, 302, 643, 650, 754; Symphony No. 2, 235, 754; Symphony No. 3, 302; Symphony No. 4, 197, 302; Symphony No. 6, 302; Symphony No. 7, 259; Violin Concerto, 643, 650

Sigall, David, 615, 630

Silja, Anja, 75, 367, 368

Silver, Millicent, 130, 131

INDEX

Sinatra, Frank, 412
Sinfonia Varsovia, 700
Sinfonieorchester des Norddeutschen Rundfunks, 71, 80
Singverein der Gesellschaft der Musikfreunde, 88
Sinopoli, Giuseppe, 417, 418–9
Sitwell, Sacheverell, 608
Skipper, Mitcham, 578
Skoda, Anton, 518, 522
Smallman, Greg, 590, 591
Smetana, Bedřich, 38, 39, 495; *Dalibor*, 38, 39; *Libuše*, 38; *Vltava*, 495
Smith, Eric, 19, 20
Smith, Fabian, 469
Smith, Ronald, 128, 129
Snape Maltings (Suffolk), 155, 623, 709, 711
Snowman, Nicholas, 269
Söderström, Elisabeth, 167, 463
Solomon, Cutner, 10
Solomon, King, 611
Solomon, Seymour, 82
Solti, Sir Georg, 52, 66, 149, 291, 326–7, 351, 353, 375, 417, 446, 447, 450, 465, 482, 483, 487, 509–10, 511, 513, 562, 564, 565, 573, 574, 675, 677, 687
Somary, Johannes, 397
Sorrell Women Conductors Programme, 251, 252
Soul Lives, 593
Southbank Centre (London), 170, 273, 502, 503, 565
South Pacific, 494
Spanish Guitar Centre (London), 580
Spencer, Lady Diana (see Diana, Princess of Wales)
Spitalfields Festival, 492
Squire, William Henry (W. H.), 603
Staatskapelle Berlin, 758, 771
Stainer, John, 108

Staines & Egham News, 760
Stalin, Joseph, 724, 725
Stanford University, 93
Stanislavski, Konstantin, 271
State Opera of South Australia, 342
Stein, Peter, 770
Steiner violins, 661
Steinitz, Paul, 315
Steinway pianos, 116, 140, 142, 239, 537, 538, 544, 554, 623–4
Stern, Isaac, 22, 26, 655, 696
Stevens, Risë, 344
Stich-Randall, Teresa, 86
Stiff, Wilfred, 392
Stiftung Mozarteum, 140
Stockhausen, Karlheinz, 68, 256, 276
Stokowski, Christopher, 186
Stokowski, Leopold, 13, 185–92, 231, 391, 395, 468, 734, 748
Stokowski, Leopold Stanislaus ('Stan'), 186
Stoll, Herr, 415
Stolyarsky, Pyotr, 634
Stradivarius violins, 565–6, 600, 658–9, 660, 661
Strasser, Jani, 390, 408, 427
Stratas, Teresa, 451
Straube, Karl, 64
Straus, Volker, 18
Strauss, Franz, 269
Strauss II, Johann, 264, 325, 494; *Die Fledermaus*, 264, *Der Zigeunerbaron*, 325; *Wiener Blut*, 494
Strauss, Pauline, 340
Strauss, Richard, 19, 55, 67, 75, 76, 77, 94, 108, 167, 174, 183, 184, 203, 210–11, 212, 213, 216, 217, 218, 239, 243, 268, 269, 270, 291, 292, 293, 296–7, 319, 329, 332, 333, 334–5, 340, 342, 344, 347, 349, 355, 356, 358, 361, 362, 368, 376, 380, 381, 400, 409,

Strauss, Richard *cont.*
436–7, 445, 448, 450, 455, 456, 458–60, 461–2, 463, 465, 474, 482, 487, 488, 505, 506, 509, 513, 527, 553, 603–4, 667, 676, 677, 684, 714, 744, 765, 780, 785, 791; *Also sprach Zarathustra*, 714; *Arabella*, 445, 448, 450, 462; *Ariadne auf Naxos*, 355, 474, 487, 676, 677; *Capriccio*, 167, 292, 450, 462, 463, 513; Cello Sonata, 604; *Daphne*, 216, 217; *Der Rosenkavalier*, 76, 212, 217, 291–2, 333, 342, 344, 347, 356, 362, 380, 436–7, 458–60, 462, 465, 474, 482, 487–8, 505, 506, 509, 513, 684, 785; *Die Frau ohne Schatten*, 203, 217, 218, 292, 780, 791; *Don Juan*, 243, 527; *Don Quixote*, 603, 604; *Ein Heldenleben*, 75; *Eine Alpensinfonie*, 183, 210–1; *Elektra*, 67, 76, 94, 212, 217, 291, 292, 329, 334–5, 342, 376, 380; *Intermezzo*, 462; *Metamorphosen*, 19, 212, 213; *Salome*, 67, 94, 217, 270, 292, 293, 329, 332, 333, 368, 380, 474, 604; *Tod und Verklärung*, 293; *Vier letzte Lieder*, 212, 213, 400, 455, 456, 461–2; *Romanze (für Violoncello und Orchester)*, 604; 'Wiegenlied', 667; 'Morgen', 667

Stravinsky, Igor, 18, 32, 51, 52, 92, 98, 167, 182, 183, 184, 194, 196, 283–4, 295, 298, 354, 428, 458, 505, 548, 640, 737, 738, 739, 770, 772; *Concerto for Piano and Wind Instruments*, 283–4; *Double Canon*, 183; *Epitaphium*, 183, 196; *Le sacre du printemps*, 32, 298, 548, 770, 772; *Movements for Piano and Orchestra*, 183; *Oedipus Rex*, 51, 52, 92; *Petrushka*, 182, 194; 'Pulcinella' Suite, 18; *Symphony in Three Movements*, 52; *The Rake's Progress*, 52, 92, 167, 428, 458; Violin Concerto, 737–8; *Requiem Canticles*, 194

Strosser, Pierre, 120
Stuttgarter Kammerorchester, 171
Suk, Josef, 46, 606
Sullivan, Sir Arthur (see Gilbert and Sullivan)
Sun Aria Competition, 345, 442
Sutcliffe, Sidney, 29
Sutherland, Dame Joan, 344–5, 351, 441, 455, 498, 504, 508
Sutton's Music Shop (Melbourne), 578
Suzuki, Masaaki, 219–31
Svetlanov, Yevgeny, 255, 262
Swarowsky, Hans, 352
Syberberg, Hans-Jürgen, 355–6; *Parsifal* (film), 355–6
Sydney, University of, 496
Sydney Conservatorium of Music, 30, 32, 343, 494, 496–7, 499
Sydney International Piano Competition, 620
Sydney Opera House, 33, 494, 497–8, 666, 688
Sydney Symphony Orchestra, 29, 31, 32, 250, 344, 666
Sydney Town Hall, 344, 494, 495
Sykes, Eric, 591–2
Symphonieorchester des Bayerischen Rundfunks, 26, 57, 58, 285
Symphony Hall (Boston), 767
Synod Concerts, 550
Szigeti, Joseph, 571
Szell, George, 23, 30, 73, 243, 529–31, 546–50, 696, 766, 769
Szell, Helen, 550
Szeryng, Henryk, 563
Szymanowski, Karol, 289, 301, 303, 741; *Stabat Mater*, 289, 303; *Król Roger*, 301

INDEX

Tachezi, Herbert, 87
Talich, Václav, 35, 36, 37
Tallis, Thomas, 100
Talvela, Martti, 336–7
Taneyev, Sergei, 595
Taronga Zoo (Sydney), 342
Tartini, Giuseppe, 741
Tauber, Richard, 30
Tavener, Sir John, 386, 598; *Protecting Veil, The*, 598
Tchaikovsky Concert Hall (Moscow), 583
Tchaikovsky, Pyotr Ilyich, 32, 118, 197, 354, 410, 414, 448, 562, 637, 640, 641, 647, 662, 665–6, 690, 736, 742, 744; *Eugene Onegin*, 354, 410, 414, 448; Symphony No. 6 ('*Pathétique*') 32; Piano Concerto No. 1, 736, 742; *Sérénade mélancolique*, 666, 690; Violin Concerto, 562, 637, 665–6; Piano Trio, 665; *Valse-Scherzo*, 666
Tear, Robert, 411, 412
Teatro alla Scala (Milan), 332, 405, 406, 429–30, 499
Teatro Comunale di Bologna, 264, 265
Teatro dell'Opera (Rome), 319, 468
Teatro Olimpico (Vicenza), 492
Tebaldi, Renata, 468, 672, 677
Technische Universität (Vienna), 520
Te Kanawa, Dame Kiri, 21, 320, 439–54, 510
Te Kanawa, Nell, 439, 440, 441
Te Kanawa, Tom, 439, 440, 441
Teldec, 639, 643
Telemann, Georg Philipp, 121, 638
Tennstedt, Klaus, 266
Terfel, Bryn, 116, 415
Test Match Special, 757
Thatcher, Baroness Margaret, 506, 701
Theater an der Wien (Vienna), 335, 337
Théâtre des Champs-Élysées (Paris), 772
Théâtre du Châtelet (Paris), 111, 465

The Great Caruso, 403
The Rats of Tobruk, 31
Thern, Viola, 521
The Sound of Music, 455
The Third Man, 523
Thielemann, Christian, 776–98
Thomas, Sally, 654
Thomasschule (Leipzig), 63
Thurston, Frederick, 10, 48
Ticciati, Robin, 479
Tillett, Emmie, 391, 392
Times, The, 700, 703
Timmerman, Leni, 68
Tippett, Sir Michael, 179, 245, 350, 392, 572–3; *King Priam*, 350; *Knot Garden, The*, 245, 350; Triple Concerto, 573
Tobis-Klangfilm, 733–4
Tomlinson, Sir John, 292, 376, 471
Tooley, Sir John, 54, 445, 453, 509
Torres Jurado, Antonio de, 590–1
Torrey Pines State Natural Reserve, 153
Tortelier, Maxime, 739
Tortelier, Paul, 597, 697, 739, 740
Tortelier, Yan Pascal, 739
Toscanini, Arturo, 10–11, 263, 529, 676, 696, 748
Tottenham Municipal Baths, 586
Tovey, Donald Francis, 596
Trobäck, Sara, 284
Ts'ong, Fou, 563
Tuckwell, Barry, 182, 194, 389
Turchaninova, Galina, 633, 634
Tureck, Rosalyn, 624–5
Turnage, Mark-Anthony, 192, 283, 302; *Twice Through the Heart*, 283
Turner, Dame Eva, 338–9, 444

Ulster Orchestra, 762, 763
UNESCO International Music Council, 697

Unitarian Church (Budapest), 570–1
United Nations, 699
United Nations Relief and Works Agency, 99
Universität für Musik und darstellende Kunst Wien, 520–1
University of Chicago Press, 407
Usher, Terry, 580

Vanderbilt, Gloria, 186
Vanguard, 82
Várady, Júlia, 116, 471, 747
Varèse, Edgard, 738
Variety Playhouse, 347
Varviso, Silvio, 416
Vaughan Williams, Ralph, 18, 53, 150, 152–4, 302, 353, 387, 398, 399, 479, 759, 764; *A Sea Symphony*, 150; *Serenade to Music*, 353, 479; Symphony No. 3, 154; Symphony No. 5, 764; Symphony No. 6, 53; *The Lark Ascending*, 150; *Tallis Fantasia*, 150
Vaughan Williams, Ursula, 387
Veasey, Josephine, 395
Vengerov, Maxim, 140, 633–49
Verdi, Giuseppe, 91, 117, 118, 159, 160, 167, 170, 193, 245, 263, 266, 268, 286, 287, 289, 294, 296, 319, 324, 326–8, 332, 347, 359, 366, 367, 368, 371, 393–4, 403, 405, 407, 408, 409, 410, 412, 415, 417, 418, 419, 442, 451, 452, 468, 496, 500, 503, 674, 725; *Aida*, 294, 296, 319, 324, 347, 366, 468, 503, 674, 725, 735; *Don Carlos*, 193, 326, 442; *Falstaff*, 167, 193, 359, 393–4; *Il trovatore*, 326–8, 332, 417, 419, 725; *La forza del destino*, 674; *La traviata*, 245, 286, 367, 371, 415; *Macbeth*, 408; *Nabucco*, 266; *Otello*, 160, 324, 368, 451; Requiem, 289, 366, 368, 418, 735; *Rigoletto*, 287, 367, 405, 407, 496, 500; *Simon Boccanegra*, 160; *Un ballo in maschera*, 326
Vickers, Jon, 393, 429, 451
Victoria, Tomás Luis de, 108; *Tenebrae Responsories*, 108
Victoria State Opera, 514
Vienna Philharmonic, 46, 70, 75, 81, 85, 114–15, 285, 480, 525–7, 678, 715–16, 777, 788, 789, 796
Vienna Staatsoper, 216, 297, 334, 336, 429, 534
Vienna Symphony Orchestra, 81, 86, 87, 88, 91, 92, 226, 528
Vienna Tonkünstler Orchestra, 81
Vienna Volksoper, 115, 295
Vietheer, Erich, 501, 513
Vignoles, Roger, 389, 434
Villa Senar (Lucerne), 729
Vinay, Ramón, 368
Violectra electric viola, 645
Viotti, Giovanni Battista, 690; *Allegro*, 690
Virtuoso String Trio, 4, 5
Vivaldi, Antonio, 41, 121, 138, 668; *Le quattro stagioni*, 668
Volkonsky, Andrei, 275
Vox Turnabout, 567

Waart, Edo de, 604
Wagner, Cosima, 339, 542, 622
Wagner, Minna, 340
Wagner, Richard, 43, 44, 51, 53, 70, 75, 94, 119, 120, 122, 152, 159, 172, 174, 210, 215–16, 259, 265, 268, 269, 270, 295, 297–8, 312, 319, 326, 327, 328–31, 332, 336, 338, 339, 340, 349, 351, 355, 356, 358, 361, 365, 367, 368, 372, 373, 374, 375, 376, 377, 378, 379, 381, 435, 447, 474, 475, 478, 481, 489, 490, 511, 534, 542, 622, 675, 677, 684–5, 725, 727–8, 744, 778, 779, 780, 788,

791, 793; *Das Rheingold*, 53, 70, 326, 376, 675; *Der Ring des Nibelungen*, 53, 70, 159, 215, 270, 297, 331, 332, 351, 361, 365, 367, 372, 373, 374, 375, 377, 381, 489, 490, 675, 677, 684–5, 780; *Die fliegende Holländer*, 75, 269, 297–8, 327, 340, 534; *Die Meistersinger von Nürnberg*, 94, 268, 269, 297, 336, 373, 779; *Götterdämmerung*, 70, 326, 328–31, 377, 474, 478; *Siegfried*, 328; *Lohengrin*, 159, 215–16, 265, 622; *Tannhäuser*, 51, 159, 331; *Tristan und Isolde*, 94, 215, 268–9, 356, 378, 379, 381, 481, 489–90, 622, 779, 780; *Parsifal*, 152, 330, 355, 356, 490, 542, 727–8, 788; *Wesendonck-Lieder*, 312, 381; *Siegfried Idyll*, 268; *Die Feen*, 298; *Die Walküre*, 327, 328, 329, 351, 368, 373, 374, 377, 447
Wagner, Siegfried, 475
Wagner, Wieland, 327, 330, 331, 332, 368
Wagner, Winifred, 355
Wagner, Wolfgang, 327, 329, 331, 416
Walker, Annie, 420
Walker, Marjorie, 343
Walker, Nina, 682
Walker, Sarah, 420–38
Walker Art Gallery (Liverpool), 755
Walmisley, Thomas Forbes, 108
Walter, Bruno, 262, 519, 529, 532, 734
Walton, William, 18, 30, 179, 495, 598, 608, 640, 646; *Belshazzar's Feast*, 495; Symphony No. 1, 30; Cello Concerto, 598, 608; Viola Concerto, 646
Wand, Günter, 780–1, 787, 788
Warfield, Sandra, 324
War Memorial Opera House (San Francisco), 543
Warner, Deborah, 294

Watkins, Paul, 299
Watts, Helen, 148, 352, 360, 478
WDR Sinfonieorchester, 67, 210, 216
Weber, Carl Maria von, 51, 117, 118, 259, 269, 272, 298; *Der Freischütz*, 51; *Euryanthe*, 269
Webern, Anton, 68, 183, 196, 275, 276, 519, 743; *Konzert für neun Instrumente*, 743
Webster, Sir David, 54, 327
Weill, Kurt, 51, 245, 246; *Aufstieg und Fall der Stadt Mahagonny* (*Rise and Fall of the City of Mahagonny*) 51, 245, 246
Weiner, Leó, 559, 561, 562
Weingartner, Felix, 72, 264, 732
Welsh National Opera, 373, 379, 417, 770
Werfel, Franz, 519
Wesley, Samuel, 108
Westminster Cathedral (London), 108
Westminster Records, 536
Wexford Festival (Ireland), 165
Wheldon, Sir Huw, 709–10, 711, 712
Whitehouse, Mary, 713
Whyte, Ian, 50
Wieniawski, Henryk, 634
Wiesenthal, Marta, 519, 520
Wigglesworth, Mark, 282–3
Wigmore Hall (London), 381, 399, 564–5, 569, 594, 619
Wilkinson, Nigel, 615
Willcocks, Sir David, 155, 157, 314
Williams, John, 237, 575–93
Williams, Len, 575–80, 582
Williams, Melaan, 576, 577, 583
Williams, Phyllis, 575, 576
Williams, Roderick, 156
Windsor & Eton Express, 760
Withers, Googie, 343
Wittgenstein, Ludwig, 704
Wittgenstein, Paul, 553

Wokingham Choral Society, 288–9
Wolf, Hugo, 400; 'Mausfallen-Sprüchlein', 400
Wood, Sir Henry J. (Joseph), 10, 59, 96, 238, 353; *Fantasia on British Sea Songs*, 238
Works Progress Administration (WPA), 542
Wright, Roger, 751–73
Wright, Simon, 751, 752, 754
Württemberg Chamber Orchestra, 567
Wyn-Rogers, Catherine, 352

Xenakis, Iannis, 276, 739, 763

Yehudi Menuhin School, The, 701
York Minster (England), 100
Young, Bertie, 577
Young Concert Artists Trust, 621, 630
Young Opera (Australia), 498
Ysaÿe, Eugène, 691
Yusupov, Benjamin, 645; *Viola Tango Rock Concerto*, 645
YWCA (London), 320

Zander, Benjamin, 581
Zappa, Frank, 713
Zathureczky, Ede, 91, 559, 560, 561, 562
Zemlinsky, Alexander von, 53; *Eine florentinische Tragödie*, 53
Zen Buddhism, 553, 627
Zhdanov, Andrei, 726
Zimmermann, Bernd Alois, 256; *Die Soldaten*, 256
Zukerman, Pinchas, 655
Zürich Stadttheater (see Opernhaus Zürich)
Zweig, Stefan, 519